Acclaim for *Making Saints*

"A fascinating and moving account of the interplay between the politics of the Roman Catholic Church and the claims of heroic virtue. A first-rate contribution to the history and sociology of religion—and a fascinating read."

—Arthur Hertzberg

"Always interesting, sometimes a little horrifying and not without comedy."

—Graham Greene

"[Woodward's] reporting—fair, thorough, and forcefully written—has earned him an international following among people who want religion to be treated as a major beat. . . . [His] professional graces . . . are on large display in this investigation of the politics, economics, and deal-making in the production of saints."

—*Washington Post Book World*

"Balanced and utterly absorbing . . . explains in fascinating detail how and why the church makes saints."

—*The Economist*

"Illuminating . . . offers a thorough, scholarly history of sainthood in the church . . . a sympathetic and yet slightly painful portrait of a church itself unsure about the nature of sainthood."

—*Village Voice*

"The book's fascination comes in the intimacy of its investigation. This is not an exposé; nothing nefarious is going on. Rather, it is the only book ever written on this highly intriguing, usually secret aspect of Catholic Church operations. . . . Books like this one, by an able journalist both qualified and devoted, perform a service well beyond their own time."

—*Minneapolis Star Tribune*

MAKING
SAINTS

*How the Catholic Church
Determines Who Becomes a Saint,
Who Doesn't, and Why*

KENNETH L. WOODWARD

A TOUCHSTONE BOOK
Published by Simon & Schuster

TOUCHSTONE
Rockefeller Center
1230 Avenue of the Americas
New York, New York 10020

Designed by Sheree Goodman

Manufactured in the United States of America

1   3   5   7   9   10   8   6   4   2

Library of Congress Cataloging in Publication Data is available.
ISBN 0-684-81530-3

Translation of *The Poems of St. John of the Cross* © 1959, 1968,
1979 by John Frederick Nims (Chicago, Ill.: The University of
Chicago Press).

But the effect of her being on those around her was incalculably diffusive; for the growing good of the world is partly dependent on unhistoric acts; and that things are not so ill with you and me as they might have been, is half owing to the number who lived faithfully a hidden life, and rest in unvisited tombs.

—George Eliot, Middlemarch

CONTENTS

There is but one sadness, . . . and that is for us not to be SAINTS.
—*Leon Bloy,* La Femme Pauvre

The world needs saints who have genius, just as a plague-stricken town needs doctors. Where there is a need there is also an obligation.
—*Simone Weil,* last letter to Father Perrin

ACKNOWLEDGMENTS

In LATE OCTOBER 1987, during the course of my interview with two Jesuit saint-makers who figure prominently in this book, there was the sudden, sickening sound of one motor vehicle crunching into another in the street four floors below—a not uncommon occurrence in modern Rome. One of the men, with a nod to the other, immediately left to see what he could do. "Excuse me," he said apologetically to me, "but we are also priests."

When I left, minutes later, I saw him conferring at the scene of the accident, which had occurred at the busy intersection outside the Jesuit headquarters at Borgo Santo Spirito, just a block from the Vatican. He was the only priest in sight.

I recall the incident here as a way of acknowledging that the men whose job it is to "make saints" are also priests, which is to say that by virtue of their calling they have responsibilities beyond those for which I sought them out in order to write this book. My first acknowledgment, therefore, is to acknowledge that they, like all people, are more than functionaries of a system. What they do does not exhaust who they are.

The same, I like to think, is true of journalists. A journalist arrives unbidden in the lives of others, asking questions, seeking information, eliciting responses. The exchange implies a bond of trust: on the one side that truth will be told, to the extent that discretion and human limitations allow; on the other that what is said will be honestly reported, given the need for concision. Not only words but context must be respected if truth is to be served. I trust the context of my questions, and the answers to them, have not only been respected but evoked. If I have chosen to view what these men do in a somewhat different light, it is because I come to their work as an interested outsider who was granted the privilege of becoming a participant-observer to the extent that the system allows. My interests are not altogether congruent with theirs, but where they differ is, I trust, made explicit. That, too, is an acknowledgment.

In a book such as this, the author is inevitably indebted to others: none of us works alone. Apart from those mentioned in the text, and those whose works are cited, I am most appreciative of those who read the manuscript as it developed, and offered critical comment. Chief among the latter is Richard Kieckhefer, professor in the Department of the History and Literature of Religions at Northwestern University; one of these days, I hope, we'll meet in person. Another is John Coleman, S.J., professor of sociology and religion at the Jesuit School of Theology at Berkeley, California, whose published work profoundly influenced my own ideas about sainthood. A third is Lawrence Cunningham, professor of theology at the University of Notre Dame, who has limned the Catholic sensibility, including the veneration of saints, better than anyone I know. Needless to say, they are not responsible for the uses to which I have put their criticism and advice.

In addition, I want to thank several people whose criticism, conversation, and encouragement sustained me through nearly four years of solitary labor. James Gollin, author, novelist, and friend, was my putative "ideal reader," generous with his time and spendthrift in his encouragement as only another harassed writer can be. At crucial points, Marvin O'Connell, Thomas F. O'Meara, O. P., and James Tunstead Burtchaell, C.S.C., all of the faculty at Notre Dame, plus Martin E. Marty of the University of Chicago Divinity School, tutor of us all, and Francis X. Murphy, C.S.S.R., that wily observer of the Roman Catholic Church, were of great help. I am beholden to Sister Radegunde Flaxman, S.H.J.C., for her close and detailed checking of the facts in chapter 8, and to Sister Josephine Koppel, O.C.D., for her invaluable assistance, both personal and professional, on Edith Stein. Thanks also to John Sullivan, O.C.D., editor of *Carmelite Studies*, for many favors. John Dunne, C.S.C., will recognize thematic debts to his thought, as would Frank O'Malley, my mentor at Notre Dame, were he still alive.

I owe a great debt of thanks to Joseph Whelan, S.J. of the Jesuit Curia in Rome—he knows why. Also to Father Thomas Nohilly of the Brooklyn diocese for his translation of the *positio* on Pope Pius IX which is the subject of chapter 9, and to the late Robert Findley, S.J., who translated several other documents from the Italian. I trust his untimely death has won him a surer knowledge of the saints than what the reader will find herein. My thanks also to Monsignor James McGrath of the Philadelphia archdiocese for his help and candid comments over two years, and to Sister Mary Juliana Haynes, President of the Sisters of the Blessed Sacrament for Indians and Colored People, for her willingness to break with tradition by supplying me with the costs of the beatification of their foundress, Mother Katharine Drexel.

Several librarians not only located books for me but winked when they were overdue. Special thanks to Jim O'Halloran at Maryknoll Seminary in Ossining, New York—your books are on the way; to Judith Hausler and her predecessor, Marilyn Souders, of the *Newsweek* library for service beyond the call of duty, and to Charles Farkas and his always obliging colleagues at the Public Library in Briarcliff Manor, New York. For listening and wondering about saints not their own, a word of gratitude to *Newsweek* colleagues Jack Kroll and David Gates, who know more about texts than most people called "reviewers." Thanks to Theresa Waldrop of *Newsweek*'s Bonn Bureau for tracking down certain people in West Germany with information on the "bombing miracle" described in chapter 6. And to my senior editor at *Newsweek* during these years, Aric Press, appreciation for recognizing inner turmoil when he saw it.

This book would not exist, of course, without the encouragement and guidance of Alice Mayhew, my editor at Simon and Schuster, who insisted that I do it, and of her associate, David Shipley, who applied the lash. Amanda Urban was all an author could ask of an agent.

Finally, to my wife, Betty, to whom this book is dedicated, yet another thousand apologies for many *fêtes* missed and absences endured. Who said patience is found only in saints?

Making
Saints

PREFACE

WHEN I FIRST went to Rome in the fall of 1988 to begin research and reporting for this book, my eye was on the process. My concern was with the way saints are "made," how that process had evolved over two millennia and what all this had to tell us about how sanctity is recognized, evaluated, and expressed. My first surprise was the discovery that the office of Promoter of the Faith—popularly known as "the Devil's Advocate"—had been abolished, and with it the centuries-old adversarial system in which canon lawyers representing the church systematically questioned the evidence put forward by lawyers representing the candidate for sainthood. Apparently the church had forgotten George Orwell's sage advice: "Saints should always be judged guilty till they are proven innocent." My second surprise was the realization of just how much the current pope, John Paul II, was using the streamlined saint-making process, which he authorized but did not initiate, to change the face of the church.

Since this book was first published in 1990, it has been gratifying to see how *Making Saints*, in its American and its seven foreign editions, has served as a reliable guide for hundreds of clergy, religious, and laity involved in promoting causes from around the world. That was not, however, my primary purpose or intent. I am also pleased that this book has served as the prime reference for countless journalists from numerous countries who have covered the many beatifications and canonizations that have occurred in the intervening years. My chief concern was to examine the saint as one of the primary figures of Western culture as well as the product of the Western world's oldest legal system. Other cultural figures—the artist, the thinker, the explorer, the ruler, and the warrior—all excite the imagination. But only in the saint do we encounter an "otherness" that ignites the sense of mystery. Miracles are a part of that mystery, and so they figure prominently in the making of saints. Indeed, it was just this point which moved Graham Greene, after reading *Making Saints* and just before his death, to write me a long letter recounting his own experiences of Padre Pio, whose story is told in these pages.

Yet, I should acknowledge that publication of the book also caused a considerable uproar within the Vatican's Congregation for the Causes of Saints. Some members of the Congregation were upset because I had dared to point out what I believe are fundamental weaknesses throughout the saint-making system as it exists today. Many of these weaknesses, as it happens, were first pointed out to me by consultants and other Vatican priests who work with the Congregation. My foremost concern remains the fact that, with the abolition of the Devil's Advocate and his staff, there now is no one charged with the responsibility to challenge the evidence brought forward by the candidate's postulator. Put another way, everyone involved in a canonization process now has a stake in its *positive* outcome. This, it seemed to me, leaves the Catholic faithful unprotected against the possibility that a powerful and influential group might manipulate this process, which the church (as I describe) had struggled for centuries to perfect, for the benefit of an unworthy candidate. Without the Devil's Advocate, who can prevent such an outcome? And without some means of making the process public, who would know?

As a case in point, I cited the questions that were then beginning to surface concerning the process on behalf of Josemaría Escrivá de Balaguer, the highly controversial Spanish priest who founded the conservative Catholic organization, Opus Dei (The Work of God), and whose cause had yet to be judged. (See pages 383–87.) Because of my questions, Cardinal Pietro Palazzini, the Prefect of the Congregation and a strong supporter of Opus Dei, presented a copy of *Making Saints*, as part of a formal complaint, to Pope John Paul II, Opus Dei's most important patron. I trust the Pope read the book and, I like to think, learned from it.

Since 1991, a few of the figures you will meet in this book have retired or been replaced—including Cardinal Palazzini himself. What hasn't changed, however, is the incredible zeal with which John Paul II has used the saint-making process to underline his vision for the church. Indeed, the one fact in the book which has been most often repeated in the media is that John Paul II has beatified and canonized more individuals than all of his twentieth-century predecessors combined. If anything, that trend has accelerated since this book first appeared. By the end of 1995, after little more than sixteen years as pope, he had presided over 208 beatifications and 38 canonizations involving some 875 individuals. By comparison, the next most active pope in this area, Pius XII, beatified 23 and canonized 33 individuals in a total of 56 ceremonies over nineteen years.

Every pope remakes the Catholic hierarchy by appointing cardinals and bishops who share his vision. (When the next papal conclave is held, a majority of the cardinal-electors—including, very possibly the new pope himself—will owe their red hats to John Paul II.) What John Paul II has also done, however, is virtually remake the calendar of saints as well. Indeed, his unprecedented determination to proclaim new saints from every corner of the globe is certain to be remembered as one of the most enduring legacies of his lengthy pontificate. And I say this in full recognition of the importance of his many encyclicals, his pivotal role in the collapse of Communist rule in Eastern Europe, and his formidable efforts, manifest in the last two years, to influence the international social policies of the United Nations.

In my Introduction, I observe that the Congregation for the Causes of Saints is not one of the power centers within the Vatican. That certainly was true under previous popes, but it can no longer be said of the current papacy. In the hands of John Paul II, the saint-making process has become a very powerful mechanism for advancing his message. Whatever else it is, religion is a symbol system. The power to decide who is and who is not worthy to be venerated as a saint is the power to define which symbols will convey to the church at large what it means to be a disciple of Christ. And no pope in the history of the church has made greater use of the church's saint-making mechanism to further his understanding of Christian discipleship.

For example:

On a cold, rainy Sunday in May 1995, the second of a three-day visit to the Czech Republic, Pope John Paul II canonized two saints in the eastern city of Olomouc. The press took note because Czech Protestants objected to the canonization of one of the Blesseds, Father Jan Sarkander, a Moravian parish priest who died in 1620 from wounds he suffered when he was tortured by Protestant forces during the post-Reformation wars of religion. To Czech Catholics Sarkander was a martyr for the faith. To Czech Protestants, he was a symbol of Catholic oppression under the Austrian Hapsburgs. In a public letter to the pope, Bishop Pavel Smetana of the Evangelical Church of the Czech Brethren, complained that Father Sarkander's canonization was an unwanted reminder of a Catholic program of forced conversions during the bloody struggles for religious and political hegemony in Central Europe. Rather than needlessly revive painful memories of the humiliations Protestants had suffered at the hands of Catholics, the bishop declared, the pope would do better to hold this obtrusive ceremony in Rome instead.

It was not the first time, nor would it be the last, that the making of a saint—a purely ecclesiastical act—was fraught with political significance. Nor was it the only time in his eighteen-year reign that John Paul II, the most political of modern popes, would use the symbolism of sanctity to transform a sticky political situation into a personal public-relations triumph. Speaking in Czech, the pope hailed the canonization of Sarkander as an honor *"for all those in this century, not only in Moravia and Bohemia but throughout all of Eastern Europe, who preferred the loss of property, marginalization, and death, rather than submit to oppression and violence."* (Italics his.) In short, he associated the martyrdom of a seventeenth-century priest with the suffering endured three hundred years later by Eastern Europeans under successive Nazi and Communist regimes. Martyrdom, he was saying, is a seamless red garment transcending time and tyranny, hardly a thing of the past.

The Polish pope then did something few of his predecessors had ever done. He apologized: "Today, I the Pope of the Church of Rome, in the name of all Catholics, ask *forgiveness* for the wrongs inflicted on non-Catholics during the turbulent history of these peoples; at the same time I *pledge* the Catholic Church's *forgiveness* for whatever harm her sons and daughters suffered." (Italics his.) By calling for healing he coopted his critics.

All this was news, of course. But what also caught my attention was a brief meditation at the close of the ceremony. In it, the pope linked the newly canonized with a long litany of Slav *sancti* and *beati* stretching across the centuries from the first apostles to the Slavs, Gorazd and his companions, through classic figures such as Wenceslaus, Adalbert and John Nepomucene, down to contemporary saints like Bishop John Neumann, a Bohemian emigrant who, in 1977, became the first—and still the only—male American saint. It was a roll call of the only royalty the church recognizes; by reciting their names, the Pope was reminding the assembled Moravians, Bohemians, Silesians, Czechs, and Poles who had crossed the border for the day that—despite wars, social conflicts, and shifting political boundaries and allegiances—"your ancient, historic lands are the homeland of saints." Holiness, he concluded, "is the only thing that matters in our life," and all are called to be saints.

Whatever else he may be—philosopher, geopolitician, leader of the world's largest body of Christians—John Paul II is an evangelist. And more than any other religious figure, he is preoccupied by the dawning of a new millennium in the year 2000. Time and again he has referred to the newly canonized as "Saints for the Third Millennium"—even when, as in the case of Father Sarkander, the saint has been dead for several centuries. As a poet and playwright, he understands the primordial power of stories; his many beatifications and canonizations are dramatic validation of this book's central argument: that *saints exist in and through their stories.*

Centuries before the canonization process achieved anything like its present-day bureaucratic form, there were martyrologies or lists of local saints who had died for the faith and whose names and stories were memorialized by the local churches. From these arose numerous calendars of saints. Not until the seventeenth century were these disparate local calendars harmonized into a universal calendar of saints for the entire Catholic church. Now, in a directive that has received virtually no attention outside the church, John Paul II has asked bishops around the world to contribute worthy names to a *new* martyrology for the church's third millennium, a list of the faithful men and women in the twentieth century who witnessed with their lives to the lordship of Jesus Christ. The list will be heavy with names—some well known, many not—from his native Eastern Europe, yes, and from the former Soviet Union, but also names of Catholics unsung outside China and other parts of Asia and of martyrs from Africa and Latin America who died for the faith in this century of almost unceasing war and religious persecution. What is unusual is that the list will include not only Roman Catholics but Orthodox, Anglican, and Protestant Christians as well. As the pope acknowledges, "Perhaps the most convincing form of ecumenism is *the ecumenism of the saints* and of the martyrs." It is by this list of martyrs for the faith, albeit honorific rather than official, that the pope wants the essential history of twentieth-century Christianity to be known. It is an act of corrective historiography, and who can say that he is wrong?

In this context, it is interesting to see what has happened to some of the recent causes, especially Americans, detailed in the following pages. The cause of Cardinal Terence Cooke of New York has been accepted by Rome, but officials are still collecting evidence of his heroic virtues and of his reputation for holiness. Every year, his successor, Cardinal John J. O'Connor of New York, hosts a lavish lunch or dinner to rally support for the cause that he himself initiated. On the other hand, O'Connor has done nothing to advance the cause of another New Yorker, Dorothy Day, co-founder of the Catholic Worker movement. At this writing, her cause remains where it was before: a fledgling effort supported by the Claretian Fathers of Chicago, where Day was born. Rome has accepted the cause of another American, Solanus Casey, a Capuchin friar who lived in New York, Detroit, and Milwaukee and was known in his lifetime for his extraordinary humility and (like another Capuchin friar, Padre Pio) for his ability to read the hearts of those who came to him to confess their sins or simply for his advice. If, as seems likely, his cause is successful, Casey would become the first native-born American male saint.

Of greater international interest is the case of Oscar Romero, the late Archbishop of San Salvador. Officially, he has moved no closer to beatification. At the end of 1994, his successor and friend Archbishop Arturo Rivera y Damas died. The new Archbishop, Fernando Saenz Lacalle, is a Spanish-born priest of Opus Dei but it is very doubtful that he could or would do anything to delay or block Romero's cause. What is certain is that Romero—easily the best-known martyr of the twentieth-century church—will be prominently mentioned in John Paul II's unofficial martyrology of the twentieth century.

Throughout this book, the discerning reader will see that causes I discuss were chosen primarily for the light each sheds on some facet of the complex saint-making process. In no instance did I use the unprecedented access I was given to the Congregation, its officials, and their *positiones*, as the candidates' official dossiers are called, to promote or retard the cause of any candidate under consideration. Among the documents I discuss is the *positio* on behalf of Pope Pius IX, to which the entirety of Chapter Ten is devoted. This document is still so secret and sensitive that to this day no Vatican official has ever publicly acknowledged its existence. The questions it raises about how a pope is to be judged worthy of sainthood are profound and far-reaching, especially since three recent popes, Pius XII, John XXIII, and Paul VI, are also candidates for canonization. Nowhere else, in short, will the reader find even a mention of this document, much less learn that John Paul II has thus far refused to beatify Pius IX, by far the most controversial pope since the Reformation.

In this context, it is noteworthy that the one *positio* that neither I nor even other members of the Congregation for the Causes of Saints were permitted to examine was the one prepared and held in secret by Opus Dei on behalf of its founder, Josemaría Escrivá de Balaguer. Since Opus Dei had regarded "The Father" as a saint even before he died and revered him accordingly, outsiders wondered what, if anything, there was to hide. This Preface would not be complete, therefore, without a brief account of the extraordinary public outcry that occurred, after the publication of this book, when Opus Dei succeeded in having their founder declared a "Blessed" of the church.

Escrivá, it should be said, was a mysterious and controversial figure long before his death on June 26, 1975. There were conflicting reports about his relationship with the Spanish dictator, General Francisco Franco, during and after the Spanish Civil War; about his own fiery and unpredictable personality; about his attitude toward the reforms of Vatican Council II and his relationships with several popes and other church figures. Opus Dei itself has been a source of considerable controversy, particularly because of what critics see as its excessive secrecy and its purported political and economic power in various countries, not to mention inside the Vatican itself. In light of all this, I was anxious to see how these issues would be addressed in the *positio*.

As it happened, Escrivá's cause was one of the first to be prepared and brought to judgment under the new reformed rules for making saints. His *positio*—6,000 pages drawn up in secret by an Opus Dei team—was the longest and, according to Father Flavio Capucci, the postulator for Opus Dei who prepared it, the most thorough ever written. Since the point of the reformed canonization process was to emphasize historical accuracy and the saint's importance as a model of holiness for contemporary Christians, I was particularly interested to learn how Capucci and his team satisfied these goals. There was, moreover, the intriguing fact that Escrivá was scheduled for beatification a mere seventeen years after his death. At that rate, he was on track to surpass St. Thérèse of Lisieux, whose canonization just twenty-eight years after her death remains a modern record. I was well aware, from my many months of interviews and research within the Congregation, that Cardinal Palazzini had given cause of Escrivá priority over other candidates. I was aware, too, that the officials of Opus Dei were counting on their founder's beatification and canonization to silence the many critics of "The Father" and to justify Opus Dei itself.

The first solid evidence that something was deeply wrong with Escrivá's cause surfaced in the first week of 1992. According to Opus

Dei, the *positio* supporting Escrivá's "heroic virtues" had been approved unanimously two years earlier by a panel of nine judges. But in the January 13 issue of *Newsweek*, I was able to report that two of the judges, Luigi DeMagistris and Justo Fernández Alonso, had in fact rendered sharp disapproval of the *positio*. Each had independently cast a "suspended" vote, demanding that certain questions be resolved before proceeding further. One of the dissenting judges, in fact, warned that the beatification of Escrivá could cause "grave public scandal" to the church. Normally, two dissenting votes (judges almost never cast a decisive "No" vote) are sufficient to halt a cause, at least until all objections can be removed. Why in this instance were the objections of these judges ignored? Further, *Newsweek* was able to break the official silence that up till then had surrounded the process. One of the Vatican's senior and most conservative prelates, Cardinal Silvio Oddi, no enemy of Opus Dei, told *Newsweek* that many bishops were "very displeased" by the rush to canonize Escrivá so soon after his death.

Reaction to the article was swift. Oddi was visited within the week by officials of Opus Dei. And shortly thereafter, a six-month investigation was inaugurated in which every member (thirty in all) of the Congregation for the Causes of Saints under the level of bishop was interrogated in a futile effort to find out who had leaked the information about the judges to me. Clearly, officials of both Opus Dei and the Congregation were upset at being found out.

In the months that followed, copies of the entire *positio* were leaked to the press, and I went to Rome to examine it first hand. In a press conference at Rome's Foreign Press Office, I was able to point to a number of facts that raised serious doubts about the objectivity, integrity, and fairness of the entire proceeding on behalf of Escrivá. Of these, two were key.

First, every cause must include testimony from witnesses who knew the candidate. Advocates for the cause are required to supply church tribunals with the names of witnesses who oppose as well as support the candidate. Testimony was given at two tribunals, one in Rome and the other in Madrid. The documents showed that the names of eleven critics were submitted to tribunal judges. Of these, only one—Spanish sociologist Alberto Moncada, a former member of Opus Dei—was allowed to testify. His remarks, a scant two pages out of a total of 2,000, were introduced in the final *positio* by a preface denying the validity of his statements.

Moreover, I was able to interview six other men and women who had lived and/or worked closely with Escrivá. The examples they gave of vanity, venality, temper tantrums, harshness toward subordinates, and criticism of popes and other churchmen were hardly the characteristics one expects to find in a Christian saint. But their testimony was not allowed to be heard. At least two of them were vilified in the *positio* by name, yet neither of them was permitted to defend their reputations. On the other hand, fully 40 percent of the 2,000 pages of testimony came from just two witnesses: Alvaro del Portillo, Escrivá's successor, and Javier Echevarria Rodriguez, who succeeded del Portillo and is the head of Opus Dei today. They were, needless to say, the two people in the world least likely to find fault with "The Father" and most likely to benefit from his beatification and canonization.

Secondly, the narrative of Escrivá's life displayed a man so favored by God that he seemed hardly human. As I argue in this book, the great weakness of *positiones* as a literary genre is their tendency to idealize candidates for canonization. Escrivá's *positio* is a classic of the kind: reading it, one would never guess that the volatile and often devious Escrivá had ever sinned, harmed others, or had any flaws of character. Only once, the authors would have us believe, did Escrivá ever lose his temper! As Eric Hoffer once observed, perhaps with the example of St. Augustine in mind, "Many of the insights of the saint stem from his experience as a sinner." But then Escrivá often claimed that his insights came directly from God.

Equally important, despite the *positio*'s exaggerated length of 6,000 pages (by comparison, the *positio* on behalf Cardinal John Henry Newman, who lived much longer and wrote much more—and infinitely better—than Escrivá, ran to only 1,000 pages), it fails to account for numerous key episodes in Escrivá's life, notably his relationship with General Franco and his dictatorship. At least nine members of Opus Dei are known to have served in Franco's cabinet. But in his haste to see Escrivá canonized, the postulator of Opus Dei was unable to document this and other crucial aspects of Escrivá's public life because the relevant ecclesiastical and state records are in archives that are still closed to researchers.

In sum, there was considerable evidence that Escrivá's life had not been thoroughly researched and fairly presented, that the tribunal judges had prevented contrary witnesses from being heard, and that officials of the Congregation had bowed to pressure from Opus Dei to speed the process through. But none of this mattered in the end. Since John Paul II had accepted the results of the questionable process, officials of Opus Dei insisted that any criticism of it was criticism of the pope himself. Thus, on May 17, 1992, Josemaría Escrivá de Balaguer was declared "Blessed" by John Paul II in a ceremony second in size and splendor only to the election of a pope. Some 200,000 Opus Dei members and friends marched like an invading army to St. Peter's Square to witness the event. For four days the festival continued, with Escrivá's body on daily display. In all, seventeen cardinals—including the papal Secretary of State and the chief administrators of the Roman Curia—celebrated masses in a dozen different languages at churches throughout the city. For Opus Dei, it was convincing proof, if proof were needed, of its ascendant power and influence on the papacy of John Paul II.

But for all the pomp and ceremony, Escrivá entered the lists of the Blesseds with a huge asterisk after his name. The legitimacy of the process by which he was judged worthy of beatification remains in permanent doubt. "The Father" may indeed be a saint in the eyes of God—and that, after all, is the only thing that really matters—but it is likely that he will be venerated only by members of Opus Dei and its friends. His reputation for holiness, it now appears, will forever be tainted by the suspicion that for his sake the saint-making process was subverted. Moreover, by failing to insure a thorough and impartial process, the Congregation has sullied its own hard-won reputation for integrity, impartiality, and independence from outside influence. With Opus Dei, the Congregation now faces the worst nightmare imaginable to Rome's saint-makers: that further information now buried in official archives—and in the memories of many who knew him well—will, like Oscar Wilde's picture of Dorian Gray, eventually give the lie to the image of holiness they themselves created.

While *Making Saints* focuses on the canonization process within the Church of Rome, it does so in the wider interest of enquiring into the nature of holiness itself. Each time a new saint is officially recognized by the church, an answer is given to the perennial question, "What is a saint?" While this book records my own journey of inquiry into the nature of sanctity, it also joins the work of numerous scholars in a variety of disciplines for whom holiness, spirituality, and sanctity have become matters of considerable interest, even urgency. The figure of the saint has become particularly fruitful for interdisciplinary studies and comparative religion. Saints are found in all the great world traditions, and, though sanctity means different things in each tradition, the quest for holiness (or its equivalent) is universal. In this respect, I have been especially pleased to see that *Making Saints* has proved useful for courses taught at several universities.

But saints are primarily figures of popular religion. This new edition of *Making Saints* arrives at a moment in American culture when popular interest is shifting from the ethereal (and often banal) figure of the angel to the more realistic figure of the saint. Since this book was first published, numerous books on saints have appeared in the United States. The young, especially, are searching for models of human behavior worthy of emulation. Among Protestants, in particular, there is a welcome reconsideration of the ancient Christian doctrine of the *communio sanctorum*, the communion of saints. That doctrine speaks to the disconnection that many Americans feel—from each other, from the past, from the earth, from themselves. The saints in the Catholic tradition cannot be understood apart from the experience of radical communion: an experience of the truth that "in God we are all connected, giving and receiving unexpected and undeserved acts of grace."

As the reader will soon discover, this is above all a book of stories. It is through the hearing and telling of stories that we come to know who we are. The same is true of saints: through their stories they are made present to us. Therefore, how those stories are told matters greatly if we are to recognize "the harmony of holiness." Indeed, it seems to me that the time has come to provide a new definition of what we mean by the word "saint" in the Christian tradition. A saint is always someone through whom we catch a glimpse of what God is like—and of what we are called to be. Only God "makes" saints, of course. The church merely identifies from time to time a few of these for emulation. The church then tells the story. But the author is the Source of the grace by which saints live. And there we have it: A saint is someone whose story God tells.

INTRODUCTION

Is MOTHER TERESA of Calcutta a saint?

To millions of people she is a "living saint" for her unselfish service to the diseased, the dying, the wretched, the homeless, the outcast. The order of religious women she founded in 1949, the Missionaries of Charity, is now a worldwide network of three thousand members, with shelters, clinics, and convents in India, Africa, Asia, North and South America, Western and Eastern Europe—eighty-seven countries in all. If this diminutive Albanian nun, winner of the Nobel Prize for Peace in 1979, were to die tomorrow—as she almost did in 1989—the pope and the whole world, one imagines, would mourn her passing.

Yet she would not be a saint—at least not officially in the eyes of her own church. Her life would have to be investigated by the proper church authorities. Her writings and conduct would be scrutinized. Witnesses would be summoned to testify to her "heroic" virtue. Miracles wrought posthumously through her intercession would have to be proved. Only then would the pope officially declare her a saint.

Roman Catholics believe in saints. They pray to them, they honor them, they treasure their relics, they name their children and their churches after them. But Catholics are not alone in their veneration of saintly figures. Buddhists venerate their *arahants*, their *bodhisattvas*, and (among Tibetans) their *lamas*. Hindus revere a bewildering range of divinely human and humanly divine figures, including their personal *gurus* or spiritual teachers. Muslims have their *awliyā'Allāh* (close friends of God) and their revered Sufi masters. Even in Judaism, whose rabbinic leaders have never encouraged veneration of human beings, alive or dead, one finds popular devotion to figures such as Abraham and Moses, assorted martyrs, beloved rabbis, and other *tsaddikim*, ("just men").

Among other Christian churches, the Russian Orthodox retains a vigorous devotion to the saints, especially the early church fathers and martyrs. On rare occasions, new names (usually monks or bishops) are grafted onto their traditional lists of saints. Since the Reformation, the cult of the saints has largely disappeared from Protestant Christianity, but even among conservative Evangelicals special reverence is attached to the prophets of the Old Testament and the apostles of the New. Something like the cult continues among Anglicans and Lutherans, who maintain feast days and calendars of saints. But while the Anglicans have no mechanism for recognizing new saints, the Lutherans from time to time do informally recommend new names (Dag Hammarskjöld, Dietrich Bonhoeffer, and Pope John XXIII are recent additions) for thanksgiving and remembrance by the faithful.

The saint, then, is a familiar figure in all world religions. But only the Roman Catholic Church has a formal, continuous, and highly rationalized process for "making" saints. And only in the Church of Rome does one find a group of professionals whose job is to investigate lives—and validate the required miracles—for sainthood. In fact, during the reign of John Paul II, the church has beatified (a penultimate declaration of blessedness allowing limited public cult) and canonized more people than under any other pope.

To the outside world, canonization is rather like the Nobel Prize: no one really knows why one candidate is chosen over another or who—apart from the pope—does the selecting. Even among Roman Catholics, the process of making saints seems as long and mysterious as the gestation of a pearl or the formation of a star. Within the Vatican itself, the handful of men most intimately involved with individual causes are neither well known nor rewarded with hierarchical rank. Among the nine congregations or ministries of the Holy See, the Congregation for the Causes of Saints will not be found on anyone's list of Vatican power centers. Its officials do not govern the church, set foreign policy, determine doctrinal orthodoxy, select bishops, or regulate clergy. Yet their work is the only activity which, in their view at least, requires the regular exercise of the papacy's unique and most awesome power: the exercise of papal infallibility.

Strictly speaking, of course, the church does not "make saints." God alone provides the grace whereby a Peter or a Paul, a Francis or an Ignatius, a Catherine, a Clare, or a Teresa attains that level of Christian perfection which, in Catholic reckoning, constitutes sainthood. And only God knows how many saints there are or have been. What the church *does* claim is the divinely guided ability to discern from time to time that this or that person is among the elect. The purpose in identifying these holy men and women is to set them before the faithful for their emulation. In this sense, the church does indeed "make saints."

The making of saints, therefore, is an inherently *ecclesial* process. It is done by others for others. In the first instance, the "others" are not bishops or professional Vatican investigators, but anyone at all who, through prayers, the use of relics, petitions for "divine favors," and similar devotions, contributes to a candidate's reputation for holiness. Indeed, by tradition and church law, every cause must originate among "the people"; in this sense, the making of saints can be regarded as the most democratic process in the church, a process by which God Himself makes known through others the identity of authentic saints. At least that is the view from Rome. In the second instance, the "others" are, in the widest sense, the current and future generations of believers. It is for their edification and, it is hoped, emulation that the church makes saints.

The saints themselves, of course, have no need of veneration. In the metaphor of St. Paul, they have already run the race and won their laurels. Canonization, in other words, is strictly a posthumous exercise. Or, to turn the matter round, a "living saint" is, canonically speaking, a contradiction in terms.

To "canonize" means to declare that a person is worthy of universal public cult. Canonization takes place through a solemn papal declaration that a person is, for certain, with God. Because of that certainty, the faithful can, with confidence, pray to the saint to intercede with God on their behalf. The person's name is inscribed in the church's list of saints and he or she is "raised to the altars"—that is, assigned a feast day for liturgical veneration by the entire church.

But popes have been canonizing saints for only the last thousand years. Since 1234, when the right to canonize was officially reserved to the papacy alone, there have been fewer than 300 canonizations. There are, however, some ten thousand Christian saints whose cults have been identified by church historians, and doubtless there are thousands more whose names are lost to history. Papal canonization, therefore, is, from the historical viewpoint, only one way that Christians have found to make saints. What's more, it may not be—even now and even for Roman Catholics—the most important.

What I'm suggesting is that formal canonization is part of a much wider, older, and culturally more complex process of "making saints." To make a saint, or to commune with the saints already made, one must first know their stories. Indeed, it is hardly an exaggeration to say that the saints *are* their stories. On this view, making saints is a process whereby a life is transformed into a text. With some early Christian saints like Christopher, whose historical existence is doubtful, the text takes the form of legend, orally transmitted. In the case of the great and prolific Augustine of Hippo, on the other hand, we have in addition to oral tradition and historical documents his own *Confessions*, an autobiographical text to which millions of Christians over the last sixteen centuries have looked for an understanding of what it means to become a saint. Moreover there are many reliable biographies in which the stories of the classic and the more recent saints have been rescued from the exaggerations of folk stories and hagiolatry.

The point is that whether through legends or folk stories, through their own writings or writings about them (including the Bible), the lives of the saints constitute an important—some theologians would say the most important—medium for transmitting the meaning of the Christian faith. Even among evangelical Protestants, for whom the cult of the saints is anathema, it is the Acts of the Apostles, and especially of Paul, which provide the core models of Christian behavior, experience, and identity. Theologians may produce theology, churches may propound doctrines and dogmas, but it is only the saint who speaks to both the common believer and the tutored elites. In their stories, history and faith, biography and ideas, time and the transcendent mix and meld.

For as long as Christianity has existed, people have told and retold the stories of saints. They have celebrated them in icons, paintings, and statues. It was the cult of the saints which transformed cemeteries into shrines, shrines into cities, and prompted that robust form of social adventure and cohesion, the pilgrimage. For better or worse, it was, as we shall see, the cult of the saints which extended the boundaries of Christianity and, even after the Reformation, continued to mediate faith and morality in Catholic countries. What happens, though, when the saint no longer registers as a cultural ideal? What happens when the stories of saints are no longer remembered, no longer told? What happens when the miracles wrought by or through saints are no longer believed? What happens when the inherited patterns of holiness by which saints are recognized and revered no longer compel the vast majority of believers? In 1988 alone, for instance, Pope John Paul II canonized 122 men and women and beatified another 22. How many Roman Catholics knew their names or cared? And outside the church, did it matter? What happens when, as one American Catholic theologian ruefully puts it, "Formal canonization procedures no longer give us the saints we need"?

Christianity is unthinkable without sinners, unlivable without saints. As recently as Vatican Council II, the church declared that "sanctity is for everyone," not just a chosen few. Yet year after year, a few *are* chosen from among the anonymous many to be held up for invocation, veneration, and imitation. Who does this, how and why—this is the subject of what follows. My inquiries took me to Rome, of course, but also to Central America, several countries of Northern Europe, and throughout the United States—to places where specific saints were made or are in the making. My journeys convinced me that the figure of the saint, though faded, is not disappearing. It is changing. So too is the process by which saints are made. That process ends in Rome but it does not begin there. It can, as I discovered, begin anywhere.

Feast of St. Lawrence, August 10, 1990

CHAPTER ONE

THE
LOCAL POLITICS
OF SAINTHOOD

CARDINAL COOKE: THE BROTHERHOOD
OF THE CHANCERY

ON THE FEAST of St. Patrick, 1984, Bishop Theodore McCarrick of Metuchen, New Jersey, wrote a letter to his colleague, John J. O'Connor, who was to be installed two days later as archbishop of New York. In his letter, McCarrick recalled that both of them had had the privilege of working closely with O'Connor's predecessor, Cardinal Terence Cooke, who had died just five months earlier. "It is, therefore, with some confidence that I make this request," McCarrick wrote, ". . . that you begin in the Archdiocese of New York a process leading, if it is God's will, to the beatification and canonization of Terence James Cooke."

McCarrick's confidence was well grounded. He had already discussed the matter with a half-dozen of O'Connor's colleagues in the New York Archdiocese, all of whom had served either Cooke or his predecessor, Cardinal Francis Spellman, as personal secretaries, auxiliary bishops, or ranking monsignori. The group's collective judgment was sufficient to convince O'Connor to set the necessary mechanisms in motion.

What began then was a concerted effort to provide New Yorkers with their first canonized saint. Since the cardinal's life would have to

be investigated, the Cardinal Cooke Archives were created at the archdiocesan seminary for the purpose of cataloging his papers and storing
his personal effects. Since the cause would also have to be publicized
and funded, the Cardinal Cooke Guild was established in an office at
the archdiocese's midtown chancery building. One of the guild's most
important functions would be to promote prayer to Cooke in the hope
that some of those prayers would be answered with "divine favors"
and the cardinal credited with the sine qua non of a canonizable saint:
the power of intercession with God. Finally, the entire project was put
in the hands of Cooke's former confessor, Capuchin friar Benedict
Groeschel, who was assigned to write Cooke's spiritual biography and
dispatched to Rome for further instructions. On October 9, the first
anniversary of Cooke's death, O'Connor officially launched his predecessor toward sainthood at a memorial Mass in St. Patrick's Cathedral.

It was an extravagant gesture, even for the flamboyant O'Connor.
Never before had an American bishop been so bold as to propose his
immediate predecessor for sainthood. But if O'Connor had counted on
enthusiasm from Rome, he couldn't have been more mistaken. For
one thing, the church's calendar of saints is already top-heavy with
clerics; what the church needs, Roman officials had been saying for
years, is more lay saints. For another, Vatican officials were surprised
to hear that someone thought the late cardinal archbishop of New
York was worthy of canonization. Cooke's reputation for holiness, it
seems, had not crossed the Atlantic. At the Congregation for the
Causes of Saints, O'Connor's emissary, Father Benedict, was given a
lesson in Roman reticence.

"What makes you think your cardinal is a saint?" asked Monsignor
Fabijan Veraja, the imperious Croatian who is subsecretary of the
congregation.

"I think he might be, Monsignor," the friar from New York carefully replied.

"Good," said Veraja. "Because if you don't think he's a saint, you
have no reason to be here. But if you're convinced he's a saint, you've
taken away my job."

If that weren't caution enough, Veraja warned Benedict of just how
treacherous the spiritual waters were that he was wading into. "Let
me remind you," he said ominously, "that the Servants of God experience much misunderstanding and detraction in their pursuit of holiness. Those who undertake to promote the causes of the Servants of
God must expect the same."

What really irritated officials of the congregation was the precipitous manner in which O'Connor and his friends had initiated Cooke's cause. In his haste to get the cause moving, O'Connor had violated both the letter and the spirit of canon law, which stipulates that a cause cannot officially be launched until the candidate for sainthood has been dead for at least five years. The rule is not a frivolous one. It is based on ancient tradition which holds that a cause for canonization must arise spontaneously among the faithful of the local church, and continue for decades to elicit their prayers and other demonstrations of devotion. It is also based on centuries of experience, as summarized by Veraja himself: "A cause of canonization is never a matter of urgency . . . He [the local bishop] should not let himself be seduced by easy enthusiasm, sometimes perhaps not so disinterested, nor should he yield to the pressures of 'public opinion'—which is quite a different thing from a true reputation for sanctity—especially when behind it all are the powers of the media."

In other words, the first duty of the local bishop—in this case, O'Connor—is to let the reputation for holiness ripen of its own accord. If it persists for five or ten years, then he is permitted to organize an official investigation into the candidate's life and works in order to determine whether the reputation is justified. By seizing the initiative himself—and so shortly after the cardinal's death—O'Connor had in fact jeopardized Cooke's cause: how was Rome to tell whether Cooke's reputation for holiness had arisen spontaneously from the people, or through the vigorous promotional and publicity efforts that O'Connor, McCarrick, and the others had set in motion?

Father Benedict returned from Rome thoroughly chastened, only to discover that word of the cause had produced resistance on the home front as well. Although the Cardinal Cooke Guild soon amassed an impressive mailing list of ten thousand supporters, not everyone in New York who knew—even loved—the cardinal was prepared to see him made a saint. Cooke's only surviving sibling, his sister Katherine, as well as several old friends of the late cardinal balked at providing testimony for his spiritual biography. To them, his death was still too fresh, their grief too resonant, to imagine him suddenly transposed into the iconic company of the saints whose marble statues and stained-glass images garnish St. Patrick's Cathedral.

More important, many priests of the archdiocese were simply not convinced of Cooke's holiness and were correspondingly skeptical of O'Connor's motives. As the more critical of these clergy saw it, O'Connor's initiative was another example of the cronyism which, they felt, had long characterized the way affairs are administered in the New York Archdiocese. In their view, the cause was a presumptuous campaign by a few close friends and protégés of Spellman and Cooke, launched without any prior soundings among the clergy, and aimed, not a few of the critics felt, at ultimately winning the church's posthumous blessing on the entire era in New York church politics. That era began with the installation of Spellman in 1939 and ended with the death of Cooke forty-four years later. No one, of course, argued this to O'Connor's face. But they did not spare Father Benedict—thus proving, in the bearded friar's mind, the truth of Monsignor Veraja's orotund forebodings.

But the biggest obstacle in the path of Cooke's canonization was Cooke himself. There could be no hope at all for the cause unless his supporters could demonstrate to Rome (a) that the cardinal had exercised the Christian virtues (especially faith, hope, and charity) to a heroic degree, and (b) that proclaiming him a saint would be an act of great importance for the entire church. It was up to Father Benedict to write a spiritual biography of Cooke which, much like the campaign biographies produced for presidential candidates, would evidence the cardinal's worthiness on both counts.

In assessing Cooke's life, Father Benedict could look to one precedent of sorts: Bishop John Nepomucene Neumann of Philadelphia, at that time the last American citizen to be canonized (1977).* At his death in 1860, Neumann was as unlikely a candidate for sainthood as Cooke was at his death in 1983. The diminutive (he was only five feet, two inches tall) Bohemian immigrant was considered an inept administrator and might never have been put up for canonization (the Philadelphia hierarchy thought Neumann's predecessor, a scholarly Irish churchman named Francis Patrick Kenrick, a more promising candidate) had he not also been a member of the Redemptorist Fathers, the religious order that eventually—and after much prodding—pushed his cause. Like Neumann, Cooke was not regarded as a strong churchman. He was a pious, self-effacing prelate, "the perfect number two man," according to one archdiocesan historian, Monsignor Florence Cohalan. Trained as a social worker and transformed into an accountant, Cooke progressed from personal secretary to Spellman to vicar-general of the archdiocese and auxiliary bishop. In addition to his formal duties, Cooke looked after Spellman's personal needs, showing him a kindness that the autocratic cardinal was not accustomed to

---

* The most recent Sister Rose-Philippine Duchesne, canonized July 3, 1988.

receiving. When Spellman died in 1968, Cooke was his surprise choice as successor. But Cooke never exerted the extraordinary national and international leadership that Spellman exercised. On the contrary, he seemed most comfortable entertaining old folks and dropping in on the sick.

But Cooke did one thing well: he died with considerable courage and grace. Three months before his death, the cardinal's office revealed that for the previous ten years he had been secretly receiving blood transfusions and chemotherapy for leukemia. Not even intimates like O'Connor knew of his painful condition. The entire city took notice as the cardinal calmly accepted his fate, citing the words of his episcopal motto, "Thy will be done." In a moving final letter, read on Sunday, October 9, three days after his death, Cooke reminded the Catholics of New York that "the 'gift of life,' God's special gift, is no less beautiful when it is accompanied by illness or weakness, hunger or poverty, mental or physical handicaps, loneliness or old age. Indeed, at these times, human life gains extra splendor as it requires special care, concern, and reverence. It is in and through the weakness of human vessels that the Lord continues to reveal the power of His love." In short, it was Cooke's affecting death that convinced his closest friends and protégés that all these years perhaps they had been living with a saint.

In preparing the cardinal's spiritual biography, Father Benedict decided to begin with Cooke's exemplary death, then show how that death was the fruition of a lifelong process of spiritual growth. It was not an unorthodox approach. It was, in fact, rather like the way the life of Jesus had been structured by the authors of the Four Gospels: from death backward to birth. The difference, among others, was that there were few stories about Cooke with which to weave a compelling narrative.

The job of documenting Cooke's life fell to the Reverend Terry Webber, a Lutheran pastor who volunteered to help Benedict and was soon appointed Cooke's archivist. As a Lutheran, and as the one person involved in the cause who hadn't known the late cardinal, Webber was well suited to function as disinterested collaborator. Even some of the officials in Rome were intrigued by the fact that a non-Catholic cleric was eager to help the project.

When I first met Webber, he was a year into his work. He was installed in the Cooke Archives at the seminary where, to simplify matters, he was called "Father" like all the other clerics. Webber showed me a room full of Cooke memorabilia: a bed, chest of drawers, and desk from his summer home; the cardinal's violin; stacks of underwear with T. J. Cooke stamped military-fashion on them; old photographs; an honorary key to the city; a pen from President Lyndon Johnson. A closet yielded an assortment of vestments and cassocks, including chamois-lined skullcaps designed especially for balding prelates. "If he is a saint, all his personal belongings will be relics," Webber observed without affect. "There'll be some old nuns who will cut his clothes into shreds and send them out as relics."

A second storage room, formerly a seminarian's bedroom, was shelved to the ceiling with documents, including fifty-one volumes of newspaper and magazine clippings devoted to Cooke. Part of his responsibility, Webber explained, was to provide a chronology of Cooke's life in terms of the major national and international events that occurred while he was archbishop of New York. The purpose of this exercise is to locate Cooke's life against the horizon of his times. For example, the day he was installed as archbishop, Martin Luther King, Jr., was assassinated, and the week he died, South Korean Jet 007 was mysteriously shot down over the Soviet Union. In between, the civil rights movement crested and declined; the United States lost its first war, in Vietnam; Richard Nixon replaced Johnson in the White House. There were Watergate and Jimmy Carter and the Reagan revolution. Throughout it all, Cooke sent and received letters to the White House, but there were no revelations in the correspondence, no evidence that he had exercised a significant influence, spiritually or politically, on any of the four presidents. Of the four, Nixon was the president who wrote Cooke most often, especially during election campaigns, but their correspondence ceased the day Nixon resigned the presidency. Cooke watched the resignation on television, then ordered all Nixon photos and memorabilia removed from his rectory.

As for his private and spiritual life, the archives had yet to yield anything fresh or arresting—or negative. With one eye Webber examined Cooke's correspondence to see if it revealed anything that could be considered out of the character expected of a saint; for example, whether he was unduly critical or overbearing with subordinates. With the other eye, Webber looked for "quotable quotes" that Benedict could lace into the cardinal's spiritual biography. "We are looking for things that are outstanding. But," he conceded, "they're not that voluminous. Many of them are pious platitudes, things we all say if you are in the business of the church. Benedict says to look for something prophetic, that would be to his credit as a saint. My big job is persistence, to keep looking."

"Do you think Cardinal Cooke was a saint?" I asked.

"Fortunately, it's not my job to make that judgment."

"Of course."

"But I do think public relations has something to do with it. I mean, you may have a very holy person somewhere, say in Des Moines, but he is in the wrong place at the wrong time. Whereas, you can have an ordinary person, like Cardinal Cooke, in the right place—that is, New York City—at the right time."

"Meaning?"

"Cooke appeared to be a man who was genuinely concerned. When he became a cardinal, that was his license to be concerned about the needs of the world, not just of New York. It was not unusual for him to travel to an area and give the bishop a check for ten thousand dollars. The bishop of Honolulu, whom I interviewed recently, told me that Cooke never came by without giving him a monetary gift. So I think he was very socially aware."

Webber paused, looked up at the ceiling, then back at me. His manner was placid, matter-of-fact. "Let's talk frankly," he said. "Cooke was able to do a lot of good from a monetary viewpoint, helping other people around the world. He was only able to do that because he had the treasury of the archdiocese to back him up. He had this huge amount of money which he could dispense and he did that. Of course the money came from the grass roots."

"Is that reason enough to make him a saint?"

"I suppose the theology of the matter is that if in His providence God wants to raise this person up, then that is what He wants. But we can't say, 'This is what God wants.' All we can do is dig and scrape and leave it up to Him."

If anyone in New York can transform Cooke's life into the narrative of a saint, that man is Father Benedict. He has studied the classic lives of the saints, has written several popular books on spiritual development, and knows well from years of counseling priests the sort of sins to which the church's celibate clergy are prone: boredom, selfishness, laziness, and, among hierarchs, the exercise of power for its own sake. As Cooke's personal confessor, he also insists that he knows the cardinal's flaws better than anyone else. In my conversations with Benedict I was especially interested in hearing about those flaws because, as the friar had been instructed, anyone who promotes a cause must provide Rome with a balanced assessment of the candidate's character and life. But in Benedict's telling, even Cooke's flaws sounded suspiciously like virtues.

"Terry's greatest flaw is that he had no stomach for controversy. He didn't like to hurt anyone. The hardest thing he ever did was refuse to meet the grand marshal of the St. Patrick's Day Parade. [The incident occurred in 1983, when the grand marshal was Michael Flannery, a prominent supporter of the Irish Republican Army.] Cooke met Flannery the day before the parade and apologized because he couldn't greet him. He was like that since the day he was ordained."

I asked Benedict for other flaws, but he had already exhausted his store of examples. Instead, he recalled his conversation with Monsignor Veraja in Rome. "He asked me if I thought Cooke was a saint and I said I thought he might be. If he were to ask me now, I would say he *is* a saint."

I ventured that others might demur on the grounds that Cooke never did anything extraordinary that might merit his being elevated above the rest of humankind as an object of imitation, much less veneration. Benedict half closed his darting blue eyes, as if wearied by the obviousness of what he was about to say. I had known him for more than twenty years and had learned to recognize his pedagogical pauses.

"Religion is supposed to be about holiness, damn it, and we forget that. This is a story about a man who became a holy man. No, he was not a great church statesman. He was not a great prelate. He didn't think of himself that way. But he was heroic. You show me another man who worked eighteen hours a day, seven days a week, with leukemia. He went far beyond the call of duty to be kind. He'd have a blood transfusion in the morning and stay to have his picture taken with an old woman. He went to his nieces' and nephews' graduations from grade school and high school. That's very charitable. *I* couldn't do that."

As I listened, I realized that Benedict was describing a world I really did not know, a clerical world in which the ordinary courtesies shown family and friends become acts of heroic virtue. I began to understand. If Cooke's close friends and protégés saw something holy in him that others had not noticed, perhaps the reason was that Cooke's ability to be courteous and thoughtful, despite his elevated ecclesiastical rank, was indeed a novelty among the clerics whose careers propel them into the church's higher circles. But surely, I pressed Benedict, there was more than this to recommend the cardinal for canonization.

There was. And his spiritual biographer was quite clear about what he regards as the importance of Cooke's cause for the church: "Cooke remained loyal and dedicated to the church in very difficult times. He is representative of a traditional Catholicism that is not going to go under. I think there will be opposition to his cause. Many clerics and hierarchs will think of him as too traditional, and that is why I am supporting the cause. He was a Catholic when a lot of other people weren't. He didn't lead progressive movements. He tried to keep the church on course at a time when huge waves broke over it."

Benedict paused again. He had one more arrow in his quiver. "The miracles," he said. "Every day we get reports from people, some of them from as far away as the Middle West, telling us of the cures and favors they've received after praying to Cardinal Cooke. Like the cause of St. Thérèse of Lisieux, this cause is going to go through on its miracles."

On October 6, 1988, Cardinal O'Connor was canonically free to open a formal process for Cardinal Cooke. But on informal advice from Rome, he elected to wait, lest the cause be jeopardized further by signs of undue haste. Nonetheless, as he told Father Benedict, of all the things he had done as archbishop of New York, proposing Cooke for canonization was the one move he was most certain of.

DOROTHY DAY: THE POLITICS OF REFUSAL

As it happened, the one New Yorker whom Cardinal Cooke himself thought worthy of canonization was Dorothy Day, cofounder of The Catholic Workers and, for half a century, one of the most compelling personalities in American Catholicism. A convert, a pacifist, in some sense even an anarchist, Dorothy Day was one of those rare Catholics anywhere whose practical holiness attracted people outside as well as inside the church.

The arguments in favor of making Dorothy Day a saint are formidable. Chief among these is the example she made of her life, which hardly requires a hagiographer's gilding. A writer, political activist, and socialist, Dorothy Day was a familiar, passionate, and quite beautiful figure among the Greenwich Village writers and radicals of the late twenties and early thirties. Her circle of intimates included playwright Eugene O'Neill, literary critic Malcolm Cowley and his wife Peggy, and Communist journalist Mike Gold, editor of the leftist monthly *The Masses*. Her conversion at the age of thirty cost her not only a network of friends ("I was lonely, deadly lonely," she wrote later of her first year as a convert) but also the love and companionship of her common-law husband, Forster Batterham, whose bed she shared near the beach on Staten Island:

It was killing me to think of leaving him . . . getting into bed, cold with the chill of the November air, he held me close to him in silence. I loved him in every way, as a wife, as a mother even I loved him for all he knew and pitied him for all he didn't know. I loved him for all the odds and ends I had to fish out of his sweater pockets and for the sand and shells he brought in with his fishing. I loved his lean cold body as he got into bed smelling of the sea, and I loved his integrity and his stubborn pride.

Conversely, Day felt a deep ambivalence toward the church she was entering. "The scandal of businesslike priests, of collective wealth, the lack of a sense of responsibility toward the poor, the worker, the Negro, the Mexican, the Filipino" distressed her. But she felt a consuming love for Christ and accepted the church for that reason:

> I loved the Church for Christ made visible. Not for itself, because it was so often scandal to me. Romano Guardini said the Church is the Cross on which Christ was crucified; one could not separate Christ from His Cross, and one must live in a state of permanent dissatisfaction with the Church.

Dorothy's new life as a Catholic took form after she met a French Catholic, Peter Maurin, whose ideas about how to build a new society she made her own. Out of their collaboration came a newspaper, the *Catholic Worker*, a network of Houses of Hospitality for the poor, and the Catholic Worker movement which continues today. As Day framed it, the principle behind the Worker movement was a simple one: Christ's Sermon on the Mount is not an ideal to honor in the abstract but the way Christians are called to live. One key was direct service to the needy. Thus, the Workers' Houses of Hospitality provided food, clothing, and shelter to anyone, no matter how crazed or belligerent. Everyone in need was Christ asking for help. A second key was pacifism: Dorothy Day not only opposed American involvement in World War II, but also mandatory air-raid drills in the fifties as well as the "conflict" in Korea and the United States' undeclared war in Vietnam. She also championed workers' movements and the rights of labor.

In sum, Dorothy Day did for her era what St. Francis of Assisi did for his: recall a complacent Christianity to its radical roots. She personally embraced the monastic vows of poverty and chastity and, by all accounts, lived them with a freedom and commitment seldom matched by members of established religious orders. Spiritually, she subsisted on prayer, the Mass, and daily reading of the Bible, which she handled almost as if it were a talisman. The point of the Catholic Workers, she had insisted more than once, was not to become "effective humanitarians" but to imitate Christ. Although her Catholicism was scrupulously orthodox, Day's circle of service and prayer functioned independently of church hierarchies and their institutional priorities. At her death in 1980, she was hailed—if a bit exuberantly—as "the most significant, interesting and influential person in the history of American Catholicism."

In the course of that history, only three Americans—two nuns, Frances Cabrini and Elizabeth Bayley Seton, and Bishop Neumann—had been canonized saints. Thus, when Archbishop O'Connor announced his intention to seek the canonization of Cardinal Cooke, many New York Catholics demanded to know why he had chosen an undistinguished prince of the church over the internationally reverenced matriarch of the Catholic Workers. If the primary purpose of canonization is to provide the faithful with compelling contemporary models of heroic Christian virtue—so the argument ran—what better choice than an independent laywoman like Dorothy Day?

Several nuns, among others, put that question directly to O'Connor in 1984 as he made his introductory round of pastoral visitations to the clergy and religious of the archdiocese. In the first week of January 1985, the archbishop finally responded. In his personal column for the archdiocese's weekly newspaper, *Catholic New York*, O'Connor wrote of his youthful admiration for Dorothy Day and allowed that she was surely one of New York's "solid gold humanitarians." But a saint? On that point he remained coyly agnostic, closing his column with this modest proposal:

> Shortly after I announced the study of Cardinal Cooke's life, several people wrote to ask me: 'Why not Dorothy Day?' I saw the same question in print recently. It's a good question. Indeed, it's an excellent question. It's almost impossible to read *By Little and By Little, The Selected Writings of Dorothy Day*, without asking it, especially if she started you thinking more than forty years ago. I would be interested in your answers.

Several people responded to O'Connor's appeal, though just how many was never made public. Neither was O'Connor's reaction. In fact, he never mentioned the idea in public again.

Perhaps it was just as well. As the former chief of chaplains for the U.S. Military Forces, as a retired rear admiral, and as one of the more hawkish members of the American Catholic hierarchy, O'Connor was an unlikely patron for an insistent pacifist like Dorothy Day. Apart from a collateral interest in "the workingman," there really was nothing in his background to suggest deep wells of sympathy for a woman whose close friends included assorted Communists, socialists, and anarchists. Indeed, the Catholic Workers' communitarian ethos was the very antithesis of hierarchical rank, order, and command which defined O'Connor's career in the military and in the church. Even Dorothy Day's legendary indifference toward the clothes she wore (they were always secondhand) contrasted sharply with the meticulously turned-out prince of the church. In any case, O'Connor shortly discovered a perfectly valid reason for washing his hands of the Day cause: someone else was already promoting it.

In September 1983, the Claretian Fathers of Chicago, a missionary order that publishes magazines devoted to lay spirituality, peace, and social justice, announced a drive to seek the canonization of Dorothy Day as "a saint for our times." Citing in particular Day's "thorough opposition to war," the Claretians appealed to their essentially liberal Catholic audience for letters of support, and offered the traditional prayer cards with Dorothy's picture and a prayer Catholics could recite in seeking "divine favors" through her intercession. Two years later, they had amassed about fifteen hundred letters, many of them recalling the spiritual influence Dorothy had had on the correspondents' lives.

But Dorothy Day's cause turned out to be as problematic as Cooke's. If the main obstacle to Cooke's cause was the suspicion that the candidate is unworthy of the process, in the case of Dorothy Day the principal objection was the suspicion that the process is unworthy of the candidate. Day's daughter and grandchildren, as well as the majority of her spiritual kin, the Catholic Workers, were either indifferent or outright opposed to the idea of having her canonized. Of Dorothy's nine grandchildren, only one bothered to respond to the Claretians' call. On recycled paper stamped with a warning, FISSION AND FUSION ARE FATAL! Maggie Hennessy, age 34, sent the following message from Culloden, West Virginia:

> Dear Folks,
>
> I am one of Dorothy's granddaughters and I wanted to let you know how sick your canonization movement is. You have completely missed her beliefs and what she lived for if you are trying to stick her on a pedestal. She was a humble person, living as she felt the best way to improve on the world's ills.
>
> Take all your monies and energies that are being put into her canonization and give it to the poor. That is how you would show your love and respect to her.

Other correspondents cited familiar words of Day herself to ground their objections to the canonization effort. Typical of these was a letter from Diane L. Stier of Vestaburg, Michigan:

> It has often been recounted to me that Dorothy Day herself, in commenting on someone's mention of her sanctity, said, "Don't dismiss me so easily!" I find it ironic, then, that persons should be engaged in working for the elevation to sainthood of a woman who insisted on being taken seriously as a peer.
>
> As long as Dorothy Day is one of us, we are challenged to be as much as she; but if she is [a] saint, we can remain passive in our sinner-hood.

Among the Catholic Workers, those who had known Day personally were torn over the issue of her canonization. She had always discouraged a cult of personality, her own or someone else's, and they were hard put to know what she would want, or what they should want for her.

On the one hand, Dorothy Day herself had been profoundly devoted to the saints. To her, the saints were like a bloodline she had inherited with her conversion, a family of familiars she found it easy to commune with through prayer and reflection on their writings. She wrote often and at length about her favorites, especially St. Catherine of Siena and St. Teresa of Ávila, two spiritual virtuosi who did not hesitate to call popes and bishops to spiritual account. She devoted an entire book to St. Thérèse of Lisieux, a contrasting nineteenth-century figure whose simplicity and ordinariness Day longed to emulate. "If sanctity depended on the extraordinary," she believed, "there would be few saints." But Day could be critical of the saints, too, citing this one's crankiness, that one's excessive or misplaced zeal. "If we imitate the imperfections of the saints," she once wrote, "we are liable to go to hell."

Dorothy Day also accepted as an axiom of faith that "all are called to be saints." She strove with great deliberation for holiness herself. The Gospel, she believed, called for revolution, but one that was within everyman's grasp. Hence her impatience with those who called her a living saint: she disliked being treated like an exception, much less an icon.

Nonetheless, Dorothy Day was quite aware that after her death there would likely be a movement to have her canonized. In fact, this prospect caused her considerable anxiety, and her intimate friends knew why. Part of her anxiety was rooted in the sense of her own sinfulness. She was given to bursts of temper, she harbored grudges, gave in to pride, was often harshly judgmental. But what bothered her most was the life she had led before her conversion. She never got over the sins of her youth, when she had several love affairs. The first of these, when she was twenty-one, ended after an abortion—an experience which she refused to discuss, even in old age. Another affair resulted in marriage which, less than two years later, ended in divorce. A third produced her only child, born out of wedlock—the event which precipitated her conversion at the age of thirty.

Day feared that if she became the subject of a canonization process, her early life would be recovered and put on public view. Worse, in her view, if her cause were successful, her complex life story would be condensed into a sinner-to-sainthood tale for popular consumption. But she preferred that her preconversion life remain buried. Indeed, after her conversion, she tried to buy up and destroy all remaining copies of her early novel, *The Eleventh Virgin*, a fictonalized account of her life up to age twenty-two that included her abortion. Later, she wrote two autobiographies, both of which elided her early sexual experiences; at her death she left behind notes for her own spiritual autobiography. The working title: "All Is Grace."

There was, perhaps, a third reason why Day was not anxious to be proposed for canonization: her family. On the one occasion when I met her, we spoke for three hours about child-rearing and the pleasures and heartaches of being a parent. She loved to talk about domestic matters—she once confounded an audience of liberal Catholic activists by observing that within the Catholic Workers' communities, the only person with any authority was the cook. What she never mentioned was the fact that despite the great comfort Day took in her daughter, Tamar Therese, both she and all her children had drifted away from the church. It was a sorrow Dorothy Day took with her to the grave.

Little wonder, then, that very few Catholic Workers spoke up on behalf of Day's cause. As far as can be determined, only two of them, Tom Cornell and Jim Forest, both former editors of the *Catholic Worker*, wrote letters supporting her canonization. Both were convinced of Day's sanctity and both had concluded, after long deliberation, that canonization was the only way that Day's extraordinary Christian witness was likely to be preserved for the benefit of believers centuries after her death.

Yet to be heard from, however, was the tribune of the Catholic Left. In a letter to the Claretians, Father Daniel Berrigan, S.J., the celebrated peace activist, put the case against canonization in characteristically pungent terms:

Thank you for that wonderful suggestion about canonizing Dorothy. I have a few suggestions along these lines, based on what I take to be Dorothy's preferences when she lived among us.

Abandon all thought of this expensive, overly juridical process. Let those so minded keep a photo of Dorothy some place given to prayer or worship. In such a place, implore her intercession for peace in the world, and bread for the multitudes.

With the money thus saved, otherwise spent on ecclesiastical lawyers, expensive meetings and travel of experts, begin here and now feeding the multitudes. Send $1, $5, $10, $20, $100 to the nearest Catholic Worker house. Better still, drop by and help on the soup line. Best of all, start a Catholic Worker house.

The above simple suggestions have a few advantages, not easily dismissed. They would restore the early custom whereby the people of the church choose their saints, in this case by a kind of modest acclamation. The suggestions would also help heal the unity between peacemaking and the works of mercy—a unity so cruelly violated by Reaganomics and mega-war.

Dorothy is a people's saint, she was careful and proud of her dignity as layperson. Her poverty of spirit, a great gift to our age, would forbid the expensive puffing of baroque sainthood. Today her spirit haunts us in the violated faces of the homeless of New York. Can you imagine her portrait, all gussied up, unfurled from above the high altar of St. Peter's? I say, let them go on canonizing canons and such. We have here a saint whose soul ought not be stolen from her people—the wretched of the earth.

The issue, then, as Berrigan framed it, was not the sanctity of Dorothy Day, or even the appropriateness of venerating her as a saint. The issue was the process of canonization itself. Expensive, intrusive, bureaucratic, canonization was to be abjured as a ritual of alienation. Let Rome honor its own through its "baroque" customs, Berrigan was saying, but let the people acknowledge the true saints by imitating their examples.

It was a tantalizing argument, more so for what it assumed than what it stated. Who could doubt that canonization is tedious and expensive? Just how tedious and expensive, however, few outside the Congregation for the Causes of Saints really knew. Again, who could doubt that Day herself would prefer imitation to veneration? But then again, St. Francis of Assisi, surely no lover of pomp and puffery, had survived the rigors of official sainthood; might not Dorothy Day do the same? Indeed, if Rome could bring itself to commend Dorothy Day to the faithful for imitation, might not the solemn declaration of her sanctity produce imitators beyond the coterie of Catholic Workers?

But Berrigan's letter was not written to raise questions, or even to offer recommendations. It was designed to make a statement. Simply put, Berrigan was insisting that the saint-makers in Rome cannot be trusted with the likes of a Dorothy Day. To put her up for canonization, Berrigan was saying, is to run the substantial risk of having her transformed into something she was not: a "church saint." And in Berrigan's view, Dorothy Day was something infinitely more precious—"a people's saint."

Is it possible to be both a saint of the church and a people's saint? The question never occurred to the early Christians because (as will be examined in the next chapter) the voice of the church was, in the matter of making of the saints, the voice of "the people." Today, however, it is the voice of the pope, speaking for a church that is no longer a sect, which determines whom Catholics may officially venerate as saints. The rule is: the people propose and the pope, after all due investigation, disposes. But the Catholic Church has always had its undeclared saints—"people's saints"—especially where the church is perceived as "the people's church."

OSCAR ROMERO:
THE POLITICS OF "THE PEOPLE'S SAINT"

AT ABOUT SIX-THIRTY in the evening of March 24, 1980, Archbishop Oscar Arnulfo Romero of San Salvador was saying Mass in the airy chapel at the Carmelite sisters' cancer hospital, where he lived. Only hours earlier, Romero had confessed his sins at the old Jesuit House outside the city so that he might, as he told his confessor, "feel clean in the presence of the Lord." It was his last confession. Just as the archbishop finished his brief homily, a single rifle shot was fired from the back of the chapel. The bullet pierced Romero's chest and scattered fragments inside his upper body. He fell behind the altar, blood spurting from his mouth and nose. Three nuns ran to him and turned him on his back while one of them, Sister Teresa of Ávila, felt for his pulse. The archbishop was already unconscious. Ten minutes later he was pronounced dead.

Romero's murderer was an expert assassin. He had fired, most likely, from the window of a car parked directly in front of the chapel, then sped away. He has never been identified and, given the volatile politics of El Salvador, it is unlikely that those responsible for Romero's murder will ever be brought to justice.*

In the days immediately following the murder, some Salvadorans claimed that the assassin was a hired killer from Cuba, thus implicating Salvador's leftist guerrillas. But the force of logic—and of circumstantial evidence—pointed to the right. Romero was known to be a target of Salvador's right-wing "death squads" and was hated by the military, from which the death squads drew their recruits. Indeed, the day before he was killed, the archbishop had used his Sunday sermon in San Salvador's cathedral to appeal over the heads of the Army High Command to the country's soldiers. "No soldier is obliged to obey an order contrary to the law of God," Romero had declared. "It is time that you come to your senses and obey your conscience rather than follow sinful commands."

Not since the murder of Thomas à Becket, the twelfth-century archbishop of Canterbury, had so prominent a prelate been cut down at the altar. Romero was only sixty-two when he was assassinated. He had been archbishop of San Salvador for only three years, but in that brief period he had become the most celebrated—and controversial— churchman in Central America, perhaps in the Western Hemisphere. His courageous defense of human rights in El Salvador had prompted 123 members of the British Parliament and 16 United States congressmen to nominate him for the Nobel Peace Prize in 1979. His assassination was reported on front pages in Europe as well as in South and North America. Roman Catholic bishops from as far away as England, Ireland, and France attended his funeral. So did Protestant representatives from the World Council of Churches in Geneva, Switzerland, and the National Council of Churches in the United States. But the presence of so many church luminaries did not inhibit Romero's enemies. Before the funeral Mass ended, a bomb exploded in the broad plaza outside the cathedral, where a crowd estimated at 150,000 had gathered. At least thirty Salvadorans died, about a third of them from shots fired by Salvadoran security forces.

Clearly, Archbishop Romero died a martyr's death. Even Pope John Paul II, who visited El Salvador two years later, has allowed as much.

---

* On February 5, 1989, the Salvadoran government claimed to have identified Romero's assassin: Hector Antonio Regalado, a dentist who became chief of security for El Salvador's National Assembly. Government prosecutors said Regalado had killed the archbishop under the supervision of Alvaro Rafael Saravia, a former air force officer, and on the orders of Roberto D'Aubuisson, leader of the rightist National Alliance party, known as ARENA. The claims were based on allegations by Alvaro Antonio Garay, who said he drove the getaway car. However, the Salvadoran Supreme Court, which is controlled by ARENA, ruled in December 1988 that Garay's testimony was too old and too inconsistent. Both Regalado and Saravia thus escaped prosecution, as did D'Aubuisson, whose ARENA candidate, Alfredo Cristiani, won the presidency in March 1989.

Just as clearly, the masses of El Salvador—and not only the Roman Catholic majority—regard Romero as a saint, their saint. Archbishop Romero's tomb inside the east transept of San Salvador's cracked and peeling cathedral has become a national shrine for pilgrims from throughout Central America. Already, several hundred cures and other "miracles" have been claimed through his intercession. And yet, seven years after his death, the church in El Salvador had yet to make a move toward the canonization of "the people's saint."

Why?

In March of 1987, I went to El Salvador to find out. The first thing that struck me was this: although Archbishop Romero had been dead for seven years, the memory of his murder was as fresh as an open wound. It still is. One reason is that El Salvador remains as divided as it had been when Romero was alive—even more so. Since 1980, many of the "popular movements," as certain of the opposition groups among the peasants, the trade unionists, the professions, students, and church workers are called, have developed ties with guerrilla forces. Another reason is the pervasive feeling that those who ordered Romero's murder—there is no doubt it was a conspiracy—remain alive and active in El Salvador. Thus, while large photographs of Romero can be found in most Salvadoran churches, anyone who dares brandish his photograph in public is likely to be stopped for questioning by the security forces. On the first five anniversaries of his death, in fact, church authorities did not permit Catholics to mark the occasion with a public procession to his tomb. When permission was granted in 1986, ten thousand people marched to the anniversary Mass at the cathedral.

At the Hospital of the Transfiguration, where Romero was shot, the Carmelite sisters pray to Romero daily, but they do so with the palpable sense that his spirit, still embattled, is very much with them. In rueful retrospect, Sister Teresa, a round, nut-brown woman with large eyebrows, recounted the curious circumstances which brought the archbishop to their chapel for Mass that fateful Monday evening.

Jorge Pinto, publisher of a weekly newspaper, El Independiente, whose offices had been bombed only days before, had asked the archbishop to say the Mass to commemorate the anniversary of the death of his mother. Apart from family and relatives, the others in attendance were mostly members of the hospital staff and a few of their cancer patients. Ordinarily, such semiprivate Masses were not publicized but, oddly enough, notices appeared in several of the city's newspapers announcing when and where the archbishop would be saying Mass that evening. Since the archbishop had received numerous death threats, his friends urged him to let another priest take his place. But Romero insisted on keeping his promise to Pinto, whom he considered a friend. Another oddity was the presence of a photographer who snapped pictures throughout the Mass, including the archbishop's dying moments. Not long after the assassination, Pinto disappeared from El Salvador and the photographer, fearing for his life, migrated to Sweden.

Like many other Salvadorans, the sisters would like to see Romero's martyrdom given more public recognition. To that end, they have proposed that a plaque be put in the chapel to commemorate the spot where he was killed. But Romero's successor, Archbishop Arturo Rivera y Damas, has instructed them to wait. Even after seven years, Rivera told the sisters, it is still too dangerous to call attention to the assassination.

The sisters have another commemorative dream: to make a museum out of the small concrete bungalow, just fifty yards from the chapel, where Romero had lived while he was archbishop. It is three compact rooms, left just as they were the day he died. The bedroom, with a small bath to one side, contains pictures of the Madonna and child, the crucifixion, and Pope Paul VI. Besides a narrow bed and nightstand, the only furniture is a small desk with a lamp in the form of a Pietà. A second room is strung with the rope hammock in which Romero liked to take his siesta. The main room, empty of furniture, displays his cassocks and skullcaps, his bishop's miter and staff, plus a shelf of books. Outside is a small garden with a shrine devoted to Our Lady of Lourdes. It was here that Sister Teresa, still director of the hospital, confided a secret.

When the physicians removed the viscera from the archbishop's body, Romero's vicar-general, Father Ricardo Urioste, insisted that the organs not be discarded. They were the organs, he said, of a saint. So the physicians placed the viscera in a plastic bag and the sisters put the bag in a cardboard box and buried it a half meter below ground in the garden. Two years later, when the sisters decided to build the shrine, the workmen unearthed the box by accident. The cardboard had rotted away but the viscera were as soft as the day they had been removed from the archbishop's body, and the blood was still liquefied. The viscera were taken to Archbishop Rivera, who agreed with the sisters that their preservation was probably a miracle, though not the kind the Congregation for the Causes of Saints would accept toward canonization. But he directed the sisters to rebury their treasure and cautioned them not to publicize what they had seen. Not only would word of the "miracle" arouse the faithful, he warned, but the powerful and wealthy elites of the city, for whom Romero is no saint, would claim that the story was invented.

Despite this official policy of caution, there were persistent rumors that the church was quietly preparing a cause for Archbishop Romero. But Father Urioste, who continues as vicar-general under Archbishop Rivera, denied that any official action has been taken. There were several reasons for their inaction, he said, but money was not one of them. "I personally think that if we asked the people for the money, they would give it to us."

"Including wealthy families, members of the so-called oligarchy?"

"Among the powerful, I think some would abandon the faith if Romero were declared a saint."

"Would all the bishops of El Salvador support the cause?"

"We have six bishops in El Salvador. Three of them are for Romero and three are against. Some people say he was manipulated, you know. But I knew him and I am convinced that he did not say anything in public or private that he did not first talk over with God. He was manipulated only by God. For me he is a saint and so I really am not interested in applying for a formal canonization process.

"You must understand," he went on, "we are so satisfied with Archbishop Romero that we don't need to have him made a saint. The people have him in mind when they suffer, are persecuted, and are killed. He is the one who gives them strength. So what else do you want from a saint?"

"Perhaps," I suggested, "it would be good for the church, as well as for the people of El Salvador, to have the pope officially proclaim him a saint."

"Being proclaimed a saint is something marvelous for the glory of God and for the church, and for so many reasons. And someday I am sure he will be proclaimed a saint. But I don't think that will happen for another fifty years."

Before I could ask him why, Father Urioste leaned forward across his desk, as if to make certain that I heard him. "You must understand," he said, "Archbishop Romero was the most loved person in the country. And the most hated."

For most of his church career, Oscar Romero was not the sort of priest who inspired passionate reactions. According to those who knew him, he was shy, conservative, stubbornly moralistic, and "churchy"—a solitary pastor who seemed more interested in the saving of individual souls than in addressing the country's deepening social crises. For these reasons, it now seems apparent, the Vatican regarded him as a safer choice for El Salvador's major see than Rivera, a far more liberal and politically astute churchman who was the preferred candidate of San Salvador's activist clergy. Certainly the Salvadoran government, which let the Vatican know of its preference for an archbishop who would mind his business, was pleased by Romero's appointment.

Three weeks after Romero's installation, however, an incident occurred which, he later said, triggered a profound change in his social outlook. A Jesuit priest Romero admired, Father Rutilio Grande, was murdered, together with a young boy and an old man, outside Aguilares, a village twenty-five miles north of the capital. To Salvador's rightists, the activist Jesuits were more hated than the Communists, and Grande's murder was seen by some as the right's retaliation for the Jesuits' part in organizing a strike against a local sugar mill in 1977. Romero was shocked by Grande's death and demanded that the authorities investigate the slayings. But the government stalled and the culprits were never found. It was not the first atrocity against the church, nor would it be the last. But it was the incident that, by his own account, emboldened Romero to accept a larger, prophetic role as the voice of the Salvadoran people.

Four months after becoming archbishop, Romero defied both the Vatican and Salvadoran tradition by pointedly refusing to attend the inauguration of General Carlos Humberto Romero as president of El Salvador. The general's election had been achieved through widespread violence and fraud, and with this gesture Romero signaled his intent to take the Salvadoran church on an independent course.

In his Sunday sermons at the cathedral, his radio broadcasts, and especially in four lengthy pastoral letters, Romero criticized successive governments for their failure to act on promised reforms, especially those designed to redistribute agricultural land to the impoverished *campesinos*. His outspokenness earned him the enmity of the landed and industrial oligarchy which had long run El Salvador in a semifeudal fashion. He was routinely criticized in San Salvador's major media. By 1978, Romero was speaking out regularly against the random killings and other violations of human rights, thereby drawing the wrath of the national security forces. Opposition politicians sought his counsel. Leaders of the "popular movements" looked to him for support.

Never before had a Catholic bishop spoken so directly, so concretely about the abuses suffered by the masses of Salvadorans. Never before had a Salvadoran bishop so identified the church with the struggle for justice. But the risks Romero took were great. He was accused of meddling in politics, of coddling "Communist" priests. Right-wing "death squads" continued to torture and kill clergy and other church personnel. Several priests were forced into exile. Repression of the church was blatant.

Romero had his opponents within the church as well. Of the six Salvadoran bishops, only Rivera could be counted on for support. An open break in the hierarchy's ranks occurred in the summer of 1978 when the six bishops met to prepare a pastoral letter on the increasingly political direction taken by the "popular movements." Some priests and many lay parish leaders were becoming involved in the movements as well. In August, with only Rivera as a cosigner, Romero issued a powerful pastoral letter on "The Church and Popular Political Organizations" which generally praised the popular movements, though not uncritically. Along with denunciations of terrorism, the letter condemned the "institutionalized violence" caused by the elite's economic oppression of the masses. Two days later, the four other bishops issued a dissenting paper, claiming that the popular movements were virtually Marxist organizations.

Throughout his three years as archbishop, Romero's actions were repeatedly criticized by the papal nuncio to El Salvador, Archbishop Emmanuele Gerarda. Gerarda's reports back to the Vatican also colored Rome's attitude toward the embattled archbishop. In 1978, when officials of Georgetown University announced that they would go to El Salvador to confer an honorary degree on Romero for his defense of human rights, Cardinal Gabriel Garrone, the head of the Vatican's Sacred Congregation for Catholic Education, tried unsuccessfully to block the ceremony. By 1979, Romero's outspokenness and the division within the Salvadoran hierarchy had so upset Vatican officials that they recommended that Romero's major duties as archbishop be put in the hands of an apostolic administrator. That recommendation was never acted upon, but in two private audiences with Pope John Paul II, Romero was subjected to close questioning and repeated cautions. John Paul II reportedly was very severe with Romero during the last audience, in 1980, because of a report the pope had received that Romero had met with a woman journalist in Spain just before coming to Rome, and had been so indiscreet as to tell her what issues he intended to take up during the papal audience.

In the view of several influential Vatican officials and diplomats, therefore, Romero's actions as archbishop of San Salvador were at best naive, at worst disruptive, and possibly hastened a victory for the country's Marxist guerrillas. When Romero was assassinated, no one from the Vatican attended his funeral.

There were, then, numerous reasons to suppose why, seven years after his death, no one in El Salvador had yet proposed Romero for canonization. One was that the Salvadoran bishops were themselves divided over the propriety of making him a saint. Another was fear of stirring up the people and angering the military. It also seemed possible that someone at the Vatican had asked that no cause be started. Or perhaps there was some secret about Romero, unknown to the public, which would rule out his canonization. But which were the operative reasons? Since Archbishop Rivera was the only Salvadoran church official who could advance Romero's cause, I put the question to him.

We met in Rivera's chancery office where the archbishop, dressed in a gray suit with a pale blue clerical shirt, spoke directly to the issue: "The problem is that his name is still being used by some people for political purposes," he said. "That's where the difficulty is. It would be easy to show that he was a martyr for the church. But now you have different groups on the left saying that he was a martyr for their particular political causes, and that makes it harder to show that he was a martyr for the church."

In descending order of political significance, Rivera ticked off on the fingers of his left hand the four kinds of groups which, he felt, would seek to make political capital out of a Romero canonization: the Farbundo Martí Liberation Front (FMLN), a Marxist guerrilla movement; the Democratic Revolutionary Front (FDR), a coalition of leftist political organizations; various other legal opposition groups and *comunidades de base*—the network of politically active Christian "base communities" formed within the church itself. "If the cause were started tomorrow," Rivera observed, "they would be out marching in the streets."

For Rivera, then, there would be no attempt to have Romero canonized as long as his memory and martyrdom could be politicized by various factions in opposition to the government. This policy, he assured me, was not for the purpose of placating the Salvadoran right, which still regards Romero as a subversive figure. The point, rather, was to depoliticize Romero. In other words, before Romero can be recognized as a saint, he must first undergo a kind of transformation: "the people's saint" must become "a martyr of the church."

I asked Rivera if he had discussed this policy with officials of the Vatican's Congregation for the Causes of Saints. He had not. I asked him if he had discussed it with Pope John Paul II. I recalled that during his visit to El Salvador in 1982, the pope had disappointed many

Catholics by not visiting the chapel where Romero had been murdered, and had made only a private visit to the martyr's tomb. Was this not a signal to the church in El Salvador to cool the people's reverence for Romero? Rivera said he had not spoken to the pope about canonizing Romero but that one of his priests, Father Jesús Delgado, had. "I could tell you what the pope told Father Delgado," he smiled, "but to be accurate you had better talk to him."

Father Delgado is a wiry Salvadoran pastor who studied history at Belgium's Louvain University in the 1950s and, with that credential, has been assigned by Rivera to marshal material against the day when Romero's cause can be safely introduced. Delgado's conversation with John Paul II took place at the Vatican in 1983, an opportunity he used to lobby for recognition of Romero's holiness. As evidence of supernatural approbation of Romero, he gave the pope a vial of Romero's blood which had been unearthed the previous year along with Romero's "miraculously" preserved viscera.

The pope's response, Delgado said, was to remind him that no miracle was needed to prove Romero a martyr. "The pope said, 'He really is a martyr.' He said that twice. So I told him, 'Holy Father, we hope that in a few years he will be canonized.' Then the pope said, 'Purtroppo'—those were his exact words in Italian—'I wish it were so. What a pity that Archbishop Romero has become a [political] banner because they say he was a guerrilla.' So long as that is so, the pope said, we should not think to canonize him as a saint. That is the pope's obsession. And that is why Archbishop Rivera has not started a process for Archbishop Romero yet."

Delgado said that John Paul II also has an "obsession" about Romero's murder. "The pope always asks who shot Archbishop Romero. That was not clear to him in 1983, but Archbiship Rivera says it is clear in his mind now. I don't know what conclusion the pope has reached. What I do know is that some people say that Romero was a politician and spoke like one at his Sunday Masses in the cathedral. But he did not die celebrating the Sunday Mass, where people say he gave political provocation. He died celebrating a memorial Mass for a woman who had died. He was not speaking about the condition of El Salvador. He was speaking about the person who died in the life of Christ, about the mystery of our faith. That is clear. And that is why the Holy Father says he really is a martyr."

"Did the pope indicate when he thought it would be safe to begin a process of canonization for Romero?" I asked.

"He thinks that once it's started it will go very quickly. That is why he said, 'I do not want a process at this time.' He wants us to wait twenty, twenty-five years, until there is no more conflict with guerrillas. But the conflict with the guerrillas is not going to end soon, so we must wait for the next generation, a new generation."

Father Delgado was, perhaps, more candid than he realized in reporting his conversation with John Paul II. If he was quoting the pope accurately, then it is apparent that John Paul II had personally interdicted, for the time being, any effort on the part of Salvadoran church officials to introduce a canonization process for Archbishop Romero. Such a direct papal intervention is highly unusual, but not unprecedented. Moreover, it would appear that the pope's reasons for doing so are essentially political rather than theological: he does not want the figure of Romero to become an advantage to El Salvador's leftist opposition movements in their efforts to gain popular support. Perhaps he also believes that Romero acted recklessly as archbishop and so is unworthy of canonization. Quite possibly, he even fears the sight of guerrilla units marching into battle behind a huge banner of "the people's saint." Whatever his reasons, it is certain that the pope would not declare Romero a martyr and saint as long as he remains a divisive figure within the Salvadoran hierarchy itself.

However, there is also a theological rationale for the pope's position. According to the church's criteria, only those who are proven to have been killed "in hatred of the faith" qualify as Christian martyrs. For the early Christians, the proof was easy to come by. But in the twentieth century, when most martyrs have been victims of political movements, as in Nazi Germany or Communist nations, the burden of showing "hatred of the faith" has become more difficult. Indeed, if Martin Luther King, Jr., had been a Roman Catholic priest, it is not at all certain that his assassination in Memphis would qualify as a martyrdom for the faith. In Roman Catholic terminology, a figure like King may well be a "martyr for justice" but not necessarily a "martyr for the church." Thus, if and when Romero's cause is taken up by Rome, his supporters will have to demonstrate that he was not simply a victim of his own outspoken criticism of government policies. On the contrary, they will have to show, as Delgado put it, that he was killed as "a man of the church."

Romero had studied in Rome and understood these theological distinctions. For example, he recognized that the murdered Jesuit, Father Grande, was a martyr for the people but not necessarily a martyr for the church. Toward the end of his life, however, Romero came to identify the church with the Salvadoran people, and anticipated what his own martyrdom, should it come, might mean to them. Here is how he put the matter in a telephone interview with a Mexican newspaper two weeks before his death:

> I have often been threatened with death. Nevertheless, as a Christian, I do not believe in death without resurrection. If they kill me, I shall arise in the Salvadoran people. I say so without meaning to boast, with the greatest humility.
>
> As pastor, I am obliged by divine mandate to give my life for those I love—for all Salvadorans, even for those who may be going to kill me. If the threats come to be fulfilled, from this moment I offer my blood to God for the redemption and for the resurrection of El Salvador.
>
> Martyrdom is a grace of God that I do not believe I deserve. But if God accepts the sacrifice of my life, let my blood be a seed of freedom and the sign that hope will soon be reality. Let my death, if it is accepted by God, be for the liberation of my people and as a witness of hope in the future.
>
> You may say, if they succeed in killing me, that I pardon and bless those who do it. Would that thus they might be convinced that they will waste their time. A bishop will die, but the church of God, which is the people, will never perish.

There is no doubt that Romero regarded himself as a "man of the church"; upon becoming archbishop he chose as his motto "To Be of One Mind and Heart With the Church." There is also no doubt that he assumed the larger role of prophet of the people, with all its attendant risks. Certainly, he would not have been assassinated if he had not spoken out as boldly as he did on political issues. Therefore, to deny or even diminish the political role he assumed at a time when an average of ten thousand Salvadorans a year were being killed would seem to falsify the central meaning of his life and death. On the other hand, to recognize that Romero was a martyr for the church precisely because he was first of all a martyr for social justice would require church officials to think in a new—or at least a different—way about the requirements for Christian martyrdom. It comes to this: Martyrs are people who die in defense of Christian beliefs or morals. But the church has yet to recognize social justice—at least in the context of the political and economic exploitation of one social class by another—as one of the moral values for which a canonizable saint may give his life.

This, at any rate, is the view taken by the community of Jesuits in El Salvador. Like their colleagues in Nicaragua, the Jesuits function independently of the country's hierarchy and, as exponents of "liberation theology," are openly opposed to the conservative wing of the

Salvadoran hierarchy. Several of the Jesuits on the faculty of their Central American University in San Salvador aided Romero in the writing of his now-famous pastoral letters. During a long afternoon visit to the university, theologian Jon Sobrino, one of several fiery Basques on the faculty and a former adviser to Romero, summarized the Jesuits' case for recognizing the late archbishop as a people's saint.

"If we want a model for the kind of saint Romero was," Sobrino began, "that model is Jesus. Not just because he was crucified in the end, like Jesus, but because he was with the people. Romero became a saint within society, not just within the synagogue, so to speak, or the confines of Jerusalem. Most saints do not get into direct contact with the people the way Jesus did. That was not the case with Romero.

"Archbishop Romero gave the people hope at a time when there was no hope. He gave them back their dignity and self-esteem, and for all those reasons he is at once a Christian saint and a Salvadoran hero. The beautiful thing that Romero symbolizes—and he is not the only one—is that for the first time in five centuries, being a Salvadoran and being a Christian converge."

Sobrino paused long enough to light the first of several cigarettes; then, at my urging, he characterized precisely those qualities which, in his view, set Romero apart as a Salvadoran saint and hero.

"Archbishop Romero was a man who told the truth and loved the people. In Third World countries like El Salvador, telling the truth is absolutely explosive. Until Archbishop Romero began to speak out, the Salvadoran people did not believe that hearing the truth was possible." For Sobrino, "the basic truth in this country is that there is no justice, there is no freedom, there is no sovereignty. For example, in El Salvador sixty thousand people have been assassinated. Those who have been killed have been called criminals, assassins, Communists, and so on. Romero would call them martyrs. It was an extraordinary thing for the poor to go to Mass at the cathedral and hear the archbishop say, 'We have martyrs in this country.'

"Secondly, he loved the people. Political parties in general do not love the people. But the Salvadoran people grasped that Romero loved them and had no ulterior motives. He even risked the institution of the church because of that love. In saying that I am not indulging in metaphor. He risked priests being killed. Bombs exploded here at this university. I remember once his saying that all these crimes are signs that the church is with the people. And it would be very sad if there were so many peasants being murdered and no priests were being assassinated. The church that does not suffer persecution is not the church of Jesus Christ. That, in so many words, is what he conveyed. As you can imagine, that is rare in the church, and in the world."

"What I imagine," I responded, "is that the pope is worried about the disunity that Romero's actions introduced into the Salvadoran church, a tension that I notice still persists. By all accounts, Romero was a highly conflicted man."

Sobrino brushed aside these objections: "The conflicted saint symbolizes a conflicted world. The Third World is not just a world that Christians should react to with mercy. Mother Teresa of Calcutta, for example, shows mercy and love. That is probably the sort of response the Vatican would like to stress. But Mother Teresa is not complete. To canonize Romero would at least logically bring out certain questions. For instance, would the Catholic Church that would canonize Romero be ready, in the last analysis, to follow in his footsteps? I don't think today the Vatican wants that. Not only in fact but in principle. There is the attitude that the best way to handle the Third World is not Romero's way. It is much better to avoid conflict with those who are in power. This is not what Romero did."

I explained Archbishop Rivera's reasons for not seeking Romero's canonization now and his fears—and those of the pope—that he would be used politically by the Salvadoran left. Sobrino conceded this was likely, but dismissed the hazard as unimportant. "That is no excuse for keeping Romero under glass as a 'man of the church.' I don't think that does justice to the Romero phenomenon."

"Do you really care if the pope canonizes Romero?"

"If he is canonized fifty years from now, a lot of historical perspective will be lost. But if he is canonized in the next ten years, in this century, it would be explosive. If you canonize Romero, you are saying by that very act that a bishop should be like Romero. And, analogously, priests and sisters should be like him too. But as a matter of principle, they [Vatican officials] do not want that type of person as bishop. And, as everyone can see, the men who are being made bishops are not like Romero.

"What is at stake is what direction the faith is taking in this country. These people are, in general, a crucified people. We hope the church will take them down from the cross. In a century or two, people will ask, who took us down from the cross? Was it the Christian believers, or was it the nonbelievers? Canonizing Romero would have this meaning. He is a symbol that brings these people into a future of faith."

March 24, 1990, the tenth anniversary of Romero's death, was marked by a number of protest and solidarity demonstrations of a political sort. El Salvador was no closer to peace than in the days of Romero. Indeed, on November 6 of the previous year, six of Sobrino's Jesuit colleagues at the university, plus their Salvadoran housekeeper and her child, were brutally murdered. Once again, as in the case of Romero, the government, could not—would not, critics said—bring those responsible to justice.

Nonetheless, Archbishop Rivera y Damas took the occasion to announce at a memorial Mass for Romero that he was initiating a formal investigation into the life, virtues, and death of his predecessor—the first step toward canonization. What the archbishop had in mind, it was clear, was an investigation designed to prove Romero's personal holiness and to secure his reputation as a martyred pastor who, in the telltale words of John Paul II, "gave himself for his flock." Coincidental with the bishop's announcement was the publication of Romero's personal diary which, in the opinion of San Salvador's Auxiliary Bishop Gregorio Rosa Chavez, revealed not only his criticism of the government but also "his severe condemnation of the rigidity, dogmatism, and abuses of groups on the left." As expected, the martyr "for the people" was on his way to becoming a martyr "for the church."

Here, then, are three contemporary Catholic figures arising out of three very different social-cultural milieus. Each reflects a different understanding of what it means to imitate Jesus Christ in the late twentieth century. Each embodies a different model of holiness. Each symbolizes a different option for the future of Catholicism. Each faces different obstacles on the road to formal canonization. None of them may officially be declared a saint. But despite their differences, all three raise the same question: what is a saint?

CHAPTER TWO

SAINTS, THEIR CULTS, AND CANONIZATION

WHAT IS A SAINT?

A SAINT IN the Christian tradition is someone whose holiness is recognized as exceptional by other Christians. In this sense, "it takes one to know one." This is not to say that the saint-makers must themselves be saints, only that Christians must be able to recognize sanctity when they see it.

In one way or another, Christians have been "making saints" for as long as the church has existed. In the beginning, the making of saints was a spontaneous act of the local Christian community. Today, for Roman Catholics, it is a protracted, painstaking process orchestrated by officials of the Vatican and governed by legal norms and procedures. How and why it got that way is the subject of this chapter.

One cannot ask, "What is a saint?" without some knowledge of the figures who have already been acknowledged as such. For the first fifteen hundred years and more of the church, saints were deceased figures around whom a popular cult had formed. Unfortunately, the word "cult" has become a pejorative in contemporary Western parlance, suggesting an irrational, idolatrous, and often totalitarian attachment to a mesmerizing spiritual crank. In this respect, it is worth remembering that Christianity itself began as a disreputable, "idolatrous" movement which gave "cult" or worship to the crucified Jesus. Indeed, had Jesus not died as a martyr, there might never have been a Christian cult of the saints.

For the early Christians, the extension of cult to other figures besides Jesus was an organic development of their own faith and experience. Venerated for their holiness, saints were also invoked for their power, especially in and through their bodily remains. The history of saint-making, therefore, is intimately connected to the history of the cult of the saints and their relics. Even in its contemporary bureaucratic form, as we shall see, saint-making is essentially a series of official acts of the church whereby the pope permits public cult or veneration of candidates proposed for his judgment. How and why the papacy gained control over the cult of the saints is also the subject of this chapter.

From even these brief observations it is clear that canonization involves much more than a solemn declaration by a pope. In its literal sense, "to canonize" means to place a name in the canon, or list, of saints. Over the centuries, communities of Christians compiled numerous lists of their saints and martyrs. Many of those names have since been lost to history. The most comprehensive works on saints, the *Bibliotheca Sanctorum*, runs to eighteen volumes (as of 1989) and lists more than ten thousand saints—many times more than the four hundred that have been canonized by popes. In any case, the listing of saints was not merely a method of keeping track of the church's holiest heroes. It also served a liturgical function: to be canonized was to be included among those mentioned from time to time during the celebration of the Mass. It was also to have a feast day in the church's calendar, alongside the feast days of Christ and his mother, the foremost of all the saints.

No one chapter, not even a single book, can capture the history and mirrorlike dimensions of the subject of saints. Indeed, recent years have witnessed a veritable renaissance in the scholarly study of saints and their lore, much of it devoted to recovering the mentalities and social patterns of ancient and medieval cultures. Without some sense of what saints have meant to the church and its people, the problems and procedures of contemporary saint-making cannot be understood.

What follows is a necessarily brief account of the main themes, controversies, and turning points in the history of the development of saints and their cults. It is by no means exhaustive. The aim is to show how and why the making of saints evolved into a highly rationalized and bureaucratic process. Along the way, we will see certain tensions develop, notably between the saint as exemplar of heroic virtue and as thaumaturge or worker of wonders. Similarly, we will trace the tension between popular saint-making and the efforts by church authorities to channel and control the proliferation of saints and their cults. These tensions still exist, as the case of El Salvador's Oscar Romero makes clear, and their presence suggests that Rome has yet to solve in a completely satisfactory matter the question of "who is a saint."

There is a tendency among critics of the modern saint-making process to dismiss it as too long and too remote from the concerns of the ordinary Catholic. And perhaps it is. But the reasons why this may be so must be sought from history. What we find at its origins is not a set of formulae for determining a priori what a saint is, but a proliferation of persons whose life and death were remembered and honored by those who knew them. And what we discover is that the procedures for making saints, however a priori they may have become, are efforts to sustain the impulse of the early Christians to lift up certain of their brothers and sisters for special recognition and veneration. In theory, at least, and to a surprising extent in practice, sanctity is still "in the eye of the beholder, and the primary beholder is the believing community."

For the history of the church is, to a large extent, the history of its saints. One might even say that the church exists to make saints of all its members, if by saints we mean those who become true imitators of Christ. That, at any rate, is how the early Christians understood the matter. And it is with them that we must begin.

Origins: Death in the Lives of Saints

INITIALLY, THE NEW Testament Christians regarded all baptized believers as "saints" (in Greek: *hagioi*). Since most of them were Jews, they regarded holiness as a quality shared by the community, not the mark of an individual. But even among the first generation of Christians, certain individuals were singled out for special acclamation—not because of their preaching or piety, but because they had witnessed to their faith by dying for it. Thus, before the first century was out, the term "saint" was reserved exclusively for martyrs (in Greek, *martys* means "witness") and martyrdom remains to this day the surest route to canonization.

It could with reason be argued that the church's first "canonized" saint was Stephen, the Jewish convert and deacon who, according to the New Testament, was the first martyr for Christ. Luke's account of Stephen's martyrdom in the Acts of the Apostles (6–7) is extremely important for understanding how, at this infant stage in the life of the church, other Christians in Stephen's community recognized his sanctity. The story is constructed in such a way that Stephen's arrest, testimony of faith, and death directly parallel the arrest, testimony, and death of Jesus. Like Jesus, Stephen is described as a wonder-worker and preacher of great power. Again like Jesus, he incites the enmity of Jewish elders and scribes. They have him arrested and tried, during which he gives a long and eloquent account of his faith. At the close, he is taken outside the city and stoned. He dies begging God's forgiveness of his executioners.

The purpose of the narrative is to show that Stephen imitated the passion and death of Christ. Since we have no other accounts of the martyrdom, we cannot know to what extent Luke's story is accurate. But accuracy is not the issue. What is crucial is that the Christian community was able to recognize Stephen as a saint *only* by way of analogy with the story of Jesus' passion and death. The story of Stephen is the story of Christ all over again. To be a saint, then, was to die not only *for* Christ but *like* him. Or, what amounted to the same thing, to be a saint was to have the story of one's death remembered and told as the story of Jesus.

From the very beginning, therefore, sanctity and martyrdom were indistinguishable in the Christian consciousness. Just as Jesus was obedient to the Father "unto death," so the saint was one who died for the sake of Christ. Just as baptism signified incorporation into the body of Christ, so martyrdom signified a dying with Christ and rising again into the fullness of life everlasting. Martyrdom was the seal of a saint's total conformity to Christ. In this regard, it is worth noting that even the twin pillars of the apostolic church, the apostles Peter and Paul, were eventually hailed as saints not because of their leadership within the communities of Christians, but because, in the end, they were martyred. And it may be for the same reason that some others among the original twelve apostles whose deaths are unrecorded were also remembered as martyrs.

For the first four centuries of the Christian era, Roman persecution was so pervasive that to become a Christian was, in effect, to assume the risk of eventual martyrdom. Indeed, to suffer and die like Christ was a grace ardently wished for, the coveted prize. Toward the beginning of the second century, for example, Ignatius, the bishop of Antioch, wrote ahead to influential people in Rome, where he was to be taken for execution, begging them not to intercede for his life: "I

AFter Constatine the
idea of saint changed.
Christians were no longer a martyred.

54   MAKING SAINTS

entreat you, do not be an ill-timed kindness to me. Let me be eaten by
the wild beasts, through whom I can reach the presence of God. I am
God's wheat, and I am ground by the teeth of the wild beasts so that
I may be found pure bread of Christ."

However, not all Christians who were imprisoned or tortured or
sent off to the imperial mines actually perished. Some were cheated of
martyrdom despite having made a public confession of their faith.
Although they survived, these "confessors," as they came to be called,
were reverenced for their public witness of faith and their readiness to
die for it. If they were catachumens (that is, people who were taking
instruction in the faith but not yet baptized), they were considered
baptized "by blood" in virtue of their willingness to suffer martyrdom
for Christ. If they were already baptized, they were offered the privileges (including stipends) and status of clerics. Eventually, in consequence of their likeness to martyrs, some confessors were venerated
at death as saints.

But with the advent of Constantine as the first Christian emperor
early in the fourth century, the church entered a new era of peaceful
relations with the Roman state. The classic age of the martyr subsided
and new models of sainthood eventually emerged alongside the old.
Chief among those models were the solitaries, hermits (called "an-
chorites"), and monks who initiated a new form of imitating Christ.
Just as Jesus had fasted in the desert for forty days and nights, so these
ascetics abandoned the "world" and its most innocent pleasures by
fleeing to the wilds of Syria or Egypt. More to the point, the ascetic
assumed a regimen of dying to the self by voluntarily renouncing food,
sex, money, comfortable clothes and lodgings, and all forms of
companionship—especially marriage. To the church, the slow "white
martyrdom" of the ascetics was the virtual equivalent of the immediate "red" martyrdom of those who actually shed their blood.

In short, to the question, "Who is a saint?" the Christians of Greco-
Roman antiquity responded by pointing to examples of exceptional
suffering. Saints were those who had died, or were willing to die, or
pursued a slow death to the world as a way of imitating Christ. Of
these, the martyr held primacy of honor—still does, in fact, to this
day. But by extending the idea of sanctity to the living, the church
gradually came to venerate persons for the exemplarity of their lives
as well as of their deaths.

Over time, the examples of recognized saints were expanded to
include missionaries and bishops of exceptional pastoral zeal, especially toward the poor; Christian sovereigns who displayed extraordinary solicitude for their subjects; and "apologists" who were noted for

their intellectual defense of the faith as well as for their personal asceticism. In the Middle Ages, the list swelled with the names of the founders of religious orders, both women and men, whose vows of poverty, chastity, and obedience were in the spiritual tradition of the early desert ascetics.

But although the numbers and kinds of saints grew, the ways in which they were categorized remained surprisingly static. Until this century, saints were identified according to categories developed during the first four centuries of the church. Saints were either martyrs or confessors. If confessors, they were typologized according to sex and state of life: bishop, priest, or monk for men; virgin or widow for women. All other (in effect, spouses) saints were "neither virgin nor martyr"—a category equivalent to "none of the above." Today, the married are acknowledged as such, but there are still no official categories for heroic Christian merchants, artists, scholars, scientists or politicians. What this typology suggests is not that the church, in the process of making saints, is blind to the candidate's real-life vocation, but that the idea of sanctity continues to be identified at root with forms of renunciation as expressive of the love of Christ. The martyr renounces his life rather than deny Christ; the confessor proclaims himself ready to die, and the virgin renounces the normal pleasures of life, particularly sex and marital companionship.

But even in the church's formative centuries, Christians saw much more in their saints than mere renunciation. Jesus, they believed, had through his life, death, and resurrection from the dead inaugurated a new age of God's kingdom. On this view, the saints—and most especially the martyrs—were witnesses to the emergence of that kingdom, here and now, against which the powers of this world were unavailing. Moreover, in them the *power* of Christ's emerging kingdom was made manifest through the working of marvelous deeds, not the least of which was the courage to accept martyrdom. In short, saints were distinguished not only for their exemplary imitation of Christ but also for their thaumaturgic or wonder-working powers. Thus, from the seedbed of Christian martyrdom, something new sprang to life within the body of the church: the cult of the saints.

THE CULT OF SAINTS

ONE OF THE earlier Christian beliefs was the "Communion of Saints." Because their witness was perfect, their renunciation total, martyrs were believed to be "reborn" at the moment of death into everlasting life. In this respect, Christians were unique in memorializing their martyred heroes not on their birthdays but on their *dies natalis* or day of rebirth. But the saints in their glory, Christians believed, were not forgetful of those still struggling on earth: between them there was a fellowship or communion linking the living with the dead. Being in heaven, martyrs could, as "friends of God," act as intermediaries on behalf of supplicants on earth, and in the course of the first three centuries, Christians increasingly prayed to them for protection, courage, cures, and other forms of spiritual and material aid. Thus, through these miracles of intercession, the worship of Christ came to embrace an ancillary—and at times a rival—cult of the saints.

It is difficult, after two millennia, to appreciate the novelty of the Christian cult of their martyred dead and the impact it had on *weltanschauung* of Greco-Roman society. According to the late Ernst Bloch, a maverick Marxist philosopher, "It was not the morality of the Sermon on the Mount which enabled Christianity to conquer Roman paganism, but the belief that Jesus had been raised from the dead. In an age when Roman senators vied to see who could get the most blood of a steer on their togas—thinking that would prevent death— Christianity was in competition for eternal life, not for morality."

Had the Christians merely asserted that only Christ survived death, their faith might not have displaced Roman paganism. What struck non-Christians—what attracted some and appalled others—was the emerging religion's vibrant cult of the martyrs. In recent years, historian Peter Brown has spelled out in considerable detail how the cult Christians gave to their martyrs challenged the "accepted boundaries" in the Greco-Roman world between the realm and role of the living and the realm and role of the dead. "We can chart the rise to prominence of the Christian church most faithfully," Brown writes, "by listening to the pagan reactions to the cult of the martyrs." As a paradigmatic case in point, Brown cites the fulminations of Emperor Julian the Apostate in the fourth century: "You keep adding many corpses newly dead to the corpse [Christ] of long ago. You have filled the whole world with tombs and sepulchers."

The primary locus of the cult of the martyrs was their tombs. After witnessing the execution, the faithful would gather the remains of the martyr, seal them in containers, and place them in the catacombs or other secret tombs. Later, on the anniversary of the death/rebirth of the martyr, friends and relatives would gather for a liturgical celebration over the remains. In this way, Brown observes, "tomb and altar were joined" in rituals that gave offense to devout Jews and pious pagans alike.

There is, of course, a paradox here. The very bodies which the martyrs so willingly sacrificed—and the ascetics treated with disciplined contempt—became for the surviving communities of Christians "dearer to us than precious stones and finer than gold." Their belief was that the spirit of the dead saint, though in heaven, was present in a special way through his remains. Thus, wherever a saint's relics were venerated, heaven and earth met and intermingled in ways that were new to Western societies, as this inscription on the tomb of St. Martin of Tours attests:

> Here lies Martin the bishop, of holy memory,
> Whose soul is in the hands of God, but he is fully here,
> Present and made plain in miracles of every kind.

To the early Christians, as later to their medieval descendants, miracles were an everyday occurrence. They were part of a reality which, though different from the modern, was no less complex. For the learned Augustine, "all natural things [were] filled with the miraculous" and the world itself was the "miracle of miracles." It was altogether "natural," therefore, that God would manifest the unusual, through prayers to and of the saints. Today, by contrast, the church is much more circumspect in its attitude toward the miraculous. As we will see, the modern saint-making process still requires miracles as signs of "divine favor." But it does not oblige Catholics to accept as a matter of "supernatural" faith any purported miracle, including those worked at shrines like Lourdes or even those accepted in support of a saint's cause. Nonetheless, "human faith" in miracles continues to be a characteristic of Roman Catholicism, including the "miracle" of faith itself. What is important for our understanding is how the attribution of miraculous events, especially at the shrines and tombs of saints, became woven into the web of requirements for canonization.

Over time, the joining of tomb and altar became even more explicit. As tombs of saints became places of pilgrimage—and considerable feasting—churches were built on the spot to house the relics and ensure a more appropriate celebration of the local "patron" saints. In this way, the walls of a Greco-Roman city were extended to incorporate cemeteries with their increasingly elaborate shrines of saints. (A major example: Vatican Hill, once a cemetery outside Rome, where the Basilica of St. Peter was erected over the grave of the apostle.) Inevitably, conflict arose between the shrines' private patrons—often, converted Roman women of noble birth—and the local bishops. The power of the bishop as local church authority was, at this early stage in the evolution of the church, rivaled by the intercessory power of the locally entombed saint. As Brown has shown, local bishops struggled to gain control of the local shrines, and eventually made them cornerstones of their ecclesiastical power. Indeed, such was the popular appeal of saints and their tombs that Brown comes close to asserting that the spread of the cult of the saints during the first millennium threatened to transform Christianity into a kind of Hinduism of the West. What he *does* assert is this:

> Wherever Christianity went in the early Middle Ages, it brought with it the "presence" of the saints. Whether this was unimaginably far to the north, in Scotland . . . or on the edge of the desert, where Rome, Persia and the Arab world met at the shrine of Saint Sergius at Resafa . . . or even further to the east, among the Nestorian Christians of Iraq, Iran and central Asia, late-antique Christianity, as it impinged on the outside world, *was* shrines and relics. (Italics his.)

Inevitably, the cult given to saints threatened to rival the worship of God. As early as the middle of the second century, Christians were well aware that their veneration of the saints was open to charges of idolatry. In the "Martyrdom of Polycarp," a letter from the Christians at Smyrna in Asia Minor to those at Philomelion in Phrygia, the author recounts how the magistrate refused to turn the bishop's charred remains over to the faithful lest they "abandon the Crucified and worship this man" in his place. The last thing the magistrate wanted to encourage was the creation of a new Christ. In fact, that is how, analogically, the Christians of Smyrna saw their bishop, and eventually they were able to recover his bones from the grave. But the letter recounting the whole episode is historically significant, among other reasons, for the care with which it distinguishes between the worship accorded to Christ and the love of the martyrs as "disciples and imitators of the Lord."

Like the Christians of Smyrna, the church fathers of the third and fourth centuries drew a sharp distinction between the *latria* or worship owed to Christ and the *doulia* or veneration proper to his saints. But this distinction, though plausible enough in the abstract, was often difficult to maintain in practice. The saints, after all, were the objects of popular devotion, and a lively intellectual controversy developed over the proper way to venerate them. For example, although the body and blood of Christ were believed to be materially present in the eucharistic bread and wine, the saints were sometimes thought in the popular imagination to be even more powerfully present in their tombs and relics. Thus the shrines and tombs of saints became the scenes of cultic practices resembling those the pagans enacted at their shrines, such as that of Asklepios. Christian families took to feasting at saints' tombs. Some also practiced "incubation" or spending the night in shrines to gain the saint's protection. Thus began yet another tradition, which lasted throughout the Middle Ages, of burial *ad sanctos* or close to the tombs of the saints. In this way, it was hoped, the deceased would enjoy the protection of the saint when he or she was ushered before the judgment seat of God.

Not only the saints' bodies but even their clothes and the instruments of their torture were venerated as sacred objects. According to one contemporary account, before the funeral of St. Ambrose, bishop of Milan, in 397, "crowds of men and women kept throwing their handkerchiefs and aprons at the body of the saint in the hope that they would touch it." Such *brandea*, as they were called, were prized as wonder-working relics. Detached from the body and placed in ornate reliquaries, relics became, in effect, portable shrines for both public and private use.

Several of the church fathers opposed the veneration of these relics on the grounds that they elicited the sort of reverence that should be given to God alone. Others defended the practice, arguing that the bodies of martyrs were sanctified—and, by extension, so were the objects they touched. Still others justified the cult of the saints and the veneration of their relics for pedagogical reasons: through them, the faithful were edified and uplifted. Eventually, the pro-relics opinion prevailed. In 410, the Council of Carthage declared that local bishops should destroy all altars set up as memorials to martyrs and not permit any new shrines to be built unless they contained relics or were established on sites known to be hallowed by the saint's life or death. By 767, the cult of the saints had became so integral to Christian worship that the Council of Nicaea decreed that every church altar must contain an "altar stone" housing the relics of a saint. Even today, an altar is defined in the church's Code of Canon Law as a "tomb containing the relics of a saint."

If saints were present in their remains, they were remembered through their stories. Apart from the Scriptures, the most popular Christian literature in the church's formative centuries were the narratives of the martyrs' passion and death. In a few instances, such as the martyrdom of Sts. Perpetua and Felicitas in the third century, the local churches were able to preserve and pass on in their *acta* of the saints the Roman notary's actual transcript of the dialogue between the magistrate and the accused. More often, the local community of believers composed "passions" of their own martyrs, which were devout and highly stylized recollections of the martyr's passion and death. Since the point of these stories was to edify the faithful as much as to exalt the saint, they were laced with legends and marvelous anecdotes dramatizing the moral courage and spiritual power of the saint. For example, what in fact had been brief, pro forma interrogations by the magistrate became, in the manner of Luke's account of St. Stephen, long and apocryphal dialogues between the accuser and the accused. To these passion narratives were attached *libelli* or stories of the miracles they worked.

The literature of the saints also came to include full-blown biographies. But these, too, were by modern standards of historiography exercises in hagiography. Among the most widely read and imitated was Sulpicius Severus's *Life of Martin of Tours*, first published in the fourth century in Latin, which contains a protracted list of miraculous healings and other prodigies worked both during his life and posthumously at the site of his tomb. Today, these texts are valued less for what they tell us about their subjects—in this regard, they are historically unreliable—than for what they reveal about the church's attitudes toward the saints, and about the ways in which sanctity was perceived, imagined, and recorded for posterity. "To say that legend has flourished luxuriantly in the neighborhood of shrines is simply to underline the importance of the cult of the saints in the life of peoples," observed Hippolyte Delehaye, this century's most accomplished student of Christian hagiography. "Legend is the homage that the Christian community pays to its patron saints."

Not all the saints, it should be noted, were Christians. In some cases they were figures out of texts. John the Baptist was but one of the pre-Christian characters from the Bible (the nameless "good thief" who died with Jesus was another) who were retroactively invested with the status of saints. Others, like St. Christopher (the name means "Christ-bearer"), were figures of ancient legend or, like St. Veronica ("Vera icon"—"true image") were confected out of the church's meditations on the Gospels—in this case, Luke's story of the woman on the way to Calvary who wiped the face of Jesus with a towel on which, in gratitude, he left the image of his bloody face. Still others, such as the Archangel Michael, were not human at all.

In sum, the cult of the saints brought the dead to life, breathed life into legend, and provided every community of Christians with their own heavenly patrons. Luxuriant in its growth, the cult of the saints took root wherever Christianity went. Eventually, the bishops saw that they would have to trim these vines because whom the people prayed to mattered greatly. Popular acclamation was well and good, but it was becoming clear that the faithful could be deceived in their enthusiasm for heavenly patrons. How were church authorities to make certain that the saints the people invoked were truly "friends of God"?

Martyrs were not a problem. Their authenticity as saints rested on the fact that the community had at one time witnessed their exemplary deaths. Martyrdom, it was believed, was more than just an act of human courage; after all, non-Christians died for noble causes too. To die for Christ, though, presupposed supernatural support. Only the power of Christ working within the martyr, it was believed, could sustain him to the bloody end. Even the sins the saint had committed were erased by martyrdom, since nothing more could be asked of a faithful Christian. Martyrdom, in short, was the perfect sacrifice and it implied the achievement of spiritual perfection. It was one thing, however, to recognize the sanctity of martyrs, quite another to do so for nonmartyrs. How was the church to know whether a nonmartyr had persevered in faith to the end of his life?

The question first arose, it seems, in connection with confessors. Like martyrs, confessors were revered even while they were in prison. Other Christians would come, sometimes at great risk to themselves, to minister to them. Afterward, as we have seen, survivors were frequently granted privileges and pride of place within the community of Christians. But, being human, not all of these confessors survived the community's adulation with their humility—or in some cases, their faith—intact.

Long before they died, ascetics too were frequently shown the deference usually accorded to martyrs. Just as the martyrs were made pure by their suffering and death, so, it was thought, were the ascetics purified by the rigor of their spiritual discipline. The analogy is quite explicit in *The Life of Antony*, ascribed to Athanasius, which was published immediately after the saint's death in 355 and remained for centuries one of the primary models for hagiographic texts. In it, Athanasius describes in exotic detail the extended fasts, silences, and other sufferings willingly endured by the desert hermit. There in his cell, Athanasius writes, Antony "was daily being martyred by his conscience in the conflicts of the faith."

By shunning the society of town and village for the bleak desert wastes, the ascetic strove for the purity of heart which, it was believed, Adam and Eve knew in the Garden before their fall from grace. Like Adam, ascetics experienced the temptations of Satan, often in the form of temptations of the flesh, and so did battle with the powers of evil who, they believed, ruled a fallen world. But these ascetics were not so removed from society that the faithful could not seek them out for spiritual counsel and cures. In a word, they were perceived, like the confessors, as "living saints," and in time the stories of their lives rivaled those of the martyrs. Indeed, *The Life of Antony* so moved the youthful Augustine that, upon reading it, he renounced his desire to marry and eventually became a saint himself.

But here again, how were the faithful to know that the ascetic, in the privacy of his cell, had not yielded to temptation? How could they be sure that any "living saint" had died in perfect friendship with God and hence was capable of interceding on their behalf?

The proof, as it turned out, was in their miracles. In addition to their reputations for personal holiness, confessors and ascetics were judged worthy of cult by the number of miracles posthumously produced at their shrines or through their remains. Augustine was particularly influential in defending the idea that miracles were signs of God's power and proof of the sanctity of those in whose name they were wrought. His conviction was especially strengthened after the discovery in 415 of the remains of St. Stephen in the Holy Land and their dispersal to various shrines in the West. Miracles quickly followed and Augustine, anxious that believers be confirmed in their faith, kept records of them. In one instance, he brought a young man who had recently been cured by Stephen's relics to testify in church, and then introduced his sister who continued to suffer from the same ailment. These and other examples are cited at great length in the concluding chapter in his monumental *City of God*, where they are introduced in the course of an elevated dialogue with Plato, Cicero, and Porphyry as unimpeachable evidence of the resurrection of the body.

By the fifth century, therefore, several elements existed which would eventually be codified in the church's formal saint-making procedure. Saints were identified as such by (1) their reputations, especially for martyrdom, among the people; (2) the stories and legends into which their lives were transmuted as exemplars of heroic virtue; and (3) their reputation for producing miracles, especially those worked posthumously at their shrines or through their relics. Although not every story was uncritically accepted, several more centuries would pass before the church would insist that these elements be verified through an investigation into the lives and deaths of saints. In the interim, saints remained objects of cult, not inquiry. It sufficed for sainthood that the deceased was remembered, venerated, and—above all—invoked.

Between the sixth and the tenth centuries, the cult of the saints expanded geometrically. As the faith was spread to the Goths and the

Franks, and then on to the Celts of Britain and the Slavs of Eastern
Europe, newly converted Christians demanded recognition of their
own martyrs and saints—often enough, the very missionaries whom
they had killed for preaching the faith. In turn, the church encouraged
the veneration of relics among the newly baptized in order to
strengthen their faith and to prevent recourse to the worship of old
idols. Popes were generous with the remains of saints in Roman cemeteries, which they treated as a spiritual treasury. Many an important
visitor to Rome came away with the gift of a saint's body.

In the East, the cult of the saints proliferated in a different manner.
Since Christian Constantinople, the "new Rome," could boast of no
martyrs of its own to match those of the old Rome, the church im-
ported them, beginning in 356 with the bodies of St. Timothy, St.
Andrew, and St. Luke. Thus began the practice of "translation" or
removal of relics from tombs to churches throughout the Christian
world. Another new practice was "invention": the discovery and veneration of hitherto unrecognized saintly remains, such as the previously mentioned discovery of the bones of St. Stephen in Jerusalem.
First in the East, and then—reluctantly—in the West, the translation
and invention of bodies were accompanied by dismemberment and
distribution of relics. Just as the soul was totally present in every part
of the body, so, it was popularly believed, the spirit of the saint was
powerfully present in each relic. Thus, detached from the whole body
and separated from the tomb, relics took on magical power of their
own.

Inevitably, this traffic in relics encouraged abuses. Relics were sold,
falsified, fought over, prompting action by church authorities. Beginning in the eighth century, popes ordered the remains of the Roman
martyrs removed from the catacombs and placed in the city's churches
to prevent further desecration and neglect. But the process was slow
and not well policed. In the ninth century there was even a corporation which specialized in the discovery, sale, and export of relics to all
sections of Europe. Monks, too, became adept at stealing relics from
each other's monasteries: the better the relics in their monastic treasury, the greater the fame of the monastery. In the twelfth century,
the commerce in relics reached a peak of sorts when the Crusaders
stripped Constantinople, Antioch, Jerusalem, and Edessa of their most
revered relics and carried them back to the churches of the West. The
appetite for relics never abated, and the abuses and trafficking continued until Martin Luther made relics—and saints—an issue of the
Protestant Reformation.

The cult of the saints, of course, was not limited to the cult of

Important.

relics. But what the preoccupation with relics confirms is the triumph of the saint as a source of miraculous power over the saint as an example of the imitation of Christ. Though venerated for their holiness, saints were invoked for their powers. Indeed, when it came to recognizing new saints, reports of miraculous healings and other thaumaturgic powers were of greater weight in Christianity's first millennium than accounts of heroic virtue. Moreover, the miracles that counted most were those received posthumously at shrines or through relics. Wizards, after all, could work miracles through the power of Satan, but only "friends of God" in heaven could intercede for the faithful on earth.

In retrospect, we can see that the joining of tomb and altar, as Brown puts it, was a process of uniting the ecclesiastical power of the residential bishops with the charismatic power of the saints. The presence of a popular saint's body or bones enormously enhanced the prestige of a local church. And within a diocese, the presence of a major shrine—especially one that attracted streams of pilgrims—was a boon to the local bishop. It is not surprising, therefore, that the history of canonization, as we now understand that process, began with the need to supervise shrines and relics. Only after the bishops achieved that control did they turn—gradually and unevenly—to the problem of validating the cults of new saints.

THE DEVELOPMENT OF CANONIZATION

ACCORDING TO AN ancient axiom of the church, the rule of worship is the rule of faith (lex orandi, lex credendi)—or, to put it another way, to know what Christians believe, listen to their prayers. Whatever else it entailed, veneration of the saints was a liturgical act. Saints were remembered, invoked, prayed to wherever Christians assembled for worship. On these occasions, their names were read out as an honor roll of the blessed. Hence the root meaning of canonization: placing a name in a canon or list of saints.

In the early centuries, such lists were numerous. Lists of martyrs, called "martyrologies," were followed by assorted calendars with the names and burial places of saints. Local churches had their own calendars, each reflecting the canon of the region, and these were sometimes exchanged with other local churches. Monasteries, too, kept their own calendars, as did nations. It wasn't until the seventeenth century, in the wake of the Protestant Reformation, that a universal

Anyone can work a miracle, but where does it come from. From a selfish place, the place of the devil or of God. From God. From God? glory.

SAINTS, THEIR CULTS, AND CANONIZATION   65

canon was established for the entire church. ✓

But the actual saint-making process, as we have seen, was far more complex, more casual, and certainly less controllable than the mere compiling of lists. From the fifth to the tenth century, however, bishops gradually assumed a much more direct role in supervising emergent cults. Before adding a new name to the local calendar, bishops insisted that petitioners provide them with written accounts (called *vitae*) of the candidate's life, virtues, and death, together with accounts of his miracles and, where applicable, his martyrdom. More exacting prelates also demanded testimony from eyewitnesses, especially of purported miracles. But these rudimentary procedures, it should be noted, were primarily concerned with establishing the saint's reputation for holiness rather than with examining his worthiness or personal virtue. Thus the *vitae* read to the bishop tended to be stereotypical accounts embroidered with legends and hagiographical excess, and the testimony of witnesses was frequently third hand—mere gossip. (Well into the Middle Ages, for example, the list of miracles attributed to saints included various raisings from the dead.) Following the approval of the bishop, or that of a regional synod, the body was exhumed and transferred (the "translation") to an altar, an act which came to symbolize official canonization. Finally, the new saint was assigned a day for the liturgical celebration of his feast and his name added to the local calendar of saints. In this informal way, canonization gradually became an ecclesiastical function.

But there were, as bishops came to realize, serious reasons for looking deeper into the lives of candidates before granting episcopal approval. Even Augustine had recognized the danger in allowing cult to heretics: in his own day, the Donatists, who were eventually condemned for heresy, were known to be so avid for martyrdom that they sometimes invited others to do them in. How could the church venerate saints whose martyrdom was not authentic or who denied the orthodox faith? As for miracles, who was to say that they hadn't been worked with the aid of the Devil? Clearly, some form of quality control was needed.

By the end of the tenth century, there was growing sentiment to have popes, in virtue of their supreme authority, do the honors. In this way, it was felt, the saint was more likely to receive recognition beyond the local community, thus adding a certain cachet to his cult. This, at any rate, appears to have been the modest motive behind the canonization of Bishop Udalricus (Ulrich) of Augsburg in 993, the first authenticated case of a papal validation of a cult. At the request of the bishop's successor, Pope John XV heard the account of Udalricus's life and miracles and authorized the translation of his remains. But another seven centuries would pass before the entire process of making saints was firmly in the control of the papacy. Before that could happen, two developments had to take place: the procedures for making saints had to be greatly refined and the papacy itself had to consolidate its authority over the church.

Neither happened instantly or without conflict. As might be expected, the extension of papal control over the saint-making process—gradual though it was—was not always welcome north of the Alps. In the first place, many saints had long since died and were already the objects of robust local cults. Who was the pope, after all these years, to deny their validity? How, in any case, were he or his legates to conduct a retrospective investigation into the saint's life to determine whether he actually merited the people's veneration? And finally, there was the inevitable tension between the church of the center—Rome—and the churches of the periphery, as is well illustrated by a celebrated incident that occurred in England after the Norman Conquest.

In 1078, Archbishop Lanfranc, a fastidious Italian enamored of Norman ways, occupied the see of Canterbury. Lanfranc was inclined to think of the Anglo-Saxons in his charge as Christian rustics whose local saints were of dubious quality. In conversation with the English monk Anselm, Lanfranc asked whether he thought the Holy See should validate the cult of a previous archbishop of Canterbury, Alphege. The latter was an Anglo-Saxon monk widely revered as a martyr and national hero. In 1011, rampaging Danes had seized Canterbury, imprisoned Alphege, and sought to extort an exorbitant sum for his release. Alphege refused and forbade the people to pay the ransom. For this, he was killed in 1012 by drunken Danes wielding the bones of an ox, thus becoming Canterbury's first, though not the last, martyred archbishop.

To Lanfranc, the evidence was not at all clear that Alphege had been assassinated for refusing to deny Jesus Christ, as tradition required, rather than for purely political purposes. Anselm, who was later canonized himself, responded with the observation that John the Baptist hadn't been killed for refusing to deny Christ either, yet he was regarded as a saint of the church. Lanfranc was immediately won over by the analogy and without further investigation authorized Alphege's cult.

In the course of ensuing decades, papal interventions in the making of saints grew more pronounced. Increasingly, the popes demanded proof of miracles and virtue in the form of testimony from reliable witnesses. Pope Urban II (1088–1099), in one notable case, refused to canonize an abbot (Gurloes) unless the monks could produce eyewitnesses who could attest to having seen the miracles attributed to their former abbot. The following century, in a letter to King Kol of Sweden, Pope Alexander III (1159–1181) upbraided a local bishop for tolerating cult to a monk who had been killed in a drunken brawl, even though the local folk insisted that miracles had been worked through his intercession. Brawling monks were not the sort of examples of holiness, Alexander observed, that the church wanted the people to imitate.

Alexander was the first in what, with some interruptions, was to become a long line of great medieval lawyer-popes who fashioned the Roman Catholic Church into Europe's most significant Medieval venture into rule under law. Like other dimensions of church activity, the making of saints was gradually placed under the jurisdiction of the Holy See and its lawyers. In 1170, Alexander decreed that no one, regardless of his or her reputation for holiness or wonder-working, could be venerated locally without papal authorization. However, his decree by no means spelled an immediate end to episcopal canonizations, nor did it quench the popular thirst for new cults. In 1234, Pope Gregory IX published his *Decretals*, or collection of pontifical laws, in which he asserted the absolute jurisdiction of the Roman pontiff over all causes of saints and made it binding on the universal church. Since saints were objects of devotion for the entire church, he reasoned, only the pope with his universal jurisdiction possessed the authority to canonize.

From this point on, the canonization process became increasingly fastidious. Essentially, the procedures called for the creation of local tribunals with delegates of the pope hearing testimony from witnesses in support of the candidate's virtue and miracles. The latter were subjected to particular scrutiny. In 1247, for example, cardinals delegated by the pope to report on the miracles of St. Edmund of Abingdon observed sardonically that if ancient saints had to submit to such strict investigation, few of them would have been canonized. At the same time, the Holy See sought to nip spontaneous new cults in the bud by prohibiting the publication of books on the miracles or revelations of unofficial local saints, as well as the public exposure of their images with halos or rays of light surrounding their heads.

Even so, it was not until the fourteenth century, with the removal of the papal court to Avignon, that the popes were able to institute standardized methods for investigating the lives of new candidates for sainthood. "Captives" though they may have become of the velvet-fisted French monarchs, the Avignoise popes (1309–1377) transformed the Roman Curia into an efficient bureaucracy. Under their canonical reforms, the procedures for canonization took on the explicit form of a full-blown legal trial between the petitioners, represented by an official procurator, or prosecutor of the cause, and the pope, represented by a new curial official, the "Promoter of the Faith," eventually to be more popularly known as "the Devil's Advocate." In addition, before a cause could be considered, the Holy See demanded letters "from kings, princes and other prominent and honest persons" (including, of course, bishops) requesting a process on behalf of the candidate. *Vox populi*, in other words, was not enough to sustain a reputation for holiness without support from the church's elites. Often, the trial itself took months and was conducted locally. For instance, the trial of the Augustinian hermit St. Nicholas of Tolentino lasted from July 7 to September 28, 1325, and heard testimony from 371 witnesses. Little wonder, then, that between the years 1200 and 1334, only twenty-six papal canonizations took place.

Despite these measures, the centuries between 1200 and 1500 saw the widest diffusion of the cult of the saints in the history of the Western church. Every village and town venerated its own patron saint, and the rise of the new mendicant orders added fresh names to the lists. Faced with an increasingly anarchical situation, the papacy introduced a distinction where before there was none: thereafter, only the papally canonized were to be called *sancti* (saints), while those who were venerated locally or only by religious orders were called *beati* (blesseds). In effect, local cults were to be tolerated but official recognition was to be reserved for those Servants of God whose lives and virtues, in the judgment of papal saint-makers, would best serve as models for Christians throughout the church. This distinction, which seems to have been born out of practical concerns, soon provoked a major theological debate which continues to this day: is a solemn declaration of sanctity—canonization—an infallible act of the pope? Canon lawyers tend to think not while theologians have generally held that it is. The issue will be discussed in detail later, but on one point the medieval theologians were unanimous. Beatification carried no guarantee that the Servant of God was truly in heaven, while canonization—depending on the theologian—probably or most certainly did. Eventually, beatification was incorporated into the canonization procedure and the theological issue of infallibility with regard to beatifications became moot.

SAINTS AND THE SUPERNATURAL:
MEDIEVAL TRANSFORMATIONS

INEVITABLY, THE POWER to canonize entailed the power to determine the meaning of sanctity. As canonization became a papal prerogative, new models of holiness emerged which not only reflected Roman values and priorities but also transformed the image of the saint. On the basis of his authoritative examination of all the canonization processes between 1181 and 1431, including many that were rejected, French medieval historian André Vauchez has been able to trace the following general shifts in the officially approved models of holiness.

Prior to 1270, sainthood was bestowed on a large and diverse company of candidates: bishops who exemplified the right use of authority and wealth; laity who labored on behalf of social justice; penitents whose conversion from sinful ways provided the ordinary faithful with examples they could readily emulate; monastic reformers; and, above all, southern Europeans like Dominic and Francis of Assisi, founders of new mendicant orders.

By the end of the century, however, the number and kinds of people accepted for formal investigation by the Curia in Rome began to narrow, reflecting both the prerogatives of the papacy and interests of their clients—chiefly the religious orders and royal houses favored by the papacy. In the course of the Middle Ages, Vauchez finds, the pious royalty and pastorally sensitive bishops "who had monopolized the attention of the faithful no longer seemed appropriate, in the eyes of popes and the 'grand clerics' of their entourage, as models to be proposed for the universal church." Martyrs, too, fell from Rome's favor. Although the church did not lack for princes and pilgrims, missionaries, and even children who shed their blood in the thirteenth and fourteenth centuries, very few were canonized. Those that were, such as Archbishop Thomas à Becket of Canterbury (can. 1173) and Archbishop Stanislaus of Cracow (can. 1253), were honored for dying in defense of the rights of the church. Later candidates, Vauchez surmises, were rejected by the papacy because their popular cults were tainted by more secular political passions. As in the case of Archbishop Alphege, it was not clear in the eyes of Rome that the victims had died purely because of their faith. Indeed, Vauchez observes that "no servants of God who had died a violent death were canonized between 1254 and 1481." And by the end of the Middle Ages, he concludes, "the identification of sanctity with martyrdom was no more than a mere memory."

To judge by the causes that succeeded, what interested the papal saint-makers were candidates whose virtue could in no way be mistaken for purely human success. In general, they favored Servants of God who embraced radical forms of poverty, chastity, and obedience—paths of renunciation which distinguished the "religious" life from that of the laity. Several of the canonized were founders of religious orders or movements through which their personal ideals were institutionalized and perpetuated. Not a few were also visionaries and mystics. Thus, as Vauchez observes, the paradigmatic saint of the twelfth century was Francis of Assisi, who was widely perceived as an *alter Christus*, not the least because he was the first person to receive in his body the "stigmata" or cruciform wounds of Christ. Francis was speedily canonized two years after his death in 1228.* His spiritual sister, Clare of Assisi, a contemplative nun and foundress of the Minoresses or Poor Clares, so impressed Innocent IV that the pope nearly canonized her on her deathbed in 1253. Innocent had to be prevented from allowing the Office of Virgins to be chanted at her funeral, as though she were already canonized. In the event, Clare was duly declared a saint two years after by Innocent's successor.

Another favored model was the learned cleric, such as St. Dominic, canonized in 1234, and his illustrious spiritual descendant St. Thomas Aquinas, canonized in 1323, forty-nine years after his death. (Scholars —even theologians—typically take longer to canonize, as we will have reason to note in chapter 12.) In part, this model reflected the rise to influence of the great medieval universities, and of the Dominicans themselves. In part, it also reflected a papal preference for clerical candidates of high birth who distinguished themselves through devotion to both the intellectual and the spiritual life. In sum, the major trend in canonizations was away from public benefactors—just kings and kindly bishops—toward world-renouncing ascetics and intellectual defenders of the faith, several of whom were also graced with extraordinary mystical experiences.

But if Vauchez is to be believed, the saints preferred by Rome were not widely popular among ordinary Christian folk. (Here, as in all things, Francis of Assisi is the exception.) In the first place, the great mass of believers were not interested in saints as moral examples, but as spiritual patrons who protected the populace against storms and plagues. Second, the moral, ascetical, and intellectual virtues exemplified by the papally canonized could not be easily cultivated outside the cloister or convent. The fact that so many of these new saints

---

* Interestingly, the stigmata of St. Frances is the only such phenomenon to be assigned its own liturgical feast day: September 17.

Saint of the poor.
Saint of the hierarchy.

AINTS, THEIR CULTS, AND CANONIZATION   71

Important page.

founded religious orders merely underlined the growing assumption
within high ecclesiastical circles that the religious life was the primary, if not the exclusive, avenue to holiness. It is not at all surprising, therefore, that religious orders became highly successful in
promoting their own members as candidates for canonization. And as
a matter of record, from the Middle Ages to this day relatively few
Catholics have been canonized who have not taken public or private
vows* of poverty and chastity, almost none at all, apart from martyrs,
who have not been promoted by religious orders.

The thrust behind papal canonizations was to present the faithful
with lives worth imitating, not saints to be invoked for miracles and
other favors. In this respect, the division between official and local or
popular saints reflected the mounting tension within the church between the saint as exemplar of virtue and the saint as thaumaturge or
wonder-worker. From the 1230s on, writes Vauchez, "preachers spread
the idea that the glory of the saints lay in their lives and not in their
miracles." The problem was not disbelief in miracles on the part of
Christianity's tutored elites. "When a toothache made him suffer or a
serious illness threatened his life, the most sober theologian invoked
his heavenly protectors," Vauchez observes, "just as the peasant did
when he was concerned about his crops or the fisherman was in peril
at sea." The point at which the elites differed from the masses was the
significance of miracles in establishing sanctity. Whereas the latter
considered miracles as preemptive signs of the presence of holiness,
the former regarded them "as effects of a moral conduct and spiritual
life on which only the church could pass judgment."

In sum, the development of canonization as a papal process meant
a shift in focus from popular concern with miracles to elite concern
with virtue. To be sure, proof of miracles remained necessary for
verifying a candidate's reputation for holiness, but only a thorough
examination of the life could establish the presence of virtue. In the
course of the Middle Ages, however, the mere "presence" of virtue
ceased to be sufficient. Pope Innocent IV (1243–1259) declared that
sanctity required a life of "continuous, uninterrupted virtue"—in effect, perfection. Thus, while reformed sinners were still eligible for
canonization, preference went to candidates whose entire lives approached the impeccable. For the postulators who compiled the dossiers on candidates for canonization, therefore, proof of virtue wasn't
enough unless it was also "heroic." Thus, as the papal criteria for

Important

* Many saints and blesseds belonged to religious orders such as the Franciscans and Dominicans as
"tertiaries" or members of "third orders" after priests and nuns. Tertiaries take private vows and have
spiritual directors but continue to live in the world and may be married.

sainthood became ever more stringent, the *vitae* of the Servants of God became increasingly idealized and stylized. On the one hand, flaws disappeared; on the other, the virtues of faith, hope, and charity were inflated by stories of supernatural gifts and prodigies of moral discipline. In this manner, paradoxically, the miraculous was restored to sainthood. Now, though, it was not the stories of posthumous healings that counted but astounding feats of moral and spiritual athleticism manifest during the saint's life. Thus, the study of canonical proceedings, Vauchez observes, "allow[s] us to see how a human life was transformed into the *vita* of a saint."

Such transformations were already evident in the thirteenth century. In pressing the cause of St. Anthony of Padua (1195–1231), each successive biographer felt authorized to outdo his predecessor in ascribing new miracles or further perfections to the famed Italian preacher. As Vauchez documents, the transformation of lives into hagiographical texts reveals an increasing emphasis on the contemplative over the active life, detachment rather than engagement with the world, the inner life over the outer—leading to the eventual redefinition of sanctity "as a state of such great interior emptiness that the soul can receive the Gift of God and the infusion of the Holy Spirit." Even the lives of activist bishops were transformed into the *vitae* of monks, as in the case of St. Thomas of Cantelupe (can. 1320), whose dossier records such a deep love of poverty and chastity that he refused to bathe or to embrace his own sisters after he became bishop of Hereford.

The comparatively few laymen and laywomen who won canonization were similarly grafted onto monastic and mystical patterns. St. Elzear of Sabran, for instance, was a Provençal count and the only layman canonized in the fourteenth century. Apart from his revelations and visions, what set this contemplative spirit apart was his deliberately unconsummated marriage of twenty-five years. Elzear's virtue was more than matched by his wife, (Blessed) Delphina of Puimichel, St. Bridget of Sweden, and St. Catherine of Siena, each of them celebrated virgins and mystics, who were the only laywomen* to be canonized in the fourteenth and fifteenth centuries.

It would be difficult to overestimate the impact of these new, papally approved models on subsequent notions of sanctity. Through them, holiness became permanently if not exclusively identified with the *intensity* and *interiority* of the spiritual life, together with the rejection of marriage and the domestic life. Thus, even though a Fran-

---

* In fact, Bridget founded an order of nuns and led a monastic life in Rome. Catherine was a tertiary and lived in a cell in her parents' home.

cis, a Dominic, or a Clare was deemed altogether inimitable in his or her particularity, through canonization these figures became either models on which other saints consciously patterned their lives or, what often amounted to the same thing, models on which their biographers relied to construct their *vitae*. In the centuries that followed, more than one *vita* of a Servant of God was written so that the candidate might be recognized as another Francis or Bridget or Catherine of Siena.

By the close of the Middle Ages, therefore, the cult of the saints was characterized by paradox. On the one hand, the gap had widened between official, papally canonized figures and local, unofficial, popular saints. On the other hand, there was a convergence between elite and popular presentations of sanctity: both looked to signs of the supernatural as evidence of holiness, though they interpreted those signs very differently. Either way, the saint was perceived as someone whom God had predestined for a life far beyond the capabilities of all but a few Christian souls. Even so, humble sinners could take hope: the perfect few, the church taught, had through their strenuous self-denial produced a "treasury" of vicarious "merits" which could be dispensed to the spiritually frail masses. It was this spiritual economy which, in due time, was effectively challenged by a conscience-driven German monk. In the name of a purer Gospel, Martin Luther would reject both the spiritual athletes put forward by Rome and the panoply of wonder-working spiritual patrons invoked by the common believer.

REFORMATION, REFORM, AND THE TRIUMPH OF THE LAWYERS

IN RETROSPECT, THE "bureaucratization of sanctity," as one contemporary Catholic scholar calls it, was both inevitable and necessary. The impulse to multiply the number of saints, after all, did not come from the hierarchy but from the faithful, who relied on their heavenly patrons for help in meeting a wide variety of needs. Indeed, to a very great extent, medieval Christianity was a culture of saints and their effects. Every town and village had its patron saint, every church its relics. Countries, too, had their patrons, such as England's St. George and Ireland's St. Patrick. Every trade and guild looked to a saint for patronage; by taking a saint's name at baptism, every Christian had his or her own advocate in heaven. Saints cured disease, and warded off calamities and evil spirits. They also punished sinners. The faithful not only prayed to saints, they also swore by them. As the number of saints multiplied, so did the feasts in their honor and the pilgrimages to their shrines. Among the literate, the lives of the saints were medieval best-sellers, fully the equivalent of the modern romance; for the illiterate, there were images and statues and iconography of every sort.

In short, Europe on the eve of the Protestant Reformation was a society drenched in saints, their effects and their lore. It was a society, Dutch historian Johan Huizinga reminds us, in which "excesses and abuses result[ed] from an extreme familiarity with the holy. . . . Too large a part of the living faith had crystallized in the veneration of the saints, and thus there arose a craving for something more spiritual." Already in the early fourteenth century, the voices of would-be reformers like the Czech Jan Hus had been raised against the promiscuous cult of the saints. Now, the same criticisms were heard from Martin Luther and John Calvin, and throughout Protestant Europe they were heeded.

There were, to be sure, many causes of the Protestant Reformation, but its most palpable effect on ordinary believers was the collapse of the mediating spiritual structures represented by the cult of the saints. Overnight, relics and statues disappeared from reformed sanctuaries. The pulpit replaced the altar, words replaced images, the eye gave way to the ear, the symbol became merely symbolic. ". . . The Reformation attacked the cult of the saints, and nowhere in the whole contested area did it meet with less resistance," writes Huizinga. "In strong contrast with the belief in witchcraft and demonology, which fully maintained their ground in Protestant countries, both among the clergy and the laity, the saints fell without a blow being struck in their defense."

Of all the Protestant Reformers, Luther's reaction to saints was the most interesting and most complicated. His decision to become a monk was triggered by a thunderstorm during which he prayed for protection to St. Anne, vowing to enter a monastery if he survived. But he eventually lost faith in the power of saints—and their relics. In 1520 he published an anonymous pamphlet parodying the relic collection of the archbishop of Mainz, listing among them "a fine piece of the left horn of Moses, three flames from the bush of Moses on Mount Sinai, two feathers and an egg from the Holy Ghost" and the like. But the archbishop's own catalog of relics was its own parody: among other holy objects, it included a clod of earth from the spot where Christ recited the Lord's Prayer, one of the silver coins Judas

Urbanu VIII
1623-1644
sets the procedure
for making saints!

was paid to betray Jesus, and remains from the Israelites' manna in the desert.

But Luther had more serious theological objections as well. Like some of the early church fathers, he thought the cult of the saints pagan and idolatrous. He rejected the mediation of saints just as he rejected the mediation of the priests. He felt that a saint had no more grace than any other Christian. Since Christians are justified by faith alone, he argued, they could not be saved through their own merits, much less those received through prayer from the "treasury" of the saints. Finally, he protested against the legendary accretions to the saints' stories as they had been handed down. Nonetheless, he appreciated those which he felt were authentic. "Next to Holy Scripture," Luther wrote, "there certainly is no more useful book for Christians than the lives of the saints, especially when unadulterated and authentic."

Rome's response was double-edged. On the one hand, the Council of Trent (1545–1563) vigorously reaffirmed the cult of the saints and their relics, declaring that "only men of irreligious mentality deny that the saints enjoying eternal happiness in heaven are to be invoked." On the other hand, it moved the church to reform. Numerous names were pruned from the overcrowded calendar of saints to make room for later additions. Detailed reform of procedures came in 1588, when Pope Sixtus V created the Congregation of Rites and gave its officials responsibility for preparing papal canonizations and for the authentication of relics. But it was only during the pontificate of Urban VIII (1623–1644) that the papacy finally gained complete control over the making of saints. In a series of papal decrees, Urban defined the canonical procedures by which beatification and canonization would take place. One of them deserves special notice. The pope strictly forbade any form of public veneration—including the publication of books of miracles or revelations attributed to a supposed saint—unless and until that person was beatified or canonized by solemn papal declaration. But he made an important exception in the case of saints whose cults could be shown to have existed "from time immemorial" or could be justified "on the strength of what the fathers or saints have written, with the ancient and conscious acquiescence of the Apostolic See [Rome] or the local bishops."

As a result, there were now only two paths to sainthood: through the narrow front door of formal papal procedure or through the narrower back door of "equipollent" (equivalent) beatification or canonization for cults that were already at least a century old at the time of

Urban's decree. In effect, the second path was a kind of edict of toleration for popular local cults of long standing, thus easing somewhat the major impact of the decree. Henceforth, any unauthorized display of public cult toward a person prior to beatification or canonization would automatically disqualify that candidate for canonization. The faithful could still gather at the tomb of the deceased and pray for divine favors. They could offer private devotions in their homes as well. But they could not invoke or venerate the deceased in a church without jeopardizing his or her chances for canonization.

Rome had spoken, and all that remained to be done was to organize and codify the Roman procedures for making saints. What was once a spontaneous recognition by the local community was now a retroactive investigation conducted by men who had never met the Servant of God. What was once a populist process was now largely in the hands of canon lawyers resident in Rome. But canon law, as we will see, is like British and American common law in that it depends on precedents, not deductions from abstract principles. And in the matter of making saints, as this brief survey attests, the precedents in one form or another stretch all the way back to the New Testament. Thus, yet another century passed before Prospero Lambertini, a brilliant canonist who had come up through the ranks of the Congregation of Rites to become Pope Benedict XIV, set himself to the task of reviewing and clarifying the church's theory and practice of making saints. His long and masterful work in five volumes, De Servorum Dei beatificatione et Beatorum canonizatione ("On the Beatification of Servants of God and the Canonization of Blesseds"), published between 1734 and 1738, remains to this day the touchstone text for the making of saints.

In subsequent centuries, refinements in the saint-making process came chiefly from outside influences. The development of history as critical science, for example, gradually affected how the congregation handled texts, though it had a less perceptible effect, as we will see, on the writing of vitae. More important, the development of scientific medicine greatly reduced the number and kinds of "divine favors" which could be accepted as miracles. But the determinant "science" remained canon law and its requirements. The primary evidence remained that of eyewitnesses, and the primary focus was on proving martyrdom or heroic virtue. Even the operative Latin term used by the church, processus, means "trial." Thus, if the purpose of papal canonization, as it emerged in the modern era, was to arrive at a theological truth—namely, the candidate is indeed with God in heaven—both the form and, what is more important, the spirit of the process were judicial.

THE MODERN PROCESS:
THE SAINT AS PRODUCT OF A SYSTEM

IN 1917, THE formal procedures for making saints was incorporated into the church's Code of Canon Law. For those who did not study canon law, or read Latin, the entire process was outlined in elaborate detail by an English Catholic cleric, Canon Macken, in a book published in 1910. Like the saints it produces, the system had, after four centuries of refinement, acquired a certain hagiographic reputation of its own for judicial precision in the discovery and verification of authentic saints. In Macken's assessment,

> The "fierce light which beats upon a throne" is as nothing compared to this most careful and elaborate enquiry. The proceedings throughout are conducted with much greater care and formality than the most important suit at law. The history of a secular jurisprudence can show us nothing approaching the extreme circumspection observed in these investigations . . .
>
> In the processes of canonization everything is reduced to an exact science. The legal procedure of civilized nations is based largely on the established methods of the Church. But nowhere else do we find the same severe regularity and strict discipline that are practiced in these examinations. The utmost care and accuracy are observed at every stage, and, looking at the matter from the purely human point of view, it must be admitted that if there is any institution, any known method of investigation, capable of arriving at a full knowledge of the truth, the calm, deliberate procedure of the Church is eminently entitled to this distinction. The great object of all the enquiries, from beginning to end, is to avoid all possibility of error or deception, and to ensure that the truth will shine forth in all its brilliancy and splendour.

Today, the saint-making process continues to inspire awe, largely because it is so poorly understood. Thus, as recently as 1985, the author of a popular study of the Vatican could write: "The mystery of sainthood and the canonic process, with all its spiritual dimensions of divine intercession, relics and miracles, probably is the Church's greatest enigma outside of the mass itself." Unfortunately, the "enigma" he went on to describe no longer corresponded to the system used by the church. Two years earlier, the procedures by which saints are made had been drastically changed. To be sure, some of the juridical formalities remained the same, but the dynamic behind them had shifted.

In order to appreciate the significance of that shift, one must understand the juridical context in which it took place. Nothing ever totally changes in the Church of Rome; thus, many of these juridical structures and procedures remain intact. What follows, then, is a description of the saint-making system, with all its "circumspection," as it existed as recently as 1982. Only after we see how the system had been operating throughout the twentieth century can we appreciate the far-reaching and little understood revolution in saint-making which has occurred under John Paul II.

Under the old rules, as well as the new, the system was designed to elicit answers to the following general questions:

Does the candidate have a reputation for having died a martyr's death or for having practiced the Christian virtues to a heroic degree?

As evidence of this reputation, do people invoke the candidate's intercession with God when praying for divine favors?

What particular message or example would canonization of the candidate bring to the church?

Is the candidate's reputation for martyrdom or extraordinary virtue founded in fact?

Conversely, is there anything in the candidate's life or writings which presents an obstacle to his or her canonization? Specifically, did the candidate hold, teach, or write anything which is unorthodox or otherwise inimical to Catholic faith or morals?

Are any of the divine signs attributed to the candidate's intercession inexplicable by human reason and therefore potential miracles?

Is there any pastoral reason why this candidate should not be beatified (that is, declared blessed) at this time?

Since the beatification of the candidate, have further miracles occurred through the candidate's intercession which can be accepted as signs from God that the blessed is worthy of canonization?

Is there any pastoral reason why the blessed should not be canonized, at least at this time?

In actual practice, the process of making saints involved—as it still does—a variety of procedures, skills, and participants: promotion, fund-raising, and publicity on the part of those who think the candidate a saint; tribunals of investigation by the local bishop or bishops; administrative procedures by Congregation officials; study and analysis by expert consultors; lawyerly disputation between the Promoter of the Faith (the Devil's Advocate) and the advocate of the cause; and advisory judgments by the cardinals of the congregation. But at all times, it is only the pope whose judgment is binding; he alone has the power to declare a candidate worthy of beatification or canonization.

Under the old juridical system, a successful cause typically passed through the following phases:

1. *Prejuridical phase.* Prior to 1917, canon law required that at least fifty years must elapse after the candidate's death before his virtues or martyrdom could be formally discussed in Rome. This was to ensure that the candidate's reputation for holiness was durable and not merely a passing phase of celebrity. Even now that the fifty-year rule has been rescinded, bishops are warned to be especially careful in distinguishing between an authentic reputation for sanctity, manifested by prayers and other acts of devotion toward the deceased, and a reputation stimulated by the media and mere "public opinion." (This wariness of the press is hardly new: a warning against taking media reputations too seriously was first issued by the congregation in 1878.)

Nonetheless, during this phase several unofficial activities are permitted to take place. First, an individual or a group recognized by the church can anticipate the formal process by organizing financial and spiritual support on behalf of the potential candidate, as we have already seen in the case of New York's Cardinal Cooke. As a practical matter, these "initiators" of a cause are usually members of a religious order, since only they have the resources, the know-how and, often enough, the institutional self-interest to guide a process to completion. Normally, a guild is formed, money is collected, reports of divine favors are solicited, a newsletter is circulated, prayer cards are printed, and, not infrequently, a pious biography is published. This is, in effect, a promotional phase, designed to encourage private devotion to the candidate and to convince the bishop or "ordinary" of the diocese in which the candidate died that a genuine and persistent reputation for holiness exists. Eventually, the initiators become "the petitioner" of the cause when they formally request the bishop to open an official process.

2. *Informative Phase.* If the local bishop decides that there is merit in the candidate, he institutes the Ordinary Process. The purpose of this process is to provide sufficient material to the congregation so that its officials can determine whether a formal process is merited. To that end, the local bishop establishes a tribunal or court of inquiry. Judges summon witnesses to testify both for and against the candidate, who is now called "the Servant of God." If necessary, tribunals may be held wherever the Servant of God has lived. The purpose of these investigative procedures is twofold: first, to establish whether the candidate has a solid reputation for holiness or martyrdom, and

second, to gather preliminary testimony as to whether that reputation is supported by facts. The original testimony is notarized, sealed, and preserved in the diocesan archives. Sealed copies (as late as 1982 special permission from the congregation was required for submitting typescript rather than handwritten copies) are sent by special Vatican courier to Rome.

The local bishop must determine that the Servant of God is not the object of a public cult; that is, it must be proven that with the passage of time, the candidate has not become the object of veneration in a public way. This requirement, formal but necessary, dates back to the reforms of Pope Urban VIII who, as we have seen, forbade cults to saints not officially canonized by the pope.

3. *Judgment of Orthodoxy.* In a concurrent process, the bishop appoints officials to collect the published writings of the candidate. Eventually, letters and other unpublished writings are collected as well. These documents are forwarded to Rome where in the past, they were examined by theological censors for any unorthodox teachings or opinions. The censors have since been abandoned but the examinations still take place. Obviously, the more the candidate wrote the longer this examination takes. Just as obviously, the more venturesome the intellect in matters of faith, the more closely will the candidate be scrutinized. Dissenters from official church teaching are, as a rule, rejected outright. Although the congregation keeps no statistics on why causes are rejected, those who work there confirm that failure to pass this test of doctrinal purity has been the major reason why causes have been halted or put on indefinite hold.

Promoters of a blocked cause, however, do have an opportunity to disprove charges of heterodoxy brought against their candidate. For example, the Society of Saint-Sulpice recently cleared heresy charges against their founder, Father Jean-Jacques Olier, who died in 1657. The Sulpicians, as they are called, are specialists in running seminaries throughout the world and through them Olier's writings on the spiritual have achieved international influence. But in the nineteenth century, a Jesuit discovered a book attributed to Olier that contained unorthodox opinions about the Virgin Mary. The volume was placed on the Vatican's Index of Forbidden Books and Olier's cause was halted. Then, in the fifties, Sulpician scholars discovered that Olier was not the author of the offending volume and marshaled evidence that his teachings on the Virgin Mary were quite orthodox. His process was recently reopened.

Since 1940, candidates have had to pass another test as well. As a kind of security check, all Servants of God must receive from Rome a *nihil obstat*, or declaration that there is "nothing objectionable" about them in the Vatican's files. As a practical matter, this means the files of the Congregation for the Doctrine of the Faith, which is charged with the defense of faith and morals, plus any of the other nine congregations (the Congregation for Bishops, for the Clergy, etc.) that would have reason to keep data on the candidate. The rationale for this procedure is the possibility that one or more congregations may have privileged information regarding the writings or moral behavior of the candidate which would preempt further action on his cause. In one celebrated case, the cause was immediately halted after it was discovered that the Vatican had conclusive evidence that the candidate, a priest and founder of a religious order, had a history of molesting children and apparently never repented his actions. In any event, objections are rarely found; since 1979, for instance, only one cause has failed to receive a *nihil obstat*.

4. *The Roman Phase.* This is the point at which real deliberation begins. As soon as the dossiers from the local bishop arrive at the congregation, responsibility for the cause is assigned to a postulator resident in Rome. There are about 228 postulators listed with the congregation, most of them priests belonging to religious orders. The postulator's responsibility is to represent the petitioners of the cause and, unless it is a charity case, he is paid by the petitioner. The petitioner also pays for the services of an advocate, or defense lawyer, selected by the postulator from among the two dozen or so canon lawyers, lay and clerical, who are trained and licensed by the Holy See to handle causes.

From the materials provided by the local bishop, the lawyer prepares a brief aimed at proving to the congregation's judges that the cause should be officially introduced. In his brief, the lawyer argues that a true reputation for sanctity exists and that the cause contains sufficient evidence to justify a fuller inquiry into the virtues or martyrdom of the Servant of God.

Next, a written dialectic ensues in which the Promoter of the Faith, or Devil's Advocate, proposes objections to the defense lawyer's brief and the advocate replies. This exchange is usually repeated several times and often many years—even decades—elapse before all the differences between the advocate for the cause and the Promoter of the Faith are satisfactorily resolved. Eventually, a printed volume called a *positio* is prepared which contains all the material developed thus far, including the arguments of the Promoter of the Faith and the advocate. The *positio* is studied by the cardinals and official prelates (the prefect, the secretary, the subsecretary and, if necessary, head of the historical section) of the congregation and, at a formal meeting in the Apostolic Palace, they render a judgment. Like the finding of a grand jury, a positive judgment implies that there are good grounds for a trial or *processus*.

Upon acceptance by the congregation, notice is sent to the pope who, unless he has reasons of his own to the contrary, issues a Decree of Introduction. But the way he does this is significant. The presumption is that if the cause has survived examination up to this point, it has a good chance of success. Still, many cases do not succeed. Thus, to emphasize the fact that at this stage the cause has only the administrative approval of the pope, he does not sign the decree with his pontifical name, Pope John Paul II, but uses merely his given first name: *Placet Carolo*—"Karol accepts."

Once a cause has been instructed, it passes into the jurisdiction of the Holy See. It is now called an "Apostolic Process." The Promoter of the Faith or his assistants draw up a new set of questions aimed at eliciting specific information about the virtues or martyrdom of the Servant of God. These questions are sent back to the local diocese where a new tribunal, with judges now deputized by the Holy See, again interrogates those witnesses who are still living. The judges may also seek testimony from new witnesses and, if necessary, they may even be brought to Rome to answer questions.

In effect, the Apostolic Process is a more exacting version of the Ordinary Process. Its purpose is to prove that the candidate's reputation for holiness or martyrdom is based on fact. When the testimony is completed, the documentation is sent to the congregation, where the material is translated into one of the official languages. (Until this century, there was one official language: Latin. Gradually, Italian, Spanish, French, and English were added, reflecting an increase in the number of causes from countries where those languages are spoken.) The documents are then examined by the subsecretary and his staff to make certain that all the juridical forms and protocols have been precisely observed. At the conclusion of this process, the Holy See issues a Decree on the Validity of the Process guaranteeing their legitimate use.

Next, the postulator and his lawyer prepare yet another document, called an *informatio* (an "information") which outlines in systematic fashion the case for virtue or martyrdom. To this is attached a summary of the depositions of the witnesses pertaining precisely to the points to be proved. After study, the Promoter of the Faith makes his objections against the cause, and the advocate, aided by the postulator, replies. This exchange is printed and the entire collection of documents is submitted to the officials of the congregation and their theological consultors for their study and judgment. Difficulties and reservations advanced at this meeting are put forward as new objections by the Promoter of the Faith, and for a second time the defense lawyer responds. This exchange forms the basis of a second meeting and judgment, this time including the cardinals of the congregation. The same process is repeated a third time but with the addition of the pope. If the Servant of God is judged to have practiced the Christian virtues to a heroic degree, or to have died a martyr, he or she is hereafter entitled to be called "Venerable."

5. *Historical Section.* In 1930, Pope Pius XI established a special historical section to take care of ancient causes and certain problems which the purely juridical process was incapable of solving. First, those causes for which eyewitnesses no longer exist are assigned to this section for historical research. Judgments of virtue or martyrdom in such cases are therefore made largely on historical proofs. Second, many other causes are referred to the historical section when controverted points require archival research and other historical investigations. Third, members of the historical section on very rare occasions investigate so-called ancient causes to ascertain the existence, origin, and continuation of a true cult to certain saintly figures, most of whom lived long before papal canonizations were performed. Such figures can, at the discretion of the pope, receive a decree of "equivalent" beatification or canonization.*

6. *Examination of the Corpse.* Sometime prior to beatification, the body of the candidate is exhumed for identification by the local bishop. If it is discovered that the body is not that of the Servant of God, the cause continues but prayers and similar private devotions at the gravesite must cease. This examination is intended for identification purposes only. But if it turns out that the body is not corrupt, this discovery can influence interest in and support for the cause. For example, when Bishop John Neumann was buried in 1860, his body was not embalmed. But when the tomb was opened surreptitiously a month later and his body found to be still intact, word spread throughout Philadelphia. His tomb became something of a shrine, prayers to him increased, and in that way his reputation for holiness spread.

Unlike some other Christian churches, notably the Russian Orthodox, the Roman Catholic Church does not regard an uncorrupt body

---

* The *Index ac Status Causarum*, 1988 edition, lists 369 names whose cults have been confirmed. Among the most recent of these to be equivalently canonized is Agnes of Bohemia, who was declared a saint by Pope John Paul II on November 12, 1989, 707 years after her death, and just in time to be invoked by Roman Catholics in Czechoslovakia during their revolt against that nation's Communist government.

as a sign of sanctity. Environmental factors, church officials believe, are sufficient to explain such anomalies. But this was not always the case. For centuries, it was believed that the bodies of saints gave off a sweet scent—the "odor of sanctity," it was called—and incorruption was taken as a strong indication of divine favor. This tradition continues to move the faithful, if not officials of the congregation. There is, for instance, the case of Pier Giorgio Frassati, an athletic young man from Turin who died of polio in 1925. At his death, Frassati was only twenty-four years old. He was a university graduate, an excellent skier and mountain climber, and, as a son of the founder of *La Stampa*, one of Italy's most powerful newspapers, he had money. Young Peter's reputation for holiness was founded on his charity: he had set about quietly giving away his money to the poor. What made his cause even more intriguing were the rumors that erupted after his death, circulated chiefly by Fascists who opposed the Frassati family's anti-Fascist reputation. Some said young Giorgio had had an illicit affair with a woman. Others said that he had been buried alive. The gossip was so persistent that the cause was halted for several decades. But when a postmortem was finally held—for medical reasons, it was said—his astonishingly preserved face appeared to be at peace. Even his eyes, observers noted, were intact and luminously clear. Soon after, the cause was reactivated and Frassati was finally beatified on May 20, 1990.

7. *Miracle Processes.* All the work done up to this point is, in the view of the church, the product of rigorous human investigation and judgment, but fallible nonetheless. What is needed for beatification and canonization are "divine signs" confirming the church's judgment regarding the virtue or martyrdom of the Servant of God. The church takes as a divine sign a miracle performed through the intercession of the candidate. But the process by which a miracle is proved is as rigorously juridical as the investigations of martyrdom and heroic virtue.

A miracle process must establish that (a) God truly performed a miracle—nearly always a physical healing—and (b) the miracle occurred through the intercession of the Servant of God.

In a manner similar to the Ordinary Process, the bishop where the alleged miracle occurred gathers the evidence and takes notarized testimony; if the data warrant, he then forwards this material to Rome where it is printed as a *positio*. At the congregation, several meetings are held to discuss, refute, and defend the evidence; often, more information is sought. This time, however, the case is studied by a panel of medical specialists whose job is to determine that the cure could not have occurred by natural means. When such a judgment is reached, the documentation is turned over to a panel of the theological consultors to determine whether the alleged miracle was in fact granted through prayer to the Servant of God and not, for example, through simultaneous prayers to some other, established saint. Eventually, the judgments of the consultors are circulated through the congregation and, upon the favorable advice of the cardinals, the pope certifies acceptance of the miracle by issuing a formal decree.

As we shall see in chapter 8, the number of miracles required for beatification and canonization has diminished over the years. The rule until recently was two miracles for beatification and two more after beatification for canonization, if the cause was based on virtue. In the case of a martyr, recent popes have routinely dispensed the cause from having to prove any miracles for beatification on the grounds that the ultimate sacrifice is sufficient for the title of blessed. Two miracles, however, are still required for canonization of nonmartyrs. The process, of course, must be repeated for each miracle.

8. *Beatification.* Before beatification, a general meeting of the cardinals of the congregation is held with the pope to decide whether it is possible to safely proceed to the beatification of the Servant of God. The meeting is largely ceremonial but the issue is real. In cases involving controversial figures, such as certain popes (see chapter 10) and martyrs who died at the hands of governments still in power (see chapter 4), the pope may in fact decide that beatification, despite the merit of the Servant of God, is "inopportune" at the moment. If his judgment is positive, the pope orders a decree to that effect and a day is set aside for the ceremony.

At the beatification ceremony, an apostolic brief is promulgated by which the pope proclaims that the Servant of God is to be venerated as one of the church's "blesseds." This veneration, however, is limited to a local diocese, a circumscribed region such as a country, or to members of a particular religious order. A special prayer to the blessed and a Mass in his or her honor are authorized by the Holy See for that purpose. At this point the candidate has passed the most rigorous part of the passage to canonization. But the ultimate goal is still to be reached. The pope symbolizes that fact by not officiating at the solemn pontifical Mass which concludes the beatification ceremony. Instead, he comes to the Basilica after the Mass to venerate the new blessed.

9. *Canonization.* Following beatification, the cause lies dormant unless and until additional divine signs are alleged and the entire miracle process is repeated. The active files of the congregation con-

tain several hundred blesseds, some of them dead for centuries, who lack the final, post-beatification miracles which the church requires as a necessary sign that God continues to work through the intercession of the candidate. When the last required miracle has been examined and accepted, the pope issues a bull of canonization declaring that the candidate must—it is no longer just an allowance—be venerated as a saint throughout the universal church. This time, the pope himself leads the solemn ceremonies at St. Peter's Basilica, thereby signifying that the declaration of sainthood has the full authority of the papacy behind it. In his declaration, the pope sums up the saint's life and briefly explains what example and message the saint brings to the church.

In essence, this is the process by which the Roman Catholic Church has been making saints for the last four hundred years. From the preparation of prayer cards to the final declaration by the pope, the entire inquiry is guided by the "exact science" of a legal system which is "arguably the oldest and certainly the most universal in the world." It was the system I expected to encounter when I first went to Rome in the fall of 1987 to observe how the saint-makers arrive, in Canon Macken's words, "at a full knowledge of the truth." What I found was something else.

CHAPTER THREE

THE SAINT-MAKERS

INSIDE THE CONGREGATION

THE CONGREGATION FOR the Causes of Saints occupies the third floor of the Palace of Congregations, an L-shaped building of bright brick and pale travertine stone on the east side of Piazza di Pio XII, just outside the wide oval arms of St. Peter's Square. By Vatican standards, it is a modern building, erected in the era of Mussolini with an eye toward modest ecclesiastical dignity. The corridors of the congregation are unadorned, shadowy in the late afternoon, and give off a mumbling echo whenever conferring monsignori hurry by. Most of the offices are small, like those university professors inhabit, and minimally equipped. Prior to 1985, for example, the only way the staff could make copies of documents was with carbon paper; now the congregation has two photocopying machines, both gifts of American benefactors.

From his corner suite, the cardinal-prefect of the congregation looks out across St. Peter's Square to the windows of the Apostolic Palace, where the walls are hung with tapestries, the Swiss Guard click to attention—and there are photocopiers readily at hand. In 1988, the four hundredth anniversary year of the congregation's founding, the man in charge is Cardinal Pietro Palazzini, a courtly, slightly stooped prelate, balding under his scarlet zucchetto. Palazzini entered the seminary at age eleven, and in a half century of service to the church has never worked outside the Vatican, nor exercised much influence within it. But he is a survivor.

When Pope John XXIII occupied the Apostolic Palace, he complained of certain traditionalists in the Roman Curia—"prophets of doom," he called them—who were uncomfortable with his decision to convoke Vatican Council II. Palazzini, author of several books on theology and frequent contributor to L'Osservatore Romano, the Vatican daily, was one of those the pope had in mind. Among other things, Palazzini's close connections with Opus Dei, a secretive and increasingly powerful movement of traditionalists, did not warm him to Papa John. John's liberal successor, Paul VI, kept Palazzini at a distance but, mainly as a courtesy, made him a cardinal in 1973. By the late seventies, Palazzini's career at the Vatican appeared to be over.

In 1980, however, there was a new pope, from Poland, and in Palazzini John Paul II recognized an experienced Vatican bureaucrat whose conservative instincts complemented his own. Unlike many Curia cardinals, Palazzini brought to his post credentials related to the congregation's work. In addition to moral theology, he had earned advanced degrees in librarianship and the custody of archives. Above all, Palazzini had a reputation for getting things done. One of his predecessors at the helm of the congregation, Cardinal Paolo Bertoli, had been so frustrated by lack of support from higher authorities that he quit when an appointment he wanted to make was not sustained. Palazzini was not the sort to back off from bureaucratic battles. At sixty-eight, he was just seven years away from mandatory retirement, and now that he was at last the head of a congregation, he would, if necessary, do everything himself.

Palazzini learned soon enough that even the prefect of a Vatican congregation does not always call his own shots. John Paul II insisted that the cardinal appoint as secretary of the congregation—second in command—Archbishop Traian Crisan, a short Romanian émigré whose entire thirty-five-year career at the Vatican was spent inside the congregation. He was considered an able if unimaginative technician. On the other hand, Palazzini's choice for subsecretary, Monsignor Fabijan Veraja, a theologian, was blocked by higher authorities; only a personal appeal to the pope overcame the opposition. Veraja is a tall, slightly hunched Croatian whose inability to get along with coworkers eventually alienated him from Palazzini as well.

These three men, along with Monsignor Anton Petti, an amiable

but inexperienced Vatican diplomat, took charge in 1982 as the officials of the congregation responsible for making saints. They set the
weekly agenda and sat in on most of the pivotal meetings. Among
them, they supervised a staff of some two dozen monsignori, priests,
and laymen, plus twenty-three lawyers and two nuns who functioned
as clerk-typists. It was a volatile triumvirate.

In structure and function, the congregations of the Vatican operate
much like committees of the United States Senate. Technically, the
only members of a Vatican congregation are its official prelates, the
cardinals and bishops appointed by the pope to advise and assist him
in the administration of the Holy See. At each crucial stage in the
development of a cause, these prelates reserve a room in the Apostolic
Palace where they render a verdict and advise the pope of their decision. As a practical matter, however, only those cardinals and bishops
who are healthy and resident in Rome—at present, about nineteen out
of thirty members—attend regular meetings. (For example, in his thirteen years as a member of the congregation, Cardinal James Hickey of
Washington, D.C., almost never appeared for a meeting.) Moreover,
since the cardinal-prefects of the Roman congregations sit on each
other's boards, an interlocking directorate of about a dozen prelates
exercise effective control of the Roman Curia, including the Congregation for the Causes of Saints.

But in the Vatican, as in other seats of government, the operative
opinions are not always those rendered by the people vested with
authority. Even more than the ministries of secular governments, the
Vatican's congregations depend heavily on consultants. Thus, in the
long and painstaking process of making saints, the determinant opinions are rendered by Vatican-appointed consultors in theology, history, and medicine from the universities in Rome who are paid by the
case for their expert opinions. Currently, the number of consultants
runs to some 128, far more than any other department of the Vatican.

When Cardinal Palazzini assumed direction of the congregation, he
inherited a juridical process that had become the longest and most
complicated in the church—and, quite possibly, in the world. But
unbeknownst to Roman Catholics outside the Vatican—and most of
the officials within—he also inherited a papal mandate to reform the
system.

A decade earlier, Pope Paul VI had established an unpublicized
commission of canonists, theologians, and prelates of the congregation to study ways in which the process of canonization could be
simplified and updated. Initially, Paul VI had two goals in mind: first,
he felt that the examination and verification of sanctity should rely

less on canon law and more on theology and the human sciences, especially history and psychology. Second, he wanted the process of making saints rethought and revised according to the principle of collegiality expounded by Vatican Council II. In light of that principle, local bishops were to be seen not merely as delegates of the pope but as successors of the original college of twelve apostles and thus coresponsible with the pope in the governance of the church.

During the council, Cardinal Joseph Suenens of Belgium, one of the leaders of the church's progressive wing, had complained that the saint-making process had become too long and too centralized in Rome. As an antidote, he suggested that the right and authority to beatify, at least, be returned to the local bishops and their national episcopal conferences. This would, he felt, speed up the process and, more importantly, provide a more diverse—and therefore more representative—company of holy men and women for the faithful's imitation. It would also restore the church's ancient practice as it existed before the papacy assumed full control over the beatification and canonization of saints.

Suenens's specific proposals failed to win any support among the other council fathers. He had, nonetheless, expressed the concerns of many bishops who felt that the saint-making process had become hostage to the Vatican bureaucracy. Because of these concerns, Paul VI established his commission. But as the proceedings dragged on, it became evident that limited change was not the answer. Proposals prepared by the canon lawyers were scrapped and fresh, more sweeping reforms put forward. When John Paul II became pope, he directed Palazzini to bring the commission's protracted and often rancorous deliberations to a conclusion. No one on the commission was entirely pleased with the results. But to this day, few outside the Vatican, and not many officials within it, realize the revolution that took place, or the ruptures it caused among colleagues.

HISTORIANS VS. LAWYERS:
THE INNER CONFLICT

ON JANUARY 25, 1983, the system was officially changed. On that day, Pope John Paul II issued an Apostolic Constitution, "Divinus perfectionis Magister," mandating the most thoroughgoing reforming of the saint-making process since the decrees of Urban VIII. The announced goals of the reform were to make the canonization process simpler, faster, cheaper, more "collegial," and ultimately more productive. It did this in two fundamental ways. First, it put the entire responsibility for gathering all the evidence in support of a cause in the hands of the local bishop: instead of two canonical processes, the Ordinary and the Apostolic, there would only be one, directed by the local bishop. Second—and far more drastic—it abolished the entire series of legal dialectics between the defense lawyers and the Promoter of the Faith. Enrico Venanzi, a layman and the newest *avvocato* attached to the congregation, was shocked when he read the new legislation. That evening he was near tears when he told his wife: "The lawyers have lost their jobs."

Indeed, not only were the advocates stripped of their powers, so were the Promoter of the Faith and his staff of lawyers. After nearly six centuries, the function of the Devil's Advocate had been eliminated. Instead, the Promoter of the Faith was given a new title of "Prelate Theologian" and assigned the largely administrative task of choosing the theological consultors for each cause and presiding at their meetings. The responsibility for demonstrating the truth about a candidate's life and death now belonged to a new group of officials, "the college of relators," who would supervise the writing of a historical-critical account of the candidate's life, virtues, and, in appropriate causes, martyrdom. To be sure, witnesses would still be called to testify on behalf of Servants of God, but the chief sources of information would be historical, and the medium by which each cause was to be judged would hereafter be a well-documented critical biography.

Thus, at the core of the reform was a striking paradigm shift: no longer would the church look to the courtroom as its model for arriving at the truth of a saint's life; instead, it would employ the academic model of researching and writing a doctoral dissertation. Hereafter, causes would be accepted or rejected according to the canons of critical historiography, not by the arguments of contending advocates. In effect, then, the relator had replaced both the Devil's Advocate and the defense lawyer. He alone was responsible for establishing martyrdom or heroic virtue, and it was up to the theological and historical consultants to give his work a passing or failing mark.

The new legislation was the climax of a long, often bitter, and—because canonization had become such a specialized procedure—unnoticed debate within the congregation. For more than two decades, proponents of change had complained that established methods for making saints had become too complex and cumbersome, that the "exact science" which Canon Macken had extolled in 1910 had proved to be too blunt an instrument in judging the subtleties of sanctity. For one thing, experience had shown that the testimony provided by witnesses was too often of limited or no value. Because it normally took decades for a reputation for holiness to mature, the only eyewitnesses available were frequently people who had known the Servant of God only in the last years of his or her life. Almost as frequently, it turned out, these witnesses were elderly themselves and therefore hard pressed to provide accurate information about a candidate whom they had met only in their own childhood or early youth. For example, in the cause of Frédéric Ozanam, the celebrated French layman who founded the Society of St. Vincent de Paul, a worldwide Catholic charity, the postulator was able to produce only one living witness who had actually known the candidate, a seventy-two-year-old woman who had met Ozanam when she was a child of ten.

The difficulty of finding reliable witnesses was especially acute in processes involving women who were founders of religious orders—a category which had increased steadily in the previous 150 years. Often, these foundresses were widows who had taken religious vows later in life. But frequently the only testimony provided the congregation was from witnesses who had known the candidates during their years as religious sisters or nuns. As a result, the entire discussion of these women's heroic virtues was often limited to how well they lived their religious vows of poverty, chastity, and obedience. How well they had lived their marriage vows—or what kind of mothers they had been—these issues, all too frequently, were not addressed at all.

As critics of the system were able to show, a disturbing trend had developed within the congregation. For lack of complete historical information, more and more cases were either being shelved—sometimes for years, sometimes forever—or they were being turned over to the four-man staff of the historical section. These historians, in turn, would attempt to fill in the gaps by sending the causes back to diocesan officials, instructing them to search for historical records, letters, and other documentation from which they could reconstruct a life. But at best, the four men could finish no more than four or five *positios* each year. Thus, every time the congregation published its index of pending causes, the list grew longer. By 1980, the backlog numbered well over a thousand causes.

Not surprisingly, the push for a radical change in method was led, in large part, by the four priests in the historical section. Among the most forceful protagonists of change was Augustino Amore, a Franciscan friar who eventually became one of the prime draftsmen of the new legislation. As president of the historical section, Amore would routinely disrupt meetings of the congregation, insisting that "we know nothing of this person's early life" when a cause under discussion had not gone through the historians' hands. In essays, and in his presentations to the commission, Amore went even further, arguing that the congregation should eliminate the word *processus* or "trial" from its vocabulary, and with it the juridical process itself.

The particular object of the reformers' ire was the repetitious debate between the Devil's Advocate and the advocate representing the cause. As we have seen, this dialectic was required before the congregation would accept the cause from the diocese, and it was repeated three times before a Servant of God could be considered for beatification. The relation between the Devil's Advocate and the advocate of the cause was—and was meant to be—adversarial. However, in the judgment of many of the saint-makers, causes dragged on for decades—sometimes even for centuries—because lawyers for both sides prolonged what was essentially an artificial process.

"The advocate's job was to take what was positive in the witnesses' testimony and make his case for sainthood," explains Father Yvon Beaudoin, O.M.I., a French-Canadian archivist who worked fifteen years in the historical section. "Sometimes he might conceal contrary evidence. The Devil's Advocate's job was to find what was negative and if he thought the advocate was hiding something he would ask to see the original testimony. Many times, however, the Devil's Advocate would pick out a word here, a sentence there, outside of the context because his job was to find something, anything against the cause."

Many of the postulators, too, were critical of the juridical system. In theory, the postulators were responsible for the cause once it was accepted by Rome. But in practice, they were essentially bystanders as long as the cause was in the hands of the advocates. Virtually all of the lawyers were Italian (a handful were Spanish), and few understood foreign languages. Yet they routinely argued points that, in causes involving non-Italian candidates, they did not always understand. "They were requiring answers to matters that were not at all necessary," says Father Paul Molinari, S.J., an Oxford-educated Italian theologian who has been the Jesuits' postulator general since 1957. "My impression was that they felt that they should produce thirty or forty pages of objections. Whether those objections were real or more or less fabricated was quite another matter. It was make-work."

"It was like a game of Ping-Pong," recalls Father Ambrose Eszer, a

Dominican friar who became an historical consultant to the congregation in 1979. "The Promoter of the Faith would hit his ball and the *avvocato* would answer back. They were exchanging these tremendous arguments and no one could stop them. There was even an official in the congregation whose job it was to clean up the interventions of the lawyers because of all the profanity and curses."

Within the commission, the advocates found few defenders. Like lawyers everywhere, they had long been objects of suspicion, even derision. To a certain extent, these feelings were fueled by long-standing antagonism between the clergy, to whom income (but not career) was a minor concern, and the laity, who sought both. For centuries, the ranks of the lawyers to the Holy See had been filled with laymen. For some of them, practicing before the Vatican's courts was an inherited career; these families not only prospered but also acquired status as papal nobility. Among those who worked within the congregation were a handful of established lawyers who regarded themselves as *patrons* of their causes.* In effect, they functioned like international law firms specializing in representing outsiders to the Vatican. These patrons were widely suspected of gouging their clients, not only through the rates they charged but also by unnecessarily prolonging causes while they lived handsomely off their fees. By eliminating the patrons, the reformers argued, the church could reduce the cost of making saints.

The office of the Promoter of the Faith, or Devil's Advocate, also came in for severe criticism. "If you look at how the Promoters of the Faith have done their work over the last forty years, what you find is that they farmed it out to less competent people," says Jesuit Kurt Peter Gumpel, who has worked with the congregation since 1960. "That had to be stopped and there were several ways to do this. Either beef up the office of Devil's Advocate with competent men and get away from this childish mutilation of texts, or allow one competent, impartial man—the relator—to be in charge of the cause from the outset. There were advantages in both approaches."

The lawyers acknowledged that some of these criticisms were true. Yes, lawyers on the Devil's Advocate's staff did sometimes make superficial objections. Yes, there were a handful of *patrons* who abused their positions. But eliminating lawyers altogether, they insisted, would radically transform procedures that had been at the heart of the saint-making process for half a millennium. In the view of Monsignor

---

* *Patrono* in Italian means "defense lawyer." Critics charged that they were also *patroni* or lords and masters of their causes.

Luigi Porsi, a twenty-year veteran of the church's legal system, the proposed reforms went too far: "There is no longer any room for an adversarial function," he complained in an unanswered letter to John Paul II. As Porsi read them, the new laws would retain some of the vestiges of a juridical process. On the diocesan level there would still be local tribunals to hear witnesses and there would be canonical forms and procedures to be observed. But the spirit was to be cooperative rather than adversarial. Everyone involved in the preparation of a cause would have an incentive to see it succeed, and none more than the relator who was to assume responsibility for the cause's success once it reached Rome. "I ask you," Porsi challenged, "who is the patron now?"

On the deepest level, the conflict within the congregation was not between two kinds of officials, or even two procedural systems. It was between two different mentalities, two different habits of craft and consciousness, two methods of getting at the sustaining spirit and truth of a person's life. The power of the juridical mentality lay in the respect it showed for good order of the church as a community of believers who have a right not to be misled by false enthusiasms or bogus miracles. But the juridical mentality was also imbued with an ahistorical sense of the church as a universal institution, everywhere essentially the same, everywhere following the same rules. It was nurtured in the language of the unchangeable—Latin—and the authority it preserved rested ultimately with the universal jurisdiction of the pope. In practice, the juridical mentality tended to seek similarities among the saints, to work off expected patterns of behavior, to fit fresh candidates for sainthood into the mold of precedent. To be sure, there was an admirable precision to the juridical approach to specific facts and assertions. But it was a precision which, in the end, presumed candidates to be guilty of ordinary humanity in a court where only extraordinary virtue was acceptable.

The historical mentality, on the other hand, was honed on limits. In this perspective, saints were individuals responding by grace to the particular challenges of time and place. They were, in the depths of the Spirit, wholly new creations, initiators in the life of faith, hope, and charity, traditional in the best sense that they reinterpreted the meaning of Christ for their own age. The historical mentality looked therefore to what was original and spare, the nub of difference. Its proofs of sanctity hinged on documentable specifics. In its mature form it was critical, skeptical of exaggerated spiritual heroics, no lover of legends. It was, therefore, a late arrival to the process of recognizing and making saints.

THE IMPACT OF THE BOLLANDISTS

IN RETROSPECT, THE real protagonists of change within the congregation were not parties to the debate at all, nor even residents of Rome. They were the Society of Bollandists, a fraternity of Jesuit hagiographers, never more than six in number, which began three centuries ago the audacious task of publishing all that could be known—and authenticated—about each of Christianity's venerated martyrs and saints. The Bollandists' original plan, still in effect today, was to provide a scholarly edition of the lives of the saints, distinguishing as they went along between legend and literary device on the one hand, and the kernel of authentic history, if any, on the other. Using liturgical calendars as their guide and beginning with January, they researched the available material on each saint who had, in whatever part of the world, been commemorated at least by some Christian churches on every date of the year. It was for its time, and remains to this day, one of the "great historical enterprises."

Initially, the Bollandists were inspired in part by the desire to defend the cult of the saints against the criticism of Protestants and the skepticism of the Enlightenment. But from the start, much of their opposition came from within the church. The learned Cardinal Robert Bellarmine, later to be canonized himself, refused to support his fellow Jesuits, observing that the old lives of the saints were so encrusted with incredible embellishments that they were better left unnoticed. The Bollandists proceeded nonetheless, examining more recent as well as ancient saints. By the time they had advanced as far as the month of April, they ran afoul of the Spanish Inquisition. They had dared to suggest that there was no historical evidence to support the story that the founding of the Carmelite friars, a religious order dating from the thirteenth century, ultimately derived from disciples of the Old Testament prophet Elijah. The Carmelites denounced the Bollandists to the Inquisition, who placed them under censure for twenty years as heretical and schismatic.

With their commitment to scrupulous scholarship and exacting standards, the Bollandists anticipated the great flowering of secular historiography in the latter half of the nineteenth century. Their ongoing series on the saints, the *Acta Sanctorum* (encompassing sixty-two volumes as of 1988) became the standard against which all hagiographic works were measured. In short, the Bollandists demonstrated that the church had nothing to fear from careful documentation and critical historical investigation. But in doing so they also destroyed the conventions of classical hagiography by which the masses and elites alike had represented saints as saints.

Among those the Bollandists impressed was Father Ambrogio Damiano Achille Ratti, a brilliant Italian professor with three doctorates from the Jesuits' Gregorian University in Rome who, as Pius XI, was to become the first scholar-pope since Benedict XIV. In 1930, with the Bollandists as his model, he established the historical section of the Congregation of Rites and urged local bishops to conduct their investigations into ancient causes according to the highest, most exacting historical-critical criteria.

Despite the pope's directive, canonization continued to be based primarily on the testimony of witnesses to the candidate's life, virtues, and posthumous miracles. By the seventies, some postulators, such as Molinari, had succeeded in producing historically nuanced material for the congregation's judgment, but the general quality of the congregation's work was highly uneven. Indeed, Beaudoin recalls, outside libraries and archives would no longer accept the *positiones* produced by the congregation, except for the few that had passed through the historical section.

By 1981, however, the proponents of history were in the ascendant. Their viewpoint eventually prevailed because the system was badly in need of repair. They also prevailed because they were able to produce what every major change inside the Vatican requires: authoritative precedent. With a little historical sleuthing of their own, they demonstrated that a string of modern popes, beginning with Pius X, had endorsed the historical-critical method. They even discovered a supportive speech written in 1958 by Pius XII, who died before he could deliver it, calling for the integration of canon law, theology, and the latest developments in the social sciences. Thus, in the first authoritative commentary on the new legislation, Monsignor Veraja saluted papal prescience "for having contributed to a change in mentality, in the sense of a growing historical consciousness at all levels." At the same time, the subsecretary sought to cloud the fact, obvious and especially painful to the lawyers, that a radical change had occurred: "And so with the new legislation we are in the presence of an evolution in procedure which has happened with continuity. It is not a revolution, as someone could be led to think from the fact that certain formalities, now having become useless, have been eliminated."

The New Procedures

WHATEVER ONE CHOOSES to call it, a new path has been laid over the old road to canonization within the Roman Catholic Church. It is a path that retains the juridical format of the old system—essentially, the holding of local tribunals so that witnesses may give testimony—but one that aims to understand and evaluate the candidate's specific form of holiness in precise historical context. In brief, it works like this:

The investigation and gathering of proofs are now under the authority of the local bishop. Before initiating a cause, however, he must consult with the other bishops of the region about the value of seeking canonization for the candidate; obviously, in the modern era of instant communications, a saint whose reputation for holiness had not passed beyond the neighborhood is hard to justify. The bishop then appoints the officials necessary to investigate the life, virtues, and/or martyrdom of the candidate. Part of this investigation still involves testimony from eyewitnesses. But the main concern is that the life and historical background of the candidate be thoroughly investigated by experts trained in historical-critical methods. Published and unpublished writings by and about the candidate are collected and evaluated by local censors as to the orthodoxy of the candidate. In other words, this judgment is no longer made in Rome. However, the candidate must still undergo a security check by the relevant Vatican congregations and receive a *nihil obstat* from the Holy See. If the bishop is satisfied with results of his investigation, he sends the materials to Rome.

With the reform, the main purpose of the congregation is to facilitate the production of a persuasive *positio*. Once a cause is accepted the congregation appoints a postulator and a relator. From this point on, the relator is in charge of overseeing the writing of the *positio*. The *positio* is to contain everything necessary for the consultors and prelates of the congregation to make their judgments as to the fitness of the Servant of God for beatification and canonization. It is, therefore, to contain a new kind of biography, one that honestly describes and defines the life and virtues or martyrdom of the candidate, taking into account all evidence of unworthiness. The relator then selects a collaborator to write the *positio*. Ideally, this collaborator is a scholar from the same diocese—or at least the same country—as the candidate, and is trained in the historical-critical method as well as in theology. For complex cases, the relator can use additional collaborators, including secular specialists in the history of a particular period or country in which the candidate lived.

When the *positio* is completed, it is studied by consulting experts. If necessary, it is given first to historical consultors. Then it is examined by a panel of eight theologians chosen by the prelate theologian. If six or more of them approve, the *positio* is passed on to the board of cardinals and bishops for their judgment. If they approve, the cause goes to the pope for his decision.

Relators have nothing to do with processes on miracles, which are judged as they were before. The difference is that under the reform the number of miracles required has been reduced by half. Thus, one miracle is required for the beatification of nonmartyrs, none for martyrs. Following beatification, both martyrs and nonmartyrs need only one more miracle for canonization.

Viewed in historical perspective, the reform represented a new stage in the evolution of making saints. Strictly speaking, the congregation is now primarily in the business of beatification, not canonization. That is to say, the congregation is essentially a mechanism for studying the life and virtues and martyrdom of candidates proposed by the local bishops. Even martyrs, as we shall see, are now examined to some extent for their virtues to see if their lives provide a message of value to the church. Although canonization remains the goal of every cause, functionally speaking it is an ancillary and sometime exercise of proving a miracle of intercession which adds nothing to the importance of the blessed or his or her meaning to the church.

It is one thing to reform the system, quite another to make it work. In anticipation of the change, all new causes were put on hold for a year and many that had been developed under the old system were sent back for fuller historical documentation. In fact, it will still be several years before the pope canonizes a saint whose cause was begun and finished under the new system. But a new era had begun for the making of saints, one whose problems and personalities I was able to examine firsthand.

THE NEW SAINT-MAKERS AND THEIR PROBLEMS

THE VATICAN HAS no shortage of canon lawyers, but where was the congregation to find men with the requisite qualifications in history to fill the new decisive post of relator? Initially, the reform envisioned a team of eight relators at the start, and several more once the new procedures became well established. According to the job description, a relator should have a doctorate in theology—but not, oddly enough, history—and be at least trainable in canon law as it applies to the congregation's procedures. Facility in several languages is crucial, since one purpose of the reform is to study the Servant of God in relation to his or her historical milieu. Thus, besides Italian and Latin, a relator should have fluency in at least three other modern tongues.

In theory, a relator can be a man or woman, cleric or lay. The post, in short, is open to any qualified Roman Catholic. But in fact the pool of available talent is severely limited. As the congregation quickly discovered, few university professors, least of all laity with families to support, are willing to give up tenure and homeland for a precarious career at the Vatican, where nonclergy have roughly the same second-class status as civilians in the employ of the military. Bishops and religious superiors also balked at allowing the congregation to raid Catholic university faculties outside Rome. For example, the congregation utterly failed in their efforts to hire a relator from an English-speaking country. Thus, given the congregation's limited budget, highly specialized work, the Vatican's low pay scale, and its traditional preference for relying on clerics, it was obvious from the start that the first generation of relators, at least, would have to be appointed from the congregation's rather short list of veteran consultors.

When the reform went into effect, the first College of Relators consisted of seven priests, all members of religious orders. Three were Italian, two German, one Polish, and one French-Canadian. They were headed by Monsignor Giovanni Papa, a former member of the historical section who, paradoxically, was only mildly supportive of the new system. He was joined by Beaudoin, the only other available man from the now defunct historical section. In the office next to Beaudoin was Ambrose Eszer, a large, garrulous German Dominican friar with fading red hair who had served as both a historical consultant and a theological judge of causes under the old system. These three men, I soon discovered, could be found every morning in their offices, but the other four seldom turned up at the congregation except for meetings.

Valentinio Macca, an Italian Carmelite and long the congregation's specialist on causes involving mystical experience, was appointed to the college despite the fact that he was recovering from a severe heart attack. He died in 1988 and was eventually replaced by Luis José Gómez Gutierréz, a Spaniard and member of Opus Dei. The third Italian was Franceso Moccia, a Pallotine father who later suffered two heart attacks. The Pole, Michael Machejek, a Carmelite with a paralyzed left arm, was also recovering from a heart attack and thus limited in the amount of work he could do. Finally, there was Peter Gumpel, widely regarded as one of the most brilliant Jesuits in Rome. Gumpel had served as an assistant to the Jesuits' postulator general, Father Molinari, for twenty-three years, and, even after the reform of 1983, the two have continued to work as an inseparable team from adjoining rooms in the Jesuits' residence at Borgo Santo Spirito, two blocks from the Vatican.

These, then, are the new saint-makers, the little-known officials whose judgments count most in determining the outcome of a cause. Of the seven, Beaudoin, Eszer, and Gumpel carried most of the load in the years that they allowed me to observe the congregation at work. They are, then, the ones I came to know best. Like most of the Vatican's middle-level management, these three priests arrived at their present position by indirection and happenstance. All three had spent most of their adult lives in Rome. None had aimed at a career in making saints, and each brings to the job of relator a different temperament, language capability, and set of work habits. Like all intellectual workers, they share a certain professional outlook, of course. But what I was anxious to know, on first meeting them, was how each feels, personally, about the making of saints and whether, in their moments away from the congregation, they found anyone else who really cared.

Of the three, Yvon Beaudoin leads the most circumscribed life. He arrived in Rome in 1947 as a twenty-year-old seminarian and has been there ever since. After pursuing the usual clerical studies in philosophy and theology, he took additional Vatican degrees in archival work and library science, then became official historian and archivist for his religious order, the Oblates of Mary Immaculate. In the late sixties, Beaudoin was assigned to the historical section of the congregation and was eventually made its archivist as well. He is responsible for some sixty-five causes, most of them French or Canadian, with a sprinkling of American and Latin American causes.

Beaudoin follows a schedule that is as precise as his handwriting. Mornings I always found him at his desk in the congregation, receiving nuns and other collaborators who were working on *positiones*. Afternoons he spends four to five hours on work for the Oblates at their international scholasticate on the Via Aurelia, a residence that was built for a hundred students but that now, with the worldwide decline in vocations, echoes with the voices of some twenty young men who are studying for the priesthood. Four nights a week he meets with groups of teenage Scouts, teaching them catechism. Weekends, he says Mass in surrounding parishes. He rarely travels, except for two weeks each summer when he visits his nonagenarian mother in Canada.

"The young," I asked him one morning, while he was working at his neatly organized desk, "do they look on the saints as heroes?" We had been discussing several of his causes, most of them nuns or priests, and I wondered whether the figures whose lives he fashioned into models of heroic virtue had any impact on the Scouts he had been working with over the last thirty years. They are, it was plain, the only regular contact he has with the world outside the church.

"Not at all," he replied matter-of-factly. "There is only one living saint for the young people of Italy, St. Francis of Assisi. After 1968, he became a kind of model for antibourgeois living, for simplicity. And since the nuclear explosion in Chernobyl, which greatly affected the crops in Italy, they saw him as a model for the ecology movement. But after Francis there is no one."

He paused. "The young do not really have models, except perhaps from television. They do not even know themselves. They want to be themselves, but in fact they all wear the same kind of clothes and they all act alike. The church is not much of an influence on them. Certainly not the saints."

Perhaps, I suggested, the church would have more influence on the young if there were more lay saints, fewer founders of religious orders. "How does it feel," I went on, "to expend so much time and energy on the causes of people who, it appears, are not realistic models for many Catholics?"

Beaudoin agreed that the recognition of vowed religious does not have much impact on lay Catholics. "Nonetheless," he said, "it means a lot to the religious orders." He cited the beatification in 1975 of the founder of his own religious order, Charles Joseph Eugene Mazenod, a nineteenth-century bishop of Marseille, saying that it stimulated a spirit of renewed dedication to the poor among his own dwindling number of colleagues. The same effect, he said, can be seen among the nuns. In response to Vatican Council II, he observed, all religious orders were instructed to renew their sense of identity and commitment in light of their founders' originating intentions. As a result, the congregation has been besieged with causes on behalf of founders, most of them women. "From 1850 on, there was a tremendous outburst of new orders of nuns," he said, "as many as six a year in countries like Spain. For a long time now we have been getting causes for these foundresses. And I expect we will continue to be flooded with them for another fifty years."

When I first laid eyes on Eszer, he was sitting in his white friar's robes astride a small stool, his thick fingers pounding an ancient Italian typewriter into submission. He had joined the Dominicans in Germany in 1952 and had taken his doctorate in theology, specializing in the seventeenth century, at the Angelicum, the Dominicans' pontifical university in Rome. Eszer was a full professor at the Angelicum when he was invited to become a consultor to the congregation. His appointment as a relator, he wanted me to know, had come as a great deliverance.

"It was too much work, being a consultor. Like other consultors, I had full-time university courses to teach. Now some might say that eighteen hours a week is not much. But remember, we are teaching in a foreign language. Anyhow, with all this the congregation would give you eighty-four different documents to study, thousands of pages, and you had to do them while you were busy with faculty, student, and other meetings." He pulled a thick-bound volume from his shelf. "For this one, I worked fifteen weeks or more, and for my vote I was paid three hundred thousand lire [$250]. And that was exceptional. Usually we were paid half that much."

I hadn't expected a lecture on clerical economics, least of all from a friar vowed to poverty, but Eszer wanted me to understand that there were limits to what the church should expect from its servants, especially university professors. "Look," he went on, "if you are assigned to the Angelicum, you get about forty-two dollars a month plus room and board. But a round-trip ticket on the bus costs twenty-one dollars a month, which hardly leaves enough for cigarettes. At the Dominican houses in Germany, they always had cigarettes. Now I never smoke in the morning at the office. I learned that from working in the archives—you cannot smoke in archives. But they should at least offer free cigarettes, and here they don't."

Now that he was a relator, Eszer went on, his economic status hadn't measurably improved, but he had more time for his work. He has about seventy-five causes, mostly from Germany and Austria; among the most intriguing are Charles I, the last of the Austro-Hungarian emperors, and Father Josemaria Escrivá de Balaguer, the controversial Spanish founder of Opus Dei, who died in 1975. Despite the crosstown bus ride, Eszer prefers to spend mornings at the office. "First of all," he explained, "I don't like people coming to my room to discuss causes. Many of them are sisters and in Rome it is not advisable to have sisters in your room. So the best place to meet is at the congregation. Second, I want to be inside the congregation because I want to know what is going on. Otherwise, you find a new prefect or a new secretary has been appointed without any warning. I like to have contact with people because, you see, a lot of people did not like it when the pope imposed us relators on the congregation. I come and I establish good relations with everybody. It is better that way."

For all his concern for perks and office politics, Eszer is deadly earnest about the importance of making new saints. In the summer of 1987, for example, he spent a marathon month of vacation visiting Germany, Austria, Hungary, and the Netherlands on behalf of his causes, including three in Vienna alone. I was surprised by his stories of meetings and conferences devoted to promoting saints. In fact, I was openly skeptical.

"Do northern Europeans really care about saints?" I asked.

"It is changing. You must remember that in Germany, the Lowlands, Scandinavia, wherever there was a Protestant civilization, they have almost no recent saints. Many German bishops in the eighteenth and nineteenth centuries were afraid to start causes because they didn't want to appear ridiculous. In Poland, too, though for different reasons, we had no saints for a long time. The country was divided in three parts and the church there had so many problems that it was only after the Second World War that they started to do something about causes."

Unlike Beaudoin, Eszer sees himself as a helmsman on behalf of holiness, using the saint-making process to steer an errant church toward a recovery of its orthodox roots. "Catholic morals have gone to pieces," he feels, and liberal European theologians are to blame. "Since there are almost no moral theologians who are abiding by the church's teaching, the pope tries to get that teaching across by making more saints." The years immediately following Vatican Council II were, in his view, "a time of desert wandering for this congregation." Eszer blames liberal clergy for denigrating homage to the saints and denying the reality of miracles. Nor did it help, he says, when Pope Paul VI removed some of the earliest and best-known names, like St. Christopher, from the liturgical calendar. "The faithful were extremely disturbed," Eszer believes. "And as a consequence, many causes collapsed. But now, they are returning."

"But," I pressed, "are the candidates you study at all interesting?"

"They are almost always interesting," he replied, "because studying the inside of the human soul is always interesting."

More than most Jesuits, Peter Gumpel dislikes talking about himself. He is shy with strangers, rather formal and unfailingly courteous. But he is also remarkably candid, reflective, and the saint-maker whose mind I got to know best. Twice exiled from Germany in his youth (to Paris and later to Holland), he joined the Jesuits in 1944, at the age of twenty. He studied four years in England and eventually took a doctorate in the history of dogma. While teaching spiritual theology at the Gregorian, the Jesuits' pontifical university in Rome, he was assigned in 1960 to assist Paul Molinari, the Jesuits' overextended postulator general, in the preparation of causes of saints. In 1971 Gumpel was appointed a consultor to the congregation, a position from which he exerted enormous influence on the shift away from a juridical approach to the making of saints. As a relator, he is now responsible for about eighty causes. Because of his facility with English, he handles most of those from countries that speak that language. But he is equally fluent in German, Dutch, French, Italian, and, to a lesser degree, Spanish. He also reads Danish and Portuguese as well as Latin, classical Greek, and Hebrew.

In Gumpel's view, one of the great weaknesses of the old system was that it relied on lawyers who rarely understood the history, culture, or even the language of the candidate they were defending. Correspondingly, the key to making the new system work, he insists, is finding the right sort of external collaborator. His eyes glisten with satisfaction every time he describes how he has found a university-trained historian from this or that country to write a *positio* under his direction. For Gumpel, I came to feel, one of the joys of being a relator is the license he has to commission scholars around the world to document the manifestations of sanctity.

But it was from Gumpel that I first learned of the difficulty the relators have experienced in finding collaborators—and, what is far more telling—in finding bishops and religious superiors who are willing to release one of their first-rate scholars to work on a saint's cause. "Doesn't that tell you something?" I asked. "If church authorities themselves are reluctant to cooperate with this congregation, that would indicate to me that they don't put a very high priority on canonizing saints. Or maybe it's just that they don't care about the candidates you are proposing. Isn't it possible," I went on, coming to the point, "that what you are doing here in Rome is digging new trenches in an exhausted cultural catacomb?"

"I want you to know," Gumpel responded, "that I am quite enthusiastic about my work. Yes, there has been a decline of interest in saints in some countries but in others we're seeing a revival. Take your own country. I have the strong impression that Americans have never really understood what is required for canonization. They seem to be laboring under the effects of an old-style hagiography in which saints are people who work miracles or experience extraordinary spiritual phenomena. But we are living in a different era now and what we are looking for are saints of the ordinary. We're trying to get the message out—this is what the Second Vatican Council said—that everyone is called to sanctity, though sanctity is not the same for everyone."

POSTULATORS: THE SYSTEM'S ENTREPRENEURS

NEXT TO THE relator, the most important figure in the making of saints is the postulator. This position, too, is now open to any qualified Roman Catholic, but in fact most are male members of religious orders except for a handful of nuns and a few former lay *avvocati*, like Enrico Venanzi, who are being retrained as postulators. Currently, the college of postulators has 227 members, but of these, only ten are real producers with 30 or more causes to shepherd.

The postulator with the most causes—about a hundred—is Molinari, the Jesuits' silver-haired postulator general since 1957. Born to Italian gentry in Turin, a graduate of Oxford, and an accomplished linguist, Molinari has, by dint of interest and industry, become the congregation's unofficial apologist for making saints. As he sees it, saint-making is under attack from two misguided factions: progressive theologians who "underestimate the saints," especially those who insist that the veneration of saints detracts from the worship of Christ, and those on the church's theological right who emphasize the miraculous, the mystical, and other extraordinary phenomena associated with certain saints. For Molinari, the church is, in its most hidden dimension, a "communion of saints."

Molinari is also, in effect, Gumpel's alter ego. The two priests have been close colleagues for nearly thirty years; they coauthor articles, answer each other's phone calls, and, in conversation, take turns completing each other's thoughts. But where Gumpel is precise and professorial in his manner, Molinari is spontaneous and enthusiastic. As a team, the two Jesuits are unmatched in their ability to get things done. Gumpel is Mr. Inside, grappling with texts, searching for the ideal collaborators and training them to sniff out of documents the stuff of heroic virtue. Molinari is a well-bred Mr. Outside: he travels widely and lectures often on the meaning and value of saints. In Rome, the two men work together from adjacent rooms, conferring often through a common door. At meals, they rarely take time to sit down.

They seldom go out socially, unless duty requires, or watch television. Evenings are reserved for serious reading. Neither requires much sleep.

To be a full-time postulator is to live with constant flux. The postulator guides the cause, pays the bills, determines which "divine favors" have a chance of being accepted as miracles. Like the relator, he handles several processes at once. He may preside at the beginning or the end of a successful cause, but no postulator in the last four hundred years has lived long enough to witness both the death of a saint and his canonization. (But it is possible: the quickest canonization since 1588 was that of St. Thérèse of Lisieux, who died in 1897 and was canonized twenty-eight years later.)

Molinari thrives on managing details. Over the years I was able to observe him, he was off to the Far East in search of Jesuit scholars who could, when the political climate is right, gather the documents on Matteo Ricci, the famed sixteenth-century Jesuit missionary to China. He was in Madagascar to arrange for a beatification during the pope's visit there in 1988. Unlike the relator, whose responsibilities cease once the *positio* has been accepted, the postulator remains with the cause down to the last ceremony. He drafts the texts for the pope's beatification and canonization homilies, and arranges for the music. When English Catholics insisted on sending their own choir to Rome in 1970 for the canonization of forty English martyrs, Molinari undertook the impossible task of convincing the Sistine Chapel's choirmaster to step aside. A postulator must also consult with the weathermen before deciding whether to hold a canonization inside St. Peter's or out: the Basilica holds ten thousand people but a popular saint will draw up to ten times that number to Rome. For the 1987 beatification of his fellow Jesuit Rupert Mayer, in Munich, Molinari helped produce a film for the occasion and did interviews on West German television. But his biggest coup was helping to convince the pope to preside in person. As a result, Molinari recalls, "instead of five thousand Germans, we had hundreds of thousands show up from many parts of Europe."

In short, the postulator is the system's only entrepreneur, and in Molinari the congregation has its most accomplished practitioner. He is an incorrigible enthusiast; listening to him, one might never suppose that to steer a cause through the congregation is to court repeated failures and frustrations. But for the majority of Rome's postulators, that is what life is like.

When I first met Father Redemptus Valabek, a gregarious Carmelite friar of disarming humility, his open American face, easy grin, and tolerance for absurdity reminded me of the late Trappist monk Thomas Merton. Valabek has worked in Rome for more than thirty years but has been the Carmelites' postulator general only since 1980. The Carmelites are Spanish in origin and noted for their asceticism and competence in spiritual direction. Besides his own priests, Valabek handles causes for the Carmelite sisters and the lay people— mostly women—attached to the order as tertiaries. But in the last three hundred years, the Carmelites have succeeded in getting only one of their priests beatified, and lost most of their other causes.

"What's the problem?" I asked him in the first of a series of meetings at his friary ten blocks from the Vatican.

"They've been blocked," he said matter-of-factly. "But I don't lament that, if there are good reasons."

Like an experienced fisherman, Valabek has good recall of the ones that got away. He went on to cite one example of what he considers bad judgment on the part of Vatican officials. He has a long-standing cause from Ronciglione, a small town north of Rome where the citizens, including the Communists, recently celebrated the 250th anniversary of the death of Maria Angela Virgili, a Carmelite tertiary and the regional patron saint. There is a school named in her honor and her house has been preserved as a civic shrine. Maria's continuing reputation for holiness rests on her good works and deep prayer life. The town still recalls how she took the indigent sick into her own home when there was no room for them in the hospital. As for her spirituality, Maria was known to spend the night on her knees in church if she had failed to complete her regimen of prayer during the day. But her cause was blocked in the 1920s by the Vatican's Holy Office after the local bishop complained that the people had made her the object of an unauthorized cult. Valabek is still trying to have that block removed so he can revive the cause. "I've read the documents," he said. "The bishop was a German and he obviously mistook the exuberant Italian manifestations of veneration as being a public cult."

What nettles Valabek is that Maria's is one cause that has deep roots and support among the people of the community. Often enough, he finds, this is not the case with the foundresses of Carmelite orders, whose causes he is expected to push. "Once one group of nuns decides to get their foundress beatified, they all want their foundresses beatified. But I tell the sisters, there has to be a swell of interest from the people—ordinary people, not just those of the cloth. My superiors tell me, 'Redemptus, you are not doing much for our mother foundresses.' And I say, 'Well, my heart really isn't in it.' And they say,

'What if they ask another order to do the work? How will that look? They belong to us but they are using another postulator. It would be a slap in the face.' But what can I say? Look, I believe that these women are holy and in heaven. I just don't believe that the church has need of that model of sanctity."

About half of Valabek's causes are for lay Catholics. Most of them are unknown outside their immediate locale. Still, he thinks, a few of them show real promise. But hard luck hounds him. In some cases he is unable to find local church officials who are able or willing to do the work. In Zaire, for instance, he has the cause of Isidor Bankanja, a black convert and lay catechist who was beaten to death by anti-Catholics in 1909 for refusing to take off the scapular he wore around his neck as sign of his conversion to Christ. It is a classic martyrdom story from mission territory and Valabek is encouraged by the fact that John Paul II mentioned Isidor during a visit to Zaire in 1985. But the cause has failed to move because there is no one in the diocese capable of acting as local postulator. In Czechoslovakia, he has another promising cause, but the priest who has been working on the case belonged to the Communist-directed Peace Committee and as such was mistrusted by Rome.

What interested me most, however, were Valabek's repeated frustrations with Western clergy—including his own Carmelites—who are not interested in making saints. In 1985, for instance, he went to Olot, a Catalonian village near the Pyrenees, to drum up support for the beatification of their local patron saint, Liberata Ferrarons, who died in 1832 at the age of thirty-nine. Liberata, it seems, had worked in textile mills for nine years, developed a disabling tumor, and spent the last thirteen years of her life confined to her bed. She learned to read, became extremely devout, and bore her sufferings for the sake of her people. In this respect, she was like many other female saint figures in Latin cultures: the vicarious sufferer. The people recognized her as such and regularly sought her out for spiritual advice. Her funeral, said Valabek, was a triumphant celebration, and a century later her centennial fiesta was conducted like an old-fashioned popular beatification.

Valabek's mission was to convince the local clergy to carry her cause to Rome. Here was a woman, he told them, who became a saint through work, and thus exemplified the Polish pope's repeated emphasis on the dignity of labor. But most of the clergy had not read the pope's labor encyclicals and failed to see the point. It was a prime instance, I could see, of a postulator trying to promote a cause by attempting to read a contemporary papal message into the life of a woman who is venerated chiefly for her embrace of vicarious suffering. He got nowhere.

"I had to appear before the bishop and priests of the diocese," Valabek recalled, smiling now at his own frustration. "And they said, 'Father, we don't want to insult you but we don't see the purpose of beatification.'" Valabek made his pitch, and the clergy listened in respectful silence. "Money was part of the problem," he has since concluded. "They figured, why put money in the Vatican's coffers—that's a bit blunt, but that is what it was. My impression was that they felt that whatever the beatification cost, it was too much. And in this they weren't at all unusual."

"Do you think," I asked, "that there would be more saints if the cost were less?"

"I'm saying that a lot people don't see the purpose and so can't justify the expense."

A year later, Valabek had the rare satisfaction of seeing one of his causes succeed. A Dutch Carmelite, Father Titus Brandsma, whose intricate cause I was already investigating, had been beatified in St. Peter's Basilica. It was Valabek's one moment of triumph as a postulator. What I hadn't realized was that a majority of the Dutch Carmelites had refused to attend the ceremony. "They didn't even want to hear about it because they said it cost too much," Valabek said. "One of the younger priests was quite blunt about it. He said that if it had been up to the younger Carmelites to start the process they would refuse. The order, they felt, shouldn't go to such lengths to hold up one of its confreres for imitation. But since the older generation had initiated it, they would go along. 'See you in Rome,' I said when I was leaving. 'For what?' he asked. 'For the beatification,' I said. And he said, 'I'm not coming.' It was tough to swallow."

ECONOMICS: THE COST OF MAKING SAINTS

EVERY POSTULATOR IS required to keep a precise accounting of expenses incurred for his causes and file them with the Vatican. But, like most Italians (and Americans) Vatican officials would sooner talk about sex than money. Despite the enduring suspicion that the making of saints is prohibitively expensive, the congregation has never published a balance sheet for a beatification or canonization. The promoters of the cause, who typically pay the bills, are free to do so if they wish, but they, too, are shy about revealing what it takes to make a saint. As a result of this silence, myths abound about the high cost of achieving sainthood.

In the summer of 1975, for example, *The Wall Street Journal* published an article on the upcoming canonization of Mother Elizabeth Bayley Seton. In it, a priest unconnected with the cause put the price tag at "millions of dollars." Vincentian Father Joseph Dirvin, who had written a biography of Seton, wrote the *Journal* protesting that the estimate was enormously excessive. But when the *Journal* pressed for the actual figures, none of the Vincentians connected with the cause was willing to set the record straight. One legitimate reason was that they still hadn't received all the bills for the canonization ceremony in Rome. The other had to do with public relations: the Redemptorists were preparing to canonize Bishop John Neumann of Philadelphia, and the Vincentians did not want to invite a public comparison of costs.

Twelve years later, the Vincentians' postulator general, Father William Sheldon, was more forthcoming. Under prodding, he estimated that from the time the cause was introduced in 1929 to the canonization on September 14, 1975, the postulation spent $225,000. This did not include such ancillary payments to the Vatican as $7,500 for the rental of fifteen thousand seats, another $12,000 for the printing of as many souvenir prayer booklets, plus such related expenses as fees for ushers and nurses, the printing of tickets, flowers, and the commissioning of a huge official painting, hung from St. Peter's, of Mother Seton in glory. In the end, then, the bill came to over $250,000.

Congregation officials, when pressed, prefer to talk in the neighborhood of $50,000 to $100,000, exclusive of the terminal celebration. But the truth is that there is no way of establishing an "average" cost for making saints. Obviously, causes involving popes, major public figures, or anyone else who either produced a large body of writing or was written about extensively cost more to complete than that of a simple cloistered nun. What's more, once any cause is launched, it is quite impossible to estimate what it will take to finance it through to a conclusion. Even in retrospect, congregation officials insist, it is impossible to arrive at an accurate accounting.

In the first place, a process typically takes several decades to complete, in some cases centuries. Many require tribunals to be held in more than one country. Thus, a fastidious accountant would have to allow for fluctuations in the value of currencies over time and between countries.

Second, saint-making is a labor-intensive industry in which much of the work is either done by volunteers or assigned to priests and sisters whose biggest expense—their time—is not charged to the postulation. In any given year, Rome has dozens of such "collaborators" who are working on the causes of their founders and are supported by their religious orders. Thus, in order to arrive at the real cost of a cause, an accountant would have to assign an arbitrary monetary value to the work of people who labor for love—or who, in any case, labor under a vow of poverty. The real expense to a religious order or a diocese, therefore, is the loss of the services of those who leave their jobs to work on a process.

Third, the saint-making process involves so many institutions of the church that even the best accountant would be hard put to track them all down. For instance, tribunals are conducted by canon lawyers and notaries in the employ of the diocese. They and the vice-postulator, who may be the pastor of a church, are entitled to recompense as well as to expenses. Archival work is done by others, usually religious, in the employ of their superiors. Witnesses and physicians are entitled to reimbursement for their travel expenses and for any loss of income they may sustain while giving testimony. All of these costs are part of the expenses a cause accrues before it arrives in Rome, but they are high enough that financially pressed bishops are not always willing to countenance them.

But what about those "Vatican coffers"? The history of saint-making offers examples of princes and other wealthy families who have plied Rome with inducements. Until the twentieth century, consultors to the congregation were paid in kind, not money. The records of one nineteenth-century cause, for instance, show that consultors were supplied with spices, sugar, chocolate, and other delicacies made scarce by the continental blockade.

Such stories, naturally enough, anger contemporary saint-makers, none of whom struck me as living in luxury. "The congregation is not a money-making concern," says Gumpel, who teaches a course on economics in the "studium" the congregation runs for postulators and their collaborators. Indeed, with the elimination of the lawyers and their fees, the Roman phase of the saint-making process appears to be a relative bargain. Postulators work for nothing, except for the few secular priests or a layman like Venanzi, who are paid on arrangement by the promoters of the cause. Relators are paid slightly less than two million lire a month (about $1,650) by the congregation. Expenses incurred by the postulator are billed monthly to the promoters. Often, causes of laity and other outsiders taken on by the postulators general of the large religious orders, such as the Jesuits, Franciscans, and the Carmelites, are handled for little or no charge.

Travel is a major expense, especially for postulators, who must check out potential miracles wherever they occur. Phone bills can accumulate as well. The printing and binding of a *positio* of 1,500 pages, an average length for those on the life and virtues, costs about $13,000 for a run of a hundred copies. *Positiones* on miracles are normally much smaller and cost about $4,000 each.* But a recent Vatican decree permitting the use of photocopies has trimmed some of this expense. Fees paid to the historical, theological, and medical consultors approach the minimum wage of a Third World country. Currently, historians and theologians are paid 500,000 lire, or about $415 for every *positio* they study. Physicians are paid about $25 more. Thus, the promoters of a cause can normally expect to pay at least $6,400 in total consultors' fees for judging a *positio* on virtues or martyrdom plus two more *positiones* on miracles.

Like a wedding, the cost of staging a beatification or canonization ceremony depends on how elaborate the celebration is. Apart from the fees already mentioned, travel, accommodations, and meals for guests account for most of the expenses. If the promoters are willing to share their saint's moment of triumph, the Vatican is quite willing to beatify or canonize more than one Servant of God at a time, thus permitting the sharing of expenses.

Figuring out who pays the bills is almost as difficult as determining costs. In rare instances, a diocese or a religious order may shoulder the bulk of the expenses. But like most things done by the church, the cost of making a saint is ultimately borne by the faithful through contributions to the promoters, either directly through contributions—the most common way—or indirectly through pass-along expenses. Popular causes, like that of Pope John XXIII, generate much more income than the postulation can ever spend. When this occurs, the money is invested on the advice of bankers. Once expenses have been met, the pope himself decides how to dispose of the excess. The standard practice is to apply them to "apostolic works" for the poor—if possible, in line with the work of the Servant of God. Under Palazzini, the congregation established a fund to aid causes from poor countries. Causes that have more than they need are asked to contribute to the fund so that the churches of the Third World, in particular, need not worry about the cost when they have a saint to promote.

Despite the almost universal reluctance of religious orders to reveal

---

* Printing of congregation documents is not done by the Vatican nor is it put up for bids. All the congregation's documents are printed by a single firm, Tipografia Guerra, Piazza di Porta Maggiore, 2, in Rome.

the expense in making saints, the Sisters of the Blessed Sacrament for Indians and Colored People, headquartered in suburban Philadelphia, provided me in the spring of 1990 with as accurate an accounting as is possible for a beatification—in this case, of their foundress Katharine Drexel, who was beatified in 1988 (see chapter 6). Since 1965, they figured, the sisters spent a total of $123,983 to process the cause. Of that, expenses by the three local postulators for travel, microfilming, and other requirements involved in the Ordinary and Apostolic processes came to $64,657. Father Molinari's bill as Roman postulator was $33,975, including payments to consultors, travel, and printing. Father Joseph Martino, the author of the *positio*, incurred expenses of $5,351.

The beatification ceremony in Rome cost more than the twenty-three-year process that preceded it. The sisters' contribution was $8,296, plus $30,587 in travel and housing for thirty of their members and an additional $10,000 gift "to the Holy Father for the poor." The Archdiocese of Philadelphia reports a total expenditure of $143,000 on the cause, most of it for travel, housing, and expenses connected with the ceremony.

In addition, the sisters spent another $90,971 for assorted services. They paid $14,768 for blacks and Native Americans invited to ceremonies in Rome and in Philadelphia. Banquets, buses, and associated expenses in Philadelphia amounted to another $16,533. Public relations cost them $22,089. In sum, the beatification of Katharine Drexel cost a total of $333,250 in ascertainable expenses.

To pay for the process and their share of the festivities, the sisters received $26,575 toward their travel expenses to and in Rome. But the remainder of their costs were paid from the interest on a fund established by Katharine Drexel's sister, Mrs. Louise Morrell, in 1927. Mrs. Morrell stipulated that the money was to be used for any "extraordinary work" the sisters might choose to undertake. The beatification of Katharine Drexel, they figured, was something extraordinary. In the end, then, the Drexel family—like many a royal family of old Europe—underwrote the cost of beatifying one of its own.

PRIORITIES: DO POPES PLAY FAVORITES?

IT IS WIDELY assumed that Rome not only gets the saint it wants, but that some saints are wanted more than others. The first assumption is false and the second, as history amply demonstrates, is decidedly true.* Like his predecessors, John Paul II has his priorities, but neither God nor the system is always obliging.

When John Paul II chose Palazzini to head the congregation, some of the pope's liberal critics interpreted the appointment as a sign that the Polish pontiff was seizing the church's saint-making machinery to ensure that only "safe" candidates would be beatified or canonized. "Palazzini's job, then, is to see that no disturbing saints get through," writes Peter Hebblethwaite, a veteran Vatican correspondent, in his recent study of the Holy See. ". . . I am not suggesting that the contemporary C.C.S. [Congregation for the Causes of Saints] is lacking in integrity or that its history is unreliable. It is simply being invited to look harder in some directions rather than in others."

In fact, neither the pope nor the cardinal-prefect of the congregation exercises anything like the control over the saint-making process which this observation might imply. For one thing, all causes, except those of popes, are initiated by local bishops. For another, several decades, and sometimes several centuries, elapse before a cause is ready for a papal decision; therefore, popes almost always beatify and canonize candidates whose processes were begun under their predecessors. Popes can and have blocked causes for a variety of reasons, but so have local bishops, and in some cases the promoters themselves have withdrawn their support. The salient fact is that a pope cannot order up a cause nor declare someone a saint (or a blessed) until the congregation has completed its work.

For example, when he was still archbishop of Cracow, John Paul II introduced the cause of a Polish nun, Faustina Kowolska. In 1983 he hoped to beatify her during his second pastoral visit to Poland. But the congregation had not finished its study of the cause, so the pope had to be content with beatifying three other countrymen, a nun, a priest, and a brother, whose processes were complete.

Nonetheless, it would be naive to maintain that popes *never* influence the saint-making process. On the contrary, controversial candidates are always watched carefully by popes, and often by the secretary of state as well. In the case of El Salvador's Oscar Romero, John Paul II demonstrated that he is not above influencing a cause even before it has started. Similarly, as we shall see, he and his political advisers raised strong pastoral objections to the demands by the bishops of Vietnam that a group of martyrs be canonized in 1988. Again, in the much argued case of his countryman Father Maximilian Kolbe (chap-

---

* In an effort to please the clergy of his former diocese, Pope Clement X "canonized their former local hero, Venantius, leaving the responsibility of knowing exactly who he might really be to the historians of the future."

ter 4), John Paul II sided with the German and Polish hierarchies in their requests that the candidate be recognized as a martyr. Moreover, for a variety of reasons which he may not explain, a pope can—and sometimes does—refuse to accept a cause that has been judged acceptable by the congregation.

Like all other departments of the Vatican, the Congregation for the Causes of Saints exists by the authority of the pope and is at his service. But it also exists to service the local church—more so, perhaps, than any other arm of the Vatican—and in light of its own experience in the making of saints the congregation has developed certain administrative priorities.

At a meeting held every November or December, the officials of the congregation schedule the Servants of God whose virtues will be discussed for the following year. In theory, causes are addressed in rotation, according to the protocol number assigned each cause on the day the congregation receives a request for a *nihil obstat* from the local bishop. In practice, the lineup is adjusted to meet various bureaucratic priorities. For instance, the closer a cause is to completion the higher its priority. Since no miracle is required for the beatification of a martyr, martyrs normally take precedence over nonmartyrs. Similarly, if a nonmartyr has a promising miracle to his or her credit, that cause will likely be discussed ahead of one that does not.

It took me several months to fathom the congregation's uneven bureaucratic rhythm. The theological consultors normally meet on every other Tuesday, except during the vacation months of July and August. At these scheduled meetings they discuss only causes based on martyrdom or heroic virtue. Causes involving miracles are inserted into the schedule—usually on Tuesdays or Fridays—whenever they are ready. In a good year, therefore, the congregation may dispose of twenty *positiones*, but the order in which they are considered is subject to a variety of papal pressures and considerations.

Far more than any of his predecessors, John Paul II is a traveling pope. And when he travels, he likes to present new blesseds to the local churches, especially to the relatively new churches of Africa and Asia. In this way, John Paul II uses the beatification of local figures to bond these young and culturally diverse communities of Catholics to the church universal—and, of course, to the Holy Father in Rome. Once his travel plans are firm, therefore, officials of the congregation canvass their relators and postulators to discover which candidates from the countries on his list they can ready for beatification. (Saints, because they are to be models for the whole church, are normally canonized at St. Peter's in Rome.) Thus, the finished *positio* on a low-priority candidate or one from the "wrong" country may sit for years while others are speedily judged.

Apart from papal visits, special situations arise when popes must choose between rival candidates to beatify or canonize in connection with certain gatherings in Rome. The most recent occasion occurred in 1987, when five beatifications and canonizations were held at St. Peter's in connection with the World Synod of Bishops. The subject of the synod was the laity, and the three years leading up to the meeting, promoters, postulators, relators, local bishops, and papal diplomats all lobbied for their favorite candidates.

Yet the feeling persists—in Rome as throughout the church—that popes do play favorites. Although some congregation officials deny it, others insist that John Paul II has conveyed to them through Palazzini that some kinds of saints are more needed than others. Whatever the source, the congregation's priorities under John Paul II are altogether predictable.

Above all, the congregation wants more lay saints. In part this priority reflects the demands of many bishops who have repeatedly criticized Palazzini for not providing the church with more models of holiness for what is, after all, the preponderance of Christians. As a result, *positiones* on behalf of nuns, such as Canadian Sister Maria Anna Blondin whose cause has been ready for judgment for five years, are routinely postponed to make room for those involving laymen or laywomen. However, women, as such, are not a priority. Although only 20 percent of the saints canonized up to the twentieth century were female, the number of canonized women has increased fivefold since. But happily married women, as will be discussed in chapter 11, are undoubtedly the rarest breed of saints.

The congregation also places a priority on causes from countries that do not yet have any saints, or those which have only a few. On the face of it, this seems plausible enough. But in point of fact, the latter category includes every country in the world except Italy, Spain, and, to lesser extent, France. It even includes Ireland, the fabled Isle of Saints, most of whom died long before there was a formal canonization process.

Finally, the congregation puts a priority on candidates who represent occupations or peoples—often immigrants—who have no saints to celebrate. It was this "pastoral" priority which inclined John Paul II in 1980 to beatify Kateri Tekakwitha, a Mohawk Indian who died in 1680, as the first Native American blessed, despite the fact that all of the miracles attributed to her intercession lacked certification.*

In effect, the congregation's priorities represent an effort to reverse the patterns of the past by making the company of the blesseds and saints more representative of an emergent world church. As the record shows, the most underrepresented group in the church is the laity. Between 993, the date of the first papal canonization, and 1978, when Karol Wojtyla was elected pope, there were 293 canonizations. Of these, only 19 percent involved laity. Of the 1,260 beatifications from the seventeenth century to the election of Wojtyla, 35 percent were laity. The underrepresentation of lay Catholics is even more striking when we observe that most of the lay saints were not canonized as individuated examples of exceptional Christian virtue but as relatively anonymous members of persecuted groups who were murdered— usually along with clergy and religious—for the faith.

Under John Paul II, the record has not changed significantly despite the congregation's priorities. Until 1987, when the church celebrated "the Year of the Laity," he had not canonized a single lay man or woman for heroic virtue. The only other lay saints were comparatively anonymous members of large group-causes of martyrdom, such as the Japanese martyrs of the seventeenth century, the Vietnamese murdered in the eighteenth and nineteenth centuries, and the Koreans killed in the nineteenth century. As might be expected, there has been a broadening of geographical representation under the traveling Polish pope, particularly in the number of saints and blesseds from Asia, Africa, and other regions he has visited.

In light of its priorities, one might suppose that the congregation would keep tabs on how well they are being met. But in fact the congregation has traditionally regarded sociological studies of sainthood as profane exercises; in the Vatican's view, saints are made by God, not the church, and any suggestion that human motives or institutions play a decisive role is unwelcome. As a result, no one at the congregation knows how many causes have reached which stage, where all candidates come from, or exactly how many are priests, laity, and so forth. In 1987, an anonymous American Catholic donated a computer to the congregation so that officials might keep better

---

* Another high-priority American figure is Pierre Toussaint (1766–1853), a Haitian slave, a layman who migrated to New York in 1787 and helped found New York's first Catholic orphanage. Toussaint has a devoted and passionate following among Haitians in the New York Archdiocese, as I discovered when I visited his grave on the anniversary of his death in 1988. A historical commission had been slowly investigating his life and virtues, but unlike Cardinal Cooke, Toussaint does not appear to be a major priority of Cardinal John O'Connor. In 1989, O'Connor finally agreed to open a formal process. .

track of the causes on the books. But the Vatican personnel office had
yet to authorize the hiring of a competent technician to program the
computer. Even so, what data are available suggest that the saints of
the future will not be significantly different from those of the past.

For instance, a scan of the latest (1988) issue of *Index ac Status
Causarum* (Index on the Status of Causes), published periodically (in
Latin) by the congregation, lists 1,369 active causes, some of them
dating back to the fifteenth century. Father Beaudoin, who compiles
the *Index*, estimates that no more than 20 percent of these are laity.
Again, as in the past, Italy, Spain, and France have more candidates
than other countries. Indeed, Rome alone has eighty-five pending
causes and Naples has seventy-five—far more, in each case, than most
other countries of the world.

More precise information can be found in a report prepared for
Palazzini in 1987 for presentation to the Synod on the Laity. The
report covered the 275 causes introduced in Rome between 1972 and
1983 and its manifest aim was to remind the bishops that they, not
the congregation, were to blame if the church was lacking lay candidates. The report revealed the following categories:

Laity: 50
  Men: 18
  Women: 17
  Children below age 18 of both sexes: 15

Hierarchy: 22
  Cardinals: 2
  Archbishops: 5
  Bishops: 14
  Abbots: 1

Secular Clergy: 55

Religious: 156
  Men: 67
  Women: 87
  Hermits (no sex given): 2

Geographical Distribution: 33 countries
  Europe: 236 (Italy, 123, Spain, 62)
  The Americas: 29
  Asia: 8 (Japan, 4)
  The Pacific: 3

In sum, of the 268 adult candidates, about 13 percent are laity and 62 percent are men. And in the future, as in the past, Italy and Spain have the most causes. For 1990, the congregation scheduled twenty-six causes on martyrdom or heroic virtue for discussion by the consultors. Of these, twenty-three were from Western Europe. Two were Canadian and one was Mexican. *Plus ça change . . .*

But in one important respect, John Paul II has made a major difference. He wants more candidates to choose from and, under Palazzini, the congregation has increased its output on several levels. Palazzini has expanded the list of consultors, both theological and medical, and won the pope's approval to divide the congregation's cardinals and bishops into two groups, thus doubling the number of causes they can judge each year. "We're becoming a factory here," says Eszer, and Beaudoin wonders whether the congregation isn't flooding the market.

As the table below shows, in his first eleven years as pope, John Paul II held more beatifications than all of his twentieth-century predecessors put together. On canonizations, he is keeping pace with the record set by Pius XII during his nineteen-year reign. (These figures include group causes, such as the 118 Vietnamese martyrs canonized in 1988, which are counted as one. Otherwize, the figurers for John Paul II would include more than 250 saints and many more blesseds.)

Pope	Reign	Beatifications	Canonizations
Pius X	1903–1914	7	4
Benedict XV	1914–1922	3	4
Pius XI	1922–1939	11	26
Pius XII	1939–1958	23	33
John XXIII	1958–1963	4	10
Paul VI	1963–1978	31	21
John Paul I	1978 (33 days)	0	0
Total:		79	98
John Paul II	1978–1989	123	23

If John Paul II has a single priority, his record suggests that it is simply to make more saints in order to multiply and replenish the church's examples of holiness. In this respect, he is merely accelerating a trend which has seen the number of beatifications and canonizations increase in each of the last four centuries. But the real change under John Paul II, as the figures demonstrate, is the vast increase in beatifications. Perhaps Eszer is right in believing that the pope is using the saint-making process as a way of countering the influence of moral theologians who disagree with his teachings. But whatever the pope's personal intentions may be, one thing is clear: although the ultimate goal of every cause is still canonization, the essential work of the saint-makers is to prove heroic virtue—or martyrdom—and thus pave the way for beatification.

Theologically, however, beatification is no warrant to the faithful that the blessed they are now permitted to venerate is, for certain, with God in heaven. It is precisely because of this uncertainty that the church requires an additional miracle of intercession beyond the one necessary for beatification before a blessed can be canonized. But a miracle is only a sign from God. What makes it "theologically certain" that a saint is with God is the pope's solemn declaration of canonization. Thus, what distinguishes canonization from beatification is, according to the congregation, an act of papal infallibility. In other words, a pope may err in declaring someone blessed. But, according to the operative theology of the saint-makers, he cannot err— in fact, they insist, no pope has ever erred—in solemnly canonizing a saint. *That* this is so, the saint-makers have no doubt. *Why* this is so remains a matter of theological debate. What has never been satisfactorily explained, however, is how this belief in the infallibility of canonization relates to the proofs of sanctity produced by the congregation.

CANONIZATION AND PAPAL INFALLIBILITY

FOR AT LEAST seven centuries, Roman Catholic theologians have argued over whether the church—and specifically the pope—can err when declaring a person a saint. Thomas Aquinas, apparently the first to raise the issue, was of the opinion that "the Honor we show the saints is a certain profession of faith by which we believe in their glory, and *it is to be piously believed* that even in this the judgment of the Church is not able to err." (Italics added.) Once canonization was firmly in the hands of the papacy, the arguments in favor of the infallibility of canonizations focused on the conviction that the pope, as the successor to St. Peter, is guided in this, as in other matters of faith and morals, by the Holy Spirit.

Interestingly enough, the church has never seen fit to issue a doctrinal statement on the infallibility of canonizations, not even at Vatican Council I (1869–1870), which defined the dogma of papal infallibility. Many theologians, therefore, do not regard canonization as an exercise of papal infallibility. But the officials of the congregation have no doubts that each canonization is an infallible and irrevocable decision by the supreme pontiff, and they point to a tradition of long-standing theological opinion to justify their position.

Their main arguments rest on logical entailment and theological necessity. At the Council of Trent, Molinari points out, the council fathers declared that the saints are to be venerated by the church. Therefore, he reasons, this teaching "has as its correlative the power to canonize. Otherwise, the faithful would not know whom to invoke as their intercessors or whom to take as models in Christian virtue." A second line of argument flows from the verbal formula popes use in canonizing saints; namely, "We solemnly decide and define that [name] is a saint and inscribe him in the catalog of saints, stating that his memory shall be kept with pious devotion by the universal church." The key phrase is "solemnly decide and define," the same words used by popes and councils of the church in defining dogmas of the faith. Therefore, another theologian concludes, "The pope cannot by solemn definition induce errors concerning faith and morals into the teaching of the universal church." A third argument considers the alternative: what would happen if canonization were not protected by infallibility? "Should the church hold up for universal veneration a man's life and habits that in reality led to damnation, it would lead the faithful into error."

It is one thing to argue that canonizations are so important that they must be protected by papal infallibility. But it seems quite rash to assert—as some theologians have for centuries—that no pope has ever been convicted of an error in declaring someone a saint. Even the best historians assume that their work is tentative, and no lawyer or judge argues that justice is always served. How does the congregation respond when evidence is discovered which suggests that a pope did, in fact, make a mistake? This is exactly what happened in the middle of the 1980s when the congregation found itself embroiled in a rare public dispute.

In March 1985, a left-wing Italian journalist, Giordano Bruno Guerri, published a sensational book, *Poor Assassin, Poor Saint: The True Story of Maria Goretti*, in which he argued that the church and the government of Mussolini had conspired to invent the martyrdom of one of Italy's best-loved modern saints. The book created headlines in Italy's anticlerical press, forcing the congregation to defend the very integrity of the saint-making process.

Maria Goretti was one of five children of a widowed peasant living in a small village in the Roman Campagna. She was barely twelve years old on July 2, 1902, when Alexander, a neighbor half again her age, burst into her home and tried to rape her. When she resisted, he stabbed her several times. The girl survived long enough to forgive her assailant and to receive a final Eucharist.

Alexander was sent to prison for thirty years and remained obdurately unrepentant until, in a dream, his victim appeared to him gathering flowers and offering them to him. From that point on, so the story goes, he became a model prisoner and was released three years early. He immediately went to Maria's mother and begged forgiveness. The story of Maria, meanwhile, caught the Italians' fancy; thousands sought her intercession and hundreds reported receiving miracles. In no time, the peasant girl became a powerful symbol of sexual purity. When Pope Pius XII declared her blessed in 1947, he appeared on the balcony of St. Peter's with her mother and two of her brothers. In an address that was reported in newspapers throughout Europe, the pope used the occasion to denounce those in the movie industry, the fashion industry, the press, the theater, and even the military, which had recently conscripted women, for corrupting the chastity of youth. Three years later, the same pope declared Maria Goretti a saint before the largest crowd ever to assemble for a canonization.

In the four decades since her canonization, Maria Goretti had become the church's most popular icon of holy virginity after the Virgin Mary herself. Indeed, wherever there are Catholic schools, Maria Goretti continues to be held up as the heroic embodiment of the church's sexual ethic. But she is also an important figure in the history of making saints. Technically, she did not die for her faith. Rather, she died in defense of Christian virtue—a significant though by now routine expansion of the grounds on which a candidate can be declared a martyr.

In attacking Maria Goretti, therefore, Bruno chose for his target a saint whose story had become symbiotic with the church's teachings on sexual purity. What's more, his book was published at a time when feminists and other Italians were clamoring for legalization of abortion. Based on his own examination of both the church's canonical process and the state's trial of Alexander, Bruno concluded that the evidence did not support the young man's conviction. He even suggested that Maria had in the end intended to give in to Alexander's demand. Bruno further contended that Pius XII had deliberately set out to make a saint out of Maria Goretti in order to counteract the sexual immorality of the American troops, most of them Protestants, who had liberated Italy in 1944.

The effect of Bruno's book was to question the integrity and methods of the entire saint-making process. For the first time in its history, the little-known congregation was faced with a major scandal. Palazzini responded by appointing a commission of nine scholars from the fields of history, secular jurisprudence, theology, and canon law to examine Guerri's charges. Months later, the commission published a "white book" which attacked the credibility of Guerri's book. He had, they argued, made hundreds of errors of fact as well as of interpretation. Guerri responded by threatening to sue the authors of the Vatican document for defamation. Eszer, who enjoys verbal combat, went on television in Rome to debate Bruno. Bruno failed to counter the Vatican's criticism and eventually dropped his threat.

What interested me about the Guerri affair was that at no time did the congregation even consider reopening the cause. To do so, I was told, would put the congregation in the untenable position of second-guessing an infallible declaration by a pope. This, then, is one important effect of papal infallibility on the making of saints: the pope's judgment is final and irrevocable and Roman Catholics are not permitted to question the sanctity of any papally canonized saint, although the infallibility of papal canonizations is very much in dispute.

On closer examination, however, it turns out that papal infallibility is not an unlimited guarantee. In the first place, it does not apply to the vast majority of the church's saints, only to those who, according to Gumpel, were canonized "after all due scientific investigations, as was the custom after 1588, when Pope Sixtus V established the Congregation of Rites." This does not mean that biblical figures like Peter and Paul, or medieval patrons such as Bernard or Francis of Assisi are questionable saints, only that the certainty of their final spiritual destination is not guaranteed by papal infallibility.

What it also means, however, is that the congregation's particular mental horizon—its operative universe—originates with its own institutional founding in 1588. For example, the first saint listed in the congregation's own guide, the *Index on the Status of Causes*, is not the protomartyr Stephen but Hyacinth, a Dominican missionary who was born near Cracow in 1185, died on the Feast of the Assumption in 1257, and was canonized by Pope Clement VIII in 1594, nearly three and a half centuries later. This institutional perspective seems to suggest that Hyacinth is the first saint whose canonization is covered by papal infallibility *because* his was the first canonization to be held after the congregation had established "scientific" methods for investigating the lives of potential saints. Yet the facts regarding Hyacinth's life and purported miracles are, as the Bollandists and others have shown, notoriously unreliable.* What can it mean, therefore, to say that popes cannot err in canonizing a saint when subsequent historical investigations show, as in the case of Hyacinth, that the pope was not in possession of the historical facts?

The answer is that papal infallibility—in the second place—does not apply to any assertions of historical fact or miraculous claims which the saint-makers may make on behalf of the candidate. Indeed, it does not even guarantee the truth of the facts which the pope himself may incorporate in his solemn declaration of canonization. In short, papal infallibility applies only to what cannot be ascertained by human inquiry—namely, that the candidate is with God in heaven—and not to anything else about the candidate's life, virtues, or miracles of intercession.

The paradox is obvious: papal infallibility applies only to saints whose causes are the products of the congregation since its activities were systematized in 1588, but the integrity of that system in no way affects the infallibility of the pope's judgment. In short, the pope's judgment is infallible because he is the pope, but the system by which saints are made is not. Indeed, were matters otherwise there would have been no need to reform the system.

Whether or not the making of saints requires the protection of papal infallibility is still a debatable issue. What is not debatable is the outlook of the saint-makers themselves. They are, as they believe, the only scholars in the world whose endeavors are aimed at achieving a final judgment which is protected by the operation of the Holy Spirit. This does not make them any less concerned for finding the truth about the lives they study. On the contrary, as the Guerri scandal demonstrated, they are keenly aware of the necessity of proving a candidate's sanctity beyond a reasonable doubt. And although their work is seldom challenged—or even read—by outsiders, their documents are expected to withstand the severest kind of scrutiny. Eventually, I was permitted to examine several causes myself and arrive at my own conclusions.

To a certain extent, Rome's new saint-makers are like secular academics, free to pursue the truth. But they do not function in anything like a modern academic environment. They cannot choose the sub-

---

* Today's saint-makers acknowledge this. But they argue, fairly enough, that the investigation of Hyacinth's cause was already ancient and not carried out according to the strict procedures established in 1588.

jects on which they work nor can they control the final disposition of their labors. Even with the reform of 1983, the relators and postulators still must respect the inherited categories by which the church has come to recognize saints as saints. How flexible are those categories? The first and most interesting test, as I saw it, was martyrdom. What, in a context of modern "total" warfare, does it mean to die for Christ?

For the saint-makers, this is not merely an abstract issue. Fifty years have elapsed since the Second World War began, the minimum time it usually takes before Rome takes up a cause. John Paul II is a man shaped by his experiences of that war. So are several of the saint-makers, notably Eszer and Gumpel, who also grew up under the Nazis. By a quirk of history, it has fallen to these men to judge whether certain well-known Catholics killed by the Nazis truly died for their faith.

CHAPTER FOUR

THE WITNESS OF MARTYRS

ON THE MORNING of May 1, 1987, the small lobby of the Hotel Gülich in Cologne, West Germany, was filled with Jews. They were members of a clan, about two dozen in all, whose German ancestors had been scattered by Hitler's pogroms to the United States, South America, and Canada. Four of those ancestors had died in Nazi death camps. One of the victims was Edith Stein—*Tante* Edith to her nieces—who, as Sister Teresa Benedicta of the Cross, was to be proclaimed a martyr that afternoon by John Paul II. But a martyr for whom? To Jews around the world, Edith Stein was one of six million Jews killed in the Holocaust. To the pope she was also—and primarily—a martyr for the church.

The beatification of Edith Stein outraged many Israelis and other Jews. Why, critics wanted to know, was the church placing the crown of martyrdom on the head of a single apostate Jew when millions of other Jews—children, grandparents, mothers, and fathers—had perished at the hands of the Nazis? Once again, it was said, the first Polish pope was attempting to rob the Holocaust of its specific intent—the genocide of European Jewry—by focusing attention on those Christians who were also Nazi victims. Was this not, it was suggested, an attempt to use the saint-making process to deflect attention from the church's own complicity through silence in the Nazis' war on the Jews? Of all the Christians killed by the Nazis, why had the church chosen a convert who had asked God, in the midst of the Holocaust, to accept her life in atonement for the "unbelief" of the Jews? "It sticks in the Jewish throat, this proposed sainthood," wrote American novelist Anne Roiphe in her (1988) reflections on the Holocaust. ". . . It disturbs not because Edith Stein chose another religion but because she could not escape her birth certificate. Her religious commitment was a private matter and from all accounts the sincere choice of an outstanding intellect, but she did not die by choice, with honor, with dignity, with purpose, religious or otherwise. She simply died like the others."

The Vatican had anticipated criticism from Jews, though not the spirited outcry that Edith Stein's name continues to evoke. Indeed, in the months before the pope's trip to Cologne, the cardinals of the Congregation for the Causes of Saints even debated whether it might not be "pastorally opportune" to postpone her beatification until the Vatican could mollify the critics. But the bishops of Germany and Poland strongly supported the idea of proclaiming Stein a martyr, and so, too, one must conclude, did John Paul II. As the archbishop of Cracow and as pope, he had on more than one public occasion invoked her name as an atoning victim of the Holocaust. Moreover, his own intellectual development as a philosopher had been influenced by Edith Stein's life and thought.

The beatification of Edith Stein, which will be examined in detail later, was one of the most controversial episodes in the papacy of John Paul II. In ways that no other recent cause had done, it focused public attention on the purpose and methods of the church's saint-making process. But the pope's decision to beatify Stein had nothing to do with the question of whether she deserved the title of martyr of the faith. *That* question was one the saint-makers themselves had to resolve. From their point of view, the cause of Edith Stein was one of three important processes—the first to emerge from the Nazi era— which allowed the congregation to expand and to a certain extent redefine its traditional criteria for proving martyrdom. Taken together, these three causes opened a new chapter in the evolution of the church's understanding of martyrdom and, as we will see, provoked new questions about the relationship between religious faith and political action.

THE NAZI AS MODERN "TYRANT"

THE ROMAN CATHOLIC Church has never issued a dogmatic definition of martyrdom. The early church, however, developed a classic model of the martyr—and of the conditions of martyrdom—by which certain individuals have since been recognized and declared martyrs of the faith. As we have already seen, the earliest Christian martyrs were perceived and celebrated as imitators of Christ's passion and death. Thus, the classic Christian martyr is an innocent victim who dies for the faith at the hands of a tyrant who is opposed to the faith. Like Jesus, the classical martyr does not seek death but freely accepts it when challenged to renounce his faith or otherwise act contrary to Christian values. Also like Jesus, the classical martyr forgives his or her enemies.

In turn, the trial of Jesus is paradigmatic for establishing the classic conditions of Christian martyrdom: ideally, the martyr is tried before judges and through his or her fidelity "provokes the tyrant" with a confession of faith. Thus, the Romans' concern for legal process, as embodied in the proconsuls' reports of their interrogations of the early Christian martyrs, was of fundamental importance to the development of the church's juridical approach to the making of martyrs. Without such documentation—or the testimony of witnesses—how could martyrdom be proved?

In most cases, martyrdom is also a political act. Jesus himself was persecuted for attacking the Temple authorities. The early Christian martyrs challenged the sacred base of Roman authority by refusing to honor the emperor as divine. Once the church itself gained temporal as well as spiritual authority over her subjects, the line between political and religious martyrdom became more difficult to draw. Thereafter, one could be a martyr for the faith by dying in defense of the rights of the church: in the twelfth century, for instance, Archbishop Thomas à Becket was quickly canonized after his murder for defending the prerogatives of the English church against King Henry II. Later, in the era of the European explorers, Christian missionaries who followed the flags of various countries were frequently killed because, in the eyes of those whom they came to convert, their intentions were often indistinguishable from those of the soldiers who came to conquer and exploit. Even when Christians killed other Christians, as in the Reformation-era wars of religion, political motives were intimately connected with confessions of faith.

Against this background, Benedict XIV established strict criteria which continue to guide those trying to prove that a candidate died a Christian martyr. Essentially, advocates of a cause must show that the victim died for the faith. More precisely, they have to prove that the "tyrant" was provoked into killing the victim by the latter's clear and unambiguous profession of faith. Therefore, advocates of a cause must produce witnesses or documents proving that a profession of faith took place, that the tyrant acted in *odium fidei* (hatred of the faith), and that the victim's motives, if not unalloyed, are clearly religious. Furthermore, witnesses are required who can testify that the victim persevered in his willingness to die for the faith right through the moment of shedding his blood.

The Nazis, however, represented a new species of tyrant. There is no doubt that they killed millions of Christians for various reasons. But the way they did it confounded the inherited categories and rules by which the professional saint-makers have traditionally judged causes of martyrdom.

To begin with, unlike the leaders of the French Revolution, the Nazis did not publicly proclaim a hatred of the Christian faith. On the contrary, Adolf Hitler was baptized a Catholic and never renounced his faith. When he came to power in March 1933, he pledged in his Reichstag speech that the government would protect Christianity. And in 1933 he even signed a concordat with Pope Pius XI ensuring "the uninhibited freedom of action for all Catholic religious, cultural and educational organizations, associations and federations." There were, moreover, Catholic and Protestant Germans who supported Hitler, who joined the Nazi movement and who became the Führer's foot soldiers. Given all this, it was difficult, though not impossible, to demonstrate by the traditional criteria that a Catholic victim of the Nazis had died for the faith. Jews were arrested and killed because they were Jews. But those Catholics who opposed the Nazis were accused of sedition or treason or other political crimes. The Nazis, in short, understood what the church means by martyrdom and were not interested in playing the conventional tyrant.

The way the Nazis disposed of their victims also caused problems for the church's saint-makers. Sometimes their victims simply disappeared. More often they were shunted off to death camps where they were killed en masse with no witnesses to testify to their steadfastness in faith. How were the saint-makers to know whether a potential martyr had not despaired of God at the last moment or, what amounted to almost the same thing, come to hate his persecutors? And finally, there were among the consultors to the congregation a handful of strict constructionists who felt canonically bound by the traditional notion that martyrs must shed their blood. Most—but not all—of these consultants had no qualms about accepting candidates who died by gas or injection, but they seriously questioned whether someone who merely wasted away in a concentration camp qualified as a martyr. Eventually, their objections were overcome by other consultants who pointed out that several of the church's earliest martyrs had also died of starvation, disease, or exhaustion in Roman prison camps.

There were, then, certain conceptual and procedural problems which had to be resolved before any Catholic victims of the Nazis could be beatified or canonized as martyrs. But these problems were not resolved by abstract reasoning or the dialectics of theological debate. Like case law in England and the United States, these issues were confronted and resolved cause by cause.

TITUS BRANDSMA: FIRST CATHOLIC MARTYR OF THE NAZI ERA

THE FIRST VICTIM of the Nazis to be proposed as martyr was Titus Brandsma, a Carmelite priest, teacher, and journalist who died in Dachau in 1942 and was beatified by John Paul II in Rome in 1985. By inclination, Brandsma was a contemplative. When the Franciscans rejected him because they felt his health was too fragile for the friars' activist regimen, Brandsma joined the Carmelites and devoted his life to expounding the writings of the order's great mystics, St. Teresa of Àvila and St. John of the Cross. But young Brandsma was hardly a passive student. Indeed, his persistent objections to the dogmatism of his Dutch professors prompted them to delay his appointment to Rome for higher theological studies. On his return from Rome he became a professor of theology and mysticism and was later one of the founders of the Catholic University of Nijmegen.

As a lecturer, Brandsma tended to bore his students; in fact, for one semester his class consisted of a single student, a woman who felt sorry for him because, she said, he was so physically unattractive and so dull at the lectern. Eventually, however, he developed one theme which made his students sit up: the "new paganism," as he called it, of Germany's Nazi party. Throughout the thirties, Brandsma lectured and wrote on the dangers of Nazism, including what he called the "cowardice" of the Nazis in their efforts to rid Germany of its Jews. By

1940, Holland itself was under Nazi control. In August of the following year, the civil governor of Holland issued a directive prohibiting children of Jewish descent from admission to Catholic schools. As president of the Association of Catholic Secondary Schools, Brandsma protested to the authorities at the Hague and won a temporary postponement of the order.

Brandsma was also the Catholic bishops' spiritual director for the three dozen or so Catholic newspapers published in Holland. He had for a time edited one of the newspapers which, unlike diocesan weeklies today, competed with the nation's secular dailies. In December 1941, the National Socialist Press Secretariat telexed every newspaper in Holland, notifying them that the Dutch press was obligated to print advertisements by the Nazi party or any of its organizations. The Dutch Catholic hierarchy responded by denouncing the Nazis and asserting the right to refuse to run Nazi advertisements or propaganda. On New Year's Day, Brandsma was dispatched to meet with each bishop and editor to explain why the directive was to be ignored and to urge them to prepare for retaliation by the Nazis.

Eighteen days later, Brandsma was arrested at his monastery for "activities endanger[ing] the prestige of the German Empire, the National Socialist ideas and intend[ing] to undermine the unity of the Dutch people." The reporting officer also added that "his hostility is proved by his writing against the German policy toward the Jews." In March, Brandsma was transferred to the prison depot at Armersfoort in central Holland where he led prayer groups and heard confessions despite harsh penalties for religious activities. In June he was again transferred, to the Dachau concentration camp, where he joined 2,700 other imprisoned clergy, most of them Catholic priests. According to witnesses, he was repeatedly beaten to the point of unconsciousness. The following month he was put in the camp hospital as a subject for medical experimentation. On Sunday the twenty-sixth, he died from a lethal injection of carbolic acid.

Titus Brandsma was not the first Nazi-era Catholic to be proposed for sainthood, but he was the first to be put forward as a martyr. His promoters, the Carmelites, were warned that they were making a mistake, that it would be exceedingly difficult to prove that he had been killed for religious rather than political reasons. Better, they were advised, to argue the case on the basis of his virtues and hope for a confirming miracle.

There was another, more practical concern as well. In 1963, less than a decade after the Ordinary Process for Brandsma was begun, Paul VI called a halt to all processes involving victims of the Spanish

Civil War. As it happened, most of the candidates for martyrdom from that war died at the hands of the Liberal (some were Communist) forces, and the victor, General Francisco Franco, was still in power. Paul VI was not in sympathy with the Franco regime, despite the general's support of the church, and neither was the liberal wing of the Spanish clergy. The pope feared, therefore, that the naming of martyrs would inflame old political passions and cause unwelcome division in the church. But his interdict angered many conservative Spanish officials in the Vatican. Among these was Father Rafael Pérez, who had served as vicar to a Spanish bishop during the Civil War and was now the powerful Promoter of the Faith. In that capacity, he vowed that Titus Brandsma would never be declared a martyr ahead of some of his deserving fellow Spaniards.

Eventually, the ban against the Spanish causes was lifted and Monsignor Pèrez was replaced. In 1980, responsibility for Brandsma's cause fell to Father Redemptus Valabek as the Carmelites' new postulator general. By then, most of the Dutch Carmelites had lost interest in the cause. (It was, the younger friars felt, a waste of money to promote new saints, and they might have dropped it if the older men hadn't insisted on seeing Brandsma through.) Valabek's predecessor had already collected sufficient evidence to prove that Brandsma willingly accepted martyrdom in a Christlike spirit. Witnesses from Dachau testified that Brandsma had urged his fellow inmates to pray for their sadistic guards, and did so himself. Even the nurse who injected Brandsma with carbolic acid came forward—with a promise of anonymity from the church tribunal—to testify that Brandsma had prayed for her as well.

"Our real problem was proving that Titus was not arrested and eventually killed for political reasons, in this case his opposition to Nazism," Valabek recalled one evening during a long conversation at the Carmelite monastery in Rome. "Of course he was opposed to Nazism but we had to prove that his martyrdom was based on other motives. Luckily, almost miraculously, the transcripts of his interrogation in front of Nazi judges in Holland were somehow saved. From these we were able to show two reasons why he was condemned by the Nazis. The first was because he had refused to get rid of the Jewish children in the Catholic schools. To do so, Brandsma explicitly stated, would be against Catholic principles. So we were able to show that he was defending the rights of the church to educate the children who were sent to Catholic schools, including non-Catholics. The second reason was that as ecclesiastical adviser to Catholic journalists, he made a personal appeal to them not to accept Nazi propaganda in their newspapers. This was the proximate cause why he was arrested and eventually killed. The Nazis were very angry with him and this comes through in the interrogatory sessions he had with the judges."

In short, given the criteria demanded by the church, Titus Brandsma succeeded in becoming the first Nazi-era martyr not just because he opposed the Nazi ideology as un-Christian—to have argued on these grounds alone would have invited the standard objection that he was only a political martyr—but also because his advocates were able to demonstrate that he was killed for defending certain Catholic principles.* Moreover, those principles—freedom of education and freedom of the press—were not, by any measure, inherent in Catholic faith and morality. But they were rights the church asserted as an institution, and Brandsma, as his advocates demonstrated, had made them his own.

This was not, it should be noted, how Blessed Titus Brandsma was presented to the faithful for their veneration. Valabek promoted him as the patron saint of journalists who, God knows, are certainly in need of one.† But it was the prerogative of the pope to establish the meaning of the church's new martyr. At the beatification ceremony on November 3, 1985, John Paul II declared: ". . . We raise to the glory of the altars a man who passed through the torment of a concentration camp, that of Dachau. It was in the midst of this scourge, in the midst of the concentration camp, which remains an infamous mark of our century, that God found Titus Brandsma worthy of Him." There was, the pope noted, an apt text from the Old Testament: "God hath tried them . . . as in gold in the furnace He hath proved them, and as victim of a holocaust He hath received them."

For the saint-makers, however, the success of Brandsma's cause had another, more precise meaning. They now had a precedent for arguing that Catholic victims of the Nazis could be officially declared martyrs

---

* This is not to say that opposition to the Nazis in defense of Catholic faith or morals cannot be a valid motive for a martyr. Father Molinari is preparing a cause precisely on those grounds. The candidate is a Berlin priest, Father Bernard Lichtenberg (1875–1943), who worked surreptitiously to help Jews escape Nazi Germany. In 1938 he went public with his denunciations of Nazi anti-Semitism and eventually died a slow martyrdom in a Nazi prison.

† How a saint comes to be the patron of a particular occupation, profession, or guild is a matter of association—often of images—rather than an exercise in logic. St. Lucy (Light, Sight), for example, is the patron saint of people with eye problems because legend holds that her persecutors plucked out her eyes. St. Agatha, who tradition says had her breasts cut off by torturers, is the patroness of wet nurses. The Angel Gabriel, who announced to Mary the "good news" of her pregnancy, is patron of postal employees, telephone operators, and radio workers. Stephen, who was stoned to death, is patron of bricklayers. Hairdressers look to St. Martin de Porres, who was barber of his monastery. The traditional patron saint of journalists is Francis de Sales, a bishop who loved books and liked to scatter pamphlets about. He wasn't a journalist but he was a lawyer, which may make his patronage all the more attractive to contemporary writers. In 1958, Pope Pius XII named the contemplative nun St. Clare of Assisi patroness of television, though she lived seven hundred years before the technology of transmitting images was perfected. Clare, it seems, once was granted the vision of a Mass which, because she was bedridden, she was unable to attend in person.

in circumstances where it could be shown that the hierarchy had provoked the tyrant into acting against the church by denouncing its unjust action. That precedent was worked into a new logic in the more controversial cause of Edith Stein.

EDITH STEIN AND THE TRANSFORMATION OF A SAINT

ON THE SAME July Sunday in 1942 that Titus Brandsma was killed, the Catholic bishops of Holland published a letter denouncing the latest Nazi scheme to deport Dutch Jews "to the East"—the Nazis' euphemism for the death camps in Poland. In retaliation, the Nazis ordered the immediate arrest of all Catholics of Jewish descent. On the following Thursday, Edith Stein and her sister, Rosa, a laywoman, were arrested at the Carmelite convent in Echt. Seven days later, they were sent to the gas chambers at Auschwitz, together with three hundred other baptized Jews from Holland.

Who was Edith Stein? The youngest of eleven children, she was born on Yom Kippur, the Jewish Day of Atonement, in 1891 to prosperous Jewish parents in Breslau, Germany (now Wroclaw, Poland). Her mother, who was widowed twenty-one months later, was religiously Orthodox, but none of her seven surviving children were observant Jews. By the time she was fifteen, Edith had ceased to pray. She was, she declared, an atheist and a feminist. Philosophy was her passion and in 1913 at the age of twenty-three she entered the University of Göttingen to study under the father of phenomenology, Edmund Husserl. There she was drawn to the Philosophical Society, an informal circle of gifted intellectuals gathered around Husserl in the years just prior to the outbreak of World War I. Edith became such an adept pupil that in 1916, Husserl invited her to join him as his assistant at the University of Freiburg, where she received her doctorate the next year with a dissertation entitled "On the Problem of Empathy."

As taught by Husserl, the phenomenological method involved a strong ethical thrust. The master himself was Lutheran and several of the other phenomenologists who impressed Edith Stein, notably Max Scheler and Roman Ingarden, were Roman Catholics. Through their influence, she began to question what she called her "rationalistic prejudice" and to explore Christianity. In 1917, she was asked by the widow of her former teacher, Adolf Reinach, who had died at the front in Belgium, to put her husband's papers in order. It was Frau Reinach's impressive forbearance during that period which moved Edith Stein emotionally toward the Christian faith. During her student years, she also fell in love with at least one member of the Philosophical Society, Hans Lipps. By 1921, however, she was beginning to feel a different kind of attraction. In the summer of that year, she read the autobiography of St. Teresa of Ávila, the great Carmelite mystic of the sixteenth century. "This," she concluded, "is the truth." On the following New Year's Day, she was baptized into the Catholic Church.

Over the next ten years, Edith continued her philosophic interests as best she could, writing a two-volume study of the philosophy of St. Thomas Aquinas. But despite a generous recommendation from Husserl himself, she could not—as a woman—obtain a professorship at Freiburg. Instead, she taught at the Dominican sisters' high school for girls in Speyer, where she also took private religious vows. In 1932, she accepted a teaching post at the German Institute for Scientific Pedagogy in Münster. The following year she was barred from her lectureship under a Nazi decree aimed at Jews, and in October she entered the Carmelites on the feast day of St. Teresa. Frau Stein was heartbroken: not only had her youngest daughter, the one born on Yom Kippur, become a Christian, she had also taken up a cloistered life that would isolate her from the family.

Despite her isolation—or perhaps because of it—Edith Stein developed an explicit sense of her continuing identity as a Jew. "My return to God made me feel Jewish again," she said of her conversion, and she thought of her relationship to Christ as existing "not only in a spiritual sense, but in blood terms." She was fully aware of what was happening to the Jews outside; in fact, she impulsively wrote a fruitless letter to Pope Pius XI in 1933, urging him to "deplore the hatred, persecution, and displays of anti-Semitism directed against the Jews at any time and from any source." In her letters and other writings, she eventually spelled out exactly how she saw the relationship between her Jewishness and her Christian faith. In one of her letters, she compared her decision to convert and become a cloistered nun to the biblical figure of Queen Esther, who sacrificed herself to help save the Israelites. "I am confident that the Lord has taken my life for all Jews," she wrote. "I always have to think of Queen Esther, who was taken away from her people for the express purpose of standing before the king for her people. I am the very poor, weak and small Esther, but the king who selected me is infinitely great and merciful." Later, in writing her last spiritual will and testament, as Carmelites are required to do, she asked God to accept her life "for the atonement of the unbelief of the Jewish people and for this: that the Lord may be accepted by His own people and His Kingdom may come in glory, for the salvation of Germany and for world peace."

Within the cloister, Edith Stein was an anomaly twice over: she was a Jew among Aryans and an intellectual among nonintellectuals. In the tradition of Carmelite spirituality, Stein devoted herself to the crucified Christ; hence her chosen religious name: "Blessed of the Cross." Significantly, her last major work was a treatise on another Carmelite mystic, St. John of the Cross, entitled *The Science of the Cross*. All this material was of major importance for her subsequent process at the Vatican. After *Kiristallnacht* (November 9, 1938), however, it was obvious that the cloister would not protect her from the Nazis' determination to rid the Fatherland of Jews. For her own safety and that of the convent, Edith Stein left Cologne on New Year's Eve for the Carmelites' convent in Echt, Holland, taking along her sister, Rosa, who had also become a Catholic.

But Holland proved to be a precarious haven for a Jewish nun. Like other Jews she was required to wear the Star of David. And when the order went out to arrest all converted Jews, the SS knew where to find her. "Come, let us go for the people," she said to her sister. Along the train route to Auschwitz, Edith Stein dropped notes at stops where she had lived. The last one, addressed to the Carmelites at Echt, contained a simple plea: "Urge Swiss Consulate to take all steps necessary to get us across the border. Our convent will take care of the expense travel."

In the immediate postwar years, Edith Stein was essentially an unknown figure. Even the circumstances of her death were unknown. Gradually, her writings were gathered together and, through the Discalced Carmelites, her story spread. Interestingly enough, the Carmelites promoted her by her given Jewish name: the Archives of Edith Stein were established at Belgium's Louvain University and her cause was promoted internationally by the Edith Stein Guild. In part this reflected the interest she had attracted under her own name as a philosopher and religious thinker. In part, too, it reflected the interest she generated as a Catholic who died like the other Jews in the Holocaust.

Twenty years passed before Cardinal Joseph Frings of Cologne opened an Ordinary Process on Edith Stein. Significantly, the process was based on proving her heroic virtue, not martyrdom. The assumption was that she had been killed because she was a Jew. Tribunals were held in Cologne, Echt, and Speyer. Of the 103 witnesses who testified, only 3 were negative and their objections were easily dismissed. One witness who knew Stein prior to her conversion testified that she was arrogant, but this was rejected as irrelevant since the church weighs the life of a convert only from the moment of baptism. A nun from the Catholic school in Speyer where Stein had taught as a laywoman recalled that she was excessive in her religious devotions. But this criticism was explained as the normal zealousness of a convert and contrasted, favorably, with the rather tepid spiritual practices of the nuns themselves. Another nun from the convent in Cologne testified that Sister Benedicta constantly defended the Jews and molested the other sisters, but this witness was shown to be an untrustworthy gossip.

On the positive side, the postulator and defense lawyer built up a strong case for heroic virtue, drawing not only on the testimony of eyewitnesses but also on Stein's published writings and personal correspondence. They argued that her particular example or message to the world was her personal, almost mystical, identification with the suffering Jesus on the cross during one of the most brutal periods of human history, an identification which allowed her to embrace death as a final act of total commitment to the imitation of Christ.

By 1983, the *positio* on Edith Stein's heroic virtues was ready for discussion by the congregation. There was little doubt that she would be judged heroically virtuous and declared "venerable." But there was considerable doubt that she would be beatified, much less declared a saint, any time soon. The reason: she lacked the necessary miracle. The problem was that the Nazi death camps left no bodies—at least no bodies that could be distinguished from the bones and skulls that were shoveled into common graves. Without a body, there can be no tomb where the faithful can come and seek divine favors through the candidate's intercession. Without a body, there can be no relics either. In the case of Edith Stein, even those second-class relics—rosaries and crucifixes she used, clothes she wore—were destroyed when the Nazis burned the Carmelite convent in Echt. Thus, without these very tangible means whereby Catholics have for millennia invoked intercession, Stein's cause seemed destined for a lengthy stay in that limbo reserved for those venerables who lack the miracles required of blesseds and saints.

But on March 3, 1983, the cause of Edith Stein was pushed in a different direction. On that day, Frings's successor, Cardinal Joseph Hoeffner, signed a Letter of Petition to John Paul II on behalf of the German hierarchy formally requesting that Edith Stein's cause proceed as a process of martyrdom. Hoeffner's request was seconded in a letter from the primate of Poland, Cardinal Jozef Glemp of Warsaw, on behalf of the Polish bishops. In their letters, the cardinals argued that the death of Edith Stein could be seen as an act of retaliation against the Catholic bishops of Holland for their public protest against the deportation of Dutch Jews. Therefore, they concluded, there were grounds for recognizing Edith Stein as a martyr for the church.

There were at least three good reasons to suppose why the bishops wanted Edith Stein declared a martyr. First, it would obviate the need for a miracle: as a martyr, she could be beatified (but not canonized) without one. Second, in the popular mind (if not in the minds of experts) Edith Stein's reputation for holiness was grounded in the story of her martyrdom; to declare her a confessor but not a martyr would, in effect, put the church in the position of questioning the significance of not only her death but also the deaths of the tens of thousands of other Catholic priests, sisters, and laymen who were victims of the Nazis. Third, to proclaim her a saint but not a martyr would suggest that the Catholic Church, as a church, had not nurtured blood witness to the crimes and horrors of the Nazis. To the bishops of Germany and Poland, this was a distortion of history that the church had to correct.

The cause of Edith Stein was of special interest to John Paul II as well. For one thing, he shared her interest in phenomenology and its relation to Christian ethics. For his own thesis in philosophy, Wojtyla had chosen to write on the phenomenology of Max Scheler and its relation to Thomistic thought. What's more, the pope had come to know well Roman Ingarden, who taught philosophy at the University of Cracow when Wojtyla was the city's archbishop. In addition to this chain of personal connections, John Paul II was genuinely moved by the figure of a modern intellectual who had come to faith in the person of Jesus through the disinterested pursuit of truth. Few candidates for sainthood in the twentieth century provided such an example for intellectuals in or outside the church.

Even so, the congregation did not act immediately on the bishops' extraordinary Letter of Petition. As it happened, the letter arrived during a period of considerable upheaval at the congregation: the reform of the canonization procedures had just gone into effect and, as a result, fourteen months elapsed before the cause was assigned to Eszer in his new role as a relator.

In essence, Eszer's assignment was to prove the bishops' contention that Edith Stein had died for the church, and therefore for the faith, and not solely because of her Jewishness. The key to his case was a collection of documents discovered in 1980 in the Royal Institute for War Documentation in Amsterdam. According to those documents, the Nazis were prepared to spare converted Dutch Jews if the Catholic bishops would agree not to publicize their opposition to the deportation order. When the bishops refused to obey, the Nazis ordered the immediate arrest of all Catholics with Jewish blood. Therefore, Eszer argued, the Nazis were provoked by the bishops' defiance into committing a specific act in hatred of the faith.

Up to this point, the case was similar to the argument put forward on behalf of Titus Brandsma. The crucial difference was that Stein, unlike Brandsma, was not personally connected to the bishops' action. Thus, it could not be argued that she had provoked the tyrant by her own act. Nor was there any evidence that, after her arrest, she had been asked for or given a profession of faith. Indeed, on the one occasion when she identified herself as Catholic (which was obvious from her habit), the concentration-camp guard who put the question to her rejected her answer. "You damned Jew," he shouted, "stand there!"

To meet the expected objections of the congregation's examiners, Eszer proposed a novel response. "The provocation of the 'tyrant,' " he argued, "was made by the action of the Dutch bishops, to which St. Teresa Benedicta definitely adhered, given the fact that she had always criticized in a radical fashion any behavior which could be considered too condescending toward National Socialism." In effect, then, the Dutch bishops' provocative act was a kind of class action on behalf of all converted Jews who died as a result. Furthermore, Eszer argued, the fact that there were no witnesses to her death was no reason to suppose that she had not persevered in her faith. In her spiritual will she had already offered herself to God as an atoning victim "for peace" and for "the unbelief of the Jewish people." In other words, Eszer argued that Edith Stein's whole life as a Catholic, as manifested by her heroic virtue, was evidence of her readiness to accept martyrdom if and when it came.

These, then, were the juridical narrows through which Edith Stein's cause for martyrdom eventually passed. But in pressing her cause, Eszer did something more: he also proposed arguments by which it could be shown that the Nazis were in reality no different than all the other tyrants who have persecuted Christians. It was an exciting prospect, especially for a saint-maker from Germany.

When I first spoke to Eszer about the Edith Stein cause it was October 1986. The panel of theologians had just passed on his *positio* and now it needed only the approval of the congregation's cardinals and bishops. We met in the Dominicans' residence at the Angelicum University, twenty minutes by bus from the Vatican. Eszer's small room was divided by a groaning bookcase, his bed on one side, two wooden desks heaped with open files and books and trays of cigar ashes on the other. Edith Stein was one of sixty causes he had assumed as a relator but it was the one which most agitated him. He was, after all, a German himself, he said, and had developed the concept of the modern tyrant as a way to deprive the Nazis of the advantage they enjoyed according to the traditional rules for making martyrs. "The modern tyrant is very sophisticated," he said. "He pretends not to be against religion or even interested in it, so he does not ask his victims what their faith is. But in reality he is either without religion or makes some ideology into an erzatz religion. We see that with the Communists and we saw it with the Nazis. In my *positio* on Edith Stein, my main argument was that the church cannot accept the arguments of criminals and persecutors of herself. We cannot give in the process [of making saints] an advantage to people who are liars just because they say they are not against religion."

I asked to see a copy of his *positio* but Eszer shook his head: until the pope made his decision in the cause it was privileged information. But he was willing to talk about the wider framework of the argument he presented to the congregation. Hitler, he said, was not only intent on exterminating the Jews. He also planned, after the war, to eliminate the Catholic Church by transforming it from within. "It is absolutely clear that he intended to found a new religion using the external trappings of Catholicism. He got this idea from Richard Wagner's *Parsifal*. Hitler considered Wagner his one worthy predecessor. You see, no one knows National Socialism who does not know Wagner. In any case, due to the overriding concerns of the war, Hitler felt that the 'final solution' of the Catholic problem was to be held off until it was over. But the Nazis' hatred of the church erupted spontaneously when the Dutch bishops protested the deportation of the Jews and so we can see that the death of Edith Stein was an act committed in hatred of the faith."

As he talked, it became clear that working on the cause of Edith Stein was more than just another assignment for Eszer. He was nine years old when she died, eleven when the Nazis surrendered, and thus of the first generation of Germans who could fairly claim not to have been Nazis themselves. To him, Adolf Hitler was a crazed outsider who had infected Germany with the Austrians' virulent racial anti-Semitism. In judging the Germans of the Hitler era—his parents' generation—distinctions had to be made, history given its due. "When Hitler came to power, he pledged to protect Christianity. Point Fourteen of the [Nazi] party program stated that the party is ideologically based on positive Christianity. Of course that was rubbish. But we must remember that there were six million jobless workers in Germany. The Catholic bishops could not sustain a protracted fight with Hitler without being reproached by the faithful.

"One also has to distinguish between the concentration camps and the extermination camps. The extermination camps were all outside of Germany. There were few real Catholics involved in the extermination camps because the SS did not want convinced Catholics. They even excluded them. They knew that convinced Catholics would not only be troublemakers but eventually they would tell others about the extermination camps which were, of course, secret."

Eszer paused to light up a cigar. As he did so he shifted in his seat, causing the small desk chair to creak under the burden. Our conversation had moved close to the skin. "Americans," he said, "don't see the diabolical character of modern totalitarian systems because they never had the experience. They are always accusing the Germans for accepting National Socialism. But it was impossible to foresee what the Nazis would do. For example, my father was in the SA, the political army, not the SS. A Jesuit advised him to go in and try to Christianize the army. But it was impossible to do. One time they sang a song criticizing the pope and he got up and refused to do it. So he went to trial. The judge let him off, but after that he was excluded from promotion. A hundred thousand Germans were killed by the Nazis but no one speaks now about that.

"Also, many, many Catholics did things for the Jews whenever they could. In my family it was forbidden to speak badly about the Jews. My mother always said they are people like us and you cannot speak against them. When other children came home with children's books which showed the Jews with big noses and fat bellies who were always making trouble, my mother said she would beat us up if we brought those books into the house. But no one writes books about these things. Today, many Jewish writers don't admit that the Catholics did anything for the Jews. But I know that in the case of Edith Stein she was killed because the Catholic Church did something for the Jews. Our critics say that she must be honored as a Jewish martyr and that we cannot accept."

Eszer felt so strongly about the Edith Stein cause that when James Baaden, an American Jew working in London on a biography of Stein, wrote the congregation explaining why he thought she had been killed solely because of her Jewishness, the Dominican incautiously responded in person—something Vatican officials rarely do with outsiders—and at considerable length. As relator of the cause, he told Baaden, there was no doubt in his mind that Edith Stein had abandoned Judaism as a student and came to value it only after she converted to Catholicism. More important, there was no doubt that in her spiritual will she meant what she said when she wrote that she was offering her life for the "unbelief" of her people, the Jews. To Eszer this meant that she was willing to sacrifice herself, as he put it, "for the conversion of all Jews to the Catholic Church." Finally, Eszer reminded Baaden in provocative terms that he was poking into matters that were none of his affair: "You are, of course, free to defend your point of view," he wrote, "but the Sacred Congregation for the Causes of Saints has outlooks which are rather different from yours. The Catholic Church is sovereign regarding matters of faith and morals and does not depend on interference from outside."

Baaden lost no time in circulating Eszer's comments. In an article in *The Tablet*, an influential international Catholic weekly published in London, Baaden sniped in return that the congregation's "allegedly exacting processes of scrutiny . . . appear scarcely to exist." Officials of the congregation were upset with Eszer for not letting them handle the congregation's public relations. Jewish leaders in Germany sought clarifications from the German bishops, fearing that John Paul II intended to use the beatification of Edith Stein to preach a message of conversion to the Jews. Eventually a group of Jewish spokesmen from around the world went to the Vatican to air their concerns to the pope himself.

The cause of Edith Stein, meanwhile, moved quickly through the congregation. At the request of the postulator general of the Discalced Carmelites—and with, no doubt, the support of Eszer—the congregation agreed to consider the process both on the virtues and the martyrdom of the candidate. In this way, the arguments on behalf of her virtues could be used to strengthen her claim to martyrdom, especially since there were no witnesses to her death. This approach was unprecedented, but on January 13, 1987, the process was approved by the congregation's cardinals and bishops. Twelve days later, in the presence of the pope, Edith Stein became the first person in the congregation's four-hundred-year history to be confirmed as both martyr *and* confessor. Whatever the theoretical implications of this novel decision, as a practical matter it meant that she no longer needed a miracle for beatification.

All that remained was for the pope to find a way of formally beatifying Edith Stein without offending Jews or denying the logic of the arguments by which her cause had succeeded. Thus, in his homily at the beatification ceremony, John Paul II deftly declared that "in the extermination camp she died as a daughter of Israel 'for the glory of

the Most Holy Name' and, at the same time, as Sister Teresa Benedicta of the Cross, literally 'blessed by the cross.' " The "cause" of her
martyrdom, the pope said, was the Dutch bishops' letter of protest
against the deportation of the Jews. But, he added, because of her great
desire to unite with the sufferings of Christ on the cross, "she gave her
life 'for genuine peace' and 'for the people,' " Prudently, he left un-
mentioned her desire to atone for Jewish "unbelief."

Maximilian Kolbe: Martyr of Charity

The Gospel of John declares that "There is no greater love than this,
that a man should lay down his life for his friends." Jesus himself,
according to Christian doctrine, sacrificed his life for the sins of all
mankind. Yet according to the criteria for making saints, giving one's
life for another is not, of itself, proof of martyrdom. To be declared a
martyr, as we have seen, it must be proven that the Servant of God
was, under one rubric or another, killed for the faith. In one of the
most controverted cases ever to come before the congregation, the
cause of Father Maximilian Kolbe, a Polish Conventual (Black Franciscan) friar who gave his life for another prisoner at Auschwitz, tested
this requirement not once but twice.

The essential facts of Kolbe's heroic gesture are beyond dispute. At
6:00 P.M. on July 30, 1941, the prisoners of Cell Block 14 were ordered
outside and to stand at attention for Kommandant Fritsch. A prisoner
from the cell block had escaped and because of this ten men would be
chosen to starve to death. Among those chosen was Francis Gajownicezek, who began to weep. "My poor wife and children," he sobbed.
When the ten were chosen, Kolbe stepped forward and asked that he
be chosen in Gajownicezek's place.

Fritsch stared at him. "Who are you?" he asked.

"A Catholic priest," Kolbe replied.

His wish was granted. The ten were marched to basement cells in
Bunker II and stripped. They had no furniture or blankets, only a
bucket to hold their urine. But according to Bruno Borgowiec, an
inmate assigned to remove bodies from the death cells, the buckets
were always dry. "The prisoners," he testified at Kolbe's church tribunal, "actually drank its contents to satisfy their thirst." For sixteen
days, Kolbe led the condemned men in prayer and hymns as one by
one they died. On August 14, the last four, including Kolbe, were
given a lethal injection.

Kolbe's heroic act of love—for a man he hardly knew—added luster to an already considerable reputation for holiness. He was founder of the Knights of the Immaculata, an international religious movement that grew out of his intense, almost fanatical devotion to the Virgin Mary. Through the movement he established a number of devotional publications, including the monthly *Knights of Immaculata* magazine which boasted a circulation of 800,000 in Poland alone in 1939. He also founded the City of Immaculata, which eventually became the largest community of Franciscan men in the world, and a similar community, the Garden of the Immaculate, in Nagasaki, Japan. Given to visions, Kolbe had a reputation among the friars for spiritual foresight: long before his arrest, he revealed to a group of his colleagues that he had been granted "an assurance of heaven." Not surprisingly, his intercession was invoked often after his death by Poles, the Conventuals, and members of the Knights of the Immaculata. When his cause was taken up by the congregation, Kolbe had two miracles of healing to his credit.

Although Kolbe's process was based on his heroic virtues, there were those who argued strongly that he should be declared a martyr. The majority of his judges concluded that the evidence did not warrant a decree of martyrdom, and so did Pope Paul VI. Nonetheless, his extraordinary act of self-sacrifice deserved some kind of attention. After beatifying Kolbe in 1971, Pope Paul VI received a delegation of Poles at the Vatican, including Archbishop Karol Wojtyla. In the pope's address to them he allowed that Kolbe could be considered a "martyr of charity."

However appropriate, "martyr of charity" had no theological or canonical standing. Strictly speaking, therefore, Kolbe could not be venerated as a martyr. The distinction, fine as it was, rankled in Poland and among many of Kolbe's fellow Conventuals. In 1982, when a delegation of bishops from Germany traveled to Poland, they were presented during a tour of Kolbe's death cell with a petition to have him canonized as a martyr. The Germans had officially supported Kolbe's original process and, under the circumstances, it was difficult to refuse. In this way it came about that Germans joined the Polish hierarchy in formally requesting that the question of Kolbe's martyrdom be reconsidered.

There was little doubt that Pope John Paul II was well disposed toward canonizing Kolbe a martyr. Auschwitz was within his jurisdiction as archbishop of Cracow, and on his first visit to Poland as pope he knelt in prayer, as he had often done before, on the cement floor of Kolbe's death cell. Still, what the German and Polish bishops were asking for required exceptional procedures. It was within his power as pope to waive the requirement for one more miracle of intercession, especially since Kolbe already had two. But the question of whether Kolbe qualified as a martyr—that had to be fully discussed.

In order to resolve that question, the pope bypassed the congregation by appointing two judges to review the evidence and arguments, one from the philosophical perspective, the other from the historical. Their reports were then heard by a special twenty-five-member commission which included Cardinal Palazzini and Cardinal Joseph Ratzinger, prefect of the Congregation for the Doctrine of the Faith, in whose salon the commissioners met to vote. Father Gumpel was the historical judge and, in his charactertically precise manner, he recounted what took place:

"The question was whether Kolbe had died as a martyr for the faith. I personally never said he was not a martyr. What I did say was we have no absolutely certain proof that he was a martyr in the classical sense, and in these cases you have to be absolutely certain. For instance, some people said that since he was picked up by the Nazis and put in Auschwitz that this was the equivalent of a death sentence. But Auschwitz became a death camp only much later and, as a matter of fact, a number of the inmates survived.

"In addition, we had to look at the circumstances of his arrest. It was part of a big operation, a large sweep. The Nazis were preparing to invade Russia, and as part of that operation they had to make sure, from a logistical point of view, that the lines of supply were safe for the transport of ammunition, foodstuffs, fuel, spare parts for tanks, and the like. So to assure the safety of all this, they arrested all the intellectuals who could possibly cause them trouble: atheists, Communists, Catholics. So Kolbe was not arrested for reasons of his faith."

The Nazis were known for their hatred of priests. The question arose, therefore, whether it was possible that Kommandant Fritsch wanted Kolbe killed because he was a priest. Gumpel responded, sensibly enough, that if that were the case, Fritsch would have picked Kolbe to die in the first place. "Furthermore," he said, "Kolbe took a risk. He stepped out of line to go up to the commander and for this he could have been killed on the spot. Now there has been a most searching investigation of the survivors who saw and heard what happened. We asked them whether they heard or saw in the commander's face or in the face of any of the guards any satisfaction that they were glad for a chance to kill a priest. There was none of this. The commander simply said to Kolbe, well, if you want to, go ahead."

Gumpel's arguments were persuasive. Despite the strong appeals from the German and Polish bishops, the overwhelming majority of the commissioners voted that Kolbe's admittedly heroic gesture did not meet the criteria necessary for a martyr of the faith. But their judgment was merely advisory. On November 9, 1982, before 250,000 faithful at St. Peter's Basilica, one of the largest crowds ever amassed for a canonization, John Paul II proclaimed: "And so, in virtue of my apostolic authority I have decreed that Maximilian Maria Kolbe, who, after *his* beatification was venerated as a confessor, shall henceforward be venerated *also as* a Martyr!"

But what kind of martyr? Nowhere in his declaration of canonization did the pope refer to Kolbe as a martyr of the faith. Neither, for that matter, did he call him, as his predecessor had, a martyr of charity. He did, however, recall the words from the Gospel of John, "There is no greater love than this, that a man should lay down his life for his friends." By using that text in making a solemn declaration of canonization, some saint-makers insist, John Paul II sanctioned the concept of the martyr for charity as a new category of saint—and with it the possibility of bestowing the title of martyr on a wider range of candidates.

The Future of Martyrdom

THE YEARS BETWEEN 1982 and 1987, then, were pivotal for the making of martyrs. They were the years in which the congregation took up the first causes for martyrdom from the Nazi era and, in resolving them, established important precedents. No longer would relators and postulators have to prove that the Nazis were ideologically opposed to the Catholic faith; that could now be assumed. As a result, causes for victims of the Nazis that had begun as processes based on heroic virtue could be transformed, if the promoters so wished, into processes of martyrdom. And with each new martyr, the church could point to fresh evidence that Catholics, no less than Jews, were persecuted by the Nazis.

The first process to benefit from these breakthroughs was the cause of Marcel Callo, a French youth who died of disease and malnutrition in the Nazis' concentration camp at Mauthausen in 1945. There were, however, no miracles attributed to his intercession and so it appeared that it would be several years, at least, before he could be beatified. Pope John Paul II, however, had scheduled a World Synod of Bishops for the fall of 1987 to discuss the role of the Catholic laity, particularly in the social and political spheres, and he wanted a selection of compelling young Servants of God to choose from for beatification and canonization ceremonies during the synod. Callo was a prime choice—if he could be judged a martyr.

Callo was born in Rennes in 1921 and as a teenager became active in the Young Catholic Workers movement. During the Nazi occupation of France he volunteered to work as a missionary among the French workers who had been deported to forced labor camps in Germany. In 1944, Callo and his Catholic coworkers were arrested by the Nazis for conducting religious activities "harmful to the German people." Surviving witnesses testified that even in confinement, Callo continued to lead prisoners in religious instruction and prayer. Like the others, he was forced to work, fed on moldy potatoes and water with sand in it. For the last six months of his life, he was often so weak that he was left to share a bed with dead bodies. Eventually he wasted away at the age of twenty-three. After the war, a French priest wrote a book about Callo that became popular among young German workers. They built a monument to him at Mauthausen, petitioned Rome for his canonization, and won the support of the bishop of Rennes, who initiated the Ordinary Process.

In January 1987, the same month that Stein's revised process went before the cardinals, Beaudoin finished his *positio* on Callo. In it, he documented the development of the youth's spiritual commitment and his exemplary heroic virtue. But in light of the Brandsma and Stein causes, officials of the congregation decided that Callo stood a good chance of being beatified as a martyr. He was, in fact, precisely the sort of example the pope wanted to hold up to the bishops at the fall synod. Cardinal Palazzini preempted other causes and scheduled the theological examination of Callo on both his virtues and his martyrdom for March. There was no doubt that Callo had led a virtuous life, or that he had properly "provoked the tyrant." But there was no hard evidence that he was willing to accept martyrdom. On the contrary, in some 150 letters to his parents and fiancée, Callo repeatedly told them not to worry, that he looked forward to marriage and a good life after the war. During the last six months of his life he sent no letters at all. Without the testimony of eyewitnesses, how could the church be certain Callo hadn't broken under torture, as others had? Beaudoin, however, was able to produce testimony from two survivors of the camp who swore to Callo's calm acceptance of his fate, including a colonel who claimed that on the day of his death Callo had the "appearance of a saint." The evidence was convincing: the need for eyewitnesses to his death was waived. On October 4, John Paul II beatified Callo as a martyr, praising him to the synod of bishops as a "prophetic sign of the Church of the third millennium."

The legacy of Kolbe as the first "martyr of charity" is still unsettled. Some of the saint-makers are not convinced that the pope intended to establish a new rubric under which candidates can be declared martyrs. The only way to find out, therefore, is to present the pope with a similar cause.

Molinari is working up a cause which he believes will do just that. It involves a young Italian national policeman (carabiniere) who, like Kolbe, gave his life that others might live. The incident occurred on September 23, 1943, at a time when German soldiers were streaming north from Rome; Mussolini had been captured, American troops had taken Sicily, and Italian authorities had begun secret peace negotiations with the Allies. About thirty miles north of Rome, a group of retreating German soldiers entered a tower to sleep for the night. Suddenly, there was an explosion. One soldier was killed and several were wounded. The Germans, assuming that the tower had been booby-trapped, took twenty-two hostages from the nearest village and announced that unless the culprit came forward the hostages would be shot. The captives were already digging their graves when the policeman, hearing what had happened, rode up to the soldiers on his motorcycle. Although he had nothing to do with the explosion—a fact he carefully did not mention to the Germans—he took responsibility for the act. Without further questioning, the Germans shot him on the spot.

"We will bring him up as a martyr of charity, now that the concept of martyrdom has been widened," says Molinari, who is postulator of the cause. "It's a beautiful, beautful case. He was later given the Medallion of Gold, the highest military decoration of the state. He was a very good Catholic, a good servant of the people, very loving, very caring. So why not offer it as an example of how to live in that profession authentically as a Christian?"

As one of the few Catholic theologians anywhere who has written on the meaning of saints, Molinari is genuinely excited by the prospect of establishing a new category of martyr. "It's like a fan opening up," he says. "On the one hand, we have the classical martyr who gives his life for the faith. On the other, we have people who have lived exemplary Christian lives of heroic virtue. Now we are asking, 'Is there not a third category of people who, presupposing a good life, out of great heroicity offer themselves at a particular point for another?' Isn't there, after all, an essential difference between people who lead up to their deaths an exemplary life and who are declared blessed and saints by way of virtues, and a case like this man's, in which it has been difficult to prove that he has come up to the standards of heroicity which are required for sainthood but who, with one act, goes to the extreme of giving his life—isn't that a category of its own, so that in the future we should take these cases according to their own proper and special procedure? If we do this, we are opening up a door."

In theory, the door has been there for a very long time, waiting to be opened. As far back as the thirteenth century, Thomas Aquines asked whether dying for the common good could be considered, from a theological perspective, martyrdom. To which he responded: "Human good can become divine good if it is referred to God; therefore, any human good can be a cause of martyrdom, in so far as it is referred to God." On a narrower scale, the church has already broadened the grounds for martyrdom to include individuals who have died in defense of certain "Christian" virtues. The most celebrated such cause is that of Maria Goretti, the eleven-year-old Italian girl who was killed in 1902 while resisting rape by a neighbor. At her beatification ceremony in 1947, Pope Pius XII called her a "martyr of chastity."

The question naturally arises: if a Catholic can be declared a martyr for chastity, why not for justice or compassion or peace—virtues on which Jesus himself laid much greater stress than on sexual purity? In this regard, it is significant that no Catholic has yet been declared a martyr solely for resisting the Nazis' obviously unjust regime or, for that matter, for protecting persecuted Jews, although many Catholics did both. It is also significant that after decades of discussion about the life and death of Franz Jägerstätter, a devout Austrian Catholic and conscientious objector who was beheaded in Berlin by the Nazis in 1943 for refusing to serve in the German army, no process has been initiated on his behalf. There is ample evidence that Jägerstätter, a sacristan at his village church, resisted the Nazis out of Christian concern. Why, then, have the Austrian bishops so far refused to take up Jägerstätter's cause, despite considerable local and international interest in his case? Is it because Jägerstätter was a "solitary witness" whose refusal to aide the Nazi cause received no support from his own Austrian bishop? Is it because many Austrians, most of whom are Catholics, still regard Jäggerstätter as a traitor to his country for refusing to fight for the Nazis? Or is it because, as one official of the congregation suggests, the beatification of Jäggerstätter "could go beyond a declaration of sanctity of one individual to imply a preference for pacifism, which would have serious implications for the [church's] just war theory." The latter appears most likely. The Austrian bishops, I was told in Rome, do not want to endorse pacifism, which they feel Jägerstätter's canonization would do.

Whatever the reasons, it is patently clear that the local bishops play a decisive role in determining who will be named a martyr. As we have already seen, it was at the request of the German and Polish bishops that the saint-makers bent to the task of transforming the causes of Edith Stein and Maximilian Kolbe from confessor to martyr. This is not to suggest that the saint-makers lack independence in investigating and evaluating causes; on the contrary, the Kolbe case demonstrates just how independent the saint-makers can be. But it is to suggest that the making of martyrs, like martyrdom itself, is also a *political* act. Even after the saint-makers have proved a martyr's cause, it is up to the pope, in consultation with the local bishops and the Vatican Secretariat of State, to calculate the consequences of proceeding to a declaration of martyrdom. Two recent decisions illustrate just how delicate those internal church calculations can be.

In 1952 the congregation accepted the cause of Father Miguel Augustin Pro, a twenty-eight-year-old Mexican Jesuit who was executed by the Mexican government in 1927 at the height of the "Christero" rebellion. Father Pro and his brother, Humberto, were members of the clandestine National League for the Defense of Religious Liberty, a militant Catholic opposition group that was part of the armed revolt against the government's suppression of the church. Father Pro denied being involved in the plot but was nonetheless executed along with Humberto and two other Catholics who were proved to be conspirators. Father Pro died in classic fashion, shouting "Viva Christo Rey" as soldiers fired their rifles, and was immediately hailed by the mass of Mexican Catholics as a martyr.

By the late sixties, Molinari had obtained an official handwritten document which proved that the secret police had found Father Pro innocent but that the government had ordered him shot anyhow. However, Molinari delayed presenting the cause to the congregation because the same Institutional Revolutionary party continued to rule Mexico, and, in the judgment of Mexican Jesuits and other local church officials, the government might respond to Pro's beatification by further persecuting the church. In 1986, John Paul II decided the church had waited long enough. In November of that year he approved a decree for the beatification of Father Pro as a martyr. Word of the pope's decision reached Mexico at a time when the Catholic bishops were charging the ruling Institutional Revolutionary party with vote fraud in the state of Chihuahua. Officials of the party warned the church not to proceed with the beatification ceremony because they faced a difficult election in 1987—as it turned out, they won a narrow and bitterly disputed victory—and they felt the beatification would be interpreted as church support for the opposition. Fearing reprisals against the Mexican church, the Vatican postponed Pro's beatification until September 25, 1988.*

In contrast, on June 19, 1988, John Paul II canonized 117 martyrs of Vietnam, including 21 French and Spanish missionaries, despite repeated complaints and threats from Communist authorities in Hanoi. Although the martyrs had been killed in the seventeenth and eighteen centuries, the Communist government of Vietnam complained that the attention given the martyrs would glorify a period of foreign domination and, what was worse, sow seeds of disunity among the Vietnamese people during a period of severe economic crisis. Three months before the ceremonies in Rome, the head of Vietnam's State Commission for Religious Affairs summoned the nation's Catholic bishops to Hanoi. "This is not merely an internal affair of the Catholic Church," he told them. "It touches upon historic issues of our nation, national sovereignty, and national prestige."

Normally, such warnings would be quite enough to persuade the pope and his secretariat of state to at least reconsider and possibly postpone a canonization. After all, the four million Catholics of Vietnam were already suspect by the Communists and functioning under severe government restraints. But the bishops of Vietnam were insistent. Between 1979 and 1987 they sent thirty-six separate letters to the congregation urging the martyrs' canonization. Despite the government's threats, they insisted that the church in Vietnam needed the example of their own official martyrs. The pope agreed.

Courageous as the Vietnamese decision was, it is politically unlikely that the church will, any time soon, beatify or canonize a martyr who died at the hands of a Communist "tyrant," despite the recent rejection of Communism in Eastern Europe. In any event, the church in the two largest Communist countries, the Soviet Union and the People's Republic of China, is in no position to conduct a formal process, much less to propose anyone for martyrdom. But even if the churches in Communist countries were free to advance the causes of their martyrs, the causes themselves probably would add nothing new to the traditional meaning of martyrdom.

The churches of Latin America, however, are a different matter. If

* There may well have been a political quid pro quo involved as well. The pope was scheduled to make a pastoral visit to Mexico, which he did in May 1990. During his visit he argued passionately for a restoration of full freedom for the Mexican church and, for the first time since the rebellion, the government agreed to an exchange of personal representatives with the Vatican.

there is to be a genuine expansion of the Catholic concept of martyrdom, the impetus for that development is most likely to come out of
the Latin church's struggle for social justice. Already, the churches of
Central and South America, plus the foreign missionaries who work
in them, have a long list of men and women—nuns, priests, bishops,
and lay church workers, not to mention thousands of anonymous
campesinos and urban slum dwellers—who are popularly regarded as
martyrs. Their stories, told and retold, already constitute a modern
Acta Martyrum; in some countries, their names are inserted alongside
those of the early Christian martyrs for remembrance at Mass. In
effect, then, Latin American Catholics are venerating martyrs who
have not been formally declared saints by the church. This is not a
new phenomenon, but it is one which the formalization of beatification and canonization procedures was designed to curtail. The bishops
can ignore or deplore the phenomenon, which some conservative prelates have, or they can treat it as a challenge to the church's understanding of what constitutes Christian martyrdom.

The challenge is at once procedural, political, and theological. On
the face of it, most of these modern martyrs do not measure up to the
church's inherited standards of martyrdom for the faith. The "tyrants" they provoke are not, like the Nazis or Communists, ideologically opposed to the Catholic faith. On the contrary, most are
Catholics killing other Catholics in countries which are culturally
and, in some cases, officially Catholic. This situation is unprecedented in the four-hundred-year history of the congregation.

Nor can the new martyrs of Latin America be easily construed as
"martyrs of charity." None of them fit the mold of a Kolbe, who gave
his life for another individual. In most cases, the "others" for whom
the Latin Americans sacrificed their lives are the poor in general, or
"the oppressed." Investigation into their lives would undoubtedly
show that they had dedicated themselves as Christians to the broadly
political process of changing social and economic structures which
the considered unjust. In any case, most were killed because they
were seen as politically subversive—possibly even agents of outlaw
guerrilla forces.

Finally, it is questionable from a traditional perspective whether
the new Latin American martyrs can be construed as having died "for
the church." In the first place, the Latin American church is itself
divided over the methods and goals of the various movements for
social and political liberation. As I discovered in investigating the
posthumous reputation of Archbishop Romero, surely the most revered figure in the new Latin American martyrology, even his fellow

bishops in El Salvador are deeply divided over the wisdom of his leadership, not to mention the meaning of his life and death. Moreover Romero identified the church with "the people" in such a way that it would be a falsification of his own convictions to suggest that he was killed out of hatred for the church. It was not "the church" that made Romero an assassin's target but rather his personal, though not exclusive, identification of the cause of Christ with the cause of liberation for the Salvadoran people.

Nonetheless, if the pope and the bishops of the church truly believe that God Himself makes known the identity of His saints through their reputations for holiness, they cannot ignore the new Latin martyrs. In other words, the problem these martyrs present to the church's saint-making apparatus is not primarily procedural or political but theological. It is a problem, moreover, which a number of Catholic theologians, not all of them Latin Americans, insist the church must address if the Second Vatican Council's commitment to justice and peace is to be credible.

Their various arguments can be summarized thus: Jesus is the model for Christian martyrdom. He accepted death out of fidelity to the Father and for the sake of His coming kingdom. The early Christians identified that eschatological kingdom with the Christian community; to die for the church, then, was to give one's life for the kingdom, and out of the same fidelity which Christ showed the Father. But the church now understands that the kingdom of God is not limited to the Christian community; rather the church is the community of Christ called to serve and extend God's kingdom. The saints are those who witness to the reality of God's kingdom in their own lives; martyrs, by making the supreme sacrifice, witness to absolute claims of the kingdom over all other values, including the value of life itself.

The signs of God's kingdom, so the argument runs, are revealed in the witness of Christ. Chief among these signs are justice and peace. To witness to these values for Christ's sake is the Christian calling. To die for them is martyrdom for the sake of the kingdom. In the present age, to witness to justice and peace is to make a political commitment to others—not simply others in the Christian community but above all to the poor and oppressed who, as Jesus taught, were the "first" in the kingdom of God. To die for that commitment is—or at least can be—to die a martyr. "It would be foolish to resist extending the range of Christian martyrdom then to those who give their lives for their neighbor in political contexts," writes Irish theologian Enda McDonagh. But, he adds, "It would be equally foolish to interpret all deaths for political causes as unambiguous instances of Christian martyrdom."

Indeed it would. For theologian Jon Sobrino of San Salvador, what the church requires is a new concept, the "political saint," to set alongside the mystic, the ascetic, and other traditional models. But just as the traditional saint is tempted by pride, lust for spiritual power, and other illusions of holiness, Sobrino soberly warns, so the political saint must be on guard lest his "political love" for others be corrupted by political concupiscence:

> By its very nature political action may tempt us, to a greater or lesser degree, to exchange the liberation of the poor for the triumph of what we have converted into our own personal or collective cause, the pain of the poor for the passion that politics generates, service for hegemony, truth for propaganda, humility for dominance, gratitude for moral superiority. There is the danger of making absolute the sphere of reality in which the struggle for—social, or political or military—liberation takes place and thus abandoning other important spheres of reality— [particularly] the reality of the poor people—which sooner or later will avenge themselves on this absoluteness.

In sum, Sobrino is calling for a new kind of holiness, a "political holiness," which would distinguish a new kind of saint. The virtues necessary for such holiness are not different in kind from those which the church has traditionally looked for in saints. However, to distinguish them from the virtues as classically conceived would require the saint-makers to think in a new key. Can they? Before that question can be answered, we must look at another kind of saint. Since the Middle Ages, the primary mark of holiness has been a deep interior life of communion with God. And in the popular mind, at least—the mind most inclined to invoke saints—the saint par excellence has been the mystic. Surprisingly, there are more causes for mystics than one might imagine in this secular age. The bigger surprise, I discovered, is that mystics cause as many problems, though of a very different kind, as martyrs do for the saint-makers.

CHAPTER FIVE

MYSTICS, VISIONARIES, AND WONDER-WORKERS

UNDOUBTEDLY THE MOST eagerly anticipated cause is that of Francesco Forgione (1887–1968), a bearded Capuchin friar popularly known as "Padre Pio." Although he rarely ventured far from the Apulian region of southern Italy, Padre Pio was, until the advent of Mother Teresa of Calcutta, Roman Catholicism's most famous "living saint." But unlike the globe-trotting angel of mercy, Padre Pio was not primarily known for his charitable work with the sick and dying. His reputation for holiness rests on works of a more wondrous nature.

Like St. Francis of Assisi, Padre Pio bore on his hands, feet, and side the wounds of the crucified Christ, the stigmata, which bled off regularly for the last fifty years of his life. From early adolescence on, he also spoke frequently in visions with Jesus, Mary, and his own guardian angel. Those were the good times. Many a night, he reported, was spent in titanic struggles with the Devil which left him bloodied, bruised, and exhausted in the morning.

Most of Padre Pio's energies were devoted to intense prayer, celebrating Mass, and, above all, hearing confessions. Like St. John Vianney, the renowned Curé of Ars, Padre Pio is credited with the gift of "reading hearts"—that is, the ability to see into the souls of others and know their sins without hearing a word from the penitent. As his reputation grew, so did the lines outside his confessional—to the point that for a time his fellow Capuchins issued tickets for the privilege of confessing to Padre Pio. Sometimes, when a sinner could not come to him, Padre Pio went to the sinner, it is said, though not in the usual manner. Without leaving his room, the friar would appear as far away as Rome, to hear a confession or comfort the sick. He was endowed, in other words, with the power of "bilocation," or the ability to be present in two places at once.

But there is more. By the time of his death, Padre Pio was credited by his fellow friars with more than a thousand miraculous cures, including the rare feat of restoring a workingman's shattered eyeball. His prophecies were less frequent, though no less striking when he was accurate. One of his predictions, it is said, came after hearing the confession of a newly ordained Polish priest who had traveled from Rome to see him. "Someday," he remarked to the youthful Karol Wojtyla in 1947, "you will be pope."

In short, Padre Pio exhibited all the charismatic gifts and thaumaturgic powers which, in the popular lore of saints, distinguish the mystic from the everyday saint. He was—and remains—Italy's most popular saintly figure after St. Francis himself. But devotion to him is not limited to Italy or Italians. The Capuchin friary in the hill town of San Giovanni Rotondo, where Padre Pio is buried, is at once a powerful magnet for pilgrims and the headquarters of a worldwide cult. More than two hundred thousand people belong to a global network of Padre Pio Prayer Groups. Books and pamphlets and videotapes—the latter filled with close-ups of his bloody hands lifting up the host at Mass—are circulated among parishes throughout the Western world.

Nor is this solely a posthumous cult. During his lifetime, Padre Pio was sought out by politicians and dignitaries of both church and state. He lived under six popes and four of them (Pius XI is the chief exception) at one time or another personally acknowledged his sanctity. John Paul II has manifested particular devotion. As archbishop of Cracow, Wojtyla wrote to the Capuchin friar in 1962, asking him to pray for a Polish woman who had survived a Nazi concentration camp but was dying of cancer. Padre Pio did as he was asked, and in less than a week, Archbishop Wojtyla wrote again to report that the woman had been cured. In 1972, Archbishop Wojtyla joined the other members of the Polish hierarchy in signing a postulatory letter supporting Padre Pio's cause. In 1974 and again in 1987—this time as pope—he made a pilgrimage to San Giovanni Rotondo where he celebrated Mass at the friar's tomb. Although the latter gesture was a personal rather than an

official act of homage, the pope's visit was widely interpreted by devotees of Padre Pio as a sign that his journey to official sainthood would
be a short one.

In fact, however, the canonization of Padre Pio is not likely to occur
anytime soon. One of the reasons, which will be discussed later, involves matters of internal church politics. But another, far more salient reason is the inherent ambivalence—amounting, almost, to
distaste—of the saint-makers when confronted with causes involving
visions, stigmata, and other "mystical" phenomena. It was an attitude
I hadn't expected.

As a rule, Catholic cultures have always been more hospitable than
Protestant cultures to the mystical, the miraculous, the supernatural.
Indeed, the cult of the saints presupposes personal experience of the
divine. And yet, precisely because the Catholic Church accepts the
reality of the supernatural (including the diabolic) its official saint-
makers are skeptical of specific claims of mystical experience. Indeed,
nowhere is the gap between official and popular ideas of sanctity more
pronounced than in the causes of mystics, visionaries, and wonder-
workers of the faith. Nowhere is popular devotion to the saints more
at odds with the rules for making saints than in cases involving mystical phenomena. Nowhere, in short, does the church's insistence on
a fastidious process seem more inappropriate—and yet, as I came to
believe, more necessary—than in judging the lives of mystics.

MYSTICS AS EXCEPTIONAL LOVERS
OF GOD

ROMAN CATHOLIC THEOLOGY is quite clear: mystics *are* different from
other saints. If all saints can be called "friends of God," mystics are
those exceptional individuals who achieve a degree of spiritual intimacy which sets them apart as extraordinary "lovers of God." These
are the men and women who experience, albeit only in moments of
spiritual ecstasy, a foretaste of the divine love to which all serious
Christians aspire—if not in this life then surely in the next. Mystics,
writes one contemporary Catholic theologian, are living "icons of
agapic love." To most contemporary scholars, the mystic is the paradigmatic religious figure, the one who recognizes that reality remains incomplete until it becomes reunited with its source.

For mystics, as for all Christian saints, Jesus is the ultimate model.
The easy familiarity with which Jesus addressed the Father, calling

him "Abba" or "Dad," his sense that "the Father and I are one" and his assertion that "he who sees me sees the Father" attest to the intimacy with God that epitomizes the mystical state in the Christian tradition. For most Christian mystics, however, it is the Son rather than the Father who is the object of mystical union. Like the Apostle Paul, the mystic proclaims: "I live, now not I, but Christ lives in me."

Although mystical experience addresses the human longing to know as well as to love God, certain affective motifs stand out in the writings of Christian mystics. Many of them speak of an overpowering divine embrace for which marital union is the only adequate analogue. St. Teresa of Ávila, for example, reports that "in genuine raptures . . . God ravishes the soul wholly to himself, as being his very own and his bride, and shows her some small part of the kingdom she has thus won." Julian (Juliana) of Norwich says of Jesus: "He is our Very, True Spouse, and we His loved wife, His fair maiden, with which Wife He is never displeased." And Catherine of Siena describes how Jesus revealed his intention of "espousing her soul to him in faith" by placing a mystical marriage ring on her finger in a ceremony attended by the Virgin Mary.

These marital metaphors are not limited to women. Male mystics, too, speak of being smitten by divine eros. Thus in his "Spiritual Canticle," a cycle of exquisite love poems in the tradition of the biblical Song of Songs, St. John of the Cross evokes the yearning of the soul that has been wounded by God's love:

> Where have you hidden away,
> lover, and left me grieving, care on care?
> Hurt me and wouldn't stay
> but off like a deer from there?
> I hurried forth imploring the empty air.

It would appear, then, that what distinguishes mystics from other saints is not the heroicity of their virtue, but their personal experience of God—or, more precisely, their experience of personal transformation through the loving action of God's grace within them. To read their autobiographical writings is to follow the soul as it treads the mystical path (though it is not always precisely the same path) through darkness and light, purgation and illumination, spiritual deserts and quenching ecstasies. What begins in ascetic discipline and contemplative prayer ends in mystical union—or, as some theologians prefer, communion—with the divine.

Although mystical union is spiritual and interior, some mystics also experience concomitant psychosomatic effects—what the saint-makers call "secondary mystical phenomena." Among the most common of these phenomena are ecstasies and visions, revelations and prophecies, the stigmata and other wounds of Christ's passion, the ability to read the hearts and secret sins of others (mystical clairvoyance), levitation and bilocation, and inedia—the capacity to forgo food for months or even years without damage to the body or brain. Needless to say, it is this dimension of the mystical life which most attracts popular attention; it is also the dimension which most vexes the saint-makers.

Many of the classical Christian saints were mystics. To cite only the most renowned: Paul, the Apostle of the Gentiles; the Evangelist John, whose Fourth Gospel and Book of Revelation are the most "mystical" books of the New Testament; Augustine, bishop of Hippo and the most influential thinker of the Western church; Francis of Assisi, founder of the Franciscans and Western Christianity's most popular saint; Thomas Aquinas, Catholicism's preeminent philosopher and theologian; Ignatius of Loyola, the soldier-saint who founded the Jesuits; John of the Cross, the greatest poet of the mystical life; and Catherine of Siena and Teresa of Ávila, two women whose writings on the soul's mystical path won for each of them the title of "Doctor of the Church."*

But just as every saint is not a mystic, so every mystic is not a saint. Such fourteenth-century figures as Meister Eckart, Jan van Ruysbroeck, Richard Rolle, Heinrich Suso, Julian of Norwich, and, in our own century, Teilhard de Chardin and Thomas Merton are but a few of the acknowledged Christian mystics who, for various reasons, have yet to be canonized by the church. Moreover, the Roman Catholic Church has gradually come to recognize that every religious tradition— Buddhism, Hinduism, Judaism, and Islam, no less than Christianity— has produced its own authentic mystics. Indeed, just as some Christian mystics have manifest on their bodies the wounds of the crucified Christ, so some Muslim mystics have produced on their backs the wounds similar to those the Prophet Muhammad suffered in battle.

Even so, in my conversations at the Vatican, I found no support for the common view, popularized by the late Joseph Campbell and other phenomenologists of religion, that mystics constitute a kind of autonomous spiritual elite within the various world religions. On this view, the mystical experience is everywhere essentially the same,

---

* Thus far, only thirty men and two women have been declared Doctors of the Church, an honorific title bestowed by popes for saints of exceptional learning and/or knowledge of the spiritual life.

differing only in the manner in which it is expressed. The theological implication is obvious: what the Christian mystic experiences as God is the same ultimate reality which the Hindu experiences as Brahman, the Muslim experiences as Allah, and so on. Only the labels are different.

The perspective of the Vatican's saint-makers is closer to the view of Steven T. Katz and other contemporary scholars of mysticism, for whom precisely the opposite is also true. They argue—persuasively, in my judgment—that mystical experience, however innovative, is inevitably pre-formed by the mystic's own tradition, language, and concepts developed in the premystical state. In other words, "the mystical moment is the conclusion of a mystical journey" which is shaped more by the mystic's specific religious patrimony and spiritual community than by his or her individual sensibilities. Far from being an autonomous spiritual sojourner who transcends the constrictions of dogma and sect, the mystic tends to confirm by personal experience what the religious community holds to be true through original revelation, Sacred Scriptures, and other elements of received tradition. Thus, if a St. Teresa experiences Christ as the bridegroom of her soul, she does so because this is what her sixteenth-century Spanish Carmelite formation has led her to expect. This is what Katz calls "the 'conservative' character of mystical experience," and it is the quality the Vatican's saint-makers look for in causes involving mystics.

Although Roman Catholicism is far more accepting of mysticism than the churches of the Reformation, Catholic theologians have always regarded the mystic with decided ambivalence. On the one hand, Catholic theology identifies mystical union with Christ as the crowning perfection of the Christian life. On the other hand, the church recognizes that those who aspire to mystical union run great spiritual risks—and not always successfully. The experience of mystics demonstrates that the soul is never so exposed to "demonic" influences as when it seeks the Absolute, never so near to despair as when it enters what John of the Cross called "the dark night" of spiritual aridity, never so tempted by pride as when it manifests extraordinary spiritual gifts and powerfully evocative charisms.

Moreover, much as mystics may certify and confirm accepted beliefs on the strength of their own personal experience, they also tend to individuate and ramify particular aspects of faith—to the point, in some cases, of challenging the prevailing orthodoxy. The mere claim to direct experience of God has, often enough, put mystics under suspicion of heterodoxy; some, indeed, have been accused of being clients of the Devil. Teresa of Ávila herself was for a time suspected of heresy; John of the Cross produced some of his classic religious poetry while languishing in prison courtesy of his own religious superiors; and Joan of Arc, whose mystical experiences took the form of heavenly voices, was condemned to death as a witch by the French hierarchy. How, then, do the church's official saint-makers judge who is the real, who the counterfeit mystic?

When I began my inquiries in Rome, I assumed that the saint-makers treat the cause of mystics as a separate category, like martyrs. If it is the gift of divine love which distinguishes the saint from ordinary Christians, then it seemed to me that these exceptional lovers of God represent a distinct species of holiness requiring a distinct set of criteria for canonization. The greatest mystics, after all, were astute psychologists of the spiritual life and reporters of their own experiences, masters of the spirit's ascent to the divine who left road maps so that others might learn how to discern between genuine experiences of God, on the one hand, and the delusions of the self and the snares of the Devil on the other. It seemed only logical, therefore, that the saint-makers would draw on this library of spiritual wisdom in weighing the causes of purported mystics.

What I discovered, however, is that the saint-makers do not regard mystical experience—by itself—as proof of sanctity. Nor, I was told, do they take into consideration claims of special mystical graces when judging a cause. On the contrary, the saint-makers seem downright suspicious of causes involving mystical phenomena, and anxious to dispel any notion that mystics are inherently different from other saints.

As a matter of theological principle, the saint-makers distinguish sharply between the interior life of mystical prayer—what some theologians call the grace of "infused contemplation"—and its secondary, psychosomatic effects, such as ecstasy, visions, and the stigmata. "Mysticism in its proper sense is simply a deep and pervasive interior awareness of God's presence," Father Gumpel told me. And Father Eszer was equally terse: "Mysticism is nothing more than a person's awareness of faith, hope, and charity operative in his soul." Since this awareness is inherently subjective, and since moreover the candidate is no longer living, the saint-makers cannot, as a psychiatrist might with a patient, pronounce on the authenticity of a candidate's claim to interior mystical graces. At most, the saint-makers can deduce the presence of these graces by the fruits they produce in the mystic's life, and by the spiritual impact the Servant of God makes on others. In line with St. Paul's dicta on spiritual charisms, Rome continues to regard all mystical gifts—the most private spiritual transports as well as the most public displays of wonder-working—as graces given for the benefit of the Christian community, not the delectation of the individual mystic. Thus, while evidence of mystical graces may be incidentally introduced in support of a cause, it is essentially irrelevant. In other words, mystics must evidence the same habits of heroic virtue required of all other nonmartyrs.

Nonetheless, Servants of God who, like Padre Pio, display unusual physical or psychic powers do require special handling. "First we have to sift through the pious ravings of the faithful to get at the truth," explained Father Sarno, a certain impatience in his voice. "If the reports of extraordinary powers appear genuine, then we have to ask whether are they of divine origin, diabolical origin, or are merely the effects of an emotionally disturbed person. While many people may consider the man or woman a saint, the church has to be sure. There must still be a solid reputation for holiness, proof of heroic virtue, and miracles of intercession. So the church stands back, waits, and demands thorough documentation."

The relators were more blunt. The fundamental problem, as they see it, is that popular Catholic piety tends to confuse genuine mysticism with unusual experiences and "supernatural" powers—a confusion which, in the opinion of the saint-makers, has given sanctity a bad reputation. "Many of the faithful do not understand that when we speak of mysticism, we do not refer to stigmata, visions, levitations, bilocations, and other such phenomena," Gumpel explained. "We do not exclude such causes, of course, but we are not inclined to propose such cases for canonization. You see, we are looking for ordinary sanctity. We are trying to counter the idea that saints are people who have had unusual experiences. Unfortunately, this idea is rooted in people with little education, especially in places like southern Italy and South America where they think that you cannot become holy unless you have these experiences. Here in Rome we are fighting this with all our might. But stories of the unusual spread very easily."

From the beginning of Christianity, however, stories of miraculous deeds and experiences have been an integral part of the cult of the saints. Jesus himself, as was noted, worked wonders and so did his apostles. The saints who followed were considered no less gifted and the stories of their miraculous deeds were regarded as normal signs of divine power and favor. Nor are such stories limited to distant, more "credulous" eras of the church. Evidence in support of unusual phenomena can be found in the *vitae*, testimony and other documents housed in the congregation's own archives. Pope Benedict XIV himself, writing at the height of the Enlightenment, devoted more than four hundred pages of his magnum opus "On the Beatification and Canonization of the Servants of God" to the proper investigation of cases involving visions, levitations, and other mystical phenomena attributed to Servants of God. According to one count, some 325 cases of the stigmata alone have been recorded (most of them women) since the death of St. Francis of Assisi, who is generally regarded by historians as the first authentic stigmatist. Of these 325, 62 have been canonized.

But there is another reason why popular Catholicism still tends to equate mysticism with supernatural powers. From the end of the eighteenth century until Vatican Council II, the church encouraged stories of the miraculous as a way of defending the supernatural against the skepticism generated by the Enlightenment. It was in this period, for example, that the church accepted no less than three miraculous apparitions of the Virgin Mary (Lourdes, 1858; La Salette, 1846; and Fátima, 1917) among several dozen sightings of the Virgin Mary by Roman Catholics. Coincidentally, this same period produced at least fifteen female mystics, most of them uneducated (like the visionary children of the Fátima apparitions), sickly peasant women whose stigmata confounded the physicians of their day and who attracted huge followings because of their visions, prophecies, and, above all, the Christlike wounds on their bodies. That some of them, like Louise Lateau (1850–1883) and Theresa Neumann (1898–1962), claimed to have lived only on the Eucharist was also part of their mystique.

Of these women, it should be noted, less than half have been proposed for sainthood and only one has been canonized. And in that case, St. Gemma Galgani (1878–1903), the church remained prudently silent regarding her purported visions of and conversations with Jesus. Moreover, in none of these cases are the women's spiritual illuminations on a par with those of a Catherine of Genoa, who lacked education herself, much less of a Teresa of Ávila. In short, the current confusion over what constitutes mysticism cannot be explained solely by the existence of two cultures within Catholicism, one official and theologically nuanced, the other popular and overly credulous. The history of the last two hundred years shows that bishops and preachers as well accepted and encouraged devotion to these rather florid figures—some of whom are still being proposed for sainthood.

THE MYSTIC AS VICTIM:
THERESA MUSCO

A WEEK AFTER my conversation with Gumpel, Enrico Venanzi motioned me into his office at the rear of the congregation. He had heard of my interest in mystical causes and wanted me to see a set of documents he had received from Caserta, a small city just north of Naples. Among the documents was a series of color photographs of assorted statues, crucifixes, and pictures of Jesus and Mary. In each picture the image was covered with blood. In some cases the blood ran from the eyes; in others, from the hands and side. In one sequence of seven photos, blood followed by tears can be seen flowing from the eyes of a cheap plaster statue of the Virgin. Altogether, about two dozen pictures and statues had been so affected; each had been registered and examined by local church authorities, Enrico said, and in some cases, the blood had been analyzed by a biologist.

The photographs had been taken in the home of Theresa Musco, a woman who had died in 1976 at the age of thirty-three. According to the documents, Theresa had experienced visions of Jesus, Mary, and her guardian angel since the age of five. From the age of nine onward, she bore the stigmata on her hands and feet. In addition, she had on occasion read the hearts of others and in one instance was credited with the miraculous cure—the victim was suffering from leukemia—through her prayers. The documentation in support of these marvels had been collected by a committee in Caserta and sent to Enrico in the hope that he would act as postulator for the cause. The young lawyer smiled as he spread the eerie photographs across his desk. "Very southern Italian," he murmured.

"Will you take the case?" I asked.

He looked up at me. "I think I will," he said.

At Enrico's suggestion I drove to Caserta to visit Theresa's home, which has become something of a shrine. At the bishop's office I inquired about the cause and was told by the vicar-general of the diocese that officially, the bishop was not involved. He fished out a dossier from his files and said that a preliminary investigation by the Archdiocese of Naples had shown that Theresa had suffered from maladies that ran in the family. He didn't say what the maladies were but added that her brother had been a victim of them, too. The implication was that whatever ailed Theresa somehow cast doubt on the validity of her extraordinary experiences.

Despite these official reservations, many Catholics in Caserta, as well as many other Italians in southern Italy and their kin in the United States, are convinced of Theresa's sanctity and promoting her canonization. According to an eighty-page popular biography, *Short Story of a Victim*, published by The Committee for Theresa Musco, she had suffered such a variety of ailments—internal and external—that her life was one of constant pain and hospital visits. Worse, her diary of more than two thousand pages reveals a lifelong emotional battle with a tyrannical father who often beat her—and her mother—and eventually threw Theresa out of the house. According to the diary, at the age of six Theresa tied a rope about her waist as a form of penance and pledged herself to a life of suffering for the sins of others. Initially, she sought to recompense Jesus for her father's habitual cursing. Later, at the insistence of Jesus, she offered her afflictions for wayward and undisciplined priests. Eventually, she wanted nothing more than to take upon herself the very sufferings of the crucified Christ. Thus, in a prayer taught her by her guardian angel, she wrote:

> Wind your crown of thorns around my head! Father, pierce my hands and feet with your nails and pierce my heart with your lance! I kneel before you, so I can feel your scourging and the bitterness of your betrayal by Judas. Accept my humble self.

Pictures of Theresa show her to have been a short, round woman with a large nose and glasses. At the age of thirteen, her biographer reports, she had a vision in which she was told to consecrate herself to lifelong virginity. Later, he records, she had to fight off the "lecherous" advances of a doctor who was attending her in a hospital. Another picture, undated, shows her attired in a white bridal gown and veil and holding a spray of flowers. Although Theresa never entered a convent, she is dressed very much like a nun on her day of solemn profession. The caption simply states: "Theresa consecrates her entire life for the Church, the Holy Father, and the conversion of sinners."

According to her diary, Theresa first received the stigmata on August 1, 1952, following a dream in which she was nailed to a cross. But apparently they did not bleed with any regularity until Holy Thursday (March), 1969. In the years that followed, she also felt scourging on her back three days a week. The phenomena which drew the public attention, however, were the statues and pictures which began dripping blood on February 25, 1975. The bishop of Caserta himself inspected the first of these wonders and later gave her permission to exhibit the bloody picture of Jesus on a small altar she kept in her home. Sometimes, her household icons would bleed for a quarter of an hour, causing Theresa to shed tears for the sorrowing Jesus and Mary. By then, she had come under the spiritual direction of two priests in Caserta—Don Giuseppe Borra, a Salesian, and Don Franco Amico, a Franciscan friar who now heads the committee seeking her beatification.

At her death—she was on dialysis and seems to have died from numerous afflictions—the bishop of Caserta presided at her funeral Mass in the cathedral. Some two thousand people turned out for the occasion. No less a churchman than the late Cardinal Joseph Siri of Genoa has endorsed her cause. In a letter to Father Amico, Siri wrote in 1979: "The Musco case possesses a documentation which I had never encountered in the anthology of other cases I had previously examined. Facts are facts, and cannot be undone by mocking or ignoring them."

Whatever the facts may be, Theresa Musco clearly does not present the sort of model of holiness which the saint-makers are looking for in the post–Vatican Council II church. Sickly and almost masochistic in her desire for suffering, she would appear to be no more attractive to educated, updated Roman Catholics than the statues that bled in her presence. But to millions of other Catholics, people like Theresa Musco represent the very essence of what a mystic is supposed to be: a figure of atonement whose stigmata and visions offer irrefutable proof of the supernatural in a world which, as they see it, no longer believes in miracles. And so long as the church insists that causes be based on a candidate's reputation for holiness, the congregation will have to deal with such cases, no matter how distasteful they may be to the official saint-makers. How do they do it?

PROCESSING MYSTICAL CAUSES

HERE, AS IN all other areas, the congregation follows the strict guidelines established by Pope Benedict XIV more than two centuries ago. In his magnum opus on the beatification and canonization of the Servants of God, Benedict discusses the problems arising from mystical phenomena, citing his own experiences as Promoter of the Faith as well as documents and discussions from the previous six centuries of saint-making. At the outset of his discussion, Benedict insists on a fundamental distinction between two kinds of supernatural graces: those which render the recipient pleasing to God (*gratia gratum faciens*) and are necessary for an individual's salvation, and special graces freely given (*gratia gratis data*) to individuals chiefly for the benefit and edification of the believing community. Among the latter are mystical experiences such as visions, prophecies, raptures, stigmata, levitation, and the like. Since these special graces can and have been bestowed on the wicked as well as on the just, Benedict argues, they cannot constitute proof of personal holiness in a canonical process.

But that is not by any means the whole of the matter. Since some candidates for beatification and canonization do exhibit mystical graces, Benedict advises that these experiences be thoroughly investigated by the congregation *prior* to taking up the question of heroic virtue, and a preliminary judgment made as to whether they are of supernatural origin, the work of the Devil, or the effect of natural causes.

In investigations involving extraordinary physical phenomena, he writes, reliable witnesses are essential. By way of example he cites a case in which he himself served as both the Devil's Advocate and, after his elevation to the papacy, as the pope who declared the candidate a saint:

> When I was Promoter of the Faith the cause of the venerable Servant of God, Joseph of Cupertino, came up for discussion in the Congregation of Sacred Rites, on the doubt about his virtues, which, after my resignation of the office was happily solved; in which unexceptional eyewitnesses deposed to most frequent elevations and great flights on the part of that ecstatic and rapt servant of God.

Joseph of Cupertino, it should be noted, was no ordinary levitator. His prolonged flights were so frequent that he was known in his lifetime as "the flying friar." According to his biographers, Joseph levitated more than a hundred times. One of the most reliably reported incidents occurred in 1645 and was witnessed by the Spanish ambassador to the Papal Court and his wife. The ambassador had been so impressed by Joseph after a private visit to the friar's cell in Assisi that his wife begged for an opportunity to speak with him. Under direct orders from his superior, Joseph reluctantly agreed to leave his cell and meet with the distinguished woman, who was waiting with her husband and their retinue in an adjacent church. "I will obey," the friar reportedly told his superior, "but I do not know whether I will be able to speak with her." In fact he didn't: just as he entered the church, his gaze fell on a statue of Mary Immaculate which stood over the altar. Suddenly, he flew about "a dozen paces" over the heads of the assembled entourage to the foot of the statue. There, after paying homage to Mary and "uttering his customary shrill cry," he flew back over the astonished observers and returned without another word to his cell. On other occasions, Joseph was observed carrying one of his fellow friars in flights about the room. And at his last Mass, celebrated on the Feast of the Assumption a month before his death, he was lifted up in a longer-than-usual rapture which was confirmed by eyewitnesses in testimony given less than five years after the event.

In general, Benedict is far less interested in validating unusual physical phenomena—he devotes only a few spare paragraphs, for example, to stigmata—than he is in supplying tests for Servants of God who claim divine illuminations. Visions and prophecies which conflict with the Scriptures, church doctrine, or sound morals cannot, of course, be attributed to God. But Benedict is willing to allow human fantasy a certain margin for error, especially in women. "Visions and apparitions are not to be rejected," he cautions, "because they happen to women," and he suggests that in judging such cases investigators rely on the testimony of the visionary's spiritual director (usually a priest), confessor, or other learned and pious men. In the case of St. Catherine Ricci (1522–1590), the pope recalls, he himself was persuaded by the postulation to overlook the fact that this otherwise admirable (and characteristically eccentric) mystic had frequent visions of Girolamo Savonarola, the fifteenth-century Dominican reformer from Florence whose fiercely apocalyptic preaching led to his burning at the stake. Catherine attributed her extraordinary recovery from poor health in 1540 to Savonarola and never ceased praying for his recognition as a saint, a fact which, in the end, did not prevent her own canonization.

What strikes the modern reader is Benedict XIV's efforts to supply the congregation with a practical psychology of mystical experience. Since most visions, apparitions, and prophecies occur during ecstasies, Benedict advises investigators to look for certain signs in trying to determine whether the visions and so forth proceed from God, the Devil, or an unstable mind. Natural causation may be presumed in cases where the ecstatic has a history of illness, or "if the ecstasy be succeeded by weariness, by sluggishness of the limbs, a clouding of the mind and understanding, forgetfulness of past events, paleness of face and sadness of mind." Ecstasies of a diabolical origin are indicated "if a man falls into it as he pleases [since] divine grace draws the soul to itself when and how it pleases." The Devil's work is also to be suspected if the ecstasies are accompanied by "indecent" bodily movements, "great contortions of the body," and especially if the ecstatic recommends the doing of evil deeds.

In contrast, Benedict finds that "a divine ecstasy takes place with the greatest tranquillity of the whole man, both outwardly and inwardly. He who is in a divine ecstasy speaks only of heavenly things, which move the bystanders to the love of God; on returning to himself he appears humble, and, as it were, ashamed; overflowing with heavenly consolations, he shows cheerfulness in his face and security in his heart; he does not delight at all in the presence of bystanders, fearing lest he should thereby obtain the reputation of sanctity." In short, a divine ecstasy is marked by an increase in the virtues of humility and charity.

To sum up Benedict's dicta: although mystical experiences do not prove sanctity, they must, nonetheless, be investigated. If that investigation shows that these experiences can be attributed to diabolical powers, the process is terminated. If the mystical phenomena are found to be purely psychological in origin, this discovery may or may not inhibit the cause from proceeding to an investigation of the candidate's heroic virtue.

In any event, the fundamental principle is clear: it is only after heroic virtue has been established that mystical phenomena may be presumed to be of divine origin. Even then, he cautions, the presumption remains just that: assertions of supernatural phenomena, even when included in a solemn declaration of canonization by the pope, never command more than human credence. They are never to be taken as matters of faith.

Although Benedict's general principles remain in force, his psychological observations on mystical phenomena are, understandably, hopelessly outdated. Obviously, in light of Sigmund Freud's discovery of the unconscious and its powerful effects on the mind and the body, the saint-makers of today have a wider range of psychological explanations to consider when investigating the origins of a candidate's mystical experiences. What, I wanted to know, has been the effect of Freud's revolution—and, indeed, of modern psychology in general—on the investigation of mystical phenomena?

Change comes slowly at the Vatican. Still, I was surprised to discover that the Congregation for the Causes of Saints has no one on its staff who is trained in psychology or psychoanalysis. When causes involving mystics do reach Rome, the candidate's personal writings, together with documents from spiritual directors and attending physicians, are given to outside experts for preliminary judgment. Most of these consultors are priests, all are Catholics. Most have doctorates in spiritual theology and, in recent years, a few have taken degrees in psychology as well. But none, I was informed, is trained in psychoanalysis. "You cannot mention Sigmund Freud at the Vatican," one clerical consultor told me. "You cannot mention Carl Jung either, because they are considered atheists. You can, of course, make use of their theories, but you must be guarded in what you write."

The "Passion Ecstasies" of Alexandrina da Costa

Although mystical causes are quite rare, I was permitted to examine the preliminary evaluation done by two consultants on the mystical experiences and writings of Alexandrina da Costa, a Portuguese laywoman who died in 1955 at the age of fifty-one. According to one popular biography, Alexandrina was born to a peasant couple in the rural village of Balasar, some forty miles north of Oporto. Shortly after her birth, her father died. According to her autobiography, which she began dictating in 1940 at the request of her spiritual director, she was a mischievous child. Her earliest memory is of an incident which took place when she was only three years old. Alexandrina reached for a jar of her mother's pomade. When her mother cried out, the jar fell to the floor and broke in jagged pieces. Alexandrina herself suffered a deep cut on her mouth and carried the scar for the rest of her life. As we shall see, the pomade was not forgotten.

At the age of nine, Alexandrina made her first confession following a sermon by a popular local preacher, Father Edmund of the Holy Wounds, whose sermon on hell made a deep impression on her. The same year, after only eighteen months of schooling, she was sent to work on a farm. Her employment lasted only three years; after her employer tried to seduce her, Alexandrina was brought back home to live. A few months later, she was stricken with typhoid fever and nearly died. Virtually an invalid, she took in sewing at home. Twice more during her adolescence, her former employer tried unsuccessfully to rape her. The second time, Alexandrina had to fight off her assailant and eventually escaped by jumping from an upstairs window. Although she fell only thirteen feet, Alexandrina severely injured her spine. Eventually, she became totally paralyzed, and on April 14, 1924, she took to her bed for life.

Over the next six years, Alexandrina turned to religion. She was especially taken by the stories of the Virgin Mary's appearances to three small children at Fatima. In 1931, she experienced her first ecstasy during which, she reported, Jesus appeared to her and gave her a lifelong assignment: "Love, suffer, and make reparation" for the sins of the world, especially sins against chastity and particularly those committed by priests. There followed an extremely tortuous period of ten years during which she reported repeated harassment from the Devil. Appearing variously as a dog, a snake, and a monkey, Satan tempted her to blasphemy, at other times to erotic and obscene acts. At times, she shouted obscenities as if possessed. On several occasions, she reported that the Devil had thrown her violently from her bed. Throughout her trials, Alexandrina revealed her experiences only to her sister and her spiritual director, Father Mariano Pinho, a Jesuit who brought her communion.

At the same time, however, Alexandrina was experiencing frequent visions and messages from Jesus. On September 6, 1934, she reported a pivotal vision. In it, she said, Jesus told her:

> Give me your hands, because I want to nail them with mine. Give me your feet because I want to nail them to my feet. Give me your head because I want to crown it with thorns as they did to me. Give me your heart, because I want to pierce it with a lance as they did mine. Consecrate your body to me; offer yourself wholly to me . . . Help me in the redemption of mankind.

Although Alexandrina did not manifest the stigmata, she did experience a most extraordinary identification with the passion of Jesus. Beginning in 1938, at the age of thirty-four, she routinely went into three and a half hours of ecstasy starting at noon on Fridays. According to eyewitness accounts—mainly physicians and priests who had received permission to be present by the local bishop—Alexandrina inexplicably gained control of her limbs during these ecstasies. Her body would rise, as if by levitation, and fall to the floor. There she would swoon and writhe, move on her knees in a hideous reenactment of the stations of the cross. As she groveled, Alexandrina would speak the words of Jesus in the Gospel accounts until, the crucifixion completed, she would fall back exhausted.

These "passion ecstasies," as they came to be called, continued until 1942, a total of some 180 times in all. Naturally, word of the extraordinary events got out and the house was besieged by pilgrims. Although Alexandrina said she dreaded being on display, church officials continued to allow select individuals to witness her Friday ritual. They even permitted the dolorous sequence to be filmed against the day when her cause would be presented to the congregation.

But there was more. On Good Friday, 1942, Alexandrina experienced her last reenactment of the passion; although her Friday ecstasies continued, she no longer left her bed. But from that day on, she refused to eat or drink anything, except the Eucharist. On June 10, 1943, she was removed to the hospital in Oporto where, for the next forty days, a team of doctors and nurses kept her under twenty-four-hour surveillance. According to her own account, the nurses several times tried to persuade her to eat and the physicians attempted to inject her with medications. She refused everything.

At the end of her confinement, Dr. Gomez de Arayjo, a specialist in nervous disorders and member of the Royal Academy of Medicine in Madrid, testified that Alexandrina's ability to survive without food for forty days was "scientifically inexplicable." Two other attending medical specialists testified that Alexandrina "retained her weight, and her temperature, breathing, blood pressure, pulse and blood were normal while her mental faculties were constant and lucid . . . The laws of physiology and biochemistry cannot account for the survival of this sick woman for forty days of absolute fast in the hospital, more so in that she replied daily to the many interrogations and sustained many conversations, showing an excellent disposition and lucidity of spirit. As for the phenomena observed every Friday at about 3 P.M. [i.e., her ecstasies], we believe they belong to the mystical order."

Alexandrina survived another twelve years. Her visions and ecstasies intensified. During one ecstasy she described how Jesus made a pomade of his heart and rubbed it on her own—a variation, it should be noted, of the exchange of hearts experienced by St. Margaret Mary Alacoque two centuries earlier. In another vision, she told how Jesus had pierced her with a golden tube extending from his body (heart) to hers. Besides the passion, she said that during raptures she had experienced the Resurrection and Ascension of Jesus as well. All these and more are recorded in her dictated autobiography, which extends to some five thousand pages of typescript.

By the time of her death, Alexandrina was the best-known religious figure in Portugal, excepting, perhaps, the children of Fatima. On some days, several thousand pilgrims would try to see her, imploring her prayers and asking for divine favors. At her death she was heralded as "the mother of the poor," "the help of the sorrowful," and "the consoler of the afflicted." According to her biography, her body did not undergo corruption but mysteriously turned into ashes—as Alexandrina had predicted. And in a final coup de grace, it is reported that the ashes give off a sweet perfume smell: the odor of sanctity.

This is not, it should be noted, a story out of the Middle Ages. It is a story that unfolded in the twentieth century in a country that, for all its rural piety, is notoriously anticlerical. What interested me, though, was not so much her own life story but how that story had been analyzed by the saint-makers. On April 10, 1973, the diocesan process was completed and forwarded to Rome. Among the documents were some 3,650 pages of Alexandrina's writings—her diary, autobiography, letters, and several volumes of her additional thoughts, revelations, and the like. To date, the only *positio* relating to her cause is the preliminary spiritual and psychological judgment on the writings rendered anonymously by two consultants.

Because they are concerned with the writings alone, the consultors are highly circumspect in their judgments. They leave to officials of the congregation any decision regarding the candidate's extraordinary ability to live without food or water for the last thirteen years of her life. They do note, however, that she rarely mentions this exceptional condition in her letters. They also offer no opinion as to why she was free of paralysis during her passion ecstasies. As for the visions and revelatory messages contained in her writings, the authors conclude—very carefully—that they "can be of divine origin." Alexandrina, they go on to say, "does not seem to be affected by a mental illness to which her extraordinary manifestations could be attributed." But, they add, "this opinion is subordinate to other arguments which could eventually be derived from a direct examination of the person in question."

In other words, as far as the consultors are concerned, there is nothing in the writings to prevent the cause from proceeding. Nonetheless, the authors do note certain concerns and caveats. The first consultor observes that Alexandrina's spirituality is of the atoning kind in which the subject seeks to suffer for the reparation of other sinners. But he objects to several passages in her writings in which Jesus tells Alexandrina that "I must take revenge in you for those [sinners] for whom you wish to atone." Indeed, he notes, Jesus seems to be bribing Alexandrina when he demands, "Either you suffer or I lose souls." The author then goes on to observe that this threatening, vengeful attitude, while theologically unacceptable, was not uncharacteristic of sermons preached at popular mission revivals in her day. Moreover, he adds, this vengeful motive disappears from her writings after 1940.

The first consultor also is concerned about Alexandrina's protracted bouts with the Devil, particularly her powerful feeling that the Devil has turned her body into an instrument of lust. "We think we should say, that although the lives of the saints are full of struggles for their chastity, we don't know of any other example in the whole of hagiography like the experiences suffered by Alexandrina." But the fact that she did not will them, he concludes, is proof of her heroic chastity.

The second consultor is chiefly concerned with psychological issues. Regarding Alexandrina's debilitating three-hour reenactments of Christ's passion, he declares, "The examination of her writings alone does not seem to be sufficient to determine the nature of these phenomena." Whatever the origin of her visions, he has no doubt that she was "subjectively sincere in believing that they came from God." He excludes schizophrenia as an explanation of her behavior, noting that on the same days in which she wrote down her visions in her diary she was also able to write letters about them that display good humor, practical sense, and even irony. "In our opinion," he concludes, "she was a person not psychically ill but one of lively intelligence, notable strength of soul and fortitude . . . with remarkable imagination."

Even so, this consultor, too, finds certain "disconcerting details." He notes that at the end of her impersonations of Jesus' passion, Alexandrina repeatedly experiences a peculiar form of consolation. The consolation takes the form of a transfusion of blood from the Sacred Heart of Jesus to her own heart. Alexandrina variously describes the exchange as taking place through a "tube of love" and "a tube that pours out love" from the body of Jesus. At other times, she describes Jesus as making a pomade from the material of his heart and using it as a balm to massage away the pain in her own breast. In a passage of massive understatement, the consultor observes: "These visions have rather strange connotations, to the point that they seem at least equivocal in their description."

Despite these reservations, the consultors' *positio* concludes that "the writings of Alexandrina Maria da Costa appear on the whole proof of uncommon virtue and of an often heroic commitment to fidelity and love of God." The consultors are particularly impressed by the candidate's humility and her readiness, even in the midst of her most consuming passion visions, to obey the commands of her spiritual director. In short, whatever one might care to make of her visions and obsessions, Alexandrina displayed the virtues of humility and obedience to a heroic degree.

By custom, consultors do not sign their reports. Nonetheless, in 1988 I was able to locate the second, psychological consultor in Chicago, where I questioned him about his judgments. Father John Lozano is a fifty-three-year-old Spanish priest of the Claretian order who has been consultant to the congregation since 1970. His doctorate is in spiritual theology and like most Spaniards, he is partial to the mystics of his native country: John of the Cross, Teresa of Ávila, and Ignatius Loyola. He has also taken advanced courses in psychology, but his acquaintance with the theories of Freud, Jung, and other "moderns," he said, was acquired on his own.

It seemed to me, I told him, that a consultant trained in psychoanalysis—even a Roman Catholic psychiatrist—would have evaluated Alexandrina differently. At the very least, a psychiatrist would have drawn attention to the obvious sexual content of some of her visions and seen connections between her employer's attempted rape and her subsequent paralysis. "What else could that tube extending from Jesus be," I asked, "other than a phallic image?"

"Of course," he said. "All the Freudian dogs were barking. It could very well be that her paralysis was a way of protecting herself from men. And look at her obsessions with the Devil. He appeared to her as a dog, a snake, a monkey—all of them Freudian symbols."

"Why, then, didn't you mention these things in your report?" I asked.

"If you notice, I put a range of responses in my report. I said there are a lot of psychological problems to be studied. The difficulty is that in Rome they don't know what to do with Freudian psychology. Most of the consultants have yet to assimilate his theory of the unconscious. The fear is that if the writings of mystics are sent out to psychiatrists, they will attribute everything to sex. Yes, that is a danger, I say, but the other danger is the tendency of spiritual theologians to attribute everything to God. The trouble is, we have very little dialogue between psychology and religion."

"But if you think a mystic's experiences can be wholly accounted for by psychological explanations, can you say so in your reports?"

"I have. I had a case of an Italian nun who was haunted by the Devil. The other sisters knew nothing about it. She died young and after her death they found her diary and thought she might be a saint because she wrestled with the Devil. To me she was clearly a psychotic personality. I found nothing positive in her experiences and on the basis of what I wrote, I was told, they killed the cause." He paused. He was marching around a long dining room table at the Claretians' headquarters in suburban Oak Park, lecturing to the air as if he were pacing a classroom. "It's a matter of intuition," he said, picking up the thread of his thought. "I don't apply norms mechanically. I look at the whole picture."

"And Alexandrina?"

"Alexandrina had a lot of problems, of course, especially her obsession with the Devil. But she kept praying. Eventually, she developed a beautiful relationship with Christ that healed the obsession. Psychologically, she was a sick person who was made whole again." He paused again, taking another turn around the table. "You know, the church does not propose as saints perfect models of normality. Jesus loved the sick. We are dealing with phenomena which may be the resonance of mystical experience or the resonance of psychological disturbance. But little by little she develops a beautiful relationship with Christ and the other stuff disappears. Severe psychological problems can help a person to focus on Christ."

"How do you distinguish between a spiritual and a purely psychological resolution of a problem?"

"With experience you get the taste. For instance, religious ecstasy and psychological trauma are similar. In both cases the connection between consciousness and the body are severed. But behind the ecstasy there is an experience of God, whereas behind the trauma there is not. In trauma, the person cannot recall what happened during the trance state, whereas the ecstatic person is extremely active and alert although the body falls into a kind of lethargy."

"How do you judge what happens during an ecstasy?" I persisted. "How do you know the experience comes from God?"

"I can only tell you how I judge these things—the other consultants are different. I always distinguish between real mystical experience and the by-products in the fantasy and the body. In real mystical experience, the presence of faith and hope and charity becomes so intense that you become aware of it. You feel moved to make acts of adoration. The core of this experience, then, is not a vision but a perception of God. To the contemplative eye, everything appears like shining. You don't see objects, you are flooded with light. So the highest mystical graces are intellectual perceptions—of the Trinity, the Incarnation, the Resurrection. There are no images connected with intellectual visions. They are given to the intellect alone, when the spirit is purified, and they are so high that the fantasy cannot follow. The more the fantasy is involved, the lower the experience."

"So visionaries are not necessarily mystics?"

"Other consultors consider all visionaries as mystics. But I do not. Some visionaries are mystics and some mystics are visionaries, but visionaries are not mystics. Visionaries are people with a predilection for suggestion. A psychopath, for instance, may see snakes, but if that person is religious or merely in a religious atmosphere, he or she may see saints instead of snakes. Seeing Jesus or Mary or some other holy person does not make the visionary a saint."

"But how do you distinguish mystical visions from merely pathological visions?"

"My rule is that graces given to the body and to the fantasy are the graces given first to the spirit. In a genuine mystic, there may be resonances in the fantasy and the body, such as the stigmata. If a mystic receives the special grace of total transformation in Christ crucified—St. Francis of Assisi, for example—this grace is reflected through the fantasy in the body."

"Through the fantasy?"

"Yes. We know that mystics who have the stigmata copy the crucifixes that they see. If the wounds on the crucifix are in the wrong place, they will appear that way on the body. Similarly, if they have seen Mary dressed in red and blue, as she appears in statues in Catalonia, rather than the standard blue and white, that is the way she will be dressed in their visions."

"I take it, then, that you do not regard visions and stigmata as proof of supernatural experience. Is that what you are telling me?"

"The church never pronounces on the authenticity of mystical experience. They know this is sandy ground. The church only asks us to determine whether the experiences look authentic. Or, do the phenomena raise questions about the psychological health of the individual? We consultors are not the final judges on the quality of the person's heroic virtues. And the church is only interested in the virtues."

At this writing, the cause of Alexandrina da Costa is still in process. The postulator is preparing her *vita* and expects it will be several years before it is completed. By that time, more than four decades will have passed since her death. Presumably her "reputation for holiness" has remained intact. What struck me, though, was the enormous discrepancy between the popular perception of Alexandrina as a privileged participant in Christ's very own passion and the tempered opinion of the consultor Lozano that she was a psychologically disturbed woman who was healed through love of Jesus. Which image, I wondered, the sick woman who was healed or the mystic, would the pope put forward if the saint-makers should conclude that she merits canonization? What, in short, is the truth of the Christian faith that her elevation to sainthood is meant to convey?

THE VISIONS OF ANNE CATHERINE EMMERICH

THE SAME QUESTIONS led me to look into the cause of another woman whose reputation as a mystic is much older and more widespread than that of Alexandrina da Costa. Anne Catherine Emmerich (1774–1824), known in her day as "the Seer of Dülmen," was one of the most widely discussed visionaries of the nineteenth century. Born to poor parents in the tiny village of Flamsche in Westphalia, Catherine was a sickly child who, at an early age, was subject to frequent visions and messages from her guardian angel, Jesus, and Mary. The visions continued after she entered an Augustinian convent at Dülmen in 1802, but the other nuns apparently did not take them seriously. In 1811, the convent was secularized by the anti-Catholic Prussian government. Catherine, who by now rarely left her bed, was assigned as a charity case to the house of an emigrant French priest. A year later, she began to bleed from a ringlet of tiny wounds around her head. Gradually, she exhibited the stigmata in her hands, feet, and side, as well as a mysterious double cross about an inch wide on her breastbone.

Word of the stigmata caused considerable excitement among the pious townsfolk of Dülmen. Some saw her as a living refutation of the rationalism which prevailed throughout much of Germany and France. Others suspected fraud. Eventually, the controversy over her prompted a pair of formal investigations. The first was conducted by ecclesiastical authorities who issued a cautious statement neither affirming nor denying the supernatural character of her stigmata. The second, which lasted from August 7 to August 28, 1818, was conducted by a civil commission composed mainly of Protestant and agnostic physicians and scientists. Catherine was removed to another house and subjected to numerous painful and embarrassing tests. At the conclusion, the commission declared that it could find no evidence of fraud. In sum, the physicians could not explain the wounds and the ecclesiastics were circumspect in claiming a miracle.

Although the stigmata eventually ceased to bleed regularly, Catherine's ecstasies and visions continued. From her bed, she foretold things that astounded her frequent visitors. She was also tested many times to see if she could distinguish between true and false relics; on one occasion, for instance, she "correctly" discerned that strands of hair encased in a reliquary brought from Cologne really did belong to the Virgin Mary. Moreover, it was reliably reported by all who knew her that for the last ten years of her life, Catherine abstained from solid food—even a spoonful of soup made her retch—and subsisted on water and the Eucharist. When she died, her body remained supple during the three days prior to burial, and when it was exhumed six weeks later to make certain that devotees had not stolen it away, it was found to be free of corruption or odor.

Up to this point, the life story of Anne Catherine Emmerich differs little from those of a number of female stigmatics who were poor, uneducated, and bedridden, and who passed much of their time in ecstasy. The pattern is familiar, except in one important respect: during her ecstasies, Catherine traveled back in time to become a contemporary of Jesus, the Virgin Mary, and other biblical figures. More precisely, she claimed to be experiencing the life and passion of Jesus as if she were a participant-observer, filling in details not recorded in Sacred Scripture.

None of these visions, however, would have reached the public had it not been for Clemens Brentano (1778–1842), a German romantic poet whose early collection of songs and poems from the Middle Ages, *The Child with the Marvellous Horn*, won praise from the likes of Goethe, Longfellow, and Heine. Brentano's private life, however, was less successful: married twice, he had drifted away from the Catholicism of his youth only to return after being spurned by a Protestant woman, Louise Hensel, who urged him to straighten out his life and return to the Catholic Church. In 1818, at the suggestion of Professor Johann Michael Sailer, later bishop of Ratisbon and in his day the most important ecclesiastical figure in Catholic Germany, Brentano went to Dülmen to visit the renowned stigmatic. Catherine immediately recognized him as the figure promised by God—"the Pilgrim," she called him—who would record the revelations she was receiving. For the next five years until her death, Brentano sat at her bedside, taking down on loose-leaf notepaper the words Catherine spoke during her ecstatic transports.

In 1833, nine years after Catherine's death, Brentano published *The Dolorous Passion of Our Lord Jesus Christ after the Meditations of Anne Catherine Emmerich*. In it, Brentano narrates in minute detail the events between the Last Supper and the Resurrection as Catherine had observed them in her visions. In an introductory sketch of her life, Brentano writes that although Catherine had never read the Bible, "her distinguishing characteristic and special privilege was an intuitive knowledge of the history of the Old and New Testaments, of the Holy Family, and of all the saints upon whom she was contemplating in spirit." In other words, Brentano presented Catherine as a mystic whose knowledge of the passion and death of Jesus was imparted directly by the Holy Spirit for the edification of the faithful. And although, at the suggestion of a bishop, Brentano inserted a saving clause disclaiming any "pretensions" that Catherine's meditations be regarded as "history," it is evident from the text that the reader was to consider them as authentic revelations of what really happened.

The text is beguiling, both for its literary qualities and for the wealth of details unknown to the writers of the Four Gospels. For example, in one typical passage, Catherine reveals the spiritual effect that Jesus had on the wife of the Roman procurator, Pontius Pilate:

> During the time that Pilate was pronouncing the iniquitous sentence, I saw his wife, Claudia Procles, send him back the pledge which he had given her, and in the evening she left his palace and joined the friends of our Lord, who concealed her in a subterraneous vault in the house of Lazarus at Jerusalem. Later the same day, I likewise saw a friend of our Lord engrave the words, *Judex injustus*, and the name of Claudia Procles, on a green-looking stone, which was behind the terrace called Gabbatha—this stone is still to be found in the foundations of a church or house in Jerusalem, which stands on the spot formerly called Gabbatha. Claudia Procles became a Christian, followed St. Paul, and became his particular friend.

The first German edition of *The Dolorous Passion* sold some four thousand copies; eventually the book went through another twenty-nine editions. It has since been translated into French, English, Spanish, and Italian and is still sold through Catholic bookstores in Europe and the United States. But *The Dolorous Passion* contains only a portion of Catherine's revelations. From his notes, it is clear that Brentano envisioned a series of books based on her visions. In 1852, ten years after the poet's death, his literary executors brought out his unfinished "The Life of the Blessed Virgin," which provides elaborate details on the birth of Jesus as well as on Mary's last days—notably, the identification of the house where she died and the revelation that her body rested three days in the grave before being assumed into heaven.

But there was more. Between 1858 and 1860, a German Redemptorist, Father C. E. Schmoger, published *The Lowly Life and Bitter Passions of Our Lord Jesus Christ and His Blessed Mother Together with the Mysteries of the Old Testament from the Visions of Anne Catherine Emmerich as Recorded in the Journal of Clement Brentano* in four volumes totaling 2,104 pages. This enormously expanded version of the visions begins with the fall of the angels from Paradise and proceeds through the fall of Adam and Eve to the lives of Abraham, Isaac, and Jacob before taking up the life of Christ. Reading these volumes, one learns that Jesus took a five-week trip to Cyprus with a group of Jewish settlers and made another, heretofore unknown, journey to the land of the Three Kings who had appeared at his birth. One also learns that Judas had been born out of wedlock to a dancer and that the couple at whose wedding in Cana Jesus performed his first public miracle immediately made vows of lifelong chastity.

In addition, Schmoger published a two-volume biography of Catherine which contains still more astounding revelations. For instance, Catherine describes the day of her baptism—the same day she was born—and claims that "I was fully conscious of all that passed around me." Again, in a later biography written by Father Thomas Wegener, the German postulator for her cause, and published in 1898, we find a further elaboration of this remarkable assertion: "At her baptism, also," Wegener writes without the least hint of skepticism, "she had the full proof of God's presence in the most holy Sacrament; she saw, besides her guardian angel and her holy patronesses, St. Anne and St. Catherine, assisting at the ceremony."

Seen in historical context, publication of Anne Catherine Emmerich's visions provided pious Roman Catholics with a powerful weapon against the rationalism and antisupernaturalism of the *Aufklärung*. This was the age of the debunking lives of Jesus by David Friedrich Strauss and Bruno Bauer. To many Catholics, the skeptics' scholarly reconstructions of the life of Jesus were no match for the supernaturally revealed truths transmitted to the humble stigmatic of Dülmen. Moreover, readers who visited the Holy Land with her books in hand marveled at the accuracy with which she described the geography of Palestine and the rituals of the ancient Hebrews. The Victorian Jesuit poet Gerard Manley Hopkins wept when Emmerich's recounting of Jesus' passion was read aloud during retreat; in the following century, leading converts to Catholicism such as the French poets Paul Claudel and Raïssa Maritain proclaimed their power to move the spirit. Bishops in Europe and the United States encouraged the faithful to read and ponder what had been revealed to Sister Catherine. Even Albert Schweitzer took appreciative note of Catherine's revealed life of Christ in his monumental volume *The Quest of the Historical Jesus*. Indeed, a century after her death, a member of the illustrious Académie Française, Georges Goyau, could look back on the collaboration between the visionary and the poet and bless them both for "bringing a fresh source of sustenance to the devout curiosity of believing souls."

Were it not for the tireless devotion of Father Schmoger, it would be difficult today to appreciate the seriousness with which learned churchmen accepted the authenticity of Anne Catherine's visions—and of her holiness. In the fourth German edition of her expanded visions, Schmoger includes a 242-page treatise on the church's teachings regarding private revelations and their application to Anne Catherine Emmerich. It is, in effect, a brief on behalf of the "authenticity" and "supernatural character" of Emmerich's visions as well as a lengthy argument for her sanctity.

In Rome, however, the visions of Anne Catherine Emmerich were not as well received. To begin with, the church has never been comfortable with private revelations, least of all those which purport to supply information that escaped the inspired writers of the four Gospels. Moreover, there was the question of how much of the published visions could be attributed to Catherine, how much to the work of Brentano. On November 22, 1928, the Holy Office issued a rare decree halting the cause for her beatification and canonization. Some of the consultors considered her a heretic. Others were simply concerned that the faithful might be misled by reading her first-person renditions of the life and death of Jesus. The promoters of the cause, however, were permitted to review the documentation and testimony they had gathered with a view to resubmitting their case.

In Germany, experts went to work. Brentano, they discovered, had left behind some twenty thousand pages of notes on Anne Catherine Emmerich, only a handful of which could safely be attributed to the mystic herself. His library was found to include maps and travel books on the Holy Land, which accounted for the typographical accuracy of the published visions. More important, it was evident that Brentano had filled out the visions with material taken from the Gospel of St. James and other apocryphal texts. The relatively few scraps of paper which could safely be identified as the words of Catherine to Brentano seemed orthodox enough.

Based on this information, Pope Paul VI lifted the ban against Catherine's cause on May 18, 1973. Six years later, the Conference of German Bishops formally requested that the process be reopened. A meeting was held in Rome at which experts testified that it would be impossible to winnow out Catherine's actual visions from the elaborations by Brentano. In a key move, Father Gumpel and others argued successfully that the visionary volumes on the life and death of Jesus should be completely ignored in judging the sanctity of Anne Catherine Emmerich. This was the break that the promoters of the cause were hoping for. No longer encumbered by the elaborate visions, they could proceed in the preparation of a positio that focused strictly on proofs of the mystic's heroic virtue. Thus, with the backing of the Augustinians and the German hierarchy, the cause was canonically introduced in 1981 with Father Eszer assigned as relator.

By the spring of 1989, the rehabilitation of Anne Catherine Emmerich was well under way. The original positio was "very disorderly,"

Eszer said, and his collaborator, a priest-historian from Germany, was preparing a new one. With regard to Anne Catherine Emmerich's extraordinary ability to survive for ten years without solid food, Eszer was confident that the stories of her inedia were genuine. "We can say that she lived only on Holy Communion for the last decade or so of her life because the reports show that all those nuns and all those anti-Catholic doctors had to accept the fact that she really could not eat." He was also impressed by Catherine's ability to discriminate between true and false relics. Whether this gift was supernatural or merely psychic, he said, is beside the point: "it is a sign that she was prudent and that her desire was to seek only the truth." As for the stigmata, it was sufficient to show that she suffered severely and that she accepted her suffering humbly "in a Christian way."

"But what of her reputation for holiness?" I asked. "Wasn't that predicated on her published visions? Aren't they the primary reason she was known as a saint?"

"They are the primary reason she was known as a *mystic*," he corrected me. "Her reputation for holiness rests on other things. Several people in Westphalia were converted to the church because of her, including Louise Hensel, who went on to establish several convents of nuns."

The "Seer of Dülmen," then, is now a lively candidate for beatification because, more than a century and a half after her death, the German bishops and some members of the Augustinian order to which she belonged continue to support her cause. Her heroic virtue still has to be proved. Should her cause succeed, one gathers, her significance will be measured not by the millions of readers who accepted Brentano's bogus visions as revealed truth, nor by the list of bishops and assorted Catholic intellectuals who once regarded her as an inspired mystic, but by the salutary effect she had on the comparatively small circle of devotees. Among the pious, however, she will undoubtedly be revered as a mystic who bore the stigmata, spoke with heavenly figures, and was miraculously able to survive without food for more than a dozen years.

PADRE PIO AND THE BURDEN OF BEING A MYSTIC

BY ALL MEASURES, the cause of Padre Pio is the most important mystical cause to come before the congregation in the last two centuries. He is, so far as historians can tell, the first Catholic priest to bear the wounds of Christ and easily the most famous male stigmatist since St. Francis. But whereas Francis bore the stigmata only the last two years of his life, Padre Pio endured them for half a century. His wounds, together with the many testimonials to his gifts of prophecy, spiritual clairvoyance, visions, bilocations, and miraculous cures, made him an international celebrity.

At the height of his fame, Padre Pio received some six hundred letters a day from around the world, and even now, twenty years after his death, he remains the object of a cult that is superseded in size only by those centered on the shrines to the Virgin Mary. Equally important, from the perspective of the congregation, his cause is supported by postulatory letters from no less than eight cardinals, 31 archbishops and 72 bishops. Here is one cause, it seemed to me, in which mystical phenomena cannot be treated as incidental to the candidate's heroic virtue. Who, after all, would have prayed to Padre Pio—or perceived his life, as some of his fellow friars do, as "coredemptive" with Christ—if he hadn't beguiled the faithful by his miraculous gifts?

As one might imagine, the Capuchins began informally to gather data on behalf of their famous brother a year after his death in 1968. But then, something mysterious happened: someone in Rome, surely with the authority of Pope Paul VI, decreed that the local process on Padre Pio could not be opened. The Capuchins would not tell me who gave the order, though they did confirm that it remained in effect until 1982, when the officials of the congregation discussed the matter and, at their urging, John Paul II permitted the archbishop of Manfredonia to institute the local process.

Neither would the friars tell me why Rome had acted as it did. But there is, of course, considerable speculation. Some members of the congregation suppose that the ban had to do with certain financial scandals surrounding the Capuchin order in the 1950s, and to a related conflict over the House for the Relief of Suffering, a modern hospital Padre built in large part from contributions he received from devotees. In order to help pay off debts the order incurred by investing money with an unscrupulous banker, the Holy See sought to take over financial control of the hospital—a move which Padre Pio's supporters protested all the way to the United Nations. Since some of the bishops who were involved in these matters are still alive—and possibly guilty of greed themselves—it was thought that Rome hoped to protect their reputations by postponing the investigation into Padre Pio's activities until after the bishops were dead.

Another view is that Vatican officials wanted to discourage expectations that Padre Pio would be canonized quickly—and, in the process, prevent the Capuchins and others connected with Padre Pio's enterprises from realizing financial gains as a result of a successful cause. A more likely reason, it seemed to me, is that Paul VI and others in Rome were concerned about the outsized cult of Padre Pio and hoped to dampen enthusiasm by putting some distance between his death and the beginning of his process.

Whatever the reason, time was needed to distinguish between Padre Pio the thaumaturge and Francesco Forgione the heroically virtuous Servant of God. If it really was true that his stigmata and the like could not be regarded as signs of sanctity, then time was also needed to let his reputation for holiness ripen along more acceptable lines. To that end, the Capuchins have published several volumes of his letters and, in 1972, they held a congress devoted to "Padre Pio's Spirituality."

In any case, it is clear that the famous friar suffered more than the wounds in his body or bruises from the Devil. For example, there was a period in his life when Vatican officials suspected that Padre Pio's stigmata were self-inflicted. At other times, they were dismissed as psychologically self-induced by the friar's persistent concentration on the passion of Christ. To this Padre Pio often responded: "Go out to the fields and look very closely at a bull. Concentrate on him with all your might. Do this and see if horns grow on your head!"

Because of his fame, Padre Pio incurred the jealousy and opposition of local parish clergy, including Archbishop Pasquale Gagliardi of Manfredonia, who denounced him to the Vatican's Holy Office. At various times, he was forbidden to say Mass except privately, and to speak with women: at the age of seventy-three, he was suspected, of all things, of taking sexual advantage of female penitents. Indeed, at one point in his life, a fellow friar, Padre Emilio, actually bugged his confessional, hoping to disprove such charges, and thereby violated the sacred seal of confession.

As late as 1960, just eight years before his death, the Holy Office severely limited his contact with the public in order to reduce what the congregation's prefect, Cardinal Alfredo Ottaviani, perceived as "acts that have the character of a cult directed toward the person of the padre." Nor was Ottaviani, the conservative defender of Catholic orthodoxy, alone in his assessment. That same year, Bishop Albino Luciani of Vittorio Veneto, who later became Pope John Paul I, dismissed the ministry of Padre Pio as "an indigestible dainty" which caters to the "craving for the supernatural and the unusual." Luciani spoke for many bishops and priests when he argued that the faithful need the Mass, the sacraments, and the catechism—"solid bread which nourishes them, not chocolates, pastries, and sweetmeats that burden and beguile."

What is the truth about Padre Pio?

"There are many things about Padre Pio," I was told, "that are still considered secret." The speaker was Father Paolo Rossi, the Italian friar who, since 1980, has served as postulator general of the Capuchins. Despite a general reluctance on the part of virtually everyone in Rome to speak about the cause of Padre Pio, Rossi graciously received me at the Capuchins' headquarters. And although the cause was technically still in the hands of the archbishop of Manfredonia, the bearded Italian priest was willing to tell me what he could.

Of the two hundred or so causes for which he was responsible, the case of Padre Pio, Rossi conceded, is probably the most difficult—but not, he hastened to add, solely because of the mystical phenomena. With regard to Padre Pio's stigmata, Rossi was confident that the congregation's consultors would confirm what several physicians had already reported during his lifetime, namely, that the wounds were not self-induced. "Not many people realize," he said, "that a few months before he died, Padre Pio's stigmata disappeared. The friars, you see, covered his hands and feet for the funeral because otherwise people would have asked why the wounds were no longer visible. There weren't even any scars on the body."

"What significance do you see in that?"

"Just this: if the stigmata had been self-induced, they would have healed slowly and left scars. But his time was up and there was no more need of them, so they were taken away. It's the principle of St. Paul: the gifts of the Holy Spirit are given for the sake of others. The same is true of his other mystical gifts. We have many people who have testified that Padre Pio was able to read the minds of others, especially in confession when he would see in their hearts what they are supposed to confess. Bilocation, too, was a gift for the people so that by this manifestation others might recognize the presence of the divine and hopefully make a change in their lives."

"Then you believe that these gifts were given by God?"

"Yes, but keep in mind that is not what the church looks for. We have to establish his heroic virtues first, then we will be able to ascertain whether his gifts came from a higher cause."

"Well, then, do you see anything about Padre Pio which would suggest that he did not live a heroically virtuous life?"

Father Rossi stopped for a few moments to consider his reply. There was, I knew, considerable difference of opinion within the worldwide family of Capuchins about the value and appropriateness of Padre

Pio's cause. The friars in San Giovanni Rotondo, especially those who knew him, already revere him as a saint. The people of the region, too, regard them as *their* saint, the latest in a long Italian tradition of "village saints" that includes St. Francis of Assisi, Margaret of Cortona, and hundreds of lesser-known local mystics and spiritual patrons. But among many other Capuchins, especially in the United States, Padre Pio is regarded as a figure of the "old" church culture which identified sanctity with the supernatural rather than with good works and political protest. Many of these Capuchins are indifferent, even hostile, to Padre Pio's cause precisely because of his mystical gifts. As the order's postulator general, Father Rossi could not take sides. I understood his position.

"Well, Padre Pio had a rough character," he said at last. "But I don't think it was something he created himself. It came from his farming background. In the past, I think, such a defect might have been enough to stop the cause. But today, when they discover a defect or flaw in a candidate's character, they study him further rather than reject him. They try to show how the Servant of God overcame his defects, or at least worked with them without necessarily overcoming them."

"How do you plan to demonstrate his heroic virtue?"

Instead of answering me directly, Rossi invited me into another room lined with *positiones* for various causes. Among them were five volumes of Padre Pio's own letters plus fourteen additional volumes relating to his life. Included were the documents prepared by two Capuchin theologians to secure the lifting of the ban against his cause in 1982. Rossi rippled through them. "The full picture of his life cannot be given until the *positio* is written," he said, "and that is years away. There are many things that the people do not understand—and can't—because they have not seen the documentation we have. But I can say this: people would better understand the virtue of the man if they knew the degree of hostility he experienced from the church, as well as from his own family of friars. I am trying to find out the source of that hostility. We have to find out what his attitude was and the way he conducted himself in the midst of it."

"I take it you are referring to the period when he was forbidden to say Mass in public or to hear confessions."

"Yes, it was a very severe punishment. The order itself was told to act in a certain way toward Padre Pio. So the hostility went all the way up to the Holy Office (now called the Congregation for the Doctrine of the Faith) and the Vatican Secretariat of State. Faulty information was being given to the church authorities and they acted on that information. Eventually, the *positio* will show what was being said about him and how he responded. That will prove his virtue."

Once more I was being told that mystical experiences would play no part in determining sanctity. Though he may have wrestled with the Devil and spoken to angels, Padre Pio the stigmatist would be judged by his response to more mundane trials—inflicted, in his case, by his own brethren in the church. Once again I was struck by the enormous discrepancy between the popular image of the mystic and the requirements of the saint-making process.

I told Rossi of my misgivings. How could Padre Pio's virtues be entirely separated from his extraordinary spiritual trials?

Rossi smiled. "You must understand, the congregation is a juridical, bureaucratic entity that still beatifies and canonizes according to the outline laid out by Benedict XIV. But I am among those who would like to get away from that approach. A better way would be to take the life of Christ and present Padre Pio in comparison, to see how he lived the life of a saint and how he made Christ come alive in his own life. Heroicity of virtue sounds too Greek, too pagan. We need to be guided by a Gospel-oriented theology."

Rossi sensed that I was still uneasy with this approach. "Come," he said, "I want to show you something." He led me to another room, unlocked the door, and took me into a small chapel. The walls, the altar, every surface in the room was festooned with small round reliquaries the size of espresso saucers and set in miniature crosses. There were about three hundred altogether and each contained bits of hair or ashes taken from Capuchins who had been beatified or canonized by the church. It had been built in 1956 before Vatican Council II by Rossi's predecessor, the aged Father Bernardino de Siena, one of the most experienced of the church's postulators.

"Relics," I observed. "Must you have relics of the saints?"

"It is the practice right now. Personally, I am against it. But it is a need created by the demands of the people." He paused and in that moment I imagined another such room, given wholly over to relics of Padre Pio. There were, I knew, more than enough pairs of the mittens he wore to cover his hands, spotted with his blood, to decorate a chapel twice the size we were standing in.

"At Vatican Council II," Rossi went on, "they recognized that devotion to the saints had taken the place of devotion to Christ, the central mystery of our faith. Even now, in Italy, you notice that when people go to church they no longer go to the Blessed Sacrament and genuflect, but kneel in front of a statue of a saint. You see this and you realize that we are losing the concept of who is who."

Although he didn't say so, I understood that Rossi was also talking about the great devotion to Padre Pio: the statues of the hooded friar which can be seen in a dozen different countries; the prayer groups and the pilgrimages; the international conferences on the spirituality of Padre Pio and yes, the millions of dollars that pour into the Padre Pio headquarters in San Giovanni Rotondo every year. All of this because he was, first and foremost, a stigmatic, a visionary, and a wonder-worker. It would be up to Father Rossi to prove that beneath it all, Padre Pio was also a saint.

The mystic, then, holds no pride of place among the saint-makers, although he represents the highest call and furthest reach of prayer. In any case, the word no longer seems to connote that perfection of the interior life which makes a Teresa of Ávila or a John of the Cross a continuing source of spiritual illumination. The saint-makers are right: mysticism has become confused with the miraculous. But that confusion is not likely to disappear as long as the church continues to demand miracles of saints. And demand it does. What counts for naught in this life is still mandatory of saints in the next. Indeed, without miracles, there would be no making of saints.

CHAPTER SIX

THE SCIENCE OF MIRACLES AND THE MIRACLES OF SCIENCE

MIRACLES AS DIVINE SIGNS

IN A SIDE ALTAR in St. Peter's Basilica lie the remains of Innocent XI (1611–1689), a reformist pope and foe of France's absolutist monarch, King Louis XIV. Although his process of canonization was initiated in 1741, the French government was so opposed to the cause that Innocent was not beatified until October 7, 1956, more than two and a half centuries after his death. Fortunately, there is no statute of limitations when it comes to the making of saints. Nonetheless, it seems unlikely that Innocent will be credited with the final, postbeatification miracle required for canonization. The reason: he no longer commands the cult which produces miracles of intercession.

Innocent is hardly alone in this state of procedural animation. The list of papally beatified people who lack a final miracle runs to several hundred, most of them—like Innocent—forgotten figures who no longer elicit prayers from those seeking "divine favors." In addition, there are hundreds of other venerables whose exercise of Christian virtue has been found to be heroic but who have yet to have that judgment of the saint-makers confirmed by a miracle. On the other hand, Pope John XXIII, who died in 1963, already has more than twenty inexplicable healings credited to his intercession, including two which his postulator is convinced will stand up to the congregation's rigorous board of medical consultants. When it comes to granting confirming miracles, God, it would appear, does play favorites.

In theory, of course, it is God alone who works miracles. But in the making of saints, it is the faithful who must take the initiative by asking His intervention in the name of the Servant of God. It is then up to the congregation's medical consultants to determine that the extraordinary healing—these days, virtually all accepted miracles are medical cures—is inexplicable by science. In the words of John Paul II, such healings, duly verified and recognized by church authorities, "are like a divine seal which confirms the sanctity of a Servant of God whose intercession has been invoked, a sign of God who inspires and legitimizes the cult being rendered to [the candidate], and [who] gives a surety to the teaching which [the candidate's] life, witness, and action embody."

No cause, as has been noted, can develop without a demonstrable reputation for holiness. In part, that reputation depends on evidence that people pray to the Servant of God in time of need and that, in their conviction, some of those prayers were answered. An essential function of the local promoter is to encourage prayers to the candidate in the hope that some of the divine favors received will turn out to be provable miracles. Ideally, by the time the *positiones* on the candidate's life and virtues have been approved, the postulator has several possible miracles ready for discussion by the congregation's medical consultants.

But not all postulators are so lucky. Some Servants of God acquire an almost instantaneous reputation for working miracles. For example, St. Thérèse of Lisieux was unknown outside her tiny Carmelite convent near the French Alps when she died in 1897 at the age of twenty-four. Yet, when word got out (mainly through her enormously popular, posthumously published book, *Story of a Soul*) that she had promised "to spend my Heaven in doing good on earth," miracles attributed to her intercession were reported from as far away as Alaska and Peru. On the other hand, as we saw in the case of the philosopher Edith Stein, the lack of a tomb or relics can seriously inhibit the kind of popular devotion which produces divine favors. In short, obtaining miracles in support of a cause is a chancy business, as the Roman postulators freely acknowledge.

There is, of course, no way to tell in advance where or when a verifiable miracle will turn up. There is, however, a rough sociology of the miraculous. Since most canonized saints are Europeans, most miracles come from Europe. But some sections of Europe are more productive of miracles than others. Southern Italy has a reputation among postulators as especially fertile territory. One reason is that southern Italians treat saintly figures as members of the family: they take their troubles to them and are not shy about demanding divine favors when a child is sick, a marriage is in trouble, or a husband is drinking too much. Another, equally important reason is that physicians from southern Italy believe strongly in miraculous healings and are well known for their willingness to cooperate on causes.

In contrast, Eastern Europe is stony turf for the harvesting of miracles. It's not, God knows, that East European Catholics don't pray to saints for miracles. The problem, rather, is that physicians in Czechoslovakia, Albania, and other Communist countries have refused—and in some cases have been forbidden—to cooperate with the church in the making of saints, though these obstacles will likely disappear with the demise of Communism. Several Marxist countries in Africa also prohibit their doctors from providing evidence of miracles. In other Third World countries, the major problem is the lack of adequate medical facilities. Since 99 percent of accepted miracles are inexplicable cures, the church is dependent upon medical records and the concomitant assurance that the patient's recovery cannot be explained by science.

There is also, as I have already intimated, a history of the miraculous. In the early Christian centuries, down through the Middle Ages, the miracles were perceived in a wide range of phenomena and presupposed a very different relationship between God, man, and the physical world than the cause-and-effect universe which came into intellectual existence in the sixteenth century. To cite one well-documented example, in the cause of St. Louis of Anjou (1274–1297), the youthful bishop of Toulouse, witnesses testified to sixty-six miraculous cures, including eight people who were deaf, dumb, or blind; six with contorted or contracted limbs; five afflicted with insanity; three epileptics and twelve who, it was claimed, had been raised from the dead.

It is not simply that Europeans of the thirteenth century were more credulous than those of today; their notions of reality were also different. Thus, while the church still requires miracles as divine confirmation of a candidate's sanctity, the types of proof required have changed because the modern sense of a miracle as divine intervention in the normal course of events is narrower than early notions of miracles. Needless to say, many of the miracles claimed in previous centuries would not be accepted today. Even so, the emphasis on healings has been consistent, in part because so many of Jesus' miracles were physical cures. The major difference is that today, as never before, the "divine science" of theology is dependent on the human science of medicine.

The irony is obvious: without modern science and medical technology, miracles are virtually impossible to prove. And without miracles there can be no certified saints. The medical consultants to the congregation, as we shall see, are anxious and proud to be of assistance to the church's saint-makers. But some of the saint-makers, I also discovered, are dissatisfied with the church's subservience to medical science when it comes to discerning the will of God in the process of proving sanctity. Just as there is more to the miraculous than medical cures, they insist, so there should be more than one method of interpreting the divine signs of a candidate's holiness.

THE CONSULTA MEDICA

EVERY OTHER WEEK from mid-October through mid-July, a panel of five physicians meet in a parlorlike room at the congregation to examine two potential miracles. The panels are drawn from a pool of more than sixty physicians resident in Rome who constitute the congregation's Consulta Medica. To judge by their professional achievements and reputations, the physicians appear to be more distinguished in medicine than the theological consultants are in theology. More than half of them are professors or department heads at one of Rome's medical schools; the rest are, with a few exceptions, directors of hospitals. Collectively, the Consulta Medica represents all medical specialties from surgery to tropical diseases. All members are Italian, all are men, and all are Roman Catholic—though, this being Italy, I was assured that no member is questioned regarding the regularity of his religious practices. Medical competence is what counts.

An invitation to join the Consulta is considered an honor among Roman Catholic doctors, rather like being tapped for the Knights of Malta. Invitees are not told who suggested them for membership, and as a rule the names of the medical consultants are not publicized outside the Vatican. For each case he studies, a medical consultant is paid a set fee of 500,000 lire—about $400 at 1990 rates—which is about what a first-class doctor in Rome charges patients for two office visits. Since the documents on the miracle can run to as much as fifteen hundred pages, requiring a month of weekend reading and evaluation, their work is in effect pro bono. Typically, the consultants donate their fees to charity.

In turn, the physicians agree not to discuss the miracle cases with outsiders. They are permitted to write them up in medical journals but not until the cause has been completed and acted upon by the pope. Since this may take a year and often longer, the consultants rarely bother to publish anything on them at all. Despite these restrictions, I found several members of the Consulta quite willing to discuss their work.

The Consulta functions much like a medical review board. By the time a case reaches them, its chances of success have usually been assessed on the local level and, unofficially, by one or more medical experts picked by the Roman postulator. A typical *positio super miraculo* includes a medical history of the patient and all the records from the hospitals, physicians, and nurses involved in the patient's treatment. In addition, there are the written testimonies of witnesses—medical personnel and the patient herself, as well as the testimony of whoever invoked the Servant of God. X rays, slides of biopsies, and other scientific evidence are crucial, and in many cases the panel will demand further evidence before making a judgment.

Procedurally, each case is submitted to two members of the Consulta who study the materials and write separate reports of four to five pages in length. Neither man knows who the other is. If both of the judgments are negative, the case is dropped. If one or both are positive, the case is submitted to two additional physicians plus the president of the Consulta and a vote of the full five-member panel is scheduled. More than half of the cases are rejected. In a typical year, therefore, the Consulta Medica reviews about forty cases and, including those that are sent back for further information, only about fifteen purported miracles survive the physicians' scrutiny.

It's easy to see why. In essence, each consultant must pass judgment on the diagnosis, the prognosis, and the adequacy of the therapy used. The cure must be complete and of lasting duration. It must also be inexplicable by all known scientific measures. Cancers such as lymphoma, renal cell cancer, skin cancer, and cancer of the breast, which have a high statistical rate of natural remission are excluded. So are all mental disorders, since the concept of cure in cases of mental illness is not easily defined. In the end, each physician on the full panel votes one of two ways on the cure: "natural" or "inexplicable." The congregation prefers unanimity. But as any patient who has ever sought a second or third opinion can attest, getting agreement from five physicians—not to mention five different specialists—is exceedingly difficult. Thus, a simple majority is usually sufficient to see a miracle through.

"It is a good method, but it is very severe," says Dr. Franco del Rosa, a professor of internal medicine at Rome's University of the Italian Republic and a specialist in infectious diseases. "Remember, when I study a cause I do not know what the others are thinking. It is only when we come together that we discover that the others may have constructed a different diagnosis. Sometimes, when I listen to the others, I change my opinion."

We are sitting in de Rosa's office on the busy Piazza del Risorgimento two blocks from Vatican City. It is a sunny Saturday afternoon and the glint from the dome of St. Peter's shines through his fourth-floor window. Dr. de Rosa is a short, thin man who has been a consultant since 1982. Of the thirty potential miracles he has studied so far—he averages about five a year—the majority were rejected.

No two cases, he insists, are alike. In one case, the patient was diagnosed as tubercular and the recovery occurred without antibiotics or other therapy. But in his own report, de Rosa argued that the diagnosis was mistaken and the case was rejected. In another case a patient inexplicably recovered from what the doctors had diagnosed as spreading skin cancer. De Rosa was able to show from his study of slides of the tissue that the skin was not carcinogenic but inflamed by another disease. Since the patient had been treated with steroids, de Rosa concluded that the therapy was sufficient to account for the patient's unexpected recovery.

He then shows me a medical dossier he has just finished analyzing. "Here is a case," he says, riffling the pages, "in which the patient was discharged from the hospital with a serious disease in the abdomen and expected to die. Instead, there was an instantaneous and complete cure at home."

"In other words," I interpolate, "it was a miracle."

"That is up to the theologians to decide. Our job as doctors is to ask whether the cure is without a natural explanation. In this case, I found there was none. But we will have to see what the other doctor has to say."

"Isn't it possible that your medical judgments can be mistaken?"

"Usually, errors are of two kinds: either I do not have all the facts on which to base a judgment, or there is an error in the memory of the attending physician. In these situations the postulator is instructed to send for more information. The documents must be very precise, or there can be no discussion."

"Do you ever contact the original physicians yourself in order to clear up an imprecise point?"

"Just recently, the congregation brought to Rome, at the postulator's own expense, five doctors from Mexico to answer questions I raised. That was an unusual situation. But I did not meet them myself. The medical consultors never meet with the doctors involved in a case they are judging. We work from the data only."

"When you read these documents, are you ever moved by the stature of the holy person invoked for a cure? Are you ever bothered by the thought that your judgment can make or break this person's beatification or canonization?"

"No, never. I don't want to know anything about the potential saint. Usually I know only the name, and most of the time it means nothing to me. I study only the technical material and that is all I want to see. The rest is up to the church." He rises from his desk and paces about the room. "This is a very serious process in the church, this making of saints. Much more serious than the process used by states for building a monument to a conqueror who killed a thousand people."

I agree. "But do you ever hear from a physician whose diagnosis you found mistaken? Have they no chance to defend themselves against your review?"

"Well, all I can say is that this has never happened to me. The congregation, you see, does not report the results of our deliberations to the physicians who treated the patient, assuming they are still living. But you know, we work very exactly because we know that our work will be stored in the archives. And the Vatican Archives don't lose a thing."

I hadn't thought of that. But obviously the doctors had. They are acutely aware, I began to see, that they are writing for history as well as for the moment. They realize that they can be second-guessed. In rare instances, in fact, a medical panel has overturned the judgment of a previous panel, but only in cases where the cure was initially rejected. Once a cure is accepted as miraculous by the church, the issue is considered settled no matter what medical science may later discover.

"Aren't you concerned," I ask, "that today's miracles will turn out to be tomorrow's common medical knowledge?"

"What has happened is that we have more sophisticated ways of studying patients than in the past. But you give medical science too much credit. Even now we don't always know why someone is cured, though we have more ways, with some diseases, to cure them. And compared to yesterday, we now have much better means for understanding what is taking place. But as far as I am concerned, in the future, as now, there will always be some cures that are not explainable by science."

Dr. Raffaello Cortesini is a man who has witnessed numerous miracles, both the medical and religious kind. He is a specialist in heart and liver transplants, procedures that were thought impossible when he began doing them two decades ago. He is a 1956 graduate of the University of Rome Medical School, where he is now chief of surgery, and one of a handful of heart-transplant specialists throughout the world. Unknown to most of his medical colleagues, Cortesini has also been, since 1983, president of the Consulta Medica and the one man responsible for studying every potential miracle that comes before the congregation's medical board. Because of his position, Dr. Cortesini was initially wary of receiving me, but eventually we met for several sessions at his private office in a Roman suburb, across from the home of the United States ambassador to Italy, and in a small consulting room at the university's medical complex. He is a tall, courtly Italian conversant in several languages.

As president, Dr. Cortesini examines each miracle process in both its medical and theological dimensions. He assigns the physicians to review each case, chairs every panel, and signs off on each decision. In about half the cures that are declared inexplicable, he says, the vote is unanimous. The hardest part of his job, not surprisingly, is casting the deciding vote when the other four consultants are evenly split. "Sometimes the sessions go on for three or four hours, sometimes we need extra sessions when the cases are especially difficult," he tells me. "Those decisions, they're the ones I pray over."

Since medicine is not the same the world over, I ask, why isn't the membership of the Consulta international?

"*Modern* medicine *is* the same all over," he responds. "Sometimes we use computers to find out the latest discoveries in various fields. So we keep up. Through the congregation we study cases from Canada, Africa, Japan—everywhere. We know from the documents that come to us what is happening medically all over the world and we are able to apply the latest scientific techniques."

"But what about cases which do not involve modern medicine? Suppose you have a case where folk medicine was applied, or where the hospital records are not up to modern clinical standards? Can you make an intelligent judgment in those circumstances?"

"We get cases not just from around the world but also from previous centuries. We recently examined one from the seventeenth century. It's amazing. Doctors then did not have our sophisticated diagnostic techniques, but they were gifted, more than the doctors of today, in describing what they saw. In addition, we have here at the University of Rome a large and very important department in the history of medicine going back to early Roman times. So you see, we have many resources for determining what the problem was."

In the weeks that followed, the Consulta Medica took up a case from southern Africa which had arrived at the congregation with no supporting scientific documentation. The cure was attributed to a French priest, Father Joseph Gérard, who had spent sixty years as a missionary among the Zulu and Basotho tribes in what is now Lesotho. Gérard died in 1914, and in anticipation of the pope's trip to Lesotho in 1988, the congregation was reviewing a potential miracle that occurred in 1928. According to the thin, forty-page *positio*, a six-year-old black girl had come down with a scale on her head that spread into her eyes, causing blindness. Ulcers formed in her eye sockets and hung from her lids like tiny, hideous bangles. An itinerant Protestant missionary doctor examined her four times and finally told the mother that the infection was incurable. Distraught, the mother went to the local Catholic church where she was given a relic of Gérard—some soil from his grave—and encouraged to seek his intercession. The missionary sisters also began a novena to Gérard. The following day, a Saturday, the local priest gave the mother another relic. That night, the girl claimed to see an old priest in a vision who told her that she would be cured. The next morning, the scales had disappeared and she could see. All that remained, according to a medical examination made forty-eight years later in connection with the cause, was a scar on one cornea indicating that it had been pierced.

The medical consultants had nothing to go on but the testimony of witnesses, including the pastor, who had written down what he saw. There was also an ophthalmologist's examination of the eye, which was done when the woman was fifty-four years old. From this meager evidence, it appeared that the girl had contracted a form of impetigo. But that alone, the consultants agreed, would not account for the pierced cornea. Despite the paucity of medical data, Dr. Camillo Pasquinangeli, a specialist in diseases of the eye, persisted with the case. Eventually, he found a disease, penthius, which matched the symptoms and could, in his judgment, account for the pierced cornea. When the full board of five consultants met on September 1, 1987, with Cortesini presiding, Dr. Pasquinangeli was able to convince the others of the plausibility of his diagnosis. Given that diagnosis and the severity of the case, the board agreed that there was no scientific way to explain the child's sudden and complete recovery of sight. The following year, Pope John Paul II beatified Gérard before ten thousand Catholics in Lesotho.

When I next visited with Dr. Cortesini he had just come from surgery and was still dressed in a white surgical gown. He was in an expansive mood and invited me to look at several red-bound *positiones* of miracles he has studied. "We get them from before the war, during the war, after the war," he said, referring to World War II. "You go back through the history of Christianity and you see. Always there are miracles."

"Doesn't it bother you, that many people do not believe in miracles?"

"There is skepticism about miracles, I know, even in the Catholic Church. I myself, if I did not do these consultations, would never believe what I read. You don't understand how fantastic, how incredible—and how well-documented—these cases are. They are more incredible than historical romances. Science fiction is nothing by comparison."

"Do you ever feel pressured when the pope takes a special interest in a case?"

"Yes, you feel it when he is enthused. Usually, this is when he is traveling somewhere and there is a rush to complete a cause. But we have to be objective. We have the power to stop a cause."

Cortesini plans to write a book on the inexplicable healings he has studied and judged. I hope he does. He knows that scientists, of all professionals, are not expected to believe in miracles—that they are expected to assume that all occurrences ultimately have a rational explanation. But he and the other doctors on the medical board are in a privileged position: they are regularly exposed to data which defy scientific explanation, yet as physicians and medical scientists, they work in a world which relies on the rigorous application of scientific methods. Their experience, their intelligence, and their testimony have to be respected. To say that they believe in miracles because they are Roman Catholics is probably true. It is also beside the point.

To assert that miracles cannot occur is no more rational—and no less an act of faith—than to assert that they can and do happen. It all depends on one's attitude toward reality. One can believe in miracles without believing in God, of course, but the two outlooks are not easily reconcilable. One can also believe in God and not in miracles, though that position, too, is difficult to maintain. A God who is not involved in his own creation—a God who is, as James Joyce imagined him, removed and paring his fingernails—is not the God of Christianity.

As a Roman Catholic, I have no trouble accepting miracles because I believe in God as Jesus came to understand "the Father," and therefore in God's grace. On more than one occasion I have experienced graced moments in my own life and in others, which have come as gifts. To believe in miracles one must be able to accept gifts, freely bestowed and altogether unmerited. Nor do I find it difficult to suppose that these gifts have come my way because someone else—parent, child, spouse, friend, or enemy—prayed to God on my behalf. In a graced world such things happen all the time; despite our inclination to credit ourselves for whatever good "fortune" we may have, "grace is everywhere." But if the world is presumed to be without grace, gifts do not make sense, least of all gifts that come through prayer. Things merely "happen" and one presumes fate or chance, nature or history, or our own merits or well-laid plans to be the cause. The "communion of saints," on the contrary, presupposes that in God we are all connected, giving and receiving unexpected and undeserving acts of grace.

In the process of making saints, however, this communion is not only presumed, it is tapped to serve a specific purpose. "Graces" received and attributed to a Servant of God are collected, sifted, tested, and authenticated as God's own proof of a candidate's holiness. It is this systematic use, and possible abuse, of divine gifts that I was trying to understand.

TWO MADE-IN-AMERICA MIRACLES

DURING THE FIRST six months of 1987, there was more than the usual sense of urgency on the third floor of Number 10, Piazza di Pio XII. John Paul II was scheduled to make his second visit to the United States in September, and in anticipation he had asked Cardinal Palazzini, a year before, if the congregation had an American Servant of God whom he could beatify or canonize in connection with his trip. There were two long-standing causes which needed only a confirming miracle. Time was growing short, however, and in the ensuing scramble to fulfill the pope's wishes, I was able to observe how the congregation operates under the pressure of a papal deadline.

The first case was an inexplicable cure attributed to the intercession of California's leading candidate for sainthood, Father Junípero

Serra. Twice before, Serra's postulator had submitted potential miracles to the Consulta Medica, and twice they had been rejected. Now he had a third and in view of the pope's impending trip Palazzini gave it top priority.

According to the documents, the potential miracle occurred in the spring of 1960 in St. Louis and involved Mother Boniface Dyrda, a Franciscan nun who was then age forty-five. Mother Boniface had developed a fever and skin rash the previous October. Initially, her doctors thought she was suffering from the flu and treated her accordingly. When her condition worsened, she underwent surgery for the removal of an enlarged spleen. For a time, her condition improved but the following January the rash and fever returned. She reentered the hospital where physicians took a tissue sample which they sent to a laboratory in Washington for analysis. But again, no one could pinpoint the cause of her ailment. After she returned to her convent, her condition deteriorated. Her weight dropped to eighty-six pounds and she could eat nothing more than a little soup. On the Saturday before Palm Sunday, 1960, Mother Boniface was given the last rites of the church and dispatched to the hospital. The attending physician told her that he saw no hope for recovery. Whatever she had was now threatening her kidneys. Short of a miracle, Mother Dyrda was not expected to leave the hospital alive.

Faced with the prospect of Mother Dyrda's imminent death, the chaplain to her convent suggested that the sisters begin a novena to Father Serra. The chaplain, Father Marion Habig, was a Franciscan priest from California and devoted to Serra's cause. On Good Friday, exactly one week after entering the hospital, Mother Dyrda suddenly felt better. For the first time in weeks she asked for something to eat. A month later, she was released from the hospital and the mysterious disease never returned.

Was it a miracle? For the members of the Consulta Medica, the major problem was that neither the doctors who treated her nor analysts in Washington could agree on a diagnosis. But without a clear understanding of what threatened her life, it would be difficult for the congregation's medical panel to be sure that her recovery was inexplicable. Moreover, the fact that she was still alive further complicated the case: theoretically, it was still possible for her to suffer a relapse, even though none had occurred for the past twenty-seven years.

In an unusual effort to clear up the mystery, the medical consultants asked that Mother Boniface be brought to Rome for a personal examination. The two primary members of the Consulta Medica assigned to assess the case, Drs. de Rosa and Vincenzo Giulio Bilotta, plus the committee's president, examined her for three days, questioning her directly about her symptoms and the circumstances surrounding her recovery. They also submitted her to medical tests of their own. From a description of her symptoms it was possible that she had been suffering from lupus erythematosus, a chronic and debilitating disease of the connective tissue which still has no known cause, cure, or single diagnostic indicator. Other symptoms suggested it was not. The medical consultants wanted to be sure.

Normally, the physicians need only six to eight weeks to reach a conclusion. But in this instance, their deliberations lasted more than six months. Meanwhile, pressure was building on the congregation. The Franciscans in California fanned hopes that the process would be completed in time for the pope's visit. Stories appeared in California newspapers that a verdict was imminent. As the only American in the congregation, Sarno was harried by phone calls from the United States. "We're killing ourselves to get the Serra miracle through," he confided one morning in May when I dropped by to congratulate him on his promotion to monsignor. "And we're late because the miracle we are working on is very complicated."

"Maybe you should try another one," I suggested, assuming that Father Serra's postulator had an assortment to choose from.

"You pick the one you think has a good chance to float," he said, and waved me away so he could work.

The final *positio super miraculo* was 445 pages long, and on June 17, the two primary medical consultants filed their reports to the congregation. Reading it, I could see why their deliberations had taken so long. In an unusual but not unprecedented decision, the doctors held that Mother Dyrda's cure was not explainable by medical science—even though neither of them was able to say just what her illness had been. In short, I learned, the medical consultants need not arrive at a clear diagnosis in order to conclude that an inexplicable cure has taken place. In such cases, the critical determination is that the patient's condition had so degenerated that she should have died. The fact that she did not—that, on the contrary, she sustained a complete and relatively instantaneous recovery that had continued for twenty-seven years—was sufficient to regard the healing as beyond natural causality or scientific explanation. Three weeks later, the full board of five physicians concurred.

The second American miracle was unusual for other reasons. The case involved a cure attributed to the intercession of Mother Rose-Philippine Duchesne (1769–1852), a French nun who came to Missouri with four other Sisters of the Society of the Sacred Heart and became a pioneer leader in Catholic education and social work. Her dream was to work with the American Indians, something she was finally able to accomplish in her seventy-second year. At her death, she was widely regarded in Catholic circles as a saint. The Sacred Heart Sisters pursued her cause. She was declared "venerable" in 1909 and, with two miraculous cures attributed to her intercession, she was beatified by Pope Pius XII in 1940.

In the years that followed, the postulator submitted two more potential miracles for Mother Duchesne's canonization. But one was rejected unanimously by the first pair of medical consultants and the other received a split vote. At that point, the Sacred Heart Sisters dropped the cause. It was the era of Vatican Council II and, like other religious orders of women in the United States, the sisters questioned the purpose—and the expense—of canonization. As far as they were concerned, Mother Duchesne could remain a blessed.

Enter Father Sarno. As the congregation's only American official, albeit a junior one, Sarno was especially responsive to the pope's 1987 red alert. After reviewing the files on Mother Duchesne, he concluded that the second cure had a good chance of being approved. "I knew enough about medicine from my doctor-brother," he told me, "to see that it showed promise."

The next step was to convince the Sacred Heart Sisters to reopen the cause. Sarno phoned Archbishop John May of St. Louis, urging him to prod the mother general of the Sacred Heart Sisters, Sister Helen MacLaughlin, an American stationed in Rome, to reconsider the order's decision. He also pitched the reluctant sisters himself. He argued that the nuns of the United States need models of sanctity and that in Mother Duchesne they had a great figure from a very difficult period in American church history. He also quieted their concern about expenses.

"Their view was, why waste the money on the process when it could be better spent on the poor?" he recalled. "I told them I respected their principle but I didn't agree with it. I figured that from the physicians' study of the miracle to the day of canonization, the most it would cost them would be ten thousand dollars. Stretch it to fifteen thousand, it still isn't much."

The order's alumnae in South America agreed to pay the expenses and the cause was reopened. But there wasn't much time to act if the canonization was to be ready in time for the pope's trip to the United States. Because of the urgency of the cause, Father Molinari agreed to suspend other responsibilities in order to shepherd the miracle through. His first step was to ask medical specialists from outside the Consulta Medica for preliminary unofficial opinions. In their judgment, the case had a good chance of holding up.

The potential miracle involved a Sacred Heart missionary in Japan, Mother Marie Bernard, aged sixty, who developed a lump in her neck and was sent for treatment to St. Joseph's Hospital in San Francisco in 1951 after a biopsy showed the lump was malignant. Surgery disclosed that the malignancy was too large to remove and too advanced for more than palliative treatment. The most the doctors could do was give her low-level radiation therapy to slow the cancer's spread, and release her. Their prognosis: she had six months, at most two years, to live.

Meanwhile, the sisters offered a novena of prayers to Philippine Duchesne, asking for a cure. The novena became a crusade involving the entire order plus the student body at the sisters' college in San Francisco. Mother Bernard herself joined in—as well she might—and took to wearing a Duchesne relic around her neck. Apparently the prayers worked. She returned to Japan and by 1960, when the miracle process was initiated, the cancer had disappeared. Ten years later, Mother Bernard died of a heart attack.

In June 1987, Dr. de Rosa and another member of the Consulta Medica reviewed the case and found no satisfactory scientific explanation for the cure. Their diagnosis was that she had been suffering from an "undifferentiated neoplasia infiltrating the thyroid gland and adjoining tissue." Although they could not say that the recovery was instantaneous, they were content that it had been relatively fast as well as complete and inexplicable. A full board of physicians concurred, adding in an unusual commentary that the healing should have been approved when it was originally submitted twenty years earlier.

THE DOCTORS AND THE THEOLOGIANS

THE RESPONSIBILITY OF the Consulta Medica is to determine whether or not a cure is scientifically inexplicable. The doctors cannot decide that it is also a miracle. That judgment is reserved for the theological consultants, whose opinions must then be seconded by the congregation's cardinals and, eventually, by the pope. The theory is that the judgment of miracles is a matter of theological and ecclesiastical discernment; to leave that judgment to the physicians would be to cede to medical science a prerogative which the church has always claimed for itself.

After reviewing several miracle *positiones*, however, it seemed to me that the role of the theologians is essentially derivative. There are sixty-six theological consultants to the congregation, but of these only a handful are regularly called upon to sit as a panel of seven to review the miracle process and determine that the cure occurred solely through the intercession of the Servant of God. Their primary evidence is the testimony of witnesses. Who invoked the Servant of God? Was it through prayer, the use of a relic, and so forth? The key elements are time and causality. It must be clear that the patient's recovery occurred only *after* the Servant of God's help was invoked. And it must be equally clear that the cure was obtained through the intercession of the Servant of God and no one else.

Obviously, these judgments do not require a great deal of theological acumen. They do, however, require familiarity with the congregation's operative theology of intercession. For instance, if a patient simultaneously prays to Jesus as well as to the Servant of God, the miracle can be attributed to the latter on the grounds that Jesus is necessarily involved in all graces granted by God. On the other hand, if more than one saint or Servant of God is simultaneously invoked, the cure will be rejected because there is no way to know whom to credit with the divine intercession.

For example, in the case of the miracle attributed to Father Serra, Mother Boniface testified that she had sought help through the intercession of several of her favorite saints: St. Jude, the traditional patron of hopeless causes; St. Frances Cabrini, the first American saint; and St. Martin de Porres, a seventeenth-century Peruvian mulatto who was known for his work with the sick and was canonized in 1962. However—and this was crucial—it was only after those invocations proved fruitless that she turned, at the chaplain's suggestion, to Father Serra. At the time, Mother Dyrda knew virtually nothing about the Franciscan Servant of God. But after her cure she wrote, "Apparently they [the other, already certified saints] were waiting to give Father Junípero Serra a chance."

Given the requirements of the congregation, this exercise in proving that the miracle occurred only through the intercession of the candidate is altogether necessary and logical. Ideally, the proof reflects the candidate's well-established reputation as an intercessor with God. But in practice the whole notion of attributing miracles to one intercessory channel rather than another is open to serious theological question. Does God really withhold a miracle until the right person is invoked? Which is more important, the healing or the intercession? Moreover, as a practical matter the system encourages prayer as a form of spiritual manipulation—of competition, even, for miracles. The chief abuse, and one that is built into the entire saint-making system, is the promotion of prayers to a candidate simply for the sake of obtaining a miracle needed to advance or complete a process. "One hears stories," Father Valabek, the Carmelites' postulator general, told me, "of nuns standing outside the emergency rooms at hospitals praying to their mother foundresses for a miracle every time an ambulance shows up." He chuckled. "They're just stories, mind you, but you see that it could happen and possibly has. God is not a fool, of course, but still there is nothing in our insistence that miracles be clearly assignable to this person rather than that which prevents such superstitious practices." And nothing, one might add, more clearly shows the derivative nature of the theologians' role compared with the judgment of the doctors.

ALTERNATIVES TO MEDICAL MIRACLES

ON NOVEMBER 19, 1988, the Congregation for the Causes of Saints opened a symposium on the validation of miraculous cures which brought members of the Consulta Medica together with members of the international Medical Committee of Lourdes, who investigate claims of miraculous healings at the famed Marian shrine in southern France. The visitors were the older hands at the science of verifying miraculous cures inasmuch as their committee—the first of its kind in the church—was founded in 1882. The Consulta Medica, by comparison, was not instituted until October 22, 1948. The Lourdes physicians were quite blunt in asserting that advances in medical science were making it increasingly difficult to prove miracles. More remarkable yet were the words of John Paul II himself in his address to the participants:

> For a long time now, the cooperation of doctors has been invaluable for assisting discernment [of miraculous cures], according to their proper level of competence. As science progresses, certain cases are better understood; but it remains true that numerous healings constitute a fact which has its explanation only in the order of faith, which the most rigorous scientific examination cannot deny a priori and which it must respect, precisely in its order.

That said, the pope went on to suggest that perhaps the mode of the miraculous was changing.

> There seems to be evidence today that the divine pedagogy is enlightening mankind by more spiritual and more intimate revelations, *and that the cases of physical healing are becoming more rare.* It remains true that God is still granting unexpected and profound gifts, responding to the supplication made in faith and charity, with confidence in the power of his love which is greater than all. (Emphasis added.)

This was the first time that any pope had acknowledged that the church was experiencing difficulty in meeting the physicians' requirements for medical miracles. Yet the trend was there to discern. The reform of 1983 had reduced the number of required miracles by half so that only one is now needed for the beatification of nonmartyrs and only one more for canonization. But even before the reform, the pope's predecessors had shown themselves increasingly willing to waive the full requirement of four miracles. Moreover, in 1980 John Paul II had beatified Kateri Tekakwitha (1656–1680), the Iroquois convert, without proof of miracles. Although Kateri had numerous miracles to her credit, the fledgling church in the United States was unequipped in the seventeenth century to carry out a formal investigative process to establish their validity. It sufficed, the pope decided, that Kateri had a reputation for producing many miracles through her intercession.

In theory this or any other pope has the juridical power to abolish the requirement of miracles in the making of saints. But should he? This was a question, I gradually discovered, which had long been simmering on the back burners of the congregation and one that, because the saint-makers are deeply divided, they were reluctant to discuss.

Gumpel was the first to broach the subject. "The question of miracles is under discussion in the congregation," he said, "and even on a higher level." As he framed the issue initially, it was a matter of practicality—and of justice. There was an unusual gravity in his voice as he reflected one evening on what he saw as the church's unbecoming bondage to the medical profession:

> On the one hand, the requirement of some divine sign is very reasonable. Even though our investigations into the martyrdom or heroicity of virtue are carried out with all human seriousness and we try honestly to arrive at a moral certainty about the candidate's sanctity, nevertheless all these investigations are human and therefore fallible. It is understandable, then, that the Holy Father, before using his supreme

power as Doctor of the Church, wants to have a confirmation of this that goes beyond the merely human level. This is at the root of the requirement, which is still valid in the legislation of the church, that before a solemn canonization takes place, some kind of divine sign is requested.

However, one may ask whether those signs should be miracles in the strict theological sense or whether we should look for signs at a different level. Right now, about 99 percent of the signs requested concern miracles of a medical nature. With regard to this issue, a number of questions have arisen.

The questions, as Gumpel summarized them, were issues which he and his fellow Jesuit, Molinari, have been pressing for more than a decade within the congregation.

First, as medical knowledge progresses, the area of the medically inexplicable decreases. Thus, some cures which are unexplainable today may in time turn out to have an explanation. As Gumpel sees it, "It is becoming increasingly difficult to ascertain exactly what is a fact which goes beyond the laws of nature."

Second, with the increased medicalization of Western societies, it is becoming more difficult to judge with certainty that none of the therapies applied in a given case was responsible for the cure. Thus, if a patient has taken several drugs, it must be proved that each failed to cure the patient. Similarly, in cases where several specialists have been involved in a case, each must testify that his or her intervention could not have produced the unexpected result. For example, Father Valabek is working on a potential miracle from Holland attributed to Titus Branasma but the process has been stalled on the local level because one of the physicians involved disagrees with the others' contention that the cure is in fact medically inexplicable.

Third, the Consulta Medica itself is becoming more stringent in its standards. Often, the demands they make in the form of medical equipment, technique, and records cannot be met by medical practitioners in developing countries. Thus, as mentioned above, the church in the Third World is put at a disadvantage when it comes to providing verifiable medical miracles.

What, then, should the church do?

A partial solution, long advocated by Molinari and Gumpel, is to expand the concept of the miraculous to include physical miracles of a nonmedical nature. One such miracle was approved in 1975 for the canonization of John Macías (1585–1645), a Spanish brother in the Dominican order who died in Peru and was beatified in 1837. The miracle occurred 309 years after his death in his birthplace, Ribera del Fresno, where Macías was known as "the Blessed" and regarded as the village's patron saint.

These were the circumstances: Every evening in the parish hall, children from a nearby orphanage were served dinner; poor families were also invited to pick up a meal at the door. On the evening of January 25, 1949, the cook discovered that she had only enough rice and meat (750 grams of each) to feed the children their evening meal. There would not be enough to feed the poor. Recognizing this, the cook implored "the Blessed" to do something and went about her duties.

Suddenly, she noticed that the boiling rice was overflowing the pot, so she ladled some of the rice into a second pot. And then a third. For four hours, she stood by the stove, as the pot continued to multiply the rice. The pastor's mother, and then the pastor himself, were summoned to witness the phenomenon. By evening's end, there was more than enough rice and meat to serve all fifty-nine children with plenty left over for the poor. In all, twenty-two people testified to the miraculous multiplication of food. And though it had cooked for hours, the last ladleful of rice was as fresh as the first. As in the biblical multiplication of loaves and fishes, everyone ate his fill. Fortunately for the cause, some of the diners saved some of the rice, which was examined by the congregation eleven years later. The consultants could find no natural explanation for the extraordinary phenomenon. And that, together with a traditional medical miracle, was sufficient for canonizing Macías.

One obvious difficulty with nonmedical miracles is procedural: in each case the postulator must find experts who can satisfy the congregation that an extraordinary and inexplicable event has taken place. This was the situation Molinari faced in connection with the cause of Victoria Rasoamanarvio (1848–1894), a married woman revered in Madagascar as the mother of Roman Catholicism for the role she assumed in preserving and teaching Catholicism at a time when all the missionaries had been expelled from that country. The miracle attributed to her intercession occurred in 1934 during the dry season. A woman inadvertently started a fire in the tall grass outside her village. Strong winds fanned the flames into a conflagration which threatened to destroy the entire community. One thatched roof had already caught fire before a young catechist went out and held aloft a picture of Victoria, asking her to save the village from the fire. At that moment, the winds shifted, and the fire ceased.

Photographs were taken of the episode, testimonies gathered, and, a half-century later, the documentation was submitted to Molinari as evidence of a possible miracle. Molinari seized the opportunity as an experiment in proving a nonmedical physical miracle. His major concern was to find an expert who could give him a preliminary scientific opinion on whether the sudden shift in the wind contravened the laws of nature. Eventually, he settled on the head of the Italian fire brigades, a meteorologist who concluded that in his view there was no natural explanation for what took place. He, in turn, submitted the documents to a panel of African and European experts at an international meeting of fire fighters. They, too, felt that there was no scientific explanation for the incident. But there was no precedent within the congregation for creating a board of meteorologists and fire experts which could function like the Consulta Medica. Nor, as it turned out, was there a need for the miracle. With the reform of 1983, only one supporting miracle was needed and Molinari, whose first responsibility was to see the cause succeed, went forward with a second, more conventional medical cure. On April 30, 1989, Victoria Rasoamanarvio was beatified in Madagascar by John Paul II.

In theory, any inexplicable happening is grist for a nonmedical miracle. Father Eszer, for instance, directed my attention to a potential miracle claimed on behalf of Blessed Maria Crescentia Höss (1682–1744), a Franciscan nun from Kaufbeuren, Western Germany, who had a reputation as a mystic and who functioned as spiritual adviser to both the lowly and the mighty, including Kaiser Karl VII and his wife, Maria Theresa. Crescentia was declared venerable in 1801 and beatified in 1900 by Pope Leo XIII. But nearly another half-century passed before her postulator could come up with another apparent miracle for her canonization.

The miracle was this: during World War II, Allied bombers flew a mission over Kaufbeuren, a small city south of Augsburg. Their goal was to level a path of destruction that included several nearby towns and military installations, among them a dynamite factory and a landing strip near Kaufbeuren. It was a cloudless day. The citizens could see the bombs in the bellies of the flying fortresses. They prayed to Blessed Crescentia, whose body is encased in glass under the high altar in the convent church, that Kaufbeuren be saved. Sister Ancilla Hinterberger, a successor to Crescentia as the mother superior, described for me what she and others witnessed:

> Bombers were above the city with open shafts. They were trying to hit Kaufbeuren but were unsuccessful. They could not see the city even though they were directly above it. From below, one could see with bare eyes the bombs hanging from the planes. But no bomb fell. Nothing happened. Kaufbeuren was spared.

Testimony was gathered from the witnesses but it wasn't until 1983, when military archives of both the United States and West Germany could be opened, that the necessary documentation could be gathered. From the Americans, the postulator collected reports of the pilots and crews and verified the purpose of the mission. From the Germans, he obtained corroborating reports. This information, in turn, was submitted separately to the historical section of the German Defense Ministry and to experts in the German Air Force. Among other things, these experts sought meteorological opinions on the possibility of a mirage and military opinions on the possibility of malfunctioning gyroscopes. They even interviewed some of the surviving bomber pilots from the United States. By the fall of 1988, Father Wilhelm Imcamp, the local vice-postulator, had his answer. "We had this wonder checked and it is no wonder," he said. "The experts tell us it can be explained by natural causes and so it is no longer under consideration."

Eszer was disappointed. But he has another promising nonmedical miracle in connection with a Swiss cause. The potential miracle involves a mountain climber who survived a fall in which all his colleagues perished. Their ropes broke but his, after he invoked the Servant of God, did not. The postulator has asked geologists and expert mountain guides for their opinions. "If they agree it was miraculous," says Eszer, "then maybe we will have a miracle process."

Must a miracle be physical? On this point, the saint-makers are divided. Molinari is of the opinion that in the search for divine signs in support of beatification or canonization, the church should accept "moral miracles"—that is, extraordinary graces which produce a moral or spiritual transformation.

The argument in favor of moral miracles is particularly appropriate for the cause of Matt Talbot (1856–1925), a figure well known among Irish—and Irish-American—Catholics. Talbot was an uneducated Dublin dockworker who overcame alcoholism while still in his twenties and went on to become a kind of laboring-class ascetic, fasting, praying, and, unknown to even the few friends he had, wearing penitential chains underneath his workclothes. At his death, Talbot was a nobody. But his story captured the Irish imagination (except for the part about the chains, which the Irish still consider a bit excessive), and in 1975 Pope Paul VI declared him heroically virtuous.

Like Paul VI, the Polish pope has said he is anxious to beatify Talbot as a saint of the working class and, equally important, as an example of how prayer and mortification of the flesh can overcome alcoholic addiction. Talbot is a popular figure in Ireland and in Poland, where alcoholism is a major social problem. In the United States there are several Matt Talbot Clubs and centers for recovering alcoholics. Talbot's Roman postulator, Father Dermot Martin, told me that he has more than a thousand testimonials claiming that Talbot's intercession has been responsible for helping alcoholic husbands beat the bottle and thereby saving marriages and preserving families.

There is, in short, ample evidence of Talbot's intercessory powers. But thus far Martin has been unable to persuade the congregation to accept this evidence as miraculous. The problem, of course, is that alcoholism is a matter of perseverance—of willpower—rather than physical cure. "Suppose we call them miracles," one of the congregation's highest officials told Martin. "And suppose we invite one of these recovering alcoholics to the beatification ceremony. And suppose that night he gets carried away by all the attention and goes out and gets drunk. Where is the miracle?"

Eszer is of the same mind. "If there is a relapse, there is no healing," he argues. "It is well known that an alcoholic can get drunk on just one brandy or beer. But if a man were healed so that he could take a glass of wine or beer without getting drunk, *that* would be a miracle."

"Yes, but that would be a physical, not a moral miracle," I interject.

"Of course. We are strict on this issue, but we have to be. Even now, critics of the congregation say we are just a factory for miracles. What would they say if we allowed so-called moral miracles?"

"So you are opposed to moral miracles?"

"For several reasons. First, in a moral miracle you have only one witness, the subject who says he or she has been changed. But suppose he lies? I know of no legal system in the world that accepts evidence from only one witness. Second, I am against moral miracles because the miracles of Jesus are not moral only but miracles in nature. You can't find a single miracle in the whole New Testament which can be called a moral miracle. The real miracle is the person's return to health or some other physical sign."

The medical consultants, too, are opposed to moral miracles. They take immense pride in supplying the church with evidence of the miraculous, and are quite firm in their belief that healing miracles, no matter how much science advances, will never cease. Dr. Cortesini, in particular, sees miraculous healings as a continuation in the saints of the cures worked by Jesus himself. "What we see are the same miracles that we read about in the New Testament," he insists. "People being cured of physical ailments. Always, when I am judging a cause, I keep these biblical precedents in mind. You must go back to the Bible to find anything comparable."

Father Gumpel concedes that the present system has certain merits. "On the merely administrative and juridical levels," he acknowledges, "it is simpler to obtain the judgment of experts in the fields of medicine or other natural sciences who can declare that a given phenomenon ascribed to the candidate cannot be explained naturally. Whereas, it is more difficult to ascertain the existence of so-called moral miracles."

Nevertheless, he insists that the church "could and should get away from the proof of physical miracles and rely more on divine science as expressed in the opinion that many graces have been granted through the Servant of God. If the bishops of a country were to declare that there are dozens or hundreds of statements made by serious people that after the invocation of the Servant of God their prayers have been answered, such a declaration would come under the direct competence of the church, and could be considered as a sign of divine work sufficient to allow us to beatify or canonize the candidate."

In sum, the fundamental issue for Gumpel is a matter of principle more than practicality. By narrowing the notion of miracles to inexplicable cures, the church has, in effect, allowed medical science to usurp its own competence to interpret divine signs. In so doing, it has lost sight of the spiritual and moral dimensions of the miraculous which are much broader than physical miracles. His solution, then, is to reassert the church's prerogatives by revitalizing the notion of "divine science."

THE NECESSITY OF MIRACLES: THE INTERNAL DEBATE

MORE THAN 750 years have elapsed since Pope Gregory IX, in connection with the canonization of St. Anthony of Padua, established the principle that neither virtues without miracles nor miracles without virtues provide sufficient grounds for canonization. And the church was to be judge of both. But in the internal debates that led up to the reform of 1983, the question of the necessity of miracles was freshly addressed.

For Father Molinari, the immediate point at issue was whether the church was needlessly delaying the completion of causes—and thus depriving the faithful of contemporary examples of Christian holiness—by insisting on a multiplicity of provable miracles. "Those medical consultants and specialists who offer their professional services," he argued, "are equally baffled, when, under the most exacting and rigorous of examinations a favorable verdict is reached, and they are told that similar evidence of a further cure or cures is required." His argument was apparently persuasive, since the reform cut by half the number of required miracles.

But Molinari and Gumpel want to go further. They see no reason why the church should continue to demand medical or even physical miracles in order to beatify or canonize a Servant of God. It is enough, they believe, that the candidate has a solid reputation for holiness, which has been duly investigated by the congregation, verified by the proof of martyrdom or heroic virtue, and authenticated by a solemn declaration of the pope.

Their position is spelled out in a long and passionate essay in which Molinari reviews the history and theology of saint-making with an eye toward ending the church's dependence on miracles as corroborating divine signs for beatification and canonization. In the early church, he argues, miracles were "in no way connected with the cult of the saints." It was only during the Merovingian and Carolingian periods (415–928) "when everyone, clerics as well as the ordinary faithful, was notoriously avid for miracle stories, and very credulous" that the church began to emphasize the miraculous. "It was a time also when [the writing of] history was in no way governed by critical or scientific standards, while the quality of medical research was not only crude, it could scarcely be said to have existed at all." But even then and in subsequent centuries, Molinari insists, the focus of concern "was not in fact on miracles as such, but on the reputation for miracle-working." Only in the last four centuries, with the development of formal procedures for canonization, has the reliance on proven miracles come to be a part of the saint-making process.

But it needn't continue, he argues. Theologically, the true "divine sign" in every cause is the reputation for holiness implanted in the faithful and manifest by their admiration, devotion, and invocation of the saint for favors. This is not, he hastens to add, a merely natural phenomenon. And once "scientific research" has established the fact of martyrdom or heroic virtue, the Servant of God should be beatified or canonized without requiring additional interventions from God in the form of miracles. If miracles are alleged through the candidate's intercession, well and good; they should be investigated and authenticated. But to demand such miracles is "extravagant and without justification," particularly in light of "the development of history as a science over the last two centuries." Therefore, he concludes, the congregation should return to the attitude of the early church toward miracles and reform its procedures accordingly:

> ... We do not believe that it is necessary or advantageous to demand a special divine sign apart from the reputation for holiness of a Servant of God ... A truly extraordinary reputation for holiness should also be sufficient proof of the divine intervention for the beatification or canonization of a Servant of God whose martyrdom or heroic virtue has already been proven.

In other words, theology and history are the only sciences required in the making of saints, and a reputation for holiness the only confirmation needed from God.

Since Molinari is one of the most influential saint-makers, his essay, first published in 1978, made a deep impression—especially among his fellow Jesuits. Its publication fed a widespread misperception that "the Jesuits," at least, no longer regarded proof of miracles as necessary to completing a process. And in one instance, this misunderstanding nearly jeopardized the beatification of one of the Jesuits' most popular wartime heroes.

Rupert Mayer (1897–1945) might have died a martyr if the Nazis had allowed it. As a young man, he joined the Jesuits at a time when the order was outlawed by the anticlerical Prussian state. He served as a chaplain in World War I, lost his left leg, and became the first Roman Catholic priest to be awarded the Iron Cross. In the twenties and thirties, Mayer worked in Munich as an inner-city pastor, preaching, baptizing, and shepherding the city's enormously popular Christian Life Movement. He also worked the beer halls, once met Adolf Hitler, and subsequently denounced the Nazi movement as anti-Christian— in part because it was also, he said, anti-Semitic. He was arrested twice for his subversive sermons and eventually was sent to the Sachsenhausen concentration camp near Berlin. But when his health began to fail, the Nazis removed him to a Benedictine monastery in Bavaria and ordered him to keep silent: better a silent adversary than a troublesome martyr. Mayer lived long enough to lead the first post-war Corpus Christi march through the streets of Munich. "So," he remarked, "a battered and exhausted Jesuit, one-legged old Jesuit, has outlived the thousand-year Reich."

In the years following his death, Mayer's flock never forgot him. Every day, between six and ten thousand people visited his tomb in downtown Munich, and this went on for forty years. Declared venerable in 1983, Mayer had by 1985 acquired a list of 104 potential miracles attributed to his intercession. And he would need one: John Paul II was planning a visit to Germany two years hence—the same trip which would take him to Cologne for the beatification of Edith Stein. But when Molinari asked the Jesuit vice-postulator in Munich for the documents supporting evidence for one of Mayer's miracles, there were none. The vice-postulator had assumed that the debate over the necessity of miracles was more than that: he had concluded that nothing more than a reputation for miracles would be needed and, aware that this was Molinari's own opinion, had decided that there was no need to follow through on promising cases. "I had told him many times that the law requiring miracles was still in force," Molinari recalled, "but he proceeded on the assumption that a change was imminent. So there was no miracle."

There were, however, some twenty thousand answered prayers. Could these not, it was argued, be considered sufficient evidence of divine intervention? In other words, could not the pope dispense Mayer from the requirement of a proven miracle, as he had done with Kateri Tekakwitha? Eszer, among others, was resolutely opposed to any dispensation. "The people would say that the Germans bought the beatification with their money," he argued.

Gumpel was dispatched to Munich to see what he could do. An Italian physician looked over the possible miracles and found one, from Germany, for which they could obtain medical documents. Because the subject was a prominent citizen of an overwhelmingly Protestant region, he was flown at his request to Rome for a confidential medical investigation. And because time was short, an emergency commission of three theological consultors—including Eszer—was created to judge the miracle. The miracle was accepted and on May 3, 1987, 100,000 Germans turned out in Munich for the pope's beatification of Mayer Olympic Stadium.

For Eszer, the Mayer incident is yet another confirmation that medical miracles are not only possible but necessary for the making of saints. He dismisses the notion that the theological consultants have become too dependent on the Consulta Medica. "The problem is that many Catholics no longer believe in the possibility of obtaining miracles through saints and Servants of God. And so for Catholics in several countries like Germany and France—and, also, your United States—miracles have become a big embarrassment. But the real problem, I think, is that many theologians no longer believe in the miracles of Jesus. They are always writing this rubbish."

In 1987, Eszer formally entered the debate over miracles with an equally impassioned essay of his own, published in a *festschrift* honoring Cardinal Palazzini and edited, coincidentally, by Gumpel. His purpose was not only to rebut Molinari and Gumpel, but to defend the very idea of miracles against any and all unbelievers.

To question miracles, he argued, was to question not just the saints but Jesus himself. Some (unnamed) biblical exegetes would reduce him to "a kind of psychoanalyst who engaged in curing only psychogenic ills." Are we to conclude, therefore, that Jesus "pretended to have powers which did not exist and would not be considered extraordinary in later epochs?"

Eszer went on to cite a saying that " 'God makes miracles to help men but not to offer some proof in the causes of beatification and canonization.' That's a witty comment. But almighty God can very well coordinate the primary with the secondary end of a miracle in view of the fact that He is also infinitely wise. Divine Providence is not limited to one purpose in its action."

Turning to the witness of science, he says that those who say miracles are impossible to modern science echo the outdated views of Newton and Karl Marx. Modern physics has shown that the laws of nature are not deterministic but function according to laws of mathematical probability. In the new physics since Max Planck, the indeterminacy of the universe leaves plenty of room for both human freedom and divine intervention.

Taking up the historical arguments put forward by Molinari, Eszer argues that St. Augustine, among other notable Christians of late Roman antiquity, was skeptical of miracles without proof. Moreover, doctors in the third and forth centuries "were perfectly able to make a distinction between normal healings and a truly great miracle." More to the point, he argues that nonmartyrs would not have enjoyed lasting veneration by the faithful if it hadn't been for the miracles produced by prayers at their tombs. If, then, the church is to return to its origins, it must reaffirm the need for miracles as divine signs of a candidate's intercessory powers.

Arguing from authority, Eszer cites Benedict XIV on the need for miracles, especially for nonmartyrs. Contemporary witnesses who testify to a candidate's virtues, he reiterates, may be unaware of private laxness. Confirmation in the form of miracles is necessary, therefore, because "only God cannot be deceived."

Eszer is not impressed by Molinari's argument that the church should content itself with a candidate's reputation for granting many divine favors. Such a reputation may in fact reveal the hand of God; indeed, without a fame for favors, "a believer in grave peril would not have recourse to the Servant of God's intercession." But reputation alone is not sufficient proof of sanctity since, in each case, what is averred is merely a divine favor granted to the individual. But miracles, he argues, are divine signs intended for the entire community of the church, not for the benefit of single individuals, and thus must be "confirmed by the authority which guides the community [the pope] and enjoys the protection of the Holy Spirit in avoiding errors."

In any other institution, a disagreement of this magnitude over fundamental theory and practice would be taken up in a formal way, studied, and resolved. But the Congregation for the Causes of Saints has no standing study committees and so the debate over miracles continues unresolved. In time, Gumpel predicts, the cardinals and bishops of the congregation will call for a formal review, and will likely seek the opinions of the national conferences of Catholic bishops around the world. But only the pope can authorize such a review, and in the judgment of the saint-makers, John Paul II is personally disinclined to initiate such a historic referendum. He has already authorized a reduction in the number of required miracles, and partially because of that he is now beatifying and canonizing at a record pace.

There is also the question of precedent. The belief in miracles of intercession—"the lying miracles of the papists"—was a major objection of the Protestant Reformers. So much so that the Counter-Reformation Council of Trent anathematized anyone who denied that miracles occur and can be "ascertained with certainty." As was noted in the last chapter, miracles were a major apologetic weapon for the Catholic Church in the nineteenth century, and in the beginning of the twentieth, Pope Pius X, who was canonized himself in 1954, included disbelief in miracles among the evils of the ideas he denounced collectively as "Modernism." The problem facing any pope, therefore, would be to find a way of affirming the miraculous while ruling that miracles are no longer required in the making of saints. Theologically, this could easily be done. But making saints is not an exercise in theology. It depends in the instance on the response of the faithful, especially their willingness to seek someone's intercession with God. Would Catholics, even in southern Italy, pray to Servants of God in time of need if they did not expect miracles?

To ask this question is to realize that the argument over miracles is, in the last analysis, not about science at all. Nor is it about the nature of divine signs. The issue is more fundamental: are saints primarily intercessors with God, in which case the granting of miracles is part of their function? Or are they primarily examples of Christian virtue, in which case the miracle requirement could easily be dispensed with?

I return in my mind to Innocent XI, lying in limbo in St. Peter's

Basilica. Once this pope had a lively reputation for holiness. Indeed, two miracles are credited to his intercession. But who today invokes his aid? With so many other saints to choose from, why should anyone bother? In what sense can it be argued that after two and a half centuries Innocent XI retains a reputation for holiness? And if someone were to invoke his name and be healed, what meaning would this "divine sign" have for contemporary Christians? On the other hand, is the craft of history sufficiently "scientific," as Molinari asserts, to prove that a reputation for holiness is truly grounded in a life of heroic virtue?

Two very different paths within American Catholicism.

New York's Cardinal Terence Cooke in 1968 with
President Lyndon B. Johnson and presidential
nominees Hubert H. Humphrey and Richard Nixon.
Cooke's cause, initiated by his successor, Cardinal
John J. O'Connor, rests on the grace with which he
endured a fatal illness.

Dorothy Day (center), pacifist, writer, and cofounder
of the Catholic Worker Movement, pictured here in
1917. Day's canonization is opposed by many of her
spiritual heirs. They regard the church's saint-making
process as inappropriate for a "people's saint."

John Paul II, who grew up during the German occupation of Poland, has had to pass judgment on the sanctity of several Catholics who were executed by the Nazis.

Edith Stein, born Jewish, was a Catholic convert and Carmelite nun who was gassed at Auschwitz. Rome's saint-makers had to argue that she was a Christian martyr, even though she was killed because she was Jewish. When Pope John Paul II beatified Stein in 1987, Jews around the world protested.

4

5

The last photograph of Maximilian Kolbe, a Franciscan priest from Poland who died to save the life of another prisoner at Auschwitz. Because Kolbe's act did not conform to the church's traditional concept of martyrdom, the pope created a new category and proclaimed him a "martyr of charity."

(*right*) Titus Brandsma, a Dutch Carmelite priest and journalist, was the first victim of the Nazis to be beatified as a martyr. Brandsma was murdered for denouncing the Nazis' deportation of Jews.

3

The politics of canonization.

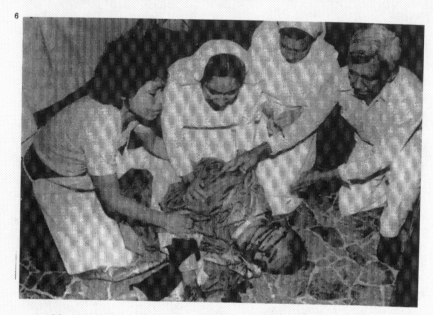

Archbishop Oscar Romero of El Salvador was assassinated while saying Mass in 1980. Although he was instantly regarded by many Salvadorans as a martyr, efforts to process Romero's cause were delayed for ten years because Pope John Paul II considered the archbishop closely identified with liberation theology and the Salvadoran guerrilla movement.

Jesuit Father Miguel Pro praying before being executed in 1919 by Mexican soldiers during the Christero rebellion. Before his cause could be cleared for beatification in 1986, the saint-makers had to demonstrate that Pro was killed for religious and not political reasons.

Vatican saint-makers are skeptical of purported mystics. Indeed, even when the mystical phenomena are judged authentic, they have no bearing on the candidate's claim to sanctity.

8

Padre Pio, an Italian friar and one of Catholicism's most popular "living saints," experienced stigmata (he's wearing gloves to cover the wounds) and had the ability to read hearts and to perform miraculous healings. Since his death in 1968, his cause has moved slowly because of financial scandal involving his brother and the Vatican's desire to curb a growing cult.

9

Theresa Musco, a stigmatic and visionary who died in 1976 at thirty-three, caused religious statues to begin bleeding. Though the bishop of Caserta, Italy, her hometown, attributed these events to an illness, Musco's promoters have succeeded in initiating a second investigation of her life.

10

Portuguese-born Alexandrina da Costa experienced "passion ecstasies" during which she reenacted the sufferings of Christ. For the last twelve years of her life, it is said, she took no food or water, a claim verified by a team of physicians.

For the last century and a half, the founders of religious orders have been the largest single category of blesseds and saints.

11

Katharine Drexel, an heiress and member of one of Philadelphia's most distinguished families, was beatified in 1987, thirty-two years after her death. Drexel, shown at her debut at sixteen in 1874, founded the Sisters of the Blessed Sacrament for Indians and Colored People and numerous missions and schools.

Cornelia Connelly, 1831. After her husband
became a priest, Connelly became a nun and
founded the Society of the Holy Child Jesus
in England. Her husband's efforts to win her
back through the English courts caused a
major scandal.

Rome rarely canonizes intellectuals, artists, or happily married people. But gradually the Vatican is trying to fill this void.

13

16

In 1990, Pope John Paul II beatified Pier Giorgio Frassati for his charity toward the poor. An athlete, university graduate, and son of the founder of *La Stampa*, Frassati was contemplating marriage before his death from polio at twenty-five.

Intellectuals, such as England's Cardinal John Henry Newman, are chancy candidates for sainthood because they tend to write too much and don't inspire the faithful to pray to them for miracles.

14

15

For the first time in four hundred years, the saint-makers are processing a joint cause on behalf of a married couple. Louis and Azélie Guérin Martin, parents of St. Thérèse of Lisieux, remained celibate for nine months after their marriage until a priest convinced them that their vocation was to raise children for God. All of their surviving children became nuns.

Only three popes have been canonized in the last nine hundred years. The question complicating their causes is this: Can the church canonize a pope without blessing his every action during his pontificate?

In 1965, Pope Paul VI announced that he was initiating causes on behalf of his immediate predecessors: Pius XII and John XXIII. Both candidates are controversial.

(*above*) Pius, shown here as papal nuncio to Germany in 1918 with Italian prisoners of war, has been criticized for failing to speak out against the Nazis in World War II.

John, photographed during his tenure as patriarch of Venice in 1958, is thought by conservatives to have been too lenient and impulsive during his brief reign.

CHAPTER SEVEN

THE STRUCTURE OF HOLINESS: PROVING HEROIC VIRTUE

PROMPTLY AT FIVE o'clock in the afternoon of November 16, 1987, eight theological consultants assembled in a small parlorlike meeting room at the rear of the Congregation for the Causes of Saints. Three of them were American, three were Irish, one was Italian, and one was Indian. They had been summoned to render and defend their opinions on whether Mother Katharine Drexel, an American nun who died thirty-three years earlier, had manifested the heroic virtues required of a saint. As in all modern causes, none of the consultants had ever met Mother Drexel; indeed, only one could recall hearing anything at all about her prior to being assigned to judge her cause. Their judgments on her holiness, therefore, were based solely on a *positio* of sixteen hundred pages sent to them for study two months earlier.

Few people outside the congregation and its consultants ever see *positiones*. Like legal briefs, they are produced for a specific purpose and copies are difficult to obtain. The main reason is expense. It can cost $20,000 or more to print a *positio* of 1,500 pages, and thus they are seldom printed in runs of more than 150 copies. Another reason is concern over confidentiality. Although *positiones* are not generally treated as secret documents, neither is the congregation anxious to have outsiders—particularly the press—looking over its shoulder while it decides the fate of a cause. This is especially true of causes involving controversial figures such as Edith Stein and Pope Pius IX (or as we will see in chapter 10), politically sensitive causes such as those of the Vietnamese martyrs and Mexico's Father Pro. In some cases, as we saw with Padre Pio, it is a question of protecting the reputations of people, especially ranking prelates, who are still alive. In others, it is a matter of protecting witnesses.

However, once a cause is successfully completed, the *positio* is available for study in the Vatican Archives. In recent decades, historians and social scientists have found this documentation—all four centuries of it—an unparalleled trove of information on such subjects as church-state relations and shifting social concepts of moral and spiritual values, as well as on the lives of individual saints. Curiously, however, *positiones* are rarely consulted by the church's professors of spirituality, a fact which puzzles and irritates some of the saint-makers. "It is very regrettable that the treasures on spiritual doctrine you find in the archives of this congregation are not sufficiently exploited," Father Gumpel remarked in the course of a conversation, "because the observations and judgments of the consultors, the postulators, and the Devil's Advocates constitute a wealth of material from which many developments in spirituality came forward." Not the least of those archival treasures, I ventured to guess, is the history of the development of the *positio* itself as the official medium and methodology for making saints.

As it happened, the *positio* on Mother Drexel's heroic virtue was the first in the history of the congregation to be executed completely in English.* And, since only a handful of the congregation's consultants are fluent in English, the panel of judges for her *positio* included five outside theologians chosen for their competence in that language. Linguistically, at least, Mother Drexel's virtue was to be judged by her peers.

The *positio* on Katharine Drexel interested me for several reasons. For one thing, although I am an American and a reasonably aware Roman Catholic, I too had never heard of Katharine Drexel. For another, thirty-three years is a rather short time for a cause to reach the judgment stage on heroic virtues, especially when the candidate is one of many founders of religious orders. What was it about this cause, I wanted to know, which prompted officials of the congregation to move it along? Far more intriguing, however, was the opportunity to study a *positio* that was one of the first—and longest—to be prepared according to the new norms established by the reform of 1983. As

---

* There was an earlier *positio* on martyrdom done in English: for 85 sixteenth-century English martyrs beatified in 1987.

such, I figured, it would be a useful prism through which to observe the impact of those reforms on the methods by which the church establishes the holiness required of a saint.

The Congregation for the Causes of Saints is quite precise in its understanding of holiness. Holiness is the grace of God operating in and through human beings. The congregation's tests for holiness are also precise—indeed, they are almost schematic. Holiness is manifested by a two-tiered structure of virtues: the three supernatural (so called because they are infused by grace) virtues of faith, hope, and charity (love of God and of neighbor), and the four cardinal moral virtues (originally derived from the ethics of Aristotle) of prudence, justice, fortitude, and temperance. Since all Christians are expected to practice these virtues, a saint is someone who practices them to a "heroic" or exceptional degree.

Because only God knows what graces a person has received and how that person responded to them, heroic virtue must be inferred from external evidence. In all "recent" causes—that is, causes for which there are still living witnesses who knew the candidate—the evidence of holiness is based on the testimony of those witnesses together with letters, diaries, books, sermons, and any other written documents attesting to the candidate's spiritual life. This material constitutes the *positio*, which is usually organized into three volumes: a *vita* or documented life story of the candidate; the testimony of witnesses and other supporting documents regarding the virtues of the candidate, his or her reputation for holiness, and the pastoral benefit the church can expect from the canonization of the Servant of God; and an *informatio* or brief summarizing the arguments and evidence for the existence of the requisite virtues.

The decisive and most difficult phase of any process on behalf of a nonmartyr is proving heroic virtue. Under the old system, the candidate's claims to heroic virtue were adjudicated by the Devil's Advocate in dialogue with the candidate's defense lawyer. Now that the lawyers have been eliminated, everything depends on the persuasiveness of the text itself.

However, the reform of 1983 intended much more than the mere elimination of lawyerly disputation. It also envisioned a shift in emphasis from the juridical to the narrative or biographical presentation of the evidence for holiness. Not only was the candidate's life to be grounded in the context of history, it was also to be presented in such a fashion as to reveal the unique holiness of each saint.

In this respect, the reform was a practical response to a new theology of saints which developed in the era of Vatican Council II and emphasizes the utter originality of each saint. That each saint *is* unique is a point on which both conservative and liberal theologians apparently agree. Thus, for the late Swiss scholar Father Hans Urs von Balthasar, reputedly the favorite theologian of Pope John Paul II, "No one is so much himself as the saint, who disposes himself to God's plan, for which he is prepared to surrender his whole being, body, soul and spirit." Moreover, von Balthasar insisted that those "representative saints" singled out by the church for beatification and canonization are "irrefutable, beyond questioning, as indivisible as prime numbers." His liberal counterpart, the late German Jesuit Karl Rahner, was of much the same mind:

> Herein lies the special task which the canonized saints have to fulfill for the Church. They are the initiators and the creative models of the holiness which happens to be right for, and is the task of, their particular age. They create a new style; they prove that a certain form of life and activity is really a genuine possibility; they show experimentally that one can be a Christian even in "this" way; they make such a type of person believable as a Christian type.

In other words, although everyone is called to holiness, holiness is not the same for everyone. The challenge for the saint-makers, therefore, is to discover and display the holiness peculiar to each Servant of God. But here they face a problem of method: what form of analysis and interpretation is best suited for revealing the holiness particular to each candidate? On this point, I discovered, there is considerable difference of opinion among officials of the congregation and their consulting theologians.

PATTERN AND PARTICULARITY

TO APPRECIATE THE scope of the problem, it is necessary to recall that in the long history of making saints, the emphasis on spiritual uniqueness is very recent. In the past, saints not only read the lives of other saints, most of them also consciously tried to pattern their lives after their favorite predecessor. To be a saint was to imitate Christ, of course, but since Christ is by definition inimitable, the operative models were, for the most part, those few truly innovative figures like St. Francis, St. Benedict, Teresa of Ávila, or St. Ignatius Loyola, each of whom created new and enormously influential systems of spiritual discipline and practice. Similarly, in the promotion of candidates for canonization, biographers tended to pattern their *vitae* on acceptable models, showing how the Servant of God either resembled an acknowledged saint or approximated an ideal type such as the holy monk, the saintly bishop, or the Christian prince. To become a saint, therefore, was to imitate an acknowledged model of holiness. And to be declared a saint was to be recognized as such according to one of the acceptable patterns.

The method of canonization also lent itself to patterns rather than particularity. The earliest form of episcopal canonization was an oral recitation in front of the local bishop of the candidate's life, together with the miracles worked by and through him. In other words, the evidence for holiness was organized and presented in a *narrative* form—or, more precisely, as a stylized spiritual saga in which the saint was cast as miracle-working spiritual hero, championing the cause of Christ against his adversaries, whether they be the Devil, the world and the flesh, or real-life enemies of the church. Thus, even in the canonization process of so cerebral a candidate as Thomas Aquinas, his *vita* was presented as a story of intellectual combat against Jews, schismatics, and assorted heretics.

In sum, the tendency in canonization up through the Middle Ages was to look for patterns rather than particularity in holiness. To be sure, the greatest saints were indeed "prime numbers"—so singular as to become models for the majority who surfaced in their spiritual wakes. But in most cases, saints were recognized as such because they fit expected patterns. Well into the twentieth century, in fact, biographers sometimes rewrote a candidate's *vita* to conform to changing patterns in acceptable spirituality.*

The official procedures for canonization established in 1642 by Pope Urban VIII solidified a genuine paradigm shift in the way that holiness was to be understood and accepted—at least by the church's authorized saint-makers. Among other requirements, Urban stipulated that candidates for sainthood must be shown to have practiced the classic Christian virtues, as these had been defined and codified by Aquinas and other Scholastic theologians. The primary purpose of this requirement was to separate genuine miracle-workers from the practitioners of magic and the black arts of the Devil. "An agent of Satan might

---

* The case of Mother Agnes of Jesus (Agnes Galand, 1602–1634) offers an exceptional opportunity to study how *vitae* are shaped to match the reigning theological and political expectations of the Holy See. In the course of three centuries, her life was rewritten four times in four different ways, each in the hope of catching the prevailing winds from Rome. When Rome wanted to stress the supernatural, her biographer underscored Mother Agnes's mystical experiences. When mysticism became suspect, she took on a spirituality and exemplarity of less exotic nature. As recently as 1963, the facts of her life were still undergoing reinterpretation.

confound the laws of nature and by wizardry lure others into the diabolical path, but someone who practiced the Christian virtues to an heroic degree could not possibly be in the devil's employ—at least so the theologians reasoned."

Whatever their initial reasons, the consequences of Urban's decrees were various and far-reaching. First, as might be expected, the saint as wonder-worker gradually receded and the saint as moral exemplar emerged in his place. This, in turn, heightened the separation between the saint as object of popular devotion and the saint as successful survivor of the canonization process. What made for a reputation of holiness among the people (and in many cases still does) were the stories—usually exaggerated, to be sure, and often apocryphal—of the extraordinary deeds and charismatic power of the Servant of God. What officially counted for beatification and canonization, on the other hand, was juridically established evidence (usually eyewitness testimony) of exemplary heroic virtue.

Second, Urban's decrees also worked a profound change in the methodology of making saints. Since the proof of heroic virtue was paramount, the life story of the candidate receded in relative significance. The events of the candidate's life were to be mined for evidence of heroic virtue and supported by the testimony of witnesses. In short, the structures for proving holiness changed: narrative organization gave way to the legal brief, comparison to analysis, story to proof texts, symmetry to categories. The pattern of holiness was no longer based on models or determined by the dynamics of narrated life story, but was dictated by the essentially static categories of the required virtues. What made a person a saint was the presence of the same heroic virtues to be found in every other saint. What made one saint different from another saint were the accidents of time and place in which the required virtues were manifest. If, in meeting the schematized requirements of an official *positio*, one spiritual candidate's profile turned out to be much like another's, the reason was that they were expected to *be* much like each other—virtue by heroic virtue.

The reform of 1983 was designed to free *positiones* from the rigidity of juridical procedures and their stereotypical approach to the manifestation of Christian virtue. Proof of virtue was to depend less on what others thought about the Servant of God, more on what could be deduced from the candidate's life. To that end, the saint-makers were to draw on all the human sciences, including psychology, to arrive at what Father Molinari called "the deeper personality" of the saint.

"Some of us had been trying to do that for years," he insisted. "Now it is official policy."

In sum, by integrating the best methods in theology, the human sciences, and canon law, the reformers hoped to produce *positiones* which would illuminate the unique holiness of the candidate, and demonstrate the Servant of God's relevance to his or her specific historical milicu. Once again the emphasis was to fall on the saint's life story, but without the narrative conventions of spiritual saga. The facts alone—scrupulously gathered, scientifically verified, and theologically interpreted—it was believed, would reveal each candidate's utterly individual spiritual fingerprint.

Just how this was to happen, however, was not spelled out in the reform. Indeed, the reform itself was a compromise insofar as it still required proof of each of the necessary virtues. On the one hand, the relators and their collaborators were to present a historical-critical life of the candidate; on the other, they were to continue to dissect that life for evidence of specific virtues—much as a physician might determine that each of a patient's life systems—the cardiovascular, the neurological, the muscular-skeletal, and so on—is working to optimum degree. As a result, there was considerable and often passionate disagreement over how the new historical-critical and the traditional juridical approaches were to be connected.

According to the congregation's own internal guidelines for saint-makers, *positiones* were to be labeled *super vita et virtutibus*—"on the life and the virtues" of the candidate. The question was, how much of the life is to be covered? Is the *vita* to be a full-blown biography, or is it to be limited to those aspects of the candidate's life which manifest his or her heroic virtue? If the latter, how was one to decide where to draw the line? Is the development of character to be treated independently of the development of holiness? If so, how are the two related? It was up to each relator to work out the answers for himself, case by case.

One evening over dinner, I asked Father Molinari to explain how he understood the relationship between the life story of the candidate and the proof of heroic virtue. As one of the most vocal proponents of the reform and as a theologian, he had long defended the notion that each saint presents a unique profile in holiness. "The virtues are like sap to a flower," he said, fashioning an uneasy simile from horticulture. "The virtues must be proved to make sure that the sap is there. But how the sap flourishes depends on the individual life. Is it a rose? Is it a tulip? Here we have a St. Francis, there a St. Benedict, over there a St. Ignatius. The flowering depends upon the unique elements in each person, and among these unique qualities are the unique gifts God has bestowed on that person. So, through the study of historical circumstances, we want to make the uniqueness of the saint emerge. Only in that way will his or her life carry a message that has meaning to the people of today. And, of course, we have to translate that message so that it does reach people, and does not remain in the convoluted phraseology of the sacristy."

It was agreed: the only way for me to understand the relation of the sap to the flower—of the virtues to the life—was to examine a *positio* myself.

THE LIFE AND VIRTUES OF
KATHARINE DREXEL

THE CAUSE OF Katharine Drexel (1858–1955) was tailor-made for the reformers' new, more organic approach to the lives of the saints. Born in Philadelphia in the decade prior to the Civil War, she died in the decade that preceded the civil rights movement of the 1960s. She was the foundress of the Sisters of the Blessed Sacrament for Indians and Colored People and, as an heiress to one of the great family fortunes of the United States, undoubtedly the wealthiest American woman ever to don a religious habit. In the course of her ninety-seven years, Katharine Drexel gave away an estimated twenty million dollars, nearly all of it to missions and schools devoted to black Americans and Native Americans, the particular objects of her—and her religious congregation's—apostolate. As founding mother superior, she was personally responsible for establishing 145 Catholic missions and 12 schools for Indians, and 50 schools for "colored people," as blacks were then called, including Xavier University of New Orleans, the first Catholic college in the United States for blacks. Until Katharine Drexel came along, it could be fairly said, the Catholic bishops of the United States tended to regard blacks as Protestants—which nearly all of them were and still are—and thus none of their pastoral concern.

To judge by the *positio*, Katharine Drexel was as holy as she was generous. Long before she died, she was regarded as a saint by the sisters of her congregation. Her funeral in Philadelphia indicated that the sisters were not alone in their assessment: thousands of mourners turned out, snarling traffic for blocks around the church. In the years that followed, more than four thousand people—white, black, and

Indian—claimed cures and other divine favors received by invoking her intercession. On March 2, 1966, little more than a decade after her death, Archbishop (later Cardinal) John J. Krol opened an Ordinary Process on her behalf. Altogether, six cardinals, nine archbishops, and forty-one bishops from the United States, plus four religious and civic associations, wrote to the congregation in support of her cause. By 1980, her writings had been cleared for doctrinal purity and the final round of testimony—the Apostolic Process—was initiated. Katharine Drexel seemed well on her way to official sainthood.

Although the Drexel cause was proceeding faster than most, serious problems emerged. In the first place, the memory of her pioneering educational efforts on behalf of blacks and Native Americans had faded in the glare of the civil rights movement of the sixties. If the United States had produced a saint who stood up for minorities, it was commonly believed, that person was the martyred Dr. Martin Luther King, Jr., a black Baptist preacher. Measured against King's dramatic struggles and achievements in leading a freedom movement based on explicitly biblical appeals and warrants (and on Gandhi's principle of nonviolence), Katharine Drexel's efforts seemed limited, institutional, rather cautious, and religiously maternalistic. By the seventies, Native Americans, too, were asserting their rights and tribal identities in ways that made her missionary work appear to be a form of religious colonization. Thus, if Katharine Drexel were to be canonized a saint, the postulation would have to rescue her from tides of historical change and demonstrate how her unique exercise of heroic virtue affected the welfare of Native Americans and blacks.

In the second place, the idea of canonizing Mother Drexel—or anyone else, for that matter—no longer moved many American nuns; in light of the needs of the underprivileged, the cost of underwriting a process seemed an unnecessary, almost self-indulgent expenditure of funds. Indeed, Katharine Drexel herself had been of the opinion that no member of her religious order would ever be canonized because the money required for the process would be better spent on helping Indians and blacks. It was hardly surprising, therefore, that several mother superiors of Katharine Drexel's own religious order professed indifference to promoting her cause.

In Rome, some of the officials of the congregation also viewed Mother Drexel's cause with glazed eyes. The list of pending causes was already heavy with the names of mother foundresses, each of whom, it could be shown, had established her religious order to meet a specific spiritual and temporal need. What, the officials wanted to know, made Katharine Drexel different? Holy though she may have been, canonization is supposed to be reserved for Servants of God whose life and work are of more than local significance. This, at any rate, is how Monsignor James McGrath of Philadelphia, vice-postulator of the cause, read reactions when he visited the congregation in 1980. "Like most Europeans," McGrath told me, "they didn't understand how deeply segregation had affected American society and culture. And so they didn't appreciate how Katharine Drexel had conscienticized the American [Catholic] church to the needs of blacks and Indians, and that because of this her example would have universal appeal."

Fortunately, by the time the results of the Apostolic Process reached Rome, the rules of the game had already changed. The new norms requiring that even recent causes be presented according to the canons of critical historiography meant that the case for beatifying and canonizing Mother Drexel could be advanced by emphasizing the uniqueness of her apostolate on behalf of blacks and Native Americans at a time when few other Americans were concerned with their fate. Given the contemporary American concern with minorities, it was argued, the Drexel cause deserved priority consideration. As Father Robert Sarno, the only American on the congregation staff, put it, "The beatification of Katharine Drexel would counter the accusation that the Catholic Church did not do much for these underprivileged people."

The Drexel cause was assigned to Father Gumpel as relator and he, in turn, insisted on the aid of a capable American scholar to act as "external collaborator" in writing the *positio*. Cardinal Krol, who was not the sort of archbishop to allow his city to lose a potential saint, found just the sort of scholar Gumpel was looking for: Father Joseph Martino, a young priest who had recently completed a doctoral dissertation in history on one of Krol's predecessors, Archbishop James Ryan, a Philadelphia prelate who had worked closely with Katharine Drexel. Even though Martino was familiar with the historical period, it took him two years to research and write the *positio*. And that was the text—all sixteen hundred pages of it—by which the holiness of Katharine Drexel was judged.

The *positio* is bound in three volumes. The first and by far the longest is a biography of 1,118 pages including documents and footnotes. Volume 2 is 406 pages of selected testimony from thirty-four witnesses, nearly half of them nuns who had known or collaborated with Mother Drexel. The third volume, 89 pages, is the *informatio* summarizing the arguments and evidence for Katharine Drexel's holiness virtue by heroic virtue.

Martino's life of Katharine Drexel is prefaced by a fifty-six-page history of the United States with special attention to the emergence of blacks and Native Americans as segregated populations. The burden of this section is to show the need for a concerted Catholic effort to evangelize and educate blacks and Native Americans, and to explain why American Catholics, most of them immigrants, were slow to respond to that need. Against this background, he introduces Katharine Drexel as a young woman of enormous wealth and social position whose family is, in the Quaker-inspired tradition of Philadelphia, bred to noblesse oblige. Her uncle, Anthony Drexel, established and endowed Drexel University for underprivileged students— an example Katharine would remember later in founding Xavier University—and her father, an immensely wealthy banker, left millions to charity when he died in 1885. But it is her stepmother, Emma Bouvier Drexel, who emerges as the most important influence on young Katharine and her two sisters. Emma, Martino observes, gained a reputation as "the Lady Bountiful of Philadelphia" for her behind-the-scenes support of many charitable enterprises; she even ran a dispensary for the needy out of her own home which her daughters helped to service. Martino, however, makes no effort to explore this mother-daughter relationship beyond quoting a few letters between them; the psychosocial origin of character, I was discovering, is still not a standard feature of positiones.

What does matter is the development of Katharine's spiritual life and subsequent religious vocation. On this score, Martino is fortunate. From a very early age, it appears, the Drexel children were expected to write personal essays. In these, as well as in her many captivating letters written while traveling abroad, and especially in the spiritual diary she kept between the ages of fifteen and twenty-five, Katharine provides her positio writer with a rather full account of her spiritual strivings. From these sources Martino is able to demonstrate the origins and development of Katharine's lifelong devotion to the Blessed Sacrament. In one letter, written when she was just nine years old, young "Katie" asks her parents that she be allowed to make her First Holy Communion long before the usual (at that time) age of twelve. In another, written at age nineteen to Father James O'Connor, a parish priest who became her spiritual adviser, she indicates how little the social life of a Philadelphia debutante meant to her. In it, she dismisses her formal introduction to Philadelphia society at a lavish gala earlier that week with a fleeting reference to "a little party the other night where I made my debut." This moves Martino to a rare burst of authorial comment: "This may well be the understatement of the nineteenth century," he observes. "Probably no one else said so little about so much."

The decade following the death of her mother in 1883 at the age of forty-nine turns out to be the critical period of Katharine's life. Although Martino is able to show that she had at least one offer of marriage—which she rejected—there is little evidence that Katharine Drexel was interested in the married life. With the death of their father two years later, the three Drexel sisters become the beneficiaries of the interest on a trust fund worth fourteen million dollars. Each sister carves out a special area for her philanthropy: Elizabeth supports orphans, Louise chooses blacks, and Katharine, for reasons Martino is unable to explain, focuses on Indians. She is particularly anxious to find a way to provide more priests for the Indian missions. The greatest injustice in the world, she feels, is to deprive any group of the opportunity for intimate communion with Christ through reception of the Eucharist.

Throughout this period, Katharine is wrestling with the problem of what to do with her own life. In a long exchange of letters with O'Connor, who was assigned to Omaha, Nebraska, in 1876 as vicar-apostolic, she reveals her desire to join an order of contemplative nuns so she can devote herself full-time to a life of prayer and penance. Above all, she wants the opportunity to receive the Eucharist daily—a privilege which, in those days, was allowed only to priests and to nuns living in cloistered, contemplative communities. In one particularly eloquent and gripping letter, written from a hotel in San Remo, Italy, Katharine—now age 25—compares herself to "a little girl who wept when she found out that her doll was stuffed with sawdust and her drum was hollow ... I am disgusted with the world," she confides, suggesting that her mother's concern that she might someday enter a convent had been one reason why she had delayed so long in making that decision.

O'Connor, however, advises against it. As a woman of wealth and privilege, he feels, Katharine is ill-prepared for the austerities of the cloister. Instead, he urges her to take a vow of celibacy and, with the wealth at her disposal, to devote herself and her money to evangelizing the Indians and other people in need. Back and forth they fight by mail until, at O'Connor's suggestion, Katharine agrees to a compromise: she herself will found a new religious order of active rather than contemplative sisters who will devote themselves to missionary work among Indians and colored people (blacks and mulattos). And to satisfy her great desire for the Blessed Sacrament, she will write into her community's rules daily reception of the Eucharist.

The remainder of the *positio* details the founding of the religious community, its expansion as a missionary teaching order, her efforts to gain Rome's approval of the constitution she drew up for the order, and her final years of suffering as a result of several strokes. Most of the material is drawn from the order's archives, including Mother Drexel's many letters and directives to her charges; from previous biographies; and from the testimony gathered during the Ordinary and Apostolic processes. Martino's primary intent in these pages is to underline Katharine Drexel's unique and, from a financial perspective alone, indispensable role in extending the church's mission to Indians and blacks, and to demonstrate how this apostolic mission was connected to her personal holiness.

Although she lived under a vow of poverty, Katharine Drexel continued to receive approximately four hundred thousand dollars a year in interest from the trust fund set up by her father. This was, by the standards of her era, an enormous sum. Where another founder of a religious order might have used this largesse to endow the order's own institutions, Mother Drexel, believing that her religious order should stand on its own financial feet, used her inheritance to support specific projects, not all of them involving the Sisters of the Blessed Sacrament. She was, in fact, a one-woman charitable foundation, the financial court of first and last resort for bishops and priests seeking money to build or staff schools for Indians and blacks. In this regard, Martino observes, Mother Drexel received more than seventeen thousand letters during her life as a nun and was as scrupulous as an accountant in evaluating each request.

The magnitude of Katharine Drexel's financial contributions to the church can be measured by two examples from the *positio*. She gave more than a million dollars to the support of the Bureau of Catholic Indian Missions (BCIM). In addition, when the United States government began in 1890 to withdraw its support to Indian schools run under contract by religious organizations—most of which were Catholic—she pledged up to $100,000 a year for their support, thus becoming the person most responsible for keeping the mission schools open. Again, in the 1920s, it was Mother Drexel's gift of $750,000 which allowed the purchase of buildings for the establishment of Xavier University of New Orleans. The total of all her donations, Martino reports, is impossible to estimate because she preferred anonymity—partly out of humility, he writes, and partly because she felt that if her generosity were publicized, American Catholics would be less inclined to support the missions themselves. Thus, when Xavier University was dedicated, Mother Drexel sat anonymously in the balcony and forbade any mention of her name during the ceremonies.

Of the two populations she sought to evangelize and educate, blacks presented the most problems. Martino takes considerable pains to explain that despite emancipation, segregation was the rule in American life, including the Catholic Church. To that end, he summarizes at considerable length a letter entitled *De miserabili conditione Catholicorum nigrorum in America* ("On the miserable condition of Catholic negroes in America") written to the Holy See in 1903 by a Belgian missionary, Father Joseph Anciaux, who was working in the black missions in the American South. In the letter, which caused a considerable stir at the Vatican, Anciaux described the abuse of blacks by whites, and the former's lack of civil rights. The lynch mob, he said, was more common than fair judicial process. More to the point, Anciaux was critical of the attitude of American Catholics, including the hierarchy, toward blacks. In Martino's words:

> Anciaux believed that most Catholic priests abhorred working with Blacks because of racial prejudice. The Blacks, he said, were confined to segregated galleries in Catholic churches, and were not welcome to attend any Benedictine, Dominican or Jesuit college. Anciaux complained that even the Catholic University in Washington, D.C., was afraid to admit Blacks for fear of giving "offense." In regard to religious vocations, Anciaux stated that Black girls were denied admission to convents, and there were also girls who had been expelled from religious communities, even years after, once it was discovered that they were actually Black.

Anciaux was also convinced that the American bishops, with three exceptions, were doing and saying nothing in public on behalf of blacks. He cited by way of negative example a bishop of Savannah who had criticized President Theodore Roosevelt for inviting Booker T. Washington to dinner at the White House. Although he applauded the work of some of the priests who chose to work with blacks, the Belgian suggested that the American bishops establish a bureau, similar to the BCIM, to coordinate the church's efforts to bring Catholicism to blacks and to support black Americans who were already members of the church. And he suggested that Mother Drexel, whose work he praised, would be willing to provide much of the necessary funding for the bureau.

Anciaux's letter was brought to the attention of the American bishops who, with Mother Drexel's personal and financial support, eventually established the Catholic Board for Mission Work among the

Colored People (CBMWACP) in 1906. But the board never succeeded in becoming what Anciaux hoped it would be—an effective administrative channel for focusing Catholic efforts on behalf of American blacks. Indeed, it wasn't until 1946—eight years before the United States Supreme Court declared "separate but equal" public education unconstitutional—that the first Catholic schools (in St. Louis) were desegregated.

Martino cites Mother Katharine's support of the CBMWACP as an example of her efforts "to achieve racial justice." Elsewhere in his biography he mentions that she was opposed to the seating of blacks in segregated galleries within Catholic churches, and he is sensitive in describing the moral complexities faced by bishops who established segregated black parishes at the request of black Catholics themselves. Curiously, however, he cites no other evidence to indicate that Mother Drexel did or said anything of a "heroic" or "prophetic" nature in opposition to racial segregation or in favor of civil rights for blacks.

In his closing section on "The Spirituality Underlying Mother Katharine's Apostolic Zeal," Martino raises the issue of civil rights but immediately argues that it is irrelevant to her cause:

> Mother Katharine died in 1955, just as the Civil Rights Movement was having real success in improving the conditions of Blacks as American citizens. Perhaps a study will be done someday to analyze the number of efforts on the part of Mother Katharine to improve the civil status of Blacks and Indians . . .
>
> The only possible danger, however, in doing a survey on Mother Katharine's role in the Civil Rights Movement is that the study might be too severely limited. Only part of the story might be told. True, Mother Katharine rejoiced at the progress any human made in this world, especially her beloved Blacks and Indians. But she had a lofty vision of humanity which made her hope for more than just improvements in the legal status of Blacks and Indians. The vision was simply this: she was consumed by love of God and she was overwhelmed by the fact that God would love us so deeply. This profound love God had for us, in Mother Katharine's view, was seen in the fact that He would choose to dwell within us in the Holy Eucharist. Mother Katharine wanted everyone to know about God's love. She wanted everyone to have a chance to love Him in return, and she feared that without the knowledge of God, our human dignity was lessened considerably. True human dignity, according to Mother Katharine, meant freedom to achieve one's potential in this world, but it signified above all else coming into union with Jesus in the Holy Eucharist. If Mother worked

against injustice in education, it was because she feared that without proper schooling, Blacks and Indians might never come to know God sufficiently, never save their souls, and never achieve anything in this world worth possessing.

In sum, the life story of Katharine Drexel, as Martino presented it for the judgment of the congregation's theological consultants, was considerably less than a full-dress biography but something more than a mere recital of facts. What the reader finds there is a chronology of her life, set in a historical and social context to illuminate the importance of her work. The development of her character, for the purposes of the *positio*, essentially stops in her early thirties with Katharine's decision to found a religious order and her training as a novice nun. From that point on in the *positio*, the report of her activities and the impressions of others take over.

The interpretive scheme, to the extent there is one, is to show how Katharine's love of God achieved fruition in her apostolate to Indians and blacks. Martino does this by allowing "the facts" to speak for themselves. That she did not address herself directly to the questions of civil rights and racial segregation is, in his judgment, essentially beside the point. Important as those issues may be, Mother Katharine was concerned with something much more significant: the salvation of souls. Indeed, throughout the *vita* Martino argues that only by giving first place in her life to the love and worship of God was she able to do good works on behalf of Indians and blacks. And that, beneath the copious historical documentation, is the meaning he finds in her life. Thus, the moral of Katharine Drexel's life story, as presented to the theological consultors, was this: by putting first things first, she achieved the kind of moral perfection which the church looks for in canonizable saints.

But the *vita* or documented life story is not the only text on which the holiness of a candidate is based. There is also the testimony of witnesses which, together with the documentary evidence, forms the basis of the *informatio*, the document which sums up virtue by virtue the postulation's case for declaring a Servant of God worthy of veneration. In the case of Katharine Drexel, the external evidence for her virtue is drawn from the testimony of thirty-four witnesses. Of these, fifteen are nuns, all but two of them members of her own religious order. Five others are priests and six are bishops. The remainder, all laity, include five blacks, two white women, and one Native American.

None of the witnesses knew Katharine Drexel before she took her religious vows, and many of them knew her only by her reputation or through the work of the religious order she founded. Those who knew her best, not surprisingly, are her religious colleagues. But what they provide by way of intimate knowledge was offset, to some extent, by the presumption of personal bias. A theological consultor to the congregation, who asked me not to use his name, put the matter this way: "The problem, I find [with nuns as witnesses for their founder's canonization], is that these women have been taught since the novitiate to revere the mother foundress as a holy person. Psychologically, therefore, it is very difficult for them to say anything critical."

As in any judicial proceeding, the quality of the testimony depends on the quality of the questions—and the expertise of the questioner. Monsignor McGrath, who—despite what appears to be an obvious conflict of interest—was both the vice-postulator of the cause and the archdiocesan official responsible for oversight of the Ordinary Process, acknowledges that he and his colleagues were rather green at conducting such a tribunal: "We were proceeding without much experience," he says. "We would have been more probing if we had been better schooled in what to ask." Father Gumpel agrees: "It was," he concedes, "one of the poorest processes I have ever had the misfortune to examine."

To read the questions the witnesses were asked is to see that the interrogation was at once very formal and very gentle. Of the twenty-one witnesses who testified during the Ordinary Process, eleven were members of her congregation. In general, the sisters were asked to establish their relationship to Mother Drexel and offer evidence in support of each of the necessary virtues. Of the 141 questions, only 9 explicitly invited the witness to consider a negative answer. (E.g., "Do you consider that Mother Katharine Drexel practiced well the virtues of Faith, Hope, and Charity? If not, where did she fail in the practice of a) Faith; b) Hope; c) Charity?") The Apostolic Process, conducted 13 years later and scripted by officials of the congregation in Rome, was only slightly more probing and precise (see Appendix). And to read the responses as Martino collected them is to get a better sense of who Mother Drexel was, in the eyes of her admirers, and what they considered heroic virtue to be.

To begin with, none of the witnesses can recall any occasion in which Mother Drexel had acted less than virtuously, with one exception: one sister remembers that "she tossed a badly shrunken woollen garment at the Sister who had laundered it." Another nun who had traveled as her companion for thirteen years allowed that "over the years there was a decrease in her imperfections," but she does not say—nor is she asked—what those imperfections were. At one point during the Apostolic Process, the judge alludes to reports that Mother Drexel did not listen to complaints of subordinates, and that during her years as mother superior the Blessed Sacrament Sisters did not pay their employees a "just wage." However, these subjects are immediately dropped after the witness disclaims any knowledge of these reports. There is also some difference of opinion as to whether the mother superior really liked children. One sister is of the opinion that Mother Drexel had no "natural affection" for children; others assure the judge with stories of "goodies" she would give to the schoolchildren. And so it goes. Every effort, however modest, to probe into even the slightest possible fault is not sustained.

The primary purpose of gathering testimony, however, is not to discover a candidate's faults but to assess the quality of her virtues. To the questions of whether Katharine Drexel practiced the core virtues of faith, hope, and charity, the witnesses are unanimous in asserting that she did. From the testimony it is clear that Mother Drexel's personal faith was rooted in the Eucharist. It is also clear that it was this faith which motivated her missionary efforts on behalf of Indians and blacks. Her sisters, she decreed, were to "make them [Indians and blacks] living temples of Our Lord's Divinity." Her hope, too, was rooted in God's Providence—and in her assurance that God's will for her was manifested in O'Connor's advice to found a congregation against her own inclination to join a purely contemplative order. Her love of God was manifested by the depth of her personal prayer life and by her desire to kindle that love in others. On this point, Martino stresses that "This desire to inform the Indian and Negro of his right to know and love God was a moving factor of her mission, not any idea such as the current civil rights movement."

There is, nonetheless, some confusion among the witnesses over what the adjective "heroic" is supposed to mean. For the most part, the judges allow the witnesses to supply their own yardstick for measuring heroicity. Thus, Auxiliary Bishop Harold Perry of New Orleans, the first black to achieve that status in the American hierarchy, observes: "I think it means doing it [exercising a virtue] to a degree that is beyond ordinary human endurance, that is, lifted up to a higher degree of love and faith. I think she possessed this because of long years of perseverance; her impeccable life and her courage supported by prayer, especially her devotion to the Eucharist, over that long period was certainly heroic. She did all this with ease, spontaneously and joyfully."

Another bishop, William Connare of Greensburg, Pennsylvania, allows that "any woman who gives herself to God under the vows of poverty, chastity and obedience and lives those vows and spends the rest of her life that way, she is worthy of canonization." Occasionally, the judge himself supplies the marks of heroic virtue. "The notes for heroism," he tells one witness, "as indicated here, are: consistency, fidelity, promptness and love. Do you think," he then goes on to ask the witness, "those notes could be found in the work that she did?" In response, Bishop Warren Boudreaux of Houma-Thibodaux, Louisiana, where Mother Katharine established schools for blacks in the bayous, offers a simple description of heroic virtue in action: "My impression was that she wanted to do everything she could, the best that she could, as long as she could."

The questions that focus on Katharine Drexel's practice of the cardinal moral virtues (prudence, justice, fortitude, and temperance) as well as the "evangelical counsels" (her religious vows of poverty, chastity, and obedience) are interesting for the light they shed on her character. When it came to obeying bishops, one might justly conclude, she was prudent to a fault. Time and again, witnesses are asked for anecdotes illustrating her docility toward members of the hierarchy, and time and again they are able to satisfy the demand.* On one occasion, a nun recalls, Mother Drexel was wont to forgo taking a medicine which, experience had shown her, brought her no relief. But at the bishop's insistence, she complied. Others testify that she taught her charges to obey all authority as coming from God, including civil laws.

The testimony indicates that Mother Drexel embraced personal poverty as only someone bred to self-sufficiency can do. She darned her own stockings, occasionally repaired her own shoes, she was known to take time out to sew up a worn washcloth, and, according to one witness, was so loath to replace her own stitched-over religious habit that the sisters had to surreptitiously buy her new ones in her absence.

Her temperance was apparently a matter of considerable whispering among the sisters. Like most members of religious orders, male and female, Katharine Drexel practiced "the discipline"—that is self-flagellation and related forms of penance and self-denial. Martino provides the theological consultants with the following testimony, taken from the memoirs of Mother Mercedes, Mother Katharine's immedi-

---

* The response of retired Bishop Joseph McShea of Allentown, Pennsylvania, is interesting for the light it sheds on Drexel's heroic obedience to episcopal authority in relation to the docility of an earlier American saint. Asked about Drexel's obedience to bishops, McShea testifies: "Excellent. I never heard of any controversy that she had. Quite the opposite with Mother [Frances] Cabrini [canonized: 1946]. She fought with every bishop along the line, but it was usually about real estate problems and things like that. But Mother Katharine, I never heard of any dissent or any disagreement with bishops."

ate successor as superior of the order, regarding the foundress's penitential practices:

> Reverend Mother always impressed me as a soul who practiced mortification in an heroic degree. In the early years, or rather in the first year of my Novitiate, having charge of the cleaning of her cell and office at St. Michael, I accidentally stumbled one day on a heavy discipline all blood stained. Later on in the same year, having occasion to sleep in the same part of her house in which her cell was located, I was many times awakened by fearful scourging which was kept up with some vigor and strength for such a long time that it fairly sickened me. Later on, the Vicar General, Mother M. James, showed me a discipline which she had surreptitiously abstracted from Mother's drawer, which was filled with small iron points and the whole almost saturated through and through with blood. I knew she practiced kneeling on her finger tips behind the main altar after night prayers from 15 to 20 minutes at a time, also with arms outstretched in the form of a cross for like or longer periods . . .
>
> Then again, she wore iron chains [a]round [her] waist and arms and the hair shirt quite frequently. At meals she was the most abstemious. For over thirty years she was never known to take a dessert or anything that was unusually palatable, such as the community had on Feast days. When the dish was presented to her, it was noticed that she always took the toughest or worst portion of meat, saying that she liked that the best. Until forbidden by the Cardinal, or her Spiritual Director, I do not know which, she fasted very severely all the Lenten season and during the other fast and abstinence days of the church . . .
>
> In kneeling she very seldom used any support, even during Mass or during the half hour's adoration before the Blessed Sacrament. In sitting, she nearly always placed herself at the extreme edge of the chair and very seldom reclined against its back.
>
> In travelling, no matter how young or robust was the Sister companion she invariably insisted on carrying the heaviest bag or suitcase, and never unless absolutely under obedience to do so would she travel in any but the cheapest way, saying that she preferred the day coaches that were crowded to their upmost capacity.

In addition to testifying to Mother Katharine's heroic virtues, the witnesses were asked, in one form or another, what pastoral benefits the church could expect from declaring her a saint. This line of questioning is especially apparent in the Apostolic Process conducted in 1980–1981 and indicates that by this time there was some concern, on the part of both the interviewers and some of the interviewees, about how her canonization would be received in the United States, especially among blacks and Native Americans. It was in this context that the question of her attitude toward racial segregation laws arose.

The first witness, retired Bishop Joseph McShea of Allentown, Pennsylvania, thought her canonization "would be a great stimulus to further missionary work among the Blacks." It would also, he said, "bring out not only the successes but the failures and the difficulties and it would show how this heroic woman was able to muster a force of other women, dedicated women, and cope with the problems and do so very, very much." But he also worried that the canonization might fuel complaints from blacks that during her long years as mother superior she "didn't accept Black candidates" as members of her religious congregation. On the other hand, he did not expect any such "protests" from Native Americans.

The second witness, Bishop Connare, was of the opinion that Mother Drexel would serve "as a great example of racial justice." In response to another question, the bishop adds: "It would be a recognition of the sincere interest that the church has had in these minorities. We are often criticized about what we have not done with the Blacks and native Americans. Here we have an example of somebody who did something positively. Out of her schools we have evidence of a lot of fine Christian families who have come from those schools. There are a lot of people like that and a good number of vocations to the religious life and the priesthood."

The testimony of a third bishop, Warren Boudreaux of Houma-Thibodaux, Louisiana, is of particular interest. Boudreaux had no personal contact with Mother Drexel, but as a priest he had served as secretary to Bishop Jules Jeanmard of Lafayette, Louisiana, which, at that time, had two-thirds of all the black Catholics in the United States within its ecclesiastical boundaries. From the questions put to Boudreaux, it is obvious that the tribunal was trying to establish the unique importance of Mother Katharine's work in providing education for blacks in that heavily Catholic area. When asked what "the church was doing for them [blacks] prior to Mother Katharine Drexel," Boudreaux responded in three ways. First he defended Bishop Jeanmard, especially his efforts in bringing black priests into his diocese. He then noted how difficult it was in the twenties and thirties to do much more than this for blacks. Racial integration of schools, he observed, was forbidden by civil law. "So I must say honestly," he testified, "that Mother Drexel did very little in the field of integration, but I think it is because of the fact that in a sense she could have suffered greatly from the law." The bishop later went on to explain why he thought Mother Drexel should be canonized:

> I think this is true, that the Church needs a witness for history's sake. The Protestants had their Martin Luther King [Jr.], but here is a Catholic woman who, at a time when it was not popular, and at a time when in general Blacks were looked down upon, truly had great success to bear witness to the love of Christ and of the Church for the most neglected of God's people, and that there was within the Church a concerned, a loved and successful work among the Blacks, and I am sure among the Indians, and that Mother Katharine was a witness to it.

One of the most obvious differences between Dr. King and Mother Drexel is their attitudes toward laws restricting the civil rights of blacks. Both, it should be said, suffered because of the laws, though obviously in very different and unequal ways. Since the laws and the mores of the United States, and of the southern states in particular, forbade the mixing of races, Mother Drexel was constrained to exclude blacks and mulattoes from joining her religious congregation. Had she done otherwise, she would have had to segregate her own convents because the law did not allow black and white adults to share living quarters. Moreover, there were already two religious orders of blacks, the Oblate Sisters of Providence and the Sisters of the Holy Family, and according to the testimony of the Oblates' superior general, Sister Marie Enfanta Gonzales, Mother Drexel did not want to draw black candidates away from the all-black congregations.

Nonetheless, nowhere in the testimony do the witnesses reveal Katharine Drexel's personal views about the nation's segregationist laws. Nor is there any indication that she ever expressed opposition to those laws or encouraged her black students to do so. On the contrary, the only witness to touch on this issue indicates that in this matter, as in others, Katharine Drexel's primary concern was obedience. Asked whether Mother Drexel was "just toward people in general," Sister Mary David Young, a former superior general of the order, replies:

> As far as I know she was. She always talked to us about trying to see that the people for whom we worked were given their rights as far as we were able to do it. Mostly it was with regard to the church and religious rights, that we should try to work with that because in most of the places where we worked there was a great disregard for the Black people, even in church. I know that one of the things that most of us resented a great deal in working, particularly in the South, was that the separation [of the races] was made so prominent. The thing I think that she did

there was that she tried to tell us not to encourage [others] to disobey the law; it was the law. But we should try to be as careful about that as we could ourselves. For instance, every place you went, even in church, the Black people had to sit in the back; they weren't allowed to go up to communion until all the white people had been given Holy Communion. She used to tell us that this was not right but that if it was the law then they had to conform to it as far as they could but that we should try to see what we could do about removing those kinds of things.

As I observed earlier in examining the life story, Martino dismisses the issue of civil rights as essentially irrelevant to his task of proving Katharine Drexel's heroic virtue. But is it? The question naturally arises: in pleading the cause of a figure whose claim to holiness rests so much on her work among American blacks, does not "heroic virtue" require something more than acquiescence in what was, after all, an obvious and malignant form of racial apartheid? The issue is a delicate one. On the one hand, it seems unfair to judge Mother Drexel or any other saint by the moral standards of a later age—in this case by the standards of racial justice established by the civil rights movement, which arose a quarter century after she retired as head of her religious order. Still, saints are expected to meet standards beyond the norms for the rest of humankind. In so doing, they remind others, in the manner of prophets, that the Gospel has standards of behavior which are not those of the world, and which all Christians are called to meet.

To judge by the *positio*, the answer seems to be this: in the church's classical hierarchy of Christian virtues, personal charity toward others ranks higher than doing justice by them. More precisely, love of neighbor rooted in love of God and manifested by personal attention to individuals more closely approximates the example of Jesus than does achieving justice for a whole class of people, particularly when justice is instanced, as in this case, by concern for the social and civil rather than the religious well-being of a subject people. As we observed at the end of chapter 4, "political holiness" would require the saint-makers to think in a new key. Thus, to give the virtue of justice more importance than Mother Drexel attached to it would do violence not only to her own understanding of the virtues but to that of the church as well. In any event, as one historian of Christian sainthood has recently observed, "The saints have not typically sought or advocated political solutions to the problems of the needy—and certainly they have not been inclined toward revolution."

Even so, it is obvious from the *positio* that everyone connected with the cause expects the beatification (and possible canonization) of

Katharine Drexel to serve a specific pastoral purpose—namely, to demonstrate in and through this woman that the Catholic Church in the United States worked heroically for the true liberation (i.e., liberation from sin through conversion) of Indians and blacks. Thus, in his introduction to Martino's *informatio*, Father Gumpel, as relator, offers two reasons, one historical, the other theological, for declaring Katharine Drexel a saint:

> The truth about a situation must be determined through a fair presentation of the objective facts. The truth and the supporting facts may indeed exist, but to become effective, they first have to be known and acknowledged.
>
> Very often, the figure of a person connected with the objective facts can be the means by which the true story is brought to the attention of others. Mother Mary Katharine Drexel is such a person. By studying her holy and virtuous life, one sees the authentic history of the evangelization of the American Blacks and Indians by the Catholic Church. Unfortunately, this history is often unknown, misunderstood or ignored. The hoped for canonization of Mother Katharine will contribute to comprehending fully the heroic efforts of so many Catholics in the United States in favor of these two neglected peoples.
>
> There is another pastoral relevance in Mother Katharine's Cause. Altruism is especially admired today, but often it is based on purely humanitarian motives. Inquiry into what inspired Mother Katharine in her work with the Blacks and Indians will show that Mother Katharine acted out of no other motive except the love of God. This love for God began in early childhood and soon became the only thing that mattered for this wealthy woman from upper class society. Precisely as she became consumed with love for her Heavenly Father, Katharine wished that others would come to the same knowledge. She was truly altruistic, and a major philanthropist. If she sought to improve the living standards of Blacks and Indians, however, two races who suffered so much discrimination in the United States, it was solely because Katharine was convinced that they had to know they were sons and daughters of God. Her works of charity and education were aimed at improving the relationship of the American Blacks and Indians with God.
>
> In a time when so many others are doing good for a variety of reasons, it is more important than ever to emphasize the specifically Christian basis for love of others, namely, God loved us first. Through the figure of Katharine Drexel, our contemporaries, especially the young, can see in the importance of God's Presence to us in the Blessed Sacrament as the starting point and support of all apostolic activity.

From this it seems apparent that the figure of Katharine Drexel has been assigned an enormous pastoral responsibility. In the first place, the church is counting on her beatification to support its claim to recognition as an institution which is and has been concerned with the true—that is, the spiritual—welfare of America's minorities. In this sense, the entire process on behalf of Katharine Drexel may fairly be seen as an act of historical recovery and redress. But do the historical facts, as found in the *positio*, really warrant such a conclusion?

On the basis of the evidence marshaled by Martino, one might well conclude that the American church, apart from Mother Drexel, did very little for their black compatriots during the century in which she lived. Indeed, it is precisely because the church was so unconcerned that Mother Drexel's missionary labors are worthy of note. It would appear, then, that by beatifying Mother Drexel the church is in fact drawing attention to the *lack* of concern for blacks on the part of the vast majority of American Catholics, including the hierarchy, in the century between emancipation and the civil rights movement.

In the second place, the beatification of Mother Drexel is expected to transmit a theological message: namely, that for Christians, altruism must be based on God's love for us, not on "purely humanitarian motives." As a statement of faith, the message is axiomatic. But precisely because it is axiomatic it is difficult to see what the figure of Katharine Drexel adds to that message to make it fresh or compelling, particularly to those who do not share her faith. On the contrary, it again appears that the pastoral purpose envisioned by the saint-makers is not altogether warranted by the facts. From her own letters it is apparent that Katharine Drexel's greatest desire was not to serve others as missionary or teacher, but to live the life of contemplative prayer and penance. Indeed, it is at least arguable that her altruism did not proceed from her perception that "God loved us first" but was ingested from the example of her family, especially her large-hearted stepmother. Since the *positio* makes no effort to account for her character apart from "spiritual" categories, there is no way to determine from the evidence provided what her real motivations were. The "higher," or religious motive is simply presumed.

These observations, if true, do not make her apostolic work less valuable. But they do tend to blur the message her beatification is meant to convey. That Katharine Drexel abandoned her desire to become a contemplative nun and accepted the compromise urged later by Bishop O'Connor was undoubtedly a noble and pious act of self-disregard, but this, it seems to me, in no way makes her the exceptional or exemplary figure that one expects of a saint.

On the other hand, if, as seems likely, the beatification of Katharine Drexel is expected to demonstrate that altruism inspired by the love of God is *superior* to altruism based on purely humanitarian motives, the *positio* plainly fails to make its case. In order to find such a message in her life, it seems to me, there would have to be evidence that Mother Drexel went beyond what one might expect, say, from a humanistically motivated nurse who also devoted her life to helping American Indians and blacks. At the very least, one might expect from a saint some evidence of transformation, both in herself and in those she touched. Yet nowhere in either the life story or the testimony is there any indication that the needy and neglected people she served had anything of spiritual value to teach Mother Drexel. Nowhere is it said or implied that she grew in love of God or neighbor as a result of serving others. All the *positio* tells us is that, in the eyes of her colleagues, she was an exemplary nun whose inherited wealth enabled her and her coworkers to meet an evangelistic need that the American church and its bishops could not accomplish without her. In short, her holiness seems to be confined to a compartment in her life that is separated, as if by a nun's veil, from her altruistic work.

None of this is to suggest that Katharine Drexel did not develop spiritually, much less that she is unworthy of beatification. But it is to question whether the *positio* accomplishes what it sets out to do. The fundamental problem, as I see it, is that the documented life story and the testimony of the witnesses do not really mesh so that a rounded, adult personality—the "deeper personality" about which Molinari spoke—can emerge. Nowhere are the virtues and the life story fused so that the reader can see, in Molinari's metaphor, how the sap produced the flower. On the one hand, we have a biography which never takes us inside Katharine Drexel after her crisis of vocation. On the other, we have testimony from witnesses which is essentially episodic, impressionistic, spiritually sterotypical—a series of snapshots rather than an integrated sequence of moving images. As a result, the relationship between her spirituality and her altruism is presumed rather than demonstrated.

In neither the *vita* nor the testimony is the reader afforded a lively sense of who Mother Drexel was for the last sixty years of her life, or how one virtue affected another. In particular, there is no way to determine from the *positio* whether Mother Drexel's apparent silence regarding racial segregation was a sign of heroic prudence, a lack of fortitude, or an excess of obedience. What is missing is any analysis of how she integrated the virtues attributed to her. In sum, I found nothing in the *positio* which shows development of character, spiritual insight achieved through doubt or adversity or moral confusion, mistakes made, weaknesses overcome—nothing, in other words, which would reveal that unique profile in holiness which the theologians tell us distinguishes one saint from another.

Perhaps I was expecting too much from the *positio* on Katharine Drexel. Certainly, I was demanding more in the way of theological insight and exploration of character than the author himself felt called upon to deliver. Shortly after his *positio* was turned over to the theological consultors, Martino reflected on his two-year assignment. His task, as he understood it, was not to prepare a full-dress biography of Katharine Drexel but "to present a balanced picture" of the candidate, keeping in mind "what is necessary to make a case for this woman being declared venerable"—namely, her virtues—and allowing whatever flaws he might discover in her character "to show through." But in fact he didn't find any flaws—nor, he told me, did he expect to. He had read, he said, a biography of Katharine Drexel while studying for the priesthood and, like other Philadelphia Catholics, he had developed a habit of praying to her. Nothing in the testimony, the letters, or the archival materials altered that early impression. "I don't know what the theological consultors will make of my work," he said, "but if there isn't heroic virtue here, then I don't know where you find it."

The morning of the consultors' meeting Martino was on hand to answer their questions and respond to any criticisms they might raise. The session lasted little more than an hour. Father Sarno—who conducted the meeting in the place of the promoter general, Monsignor Petti, because the latter does not speak English—insisted that each consultor take at least five minutes to express any reservations he might have regarding the persuasiveness of the *positio*. There was a brief discussion of whether Martino had included sufficient material on how Mother Drexel had governed her religious community. Sarno himself asked Martino if he thought he had included enough documentation on Mother Drexel's spiritual perseverance during her last fifteen years, when she was sickly and semisenile. But there were no questions raised about her stand on racial segregation or civil rights, no doubts about her holiness or the proofs of heroic virtue. When the votes were read, all nine of the consultors (including one who was absent) approved.

I was anxious, of course, to check my own reactions against those of the theological consultors who judged her *positio*. But the congregation's rules forbid consultors from discussing pending causes, or why they voted as they did. I could only conclude, therefore, that my reading of the *positio* was essentially out of tune with those of the experts.

Once again, I was wrong.

Several of the congregation's theological consultors, I discovered, had in recent months voiced many of the same objections I found with the structures used in proving heroic virtue. Their criticisms were not directed at any one *positio* but at the received methods and assumptions by which the evidence for holiness is conventionally organized and judged. Although their criticisms were kept strictly within the congregation, Gumpel himself later alluded to some of them in print:

> It is common knowledge that a number of highly competent theologians who are conversant with the work of our Congregation question the wisdom of dealing with the individual virtues by following the classical system of the Scholastics. They are of the opinion that by dividing and subdividing the virtues, one runs the risk of losing sight of the spiritual unity of the life of a Servant of God. They fear too that this schematic approach impedes one from highlighting and grasping the most typical and personal elements in the spirituality of the person whose life is under examination.

One of the critics eventually agreed to talk with me providing I did not use his name. Like many of the theological consultants to the congregation, he is an Italian, a member of a religious order, and a professor of spirituality at one of Rome's pontifical universities. In the course of a two-hour conversation at his monastery one evening, he outlined a series of interlocking issues which, he said, have produced considerable differences of opinion among the congregation's corps of consultants.

In the first place, he said, there is a general concern that too many of the men and women proposed for sainthood are "archaeological figures only—good people who were founders or members of religious orders, but whose holiness does not inspire people of today. The problem is that we do not know how to present these people so that they will have value for our culture."

What's more, he said, "many of the consultors themselves live in a rather closed clerical world and so have a rather static idea of holiness. They are archivists, really, rather than theologians. They are quite content to consider the proofs for each of the virtues one by one rather than in relation to each other because that is what they are used to. In some *positiones*, the proof of virtue is almost a quantitative measure: so much testimony for this virtue, so much for that. The problem with this approach is that it focuses on the quantity of faith and hope and so on and not on the process. This approach I cannot accept."

"Why not?" I asked.

"Because it is not natural. A person becomes a saint by living out a project of holiness, always tending toward greater spiritual synthesis. In this process, the virtue of purity may stand out at one stage of life, charity in another, contemplation in a third, and so on. The spiritual life, if it is dynamic, passes through different phases, with a certain virtue emphasized in each. What we as consultors have to discern in people is this process of holiness as it is being lived out. But in most *positiones* we can't see this."

"Is the problem with the schematized way the virtues are presented or with the way the life story is organized and written?"

"Both. Occasionally, a relator and his collaborator will use the documentation to interpret the life in a dynamic way, but the form used by the congregation really doesn't allow that. When I receive a *positio* from the congregation, I personally try to read it in a dynamic way. I try to see what spiritual process is at work. But when I give my vote, I have to stick to the traditional format. If I want to speak up at the meetings, I have to follow the rules."

"Can't you challenge the material? Can't you veto a *positio* that fails to provide the dynamic you are looking for?"

He smiled. "You misunderstand. Many consultors are very comfortable with the juridical way of presenting the virtues and the traditional categories for thinking about holiness. Their own spiritual formation was very clerical and they look at the documentation in a very clerical way." He paused, trying to explain. "I'm talking about two different worlds—theirs and ours—two different sensitivities, two different cultural attitudes. In the world they come from holiness exists in a certain way and always will. Whereas we . . ."

"How would you change the way *positiones* are written?" I interjected.

"I haven't thought that through. What we are asking for is something new, a deeper interpretation of the life and the virtues. All we can do, we have been told, is to insist on change. And if enough of us insist, perhaps change will come."

The writing of *positiones*, it appears, is a genre in search of its proper form. Once its form was determined by convention—the spiritual saga—then by an essentially alien method, the juridical. Now, with the reform, it lacks its own specific canons of science or of art. The genre it most closely approximates is biography. Like biography, a *positio* transforms a life into a text. But unlike most biographies, it attempts to illuminate what is hidden—namely, the movement and moments of grace. For this kind of biography, what is needed is not just critical historiography but theological imagination. In this sense, the writing of *positiones* resembles the translation of a poem from one language to another: to be concerned only with the message is to lose the poetry. It is to suppose that the meaning of holiness can be extracted from its particular sounds, shape, music.

What the theological consultant I spoke with was looking for—what the whole movement of reform was straining to capture, it seemed to me—is the melody of grace particular to each life that is lived with the spiritual integrity required of a saint. And that is what I missed in reading the *positio* on Mother Drexel. It's not enough, I thought, to be able to identify the notes of holiness, nor to arrange them according to a theologically acceptable pattern. One had to listen for the music, the combinations of tones and halftones and overtones, of rests and pauses and silences, of motifs and leitmotivs, that make for the harmony of holiness.

CHAPTER EIGHT

THE HARMONICS OF HOLINESS: INTERPRETING THE LIFE OF GRACE

EVERY YEAR, THE Congregation for the Causes of Saints processes a number of "ancient" causes—that is, Servants of God who died so long ago that there are no longer any witnesses who can testify to their heroic virtues. Some of these causes are so ancient—Queen Isabella I of Spain, who died in 1504, is an example—that it is difficult to imagine what "pastoral purpose" would be served by making them saints. Others, such as Father Junípero Serra (1713–1784), the Franciscan friar who founded a string of missions in California, have retained such popular devotion and historical interest that their beatification seems almost superfluous.

From the perspective of the saint-makers, ancient causes have certain disadvantages. If the candidate is not a well-known figure, the canonization process may appear to be a needless exercise in archaeological hagiography. On the other hand, if the candidate is of substantial historical interest, then the postulation must deal with secular opinion, both popular and expert, which is typically skeptical of saintly reputations. For example, in the case of Isabella, whose *positio* is ready for judgment , the church will have to explain how a monarch who revived the Spanish Inquisition and expelled the Jews from Spain merits canonization as a saint. As for Father Serra, when the Vatican announced in 1985 that he was ready for beatification, certain Native American activists, supported by a few historians, charged the Spanish missionary with mistreatment of the Indians. Although their criticism did not alter the judgment of the congregation, the threat of an unseemly protest did force Pope John Paul II to cancel plans to beatify Serra during his pilgrimage through California in May 1987. Instead, the ceremony was held on September 25, 1988, in the safer surroundings of St. Peter's Square.

But ancient causes also offer saint-makers an important opportunity to identify with greater clarity the candidate's unique claims to holiness. Precisely because there are no witnesses to testify to the candidate's heroic virtue, the case of holiness must be made solely through the documented life story. Thus the writer of the *positio* must rely on the candidate alone to provide both the evidence of heroic virtue and the way in which those virtues were manifest in concrete historical circumstances. In short, historical causes by their very nature impel the postulation to reveal the candidate's unique response to grace by providing a genuinely theological as well as historical interpretation of the subject's life.

Of all the historical causes to reach the congregation since the reform of 1983, none is more arresting than the case of Mother Cornelia Connelly, founder of the Society of the Holy Child Jesus. Certainly it is one of the most delicate and complicated to confront the congregation's judges. Long before her death in 1879, Cornelia Connelly had aroused considerable controversy and, at times, even embarrassment within the church. She was at one and the same time a wife and mother and a nun. Her husband, Pierce, was a priest who eventually died apostate. His insistence that he was called to the priesthood had devastating effects on their three children, and his wife became the object of a scandalous lawsuit, *Connelly* v. *Connelly*, in the courts of Protestant England when he demanded the restitution of conjugal rights long after the church had agreed to separation and she had made a vow of perpetual chastity. Nearly seventy years after her death, Cornelia's reputation was such that some English bishops and priests stoutly opposed the society's efforts to open a process for her canonization. It took another thirty years to gather and assess the historical documentation and to produce a three-volume life story of 1,637 pages. But even then there was serious concern among the saint-makers that the life of this extraordinary woman would, if made known through canonization, scandalize Catholics of the late twentieth century. After all, the church has never before canonized a nun who was married to a priest.

I first became aware of Cornelia Connelly in the fall of 1986.

Gumpel and Molinari, who were in charge of her cause, suggested I speak with Sister Elizabeth Mary Strub, an American and former superior general of the Society of the Holy Child Jesus, who had been assigned to write the *informatio* proving her foundress's heroic virtue. Strub, it turned out, is a pioneer: the first woman to prepare a document for the congregation's judgment.*

"Let's face it," Elizabeth said one afternoon over lunch, "Cornelia's life story reads like a Victorian soap opera. The fact that she survived at all is, I think, heroic." The wine arrived and then the pasta. By the time we had finished our salad, fruit, and espresso, an hour had passed and Elizabeth was still only at the halfway point in Cornelia's long and fitful life. Rather than hear the story secondhand, she urged me to read the *positio* myself. "I think you'll see that Cornelia speaks to every woman who has suffered from ruptured personal relationships through divorce, alienation of children, and so on. In this sense she really is a very contemporary woman. A saint for our times."

To read the *positio* on Cornelia Connelly is to recognize at once that she is not a conventional candidate for sainthood. Theology aside, her life appears to be so relentlessly episodic that it challenges even the most adroit biographer's efforts to find a coherent thread.

The Good and Bad Times of Cornelia Connelly

BORN IN PHILADELPHIA in 1809, Cornelia Peacock was raised a Presbyterian. At the age of fourteen she went to live with a half sister, Isabella, after the death of both her parents. In 1831 she was baptized into the Protestant Episcopal Church and, over the objections of Isabella, married the Reverend Pierce Connelly, an Episcopal priest. Like Katharine Drexel, Cornelia was well educated by tutors at home. She was slight, poised, and, as her photographs reveal, quite beautiful. Pierce was five years her senior, a graduate of the University of Pennsylvania who studied law briefly before turning to the ministry.

Shortly after their wedding, the Connellys moved to Natchez, Mississippi, where Pierce became rector of Holy Trinity Church, serving the established planter and merchant class. By all accounts they were an immensely happy, devoted couple and well received by their par-

---

* The rest of the *positio* was also prepared by a woman, the late Sister Ursula Blake, the first collaborator on the cause, whose work Strub completed.

ishoners. Pierce's salary was soon raised and, guided by parishioners, he invested advantageously in land. Within four years, Cornelia gave birth twice, to a son, Mercer, and a daughter, Adeline. In 1835, Pierce was appointed chairman of the Episcopal Convention of the Southwest, a position which augured well for a future bishopric.

But in the same year, a wave of anti-Catholic hysteria swept across the United States in reaction to massive Catholic immigration from Europe. Wild accusations against Catholics prompted Pierce to take up a detailed study of Roman Catholic beliefs and practices. Cornelia joined him in his studies and by the end of the year, Pierce had become so uncertain in his own beliefs that he resigned his parish and journeyed to St. Louis to consult with Bishop Joseph Rosati about conversion. In doing so, Pierce sacrificed a promising career, and with it, an assured financial future for his family. But he had the full support of his wife: "I have perfect confidence in the piety, integrity and learning of my dear husband," she wrote to her half sister. "I am ready to submit to whatever he believes to be the path of duty."

As it turned out, Pierce saw his path leading to ordination as a Roman Catholic priest, despite the fact that he was a husband and father. The Catholic Church, he was told, does occasionally ordain married men, but such exceptions are rare and require Vatican scrutiny. After seeing Rosati, Pierce took his family to Rome in order to study the church more closely before committing himself—and to present his plea for ordination to the authorities at the Vatican. While the family waited in New Orleans for passage to Italy, Cornelia decided not to wait for her husband's decision. She presented herself for instruction in the faith and was received into the Roman Catholic Church.

In Rome, Pierce petitioned the Vatican's Holy Office for admittance to the church, and to consideration for the priesthood. His petition was so compelling that, after receiving Pierce in a personal audience, Pope Gregory XVI was moved to tears. Two months after his arrival, Pierce was received into the church. But the question of ordination was not so easily resolved. Since celibacy is required of priests in the church's Latin rite, Vatican officials suggested that he consider the Eastern (Greek) rite, which ordains married men. Pierce ignored this proposal. There were no Eastern-rite parishes in the United States for him to serve, and his career horizons would be limited, since only celibates can become Eastern-rite bishops.

Pierce Connelly was a charismatic young man who immediately impressed the Vatican's ranking churchmen and the Roman nobility; Cornelia, for her part, impressed with her quick intelligence, charm, and a classical profile that reminded others of Greek statues. Together, the Connellys were welcomed into Rome's international high society. Among their most important friends were the English Catholic John Talbot, earl of Shrewsbury, who took Pierce with him to England for five months and introduced him to influential British Catholics. In her husband's absence, Cornelia tended the children while staying at Lord Shrewsbury's Roman palazzo. During this time, she also studied languages, music, and painting—she had both a good voice and a good eye—and worked among the poor alongside Talbot's saintly daughter, Gwendalin, who had married into the noble Borghese family.

But at heart Cornelia was profoundly disturbed. She came from a Protestant tradition which not only ordained married men but preferred them to be married. It gradually dawned on her that if Pierce became a Catholic priest, she would have to give him up. She took her troubles to Father John McClosky, a young priest studying in Rome who was later to become cardinal archbishop of New York. "Is it necessary for Pierce to make this sacrifice and sacrifice me?" she asked. "I love my husband and my darling children. Why must I give them up? I love my religion and why cannot we remain happy—as the earl of Shrewsbury's family? Why?"

After her husband's return to Rome, Cornelia became pregnant with their third child. Pierce had two more audiences with the pope, including one with Cornelia at his side. The family them moved on to Vienna where the irrepressible Pierce had a twenty-minute visit with Prince Metternich, Europe's leading diplomat, and another with the Archduke Maximilian, who treated him as a friend. In Vienna, a second son, John Henry, was born. In July, a bank crisis broke out in the United States and Pierce was forced to return to Natchez to find employment. At the invitation of the Jesuits, he and Cornelia decided to serve the church as schoolteachers. Pierce accepted a position teaching English at a Jesuit college in rural Grand Coteau, Louisiana, in exchange for a small house and a free education for their elder son, Mercer. Cornelia supplemented the family income by teaching music at an academy for girls run by the Religious of the Sacred Heart. She was twenty-nine and the mother of three children under age six. For the first time in their married lives, the Connellys were poor but, by all accounts, quite content.

There began then a series of incidents which were to totally transform the lives of Cornelia and her husband. In the summer of 1839, their fourth child, Mary Magdalen, died six weeks after birth. Just before Christmas, Cornelia made a four-day retreat with the Sacred

Heart Sisters at which she was introduced by the Jesuit retreat master to the *Spiritual Exercises* of St. Ignatius. Later, she would insist that during these three days she experienced a profound conversion of heart. She would need it. In February, a playful Newfoundland dog knocked John Henry, just thirty months old, into a boiler of scalding cane syrup. There were no doctors available and so for two days Cornelia held the child in her arms until he died. Eight months later, while making a retreat himself, Pierce told his wife that he was now certain God was calling him to the priesthood in the Roman Catholic Church and asked for her support.

Cornelia had been expecting—and dreading—Pierce's declaration. By then she was aware that to agree to his wishes would mean their separation for life and thus the breakup of the family. It would mean that she herself would have to take a vow of perpetual chastity and never remarry. In light of this, Cornelia's response, duly authenticated, was heroic in its selflessness and restraint. She reminded Pierce that the choice he was urging on both of them was a weighty matter and urged him to consider it deeply and twice over. If it still seemed to be God's will—and only then—she would agree: "Great as the sacrifice is, if God asks it of me, I am ready to make it to Him with all my heart."

As a test of his resolve, Pierce and Cornelia agreed to a period of sexual abstinence. She was, in any case, already pregnant with their fifth child, Pierce Francis, who was born in the spring of 1841. Just before and after his birth, Cornelia made two eight-day retreats, during which she began to think seriously about taking religious vows if Pierce were to follow through on his plans to become a Catholic priest.

The following year, Pierce broke up the family unit—against the advice of Bishop Anthony Blanc of New Orleans, a friend of the Connellys. He sold their home and went to England, stopping along the way to give major addresses to churches in Baltimore as a fairly prominent convert. In England he placed Mercer, age nine, in a boarding school and applied—unsuccessfully—to enter the Jesuits. Cornelia moved with the two remaining children into a two-room cottage on the convent grounds at Grand Coteau and for the next fourteen months took up a routine of prayer and work patterned after the sisters' spiritual regimen. Pierce, meanwhile, became a traveling tutor to Robert Berkeley, the scion of a wealthy British Catholic family, a position which brought him to Rome in 1843 where he pressed his request for ordination. By now, Pope Gregory regarded Pierce as an old friend and, seeing that the American convert had been a Catholic for seven years, instructed Pierce to bring his wife and children to Rome so that officials could discuss the matter with Cornelia personally.

Pierce returned to London, then sailed to Philadelphia to collect Cornelia and the children. They returned to England and, as guests of Lord Shrewsbury, they met members of the Oxford Movement. With young Berkeley in tow, they spent a month in Paris and then settled into a large apartment near the Palazzo Borghese in Rome. Carnival time found the Connellys once again in social demand. No one was aware of their plans to separate; in any case, Pierce assumed that it would be several more years before he received permission to prepare for ordination.

But the pope, after receiving Cornelia's personal consent to her husband's ordination, moved swiftly. Permission was granted and after only three months' time Cornelia and Pierce signed a decree of formal separation. Cornelia moved with Frank and his nurse into a retreat house at Trinità dei Monti, a convent of the Sacred Heart Sisters at the top of the Spanish Steps. She was to live as a laywoman for as long as her small son needed her, and not yet as an official postulant to the community. Adeline was enrolled in the convent school where her mother taught English and music. Pierce, meanwhile, took up his theological studies, received the tonsure, and donned the garb of a Roman Catholic priest. On May 1, 1844, he was admitted to minor orders. Pope Gregory showed his approval of the "big catch" for the church by sending them a very large fish freshly pulled from the Tiber.

At the Trinità, Cornelia lived her life within the enclosure, but the Vatican had arranged that once a week Pierce could visit his wife and children. He hoped—and Cornelia counted on it for him—to become a Jesuit. But the hope was put aside when the father general of the society accused him of visiting her too often. Later, Pierce found it convenient to say that during their visits he was sometimes too familiar with his wife. Cornelia, as the day approached for her husband to take major orders, had one final talk with him. She pleaded with him to consider once more the sacrifices he was demanding of himself, herself, and their three children. She even offered to renounce what was by then her own desire to become a nun, and to return with him to a normal family life. But Pierce insisted on taking Holy Orders. In keeping with the requirements of canon law, Cornelia pronounced a vow of perpetual chastity, thus releasing her husband for ordination. In June, Pierce was ordained and said his first Mass: he himself gave his daughter her First Holy Communion and Cornelia sang in the choir.

In the eyes of the church, as well as in their own eyes, the Connellys were still married, but she had given her husband to the church. Her attitude was captured neatly in a letter she subsequently wrote to Pierce's brother John: "He [Pierce] is well & deeply engaged in the duties of the ministry, instructing, preaching, hearing confessions &c., &c. So you see it is not for nothing that I have given him to God. You may be sure this thought gives me much consolation & we ought to look for a greater share of the divine love in proportion as we are willing to sacrifice our natural happiness . . . and look for more in eternity . . ."

Cornelia was now thirty-six and and faced with the problem of working out her future. Her belief and intention when she agreed to separation had been that in religious life she would have her children under her own eyes "as much as if" she had never "left the world." At the Trinità there were aspects of the cloistered way of life which she found too restrictive, not the least of which were rules that would limit access to her children. Adeline, at age ten, was not yet ready for boarding school and Frank was only five. Although the sisters pressed her to join the community, to Cornelia's great relief the cardinal vicar of Rome assured her that her duty was to care for her children. And he told her something Cornelia hadn't realized: even though she now wanted to become a religious, she was under no obligation to do so.

With the help of Father Giovanni Grassi, an Italian Jesuit in Rome who had spent many years in the United States, Cornelia found a solution. She would found a new, noncloistered congregation of religious women which would permit her to keep her children under her care. Grassi urged her to take up her work in the United States, but word of her decision reached England, where Lord Shrewsbury and Bishop Nicholas Wiseman had decided that Cornelia was the right sort of person to help educate Catholic girls and the poor. Because the invitation to come to England was presented to her as the wish of Pope Gregory, Cornelia complied. With the help of Pierce, who was headed for England himself as chaplain to Lord Shrewsbury, she drew up a preliminary set of constitutions or rules for the new religious congregation. Cornelia had already thought of a name: "Society of the Holy Child Jesus."

As the *positio* makes clear, midcentury in England was a volatile era for Roman Catholics. The Oxford Movement was afoot: John Henry (later Cardinal) Newman had just made his spiritual journey from Canterbury to Rome and the Catholic hierarchy was about to be restored. After 150 years of suppression, English Catholics were allowed to vote and sit in Parliament. The darker side of all this was that the English church was poor, its clergy ill-educated, and its pastoral needs enormous. Five million Catholics, most of them penniless and untutored, had emigrated from Ireland and were looking to the church for support. No one, least of all the Protestant majority, was certain what political emancipation would mean for the body politic. What's more, the restoration of the Catholic hierarchy revived anti-Catholicism in England. Once again, "popish" practices were under public scrutiny: the secrecy of the confessional, the dark goings-on in convents, and above all, the political machinations of Rome. William Taylor, author of *Popery: Its Character and Its Crimes,* reflected the wariness of English Protestants: "We do not ask what Romish priests are when surrounded by Protestantism," he declared in 1847, a year after the Connellys—now priest and nun—arrived in England, "but what [they are], where the system develops itself without restraint."

To avoid scandalizing English Protestants, Bishop Wiseman refused to continue the visitation permission that Pierce had enjoyed in Rome. Communication between husband and wife was limited to correspondence. For much the same reason Wiseman also insisted, to Cornelia's great maternal anguish, that she send the two younger children away to boarding school while she completed her training as a novice. Mercer was already boarding away. In any case, Cornelia was busy enough. Wiseman had found her a large convent at St. Mary's Church in Derby, a factory town, and given her a mandate to begin an ambitious program there in women's education. In no time, Cornelia was running a day school for two hundred pupils, a night school for factory women, and a crowded Sunday school program—and training novices to the Society of the Holy Child Jesus.

After a year of total separation, Pierce arrived unannounced at the convent to see his wife. Even though Cornelia was longing to see him too, she angrily criticized Pierce for violating Bishop Wiseman's command and told him not to repeat his visit. He wrote her a letter of reproach and she responded, acknowledging his continuing physical attraction for her and the difficulty she was experiencing in trying to overcome it. ("You have not the violent temptation that I have in thinking of the little Bethlehem room [their bedroom in Natchez] nor have you, perhaps, gone through the struggles of a woman's heart," she writes. "No, you never have.") In December 1847, Cornelia took her perpetual vows as a nun and was formally installed as superior general of the society. Pierce did not attend the ceremony. He had become jealous of Wiseman's growing ecclesiastical jurisdiction over Cornelia. He decided to take action to bring Cornelia under his own control.

In January 1848, without telling Cornelia, Pierce removed the children from their schools. He put six-year-old Frank in a secret home. Pierce took Mercer and Adeline to the Continent, hoping that Cornelia would follow. Instead, on the advice of her Jesuit spiritual adviser, Father Samuele Asperti, an Italian, she made a private vow not to let communication with her husband and children deflect her from what she had come to regard as the claims of God upon her. In other words she meant to be faithful to the celibate separated state in which the church has placed her, faithful to her recent religious vows, and faithful to the obligations now laid on her as superior of a new community in the church. The next move was Pierce's. He went to Rome and, posing as founder of the Society of the Holy Child Jesus, presented to the Congregation for the Propagation of the Faith (which at that time had jurisdiction over religious institutes in Great Britain) his own version of the society's constitutions or rule of life. His hope was that if the constitutions were approved with himself as founder, he would have the power to override Wiseman's authority and gain control over Cornelia. When they heard of this ploy, Cornelia and Asperti wrote to the congregation and thwarted Pierce's immediate efforts. Nonetheless, from that point on officials of the congregation assumed that Pierce was the society's cofounder and retained his version of the institute's rule—an error which was to cause considerable confusion in the future. Upon his return, Pierce called on Cornelia, bringing her a gift from the new pope, Pius IX. But she refused to see him unless he agreed to return Adeline to her care. Pierce argued for six hours with Asperti while Cornelia remained kneeling on her prie-dieu upstairs.

Pierce was not the only problem complicating Cornelia's life. She also faced the first of a series of financial and legal problems which would plague her the rest of her life. Although her schools were going well, the factory girls could not afford to pay for their education and the church itself was too poor to give more than occasional subsidies. Bishop Wiseman, who at the beginning wrote that he would "take the whole convent and its liabilities" on himself, was unable to follow through fully on this; when Cornelia could not meet expenses she found herself threatened with eviction by the mission priest in Derby. Bishop Wiseman, who had been given a new assignment as vicar apostolic for the London district, urged Cornelia to move her sisters to property within his district at St. Leonard's-by-the Sea on the Sussex coast. She agreed.

Pierce was livid when he heard that. He moved out of Lord Shrewsbury's establishment and into the home of Henry Drummond, a fanatical anti-Catholic and Member of Parliament. Pierce was obsessed with hatred for Asperti and Wiseman, convinced that the bishop was removing his former wife to Sussex to exercise greater control over her. Defying canon law and his own priestly vows, he began legal proceedings for the restoration of his conjugal rights.

Connelly v. *Connelly* threatened to embarrass the entire Catholic Church in England with major scandal. Cornelia could avoid it, Pierce suggested, only by returning to live with him. She refused. Shrewsbury suggested a compromise to Cornelia: leave England, or at least Wiseman's district, to avoid scandal. Again she refused, believing this would betray both her vows and her fledgling religious institute, which by then numbered some twenty members. Wiseman supported her decision and provided lawyers for her defense.

In February 1848, Pierce's lawyer presented the judge with his client's statement of marital defection against Cornelia. It was a Protestant court. The statement signed by Pierce entirely omitted his conversion to the Catholic Church, the separation, and his ordination to the Catholic priesthood. It pled their original, Protestant Episcopal marriage and the birth of five children; and having claimed that Cornelia "withdrew herself from bed, board and mutual cohabitation" it petitioned that she be "compelled by law to return and render him conjugal rights." Cornelia's lawyers presented her answering allegation giving the omitted facts. The judge took his time and after a year pronounced against accepting her allegation on the ground that Roman law is not binding in England. Cornelia was faced with two options: forcible return to her former husband or prison. To avoid either alternative, her lawyers immediately appealed the case to the Privy Council. *Connelly* v. *Connelly* became a running scandal in the British press. Popular opinion, which had always been suspicious of what went on behind convent walls, favored Pierce: on Guy Fawkes Day, for example, marchers carried effigies of Wiseman and Cornelia through Chelsea. Cornelia and the bishop were denounced from Protestant pulpits and, understandably embarrassed by the scandal the Connellys were causing, some English Catholics urged the two Yankees to go back to the United States.

Bishop Wiseman then added a new complication to Cornelia's life. He fancied the well-stocked library at St. Leonard's, and when the owner—a priest—died he sent workers to the premises to construct a "marine residence" where he could spend his leisure moments. Cornelia sent them away; apart from the impropriety of having these two now notorious Catholics occupying the same property, there was the bubbling question of who had the legal right to do what with the land. Cornelia's defiance of Wiseman was the beginning of a process of alienation between the bishop and the mother superior. Their personal falling-out became a threat to the survival of Cornelia's community.

In September 1850, the Catholic hierarchy was restored in England; Rome appointed Wiseman Cardinal Archbishop of Westminster and therefore Catholic primate of England. The archdiocese was divided and a new bishop put in charge of overseeing Catholics in the south. But Wiseman did not divide the assets of the archdiocese proportionately and thus exacerbated the financial problems which were to cause Cornelia thirteen years of strife at St. Leonard's.

The following June, the Privy Council finally heard *Connelly* v. *Connelly* and, though no definitive verdict was pronounced, the previous judgment favoring Pierce was suspended. The court was ordered to admit Cornelia's counterallegation. The judges signaled their opinion that Pierce could prevail but ordered him to pay the costs to date of both parties as a precondition for a second hearing in the lower court. In order to prevent further scandal to the church, Cornelia paid Pierce's court costs, which he could not afford. But she was in effect the winner and could not be forced to return to her husband.

On the other hand, neither could Cornelia regain custody of her children since, under British law of the time, a man's wife and children were considered his property. Thus, the three oldest children continued to live with Pierce on the Drummond estate until the eldest, Mercer, was sent to an uncle in America and Frank was placed in a school for children of clergy. For several years Pierce supported himself by writing scurrilous tracts against the pope, the Jesuits, Catholic morals, Cardinal Wiseman—all of which kept Cornelia in the public eye and required her to take precautions against abduction by her irate husband. When the case was finally dismissed by the Privy Council in 1857, Pierce took Adeline and Frank with him to the Continent. Cornelia never saw Mercer again: he died at the age of twenty of yellow fever in New Orleans. Adeline remained with her father, who kept her dressed in the clothes of a young girl and otherwise dependent on him. Pierce spent the last seventeen years of his life as the rector of the American Episcopal community in Florence. After his death in 1883, Adeline visited her mother twice and eventually returned to the Roman Catholic Church. Frank settled in Rome where he became an internationally renowned painter. He remained devoted to his mother but developed a lasting hatred for the Catholic Church which—understandably—he blamed for destroying his childhood home and his parents' lives.

All of this material consumes less than half of the three volumes containing Cornelia Connelly's documented life story. The remainder, covering the last quarter century of her life, is too long to summarize in similar detail. Nonetheless, a brief look at Cornelia's triumphs and failures as a founder and educator is essential in order to appreciate the full scope of her life and the difficulties that her continual conflicts with church authorities presented for her cause.

Founding a new religious institute is seldom easy. In Cornelia's case, it was nearly miraculous. For much of her life as a superior general, she was embroiled in a complicated legal battle over the real estate at St. Leonard's which added to her already questionable reputation among some of England's bishops and priests. The property of St. Leonard's had been intended by its owner for the use of the sisters, not for the mission parish of All Souls which also developed there. One powerful layman influenced the very small mission congregation, demanding that the partly constructed church be completed by the sisters and turned over for the congregation's exclusive use. Cornelia's own bishop, Grant, and Cardinal Wiseman both supported his demand. He was opposed by the legal heir to the property, Colonel Towneley, a Catholic, a Member of Parliament and a justice of the peace. The trust which Towneley had established and under which the sisters lived and worked did not permit any use of the property except for education—not even if demanded by the bishop or the cardinal. Cornelia was caught between two legal systems: canon law, which dictated that she obey the local bishop, and English civil law, which forbade her to do anything which violated the trust. In the course of thirteen years, the lay leader of the congregation, supported by the cardinal, sent seven appeals to Rome. Accompanying the appeals was damning and—as it turned out—false testimony regarding Cornelia's character and judgment. Cornelia, who stood by the trust, was vilified as an insubordinate, self-willed, grasping woman—a reputation that continued well after her death.

At one point in the 1850s, matters became so inflamed that Cardinal Wiseman, along with others, plotted to have Cornelia summoned to Rome on a pretext and then shipped back to the United States. Although she saw through the ruse, Cornelia went to Rome anyhow, trusting that God's will for her would be done. But thanks in part to a Roman cardinal who had known her in the past and respected her integrity, the scheme failed and she returned to England.

Cornelia's honesty and integrity were impugned again when she refused to use the society's funds to pay off a debt incurred without her approval by Sister Emily Bowles, one of her earliest and most gifted colleagues. Like Cornelia, Emily Bowles was a convert and was devoted to education. In order to purchase a building in Liverpool for use as a teacher-training school, secretly Emily borrowed six thousand British pounds from her brothers against an expected grant from the Catholic Poor Schools Committee. But the grant failed to materialize and the Bowles brothers threatened legal action to force Cornelia, as head of the order, to make good Emily's debt. Emily left the society and Bishop Grant, fearing her tongue would create more scandal for the church, pressed Cornelia to meet all the Bowles family's demands—which she did, though she preferred to fight in court. Wiseman's sympathies were with Emily, who succeeded in manipulating opinion in her own favor. Although Cornelia lost her financial struggle with the Bowles family, she and Towneley were eventually vindicated in the St. Leonard's property dispute when officials in Rome finally learned the facts.

Perhaps Cornelia's most trying experience was her effort over three decades to gain the Vatican's approval for the constitutions she had drawn up for her religious institution. Constitutions embody the particular spirituality and vision of the founder by establishing the rules under which the members are to live. They are also the charter which allows the institute to survive as a self-governing religious order within the Roman Catholic Church. Time and again, Cornelia was ordered to revise the rules she had written. And in 1870, just as it appeared that the Vatican would finally grant its approval, a dissident faction of her sisters in Preston, England wrote to Rome, charging Cornelia with acting autocratically and asking Vatican officials to intervene against her.

In addition, there was lingering confusion among officials at the Congregation for the Propagation of the Faith over the role that Pierce had played in drawing up the original constitution; so long as he was alive, at least some Vatican officials were unwilling to grant approval lest it appear that a renegade priest was the cofounder of a Catholic order of nuns. Once again, Cornelia was vindicated: the society's constitutions were eventually approved substantially as Cornelia had originally drawn them—but not until eight years after her death.

Despite her many difficulties, Cornelia Connelly not only expanded her religious order, she also developed a system of education which challenged many of the dogmas of Victorian education. She established a college for training schoolmistresses, one of only two such institutions in England for men or women. Despite pressure from Lord Shrewsbury and some members of the English hierarchy, who wanted her to focus on improving schools for the better-class Catholics of Britain, she insisted on maintaining both day schools for those who could afford tuition and free schools for those who could not. For her brightest female students she introduced Latin and Greek authors in translation—courses the British reserved only for males. In the midst of the Darwinian revolution, she insisted that her students be taught geology. Equally important, she encouraged her teachers to allow their charges to express themselves through art, music, and drama. But her greatest challenge to the British system was her atti- tude toward discipline. The school, in her view, was a home and her nuns mothers who must respect, trust, and love their students. To the discomfort of some of the English bishops, she even encouraged the sisters to teach their pupils to waltz and polka—and to play whist.

Her vision for the society was also liberating. As a convert—and as an American—she found the customary convent rules of stiffness and constant surveillance spiritually alien. The society, she insisted, must encourage mutual trust and respect for diverse talents. She pushed the sisters to take on new challenges, especially in the arts. And although she could be stern, she never lost her sense of play. Thus, when it came time to distribute the "disciplines" (small whips for flagella- tion) to her protégés, she wrapped up the leather thongs, and handed them out as Christmas gifts.

Cornelia's declining years were not especially happy ones. In 1874, Cornelia was elected mother superior at the society's first chapter meeting. But at the meeting Bishop Danell of Southwark, responding to criticism of Cornelia from the Preston group, imposed his own constitutions on the society which made him the de facto religious superior and reduced Cornelia to a mere figurehead. The new consti- tutions were unpopular and in America the sisters ignored them. The bishops of Liverpool and Philadelphia, however, refused to acknowl- edge her authority over the Holy Child sisters in their dioceses. Schism threatened. Cornelia worked for a concerted reaction to the new rule, hoping that when elected delegates from the whole society met at the next chapter, the old, much-loved rule could be retrieved. They met in 1877 and expressed their unanimous opposition to Danell's rule. Danell, however, insisted that they continue to live by it. Cornelia was again elected mother general but she did not live to see the next chapter.

Her health failed. Never robust, she was gradually reduced by chronic nephritis to being wheeled about the garden in a wicker bath chair. The "gout," as she called it, produced a rash that disfigured her skin and eventually affected her brain and spinal cord. After a night of intense pain during which she called out three times, "In this flesh I shall see my God," Cornelia Connelly died on the Friday after Easter, 1879.

THE FIGHT FOR A CAUSE

IN HISTORICAL CAUSES, the postulation must not only show that the Servant of God has a reputation for holiness (*fama sanctitatis*), but also explain why the cause was not initiated sooner. In the case of Cornelia Connelly, her *positio* argues, it was not at all surprising that a century elapsed before English Catholics took the first steps toward her canonization.

For one thing, the recently restored English hierarchy had many more pressing problems to address than the making of saints. Moreover, the *positio* argues, as practical, nineteenth-century Englishmen, the bishops would have found the Vatican's intricate procedures odd and hopelessly convoluted. In any case, they would not have considered Cornelia Connelly the sort of material that saints are made of. Although many of the Sisters of the Holy Child Jesus thought of their foundress as a holy person, the English Catholics at large remembered her chiefly as the notorious "Mrs. Connelly" whose husband's lawsuit heaped considerable embarrassment on the church. Among the clergy of Sussex, the name of Cornelia Connelly conjured up stories of an intractable American nun who, as the oral tradition had it, was constantly defying the directives of her ecclesiastical superiors. Indeed, as late as 1946, the centenary of the society's founding, the bishop of Southwark refused the sisters' request to open an Ordinary Process on behalf of their foundress. The church, he insisted, would never canonize her; just to make sure, he removed the relevant documents from the diocesan archives and locked them away in his private quarters. In short, Cornelia's local reputation was not the sort that makes for *fama sanctitatis*.

But the *story* of Cornelia Connelly was something else. Those who read it or heard it were drawn to the figure of a wife and mother whose children were taken from her and who, despite enormous heartache and misunderstanding, persevered in her religious calling to establish an international congregation of religious women. The first biography of Cornelia was completed by one of the sisters seven years after her death but was never published—partly out of consideration for the Connelly family, and partly because the Vatican still had not approved Cornelia's constitutions. In 1922, a life of Cornelia Connelly written by another nun was published in England and the United States, and the response was such that the sisters began circulating a prayer for Cornelia's eventual beatification. In 1930, a new biography was published in France and two years later an Italian edition appeared. Nor was interest limited to church circles. In the sixties, *Connelly Versus Connelly*," a play based on the lawsuit, was written and performed at the Blackfriars in New York and Los Angeles; a radio drama, "Roses among Lilies," was broadcast over British public radio; a six-part television series was written but never produced for British television.

Officially, Cornelia's cause began in 1953 when a new bishop of Southwark established a historical commission to collect and evaluate her writings and all other documents relating to her well-publicized life. Of the fifty-six volumes of her personal writings, those reflecting her spiritual response to the major crises in her life and her correspondence revealing her reactions to episcopal directives were the key in evaluating the evidence of heroic virtue. Six years later, an Ordinary Process was begun to investigate her reputation for holiness. This investigation took ten years and, since there were no firsthand witnesses to provide testimony, judgment was based on the opinions of the three historical commissioners, plus seven nuns and laywomen and four priests of the diocese of Southwark.

The research reveals that two of the four diocesan priests felt that Cornelia's reputation for holiness was essentially limited to members of the society. In fact, the vicar-general of Southwark testified that the prevailing opinion among the clergy was "skeptical cynicism" regarding her cause. Another seriously doubted Cornelia's "spiritual motivation" and dismissed as "wishful thinking" the assertion that there was widespread devotion to her among bishops and priests. The archivists of the society countered with hundreds of letters, many of them from people living outside England who had come in contact with the society and its schools, attesting to a belief in her holiness. For their part, the historians were unanimous in their praise for Cornelia; as one of them put it, "In the character of Cornelia Connelly we find a new attitude brought from America. She combined freshness and firmness with respect for [the bishops] as ecclesiastical superiors."

The questions put to the historical witnesses reveal a certain uneasiness about the cause. Never before had anyone sought the canonization of a nun who was married to a priest. The judge was particularly concerned that, given the sensational events of her life, the publicity generated by the cause would provoke serious criticism of the church by "unscrupulous writers." At the very least, it would refocus unwanted attention on the church's policy of demanding separation of men from their wives and children as the price for the ordaining convert clergy to the Roman priesthood.

Each witness was pointedly asked if there was anything about Cornelia which they did not find admirable. The negative responses indicated some uneasiness about the way she raised her children, about her "strong character," and particularly about her attitude toward authorities of the church. But despite these misgivings, even one of the skeptical diocesan priests was moved to observe that "she made the greatest sacrifice any woman could be asked to do on the advice of the Church in giving up her husband and her children." The proceedings were then forwarded to Rome with the opinion that there was nothing in the historical material or testimony that would undermine Cornelia's reputation for heroic virtue.

It remained, however, to produce a *positio* that would not only document the twists and turns of Cornelia's life but—what was more important—make a convincing case for her heroic virtue. The job was begun in 1973 by Sister Ursula Blake from the society. The project was guided by Monsignor Veraja as head of the historical section of the Congregation for the Causes of Saints and, because of Cornelia's long involvement with the Jesuits, Molinari was appointed postulator.

From the outset it was obvious to everyone involved in the cause that the central issue to be resolved concerned Cornelia's responsibility for the dissolution of her family and its malignant consequences for her husband and children. Could some or all of these consequences—Pierce's misguided decision to become a Catholic priest and his subsequent apostasy; the alienation of the children from their mother and church; Mercer's early death; Adeline's overdependency on her father; and Frank's rejection of his faith—have been avoided if she had acted otherwise? To be sure, there were also serious questions about the hostility she provoked among certain members of the clergy, especially the English bishops; about the factions within her own religious order; and about her prudence (or stubbornness) in handling her many legal disputes. But none of these issues touched the quick of her character—and therefore her claims to heroic virtue—in the way that the breakup of her family did.

In the first place, there was the question whether Pierce or Cornelia had first proposed that the two of them separate. After he left the Catholic priesthood, Pierce insisted in public and private that the idea originated with Cornelia at the suggestion of her spiritual directors. This argument was central to his accusations in *Connelly* v. *Connelly*, and to the anti-Catholic pamphleteers who claimed that Rome had forced Cornelia "by priestly art [to] forget the children whom she has borne, as well as the husband whom she has sworn before God to obey."

The *positio* resolves this question with relative ease by showing that Pierce was considering separation as early as 1835 when, still an Episcopal priest, he went to St. Louis to discuss his chances for ordination with Bishop Rosati. In addition, the *positio* marshals considerable evidence which proves that Cornelia dreaded the prospect of separation from her husband, pleaded with him to consider his decision carefully, and definitively chose the religious life for herself only on the eve of his ordination.

Next, the question arises: should Cornelia have signed the required Decree of Separation which freed Pierce for ordination? Should she not have foreseen that he was too unstable to sustain his vows as a priest? Here the *positio* recalls that Cornelia was hardly alone in judging her husband fit for the celibate Roman priesthood. Among those who supported his candidacy were Pope Gregory XVI himself, plus two of his cardinals, two American bishops, and five Jesuit priests. If mistakes were made in assessing Pierce's character, the finger must be pointed first to these men who, Cornelia had every right to assume, were specialists in measuring a man's fitness for the priesthood.

As might be expected, Pierce Connelly does not come off well in a *positio* devoted to proving his wife's heroic virtue. Indeed, that Cornelia needed the virtues of a saint to cope with his jealousy and almost paranoid suspicions of Bishop Wiseman and Father Asperti is part of the argument for her holiness. Even so, Pierce is treated here more as a failure than a villain, a man of exceptional gifts and education who, emotionally, never grew up. Included in the documentation is a psychological interpretation of Pierce by a French Jesuit, Father George Cruchon, who suggests that he was a man of "attractive, brilliant character" whose "ill-conceived ambition" was satisfied so long as he had the sustained admiration of his wife. But in his three short years as a Roman Catholic priest, he never achieved the eminence he craved and, Cruchon surmises, was overwhelmed by jealousy when it appeared that his wife was likely to establish a greater career in the church as a foundress and educator than anything he was likely to achieve as a priest.

The next issue is whether Cornelia put her own desire to become a nun ahead of the welfare of her children. The burden of the *positio* is to show that in becoming a nun, Cornelia Connelly did not abandon motherhood; rather, her children were taken from her—first, for the year of her novitiate by Bishop Wiseman, and then, before that year was over, by Pierce, who took them without her knowledge to the Continent in the hope that she would follow. The greatest suffering Cornelia endured, the *positio* concludes, was the alienation of her children from herself and from the church. As Cornelia herself put it, the Society of the Holy Child was "founded on a broken heart."

But to judge by the *positio*, the most troubling issue raised by the cause is whether the canonization of Cornelia Connelly would edify or scandalize contemporary Catholics. This issue has nothing to do with Cornelia's holiness or lack of it, but whether the church itself acted wisely in its treatment of her, her husband, and her children. Would it not appear that the church's highest authorities, beginning with the pope himself, willingly tolerated—supported, even—the breakup of the Connelly family in the belief that the religious life is a higher calling from God than Christian marriage? Would not the act of canonizing Cornelia Connelly reaffirm the view, long held by critics of Catholicism, that the church prefers celibacy to sex? For all of that, might not the more liberal Catholic faithful read the story of the Connellys as yet another proof that the church is wrong to demand celibacy of its priests?

As we have seen, some of these concerns emerged as early as the Ordinary Process (1959–1969), when several of the priests of the diocese of Sussex testified that in their opinion the cause of Mother Connelly would be bait to "unscrupulous writers." As the cause gained momentum, theologians took notice—and sides. In 1963, an exchange of strongly worded opinions enlivened the pages of *The Homiletic and Pastoral Review*, a monthly published for clergy. In the initial article, Father Leonard Whatmore, one of the historical consultors for the cause, took issue with various critics for whom the separation of Pierce and Cornelia demanded by church authorities is, in his words, "an outrage to parental feelings, natural humanity, priestly discretion, and elementary common sense, so fantastical, so unsavory and even nauseating." In response, a Canadian priest, Father Joseph H. O'Neill, argued that ecclesiastical approval of the Connellys' plan to separate was possible only because the church at that time had an underdeveloped "theology of Christian marriage."

The debate widened when Father Molinari, as postulator of the cause, responded with a long article, "Commitment to Love—a Reply to Cornelia Connelly's Critics," in which he outlined what he took to be the theological principles governing such cases. In essence, Molinari defended the principle that God sometimes calls a parent, married or widowed, to a second vocation as priest or nun. "We simply cannot set a limit to the rights of God," he insisted. Such a vocation, he went on, requires a "firm and indeed heroic love of God above all things" not only on the part of the person called to "higher perfection" but also the spouse and children that he or she may leave behind. As for the latter, Molinari declared: "He [God] will also supply (though not always in a way visible to our human eyes) for the needs of that parental care and love that the parents concerned will no longer be able to give to their children."

Molinari then went on to cite two examples of widows who became cloistered nuns despite the entreaties of their adolescent sons. In the case of one of them, St. Jane Frances de Chantel, the mother literally stepped over her fifteen-year-old boy, who had thrown himself across the doorway in grief at his mother's departure for the cloister. Molinari's point was that in each case, the church had examined the circumstances of the mother's second vocation and concluded that she had practiced heroic virtue as both a mother and a nun. Each went on to found a new religious order and in each case, he concluded, the hand of Providence could be discerned by "the fruits in the order of grace which flow from the second vocation." In other words, the good works subsequently performed by their respective religious orders proved that each woman had truly responded to the will of God.

By 1987, the theological arguments were, as a practical matter, essentially moot because the church had since altered its policy to permit the ordination of qualified convert clergymen like Pierce Connelly without requiring them to separate from their spouses and children. But this change in policy only made the church's handling of the Connellys seem more arbitrary—and enhanced the possibility that Cornelia's canonization might scandalize contemporary Catholics. If the cause was to pass the panel of theologians—and especially the panel of cardinals, who are particularly sensitive to pastoral impact—the decisions of both Cornelia and the pope had to be defended.

As relator of the cause, Gumpel elected to confront these issues directly. In September of 1987, he wrote a long preface to the *informatio* in which he acknowledged "a problem that, both during the lifetime of the Servant of God and up to our present day, has caused bewilderment on the part of some people. I refer to the fact that Cornelia Connelly, a married woman and mother of young children, left her state of life in order to become a religious." He then goes on to defend Cornelia by pointing out two facts: (1) that it was Pierce who initiated their separation because he felt called to the Roman priesthood, and (2) that "the highest ecclesiastical authorities . . . not only approved but practically imposed on the Servant of God, the dispositions regarding her young children whom she loved dearly. Not much imagination or psychological insight is needed," Gumpel remarks, "in order to understand the greatness of the sacrifice required from the Servant of God." At the same time, however, he reminds any consultors who might be inclined to fault the decisions of the church authorities in this matter just who they are second-guessing:

> It is abundantly clear to anyone possessed of the full information on these matters, that any criticism in this area is ultimately not criticism of the Servant of God but, directly, formally and explicitly, criticism of the Holy See and the Supreme Pontiff of the time. The decisions accepted by the Servant of God were accepted in the strength of her faith in God and in his representatives on earth. The manner of her acceptance can be judged only as exemplary. Naturally, decisions of this kind are not infallible. They have to be seen and judged in light of the times, and, what is even more important, in the light of the humble attitude of faith, reverence and obedience, with which they were accepted by those to whom they were communicated.

Finally, Gumpel anticipates objections to the cause's pastoral opportuneness, principally the fear that her canonization might be interpreted as a denigration of marriage and, what is worse, as an invitation for other pious couples to abandon their children for the religious life:

> . . . [T]he question may be raised as to whether the Canonization of Cornelia Connelly is opportune in the concrete circumstances of our times which, under so many aspects, are different from those of the 19th Century. Perhaps some theologians (or would-be theologians) will argue that the Second Vatican Council and post-conciliar theological and pastoral teaching have so extolled Christian marriage and Christian parenthood that it would be inopportune to propose today for canonization, and thus as an example of Christian virtue, a woman who, a wife and a mother, abandoned everything and entered the religious life. As a professional theologian and a professor of spirituality I cannot agree with such a standpoint because it seriously neglects and underestimates tenets of Catholic dogma and theology. In this connection I must first of all point out that the canonization of Mother Connelly would not in any way be a slight to the Catholic doctrine on marriage and parenthood. Still less would it be an indiscriminate invitation to Christian couples to follow her example. Her vocation was indeed a highly personal and quite exceptional one, just as was the vocation of other canonized men and women who are asked by God to renounce for his sake

all legitimate family ties and to follow unconditionally, though with a breaking heart, the Will of God clearly manifested to them.

On the other hand, Gumpel is not about to allow the figure of Cornelia Connelly to become hostage to proponents of marriage for Roman Catholic priests. Echoing Molinari's defense of "the right of God" to call some parents to "second vocations," he writes:

> Precisely in this context it would in my opinion be most opportune to proceed with the canonization of Mother Connelly. In our times, in fact, the state of married life, which indeed is to be highly esteemed, is presented not rarely as an absolute and even supreme value, to the detriment of celibate priesthood and consecrated life in the church. What is easily overlooked by those who defend such views, either in writing or by word of mouth, is the fact that God's ways are not our ways; that in his infinite Wisdom and Goodness he can and does make demands on men and women which may seem to be folly according to purely human criteria. In reality, these are his means to further the greater good of the Church and of humankind at large.

Here, as in the *positio* for Katharine Drexel, the relator's preface provides the sort of argument for the defense which, under the old juridical system, used to be advanced by the *avvocato* of the cause. It is, in effect, a series of directions to the jury of consultants on how to interpret the facts and how to assess the larger pastoral issues for the church raised by the life of Cornelia Connelly. But they do not make the case for her holiness. That is the burden of the *informatio* itself.

From what we have seen so far, there could be little doubt of Cornelia Connelly's uniqueness as a candidate for canonization. The events of her life in themselves easily set her apart from other Servants of God. The problem for Sister Elizabeth Strub, as the author of the *informatio*, was to elucidate the harmonics of holiness in what appeared to be a very discordant life.

THE MELODY OF GRACE

WHEN I HAD first spoken to Sister Elizabeth, she was still in the throes of writing the *informatio*. She had, however, established a number of guiding principles which differed from those of traditional *informationes*. In the first place, she insisted on examining Cornelia as a "whole person," gifted by nature as well as by grace. Not the least of those natural gifts, Elizabeth believed, was "the delight she took in life"—a quality, she felt, that Cornelia had also infused into the society and its schools, but one that does not appear in the congregation's catalog of Christian virtues. Second, she intended to search the full range of her adult life for evidence of holiness. "I don't see Cornelia," she said, "as just a nun or a wife or mother, but a woman who was a saint in all three stages of her life." Third, she was determined to present Cornelia's case for holiness without subjecting her spiritual integrity to the solvents of classification according to the conventional method of proving heroic virtue. "I've decided that the categories I use will be those Cornelia dictates to me, not what I dictate to her," she told me. "I want to present the evidence for holiness according to her own inner logic and experience of grace."

The *informatio* was completed a year later, and to read it is to recognize at once that it is a spirited departure from the past—perhaps because it is the first one conceived and written by a woman. There is, to begin with, a four-page appreciation of Cornelia's character and natural gifts: her physical beauty, charm, and "remarkable powers of attraction"; her intelligence, artistic discrimination, and talent; her industry, initiative, and capacity for innovation, especially as an educator; and—what is rarely remarked upon in the formal presentation of a candidate for sainthood—her capacity for "fun." Also rare is the author's acknowledgement that not everyone found Cornelia's character so winning—that critics accused her of being overbearing, insolent, autocratic, obstinate, and even devious. "Rose water will not do with her," Elizabeth quotes one bishop warning another.

What impresses Elizabeth most is Cornelia's "exceptional balance, integration and consistency as a human person" despite the tumult of her life. These qualities, she argues, "derive from her being fixed on God. Her whole life holds together only in God. All that one might call virtue in Cornelia—and she practiced virtue systematically and of set purpose—is the consequence of her clinging in love to a single point of reference: God, who fills all compartments of her life and breaks down in her all walls of separation."

The burden of the text is to identify "the core of Cornelia's holiness" and thus individuate her sanctity. The key is to be found in a ten-month period at Grand Coteau during which, Elizabeth argues, Cornelia was raised from "ordinary goodness" and given the capacity for "heroic goodness." Her goal, then, is to reconstruct from external evidence what is essentially the hidden movement of grace.

The pivotal period begins in December 1839. The Connellys have just returned from Europe, where they have been lionized by international celebrities and exposed to the sophistication of the Papal Court and the splendors—artistic and liturgical—of Catholic Rome. After much prayer, they opt for the simple, financially precarious life as Catholic schoolteachers in rural Louisiana. They are a family living among priests and nuns in a rather isolated community, but they are buoyant and intensely happy. In their enthusiasm for their new faith, both Cornelia and her husband select spiritual directors from among the local Jesuits and, during the course of the year, each makes a crucial spiritual retreat.

Cornelia's retreat is in late December and lasts only four days. She becomes aware—and is deeply disturbed—that her husband is still thinking of becoming a priest. She realizes now that his ordination would mean their separation and the breakup of the family. During the retreat, Cornelia experiences what she regards as a "conversion," a personal turning to God in love and the acceptance of His will for her, whatever that may be. Subsequently, she puts this experience in the form of a prayer, recorded in her notebook: "O God, trim Thy vine, cut it to the quick, but in Thy mercy root it not up yet."

A month later, the trimming begins. On February 2, her infant child, John Henry, dies in her arms, three and half days after the terrible scalding. In her grief, she turns to prayer and meditation and makes another retreat. In October, her husband makes his own retreat during which, he tells her, he has discerned that God is definitely calling him to the Roman priesthood. He asks her consent. She urges him to consider the decision twice over, and in preparation they agree to asbstain from sexual intercourse. Cornelia is still just thirty-two years old, pregnant with their fifth child. Her thoughts are far from convent life. Yet many years later she will cite the first day of sexual separation from her husband as the day the Society of the Holy Child Jesus was founded "on a broken heart."

So much for the known facts. Utilizing what few notes Cornelia made in her spiritual journal during this sequence of events, Sister Elizabeth offers a theological interpretation of how this crisis in her life produced a unique and, for Cornelia, paradigmatic experience of divine love. Instead of turning against God or wallowing in her own grief, Elizabeth argues, Cornelia grafted her own experience of death and bereavement onto the story of Jesus' death and the consequent suffering of his mother, Mary. This sort of transposition is not at all unusual for devout Christians who encounter tragedy, but in Cornelia's case it was to generate the sustaining vision of her life.

Elizabeth makes much of the fact that on the day of her son's death, Cornelia made only a single, terse entry in her journal: she drew an outsized monogram of the Virgin Mary in the form of an interlocking

M and *A*. Below that she listed in order the names of Jesus, Mary, and Joseph, followed by John Henry's initials. Below that she wrote: "Fell a victim on Friday—Suffered 43 hours and was taken 'into the temple of the Lord' on the Purification."

Elizabeth regards this cryptic text as the key to understanding Cornelia's unique spirituality, and proceeds to tease out meanings as if she were explicating a poem. On one level, it is apparent, Cornelia is recording the fact that John Henry's death occurred on Friday, the day Jesus died, and on the Feast of the Purification, the day in the church's liturgical calendar when Catholics celebrate Mary and Joseph's presentation of the child Jesus in the Temple as prescribed by Jewish law. On another level, Cornelia is using this configuration of biblical images to locate the shocking loss of her son within the transforming symmetry of faith. Like Jesus, John Henry's death was preceded by a three-day agony; like the Mary of the Pietà, Cornelia had held him in her arms, and like the ritual presentation of their own son in the Temple, Cornelia seems to be invoking the Holy Family to join her in presenting her dead son to God the Father.

Elizabeth is particularly anxious to demonstrate how, in the mind of Cornelia, these identifications with the suffering Jesus and his sorrowful mother conflated into the controlling image of her subsequent devotional life as a nun—"the Holy Child":

> In Cornelia's experience, Calvary is superimposed on Purification, just as the Pietà is superimposed on her own projection of the mother holding her Child in Bethlehem. It is worth noting that her thoughts as she records them are carried backwards from Good Friday to the Purification—from Jesus' adulthood and passion to his infancy. John Henry becomes for her a sign that Jesus' passion would always lead her back to the Child. In fact, Cornelia came to the Holy Child as the center of her Society's devotional life by way of suffering and separation—by way of her own Calvary . . .
>
> Any devoted mother holding a dying child for forty-three hours would be cut to the quick by almost unbearable suffering. Cornelia went beyond personal grief in that space of time, and, through the compassionate holding of the little body in her arms, received the grace of suffering with Christ and of knowing his sorrowing mother as an *alter ego*. In the course of her prolonged meditation, she reinterpreted all that had happened as part of the mystery of Christ. Her personal tragedy was illuminated and transposed by the Passion of Jesus explicating the infancy of Jesus.
>
> Because of John Henry, Cornelia was made to see clearly. In him she saw Jesus, the suffering Child of the Father, her own child in his need. There was a very physical base to her understanding of this mystery by

which Christ identified himself with humanity. It involved touching, holding, mothering, comforting and suffering with the child of her own womb. It is not surprising that the Incarnation [imaged in the figure of the "Holy Child"] came to be the mystery she pondered most deeply.

Elizabeth then goes on to argue that out of Cornelia's response in faith to her son's death, her friendship with God was deepened and a spiritual personality formed.

> Looking back over this period, it is possible to see that the graces of Cornelia's thirty-second year were at the same time purifying—her vine was trimmed and cut to the quick; illuminative—she was given to understand John Henry's death as her share in the Paschal Mystery; and unitive—she was joined to God by desire and love and she was faithful to that unitive gift in ordinary time and in seasons that were extraordinary . . .

> It is noteworthy that Cornelia's holiness was given its definitive shape while she was living a married life. By degrees her context would shift, she would make religious vows and her life's devotion would center more heavily in the Incarnate Word, the Holy Child. But her love for God which was ignited at Grand Coteau would continue to express itself in all the same characteristically active ways.

Purgation, illumination, union—the categories are taken from the literature of mystical experience and used here to suggest that, in her own way, Cornelia traveled the same spiritual path in the space of ten months and was thereby transformed through love of God. "Desire for God" and "receptivity to grace," Elizabeth goes on to say, were the twin points of Cornelia's holiness, but instead of driving her into withdrawal from the world, they fueled her engagement with it.

From this point on, Elizabeth's method of proving Cornelia's heroic virtues is to show how they spring to life as a result of her experience and understanding of divine love. All the required virtues—plus a few more—are present and accounted for, but in a fluid rather than categorical manner. For example, the virtue of poverty becomes a form of hope and is manifest as surely in Cornelia's willingness to forgo a comfortable life in Natchez for the Spartan surroundings of Grand Coteau as it is in her self-denial as a nun. Hope, in turn, begets forbearance and both are manifest when Cornelia is betrayed by Pierce, by some of the bishops, and by some of her own sisters. Temperance takes on the features of "supernatural calmness" in the midst of recriminations and scandal. And so it goes. Chastity loses its negative connotations and manifests itself as heroic generosity when Cornelia bows to the wishes of her husband—and the demands of the church—

that she separate from him so that he can become a priest. Obedience to church authorities is tempered by patience with their blind spots. And to account for Cornelia's prodigious enthusiasm—her ability to transform hardship into opportunity, her readiness for action, her sheer apostolic exuberence—Elizabeth devotes a dozen pages to examples of an often neglected virtue: zeal.

Appropriately enough, nearly half of the pages are given over to a discussion of charity, or fructifying love of God. Here the proofs are organized as variations on two themes: love of God as identification with Christ in his sacrificial passion and death, and love of others as inspired by the Incarnation of God as the child Jesus. Drawing on Cornelia's letters and other written documents, Elizabeth argues that these two great mysteries of the Christian faith became the poles that defined the axis of her spiritual experience and development. Along that axis, Cornelia's experiences of marriage, motherhood, death, separation, religious vocation, innovation in education, the development of a religious sisterhood—all her moments of suffering and joy—are transposed as a rhythmic movement between Cross and Crib. The images are appropriated from religion but they are rooted in Cornelia's experience as wife, mother, and nun.

In May 1988, the *positio* on Cornelia Connelly was approved by a panel of historical consultors. But because the cause lacks a potential miracle, because it meets none of the congregation's other pastoral priorities, and because the saint-makers still regard Cornelia's life story as potentially scandalous, it has yet to be turned over to the theologians. Whatever their judgment turns out to be, however, it is clear that the argument for her holiness represents a significant departure from the past.

First, by allowing the person and life of the candidate to determine the form—and content—of the virtues, the *informatio* permits Cornelia Connelly to emerge as an individual rather than a type. Second, by interpreting the virtues in a fluid rather than a rigid way, it is possible to see how they actually functioned in relation to each other. Third, by relating the official "evangelical counsels" of poverty and chastity and obedience to her whole life, and not merely her religious vows, the *informatio* imbues these categories with more than institutional relevance. Equally illuminating is the way the text goes beyond the list of required virtues to include others which the candidate actually practiced. On the other hand, the *positio* as a whole still remains something less than a full-scale study in spiritual development because no account is provided of the moral faults or other weaknesses of character others saw in her. For all her trials and hardships, the Servant of God still inhabits a moral Eden where serious personal sin has yet to spoil the landscape.

But the most important contribution of the Connelly *positio* is theological. Although Elizabeth's *informatio* respects the congregation's requirement to prove heroic virtue, the case it makes for Cornelia's holiness does not rest primarily on the virtues themselves. Rather, it is her friendship with God—and the grace that fuels that friendship—which gives birth to her heroic virtue. Indeed, the thrust of Elizabeth's argument is that what makes Cornelia's virtues "heroic"—what makes her response to adversity seem beyond ordinary morality—is precisely the fruit of a love that transforms the ordinary into the extraordinary. It is difficult not to conclude, therefore, that the harmony one finds in her life, the uniqueness and integrity of her virtues, the calm in the eye of so many storms, is not the mastery of moral skills but the gift of God's love. In short, the theological message appears to be that saints are not holy because they are virtuous, but virtuous because they are holy.

If this is in fact the case, then it would seem that there is no structure of virtues by which saints can be adequately measured. They measure us, not we them. Moreover, it seems that historical investigation alone, however "'critical'" or "scientific" its method, cannot reveal sanctity apart from a disciplined theological imagination. All "facts" demand interpretation, and never more so than when the goal is to track the yeasting of grace.

Nonetheless, so long as saints are made "by others, for others," some procedures must be followed, some standards applied. And nowhere is this more necessary—or complicated—than in causes involving popes.

CHAPTER NINE

POPES AS SAINTS: CANONIZATION AS CHURCH POLITICS

THE COVERT POLITICS OF CANONIZATION AT VATICAN COUNCIL II

IN OCTOBER 1963, the twenty-five hundred fathers of Vatican Council II opened discussion on "The Vocation to Sanctity in the Church," a brief "schema" or draft document on saints and sanctity. There were many issues on which progressives and conservatives within the council were deeply divided, but the subject of saints was not considered one of them. Not, that is, until Cardinal Leo Joseph Suenens of Malines-Brussels, one of the leaders of the council's progressive faction and a close friend of the late Pope John XXIII, rose to address the question of how saints are made. The church's formal canonization process, Suenens complained, is much too slow. It would be wise, he argued, to expedite the saint-making process in order to provide the faithful with contemporary examples of holiness rather than wait many decades, even centuries, to put forward figures whose moral relevance had inevitably faded with age.

Although Suenens did not mention any names, other progressive bishops knew that the "contemporary example" the Belgian cardinal had in mind was Pope John XXIII. John had died of cancer just five months earlier after the first session of the council, and now a move-ment was afoot to have the assembled fathers of the church—with, of course, the approval of Pope Paul VI—canonize John the old-fashioned way: by popular acclamation.

To the world outside the council, the idea of proclaiming John XXIII a saint seemed altogether appropriate. In less than five years on the throne of St. Peter, "good Pope John" had, through sheer force of personality, won what seemed like universal love and admiration. Indeed, no pope since before the Protestant Reformation had so cap-tivated the hearts of non-Catholics—including secular humanists, Marxists, and even atheists. John's personal warmth, wry peasant's humor, and evident trust in humanity were in stark contrast to his aloof, aristocratic, intellectually daunting predecessor, Pius XII, who had occupied the papal throne for nearly two decades. But the contrast was more than a matter of mere personality. John's encyclicals, espe-cially his last, inspired plea for world peace, *Pacem in Terris*, ad-dressed the Cold War world in a way that drew accolades from the Communist bloc no less than from the West. Moreover, the council itself was the fruit of John's inspiration: he had announced it without first consulting with the Roman Curia, and through it, the entire church was plunged into the heady experiences of *aggiornamento* (updating) after two centuries of suspicion of the modern world. Now, with the memory of John's invigorating spirit still fresh, some of the council fathers hoped to complement the world's opinion of this much loved pope by having the assembled prelates affirm that John was not just a good man but a saint of the church.

From the perspective of church history, however, the initiative on behalf of John was not only bold but radical. Although popes are expected to set a spiritual example for the church, very few of them have actually been found worthy of formal canonization. Indeed, if the history of canonization has any lesson, it seems to be this: the church's highest office is no place for anyone who aspires to the heroic virtue required of a canonized saint.

Of Pope John's 260 predecessors as bishops of Rome, 81 are regarded by the church as saints. But this figure is grossly misleading. In addi-tion to the Apostle Peter, it includes 47 of his first 48 successors as leaders of the Christian Church in Rome—half of whom were martyrs and all of whom died before the year 500. Of the remainder, 30 died before 1100, more than a century before the church developed even rudimentary procedures for investigating the lives of potential saints. In short, they were proclaimed saints by popular acclamation.

In the last nine hundred years, therefore, only three popes have been declared saints. The first of these, moreover, was hardly a model pope: Celestine V, an ascetic hermit who was ill-cast and inept as Supreme Pontiff, abdicated the papacy in 1294 after only five months in office. He was declared a saint in 1313, still some two and a half centuries before formal canonization processes were organized under the Congregation of Rites in 1588. In effect, then, only two popes— Pius V (1566–1572), a Dominican who implemented the reforms of the Council of Trent, and Pius X (1903–1914), a personally pious man who unleashed a crippling suppression of thought and scholarship in the church—have been canonized according to modern methods of making saints, and only eight others have been beatified.

There was, therefore, scant precedent in 1963 for making a pope a saint—and none at all in the previous four centuries for circumventing the established canonization process. But it was within the power of Paul VI to allow the council to do so and, one way or another, John's proponents hoped to persuade him to act.

By the time the third session of the council opened in the fall of 1964, the movement to canonize John by acclamation had attracted considerable outside support. In the Diocese of Bergamo, where John was born, fifty thousand priests and lay people signed a petition for his canonization and delivered it to the bishop. Vatican Radio reported that several non-Italian bishops had also joined the petition drive and that the Holy See had received formal requests from various other countries. The issue was brought up twice that November while the council was in session. In a commentary to the council on the influence of saints and the development of culture, Auxiliary Bishop Bogdan Beize of Lodz, Poland, suggested that "the church would exert deeper influence on the culture of our time if John XXIII were to be inscribed in the List of the Blessed." A few days later, in a lecture in Rome, Brazil's charismatic champion of the poor, Archbishop Dom Helder Câmara of Recife, proposed that, in response to worldwide expectations, Pope John should be canonized at the close of the council as "the prophet of new structures, God's friend, and friend of all the people."

At this point, the movement had garnered the support of a number of high-ranking churchmen, all identified with the council's progressive or reformist camp. Among the most influential were Cardinals Franz Koenig of Vienna; Bernard Alfrink of Utrecht, Holland; Achille Liénart of Lille, France; and Giacomo Lercaro of Bologna; as well as Suenens of Brussels. There was no doubt that these men regarded John as a saint. There was also no doubt that they regarded themselves as his true spiritual heirs, called to complete the revolution in church structures and attitudes which he had initiated.

The progressives, however, were deeply concerned that the openness John had shown—toward the church's separated Christian brethren (John had insisted that non-Catholic Christians be invited to sit in on the council as official observers), toward nonbelievers, and even Communists (shortly before his death he had scandalized Catholic conservatives by receiving the son-in-law of Soviet Premier Nikita Khrushchev at the Vatican), and toward the entire modern world—would be blunted by conservatives who did not share the late pope's optimistic outlook. Although John's successor, Paul VI, was regarded as a moderate progressive, he was already showing signs of personal agony over the evident ideological divisions within the council. Proclaiming John a saint, progressives felt, would be one way of ensuring a reformist council: after all, the fathers could hardly canonize John as a saintly example to all the bishops of the church and then repudiate that example by producing conciliar texts that contradicted John's hopes for renewal.

In sum, the motives for acclaiming John's sainthood were as political as they were pious. That much was evident from the lengthy intervention which leaders of the progressive faction circulated among the council fathers. Addressing both the "why" and the "how" of acclaiming John a saint, it read:

> Under Pope John, a man of genuine faith as well as true humanity, the church once again made this love of the world its emblem, rejecting severity towards prodigal brothers and, with its loving Father showing mercy even though this same world tries hard to appear agnostic and atheistic . . . From Pope John the world has learned that it is not so alienated from the church after all, nor is the church from the world. Maybe now the world expects us to declare that we do not consider Pope John a dreamer, or as one who has rashly overturned everything that, with long and patient effort, will have to be put back in order . . . but on the contrary, that we see him as a true Christian, indeed a saintly one, a man filled with true love for the world and for all mankind. And that his attitude, adopted and lived by Pope Paul VI from the beginning of his pontificate, is the attitude we too, the bishops he has assembled in the Council, wish, together with all Christendom, to adopt and live with ever greater commitment. What prospects for pastoral renewal, what hopes for dialogue will be fulfilled if this Council, which in so singular a way represents the whole church here on earth, were to proclaim, without the usual long delay, in an unusual but not new manner, the sainthood of its Pastor!

As for the "how," the authors noted that for centuries the church had made saints without a juridical process and could do so again in the case of Pope John:

An ad hoc Commission [of Council fathers] could carefully and expeditiously examine all matters with objectivity. After all, we bishops have ourselves all known Pope John's positions and intents from his very words and writings. All of us have witnessed in awe the admiration and affection expressed for Pope John in his life and especially at his death by everybody regardless of race or religion . . .

Now why should it not be that the Sacred Council, just as it proclaims other truths of faith, might petition the Holy Father to empower it to proclaim, with him and under him, Pope John XXIII a model of sainthood that is both new and ancient, to be presented to all, and especially to us bishops, as pastor and guide in our recognition of God's hidden but operative presence in the world and in all persons of good will?

It did not require a doctorate in exegesis to recognize that the text of the progressives' intervention was aimed at silencing the criticism of Pope John emanating from the council's most reactionary bloc. From the very beginning of the council, a core of some 250 prelates had resisted John's call for aggiornamento. Chief among them were the most powerful cardinals of the Roman Curia, who had greeted John's decision to convoke an ecumenical council with stony silence. These prelates, who had grown accustomed to running the church from Rome, clearly did not consider John's brief pontificate a benefit to the church—and for that reason alone they did not regard him as a model of sainthood to be imitated by other bishops. Privately, some of them had indeed dismissed John as a "dreamer," and now, as a group, they did in fact feel obliged to restore the good order of a church which, they believed, the late pope had "rashly overturned." In short, they were not about to cooperate in what they regarded as a purely political ploy.

Progressives hoped to introduce their intervention on November 5, 1964, the day on which the council was scheduled to discuss the proposed "Pastoral Constitution on the Church in the Modern World." Of all the conciliar documents, this was the one which most breathed the world-embracing spirit of John XXIII. Council protocol, however, required that an intervention must bear the signatures of at least seventy fathers, and this one had only fifty. Supporters scrambled to enlist another twenty prelates, but the complete list was received too late. Thus, although the written text was submitted to the council moderators, the progressive faction was frustrated in its effort to have John's canonization taken up for debate or vote. They were, however, determined to have their day during the council's fourth and final session.

As it turned out, the intervention never reached the council floor—and thus intense political drama surrounding the canonization of Pope John XXIII escaped notice by the three thousand reporters who covered Vatican II. Much of that drama took place off the council floor in the offices of the church's official saint-makers. Several delegations of bishops visited the congregation to obtain its views on the progressives' proposal to let the council assume extraordinary saint-making powers. Understandably, congregation officials were smarting from the criticism of Suenens and other council fathers who coupled their call for John's canonization with complaints about the length of canonization procedures. Though some of the saint-makers agreed that the process was too long, they interpreted the move to have John's sanctity proclaimed by the council as a reproof of the congregation itself.

But the saint-makers had more substantive objections as well. In part, they were opposed to the method of popular acclamation. It was not the business of a council, they said, to canonize anyone. Whatever John's reputation at the moment, they argued, it would be imprudent to proclaim his sanctity without a thorough investigation of his life and virtues. Popes, like all candidates for canonization, they explained, have private as well as public lives which require the congregation's meticulous scrutiny. As one of them reasoned, "a definitive biography cannot be written until fifty years after the death of a man if he has any importance. And in the case of popes, it takes years just to collect all the documents."

Equally important, some of the saint-makers were deeply suspicious of the progressives' motives. "They were using John to get at Pius," says Molinari, who was also an official *peritus* (expert) during Vatican II. "They were creating an opposition between the two popes which was totally contrary to the thought of John XXIII. As a matter of fact, his last few hours were an agony for Pope John because he knew that some theologians—and not only theologians but bishops as well—were trying to push liberal ideas through the council by presenting them as if they were John's own ideas."

Indeed, many of the council conservatives felt that if any pope should be declared a saint, it was Pius XII. Pius had been dead only four years when the council opened, and there was considerable sentiment to open a formal process on his behalf. To conservatives, Pius was everything a pope should be: disciplined; authoritarian; awesomely informed on a wide range of technical subjects; suspicious—at times almost contemptuous—of the modern world (especially Communism); self-contained to the point of aloofness; monarchical in his conception and administration of the church; and, above all, resolute in condemning a wide range of progressive "errors" within the church. During his reign, for example, a number of the church's most prominent theologians were censured or silenced,* and some conservative cardinals wanted the council to reiterate the church's opposition to their errant theology. John, on the other hand, had lifted the censures and now these same theologians were loose in the council's corridors as official *periti* to the ascendant progressive faction. Thus, conservatives were convinced that the move to canonize John was actually a covert effort to discredit the pontificate of Pius XII, as well as their own views, and to vindicate the theological "errors" which Pius had suppressed.

In sum, the conflict between progressives and conservatives within the council became crystallized around the contrasting figures of John XXIII and Pius XII. They, in turn, symbolized two different conceptions of the church, especially in its relations with the outside world. No one understood this better than Paul VI, who had served under both popes. He was also aware, as the last session of the council opened in the fall of 1965, that the progressives were determined to present their intervention to the assembled fathers. If that happened, there would likely be a spontaneous demonstration on John's behalf. The story of the demonstration would produce immediate headlines around the world. The pressure to accede would be great, Paul knew. As gauged by world opinion, John was, quite simply, the most popular figure in the church.

What to do? By temperament and training, Paul was not inclined to sidestep established procedures. On the other hand, he could ill afford the appearance of denying John's holiness. In a matter of days, he was told, the progressives would make their move. He would have to act first. Privately, he called on two saint-makers whom he knew well and whose judgment he trusted. Their advice to him became public knowledge on November 18, 1965. In a Solomonlike decision, Paul announced that he would instruct the congregation to initiate processes on behalf of *both* John and Pius—according to established procedures.

The progressives were disappointed, some of them bitterly so. Con-

---

*Among the most important: Jesuits Henri de Lubac, Henri Rondet, and Henri Bouillard, and Dominicans Marie-Dominique Chenu and Yves-Marie Congar, all French.

servatives were pleased: indeed, without the push on behalf of John, Paul might not have instituted a formal process so soon for Pius, whose reputation for holiness had considerably faded during the reign of John. But the real victory belonged to the congregation. Its role in the making of saints had been vindicated.

It soon became clear, however, that in yoking the causes of Pius and John, Pope Paul had not solved a delicate issue of church politics; he merely postponed it. By initiating the two causes with the same papal stroke, had Paul not also linked their outcomes? Juridically, the causes were separate: each Servant of God was to be judged on his own merits. But as a matter of ecclesiastical politics, could the church canonize one pope without the other? In the history of the congregation, the question had never come up.

JUDGING POPES AS SAINTS

IN THEORY, THE cause of a pope is no different from that of any other candidate. The same procedures are followed, the same virtues must be proved. In practice, however, papal causes do receive special handling and present special problems.

First, papal causes are introduced only by another pope. At least this is the force of precedent.* In any event, from the very beginning of the process, papal causes are under papal control; even the promoters of a pope's cause are assigned by the reigning pontiff.

Second, since a pope is presumed to be orthodox, his published writings (such as encyclicals) as supreme teacher of the church are not subject to the usual preliminary scrutiny by theological censors. Nonetheless, they are open to criticism by the congregation's consultors on the grounds that a pope's words—like his actions—may have been imprudent and possibly even harmful to the church. Moreover, there may be certain politically sensitive documents—papal diaries are a prime example—which only the postulator and relator are permitted to read. However, a pope's personal letters and other private papers *are* grist for the examiners, since they may bear directly on the candidate's spiritual life.

Third, by the very nature of their office, popes generate much more

---

* If a pope were to die while visiting another diocese, technically the bishop of that diocese would be the one to introduce the cause. But in fact he would waive his right in deference to the Holy See.

written material—by and especially about themselves—than most
other Servants of God. Not all of that material can be retrieved and
examined, of course, and in some cases it has been alleged that negative documents have been withheld or conveniently lost.* But postulators are morally bound to consider all relevant material and may
in fact jeopardize their case if they fail to do so. Moreover, since popes
are by definition key players on the stage of history, postulators are
expected to examine the varying historical interpretations of the pope
as well as the primary documentation. In the case of a pope like Pius
XII, who held key diplomatic posts for twenty-two years prior to his
election, the range of potentially relevant literature is staggering.

Fourth, unlike most saints, popes tend to make many enemies,
especially among those who work closely with them in the church. It
goes with the territory. Thus no papal cause, especially that of a controversial figure like John or Pius, is apt to move quickly as long as
any of his opponents remain alive and influential in the church.

But the major difference, the one which definitively separates papal
from all other causes, is this: a pope must be judged not only on his
personal holiness but also on his stewardship as supreme teacher and
head of the church. Benedict XIV is quite clear on the matter. In his
treatise on beatification and canonization, he devotes an entire section to those duties of office which investigators should consider in
appraising Servants of God who occupied the Chair of Peter. As Benedict saw it, a pope's claims to holiness should be measured by his
"zeal for the preservation and propagation of the Catholic faith, for
the encouragement and restoration of ecclesiastical discipline, and
the defense of the rights of the Apostolic See." His main model was
Pius V. Elsewhere, he counsels investigators to be on the lookout for
manifestations of humility, citing with approval St. Bernard's judgment that "There is not a more splendid jewel among all the pontifical ornaments." Thus, for example, Benedict declares that popes
should not seek out the church's highest office and should offer to
decline it when elected—which may be one reason why most modern
popes routinely do.

To judge by the last three popes canonized by the church, Benedict's norms were closely followed in each case. Both Celestine V and
Pius V were extreme ascetics, even as popes, and the evidence suggests that their holiness was largely predicated on their monastic

---

* This allegation has been made, in private conversation with the author, by church historian Francis
Xavier Murphy, C.S.S.R., in connection with the process on behalf of Pope Pius X.

virtues. Certainly in the case of Celestine V, it is obvious that his dismal record as pope was no obstacle to his cause.* In the case of Pius V, the evidence from Benedict XIV indicates that Pius's resolute program of church reform and sturdy opposition to heretics and nonbelievers were also pivotal considerations in his cause. On the other hand, both Pius V and Pius X were notorious for their fierce and often unjust crusades against Catholics of culture and distinction whom Roman inquisitors regarded as real or potential heretics. In addition, there is considerable evidence of anti-Semitism in Pius V's expulsion of all but a handful of commercially useful Jews in Rome from the Papal States. In short, a glance at the three most recent papal canonizations suggests that excess "zeal for the preservation and propagation of the faith" is no vice in judging a pope for heroic virtue.

But the world was vastly different in the age of Pius XII and John XXIII, and so were the demands on the papacy. Both men had been Vatican diplomats; both played crucial roles during and after World War II, and both were instrumental in the reshaping of the church that found expression in Vatican Council II. Each, on the other hand, possessed very different temperaments and outlooks. They addressed the world at large in different ways—almost, one might say, in different languages. Equally important, each represented very different tendencies within the contemporary church and each was championed, so far as I could tell, by opposing factions.

For all these reasons, then, it was difficult to see how Pius XII and John XXIII could be judged by the comparatively parochial norms developed for their predecessors. Both were world figures whose words and deeds had important consequences for international affairs, and the world surely takes more than passing interest in the outcome of their causes. Nor, it seemed to me, could the differences between the two popes be easily reconciled. Both causes had been initiated in the context of fevered ecclesiastical politics, and whatever their individual claims to heroic virtue, each presents the saint-makers with a delicate political problem: how can the church canonize either one of them without also endorsing the secular and ecclesiastical politics which each pope continues to represent? Or, to put the question somewhat differently: how can the church declare a pope "blessed" without, at the same time, blessing what he did as pope?

---

* Very much in his favor was the political quarrel between his successor, Boniface VIII, and King Philip IV of France. Clement V's canonization of Celestine in 1313 was due in no small measure to pressure by the French king, who regarded it as a disparagement to Boniface.

THE BLENDING OF TWO PONTIFICATES

WHEN I FIRST began my inquiries into papal causes, the processes on John and Pius were nearly a quarter-century old. But neither was ready yet for discussion by the congregation. Pope Paul VI had entrusted Pius's cause to the Jesuits, John's to the Franciscans. Pius had always displayed a special affinity for the Society of Jesus; from his earliest days as apostolic nuncio to Germany to his last days as pope, his closest advisers were principally Jesuits. But that was not the only or primary reason why Paul chose the Jesuits. Pope Paul also had a long and close friendship with Father Molinari—their parents had been friends—and Montini knew Molinari to be one of the most accomplished of the saint-makers.

The pope's reasons for giving John's cause to the Franciscans were also based to some extent on personal considerations. The Franciscans' equally experienced postulator general, Father Antonio Cairoli, was in charge of the cause of Cardinal Andreas Ferrari (1850–1921), one of Paul's predecessors as archbishop of Milan. Pope Paul had a keen interest in the cause because Ferrari had defended his father, Giorgio Montini, a Milanese newspaper publisher, against charges of heresy during Pius X's anti-Modernist crusade.* Cairoli's work in clearing Ferrari's name, and thus paving the way for his beatification, moved a grateful Paul VI to name the Franciscan postulator for John XXIII.

As it happened, Ferrari was beatified on May 10, 1987, while I was doing research in Rome. A week later, I had my first visit with Cairoli at the Franciscan college some twenty minutes by taxi from the Vatican. A short Italian friar in his late seventies, Cairoli was reading his breviary in the parking lot when I arrived. He was in high spirits: Ferrari was the latest of ninety-one Servants of God he had escorted through the congregation and now he had only his beloved "Papa John," as he called him, to work on.

We spoke briefly of Ferrari. There was poetic justice in the cardinal's beatification, I suggested, since Ferrari, too, had suffered at the

---

* During the reign of Pope Pius X, the elder Montini was subjected to unwarranted and financially debilitating attacks by friends of the pope as part of the latter's assault on suspected Modernists in the church. As a result of these attacks, the elder Montini lost so much money that his son, the future pope, had to interrupt his studies for the priesthood for a year. Through Ferrari, Giorgio Montini's name was eventually cleared. But when the local process for Ferrari was initiated, the Modernist stigma was still attached to the cardinal's reputation. To Pope Paul's great delight, Cairoli saved the cause when he discovered a letter in support of Ferrari written by Ambrogio Damiano Achille Ratti, who later became Pope Pius XI. That document proved crucial in clearing Ferrari for beatification—a ceremony over which Pope Paul hoped to preside personally in Milan but did not live long enough to do. Nevertheless, Paul was so grateful to Cairoli that he awarded him the cause of Angelo Giuseppe Roncalli, John XXIII.

hands of Pius X's witch-hunt. I wondered if the two men, one blessed, the other a full-fledged saint, were on speaking terms in the hereafter. The old friar smiled. The fact that these two adversaries had been found heroically virtuous, he said, was proof that the congregation judges each cause on its own merits.

"And what of Pius and John?" I ventured. "In the minds of many people, including Catholics, their merits are not only different but in some ways opposite."

Cairoli demurred. "Every pope completes the pontificate that went before," he said. "I am convinced that there was no division between these two popes. Their pontificates were very united. What differences there were between them have been exaggerated."

"Do you see the two causes as interconnected, then?"

"No, they are completely independent. I know Father Molinari very well. I see him very often. But we never ask each other how our causes are going." At that point, Cairoli reached inside his brown friar's robe and pulled out his wallet. He showed me a picture of Pope John which he carries with him. "Every day I pray for the cause of Papa John," he said. "And every day I say a prayer for the cause of Pius XII too. If Pius is canonized first—good. Every saint is different."

John and Pius may have been different men with different personalities and separate claims to sainthood, Cairoli was saying, but as popes they formed a continuum. History, of course, has a way of discerning continuities which, to contemporary eyes (especially the eyes of journalists, who are trained to look for contrast and change), appear to be disjunctive. But the idea that "one pope completes the pontificate of another" is hardly an axiom supported by hard facts. Like the doctrine of apostolic succession, it proceeds from a deeply ingrained Roman impulse to emphasize continuity in the church, especially among the successors of St. Peter. To be sure, every pope inherits his predecessors' unfinished business, and by the very nature of his office is constrained to uphold tradition. But many people, including the rival factions at Vatican Council II, claimed to see a real difference between the pontificates of John and Pius. Were these men, and millions of others besides, really so mistaken?

Molinari and Gumpel think they were. Indeed, in the early summer of 1987, Molinari attended a conference in France where he read a paper arguing just that point. "During Vatican Council II," Gumpel said one evening while his colleague was still away, "writers presented things as if there was an absolute break between the two popes. Now, a lot of studies show that this was not so. No serious scholar can claim there was serious opposition between them."

"But surely John was more liberal than Pius," I interjected.

"That's not true. After the death of John, whom I liked very much, a kind of legend sprang up, due mainly to journalists. Pius was more distant, more remote, than John, it is true. But really, John was much more conservative. People forget the Synod of the Diocese of Rome, which John called as a preparation for Vatican Council II. At that synod John, as bishop of Rome, tightened up things that Pius XII had loosened."

To Molinari and Gumpel, the real progenitor of Vatican Council II was not John but Pius. Although it was John who actually convened the council, they argue, it was Pius who first had the idea for an ecumenical council. In fact, history now shows that in the 1940s Pius secretly instructed leaders of the Roman Curia to draw up preparatory schemas for a council. "Not many people realize that Pius had already thought of calling a council," said Gumpel. "But he did not do so for three reasons. First, after World War II he felt that the world needed to quiet down before a council could be called. Second, he felt that a very gradual and progressive preparation of the faithful was necessary to prevent too radical a change in the church. He was very aware of the changes that were necessary in the church but wanted psychological preparation. Third, he felt that he was getting too old to carry out a council. These are the facts."

Characteristically, Molinari casts the relationship between the two pontificates in organic terms. "Pius felt the soil was not yet ready," he said. "But in every field he planted the seed which began to germinate in the days of John XXIII. But the seed had been planted and John, conscious of all that, felt that the time had reached the maturity needed for a council. His intention was not to go against Pius but on the contrary, to proceed along the lines Pius had established and to go even further."

As Molinari sees it, Pius XII also laid the intellectual foundations of Vatican II. His encyclical, *Divino afflante Spiritu,* was the basis for the council's important declaration on the source of revelation. His encyclical *Mystici Corporis* was the basis for the council's dogmatic Constitution on the Church. Pius also anticipated the conciliar documents on missiology and the laity. "Without Pope Pius XII, Vatican II would not have been possible," Gumpel summed up. "Apart from the Bible, no author is quoted more frequently in the council's texts."

"It seems to me," I said, "that when Pope Paul VI introduced the two causes, it was John, not Pius, who had the reputation for holiness." Even secular newspapers and journals, I recalled, treated his passing as the death of a saint. It would appear, then, that Pius's cause was piggy-backed on that of John.

Molinari disagreed. "Both men had great reputations for holiness while they were alive," he said. "But the times were different. Remember, Pius reigned through World War II. Rome was bombed. Armies were in Italy. The faithful could not come round to see Pius the way they could when John was pope. But after the war, they came. It was quite a sight. So many soldiers came, not only officers but ordinary soldiers—British, American, Canadian, Polish. They all wanted to approach this holy man who always spoke of peace. And when he died in 1958, there was the same phenomenon as at the death of John. I was here in Rome when both popes died. And there was the same phenomenon: the people assembling at Castel Gandolfo where Pius was dying, watching the little light in the pope's bedroom, waiting for news. And afterward, I can tell you, priests celebrated Mass from six in the morning until noon at Pius's tomb. Pope Paul VI was conscious of all this, and of the requests for Pius's cause that continued to come in. So it was not a case of Pope Paul saying it would be nice to canonize Pius. It was the response of a pope who must be attentive to the signs of God that come from the people."

The message from both postulations was the same: Pius XII and John XXIII are not to be seen as rivals, either in their lifetimes or in their posthumous journeys toward sainthood. They are different popes with separate claims to sanctity, but their pontificates are to be treated as two phases of a single movement, two tides producing different but successive waves upon the shore. This, at any rate, was the effect of introducing the two causes in tandem.

But it occurred to me that Pius had nineteen years as pope in which to establish his reputation for holiness, while John had less than five. Yet the memory of John had so thoroughly eclipsed that of Pius that it was difficult for anyone who hadn't grown up in the era of Pius XII to realize how completely that noble-looking Roman pontiff had managed to identify the fortunes of the church with himself. He was the last (so far) of the popes to be perceived as a spiritual monarch, a man who—to paraphrase the French Sun King, Louis XIV acted as if he truly believed that *L'église, c'est moi.*

Listening to Molinari's recital on behalf of Pius XII, I was reminded of my own childhood images of that pope. There were the bland official portraits of him that hung in every Catholic church and school, the way that Washington or Lincoln presided over public schoolrooms. But there were also the papal prayer cards, like those for saints, which we tucked inside our missals. On these, Pius appeared in profile: ascetic, hollow-eyed behind his silver-rimmed glasses, the long lean figures of both hands pressed for prayer in the tentlike way the nuns required of all us children during Mass.

But what I remembered most was a mental image shaped more by piety than pictures. I imagined him alone in a distant palace called the Vatican, in touch as only popes can be with God, receiving divine wisdom which he passed along from time to time. I had heard his voice on the radio, and he seemed—to Catholics, at least—like a prophet come down from the mountain to tell the world what God was thinking.

During the war, I kept a scrapbook of newspaper headlines and pictures from the battlefields. Among them were grainy pictures of the pope, always dressed in white and pleading for peace, Christ's vicar on earth yet captive in Rome, our saintly and suffering link with the Lord in a world at war. I saw him on newsreels in darkened movie theaters, ivory white and ramrod straight as he turned now this way, now that, his bony fingers carving crosses in the air over heads bent to receive his benediction. "*In nomine Patris, et Filii et Spiritus Sancti . . .*" I recognized the Latin from the Mass: it was our language, church language only Catholics understood. That was what a pope looked like, sounded like, and for the first twenty-three years of my life that was the only pope I knew.

And when, in the winter of 1960, I marched into St. Peter's Basilica for the first time, I was shocked. The figure on the papal throne was round and jowled and smiling hugely, a figure so short it seemed to me his papal slippers did not quite touch the floor. The man was John, but he did not look like a pope to me. I did not know it then but there were others who, for decidedly different reasons, thought so too. For them, the real pope had died and gone to heaven. That was the feeling—so distant now, so buried under layers of intervening time—that Molinari and Gumpel were trying to summon forth on behalf of Pius. And it would be up to them to demonstrate, with no prejudice to John, that the object of that feeling—that primal, powerfully channeled feeling for an erect and isolated leader of the church—was truly a saint.

BUILDING A CASE FOR PIUS XII

BY EVERY MEASURE, the cause of Eugenio Maria Giuseppe Pacelli is the most complex and daunting that the two Jesuits have taken on. Descended from a long line of jurists and papal (black) nobility, Pacelli entered papal service in 1901 at the age of twenty-six. For twelve years he was Cardinal Pietro Gasparri's chief assistant in codifying the canon law. In 1917, he began more than a decade of diplomatic service in Germany, first in Munich and then as nuncio to the new German Republic. In 1929 he was named cardinal and succeeded Gasparri as Vatican secretary of state. In that capacity he negotiated treaties with Austria and Nazi Germany.

In March 1939, with war in Europe imminent, Pacelli was elected pope, receiving all but five of the fifty-three ballots cast. In intellect and experience, he was the match of Roosevelt, Churchill, and the other strong-willed wartime leaders. Like his immediate predecessors, Pius sought to play the role of international peacemaker, spelling out in his first Christmas message to the world what he regarded as sound, "natural law" principles for a just resolution to international differences. But, again like his predecessors, he failed. Throughout the war he maintained a stance of "impartiality," a position which put him under considerable pressure from both the Allies and the Axis. He tried in vain to prevent Italy from entering the war but was more successful in keeping Rome an "open city." When the Nazis finally did occupy Rome in 1943, Pius managed to harbor thousands of refugees, including numerous Jews, in the Vatican and Vatican-owned buildings throughout the city. But because he feared that direct criticism would only intensify persecution of Jews as well as Catholics, and because he preferred to rely on Vatican diplomacy, Pius spoke in only general terms about the Nazis' genocidal pogrom against Europe's Jews. At war's end, he was hailed by several Jewish leaders, including Israel's Golda Meir, later Premier, for his aid to Jews. In the first decade after his death, however, he was widely denounced in Jewish and other circles for his "silence" during the Holocaust.

Despite his preoccupation with the war, Pius XII was amazingly active as the church's Supreme Teacher. He was by turns liberating and restrictive in his guidelines to church scholars. In *Divino afflante Spiritu* (1943), for example, he reversed the prohibitions of his predecessors by endorsing the careful application of historical-critical methodologies to the texts of Sacred Scripture. On the other hand, in *Humani Generis* (1950), his warnings against new theological tendencies—including the view, now widely accepted among Catholic scholars, that humankind did not descend from a single set of parents—initiated a period of repression against the church's more venturesome thinkers. That same year, he became the first pope in a century to define a new dogma of faith: the Assumption of the Virgin Mary into heaven. But like many autocratic rulers—he acted as his

own secretary of state from 1944 on—Pius grew increasingly withdrawn in his later years. Never very approachable, he spent his last
years as a virtual recluse within the papal apartment. Indeed, his
chauffeur claimed that Pacelli never greeted him in all his years of
service.

As soon as the Jesuits were assigned Pacelli's cause, Molinari assembled a four-man team, including Gumpel, to contact everyone
they could think of who might have letters from the pope. The list
came to more than a thousand names. Bishops and heads of religious
orders were asked to search their archives and forward notarized copies of any private letters from the pope in their possession. Those who
failed to reply to the first request were queried again. This process
alone took two years.

A second list was drawn up of people who were known by reputation to have had dealings with Pacelli, beginning with his family.
Eventually, several thousand documents were collected, including
compositions he had written as a student. One thing was peculiar: in
1930, when he became secretary of state to Pius XI, Pacelli had made
a firm decision to limit his personal correspondence. For example, he
rarely wrote to his sisters and when he did, it was merely to send a
birthday or Christmas greeting. And his sisters rarely saw him except
on a few occasions when they attended a Mass he was celebrating. In
short, Pius was not the sort of man who divulged his private thoughts
and feelings, even to his kin.

Finally, the Jesuit team assembled a third list of potential witnesses. Tribunals were held in Rome, Munich, Berlin, and other stops
in Pacelli's life so that testimony could be taken. Both Molinari and
Gumpel make no bones about the fact that in their eyes they are
dealing with a saint. Gumpel had met him as a boy in Germany, he
said, and both men met him in Rome when he was pope. But their
attitude, they hastened to add, is merely subjective. Their job is to
view his life objectively.

In that case, I wanted to know, how did they go about locating
negative witnesses?

Their answers were generalized and circumspect—this was, after
all, a pope I was asking about. "Well, you may know someone who
was silenced or otherwise hurt in his life or mission or career in the
church," Molinari said. "Someone who might have a grudge against
the candidate or at least a divergent opinion."

I asked for names but, as I expected, Molinari said he was bound to
secrecy on pending causes, especially this one. "I can say that a postulator who takes his job seriously does it to seek the truth. It would

be against conscience to brush damaging evidence aside. Besides, the church would gain nothing if it did not have the truth. And the truth means putting all of the cards on the table."

"But surely," I persisted, "you can anticipate some points where the cause may run into problems." I recalled that Benedict XIV had invited investigators to pay particular attention to how authorities in the church, especially popes, treated subordinates. I recalled, too, that the way popes made decisions was as important to a cause as the content of those decisions. In this regard, I mentioned Pius's legendary distrust of others, especially in the last years of his pontificate when he was infirm, seeing visions of the Virgin Mary, and barely communicating with anyone except by phone. The solitary figure I had imagined as a boy was, I had long since come to realize, almost pathologically insistent on running the church himself. And all those speeches—the innumerable locutions, addresses, and encyclicals touching on a bewildering array of subjects—all these, it was now clear, were the work of an intellectually prepossessing pope who apparently felt little need to consult anyone else.

"Yes, Pius was a very sensitive man and he had a very strong temperament," Molinari acknowledged. "Theoretically, these are areas which would create problems for his cause. Sensitivity can be a two-edged sword. Sensitivity to suffering, for example, can lead to overreaction as well as to good things. Pius was very sensitive to intellectual matters and that sort of sensitivity can lead to a certain diffidence toward individuals. He was, we know, slow to give his trust to people and this can lead to an exaggerated independence."

But the major issue concerning Pius's claim to holiness is not personal but political: did he do all he could have, or should have, to counter the Nazis' genocidal pogrom against Europe's Jews?

Gumpel anticipated this line of questioning and was eager to respond. It is an issue about which he has especially strong feelings. He had, he reminded me more than once, twice been exiled from his native country because of the Nazis. What's more, he had been a student in Holland when the Nazis took over that country. His admiration for Pius ran long and deep: it was because of Pius XII, he confided during one long evening session in his rooms, that he had decided to become a priest.

"There are," I pressed, "some people—perhaps many people—for whom Pius XII remains the pope who chose to remain silent about the Holocaust because he feared that in speaking out he would only incite a greater persecution of Catholics. How do you intend to deal with this issue in the cause?"

"You forget," he began, "that these accusations are of compara- tively recent vintage. During the war, Pius was regarded on all sides as the pope of peace. It was only after 1963, when the German writer Rolf Hochhuth published his foolish play *The Deputy*, that Pius's reputation changed, at least among some people. I recall that at that time we were asked to take issue with it. But we refused because we were convinced that with the passage of time these things would sort themselves out. And that is exactly what happened. History is a se- vere but just taskmaster, and nowadays I doubt there is a serious scholar who takes Hochhuth seriously."

Nonetheless, Gumpel acknowledged that "the Jewish question" was the most serious issue that the *positio* on Pius would have to address. I pressed him and Father Molinari to tell me how they intend to deal with it.

"There is," Gumpel said, "plenty of evidence on this subject which is not yet known publicly but which we have to gather so as to re- spond with certainty to the doubts about Pius's course of action which continue to exist. But there are already many facts which are known. For example, in 1937, Pope Pius XI issued a very strong encyclical [*Mit brennender Sorge*, written in German, not the customary Latin and printed as a precaution on clandestine local presses and throughout Germany], denouncing Nazism as fundamentally anti-Christian. The letter was drafted by Cardinal Pacelli, the secretary of state, who had served as nuncio in Germany for many years and had no illusions about the Nazis. Absolutely none. And there were numerous protests on the diplomatic level which people did not know about."

"But if he was so well informed why did he not protest more di- rectly after he became pope?"

Gumpel threaded his fingers, leaned forward, and placed both el- bows on his desk. He was wearing the dark blue woolen sweater that he often put on in evenings, the kind one sees quite frequently on Germans. "I put the question to you very frankly," he said. "If you had known Nazism as he knew it, and as I knew it, are you so sure you would have made a stand? Perhaps by doing so you will appear as a hero to posterity. That is one thing. But if you have any experience in government you have to consider the consequences. Are the persecu- tions going to be even cruder? How many people are going to suffer for it? Pope Pius came out with strong statements against the Nazi treat- ment of the Jews. But he did not do so after the experience of the Dutch hierarchy."

Gumpel then went on to recapitulate what happened to the Jewish converts to Catholicism, including Edith Stein, after the Dutch bish-

ops denounced Nazism in 1942. "This was an example to the pope
that public protests would do no good," he said. "Moreover, the Polish
episcopate asked him not to do anything. They warned him that a
protest would only make matters worse. So did other episcopates. So
the question of the so-called silence of Pius XII is extremely delicate.
The question was, would it do any good or would it only make matters worse? There are a number of documents which make it clear
that it would have only worsened matters—including pleas from Jews
not to say anything that would encourage greater persecution. To
allay this accusation that the pope did nothing, the Holy See has
already published twelve volumes of his official acts issued during
World War II."

It is obvious that in making a case for Pius XII's heroic virtue—
especially the moral virtues of prudence, justice, and fortitude—
Gumpel and Molinari have to examine not only the actions of Pacelli
but also those of the Vatican's diplomatic corps as well as of the
European episcopates during the Nazi era. In this respect, they said,
their work is dependent on the availability of previous classified material in the wartime archives of the Germans, Italians, Americans,
and other participants in World War II. By way of example, they drew
my attention to the work of British historian Owen Chadwick in
reconstructing the various diplomatic pressures brought by both the
Allies and the Axis powers to move Pius XII away from his position of
neutrality during World War II. "Father Molinari and I are aware that
Pius XII is a controversial figure," Gumpel said. "We want to present
the cause in the way that really first-class scholars deal with different
aspects of his pontificate. This means we need lots of time. We don't
want to rush it through."

Indeed, as the two Jesuits talked about their project, they revealed
an aspect of the saint-making process which I hadn't noticed. Unlike
most other *positiones*, the one on Pius XII will be a collaborative
effort containing material from dozens of outside historians. Gumpel
has already sketched out an overview of Pacelli's life and isolated
several areas requiring collaborative material from specialists. In some
cases, Gumpel has written to experts asking them to respond to questions; in others, he has asked for lengthy monographs. "Thus far," he
confided, "we have far more than two dozen of the first kind, and
more than fifteen of the second. People are quite willing to do this.
You see, there is great collaboration in the field of scientific history.
People who are seriously interested in historical subjects are willing
to help us because it's an exchange. They help us and we facilitate
things for them. And today there are so many scientific writings on

Pius XII that it is not hard to find collaborators willing to write certain sections."

But how, I wanted to know, did they decide which outside experts to consult? What criteria do they use in picking one historian rather than another? I recalled the criticisms of Father Luigi Porsi, the canon lawyer and former advocate, who argued that the reform of 1983 did not provide for systematic criticism of a cause as the process developed. Since Molinari and Gumpel were, as they acknowledged, subjectively convinced of the pope's holiness, were they willing to incorporate into their *positio* the work of scholars who may be critical of the pope? I cited by way of example the American sociologist Gordon Zahn, whose study *German Catholics and Hitler's War* was highly critical of Pius XII's conduct in the Nazi era.

"First of all," Gumpel said, "we have access to everything that concerns the pontificate of Pius XII. Therefore we already have a great number of ascertained facts. With these in your head, you read a book and see perhaps that a man deals with a question but that he ignores a great or essential amount of the historical evidence. In that case we can see that his judgments are based on scanty and sometimes erroneous evidence. For example, we will not consult Gordon Zahn because he does not have the facts."

"But," I objected, "is it really so easy to separate facts from their interpretation? It seems to me that in history there are no facts apart from interpretation. Even the choice of which facts are relevant is an exercise in historical interpretation."

"It is not easy," Gumpel replied, "but neither is it impossible. If you read an author who says that Pius XII said this or that, and you have the original document in front of you, you can see whether the author misquotes or speculates. It is simply a matter of whether he knows his material or not—does he have the evidence for talking about the pope's motivation in this or that case."

"So you choose your collaborators on the basis of how they treat materials which you already have in your possession?"

"Yes. You see, with regard to this case we have access to all the German archives as well as to those of the Vatican. And recently the archives of the British Foreign Office regarding World War II have been opened so we have those as well. So when we read a book touching on some important aspect of this cause, we write to the author saying, your work inspires confidence because you quote documents and we have access to those documents. We have a real doubt with regard to a certain issue and we would like your opinion on this. As you might imagine this is an enormous amount of work. And in the case of a pope you have to go to the utmost limit in ascertaining what happened."

I was aware, of course, that this was not the only cause Gumpel and Molinari are working on. But even if it were, I suggested, it seemed unlikely that either of them would live to see it finished.

Gumpel smiled a weary smile. Although the Vatican has no mandatory retirement age for people who do his sort of work, Gumpel allowed that "I really don't know if I will live to see the conclusion of it." In any case, he said, there is no pressure on them to meet a deadline. If anything, he added, the political climate of the church remains such that neither Pius's nor John's cause would be acted upon even if the *positio* were written. "The fact is, neither *positio* is going to be finished in the immediate future. We are very friendly with Father Cairoli and we certainly do not want to have a kind of horse race. But we do have a kind of gentlemen's agreement with him that we will proceed with the causes contemporaneously."

There it was: the first acknowledgment by anyone in the congregation that the fates of the two causes are procedurally linked. Previously, everyone I had spoken to had danced around the question because it touches on the most sensitive side of saint-making—ecclesiastical politics. But Gumpel was quite frank about their informal arrangement and the reason for it.

"To put it bluntly," he said, "if at this moment this pope were to beatify Pius and not John, there would be a certain section of opinion which would say that he prefers the line of Pius to that of John. Exactly the opposite would happen if he beatified John instead of Pius."

THE CASE FOR JOHN XXIII

UNLIKE PACELLI, ANGELO Giuseppi Roncalli was born far from cultured Rome—and from his predecessor's privileged circumstances. His parents were sharecroppers in Sotto il Monte and he served in the military before becoming a priest. Awarded a scholarship to study in Rome, he completed his doctorate (with Pacelli as one of his examiners) and returned north to teach in a seminary and become secretary to Giacomo Radini-Tedeschi, the politically active bishop of Bergamo. These were the later days of Pius X's furious efforts to uproot Modernists in the church and the era of the *Sodalitium Pianum* (Sodality

of Pius, named in memory of Pope Pius IX), a network of spies run out
of the Vatican whose members reported on suspected Modernists.
Among those who fell under suspicion were the young Roncalli's
superior, Bishop Radini-Tedeschi, whom Pius X liked to ridicule, and
Roncalli's elder friend, Cardinal Ferrari of Milan—and Roncalli himself. Among other things, Roncalli was accused of reading and approv-
ing of French Catholic historian Monsignor Louis Marie Duchesne,
whose three-volume *History of the Ancient Church* was placed on the
Vatican's *Index of Forbidden Books*. Roncalli hastily worked to clear
his name. But the incident so unnerved him that it may account for
his distaste as pope for intellectual repression.*

During World War I, Roncalli served as sergeant in the medical
corps and saw service at the front. For several years he worked in
Rome, then was sent to Bulgaria to deal with problems between Latin
and Byzantine Catholics and the Orthodox. In 1934, Archbishop Roncalli was appointed apostolic delegate to Turkey where, after the outbreak of the war, he managed to aide countless Jews and other refugees
from Nazi Germany. A decade later he became papal nuncio to France
and deftly dissuaded de Gaulle (who later gave written testimony on
behalf of Roncalli's canonization cause) in his efforts to force Rome to
remove twenty-five French bishops—including three cardinals—
whom the government accused of collaborating with the Pétain regime. While in Paris, he inaugurated a seminary for training German
prisoners of war and tried to soften Pius XII's condemnation of the
French priest-worker movement.

Created a cardinal, in 1953 Roncalli was awarded the patriarchal
see of Venice where he had every reason to expect he would end his
ecclesiastical career. He was seventy-seven years old in 1958 when, as
a compromise candidate, he was elected pope. He took the name of
John, he said, because he wanted to imitate the Baptist who made
straight the path of the Lord. An outsider to Vatican politics—"I'm in
a bag here," he once complained—John plunged ahead with Vatican
Council II, knowing full well that there was opposition to the idea
from his own advisers in the Roman Curia. His opening speech to the
council fathers was revelatory of the man. Whereas past councils had
used severity in confronting the contemporary world, this time it was
understanding that was needed. John thought the council would last
only a few months. Instead, it was drawn out over four years. He
didn't live to see its finish, but in his five brief years he had already

*After he became pope, Roncalli asked for a secret dossier that had been compiled on him. He read it,
then returned it to the files—unlike his predecessor, Pius XII, who removed a dossier of complaints
against himself from the Vatican's files.

transformed the image of the papacy—and of the church. His passing was mourned, in the words of one newspaper headline, as "A Death in the Family of Mankind."

Compared to Molinari and Gumpel's elaborate team approach, Father Cairoli was running an old-fashioned, one-man operation on behalf of John XXIII. Roncalli was the aging Franciscan's last and only cause, and though through illness he had fallen far off the pace set by the Jesuits, he relished doing everything himself.

For example, he visited all the places Roncalli worked as a diplomat. In Bulgaria, he was shadowed by the police. In Turkey, he interviewed a Jewish newspaper editor who told him that Roncalli funneled money to him twice a week during the World War II so that Jewish refugees from Hitler could purchase food. What interested Cairoli even more was that the money came not from the church but from Franz von Papen, Hitler's ambassador to Turkey.

"I had never heard this story before," Cairoli said. "But I needed to confirm it with von Papen himself. He was still alive, then living in southern Germany near the Black Forest. So I went there and he told me that yes, it was all true. Hitler had given von Papen a lot of money to use in order to help convince the Turks that they should side with the Axis. Von Papen was a Catholic and he would attend Roncalli's Mass. Afterward, they would talk. Both believed that Germany and Italy would lose the war and both were worried that if the Turks sided with the Axis, the Soviet Union would invade Turkey. So instead of spending the money to bribe the Turks, von Papen gave it to Roncalli who gave it to the displaced Jews. That was the sort of diplomat Roncalli was."

Though he was willing to travel on behalf of the cause, Cairoli wanted no part of handling its finances. He insisted that the Vatican's Secretariat of State handle the considerable funds donated on John's behalf. Cairoli was also frugal. For instance, officials of the secretariat urged him to investigate an inexplicable cure in Chicago. A miracle from there, they felt, would help to show the universality of John's reputation for holiness. But Cairoli, who had more than twenty potential miracles to choose from, picked one from Naples, another from Sicily.

"You see," he explained, "a trip to Chicago would mean the cost of an international flight. Hotels are more expensive in your country than in mine. Doctors are paid much more and I must at least offer to compensate physicians for their time. But in Italy," he explained, "I can travel cheap by train, stay in a *pensione*, and the doctors here do not charge when they testify on a miracle."

I found it odd that after nearly twenty years of working on the cause Cairoli did not yet have a relator. He didn't want one, he said, nor did he want any collaborators in the daunting task of writing the pope's *positio*. He had already collected some six thousand documents by and about the late pope, including testimony from some three hundred witnesses, and altogether they ran to more than twenty thousand pages. "I will write the *positio* myself," he told me one afternoon when we met at the congregation, "because I am working with reserved documents which I cannot show to a collaborator." His prize document, one on which he was counting to reveal the pope's sustaining heroic virtue, is the personal diary Roncalli had kept for most of his adult life. "I keep it locked in an armoire," Cairoli explained. "Then I put the key inside another armoire and keep the key to that one always with me." He chuckled at his elaborate precaution. "It belongs to the Holy See, but I doubt that they will ever publish it. I don't even think they will put it in the Vatican Archives."

"Why?"

"Roncalli wrote in it about many politicians. When he was in Istanbul, for example, as papal nuncio to Turkey, there were many international spies there from Germany, Russia, and every other country. He wrote down what he saw, what he heard from them. And he continued to do so when he was pope. All the names are there, so I don't think the Holy See wants his diary made public. But I can tell you this: never once have I read something in it that was against another person."

"So you think the diary will be important evidence to his heroic virtue?"

"Yes, certainly. You see when people have notorious enemies, it is heroic when they respond with love. Papa John always responded with love."

Cairoli then went on to tell the story of Cardinal Domenico Tardini, a carryover from the administration of Pius XII, who had complained to some journalists that he could not work with the new pope. But when Tardini went to John and offered to resign, the pope insisted that he stay on as his secretary of state. Cairoli relished the end of the story: "Papa John said, 'I know you do not have great esteem for me—and for good reason—but I have great esteem for you. You have worked at the center of the church and know well the major problems. I was not at the center of the church but at the periphery and I know what the periphery wants from the center. So you will complement me and I will complement you and together we will work for the church.' You see, Papa John never spoke against people who spoke against him. Not one word. Never. During his whole life, he was like that—heroic in his charity."

I knew that John had numerous enemies during his lifetime, especially detractors inside the Roman Curia. But, what I wanted to know was whether any of his enemies had gone so far as to testify against his cause.

Cairoli began fingering the knotted rosary that all Franciscans wear at the waist. "To collect testimony we held tribunals in many places: Bergamo, Paris, Sofia, Venice, wherever Roncalli lived. The first was in Rome, where he died, and the first witness I presented was Cardinal Eugene Tisserant. You see, we must present all the witnesses who are against the cause and I had heard that Tisserant had spoken against Papa John. So I asked him to explain. Tisserant had been prefect of the Vatican Archives as well as prefect of the Oriental Congregations. When John became pope he didn't see why one man should hold two important jobs, so he told Tisserant to choose one of them. Tisserant became angry. But his anger was just over this single incident. As it turned out he was not at all against Papa John's cause."

"Were there others?" I pressed.

There were. One of them was Cardinal Giuseppe Siri of Genoa, a reactionary by any standards and one of the principal opponents of reform at Vatican Council II. Pope Pius XII, his hero, had given him the red hat in 1953, when Siri was just forty-six years old, making him one of the youngest cardinals in the church. For decades Siri was a power in the Italian episcopate. Three times his name had been placed in nomination for the papacy, and three times he had been passed over.

As Cairoli told it, Siri had been widely quoted in the press as saying that it would take forty years to repair the damage Pope John had caused by calling Vatican Council II. "People told me that Siri was against Papa John's cause, so I went to him in Genoa and said, 'Your Eminence, I know you are against this cause. Please, will you testify at a tribunal?' And he said, 'They say I am against the cause and that is not true.' He even denied that he had spoken against Pope John's calling of the council. So then he agreed to tell this to the tribunal."

It was clear that Cairoli regarded criticism of John, however limited or mild, as grist for the cause. What concerned him, however, was the pope's reputation for making spontaneous judgments. Indeed, this characteristic—which endeared him to ordinary Catholics and charmed the non-Catholic world—was something which his postulator obviously felt might be cited against the cause.

"They say he was *impulsivo*. But that's not true. What he did was never simply *impulsivo*. Take, for example, his strong desire for re-union with the Orthodox churches. In 1925, when he was a papal representative to Bulgaria, he attended the Holy Synod of the Ortho-dox Church. In Rome his presence was regarded as a scandal. The Secretariat of State and the Holy Office wanted to know what he thought he was doing. So Roncalli wrote to his friend Gustavo Testa, later a cardinal. 'Please tell me, Gustavo, what have I done wrong? They are bishops as we are. They are priests as we are. Their sacra-ments are as valid as our sacraments. They believe in one God as we do. They honor the Mother of God as we do. And if from the law of Gospel I must love my enemy, can I not also love these my brothers?' Therefore, when he invited the Orthodox to come sit in at Vatican Council II, it was the same as in 1925. It was not, as I said, something *impulsivo*."

"But what about the council?" I asked. "Didn't John himself say the idea of calling it came to him as a sudden inspiration of the Holy Spirit?"

Cairoli's eyes widened behind his rimless glasses. He had yet an-other story. In 1905, when Roncalli was just a young secretary to the bishop of Bergamo, he accompanied his boss to Milan on a visit to Cardinal Ferrari. In the archives of the Milan archdiocese he discov-ered five books that the great Cardinal Charles Borromeo had written on applying the teachings of the Council of Trent to the local church. Roncalli thought a critical edition of the texts should be published and for the next fifty years—until he became pope—he worked on it.

"During World War II, when Roncalli was in Istanbul, his secretary wanted to fly to Italy to see his parents. Roncalli told him it was too dangerous; the British or the Americans might shoot the plane down. 'But if you go,' he said, 'please bring me these books.' The books were about the Council of Trent. So you see, he was always studying the council. And in 1944, in the Church of the Holy Spirit in Istanbul, with Germans and Americans and others present, he talked about how the church should deal with the world after the war. There he talked about a council and the need to prepare ourselves to enter this new world. He never imagined that he would be pope. But when he was elected it was natural for him to think of calling a council. He had been preparing for it for fifty years. He was not *impulsivo*."

I never saw Cairoli again. He died in March of 1989. In these cir-cumstances, the congregation could be expected to turn over a cause as important as Pope John's to another postulator of long experience. But that did not happen. Instead, it was given to the Franciscans' new postulator general. The reason was that the material Cairoli had collected was so sensitive, a congregation official explained, that they didn't want too many people to see it.

Although Cairoli had given me no hint of any problems with John's cause, rumors were circulating within the congregation that John's process was in serious trouble. "Before it was the cause for Pius that had the problems," said the archivist, Father Yvon Beaudoin, a few months after Cairoli's death. "Now it is John's. You hear people say it, you read articles. Now he is being blamed for everything that has gone wrong in the church since Vatican Council II." Others within the congregation spoke more ominously. Investigation into Roncalli's life, I was told, had turned up impediments far more serious that the reputation for impulsiveness which Cairoli had been so anxious to combat. The miracles that the lire-conscious friar had culled on John's behalf were of no avail so long as there was real doubt about the pope's heroic virtue. For the moment, at least, the cause was stymied, but not officially stopped.

In contrast, by the end of 1989 Pius's cause was ready for the writing of the *positio*. Yet Molinari and Gumpel appeared to be in no hurry to finish their task. The reason, presumably, was that Pope John Paul II still wants both causes processed simultaneously.

Whatever the case, it is clear that the two popes and their pontificates are still much too sensitive politically to allow either cause to come to judgment soon. In this respect, both causes are hostage to the future as well as to the past: John's fate depends in part on the interpretation that is placed on the council he convoked, Pius's on the still simmering controversy over his highly circumspect public reaction to the Holocaust. Indeed, the 1989 crisis in Jewish-Catholic relations precipitated by the building of the Carmelite convent at Auschwitz was a potent reminder of just how deep feelings run among Jews concerning the Holocaust and Pius XII's decision not to address it directly. In both cases, the ultimate disposition of the causes will be greatly influenced by how the prelates of the congregation eventually weigh the "opportuneness" of each cause—in other words, its impact on church and world opinion.

What was not yet clear to me, however, was how the consultors themselves judge papal causes. In weighing the candidate's performance in office, do they focus mainly on his zeal for preserving and propagating the faith, as Benedict XIV proposed? To what extent is a papal Servant of God also held accountable for his social and political doctrine? His treatment of theological dissenters? His administrative decisions? His relations with foreign governments? His reading, to use a favorite phrase from Vatican Council II, of "the signs of the times"? Certainly these are important issues in the causes for Pius and John. What I had yet to discover is that they are major issues in the cause of another papal candidate as well.

CHAPTER TEN

PIUS IX
AND THE
POSTHUMOUS POLITICS
OF CANONIZATION

INSIDE THE VATICAN, knowledge is power and a secret is something you tell one person at a time. After a year and more in Rome I had become a familiar figure in the corridors of the Congregation for the Causes of Saints. But even then I was slow to learn that John Paul II had established a secret commission of scholars and prelates to advise him on the "opportuneness" of beatifying one of his most controversial predecessors, Pius IX (1846–1878). Members of the commission were sworn not to discuss the panel's deliberations or even to acknowledge its existence. Indeed, almost no one outside the congregation was aware of the commission or what the pope was up to. It was one of those rare things in Rome: a well-kept secret.

For that matter, few bishops outside Rome even knew that in 1985, John Paul II had approved the heroic virtue of Pio Nono, as he was popularly known, and a year later had approved a miracle of intercession as well. Normally, beatification follows as a matter of course unless—as in this case—the pope has problems with the cause.

The problems, I was told, were chiefly political. To this day, Pio Nono is regarded within Italy's liberal and anticlerical circles as the retrograde Roman pontiff who resisted the unification of Italy and its eventual emergence as a modern nation-state. Understandably, some cardinals and others within the Roman Curia feared that the beatification of Pius IX would inflame this influential segment of Italian opinion and thus produce more harm than good for the Italian church.

But there were reasons for thinking that the beatification might also embarrass the universal church, especially in Western democracies. For one thing, it was Pius IX who in 1864 issued the notorious Syllabus of Errors, which condemns such liberal ideals as freedom of conscience and separation of church and state. To beatify him a century later when these values are widely accepted as the foundation stones of liberal democracy—indeed, as human rights and values now promoted by the papacy itself—would be to invite ridicule of the church. For another, Pio Nono was the pope who convoked Vatican Council I with the express purpose of having the doctrine of papal infallibility defined as dogma of faith. Since this dogma is the major obstacle to reunion of the Christian churches, beatification of Pius IX might well be interpreted as a rejection of the contemporary ecumenical movement. In addition, there are many Roman Catholics, including scholars of the nineteenth-century church, who simply do not regard Pius IX as a saint—much less a worthy example to be put before the faithful—despite the congregation's judgment to the contrary.

On the other hand, Pio Nono was deeply loved by the ordinary Catholics of his day and his cause has attracted powerful supporters. Since 1972, its promotion has been in the hands of an association of more than five hundred prominent church officials and lay Catholics, including 30 cardinals, 60 archbishops, and 150 bishops. Among them, at the time, were more than a dozen officials of the Roman Curia, including Paul VI's former secretary of state, Amleto Cicognani; Cardinal Paolo Bertoli, then the prefect of the Congregation for the Causes of Saints; and two of his successors in that post, Cardinals Luigi Raimondi and Pietro Palazzini. Indeed, by 1987 Palazzini had assumed the role of Pius IX's chief proponent inside the Vatican.

It was widely assumed that John Paul II personally approved of the cause. Historians, in fact, could see a certain rough symmetry at work: Pio Nono's cause had been initiated by Pius X, a soul mate in condemning liberal heresies. Pius X, in turn, was canonized in 1954 by Pius XII when the Vatican was again condemning some of the church's most distinguished theologians. By the mid-eighties, John Paul II had proved himself equally disposed toward disciplining dissident thinkers in the church. Surely, it was said, he would welcome the opportunity to declare Pio Nono among the blesseds of the church.

What the pundits had no way of knowing is that the cause of Pius IX had experienced rough going from the start. Pius X was himself dubious of some aspects of his predecessor's character. All the firsthand witnesses interrogated by the investigating tribunals testified that they had objections to the way Pio Nono had run the church. Twice, under the old juridicial system, the cause had gone to a vote of consultors and prelates of the congregation, and twice it had received considerably less than unanimous approval.

My own interest in the cause was driven by the singular opportunity, as I saw it, of seeing precisely how a modern pope is measured for heroic virtue. For that I needed to study a papal *positio*. The only other candidate was Pius X, but the documents on his cause—or at least the last, clinching *positio*—were embargoed by the Vatican because some of the material is still considered sensitive. The secrecy surrounding the commission on Pius IX, however, gave me little hope of examining his official papers.

As it happened, the last in a long line of Pius's advocates was still alive. Carlo Snider, a Swiss layman with long experience in the congregation, had been assigned by Paul VI in 1975 to undertake yet another defense of Pio Nono. His task was not to write a whole new *positio*, but to respond to the cumulative criticism of the Servant of God, as summarized by the Devil's Advocate. I wrote to Snider, asking him to receive me so that I might find out how he marshaled his defense. Snider refused to discuss the case with me unless ordered to do so by Cardinal Palazzini. It was only then that a trusting Vatican official gave me a copy of Snider's *positio*. It was the third and last argument on behalf of Pius IX, the one which finally convinced the consultors and prelates of his heroic virtue.

THE FIRST MODERN POPE

GIOVANNI MARIA MASTAI-FERRETTI reigned for nearly thirty-two years, longer than any pope before or after him. He was the last pope to rule the Papal States and therefore the last to exercise the temporal powers of a secular prince. Conversely, he was the first of the "modern popes"; that is, the first to be officially recognized as exercising infallibility in matters of faith and morals and primacy of jurisdiction over every Roman Catholic in the world. He was also the founder of the modern papacy in the sense that in and through him the Holy See developed into a spiritual monarchy buttressed by a highly centralized Vatican bureaucracy. Above all, he was the first pope to inspire "the almost mystical awe that modern Catholics associate with the papacy."

By temperament and intellect, Mastai was poorly prepared for the church's highest office. He suffered from epilepsy as a young man, a fact which will figure significantly in Snider's defense. His education was modest, and apart from a brief diplomatic visit to Chile, he knew little of the world outside the northern Papal States, where he served successively as bishop of Spoleto and as cardinal of Imola. He was a youthful fifty-four in 1846 when he was elected pope.

Upon his accession, Pio Nono gained a surprising reputation for liberal reform. He proclaimed amnesty for political prisoners in the Papal States, relaxed censorship laws, and granted Rome a constitution with a prime minister. These measures so shocked Prince Metternich, the Austrian foreign minister whose troops occupied several northern Italian territories, that he exclaimed that he "had allowed for everything in Italy except a liberal Pope!"

Papa Mastai's liberal reputation dissolved in the political upheavals of 1848. He refused to support the Italian war of independence against Austria, arguing that to do so would compromise his religious mission as father of all the faithful. This outraged the revolutionaries in Rome, who murdered his prime minister and besieged the new pope inside the Quirinale. Disguised as a layman, Pio Nono fled to Gaeta and took asylum with the king of Naples. He returned in 1850 as a political reactionary. Twenty years later, armies of the Italian Risorgimento occupied Rome and abolished the Papal States. Pio Nono refused to negotiate with the insurgents; they were, after all, secularizers who had closed convents and monasteries and were bent on rooting religion out of Italy's schools. Instead, he retired to the Vatican and its surrounding gardens where he and his successors remained voluntary "prisoners" until the Vatican pact with Benito Mussolini in 1929. For the rest of his pontificate, Pio Nono's foreign policy was predicated on gaining the return of the Papal States. Without them, he insisted, the independence of the church could not be assured.

Politically, the old order was passing away, but Pio Nono refused to accept it. Everywhere he looked, he saw the rise of popular sovereignty, which appalled him, and parliamentary governments, which he mistrusted. Worse, in his view, was the triumph of "Liberalism," a synthesis of heresies which he rejected as a denial of divine revelation and which he came to regard as literally the work of the Devil. In 1864, he set the face of the church against the main currents and ideas of the nineteenth century with the publication of an encyclical, *Quanta Cura*, to which he appended the eighty propositions entitled "A Syllabus of Errors." Both documents bristled with condemnations. Not only liberalism, pantheism, and rationalism, but progress, sepa-

ration of church and state, a free press, freedom of conscience, civil
rights, and even modern civilization itself were identified as evil and
declared anathema. Unwilling to distinguish the gold from the dross
in liberal ideals and movements, the pope rejected them all.

The effect of these fulminations was to create an enormous abyss
between the church and contemporary Western societies. Loyal liberal Catholics who saw positive value in such ideas as separation of
church and state were either discouraged or silenced. Outside the
church, Catholicism was seen as retreating into black reaction. In
democratic but largely Protestant countries like England and the
United States, Catholics were hard put to defend themselves against
charges that their religion was inimical to the good of the country. On
the other hand, Ultramontanist Catholics cheered the pope's aggres-
sive rejection of the modern world and demanded more of the same.
The future of civilization, these hyperpapalists believed, depends upon
preserving and emphasizing the authority of the papacy.

There was more. In 1869, Pius IX convoked Vatican Council I.
Among the Roman theologians assigned to draw up the agenda, there
were some who wanted the council fathers to define the Syllabus of
Errors as doctrines of faith. But Pius IX had a more encompassing goal
in mind: he felt the times called for the council to define—explicitly
and solemnly—the doctrine of papal infallibility as a dogma of the
church. Already in 1854 he had, after consulting with members of the
episcopate, invoked papal infallibility by declaring the Immaculate
Conception of Mary a dogma of faith. Most of the council fathers had
no quarrel with the idea that a pope can, when speaking as head of the
universal church, pronounce infallibility on matters of belief and morals essential to the faith. But a sizable minority of them felt strongly
that it was inopportune to define this doctrine as dogma, thereby
giving it the status of divinely revealed truth. Some wanted restrictions written into the declaration which would prevent a pope from
issuing infallible statements based on his personal theological opinions. Others quarreled with the concomitant notion of the pope's
universal jurisdiction over all Roman Catholics; they wanted the
council to make clear that bishops rule by divine right as successors
to Christ's apostles, not as mere representatives of the pope.

Pius IX, however, was in no mood for temporizing. Although the
fathers engaged in strenuous debate, the pope was not above applying
pressure to opponents of the infallibility document. When Cardinal
Filippo Guidi, a distinguished theologian, protested privately to Pio
Nono that "European tradition is unfavorable to the dogma," the pope
exploded: "*I am Tradition.*" Whereupon he sentenced Guidi to a con-

vent until he could pray his way to accepting the pope's position. In the end Guidi voted with the infallibilist majority.

In short, what Pius IX lost in the way of temporal power he more than gained in spiritual provenance. As subsequent history shows, papal infallibility has so far turned out to be a sheathed sword: since Vatican I, it has been invoked only once, and then only after wide consultation with the bishops, when Pius XII proclaimed the dogma of the bodily Assumption of Mary into heaven. On the other hand, history also shows that as a consequence of papal infallibility, a "cult of the Pope" emerged among the Catholic faithful which sustained the steady centralization of power in the Vatican throughout the twentieth century and made the person of the reigning pontiff an object of almost idolatrous piety. Pius IX was the first pope to enjoy such adulation: indeed, his contemporary and friend, St. John Bosco, was not along in thinking that "the Pope is God on earth. Jesus has set the Pope above the prophets, above his precursor, above the angels. Jesus has placed the Pope on a level with God." So did the Jesuits in Rome, who likened the pope to "Christ, if he were himself and visibly here below to govern the church."

Liberal historians have not been kind to Pio Nono. They note, for example, that he virtually eliminated all serious intellectual discourse within the church and failed utterly in his foreign policy; at his death only four countries still maintained representatives to the Vatican. More recently, however, his pontificate has been placed in a brighter light. The church did not collapse into irrelevance, as some critics had predicted, but retrenched and survived, albeit at the price of losing considerable influence in world affairs for seventy-five years. In retrospect, Pio Nono must be regarded, for better and worse, as the man who shaped the modern papacy. In this regard, a judgment on his pontificate involves, at least implicitly, a judgment on the whole course of the church since his reign. Snider, as I was to discover, was well aware that his defense of Pio Nono would have to rest on the pope's own conviction that his actions, however they may be measured by human standards, were dictated by Divine Providence.

But what of Mastai's personal virtue, the stuff that canonized saints are made of? There was, as has been noted, ample evidence of his irascibility and impulse to bully. On the other hand, there was considerable evidence of his warmth, charm, quick wit (which he often turned on himself as well as on others), energy, and, above all, personal piety. His faith was rock solid and his fortitude beyond cavil. "Prisoner" though he was, he was the first pope to hold regular audiences at the Vatican, and faithful throughout Europe traveled by train to see him. Less than a week after his death, the Vatican received the first request—from Franciscans in Vienna—for his speedy beatification.

How, then, to measure Mastai's claim to sanctity? What episodes out of so crowded and controversial a life would the consultors focus on? What weight would they give in their deliberations to his performance as pope? Dare they second-guess his pressure tactics during Vatican I on behalf of the infallibility dogma? For that matter, how would they judge the Syllabus of Errors, which was thoroughly repudiated by the declarations of Vatican Council II? How, finally, would theologians and prelates schooled in the teachings of Vatican II judge the father of Vatican I? I knew the result, but only Snider's *positio* would reveal how it was obtained.

THE OBJECTIONS AGAINST PIUS IX'S CAUSE

UNLIKE OTHER POSITIONES I had read, Snider's did not follow the usual outline of attempting to prove each of the required virtues. His specific assignment was to answer the objections which had been made by the consultors in the two votes on the cause. Fortunately, these objections were well summarized in a brief by Father Rafael Pérez, the former Devil's Advocate. Reading them, one finds a curious mix of issues, some personal, some political, and some gravely suggestive of improper conduct by the head of the universal church.

Several of the consultors and prelates were struck by Pio Nono's apparent lack of "meekness." Witnesses had testified that he frequently broke out in "rages," addressing "abrasive remarks to persons of decent reputation." He was "impulsive," quick to ridicule, to show resentment and disapproval without regard for the effect his sharp tongue had on the recipients of his sarcasm.

For some of the consultors, this abrasiveness amounted to a serious lack of "charity toward neighbor." As bishop and as pope, Mastai failed to practice "the fundamental norm of evangelical charity—not to do unto others what you would not want them to do unto you." He appeared much too willing to accept accusations against third parties at face value, and to punish or dismiss them from service without first granting the accused a hearing. In particular, the Devil's Advocate cites the pope's refusal to commute the death sentences of two anarchists, Monti and Tognetti, who had blown up a barracks housing papal soldiers in 1862. Their executions had apparently scandalized even the pope's supporters. Indeed, the Devil's Advocate notes, Pope Pius X himself "was known to say, 'This fact alone would impede the canonization of the Servant of God.' "

The brief also accuses Pius IX of lacking "prudence in government." The Devil's Advocate cites six cases in which Pio Nono promoted unworthy, inept, or "excessively ignorant" men to important posts in the papal government. The pope is also accused of "call[ing] to government persons who were hostile to religion." The brief makes special note of Cardinal Giacomo Antonelli, who served as Pio Nono's powerful secretary of state for twenty-six years. According to some historical accounts, Antonelli was a skilled fund-raiser who not only replenished the Vatican's accounts but, at the same time, amassed a huge private fortune for himself. Although the brief does not specifically mention profiteering, it does ask for more information regarding "unanswered questions" about Antonelli's public and private life.

Pope Paul VI was particularly interested in Pio Nono's treatment of Father Antonio Rosmini-Serbati, one of the few outstanding intellectuals of the Italian church and also one of its holiest men. The brief asks whether Pius IX manifested "sufficient charity" toward Rosmini. It notes that Pio Nono repeatedly promised Rosmini that he would make him a cardinal but failed to do so. More important, the brief asserts that the pope "lulled and assured Rosmini" that several of his political writings were under examination when in fact he had already signed a decree of the Congregation for the Index condemning them. Rosmini, it should be said, was one of the few intellectuals in the church who supported the unification of Italy. Why, then, the Devil's Advocate asks, did the pope reject the counsel of Rosmini in favor of the antiunification policies of Antonelli?

Several objections question the pope's own political judgment. Pio Nono claimed to be neutral in the 1848 conflict between Austria and the Piedmontese, but on several occasions he violated that neutrality in favor of Austria. Similarly, the brief criticizes Pio Nono's abrupt and politically disastrous about-face with regard to Italy's independence movement. There was a "strident contrast," the Devil's Advocate notes, between his initial, favorable attitude toward the independence of Italy and his subsequent "intransigent opposition." He seemed to misjudge the movement toward liberal government which "appeared to everyone as irreversible."

In the eyes of some of the consultors, Pio Nono seemed to suffer from "a certain confusion of ideas," particularly the distinction between "divine and human law." The Devil's Advocate then goes on to cite one historian who charges that Pio Nono's intransigence in the face of inevitable political change—notably his decree forbidding Italian Catholics to hold public office or even to vote as citizens of the new Italian state—made him personally responsible for a number of harmful effects to the church: notably, the "violent " loss of the Papal States, the "more violent" continuing conflict between church and state in Italy, and "unrestrained anticlericalism." In addition, the brief criticizes the pope for failing to deal with "the social question"—that is, the needs of Europe's emerging working class, which fell under the increasing sway of the socialists and communists. These needs "seemed to be very far from his cares and pastoral preoccupations."

The brief then goes on to demand an explanation of three major events which affected the universal church. It asks, first, whether the pope displayed the proper "fortitude of soul" in fleeing from Rome to Gaeta—"one of the saddest and least glorious pages of his pontificate." Second, it questions the "opportuneness of some of the positions he took in the Syllabus of Errors, which were criticized even by Catholic authors." Third, some of the consultors questioned whether the pope allowed the fathers at Vatican Council I "full freedom" to study and deliberate the dogmatic definition of papal infallibility. Did the pope show himself decent and respectful toward those who opposed the infallibility question, and, after the council, did he not display a certain resentment toward the dissenting bishops despite the fact that they all eventually accepted the definition?

These, then, were the last bones, as it were, which stuck in the throats of the consulting theologians and cardinals. Some of the issues, it should be noted, especially those involving the Syllabus of Errors and the freedom of the bishops at Vatican Council I, were questions which had long vexed church historians. It is not surprising, therefore, that the brief suggests that some of these nettlesome issues be referred to the congregation's historical section for further documentation.

In addition to these questions of character and competence, the Devil's Advocate reports that several of the theologians and prelates were deeply concerned about the impact the beatification of Pius IX might have on the church. Some felt that however deserving Pio Nono might be of "eventual glorification," now was not the time to proclaim him blessed. Some feared it would "unleash a new campaign by Liberals and other anticlericals." Others worried that his beatification might be misinterpreted as implying church approval of Pio Nono's blanket condemnations of liberal democratic institutions and principles. In any case, the general feeling was that the cause should not be rushed.

It wasn't. Snider took nine years to construct his reply. Moreover, he did so without asking the aid of the congregation's historians. Historical evidence is one thing, he was to argue, but theology is something else. And it was theology—or, more precisely, the designs of Divine Providence—which he ultimately invoked to prove Pio Nono's heroic virtue.

THE ARGUMENT FOR THE DEFENSE

SNIDER'S RESPONSE IS 223 pages long and organized around fifteen questions, plus an appendix. The style is lawyerly, full of long sentences and sweeps of Italian rhetoric. To read it is to imagine the advocate leaning on a jury box railing, addressing the consultors and prelates as if he were conducting a courtroom trial. He is by turns ingratiating and condescending toward his client's critics. The astonishing thing is that he prevailed.

In the first four chapters, Snider surveys the cumulative objections to the cause and outlines the method he will use to refute them. He is concerned not only with the issues enumerated by Father Pérez but with all the objections which have been made by various consultors in the course of the process. He notes, for example, that every witness interviewed by the investigating tribunals "had some kind of problem with Pius IX's conduct of his pontificate." Further, he observes that the process has reached a critical impasse. The consultors in favor of the cause feel that the evidence in support of the pope's heroic virtue outweighs the negative evidence. The critics take the opposite view. "Neither side is correct," Snider argues. There is a middle ground, which he will establish and defend by recourse to the historical-critical method.

Next, the advocate observes that many of the consultors, including those who consider the candidate heroically virtuous, question the opportuneness of beatifying him. This view is too timid, Snider asserts, and in a rhetorical aside, he wonders whether "the fear of opportuneness" could not have been raised as well against the previous eighty-nine popes who have already been canonized or beatified—especially those whose boldness of action make them "stick out from the pack." What worries the faint of heart, he argues, is that the beatification of Pius IX will send the wrong signal to the contemporary world. Snider acknowledges that since Pius IX symbolizes rejection of certain political, social, and cultural movements of his day, honoring him now might well be interpreted as support for those antiliberal positions by the contemporary church. This concern, he counters, shows a lack of trust in the "magisterium of the church"— by which he means Pope John Paul II. Nonetheless, he concedes, there is a real danger, not from John Paul II, but from those (presumably ultraconservatives) who "by excessive concepts of their own knowledge and authority, believing themselves the only sure interpreters of said magisterium, would use the pastoral conduct of Pope Pius IX . . . in order to justify and in some cases impose their own spiritual, intellectual and pastoral direction" on the church, condemning every other direction other than their own . . ." This has happened before, Snider acknowledges, and the temptation to abuse the beatification of Pius IX is manifest among some people who are "rather strict of conscience and spirit."

But, he contends, the possibility of abuse is no reason to stop the cause of Pius IX. As he will demonstrate, there are sound reasons for celebrating the pontificate of a pope whose "importance and value are prolonged into our time, most especially because through them and with them the church entered into the contemporary history of man with the patrimony of its perennial values and doctrine intact." The echo here of Benedict XIV's dictum on zeal for the faith is obvious. Indeed, Snider says he will demonstrate that the pontificate of Pius IX "shows nothing other than the path walked by the church from the time of Pius IX to today in its uninterrupted pilgrimage through the history of mankind."

To do this, says the advocate, it is not necessary to submit the cause, as was urged, to further investigation by the congregation's historical section. That would only prolong the process unnecessarily and deflect attention from the primary goal of investigating his heroic virtue. "Look as you might to any known or unknown document," he writes, "you are not going to find anything to give the final formulation of a moral judgment, positive or negative, on Pius IX."

Snider then sets out what he sees to be the task of anyone who would sit in judgment on Pius IX's claim to sanctity:

> Whoever studies [this cause], and moreover, whoever judges it, must know how to see Papa Mastai in his exact position with regard to the history of the church and civil history of his time. Whoever does that must interpret exactly his thinking, in relation to the reality to the times which were lived by him, and therefore to the real needs of the church and of society. One must understand the spirit with which he undertook his pontifical mission, ordered as it was to the particular charism [as pope and Supreme Teacher of the church] conceded to him

by divine wisdom, the charism which to us reveals the supernatural reason for his pontificate. We must not forget that the reason for any pontificate is not simply for purely human causes. The reason for a pontificate is read in the designs of Providence and it is necessary for that to understand within the limits of our intelligence the plan of God ordered toward the good of the church and of society, actuated with the coming to the pontificate of Pius IX and in the acts of doctrinal and pastoral magisterium.

In short, Pio Nono must be judged as head of the universal, not just the Italian, church; as a spiritual leader, not simply the sovereign of the "moribund" Papal States; and as a man of his times who nonetheless is "involved in the unfolding history of salvation, and who sought to find the traces of divinity in the unfolding history of humanity." To take a more restrictive view—specifically, to condition his cause upon his human limitations as a temporal sovereign—Snider says, is to ignore "the sacred nature of his pontificate." In other words, the advocate is arguing that the ultimate context for judging Pius IX is not profane history but the history of salvation, the domain in which the "designs of Providence" are revealed through the activities of the church. In his own words:

> The pontificate of Pius IX must be seen as a continuation of the perennial mission of the church as the introduction of that mission in a successive age. Having done this we obtain the most secure indications not only for historical judgment but for the purposes of our investigation which has as its object, the correspondence of mind, of the tenor of life, of the private and public acts of a pontiff toward his responsibilities to God and to the Church at whose helm he found himself positioned at an important moment in contemporary history.

Snider then goes on to paraphrase—though he does not cite—the advice of Benedict XIV regarding the virtues to look for in a papal candidates for sainthood.

> The exemplarity of the virtues of a pope must be seen also in the constant obligation to spread the reign of Christ in the world; to maintain the unity of his flock, to care for the deposit of the word of God and to work untiringly so that this work might run and be diffused throughout the whole world; to consolidate the human community according to the divine law; to inculcate in the clergy an even deeper consciousness of the dignity of sacred orders and the obligations of priestly ministry; to give firm testimony to the gospel; to impress upon men the meaning of their existence and to enable them to comprehend fully the value of the human person; to fulfill in every circumstance and condition the will of God.

The Personality of Mastai-Feretti

HAVING LAID OUT the terms and context of his analysis, Snider then turns to a discussion of the personality of Pius IX. He was a man like others, he writes, a mixture of "joys, uncertainties, fears, hopes, impulses to rebellion, pains and sufferings." What set him apart, however, was his epilepsy, a handicap which, Snider notes, Pius IX shared with Napoleon, Bismarck, Alexander the Great, and other great figures of history. Contrary to some hagiographers, Snider insists, Mastai's epilepsy continued to plague him throughout his adult life, and his personal battle to control its effects, he argues, "helped him to acquire virtue." Because of this handicap, he writes, Mastai was highstrung and often irascible, especially in moments of stress. But he assures his readers that the pope never intended moral or material damage to his neighbor. If he did harm anyone—as assuredly he did— it was merely the unfortunate effect of his infirmity.

On the other hand, Snider argues, Pius IX manifested a number of endearing qualities: he had "an open face and an open heart"; he "wanted to love and be loved"; and throughout his life he showed 'a lovable and youthful attitude." True, he was at times pessimistic, but so were other saints. If he was impulsive, this was because he was also passionate and enthusiastic, especially in his "desire for the kingdom of God." He was also courageous, the advocate avers, as can be seen in his determination to convene Vatican Council I and oversee the dogmatic definition of papal infallibility "in the teeth of an unbelieving era."

Though not an intellectual, Mastai did have a masterful gift for "simplifying" complex issues. What some critics regard as a "retrograde" refusal to recognize new realities was, in fact, a keen ability to get to the heart of a question and to recognize the necessary steps to be taken "in obedience to truth." Indeed, Snider assures us that Pius IX "had the intelligence to see things in the manner of God, which means that in some manner he participated in the same horizon as God has." He never relied on human reason alone to resolve problems, Snider asserts, but always "felt the need to be guided by the charisma which, as pope, he knew he had." Thus guided, this "conservator pope, who has been seen [by his critics] as enclosed in a desperate defense of the past, [was actually able] to see better times for the church with a lucidity and an exact attitude which is quite remarkable."

What is remarkable about all these assertions is not merely that

they contradict accepted historical judgment, but that they are made
with a paucity of footnotes. Apart from a few references to appreciative biographers, there is no supporting evidence from any of the witnesses interviewed for his cause. Essentially, Snider is presenting Pius
IX as the pope saw himself. When, however, he goes on to describe the
pope's ecclesiastical mission in the middle of the nineteenth century,
the language he uses is not that of Mastai but of the fathers of Vatican
Council II.

LIBERALISM, PAPAL INFALLIBILITY, AND THE FIRST VATICAN COUNCIL

FIRST OF ALL, Snider reminds the consultors that the pope's mission
was to be "the pastor who diffuses the message of Christ from the
highest throne of the ecclesiastical magisterium, giving testimony to
the truth, being the voice of the spirit of truth which guides on its
earthly journey the church, the community of faith, hope and love,
especially as a social organism, a priestly, kingly and prophetic community." Far from being a reactionary bent on restoring the papacy's
temporal powers, he argues, Pius IX was actually a reformer who
prepared the church for a new era by establishing new structures and
new means of governing the church—in short, a distant precursor of
Pope John XXIII.

Second, Snider asserts, Papa Mastai set himself the task of reconstructing the social order. This is, it should be noted, an extraordinary
assertion, one that contradicts the consensus of historians. According
to that consensus, the papacy did not begin to address "the social
question"—that is, the rise of the bourgeoisie and the development of
an urban proletariat—until the reign of Pius IX's successor, Leo XIII.
But in a flourish of rhetoric, unsupported by any evidence, Snider not
only describes Pius IX as a forward-looking reformer of secular society, he also suggests that Mastai anticipated the progressive ecclesi-
ology of Vatican Council II:

> One could even say that the pontificate of Pius IX spoke of the church
> and service, the church and poverty, the church and reform, the church
> and adaptability and—we should not hesitate to say—of the church in
> dialogue, the church and earthly realities, of the dynamism of faith and
> the integration of human history with the history of salvation; in a

word, [he spoke] of the church and the world in the same sense, and with the same fullness of demonstrative argument, and in the same words and terms that a century later would be spoken of in the Second Vatican Council.

It would appear that at this point Snider has abandoned the historical-critical method. In fact, he has merely invoked the language and concepts of Vatican II to put the plight of Pius IX in a more favorable light. If, as he has already suggested, the mission of the pope is always the same—to preach the Gospel, guide the church, and defend its religious patrimony and principles—then it needs only to be demonstrated how Pius IX did this within the horizon and challenges of his own epoch.

Surveying the social upheavals that preceded Mastai's pontificate, Snider observes that the French Revolution and the industrial revolution had produced a "completely new social class," the bourgeoisie,"which did not have the kind of religious and spiritual formation" that the displaced aristocracy enjoyed. The church had no social teaching for this new class and the fact that Pius IX did not formulate one, Snider argues, should not be judged as a lack of prudence or justice. Again, he reminds the consultors that Mastai's primary responsibility as pope was not intellectual but pastoral. Therefore, whatever errors of judgment he made on the administrative, political, or diplomatic level should not be confused with his prudence as chief pastor and teacher of the church.

Snider concedes that there is some truth to the charge that the papacy under Pio Nono remained intransigent in the face of Liberalism. Mastai, after all, grew up in northern Italy and even as bishop of Imola was far from the new ideas of institutions that were remaking the face of Europe. In the realm of ideas, he notes, the influence of Enlightenment thinkers had given rise to a new sense of the natural rights of man and even to a new figure—the citizen. New states came into being based on popular sovereignty and equal rights before the law. Democratic constitutions were written, public organizations were laicized, and nationalism was in the air. To some, especially the Ultramontanists, "all things appeared to be the work of Satan." In any event, he acknowledges that during the pontificate of Pio Nono, Roman authorities judged Liberalism in general "from afar" and altogether misunderstood the Catholic Liberals in France and Germany.

Nonetheless, Snider argues, the fact that Pius IX did not possess a "deeper perception" of all the events that were unfolding in his time should not be counted against him. Nor should he be held personally responsible for all of the "negative consequences" for the church that resulted from his policies. Like other popes, he had to rely on his lieutenants. What he can and should be held accountable for, says Snider, was his "responsibility for helping the church to listen beneath all these changes to the Voice of God which expresses itself continually in the voice of the times in which one lives."

The question, then, is whether the pope showed spiritual discernment in his response to the ideas and movements of his era. On the face of it, Snider concedes, it appears he did not. He seems not to have recognized that Liberalism contained within itself principles of freedom and social justice which the church would, as a matter of fact, eventually come to embrace. On the contrary, Pius IX has long been criticized for his constant repudiation of new ideas, especially in the apodictic Syllabus of Errors.

But, says Snider in Mastai's defense, a careful reading of all the pope's writings shows that "he did not intend to condemn liberty, which in human beings is the sign of divine image, and because of that is an expression and guarantee of man's dignity, and of the respect for the values of the human spirit." What he did denounce, says Snider, are principles and programs of rationalism and naturalism "which would have led to an oppressive and repressive absolutism." In this sense, he condemned Liberalism "as a way of reminding people not to exalt human reason and human institutions to such an extent that they forget the One from whose hand they come, or at least the gifts that God has given us to make us realize these liberal dreams."

Having offered a rationale for the pope's condemnation of Liberalism, Snider then turns to the issues surrounding Vatican Council I and the dogma of papal infallibility. Pio Nono, he argues, regarded infallibility "as the very reason for the presence of the church in the history of humanity." As such, he continues, Mastai did not regard infallibility as a power centered on the person of the pope for the latter's self-aggrandizement, but for the unity of the church. "The church is known to be infallible," Snider reminds his readers, "in as much as it is united with the Holy Father who acts as shepherd of all the faithful."

The question remains, though, whether Pius IX allowed the fathers of Vatican Council I to act freely when they voted to define papal infallibility as a dogma of the Roman Catholic faith. Here Snider concedes that the organization of the council, and particularly of its preparatory commissions, followed "a mentality that no assembly, whether civil or ecclesiastical, would today accept." Moreover, he reminds the consultors that even as recently as Vatican Council II, the bishops rebelled against organizational principles and procedures which they regarded as hindering the freedom and full use of their faculties. In addition, he notes that at Vatican I there were bishops both for and against the infallibility doctrine who had eloquent things to say but no opportunity to speak. Much as this is to be regretted, he says, the fact remains that there wasn't enough time for everyone to be heard. Nor, says Snider, was it necessary. The majority was in favor of the dogma and the majority ruled.

But there is more to the issue of papal infallibility than the question of the council fathers' freedom, Snider asserts. "One has to ask oneself," he writes, "whether as a matter of fact the doctrine of papal infallibility was not of incalculable importance for the future history of the church, [an event] in which is seen expressed the supernatural and historical reasons for Pius IX's pontificate." The idea of papal infallibility came very early in Mastai's life, long before he was elected pope, Snider contends. He invoked it in 1854 when he proclaimed the dogma of the Immaculate Conception. "It seemed to him and to others that the proclamation of the Immaculate Conception was a mission assigned to him by God, and operating in such a way it led naturally to the dogmatic definition of papal infallibility." For Pius IX, Snider says, "the basic purpose of papal infallibility was to safeguard the mission of the pope and the church" in a time when the papacy had lost its temporal power. In addition, he saw infallibility as a repudiation of Gallicanism—that is, various efforts, not limited to France alone, of governments and/or local churches to circumscribe the authority of the papacy, especially in the appointment of bishops. In retrospect, Snider suggests, the design of Providence might well be seen in the fact that Vatican Council I was prematurely suspended after its first session—thereby postponing for another century consideration of the correlative authority of bishops—because "it actually reinforced the universal prestige of the mission of the pope as a necessary condition for the life of the church in the course of history."

Snider then turns to a number of issues which bear on Mastai's prudence in office, both as pope and as head of the Papal States. Several consultors, for instance, were of the opinion that Pius IX had overreacted in issuing the Syllabus of Errors, particularly since there were a number of outstanding Catholic intellectuals who embraced the principles of political Liberalism and sought to reconcile them with the church's doctrines. Snider concedes that "today, of course, we would never adhere to some of the formulations of the Syllabus because they do not fit the social, cultural, or political realities of our time." He also concedes that the language the pope used to deplore the evils he saw in his own time "seems perhaps a little dramatic to us." But he argues that Pio Nono was not the last pope to criticize the rationalistic premises of Liberalism. That, Snider argues, is what popes as "guardian[s] of the values of the spirit" are supposed to do.

Nonetheless, the advocate does acknowledge that Pio Nono condemned a number of outstanding Catholic Liberals whom history has shown to have been loyal sons of the church. The truth is, says Snider, that the pope's condemnations were based on ignorance: he never got to know these men or their works, nor did he understand the political circumstances in France, Germany, and other countries where Liberal Catholic intellectuals and activists were attempting to integrate the positive aspects of Liberalism with church doctrine. But again, in the pope's defense, Snider insists that there was no unanimity in the church as to how to deal with Liberalism, nor even on the political responsibilities of Catholics under Liberal governments. "Pius IX could not be clairvoyant," Snider writes, and even though his measures were harsh (he forbade Italian Catholics to hold office or even vote), "history shows that there was a providential design at work that he was part of."

THE MORALITY OF POPES
AS TEMPORAL SOVEREIGNS

AT THIS POINT, Snider takes up the special case of Father Rosmini, whose life and work were especially admired by John XXIII and Paul VI. It is clear from the brief of the Devil's Advocate that several consultors saw Pio Nono's treatment of this saintly figure as a glaring example of his lack of prudence and justice. Snider acknowledges that Rosmini was not only a brilliant thinker and holy man, but also a fit candidate for canonization himself. Why, then, did Pio Nono deny him a promised red hat, and why did he condemn two of his most distinguished works, *The Five Wounds of the Church* and *Constitution According to Social Justice*—condemnations which to this day have prevented Rosmini's cause from moving forward in the congregation?

The answer, Snider argues, must be found in the difficult political position of the pope. Rosmini championed an independent and unified Italy, a position which put him at odds with Catholic Austria, which regarded itself as the protector of the church's liberty in Europe. He also attacked the system of ecclesiastical benefices whereby the Austrian emperor and other European monarchs were able to control the bishops within their jurisdictions. Rosmini, therefore, had many enemies within the church who felt threatened by his ideas. They mounted a campaign against Rosmini, vilifying him as another Calvin or Luther.

Under these circumstances, Snider argues, the pope could not make good his promise to elevate Rosmini to the cardinalate, much less make him his secretary of state, as he once planned to do: this would have alienated the Austrians, whose support the pope coveted in his conflict with the anticlerical leaders of the Risorgimento. Moreover, Snider insists, the pope's decision to put Rosmini's writings under scrutiny by the Vatican's theological censors was actually designed to protect Rosmini! By doing so, Snider says, in what is clearly the weakest and most paradoxical argument on the pope's behalf, Pio Nono hoped to end the ideological struggle within the church which Rosmini's writings had occasioned. In short, he punished Rosmini to silence his critics, though in fact they continued their campaign against him.

Snider's discussion of the Rosmini affair turns out to be a prelude to a much broader question: in his exercise of temporal power as head of the Papal States, did Pius IX manifest the virtues of prudence and justice to the heroic degree required for canonization? In the course of the process, the consultors had raised nineteen specific objections to Mastai's prudence. Among them: the extraordinary influence exercised by his secretary of state, Cardinal Antonelli; the ill-treatment of several capable and worthy individuals; the assignment of inept and poorly trained people to offices in the Papal States; and the decision to forbid Italian Catholics to participate in Italian politics after the loss of his temporal power in 1870.

Snider's initial response to these objections is to accuse the consultors of serious misconceptions. In each case, he says, they presume that the pope alone was responsible for all the administrative acts which took place during his pontificate, blaming each of them on Mastai's impulsivity, intransigence, or lack of political wisdom. In doing so, he argues, they fail to recognize that in some instances the pope's lieutenants were to blame; even when the responsibility is the pope's alone, the objectors fail to take into consideration his intent and attitude.

For Snider, the real issue is twofold: in considering the cause of a pope, what weight should be given to his exercise of temporal power, and by what criteria should his decisions as head of a political state be measured? "In the design of God," he argues, "neither Pius IX nor any of the popes who preceded him were placed at the head of the universal church solely to exercise a purely temporal sovereignty with the sole [aim of] providing for the private and common good of the subjects." On the contrary, he argues, popes are elected to guide the church on a religious mission to which issues of a political, economic, or social character are distinctly subordinate. To be sure, the way in which a pope addresses temporal issues is relevant in judging his prudence and justice. But, he argues, the issue here is not his practical wisdom but his morality. In other words, his "sincerity."

Snider concedes that Pius IX made errors of practical judgment, though like a good defense lawyer he does not specify what those errors were. After all, he observes, papal infallibility does not make a pope omniscient. But, he argues, every pope *is* promised the assistance of the Holy Spirit, "filling up the lacunae in his knowledge, repairing the breaches and errors which are not deliberate, granting him the necessary lights so that by his pontificate, the People of God might see (as in this case) in the Roman Pontiff the Vicar of Christ and the visible head of the church, the principal, perpetual, and visible foundation of the unity of faith and of the community [of the faithful]." Indeed, Snider boldly asserts, Pio Nono's very shortcomings as a temporal sovereign are proof that he was divinely guided since, in the advocate's view, history shows that he did in fact maintain the unity of the church and integrity of the faith in a time of great crisis.

In other words, Snider is arguing, as long as it can be shown that a pope did the best he could as a temporal ruler—as long, that is, as he was sincere and intended the good of the church—the judges should give him the benefit of the doubt regardless of the effects of those decisions and acts on the life of the church.

Having established this general principle, Snider takes up the specific questions raised against the pope's conduct as a head of state. And in each instance he finds the pope's actions were either justified or at least excusable. The major accusation is that Pio Nono was so preoccupied with the loss of the Papal States that he failed to realize that this loss, in fact, liberated the papacy from political responsibilities and entanglements, allowing future popes to exercise the power of spiritual suasion more in keeping with the Gospel. Snider counters this objection by arguing that Mastai's unwillingness to accept the loss of the Papal States was thoroughly understandable as "the experience of an old man who was seeing the passing of a world he grew up in, was used to and which formed his whole life as a human being and as a priest." In any case, Mastai did not covet temporal power for its own sake but regarded the papal monarchy as indispensable to the freedom of the universal church.

As for his handling of political appointments and related issues bearing on his prudence and justice toward others, Snider finds reasonable grounds for each of the pope's actions. His governing principle, however, is that such questions are essentially irrelevant to proving his candidate's holiness. To suggest otherwise, Snider says, would require the cause's critics to demonstrate that no other pope, only Mastai, permitted such things to take place. Moreover, he declares, "If we are going to stop the cause of Pius IX, we will have to decree the prohibition of every form of public cult for the holy and blessed popes who preceded Pius IX" because they, too, were imperfect custodians of temporal power. In short, Snider holds that the pope's conduct as temporal sovereign does not supply serious criteria for judging his moral virtue.

THE POPE AS REFORMER
OF CHURCH AND SOCIETY

NEXT, SNIDER ADDRESSES the objection that Pio Nono failed to recognize, much less deal with, the "social question"—that is, the social and economic upheavals created by the disintegration of Europe's nobility and gentry. His response is that few people in the church, least of all Mastai, recognized the social transformations that were taking place. If the pope was "timorous and slow" to respond to the needs and aspirations of the new social classes, it was because he realized that his knowledge and experience of secular affairs were limited. He failed to recognize the emergent "class struggle" in Europe, Snider argues, because such concepts did not become widely known until the pontificate of his successor, Leo XIII. Nonetheless, Snider concludes, seen in the context of his times, Pius did what he had to do: "he prepared[ed] the necessary spiritual and moral conditions and the doctrinal premises" which allowed his successor to "present the social question as the fundamental problem for the universal church."

Finally, Snider takes up repeated objections that Pius IX neglected necessary reforms and renewal in the church. He concedes that Mastai did not have the cultural or social sophistication of a Rosmini, a John Henry Newman, or other leading lights of the nineteenth-century church. However, Snider argues that in his own way Pio Nono did call the church "to a deeper purification" and sought through the exercise of his magisterium to raise the moral and spiritual tenor of the church.

First, he says, Mastai sought personal renewal through his own spiritual dedication. Here, Snider observes how much more difficult it is to demonstrate the heroic virtues of a pope compared to those of an ordinary priest. The latter, he observes, are better positioned to intervene personally in the lives of individuals and change them for the better. But popes, because of their elevated status in the hierarchy, are less able to deal with individuals on an intimate basis. Thus, the heroism of a pope is apt to appear "somewhat cloudy and difficult to demonstrate with precise arguments and examples."

Even so, Snider asserts, it is possible to see in his "whole magisterium" Pio Nono's "constant and ever deeper preoccupation with the dignity of the human person, the duties and coherent life of faith which allowed the Christian to be a light to the contemporary world." Snider then goes on to list the major pastoral accomplishments of Pius IX's pontificate: the creation of many new dioceses, metropolitan sees, vicariates, and apostolic prefectures around the world; the reestablishment of Catholic hierarchies in England and Holland; his "haste" in celebrating diocesan and provincial synods; the opening in Rome of several seminaries and colleges for students from foreign nations; and "the enrichment of Catholic culture," especially in philosophy and theology through the promotion of the study of St. Thomas Aquinas. Compared to these accomplishments, Snider goes so far to suggest, the negative impact of the much-criticized Syllabus of Errors is of relatively small account.

In light of all this, Snider demands to know, why do the negative consultors insist on seeing Pio Nono as an obstinate man? Why must the pope's stout resistance to the changing social order and the regnant ideas of Liberal thought be attributed to "overbearing pride"? Why not, rather, see in his slowness to change his mind in the face of the overwhelming disequilibrium of this age evidence of the virtues of prudence, temperance, and humility? The point of renewal, he argues, is not to change the church in response to the changing realities of the times, but to "change the church so that it might change the face of the times."

THE DEFENSE RESTS

AT THIS POINT, the reader can almost hear Snider's voice rising as he moves toward the summation of his defense. The questions the judges must consider, he says, are:

What did the pontificate of Pius IX contribute to the actualization of the plan of salvation conceived by God in its visible insertion in history, and in what way did the history of salvation visibly continue in the church governed by Pius IX? In what way did his pontificate allow the human history to be integrated into the story of salvation which continues toward the future?

This, he argues, is how Mastai understood the mission of the church and how, therefore, he must be judged.

As a young priest, he wanted to have an understanding of events that took place on the street in terms of whether they were a manifestation of the will of God, and this grew in him in terms of having a clear concept of the church advancing through time with the security of infallibility which comes from God but also comprises the fallibility to which its members are subjected. The famous proclamation of infallibility [therefore] is just the full flowering of this concept.

With regard to mistakes and shortcomings of Pio Nono's pontificate, Snider would have the judges understand that the pope "could not foresee or foreshorten" the events of his time. But what he could and did do was "constantly respond to [those events] with the same consciousness of the work of the Spirit through the church [so] that the church should be the light of the world." To be sure, Snider concedes, the church in Italy may have suffered by his ban against Catholics participating in the public life of their country, and he acknowledges that this represents a "difficulty" to his cause. "But," he argues, "the reality is that while the church may have seemed to be a kind of relic of the past defending a truth that intellectuals of the time were not interested in, it was no longer sustained by the kinds of support systems" that existed in Europe prior to the French Revolution. If outsiders "viewed the church as a private society defending its own cause," the truth is, Snider maintains, that it was actually "regrouping and gathering strength."

Given these realities, Snider goes on, Pius IX found himself confronted with a double responsibility: "to continu[e] the work of restoration undertaken by his predecessors" and "to erect a kind of wall against the diverse forms of modern irreligiosity." Whatever his successes and failures, Snider concludes, one must recognize that Pius IX "always understood that his supreme duty was to guide the church in its walk through history, allowing it to follow through to the future with the certainty that the gates of hell would not prevail."

The significance of Snider's *positio* on behalf of Pius IX is not that it was successful, but the way in which it succeeded. Although each cause is judged on its own merits, precedent is very important to the saint-makers. In this case, we have the freshest and only contemporary example of how the congregation weighs papal causes. And on the basis of this evidence, a number of conclusions can be drawn.

First, it is clear from the objections to the cause that popes are not immune to close scrutiny. To take but one example: the question of whether Pio Nono allowed full freedom of deliberation to bishops at Vatican Council I. This issue, it should be noted, is highly sensitive, one that has been advanced by dissenting Catholic theologians as grounds for rejecting the dogma of papal infallibility. That the theologians and prelates of the congregation, who can hardly be classified as liberals, insisted on reprising this issue testifies to the independence and integrity of the process. Whatever one might make of Snider's rebuttal on this point, the fact remains that the process itself demanded that Mastai's apparent lack of simple charity toward neighbor be investigated.

In a similar vein, it is clear that popes must be held accountable for their bureaucratic and administrative decisions. In other words, it is not enough that they are personally pious; they must also be prudent and just. It is less clear, however, that a pope's virtues must include wisdom in assessing and addressing the drift of ideas and movements in the secular world. The fact that the negative consultors held Pio Nono accountable for the deleterious impact of the Syllabus of Errors surely indicates that this dimension of a pontificate is germane in judging a pope's heroic virtue. On the other hand, the logic of Snider's successful defense suggests that a pope's intentions—if moral—are sufficient to overcome the negative impact of his pronouncements. In short, it is enough that he "did the best he could."

What this suggests is that the "perfection" required of a saint does not extend to every facet of a pope's ecclesiastical responsibilities. Indeed, it is hard to imagine how it could. Snider himself argues that it is enough that on balance a pope's positive virtues outweigh the negative. For that matter, part of his defense depends upon showing that Mastai needed all the divine guidance he could get since he had so many human shortcomings. In this respect, his *positio*, precisely because it is limited and specific, reveals a much more rounded, more "human" figure than those on behalf of Mother Drexel and Cornelia Connelly.

On the other hand, the thrust of Snider's defense is that popes ought to be judged differently from other Servants of God. It is not simply that a pope should be measured by his zeal in preserving and propagating the faith. But rather, he argues, because a pope is a pope—that is, because he is endowed with the "charism" of his office as supreme pontiff—he must be presumed to be fulfilling the "design of Divine Providence." This is dubious reasoning at best. Nowhere does he suggest that a pope may in fact thwart the designs of Providence or, to employ more theological terms, that he may fail to respond to the graces offered him. Instead, Snider asks the judges to assume that Pio Nono was ever obedient to the will of God and acted accordingly in exercising the duties of pope. That the direction he chose to take the church caused many devout and distinguished Catholics to suffer, that he precipitated a cultural retrenchment that severely crippled Roman Catholicism's ability to respond to the challenges of modern thought and social movements, that he needlessly burdened Catholics with the suspicion that they could not be responsible citizens of democratic states, that he fathered the constricted mentality that eventuated in the intellectual pogrom against Catholic scholars under Pius X—such matters are, in the end, to be given little weight in measuring the impact of Pio Nono's pontificate. In short, Snider invites the judges to accept Pius IX as a necessary and exemplary figure in salvation history, against which his mundane shortcomings are to be held of no account.

What the judges made of Snider's various arguments cannot be known until they are made public. Certainly they did not have to accept all of them in order to find the candidate heroically virtuous. What intrigued me, though, is that the most distinguished biographer of Pius IX, Jesuit historian Giacomo Martina, was not appointed to be a judge of his cause. Martina is a professor at the Gregorian University in Rome and a sometime consultor to the congregation. His three thick volumes (so far) on the life and personality of Pio Nono is the most detailed biography of the pope yet produced, and is referenced more than once by Snider. I sought Martina out one afternoon at the university and questioned him directly: "Do you think Pio Nono was a saint?"

"No, I do not," he said.

"Do you think that is why you were not asked to judge the cause?"

"That I don't know. Why don't you ask the officials of the congregation who appoint the consultors?"

I did. What I was told, though not for attribution, was that Martina has a reputation in Rome for "unbalanced opinions." The fact that he has spent much of his life writing about Pius IX did not, I was told, make him particularly qualified to judge his virtue.

"It looks to me," I said, "that he was purposely excluded because he is known not to regard Pius IX as a saint."

"That's not true," the official insisted. "We've had many consultors who were burrs under the saddle. There's no problem with that. We do demand that our consultors be more than just good theologians. They have to be balanced as well."

Obviously, I had touched on a very sensitive point. The Promoter of the Faith may have lost his role as Devil's Advocate, but he still retains the power to appoint the theologians who judge each cause. He can, therefore, avoid theologians known to be critical of the candidate and select those known to be favorably disposed. Unlike the various tribunals of the Vatican, the Congregation of the Causes of Saints does not assign its judges according to an impersonal, rotating procedure. Therefore, the opportunity to abuse the process exists, and Father Gumpel, for one, concedes that in a few cases he has seen consultors chosen for their sympathy to a cause. My own suspicion is that when an important cause has powerful supporters—especially a pope—the prefect of the congregation and the Promoter of the Faith are under great pressure to choose only accommodating theological consultors. And given the secrecy and subjectivity of selecting judges, it would be very difficult for anyone to prove that the process had been thus manipulated. To suppose that congregation officials never resort to politics of this sort would be to presume that they, like the saints, are men of heroic virtue.

Martina was, however, found sufficiently "balanced" to be appointed to the pope's commission to advise him on the opportuneness of beatifying Pio Nono. How many other commissioners there are, and their identities, are still closely held secrets. What is known is that the commission has been in existence since 1985 and that Pius IX remains unbeatified. By 1990, the feeling within the congregation was that the cause had been put on indefinite hold.

Snider, it seems, won the battle of proving Pius IX's virtue but lost the war of justifying his candidate's "opportuneness." The same might be said of Cardinal Palazzini, Pius IX's chief promoter. In 1989, he was retired from the Curia at the age of seventy-five without seeing his beloved Pio Nono declared blessed. As for Pio Nono, it appears that he is a victim of the posthumous politics of making saints. Whatever his place in "sacred history," it is his record as a figure in human affairs which apparently now stands in the way of beatification. For the time being, at least, his cause has been cast into that special limbo reserved for those very few Servants of God whose personal virtues, however heroic, are not enough to overcome the perceived harm that might come from according them the church's highest honors.

Conceivably, the causes of Pius XII and John XXIII could meet the same fate. In any case, there are those among the saint-makers who feel that it would be unwise to canonize too many popes. Including Pius IX, they note, six of the last eight popes have been mentioned for possible sainthood."I think we should not give the impression that the pope is necessarily a candidate for sanctity," says Gumpel. Perhaps not, but given the history of the modern papacy, with its strong "cult of the pope," the tendency to regard Supreme Pontiffs as saints remains powerful. The very office itself excites a "frenzy of renown" among the faithful, as the frequent pilgrimages of John Paul II attest.

But according to the Gospel, heaven is reserved for the least of the brethren. And it is time to take a closer look at Rome's candidates for sainthood to see what kinds of people the saint-making process—for various reasons—tends to leave out.

CHAPTER ELEVEN

SANCTITY
AND SEXUALITY

As IN ANY investigation, what doesn't happen is interesting, and the kinds of people who do *not* get canonized reveal as much about the saint-making process as those who do. If one examines the company of holy men and women who have been beatified or canonized since 1588, certain categories are notable by their limited representation or their absence altogether. Popes are rare, as we have seen, and so are cardinals.* Men outnumber women by about two to one—though this ratio has changed significantly in the twentieth century, chiefly because so many religious orders of women have successfully put forward causes on behalf of their foundresses.

But the one group which is clearly underrepresented is the laity. Between the year 1000 and the end of 1987, popes held 303 canonizations, including group causes. Of these saints, only 56 were laymen and 20 were laywomen. Moreover, of the 63 lay saints whose state of life is known for certain, more than half never married. And most of these lay saints were martyred, either individually or as members of a group. One might conclude from the lack of married saints that the emotional and sexual satisfactions of a good marriage somehow conflict with the heroic virtue required of a saint.

---

* Since 1588, only about six cardinals have been canonized.

What is it about the passionate life of the body which the church finds unbecoming in a saint? Why, in particular, are there no examples of happily married saints?

VIRGINITY AND HEROIC VIRTUE

The history of Roman Catholicism exhibits a profound ambivalence toward human sexuality. Throughout that history, the church has placed a higher value on virginity than on marriage, even though marriage has the status of a sacrament while virginity does not. The roots of this ambivalence go back to the New Testament, but it has become commonplace to blame the writings of the church fathers of the third, fourth, and fifth centuries for establishing a tradition of associating sexuality with sin. To a great extent, the blame is justified. Some of the fathers were plainly misogynistic: Tertullian, for example, thought of women as "the Devil's gateway." And St. Augustine, who before his conversion became thoroughly experienced in the passing pleasures of the flesh, later taught that sexual intercourse was the means by which original sin was transmitted from generation to generation.

But as Peter Brown, foremost historian of Christian antiquity, and other scholars have amply demonstrated, the church fathers' tendency to identify sex with sin can easily be overstressed and should, in any case, be understood against a wider range of socioeconomic attitudes involving the relationship between "the body and society" in Greco-Roman culture. After all, most Christians (including clergy) *did* marry and reproduce, and when faced with Gnosticism, an early Christian heresy which rejected the body along with all material reality, the church eventually asserted as orthodox the view that marriage is an acceptable, though lesser, calling for Christians than perpetual virginity.

The issue for the church fathers, it is now clear, was not so much the identification of sin with sex, but the positive identification of sanctity with virginity. Their Christianity was imbued with neo-Platonism, which regarded the body as an unruly appendage to be subdued in order to liberate the higher life of the mind and spirit. Augustine, who knew whereof he spoke, pointed to the inability of males to produce a timely erection—and the inability to restrain one at inopportune moments—as comic proof that the body of fallen man cannot be trusted to play servant to the will. For Augustine, the very act of intercourse itself was regrettable because "at the moment of time in which it is consummated, all mental activity is suspended . . . "What friend of wisdom and holy joys," he goes on to ask, ". . . would not prefer, if this were possible, to beget children without this lust . . . ?"

In their amalgam of Greek and biblical ideas, the fathers believed that human perfection lay in recovering, as nearly as possible, the spirit's control over the flesh, which they imagined Adam and Eve enjoyed before the fall. Looking ahead, they imagined life in heaven—where, as Matthew's Gospel says, "there will be no giving and taking in marriage"—as a restoration of Adam's primitive integrity. In the present state of fallen human nature, therefore, virginity was more conducive than marriage to the quest for spiritual *perfection*, which they identified as the specific calling of the saint. Gregory of Nyssa sums up the issue nicely: "The more exactly we understand the riches of virginity, the more we must bewail the other life [marriage] . . . how poor it is." Elsewhere, he adds, "Marriage, then, is the last stage of our separation from the life that was led in Paradise; marriage, therefore . . . is the first thing to be left; it is the first station, as it were, for our departure to Christ."

For the most part, the fathers were merely justifying theologically the ascetic practices already evident among individual hermits and groups of consecrated virgins, both male and female. However, what the learned fathers wrote for their rather limited circle of literate colleagues was of less consequence than what the early Christian communities themselves understood to be the virtues of a saint. These were, after all, the same centuries which saw the rise of the cult of the saints as a distinguishing feature of Christianity, and it was to the saints—nearly always celibates—that the learned and illiterate alike looked for models of human (Christian) perfection.

As we saw in chapter 2, Christian notions of sanctity were, from the very origins of the church, identified with renunciation: of life in the case of martyrs, and of "the world" in general and of "the flesh" in particular in the case of ascetics. But to embrace virginity was not simply to flee the flesh, any more than to embrace martyrdom was to flee life; it was also to open one's self fully to the transforming power of God's emergent kingdom and to the expected life in heaven. There was virtue in a chaste Christian marriage, but only in virginity—for women and men alike—was there the heroic virtue of the saint.

Again and again, this is the message of countless saints whose stories and legends have catechized the faithful down the centuries far more powerfully than the writings of learned bishops and theologians.

Among the earliest, most popular, and long-lived legends of the saints are those of the virgin-martyrs like Agatha, Lucy, and Agnes, young women espoused to Christ who were variously stripped, maimed, dispatched to brothels, and eventually killed in defense of their sexual purity. Although these legends date from the fourth and fifth centuries, they were repeated, embellished, and celebrated throughout the Middle Ages (notably in Jacobus de Voragine's widely popular collection, *The Golden Legend*), and continue to function as models for Christian sainthood today, as we will see, even though Agatha, Lucy, and Agnes are no longer regarded as historical figures. Indeed, the names of these women and numerous other virgin-martyrs are still honored with feast days and, until the Roman Catholic liturgy was reformed in the 1960s, they were remembered every day in the canon of the Mass.

Among male saints of the same vintage, a typical story is that of Alexis, a well-born youth who, desirous of serving the poor, leaves his wife on their wedding day to wander as a beggar for seventeen years. Summoned home by a vision, Alexis takes a room under the stairs of his father's house. For the rest of his life he works as a humble gatekeeper, unrecognized by his father or by the woman he has abandoned, and achieves a reputation as a wise and holy man. The legend varies in details, some stressing his poverty, some his wisdom or his service to the poor. What has not changed over the centuries or among various versions of the legend is Alexis's repudiation of marriage.

The point, once again, is that if saints are known by their stories, it is also through their stories that sanctity is recognized and understood. Thus, if the church has canonized few married people, one reason is that there are, even today, no compelling stories of married saints to match those ancient Christian figures whose legends embody a jaundiced view of marriage and human sexuality. To be sure, hagiography itself is no longer what it was when the stories of saints were, like those of the early virgin-martyrs, the products of rich oral and community traditions and designed to edify and instruct. But even in secular literature, the quotidian virtues of domestic life have never inspired legends or myths—unless an exception is made for the transformation of the wandering Ulysses into James Joyce's cuckolded Everyman, Leopold Bloom.

Even so, the church's unique ability to make saints is the ability to translate lives into stories. Now that the church no longer teaches that marriage is inferior to virginity or consecrated celibacy as a path to holiness, it could put forward saints whose lives embody the virtues of Christian marriage. Indeed, one might suppose that the virtues needed to sustain the lifelong fidelity expected of Catholic spouses have become, in the face of widespread infidelity and divorce in modern secular societies, every bit as "heroic" as the virtues demanded of celibate nuns and priests. Why, then, at a time when the church is making more blesseds and saints than ever before, are so few of them married men or women?

MAKING SAINTS IN "THE YEAR OF THE LAITY"

THE QUESTION OF marriage and its relationship to sanctity emerged in October of 1987 in Rome. The occasion was a World Synod of Bishops convoked in Rome by Pope John Paul II to discuss the role of the laity in the church and in the world. The question was not on the bishops' formal agenda, which was primarily concerned with the laity's function as Christians in society, but it was on the minds of some bishops who wondered aloud why the church has found so few married men or women worthy of veneration as blesseds and saints. As prefect of the Congregation for the Causes of Saints, Cardinal Palazzini anticipated criticism on this point. Once before, in 1980, he had sought to defend the paucity of married saints by arguing that all saints come from families, "and therefore their parents were honored when they were honored." This time round, the cardinal sought to forestall criticism by showing the bishops that the congregation is in no way prejudiced against lay causes. He instructed Monsignor Sarno, the official responsible for tracking causes, to provide him with a list of lay causes on which there had been some action by the congregation in the previous year. Sarno came up with seventeen candidates, of whom four had been married. What mattered, however, was not Palazzini's words to the bishops but the actions of the congregation.

The synod was the capstone of a twelve-month period which John Paul II had designated as "The Year of the Laity." In honor of the occasion, the congregation had labored for more than two years to provide the pope with a variety of examples of lay sanctity suitable for beatification or canonization in conjunction with the bishops' month-long deliberations in Rome. Postulators pressed their causes, bishops lobbied for local candidates. There were fifteen candidates ready for the pope's consideration, far more than there were Sundays in October on which to celebrate them. Indeed, some officials feared the pope would do too many and thus blur the individuality of each new saint or blessed. In the end, three candidates were chosen for beatification, two (one was a group cause) for canonization, and their collective biographies said more about the church's attitude toward marriage, sexuality, and sainthood than all the tired synod speeches about the laity's calls to holiness.

On October 4, the first Sunday of the synod, the bishops gathered inside St. Peter's Basilica for the beatification of three lay martyrs. Since one of the major issues at the synod was the role of lay movements, such as Italy's Catholic Action, the trio of new blesseds were evidently selected as examples of the holiness that can be attained by working "in the world" through such organizations. "All three are lay persons, are young, are martyrs," the pope stressed in his homily, and together they constituted nothing less than "a prophetic sign of the Church of the third millennium."

What the pope did not mention is that none of the three was married. Only the male among them, Marcel Callo, the courageous French youth who died in Mauthausen, had even intended marriage. Callo had left behind "a fiancée whom he loved tenderly and chastely," the pope noted, though it was for his courage as catechist, not for his chastity, that he was being honored. But chastity was precisely the point of the other martyrs' stories. Both were young Italian women who died resisting rape. Antonia Messina, twenty-five, was a grade-school dropout who lived at home in Sardinia and was fatally attacked by a "peasant youth" while gathering wood for baking bread. She was hailed by the pope for defending "the beatitude of purity." Pierinia Morosini, twenty-six, worked in a cotton mill in the Bergamo region. She had wanted to become a nun, but because her family needed her income, she had settled for taking private vows of poverty, chastity, and obedience at the suggestion of her spiritual director. In this way, the pope observed, Pierinia discovered that "she could become holy without entering the convent." The only time Pierinia ventured outside her native region was in April 1947, when she went to Rome for the beatification of Maria Goretti, Italy's modern martyr for chastity. Ten years later, Pierinia died—as she had hoped she might—in the same defense of virtue. It was the story of Agatha, Lucy, and Agnes all over again.

These were the first three figures John Paul II chose to exemplify the sanctity of lay Catholics on the eve of Christianity's third millennium. But lest the synod fathers miss the larger significance of these short and circumscribed lives, the pope went on to extol the new blesseds as "young and courageous citizens of the Church and of the world, brothers of a new humanity, free and nonviolent builders of a fully human society . . ." Fourth-century Christians would have understood exactly what he meant.

On Sunday, October 18, the synod fathers were again assembled outside St. Peter's, this time for the group canonization of Blessed Lorenzo Ruiz and his Companions, sixteen men and women from eight countries who had been martyred by the Japanese in the seventeenth century. It was Mission Sunday according to the liturgical calendar, and the point of the celebration, apparently, was to present new saints who exemplified the true spirit of the Christian evangelization. Just what this canonization had to do with *lay* sanctity, however, was not immediately apparent. All of the martyrs were identified with the Dominicans and the canonization was, if anything, a tribute to that religious order. Nine were priests, two were brothers, and the two women were Dominican tertiaries. Of the three laymen, two were unmarried catechists recruited by the Dominicans. Both had broken under Japanese torture—one betrayed the priestly identity of a colleague, the other renounced his faith—but later they had recovered the courage to embrace martyrdom for the faith.

It was Lorenzo Ruiz who caught my attention. The cause was identified by his name and it was his image that dominated the group's official canonization portrait that hung over the entrance to St. Peter's. Why was Ruiz, also a catechist, so singularly favored? There was nothing in the account of the group's grisly martyrdoms to suggest that he was any more heroic than the others. He was, however, the first Filipino to be canonized—a point the pope stressed to the legions of Filipinos in the crowded square—*and* he was the only member of the group who was married. Not only that, he was the father of three children—a *paterfamilias*, as the canonization brochure put it. But Ruiz was being canonized as a martyred missionary, not as a devoted husband and father. Indeed, to read his capsule biography as it appeared in *L'Osservatore Romano* was to realize that he had in fact *abandoned* his wife and children to join the Dominicans in their fateful missionary expedition.

On the final Sunday of the synod, John Paul II canonized one more lay saint, Blessed Giuseppe Moscati, a well-respected physician from Naples who died in 1927 after attending patients. Moscati was the first lay Catholic to be canonized individually since 1968 and was one of the few saints canonized in this century who had achieved a measure of eminence in a secular career: he was head physician in his hospital, a university professor of human physiology and physiological chemistry, and an exemplary mentor to medical students and nurses. As the pope noted in his homily, Moscati had earned an enviable reputation for concerning himself with the souls as well as the bodies of his patients and was singularly devoid of self-promotion. He was, it seemed to me, exactly what John Paul II had often said Catholics should look for in a lay saint: a man who integrated faith with professional competence and zeal in "collaboration with the creative and redemptive plan of God." But like nearly all unmartyred laymen the pope has canonized, Moscati never married. He had, in fact, taken a vow of chastity at the age of seventeen and had patterned his life like a celibate monk.

In the week following the synod, I stopped by Gumpel's room to discuss the congregation's choices. For months, I had heard from him and other saint-makers about the priority John Paul II has placed on lay causes. The congregation, I observed, had nearly three years to come up with appropriate candidates to beatify or canonize during a synod devoted exclusively to the laity. And in the end, the congregation delivered two virginal rape victims, another young martyr who never got the chance to marry, a lifelong bachelor, and a man who left his wife and children behind to go to the missions.

"The message couldn't be more obvious," I said. "When it comes to sanctity, sex is still something to be avoided and celibacy is preferable to marriage. What good is all the talk about the sanctity of marriage if the congregation cannot come up with even one example of a holy and happily married saint?"

Gumpel looked at me with eyes that suggested he was about to defend the indefensible. "In the past," he reminded me, "the ancient and the medieval church did not look upon married people as candidates for sanctity, though there were exceptions. Like martyrdom, consecrated chastity was considered a more perfect state. It wasn't just this congregation that felt this way, but the whole culture of the church."

"It seems to me," I replied, "that the culture of the church hasn't changed much in the twentieth century either. In your youth and mine, and surely in that of the pope, to be a priest or nun was still considered more pleasing to God than marriage." In 1954, I reminded him, Pope Pius XII issued an encyclical, *Sacra Virginitas*, which reiterated the traditional Catholic teaching that celibacy is a higher calling than marriage. "And if the present pope's words of beatification are to be taken seriously," I added, "that is the culture he hopes the church will carry into the next millennium."

The Jesuit saint-maker said he couldn't speak for the pope. But the lack of married saints, he argued, was the fault of the Catholic laity itself, not of the congregation. "We all regret that we don't have more candidates who are married. But as you know, causes depend on a reputation for holiness, and as long as lay Catholics do not have a full and total appreciation of marriage as a way to sanctity, then people seeing married people will not even think of them as saints. Unless this happens, there can be no *fama sanctitatis* and thus no causes of married people sent to Rome."

He was right, of course. If the laity themselves do not connect sanctity with marriage, the congregation cannot do it for them. Thus far, I had found no reason to doubt the congregation's desire to beatify more married saints: in this respect, the fact that all of them are celibate clerics is not, I felt, reason to suspect them of a hidden bias against married candidates. On the other hand, I had found no evidence that the church's new and more enlightened view of marriage had in any way affected the way in which the congregation evaluates sexual love and intimacy in the lives of those few married candidates whose causes have reached Rome.

Since no one has ever been beatified or canonized precisely for being an exemplary Christian spouse, it is obvious that a holy marriage alone is not enough to ensure a successful cause. On the other hand, the evidence suggests that a bad marriage patiently endured can go a long way toward establishing heroic virtue. For example, in 1988, John Paul II went to Madagascar, where he beatified Victoria Rasoamanavivo (1848–1894) for her singular role in preserving and passing on the faith during a period of political persecution when the Catholic clergy had been expelled from her native land. One of the arguments in support of Victoria's heroicity of virtue, however, was the manner in which she bore her husband's debauchery. Victoria was the daughter of a royal family, he the son of the prime minister. Their marriage was arranged between their parents and despite her husband's drunken rages, Victoria refused, as a Catholic, to divorce him. "I gave my life to this man," she is reported to have said, "and through him to God." Victoria had every moral reason to desert her husband; even the church could not have faulted her for that. But had she done so, it is an open question whether the saint-makers would have judged her virtue sufficiently heroic.

Obviously, a person who fails to honor his or her marriage vows would not be a strong candidate for sainthood. But what about widows or women who leave their husbands to enter the religious life? Does the second vow—the "higher calling"—override the obligations incurred by the first?

Among foundresses of religious orders such cases crop up more often than one might expect, and as several recent causes suggest, the reactions of saint-makers are not always uniform. Father Beaudoin has the historical cause of an Argentinian nun, Catherine Marie Rodriguez (1823–1896), who was married for fifteen years to an army colonel. After her husband died and her children were grown, she founded a congregation for religious. But the documentation sent in by the local bishop focused solely on the candidate's life as a nun. The assumption, obviously, was that her vows of poverty, chastity, and obedience were the ones that mattered most in proving her heroic virtue. In this instance, the congregation instructed the postulator to go back and produce evidence of virtue from Catherine's years as a wife and mother. At this writing, the nun-collaborator is still scouring the archives for information on Catherine Rodriguez's buried life.

But in another recent cause, the judgment was different. The candidate in question had been married only two years when—with her husband's permission—she made a vow of permanent chastity, left her home, and founded an order of nuns. Their marriage was childless and the husband, of course, was not permitted to remarry. After her death, the nuns proposed her for beatification.

When the cause arrived in Rome, one of the theological consultors, who asked to remain anonymous since their discussions of cases are secret, complained that the documentation was incomplete. "The entire *positio* focused on her later life as a nun," he recalled. "So I asked for an explanation of the value of those two married years. Why was there no child? If the marriage did not go well, I argued, maybe there was a moral or psychological problem we should look into."

"Did the postulator give you a satisfactory answer?" I asked.

"No. But the other consultors thought it strange for me, a priest and a member of a religious order, to question her decision to leave her husband. Their attitude was that this woman had decided after two years to devote herself completely to God, and since her husband approved there was no reason to investigate the marriage. I was overruled."

In this case, then, the particulars of the woman's marriage were deemed to be of no consequence in judging the candidate's heroic virtue—perhaps because it was so short and certainly because it was superseded by her "higher calling." That "love of God" should take precedence over love of spouse is a principle the church has honored from its earliest centuries. But by continuing to beatify such women as examples of heroic virtue, the church is clearly reenforcing its ages-old preference for virginity over marriage. How else can one explain so recent a case as that of Benedetta Cambiagio Frassinello (1791–1858), beatified by John Paul II on May 10, 1987? This quixotic

Italian woman was married two years, then took the veil with her husband's consent. But two years later she abandoned convent life to rejoin her husband. This time, however, she renewed her vow of chastity—again with her husband's consent. Thereafter, they lived as brother and sister while devoting themselves to caring for orphans and abandoned children.

Regardless of the church's heightened view of marriage, it would be difficult to conclude from those it raises to the altar that marriage is a life fit for a saint. Sexual intimacy, it would appear to anyone who looks to saints for instruction in heroic virtue, had best be avoided or failing that, endured for the sake of begetting children. For this the laity alone are not to blame. It is well within the power of the saint-makers to choose or reject candidates on the basis of the example they set for the faithful. Indeed, this is one of the conditions for accepting causes. But so far, they have shown no inclination to take advantage of their opportunity.

What would happen, though, if the pope were to canonize a married couple? Would this not provide an opportunity for the pope to do what no pope has done before—celebrate marriage as a path to holiness and lay to rest the suspicion that the church still mistrusts human sexuality?

"TWO IN ONE FLESH": A TEST CASE

JOHN PAUL II is likely to have that opportunity. For the first time in four hundred years, the congregation is processing a *joint* cause on behalf of a married couple. The candidates are Louis and Azélie Guérin Martin, who owe their reputation for holiness to the fame of their youngest daughter, St. Thérèse of Lisieux, the Carmelite nun who died at the age of twenty-four.

Just before her death in 1897, Thérèse completed her brief autobiography, *The Life of a Soul*, in which she celebrated the mundane details of her family life and her brief life as a nun. Thérèse's spiritual message was simple: anyone could become a saint by doing the most inconsequential, self-effacing tasks for the love of Christ. What caught the imagination of her more romantic Catholic readers, however, was the way in which this childlike nun dramatized that message by her own cheerful acceptance of an early and painful death from tuberculosis.

Thérèse's *Life of a Soul*, edited by her sister, Pauline, and published by the community, became an instant best-seller among Roman Catholics. Within two years of her death, she was the object of an extraordinarily powerful cult which led to a worldwide reputation for granting miracles. Pope Pius X, under whose regime her cause was initiated, proclaimed Thérèse "the greatest of modern saints." Just twenty-eight years elapsed between her death and her canonization—a record for a modern process.

Thérèse's autobiography was also a powerful advertisement for her parents. She considered both of them saints—especially her father, to whom she was deeply attached. Thérèse was manifestly her father's favorite among his children and she returned his doting devotion. He called her "my little Queen" and she, in turn, addressed him as "my King." When Louis Martin suffered a mental breakdown after she entered the convent, Thérèse saw it as a form of "crucifixion," and as her own death approached, she often addressed God in her prayers as "Papa." Gradually, after the publication of her *Life of a Soul*, a minor cult developed around Louis Martin as well, and through him, apparently, his wife. Pope Benedict XV hailed Louis Martin as "a true model of a Christian parent." Decades later, in a speech dedicating a basilica to St. Thérèse in Lisieux, the future Pius XII allowed that "as a daughter of a wonderful Christian, she learned at her father's knee the treasures of indulgence and compassion contained in the heart of God."

There is, it should be noted, a popular impulse among Catholics to impute holiness to the parents of saints, an impulse that goes back to the early church and its attitude toward figures in the Bible. Saint Anne, the otherwise anonymous mother of Mary, is a classic case; so is St. Elizabeth, the mother of John the Baptist. Indeed, if it weren't that their son turned out so well, Mary and Joseph would not be venerated as saints either. But unlike these biblical figures, the Martins' reputation for holiness has to survive the modern canonization process. Their joint cause was formally introduced in 1974 and entrusted to the historical section. The *positio* was completed in 1989, but because it had not yet been judged by the consultors, the relator, Monsignor Papa, felt he could not permit me to analyze the text. Nonetheless, several officials of the congregation were willing to discuss the cause and the novel issues it raises.

As the first modern process on behalf of a married couple, the Martins' cause presents the saint-makers with a unique procedural question: since it is a *joint* cause, must both parents be found heroically virtuous? The only recent precedents in this regard are group causes on behalf of martyrs. In those cases, however, the congregation easily can—and often does—eliminate one or more of the candidates

for whom evidence is lacking without prejudice to the cause. But in
the Martins' case, the spouses are being proposed as a conjugal unit; to
eliminate one would destroy the example of Christian parenthood
which the church wants to promote. On the other hand, if one spouse
fails to be declared heroically virtuous, should that fact alone block
the other spouse's path to sanctity?

To judge by the way the cause is being handled, the congregation
has not resolved this issue and is keeping its options open. The *Index
ac Status Causarum*, for instance, does not list the Martins together.
Although both were formally introduced on the same day, each has an
individual protocol number and Zelie, as she was called, is listed
separately under her maiden name. Each *positio* is also a separate
document, but the two are bound in the same book and will be judged
together. Yet there is some confusion among congregation officials as
to whether the fate of one spouse depends on the fate of the other.

The person to clear this up, I felt, was the prefect of the congregation. When I broached the subject to Cardinal Palazzini one afternoon
in his office, he conceded that "technically, yes, the two candidates
are separable." But he insisted that the cause itself is indivisible.
Given the Catholic conception of marriage as the intimate union of
two people—"two in one flesh"—Palazzini was of the opinion that a
cause promoting spouses *as spouses* requires that both be found heroically virtuous. "If one of the spouses fails," he said, "I would have
to question whether there was enough love and support there to beatify the other."

But Father Gumpel takes a different view. In principle, he rejects
the assumption that if one spouse is found unworthy of beatification
the other is automatically disqualified. "It is not a cogent approach,"
he insists, "to say that if one spouse fails, the other must also fail
because both are responsible for a marriage. If, for example, the husband did not behave properly, we must ask whether this was due to
the wife's coldness or perhaps to a misunderstood religiosity which
prevented her from responding sexually in a state of life where you are
supposed to give of yourself—though, of course this may turn out not
to be the case."

My own hunch is that Palazzini's view will prevail. The purpose of
promoting the Martins, it appears, is not to celebrate the virtues of
marital companionship, but to emphasize the obligations of Catholic
parents. "The Martins are being promoted for the upbringing they
gave their children," says Father Beaudoin, and in this respect no
parents could be more Catholic. Besides Thérèse, the Martins had
eight other children. Four of them died in infancy or early childhood,

and all the survivors took vows as nuns. One daughter, Pauline, became mother superior of the convent and was, in the view of Beaudoin, "possibly more holy than St. Thérèse."

Regardless of the purpose behind the Martins' cause, their life together deserves scrutiny for what it reveals about the church's attitude toward marriage and human sexuality. Are these nineteenth-century spouses really figures whom contemporary Catholics can take as models of holiness in marriage?

From what has already been published about the Martins, sex was a serious problem early in their marriage. Zelie's first ambition was to become a nun like her elder sister, Elise, but her application was rejected. At the suggestion of the Virgin Mary, so the story goes, Zelie took up lace-making, and she became so proficient that she eventually established a lucrative business. For Louis, too, marriage was a decidedly second choice. A dreamy young man, he tried at the age of twenty-three to join an Augustinian monastery, but was rejected for insufficient education—notably a lack of Latin. He became a watchmaker and after ten years of bachelorhood, he married Zelie. But on their wedding day, Zelie fled to her sister's convent, sobbing at the cloister's iron gate that she still wanted the life of a nun.

For the first ten months of marriage, that is how Zelie lived. The Martins had no sexual relations, though it is not clear from published material whether this was Zelie's idea, Louis's, or an arrangement arrived at by mutual consent. What we do know is that Louis was prepared to formalize their mutual virginity by establishing a "Josephite" marriage—that is, a lifelong, nonconsummated union patterned after the marriage of Mary and Joseph. Louis found theological justification for this arrangement in a passage from a Catholic theology book which he copied out for Zelie and kept among his papers for the rest of his life. The passage cited precedents among the saints (notably St. Cecilia and her husband, Valerian, both figures of legend) and reiterated the traditional Catholic view that a sexless marriage is superior to a normal one because it "represent[s] more perfectly the chaste and wholly spiritual union between Jesus Christ and His Church."

The Martins abandoned the idea of marital celibacy on the advice of a priest who convinced them to regard their marriage as a call to produce children for the greater glory of God. One month later, Zelie was pregnant with the first of the nine children she was to bear over the next thirteen years. All the girls were given the dedicatory name "Mary," all the boys, "Joseph." Louis and Zelie hoped at least one of the boys would be a missionary priest. What they got, instead, were five cloistered nuns, including Thérèse, who—by the alchemy of attribution—would be posthumously declared a patron saint of missionaries.*

By all accounts, the atmosphere of the Martin home was pervasively religious—"rather like a convent," in the judgment of one of Thérèse's most recent biographers. Zelie presided like a loving mother superior: she was particularly concerned with teaching her children how to make a rigorous examination of conscience. Louis loved to take his children on walks to all the local churches. On Sunday evenings after checkers, he would read aloud to the children from a book which explained the liturgical feasts of the church. If marriage was seldom discussed, it was because the religious life was always held out as the preferred calling.

The Martins' social life was also structured around the church. The parents attended Mass early each morning. Zelie was a Franciscan tertiary and her husband was active in at least four church groups. As members of the provincial bourgeoisie, the Martins could afford to protect their children from outside secular influences. The homes they lived in were large and comfortable; there were servants and, when necessary, private tutors. By 1870, Louis had apparently amassed a small fortune. The following year he sold his watchmaking business to a nephew and settled into a routine of gardening, fishing, and frequent visits to churches. In 1887 he took Thérèse and Celine on a grand tour of Europe, including a memorable visit to St. Peter's in Rome, where Thérèse importuned the pope for permission to enter the convent before the usual age. With Louis's encouragement, Zelie continued to make lace at home and to look after the children when they were not away at school.

When Zelie died of cancer in 1877, the Martins had lived together for only nineteen years. She was forty-five, he, fifty-five. Without questioning their individual claims to sanctity, one has to wonder whether their experience as parents is sufficiently deep and varied to recommend them as models for Christian spouses and parents. In the first place, at the time of Zelie's death, the three eldest children were still teenagers; Celine was only eight and Thérèse only four. Although children matured faster in the nineteenth century than they do today, it is still obvious that for the Martins—as a couple—child-rearing ceased just when, for most parents, the going gets difficult. Moreover, the Martin children were by the standards of any age curiously insu-

---

* Thérèse had wanted to be an overseas missionary but her health was considered too delicate. Her status as a patroness of missionaries is rooted in her correspondence with two missionary priests she conducted from the cloister.

lated from outside influences. Their entire lives were lived within the concentric circles of family and church.

Second, although Louis outlived his wife by seventeen years, he seems to have been a rather passive parent after Zelie's death. Zelie herself was so concerned about her husband's inability to care for the children that before she died she arranged to have the family move from Alençon to Lisieux so that her sister and brother-in-law could take custody of the children. Thereafter Louis was as much cared for as he was caring. In 1887, he suffered the first of a series of strokes which eventually made him a mental invalid for the last seven years of his life.

No doubt there is much that is admirable in the lives of Louis and Zelie Martin. And I, for one, have no reason not to wish their cause success. But as examples of Christian marriage, their lives and outlook are still redolent of the cloister—and of a Catholic culture which still cannot connect sanctity with sexuality. What, after all, are married Catholics to make of a couple who preferred the religious life to marriage, who were willing to forgo sex even after marriage, and whose children all opted for the convent over married life?

Moreover, there is something sentimental about the entire saga of the Martin family—parents as well as children—which lies at the foundation of the present cause. Theirs is the affective nuclear family redeemed and at prayer—a domestic convent in which the inner life and exquisite sentiments are nourished and protected. Apart from Zelie and the servants, no one really works. The outside world, menaced as it was by French secular anticlericals, is kept at a distance. Thérèse herself—the Little Flower, as she is popularly known—is authentic in her consuming love of God, her compassion for others, her missionary zeal, and her final struggle to maintain confidence in God in the face of an early, painful death—all of which is manifested better in her letters than in her popular autobiography, which was edited and embellished by her sister, Pauline. But she barely reached adulthood. She is, however, every father's dream of a devoted child, just as Louis is every child's dream of a perfect "Papa"—on earth as well as in heaven. Despite a piquant streak of girlish impulsiveness, the Thérèse cherished by popular devotion and the hierarchy is above all else an alert and obedient child—to parents, to superiors in the order, and to the fathers who preside over families and church. No wonder Pius X considered her the greatest of modern saints. Nor is it any wonder that her parents, misplaced monastics, are being promoted as examples for others to imitate. But there is no hint in their lives of mutual pleasure or passion, no sense that, apart from producing children, their being "two in one flesh" was something they understood as a source of grace or even happiness.

For them, as for Augustine, producing children was the sole justification of sex. And the message of the Martins' cause is that human sexuality is fine as long as the children turn out well. Whatever the outcome of their cause, human sexuality still awaits its vindication in the form of uninhibited, happy-to-be-married saints.

CHAPTER TWELVE

HOLINESS
AND THE LIFE
OF THE MIND

IN A COMPARATIVELY quiet ceremony at St. Peter's in 1988, Pope John Paul beatified a Danish bishop, Niels Stensen, who had died three centuries earlier. What made this beatification unusual is that Stensen is one of the very few genuine intellectuals to be beatified in the four-hundred-year history of the congregation, although many of the early church fathers and medieval theologians (such as Thomas Aquinas) now venerated as saints were great teachers and scholars. A scientist of international repute, Stensen was a polymath genius in paleontology, geology, medicine, and mathematics whose pioneering contributions ranged from explanations of how fossils and mountain ranges are formed to the discovery of the law of constancy in crystalline angles. Stensen converted to Catholicism in his thirties, later took Holy Orders, and eventually became a bishop. However, it was not for his scientific discoveries or even his ecclesiastical accomplishments that Stensen was beatified, but for his personal asceticism, his manifest help to the poor, and his profound prayer life. His cause, which wasn't initiated until 1938, was finally introduced in 1984 and, under the guidance of Molinari, was completed in time to coincide with John Paul II's visit to Denmark in 1988.*

---

* Denmark's tiny Roman Catholic population hasn't had an official saint since Pope Paschal II approved the veneration of King Canute IV and his relics in 1101. Stensen's candidacy, therefore, was very opportune from a pastoral perspective. But out of deference to the majority Lutheran Church of Denmark, which Stensen had rejected for Catholicism, the pope beatified the bishop-scientist in Rome.

Saints, of course, are not canonized for the excellence of their intellects but for the excellence of their lives. Charity, not wisdom, is the noblest of Christian virtues. Still, anyone who examines the papal canonizations since 1588 is immediately struck by the absence of outstanding thinkers and writers, other than a few monastic theologians. How is it that a church which has, at least since Aquinas, insisted on the inherent compatibility between faith and reason has found no distinguished philosophers or other thinkers or writers to add to its list of saints? What is it about the passionate life of the mind which—like the passionate life of the body—seems to create obstacles to sainthood?

One reason is historical: since the French Revolution, the main currents in modern thought have developed outside the church, and frequently in opposition to it. In the same period, Rome had been markedly inhospitable to its own intellectuals and scholars. The reaction of Pope Pius IX to political Liberalism and its attendant philosophies, St. Pius X's subsequent reign of intellectual terror against suspected Modernists in the church, and, as recently as the 1950s, Pius XII's silencing of noted Catholic theologians and biblical scholars all manifested Rome's profound suspicion of untethered intellects.

For genuine intellectuals, to think seriously is to enter into critical conversation with one's own tradition as well as with thinkers of other traditions. But until the latter part of this century, the Church of Rome so identified tradition with the pronouncements of the papacy that even devout Catholic thinkers and writers were unlikely to be held up as examples of heroic virtue if they challenged the prevailing papal orthodoxy.

Another reason is cultural. Intellectuals and scholars, however strong their reputation for holiness among those who knew them, do not appeal to those who invoke the intercession of the dead for miracles. Hence, intellectuals are unlikely to acquire the sort of posthumous cult which the church requires before instituting a formal cause. Conversely, however much Catholic intellectuals may uphold the idea of sanctity—and strive to be holy themselves—they are not inclined to show devotion or otherwise do what is necessary to promote the cause of a deceased thinker or scholar. "It is difficult to move a cause if one has to depend on intellectuals," says Father Eszer. "They don't pray to the saints—they never put a simple flower on a candidate's tomb." Then he paused, swiveling around in his chair to face me. "Saints are for modest people, you see. Not for stupid people, but for devout people. Arrogant people do not accept saints because they must admit that there are people who are more perfect than themselves."

In sum, the culture of Catholics who invoke saints—and thus make saint-making possible—is not the culture of those Catholics who revere saints for what they thought or said.

But John Paul II is a man of both cultures: a philosopher and playwright as well as a pope who seems genuinely at ease on his knees praying at the tomb of Padre Pio. On several occasions he has gone out of his way to beatify figures who, in his view, can serve as examples to Catholic intellectuals and artists. The belated beatification of Niels Stensen was intended in part to serve that purpose. So was the beatification of Edith Stein: by designating her a martyr, rather than a confessor, the pope was able to overcome the lack of a miracle attributed to her intercession.

But the most egregious example of the pope's readiness to reach out to the world of culture occurred on October 3, 1982, when he used papal prerogative to confer equivalent beatification on Fra Angelico (Guido di Pietro, c. 1387–1455). Fra Angelico was a Dominican monk and painter whose radiant, often mystical frescoes and paintings of biblical figures and events are among the religious ornaments of the Italian Renaissance. He had once been venerated among his fellow Dominicans as a saint, but his cause had lost popular impetus until John Paul II, less than four years after his election to the papacy, exercised his option to declare the friar a blessed. In doing so, however, the pope bypassed the official saint-makers.

"The congregation was angry because they weren't asked for their opinion," Eszer said, recalling the turmoil in the office. "And if they had been asked, I don't think they would have been in favor. They would have said that Fra Angelico no longer has a *fama sanctitatis*. But what can you do? This pope wants to bring together the world of the church and the world of the fine arts, science, and all that intellectual stuff. He saw an opportunity to do this and he did."

Above all, Pope John Paul II would like to be the pope who beatifies, and perhaps even canonizes, John Henry Newman, the best known and certainly the most influential Catholic thinker and writer of the nineteenth century. In his own lifetime, which spanned virtually an entire century (1801–1890), Newman was something rare in Roman Catholicism: a "public thinker" who addressed the most controversial issues of his day and in doing so sometimes set himself forthrightly against the prevailing winds from Rome. He was an eminent man of letters, a master prose stylist, perhaps the finest preacher of his day in the English language, an editor, a superlative educator, a minor poet and novelist. He was also a priest—first of the Church of England, then of the Church of Rome—and he recognized that his were not the gifts the church prizes in its saints. "Saints are not literary men," he wrote after hearing that a friend considered him a living saint; "they do not love the classics, they do not write Tales."

Newman did not regard himself as a theologian, either, and it would distort his accomplishments to call him one. He was that rarer and more comprehensive figure, a Christian humanist, who set his face against utilitarians of both the mind and the spirit. The spirit of Newman sought wholeness of vision: the integration of faith with knowledge, history with human experience, continuity with change. As a thinker and writer, he addressed that zone of controversy and concern where religion and culture fuse and overlap. Although Newman was unmistakably a man of his times, he alone among the Roman Catholics of his era anticipated the direction his adopted church would take—in part because of his own influence—a century later at Vatican Council II. Where Vatican I emphasized the sovereignty and infallibility (albeit circumscribed) of the pope, Vatican II stressed—like Newman—the collegiality and coresponsibility of the other bishops in the governance and magisterium of the church. Where Vatican I focused on obedience to church authority, Vatican II recognized—again like Newman—the role of individual conscience. Such was Newman's reputation for personal integrity and holiness that at his death even the secular *Times* of London declared in an editorial, "Whether Rome canonizes him or not, he will be canonized in the thoughts of pious people of many creeds in England."

Despite such sentiments, Newman's cause was slow to start and slower yet to reach Rome. And when it did, liberal Catholics suspected that Newman was much too progressive to find favor with John Paul II, and particularly with the conservative prefect of the congregation, Cardinal Palazzini. The latter, they pointed out, was the champion of Pius IX, who represented much that Newman had found needlessly obscurantist and reactionary in the Church of Rome. But liberals failed to remember that Newman was in many ways a conservative himself. Although he recognized that church doctrine develops in response to historical events, he was cool to those scholars of his day who were applying the same ideas of development to the Bible as well. Moreover, Newman was more critical of the religious Liberalism of his era—"false liberty of thought," he called it—than he was of the reactionary ideology of Pius IX.

In any case, long before the election of John Paul II, Newman was considered orthodox enough to be taught in Rome's pontifical universities, and by 1987 was considered safe enough to be enlisted—albeit selectively—in the Vatican's battle against Catholic couples who in conscience cannot accept the papal ban on contraception. Indeed, in that same year, some conservatives in the Congregation for the Causes of Saints were insistent that Newman might well have been canonized already if England's Roman Catholic bishops had been more vigorous in his support. Eszer, for one, assured me that the problem with Newman's cause was that the English bishops had hesitated to press it out of fear of Anglican resentment. "They are just handling it, like a parcel," he said, chuckling at his own simile. But in fact the English Catholic bishops were on record in support of the cause and the Archbishop of Canterbury had already assured them that he had no objections.

Obviously, Rome was not the place to get at the truth of the matter. My own hunch was that Newman, a prolific writer, presented the saint-makers with unique problems. If I wanted to know what lay behind Newman's slow march toward official sainthood, I needed to get behind the usual web of rumors and gossip of the Vatican. I would have to go to England.

NEWMAN: THE LIFE OF A THINKER IN THE CHURCH

THE LIFE OF John Henry Newman has been told and retold many times, beginning with his own celebrated intellectual autobiography, *Apologia Pro Vita Sua*, which he published in 1864 at the age of sixty-three. His latest biography, which draws heavily on the more than 20,000 letters Newman wrote, runs to 789 pages. One reason why causes on behalf of intellectuals take a long time to develop is therefore clear: everything they write—and, what is more, everything written *about* them—must be collected and examined. And the more a person reveals himself in print, the greater the risk that he may betray a fatal flaw in virtue or an equally fatal opinion that runs counter to the accepted teachings of the church. Unlike popes, whose official writings can also run to several volumes, intellectuals are not protected by the doctrine of infallibility.

Newman was an Anglican for forty-four years. Technically, what a candidate for sainthood says and does prior to conversion is considered irrelevant in proving heroic virtue. But Newman himself was loath to so divide his life into "before" and "after" phases. From adolescence onward, he had a profound sense of being led by God, an intuition he later dramatized in his best-known verse: "Lead, Kindly Light."

Influenced by Protestant evangelicalism, Newman underwent what he himself always regarded as a personal conversion experience at age fifteen. Again, as a young man traveling in Sicily in 1833, he felt a similar call to work for reform of the Church of England. Between these two religious experiences, Newman had been a student at Trinity College, Oxford, and had won a fellowship to Oriel College, the most coveted appointment within the university. Of all human institutions, Trinity and Oriel were the two Newman loved most. His genius was apparent to his professors and colleagues and in his twenties, he later wrote, he "was beginning to prefer intellectual excellence to moral."

Oxford was in those days Anglicanism's seat of learning; admission was prohibited to Roman Catholic and Protestant nonconformists. It was in this environment that Newman, now ordained a priest and vicar of St. Mary's Chapel, began an intensive study of the early fathers of the church with a view toward rooting the Anglican "middle way" between Catholicism and Protestantism in the early history of Christianity. Against the views of theological Liberals, Newman upheld the importance of revelation in Christianity and of the historical experiences of the church as the matrix in which doctrine properly develops.

Newman's research had a polemical edge. Together with a group of talented university colleagues, he launched the Oxford Movement, a theological and spiritual revival which eventually precipitated his conversion to Rome. Newman and his colleagues were concerned, among other things, with recovering Anglicanism's pre-Reformation roots. They pressed their program in a series of short anonymous "Tracts for the Times." In number 90, Newman went too far, arguing for a Catholic interpretation of the Thirty-nine Articles of the Church of England. The result was his censuring by the university and by twenty-four of the church's bishops. In 1841, Newman retired to a small church community at Littlemore. There, in the course of preparing his far-reaching "Essay on the Development of Christian Doctrine," Newman concluded that "truth" was on the side of Rome. In 1845, he and a group of like-minded friends were received into the Catholic Church.

Newman's change in spiritual allegiance cost him dearly. He was banished from his beloved Oxford, an exile he described in his novel

Loss and Gain, an account of an Anglican convert to Rome. His family and his closest Oxford friends remained Anglicans. Conversely, he would never be completely accepted by English Catholics, his talents never fully appreciated or utilized by the bishops of his adopted church. But for Newman there was more than compensation in his sense of having discovered, at last, "the true church of the Redeemer." Like Augustine, Newman saw in his own spiritual questing and questioning the mirror and movement of history, and history would be his vindicator. But for long periods of his life as a Roman Catholic, Newman felt misused, dried up, spent in petty quarrels. At one low point he confided to his private journal: "O how forlorn and dreary has been my course since I have become a Catholic! here has been the contrast—as a Protestant, I felt my religion dreary, but not my life—but, as a Catholic, my life dreary, but not my religion."

After ordination in Rome in 1847, Newman settled in Birmingham with a commission from Pope Pius IX to establish a community of Oratorians, a religious congregation founded in Rome by St. Phillip Neri in 1564. Unlike religious orders, members of the Oratory take no monastic vows but live in common and fraternal charity. Living this way, it was felt, Newman could incorporate other converts into a new community of priests and brothers devoted to the parochial needs of local Catholics. In view of Newman's evident intellectual gifts, the Birmingham Oratory was given special leave to cultivate scholarship as well. But it was all Newman could do to keep the community together. Money was hard to come by—English Catholics were hardly well-to-do—and at times the former Oxford don could not afford a new pair of shoes.

In 1850, the pope restored the Roman Catholic hierarchy to England, which had been without residential Catholic bishops since King Henry VIII proclaimed himself head of the Church of England. The move incited public protests against the resurrection of "popery" in Protestant England. As the most prominent convert to Rome, Newman was a special target of abuse. In 1851, he was tried for libel for exposing the sexual seductions of an ex-Dominican priest, Giacinto Achilli, who was posing as a victim of the Inquisition to Protestant audiences. Newman also had a painful falling-out with his friend F. W. Faber, another Anglican convert, over the direction of a second Oratory in London. Among their differences, interestingly enough, was Faber's penchant for translating the most outlandish stories of the Catholic saints, which Newman found preposterous and damaging to the credibility of the church.

But the chief frustrations of Newman's middle years came at the hands of assorted Catholic bishops. In 1851 he was invited by Archbishop Paul Cullen of Armagh to establish a Catholic university in Ireland. In preparation, Newman delivered a series of discourses which eventually became his classic work on education, *The Idea of a University*. What the church of Ireland—and for that matter, England, Newman believed—needed was an educated laity. But Newman's idea of education was not the bishops'. They had in mind a university run like a seminary, narrowly focused in its curriculum and under the firm direction of clerics. Newman's vision of university education was more liberal, more classic, and more collegial—more like Oxford but with a Roman Catholic tradition. Cullen would have none of it. Neither would Cardinal Manning, England's Roman Catholic primate, who, when Newman was invited by his bishop to establish a collegiate "mission" for Catholic students at Oxford, worked quietly behind his back to defeat the project. Like Newman, Manning had converted from the Church of England, but unlike Newman, he feared that Oxford-educated converts might become an Anglican fifth column in the Roman Church. "I see much danger of an English Catholicism of which Newman is the highest type," Manning wrote to a colleague in Rome. "It is the old Anglican, patristic, literary, Oxford tone transplanted into the Church." Newman, on the other hand, felt that "the church must be prepared for converts, as well as converts prepared for the church." By preparation he meant nurture through genuine education. After all, he observed of his own conversion, "Catholics didn't make us Catholics; Oxford made us Catholics."

It was Newman's fate to become a Roman Catholic at a time when the leadership in Rome was viscerally opposed to contemporary thought. In 1864, Pope Pius IX published his notorious Syllabus of Errors, which Newman found airy and abstract, but the English hierarchy, so recently restored, echoed Rome's conservatism. Newman set great store by ecclesiastical obedience, much as he chafed under Manning's "tyranny," and kept many of his opinions to himself. For example, Newman's theory of development in religious matters inclined him to accept Darwin's argument in *The Origin of Species* (1859). "I will either go whole hog with Darwin," he confided to his notebook, "or dispensing with time & history altogether, hold, not only the theory of distinct species but that also of the creation of fossil-bearing rocks." But as a practical matter, Newman felt he had to be circumspect in his public utterances; Pius IX's sentries were scanning the northern provinces for incipient heretics.

Even so, Newman was caught unawares by Rome's response to an article he wrote in 1859 as editor of the *Rambler*, an English Catholic magazine. The article was entitled "On Consulting the Faithful in Matters of Doctrine," something Rome was not inclined to do. Newman was immediately "deleted"—that is, secretly reported—to Rome by Bishop Thomas Joseph Brown of Newport on suspicion of fomenting heresy.

When informed of his transgression, Newman offered to clarify any offending passages. Eventually, the matter was smoothed over. But Newman was forced to resign his editorship and his reputation remained under a cloud in Rome. Monsignor George Talbot, the agent of the English bishops at the Vatican, denounced him as the leader of a dissident Liberal party within the English church. "If a check be not placed on the laity in England, they will be the rulers of the Catholic Church, instead of the Holy See and the episcopate," he warned Vatican officials. Talbot then offered his own view of the matter. "What is the province of the laity? To hunt, to shoot, to entertain. These matters they understand. But to meddle with ecclesiastical affairs they have no right at all . . . Dr. Newman is the most dangerous man in England, and you will see that he will make use of the laity against your Grace."

Five years later, Newman was attacked from another direction. Writing in a London review, Charles Kingsley, a popular literary figure and chaplain to the queen, gratuitously slandered Newman's integrity and, by extension, the honesty of all priests of Roman persuasion. "Truth for its own sake has never been a virtue with the Roman clergy," Kingsley wrote, and he supported his remarks by citing one of Newman's sermons. As it happened, the sermon was one he had delivered decades earlier when still an Anglican. But when Newman wittily pointed this out in print, Kingsley responded with an even more intemperate pamphlet.

This was Newman's opportunity, as he saw it, to "vanquish not only my accuser but my judges." For ten straight weeks, often with the printer's messenger at his side, Newman wrote in weekly installments an account of his thinking that led to his conversion. The result, five hundred pages long, was his classic *Apologia Pro Vita Sua*, a work so powerful, subtle, and persuasive that Newman won not only vindication for himself but for the entire English Catholic Church. Newman's reputation was henceforth secure, at home and abroad, save for a few reactionary Catholics like Cardinal Manning, who still thought him much too free an intellectual spirit. In 1870, Newman followed the *Apologia* with his equally exquisite *Grammar of Assent*, a philosophical and psychological study of the relationship between faith and reason. Like it or not, Manning had to concede that

Newman was now and would remain *the* Catholic voice in contemporary religious thought as well as in English public affairs.

Vatican Council I opened in 1869 and saw Manning leading the Ultramontanist party in its determination to wring from the conclave the strongest possible definition of papal infallibility. Not only did the Ultramontanists want a pope who could pronounce infallibly on virtually every serious moral and intellectual matter, they also wanted Pius IX's condemnations of Liberalism, church-state separation, progress, and the rest of the Syllabus of Errors made matters of faith for all Catholics. Newman, however, disliked factionalism in the church, even papal factions. And in matters of controversy, he opposed blunt condemnation. "Mere error in theology should be met with argument," he insisted, "not authority, at least by argument first."

Despite his advanced views, three bishops (including Brown, who had reported him to Rome) invited Newman to attend Vatican I as a consultant. But after weighing the pros and cons, Newman elected to stay home. He was never very good at working on boards and commissions, he told himself, nor did he feel free to speak candidly in the presence of bishops. As he wrote in his diary at the time, "I have never gotten on intimately with my ecclesiastical superiors. It arises from my shyness, and the sort of nervous continual recollection that I am bound to obey them, which keeps me from being easy with them, speaking my mind without effort, and lucidly and calmly arguing with them. I never could make my presence *felt*."

Newman knew that Pope Pius IX was determined on the matter of infallibility and, though Newman believed it himself, he opposed a formal definition of the doctrine as unwise and inopportune. He saw no heresies on the horizon which required so severe a decision. Besides, he thought infallibility should be exercised through a pope pronouncing on matters in conjunction with an ecumenical council of all the bishops, and feared that a declaration of papal infallibility would encourage a pope to act alone. Above all, he saw the church as an organism: to be a thinker *in* the church was to think *with* the whole body of the church, and not just with whomever occupied the Chair of Peter. These views, he knew, still made him suspect at the Vatican.

After much maneuvering and under considerable pressure from Pius IX, the council fathers passed a constitution, *Pastor aeternus* (Eternal Pastor), defining the infallibility of the pope and his immediate jurisdiction over all Roman Catholics. But the final wording of the document was cautious, limited, and purposely vague: to the consternation of Manning and other Ultramontanists, it did not extend infallibility to every papal utterance, nor did it suggest that popes were divinely inspired. Nonetheless, upon his return to England, Manning issued a pastoral letter on the council which exaggerated the meaning of the council's definition. Newman knew it was an exaggeration, but his faith in the church was such that he could not despair of what Pius IX had wrought. To his diary he confided:

> It is not good for a pope to live twenty years. It is an anomaly and bears no good fruit; he becomes a god, has no one to contradict him, does not know facts, and does cruel things without meaning it. For years past my own consolation personally has been in our Lord's Presence in the Tabernacle. I turn from the sternness of external authority to Him who can immeasurably compensate trials which after all are not real . . .

And to a friend, he offered words that, in light of Pope John XXIII's decision to convoke Vatican Council II a century later, would prove prophetic: "Let us be patient, let us have faith, and a new Pope, and a re-assembled Council may trim the boat."

Newman had not planned on addressing the infallibility issue publicly. But news of the dogma inflamed Protestant England. Former English prime minister William Gladstone published an essay charging that, in light of the council's definition of papal infallibility, Catholics could not be loyal subjects of both the pope and the British crown.

Gladstone's attack demanded a reply, and at age seventy-three, Newman took up pen once more. In his famous "Letter to the Duke of Norfolk," Newman held the Ultramontanists responsible for Gladstone's misunderstanding of the Catholic position. Popes do not act on personal inspiration from God, he argued. If a pope made a decision which proved to be immoral, Catholics would not be bound by it. "As private men," he wrote, the weight of the pope's hand "is absolutely unappreciable." And nothing in the council's declaration, he held, could subvert the inviolability of personal conscience. "Certainly, if I am obliged to bring religion into after-dinner toasts (which indeed does not seem quite the thing) I shall drink,—to the Pope, if you please,—still, to Conscience first, and to the Pope afterwards."

Newman's response not only won over the suspicious English public, which now regarded him as a proud national possession, but even Manning himself accepted his adversary's interpretation. In 1878, Newman's old college, Trinity, gladdened his declining years by naming him its first honorary fellow. Though Oxford still refused degrees to Roman Catholics, Newman had always cherished Trinity and taken the snapdragon that grew on the walls opposite his fresh-man rooms there as the emblem of "my own perpetual residence even unto death at the University." He gladly returned for dinner. That same year, Pius IX died and in 1979, at the instigation of several prominent lay Catholics—and despite some maneuvers by Manning—the new pope, Leo XIII, named Newman his first cardinal. It was, for the aging controversialist, a final vindication of his life as a Catholic, and he went to Rome in person, despite increasing disability, to re-ceive his red hat.

At his death, Newman was hailed as a Victorian sage. His reputa-tion was such that obituaries appeared in fifteen hundred newspapers around the world. In Birmingham, a crowd estimated at ten to fifteen thousand lined the streets as his coffin passed from the Oratory to his grave at Rednal, the Oratorians' retreat seven miles distant, where his body remains to this day. *The Times* of London was not alone in remarking on Newman's potential for canonization. Among others, the sturdily Protestant *Evangelical Magazine* reckoned that "Of the multitude of saints in the Roman calendar there are very few that can be considered better entitled to that designation than Cardinal New-man."

THE LONG MARCH TOWARD ROME

GIVEN THIS REPUTATION for holiness, why did it take a full century for Newman's cause to reach Rome? Three reasons are immediately ev-ident.

First, the English church was too small, too poor, and altogether inexperienced in the intricate protocols of making saints. Moreover, in the fifty years following Newman's death, England itself was twice threatened in two world wars, which is not the sort of context in which to launch a canonization process.

Second, with the passing of those who had known him well, New-man's reputation survived chiefly through his writings. Which is to say, he was admired for the quality of his mind and the elegance of his prose—for his integrity, too—but not necessarily for heroic virtues on which a popular reputation for holiness is built. Indeed, his first major biographer, Wilfrid Ward, who had known Newman, presented him as rather wintry and hypersensitive—not the sort of profile one expects of a saint. When Ward's two-volume biography appeared in 1912, re-viewers did not dwell on Newman's holiness.

Third, the clouds that hung over Newman in his heyday as a controversialist were not altogether dispersed by his elevation to the cardinalate. In England, church leadership remained more in the mold of Manning than of Newman. In Rome, Leo XIII died and was replaced by Pius X, whose 1907 encyclical *Pascendi* unleashed a ruthless vigilante campaign to identify—and in several cases, excommunicate—intellectuals and scholars tainted by an assortment of liberal ideas he labeled Modernism. To both the hunters and the hunted, Newman qualified as at least a proto-Modernist. Wilfrid Ward read *Pascendi* and thought the pope's condemnations surely applied to Newman. So did the Irish priest George Tyrrell, one of the chief exponents of Modernism, who was excommunicated in 1907. The Oratorians defended Newman and eventually cleared his name. Still, Newman's most progressive ideas—notably his insistence that church doctrines are developmental and cannot be properly understood apart from historical context; his regard for the laity as active rather than passive instruments in the hands of clerics; his emphasis on the priority of individual conscience; his openness to modern thought and distaste for the arid scholasticism that dominated Roman theology; and his reservations regarding the doctrine of papal infallibility as defined by Vatican I—all these troubled Rome for the first half of the twentieth century and were not officially accepted until Vatican Council II. Newman remained a nonviable candidate for sainthood because Rome does not canonize thinkers whose ideas it has not yet made its own.

Significantly, it was among Catholics in North America, so unlike both the English or the Italians in their efforts to relate faith to culture and politics, that the first movements on behalf of Newman's canonization surfaced. The first prayer cards promoting a cause for Newman appeared in Toronto, Canada, in 1935 at the direction of Archbishop George McGuigan. And the first genuine public clamor arose six years later when *America*, the Jesuit magazine edited in New York, published a letter to the editor urging Newman's canonization. For four consecutive months, the magazine ran letters supporting the idea. It was not Newman the cardinal of the church they were promoting, or Newman the man of prayer, but the Catholic thinker whose wrestling with the demands of faith and intellectual honesty mirrored their own.

This was, at any rate, the Newman I had known from reading him as a student. And of all the figures the congregation was preparing for judgment, Newman was the only one, it seemed to me, whose life and virtues still spoke to Christians of the late twentieth century. I went to England, therefore, animated in no small way by the anticipation all pilgrims feel when they set out for the shrine of a favorite saint.

The Birmingham Oratory remains as Newman built it, a mass of bricks—1.7 million, by Newman's own count—encompassing a church, library, and quarters for the community of a dozen priests and brothers. Newman's own small room, a bed along one side and bookcases against another, has been left as it was the day he died. This is where he had lived from 1852 on, wrapped against the cold in his favorite garment, his academic cloak and hood from Oxford. Framed against one wall are a collection of portraits of the Oxford men who accompanied him into the Church of Rome. His desk is illuminated by a lamp Gladstone gave him as a gift. On the desk is a letter he wrote to his parents at the age of seven, the hand clear, formal, and precise. Another exercise book contains jottings he made between 1812 and 1834. His cardinal's hat, cross, and cassock hang in one corner, and near his bed is the prie-dieu. His books, as I examined them, were devoid of marks—he respected books too much to write in them, apart from signing the inside cover with his name. I fished at random through some letters and picked one out from 1867 which, characteristically, is in response to a personal attack: "We are taught by holy men that any insult addressed to us may be meritoriously borne in silence," it began, "except such as has reference to our soundness in the Catholic faith." I handled it gently, as if it were already a second-class relic.

"I suppose we'll have to lock this room up once they've made him a saint," said Brother Martin, who showed me about. "Awful nuisance. We'll have to put up some sort of exhibition of his clothes and pictures, that sort of thing, downstairs for the tourists. Can't have crowds of people coming up here."

Like many others in the Oratory, Brother Martin is a convert from the Church of England, mainly because of reading Newman. "His way of thinking became my way of thinking," he explained crisply. I asked to see the library and he showed me an elliptical room with 20,000 books, most of them Newman's own. To one side is the writing stand on which Newman composed his *Apologia*. Like Hemingway, Newman preferred to write his longer works standing up. The Newman archives are shelved throughout the house. Altogether, they contain 120,000 separate items which constitute the copious foundation for his cause. Scholars have been coming to the Oratory for decades to do research on Newman, and the collection, editing, and publication of his letters alone have sustained a cottage industry.

Even so, the Oratory is more than just a shrine to its famous founder, and the provost, Father Gregory Winterton, sizing me up as yet another star-struck pilgrim, gently set me straight. "This house *is* Newman, make no mistake," he said over lunch in the refectory. "But our apostolate is to the people on our doorstep. This is a parish. We run a school, say Mass, hear confessions, lots of them. Newman did too, but that's a side of him most people who come here don't know about. Oratorian spirituality is low-key. Keep a low profile, we say, and that's why the community here has never been keen on blowing Newman's trumpet."

"Then who did?" I asked. "The North Americans?"

"No, the man who got it going was Father Henry Francis Davis, who was teaching Newman at the diocesan seminary here in Birmingham. About 1944, he came across a book, in French, by Louis Bouyer, a convert and a priest of the Oratory in France. It was the first book to treat the spirituality of Newman the man, not just Newman the thinker. This gave Davis the idea that Newman should be made a saint, so he wrote an article urging the introduction of Newman's cause and sent it to all the English-speaking bishops in the world asking their support. He got a favorable response, enough anyway that he came to the Birmingham Oratory and asked the fathers to promote the cause. A lot of the old fathers were against it. Some thought it would disturb the pastoral ministry of the parish. And, as I said, pushing one of our own was not an Oratorian thing to do."

In 1955, the Oratory finally voted to support the cause and sent a letter to Bishop Francis Grimshaw of Birmingham asking him to initiate the Ordinary Process. But Grimshaw, worried about the cost to the diocese, dithered over the proposal for three years before agreeing to go along. From the start, though, the cause encountered major problems.

"The Italians know all about making saints but we didn't have the hang of it," Winterton recalls. "For instance, we appointed four men to the diocesan tribunal instead of three, as required by canon law. They started out interviewing some of the people who had known Newman but all they knew about was the cardinal in his old age. Not much we could use. Davis was the vice-postulator. But he was too gentle, not the sort to knock heads among the bishops to get them behind the cause. Anyhow, the tribunal only lasted nine months and didn't accomplish much. Then Rome wrote and said, look, an Ordinary Process won't work. Newman's been dead too long and if he is to be beatified it will have to be through an historical process based on written documents."

Throughout the sixties and into the seventies, Father Charles

Stephen Dessain, the Orator's archivist, whittled away at the mountain of Newman's writings, preparing scholarly editions of Newman's correspondence. But the cause itself was dormant. In 1973, Pope Paul VI asked the Oratorians how far along the process had progressed. He wanted, he said, to beatify Newman during the upcoming Holy Year of 1975. The pope's interest prodded Winterton to action. Besides the preparation of documents, what the cause needed was a vigorous promotion, something that seemed alien to the reserve of English Catholics. In 1974, two nuns from "The Work," an international institute of religious women, showed up at the Oratory. Their mother superior, it seems, had been reading Newman and found him a congenial spirit. With the Oratory's permission, she opened a Newman center in Rome. The next year, the center sponsored a symposium on Newman, complete with a Mass at St. Peter's attended by seven cardinals. Rome was impressed.

"It was time to get on with it, I felt," said Winterton, who has been superior of the Birmingham Oratory longer than anyone since Newman. "We went to Archbishop George Dwyer of Birmingham and, after some dithering, he named a new vice-postulator to raise money and in 1979 set up a new historical commission to investigate Newman's life, virtues, and reputation for holiness. We also established the 'Friends of Newman' to promote prayer to Newman, the sort of thing one does to collect divine favors."

The new commission was chaired by an American historian, Jesuit Father Vincent Blehl, a Newman specialist from Fordham University in New York City, and included Father J. Derek Holmes, an ecclesiastical historian from Ushaw College in England, and Mr. Gerard Treacy, a historian who had replaced the deceased Father Dessain as the newly appointed archivist of the Oratory. Their task was formidable. Apart from examining all of Newman's own writings, which run to ninety volumes, for their theological and spiritual significance, the commission had to research the letters, memoirs, autobiographies, and biographies of his friends, associates, and enemies. The letters written to or about Newman during his lifetime alone numbered between 50,000 and 70,000. In addition, the commission collected such occasional secondary material as newspaper and magazine articles, biographies of Newman, and even their reviews. As of 1980, the bibliography of secondary Newman studies, not including newspaper articles or short notices, numbered 5,000 titles. Finally, the commission sifted between 70,000 and 90,000 other letters about Newman written after his death to his literary executor, the Oratory, and the vice-postulators for evidence of a continuing reputation for holiness. In

May of 1986, the commission completed its work and submitted 6,483 pages on Newman's life, virtue, and reputation for holiness to the diocesan tribunal.

Among the Oratorians, there is no doubt of Newman's sanctity and their expectation is that Rome will agree. They are divided, however, over what to do with Newman's body once he is beatified. Newman had stipulated that he wanted to be buried at Rednal, in the same grave with the body of his closest friend and fellow Oratorian, Father Ambrose St. John. But already pilgrims are arriving by the busloads from as far away as Germany and the Ukraine, and the Oratorians must make a choice: should they continue to honor Newman's wishes or build a chapel inside their parish church where the body can be both venerated and protected? "Awful nuisance," said Winterton. "There's no way we can keep a man at Rednal all the time." But turning the church into a shrine, he knows, would not be Newman's way. As an Anglican and as a Roman, Newman was never keen on ritual and fuss.

Newman cared even less for Catholic hagiography, and on my return flight to Rome I tried to imagine how he would have reacted to the enormous effort now under way to transform his life into a text suitable for judgment by the congregation. Among Newman's collected writings is a controversial piece on "Ancient Saints," initially published in the *Rambler*, in which he dismisses the standard Catholic biographies of saints as a form of moral vivisection:

> I ask something more [of saints' biographies] than to stumble upon the *disjecta membra* of what ought to be a living whole. I take but a secondary interest in books which chop up a Saint into chapters on faith, hope and charity, and the cardinal virtues. They are too scientific to be devotional . . . They do not manifest a Saint, they mince him into spiritual lessons . . .
>
> And I have a parallel difficulty in the case of hagiographers, when they draw out their materials, not according to years, but according to virtues. Such reading is not history, it is moral science; nay, hardly that: for chronological considerations will be neglected; youth, manhood and age, will be intermingled. I shall not to be able to trace out, for my own edification, the solemn conflict which is waging in the soul between what is divine and what is human, or the eras of successive victories won by the powers and principles which are divine. I shall not be able to determine whether there was heroism in the young, whether there was not infirmity and temptation in the old. I shall not be able to explain actions which need explanation, for the age of the actors is the true key for entering into them. I shall be wearied and disappointed, and I shall go back with pleasure to the Fathers.

Newman delighted in reading the personal letters of the early church fathers such as Basil, Augustine, and John Chrysostom because in reading them he felt he was encountering the "real, hidden but human life" of saints as they wrestled with the controverted issues of their day. "I want to hear a Saint converse," Newman wrote. "I am not content to look at him as a statue . . . Instead of writing formal doctrinal treatises, they wrote controversy; and their controversy, again, is correspondence . . . They wrote for the occasion, and seldom in a carefully-digested plan."

Newman, of course, was just that kind of writer. But whereas the ancient church fathers were canonized by popular acclamation, Newman and his writings would have to be abridged and cast into the mold of a formal *positio*, the requisite virtues noted and numbered like the fingers on his hands. I had, by now, examined enough *positiones* to know that the authors were seldom successful in presenting candidates whole and entire. Would the "real" Newman, I wondered, the engagingly human figure whose personality was so powerfully alive in every page he wrote, survive the process for his canonization? What could a *positio*, however long and detailed, contribute to what was already present and engagingly accessible in his writings?

I put these questions to Father Blehl, the postulator of the cause and, as Gumpel's collaborator, the man charged with writing Newman's *positio*. Blehl had edited a volume of Newman's letters for his doctoral dissertation at Harvard in 1958, and has been absorbed in Newman ever since. Graying and rather formal for an American Jesuit, Blehl wants nothing more than to be the scholar who presents the "objective evidence" for Newman's sanctity. But he is a neophyte in the craft of making saints, and at lunch in Rome, talking over a robust bottle of Nebbiolo d'Alba, he seemed awed by the fastidious demands of the saint-making system—as well he might: the congregation rarely gets a candidate who wrote so much, or about whom so much had been written.

There was no need to remind Blehl of the repugnance Newman felt in reading the dismembered lives of Catholic saints. The Jesuit knew the passage well. He then reminded *me* that a *positio* is not a biography but a document whose purpose is to make a convincing case for personal sanctity. In doing so, however, Blehl felt he could not ignore the Anglican half of Newman's life, even though the congregation usually considers only a convert's life as a Roman Catholic. "I see a great continuity in Newman's life," he said. "His spiritual journey began within the Anglican church and he never gave up anything that he felt was compatible with what he believed. His personal endeavor was to follow 'the light and the call,' as he put it. My job is to go through his life and his writings from the perspective of his attempts to serve God, and to follow the instructions which he received from the pope in setting up the Oratory at Birmingham."

It was good that the investigation of Newman's virtues had not been started until all his letters and diaries had been published, Blehl said. Without these, Newman's inner life, the dimension that was not evident from his writings, could not be fully documented or appreciated. Among Newman's virtues, Blehl stressed his humility in the face of repeated frustrations as a Catholic, especially at the hands of Manning and other English bishops. Newman never complained of these to his colleagues at the Oratory, who were astonished to read of them after his death. "This to my mind is why he is a saint," he said. "People said he was a skeptic, a fideist, a liberal—there were so many slanders against Newman in his day that by the time we got round to doing his cause we found that other scholars had cleared up most of these problems."

There is, however, one aspect of Newman's life which Blehl expects the *positio* alone adequately illuminates: his dedication to the spiritual ideals of the Oratory. This is the side of Newman about which the reading public knew or cared little about, but it is the side which the congregation would examine closely for evidence of heroic virtue. "You see, Oratorians were expected to work quietly and without fanfare," Blehl observed. "They were to heal divisions in the Catholic community, not increase them. And they were to immerse themselves in the environment of the city in which the Oratory was located."

Much of the *positio* will concentrate on showing that Newman, far from being individualistic in his quest for personal holiness, did all the things expected of an Oratorian and did them well. Despite his eminence and great intellectual gifts, Blehl argues, the evidence shows that he was always willing to assume the tasks of others.

"He kept the accounts of the Oratory school, wrote letters to parents of the pupils about their children's performance, directed Latin plays, even dusted the books in the library. He was at the service of the parishioners, most of them poor, hearing confessions daily, preaching and directing the various missions to the jail, the workhouse, and the orphanage. And in the last year of his life, he went out into the slush and mud to mediate a dispute between the Catholic workers in the Cadbury chocolate factory who were being forced under threat of losing their jobs to attend daily Bible instruction from the Quaker masters. As one old Oratorian remembered him, 'Newman carried the art of being ordinary to perfection.' "

Blehl's personal assessment is even more generous. "There is evidence," he says, "that Newman always lived in the presence of God." The issue, though, is demonstrating that others thought so too. Like other postulators, Blehl must show that his candidate has enjoyed a continuous reputation for holiness. And here again, Blehl thinks the work of the historical commission has produced the goods.

"Newman's spiritual influence on others began in his lifetime," he said. "We have letters, thousands of them, from Catholics, Anglicans, Methodists, Presbyterians—who write things like, 'under God, I owe my soul to Newman.' Now that's a pretty strong statement. And since his death, and especially since the cause was introduced, we've gotten letters from a number of people saying they were converted [to Catholicism] because of Newman. There are letters saying he ought to be canonized, letters that say we ought to pray not *for* Newman but *to* him. To my mind—and in the judgment of the historical commission—this spiritual influence is a moral miracle."

The Jesuits, I knew, are keen on moral miracles, as Eszer and other Dominicans are not. "Miracles became a prerequisite for canonization only in the Middle Ages," Blehl reminded me, but he thought it unlikely that the congregation would accept Newman's spiritual influence as the equivalent of a physical healing. The postulation, he said, had collected testimonies of numerous "graces" and "divine signs" attributed to Newman's intercession, but nothing which would pass muster as a genuine miracle. Ironic as it may seem, one was found for Dominic Barberi, the Italian priest who received Newman into the Catholic Church in 1845. Barberi was beatified in 1963.

From my conversations with Father Winterton, I knew that at one time he had hoped that Newman would be beatified in 1988, canonized in 1989, and declared a Doctor of the Church in 1990, the centennial of his death. But this schedule turned out to be much too optimistic. Blehl did not finish the *positio* until the summer of 1989.

Newman may have been the greatest Catholic thinker of his time. He may have occasioned hundreds of conversions through the example of his life and writings. He may have, through his personal courage, the boldness of his thought, and his elevated gift of language, enabled countless Roman Catholics to persist in faith despite the recklessness of certain papal policies. He may have proved more durable and prescient than the church's more cautious professional theologians. He may, as has been said, have been the distant father of

Vatican Council II. But until someone comes forward with a demonstrable miracle through Newman's intercession, his cause will remain in a state of arrested development.

John Paul II, or a successor pope, could, of course, waive the miracle requirement in Newman's case. But that would set more precedents than one. None of the great fathers of the church whose writings Newman prized were considered saints primarily for their intellectual contributions to the faith. For example, St. Jerome, who translated the Bible into Latin, was an ascetic and Augustine was bishop of an important see. Even the cause of Thomas Aquinas, now regarded as the church's foremost philosopher and theologian, floundered temporarily when the Devil's Advocate discovered that he had worked too few miracles during his lifetime.* At his canonization, Pope John XXII praised not only Aquinas's intellectual accomplishments but also his perpetual virginity—and his having no less than three hundred posthumous miracles to his credit. Indeed, Aquinas's reputation for wonder-working was such that long before his canonization, rival groups of friars fought over his body: one group cut off his head, another a hand, and before his mangled corpse was finally laid to rest, the flesh was boiled away so that his bones could be conveniently contained in a reliquary.

It is unlikely that Newman will ever attract the same frenzy. (His body, one assumes, is safe.) But who can say that an acceptable miracle will ever be found? The question, of course, is does it matter? What can canonization add to a man whose influence is equal to that of any other saint created by the church in the last four hundred years? Will Newman's reputation for holiness diminish if the miracles needed for beatification and canonization are not forthcoming?

What matters is that much as the church needs saints like Newman, the canonization process still does not readily comprehend the worth of the intellectually gifted. Religious intellectuals and artists mediate Christ in ways that only powerful thought and art can do and therefore serve as models of holiness within high culture. Their asceticism is not the asceticism of the cloistered monk, their insights are not the insights of the mystic, their suffering, though often great, is not the suffering of the martyr.

---

* At one point, supporters of his cause argued that Thomas's books were themselves miraculous in their wisdom.

CONCLUSION: THE FUTURE OF SAINTHOOD

AN UNDISCRIMINATING SYSTEM

IN APRIL 1989, Cardinal Joseph Ratzinger, prefect of the Congregation for the Doctrine of the Faith and John Paul II's closest adviser on theological matters, offered some rare public remarks critical of the church's saint-making process. The occasion was a question-and-answer session following an address by the cardinal at a Catholic cultural center in Seregno, a small town near Milan. Ratzinger was asked whether he thought the church was making too many saints. In response, he acknowledged that the number of saints and blesseds had increased in the previous decade, adding that among these were some "who perhaps mean something to a certain group of people, but do not mean a great deal to the great multitude of believers." Ratzinger then went on to suggest that priority ought to be given to saints whose lives carry a more universal and relevant message for contemporary believers. By way of example, he cited Edith Stein and Niels Stensen, as two saints who speak to the modern condition, even though the latter has been dead for three centuries.

Brief and circumspect as they were, Ratzinger's observations produced headlines in the Italian press and stories in *The New York*

Times and other newspapers around the world. The Italians, in particular, interpreted the cardinal's remarks as a criticism of the pope's penchant for increasing the number of saints and as a confirmation of those critics of the church who have long ridiculed the congregation as a "saint factory." Not surprisingly, Ratzinger's comments occasioned considerable anger among the saint-makers as well. The cardinal had been a member of the congregation for four years, and if he considered the system deficient, some of the saint-makers felt, why hadn't he voiced his criticisms to the staff? In a brief and conciliatory public response, Archbishop Traian Crisan, secretary of the congregation, allowed that "It [saint-making] is like anything else that's done every day—it can lose some of its value. We need to be careful." But word was passed to the rest of the congregation that no one else was to discuss Ratzinger's comments with the press.

I could tell the saint-makers were smarting. One of them complained that Ratzinger was taking a typically Eurocentric perspective: both Edith Stein and Niels Stensen, he noted, were northern Europeans. "Who is the cardinal to say that they are world figures and others are not?" he asked rhetorically. "Besides, if we are to canonize only saints with global reputations, who apart from an occasional Mother Teresa would qualify? If Ratzinger's advice is to be followed, we might as well close this congregation down and let a handful of cardinals decide who will be saints."

For his part, Ratzinger, too, was upset by the speculations his remarks fueled in the secular press. In a subsequent interview with a friendly publication (*30 Days*, a conservative Catholic monthly which he frequently uses to air his views), the cardinal attempted to clarify his thoughts:

> In fact, I said that this problem had not existed up to now, but that it was a problem that now gradually required to be confronted. This statement, which was in fact very cautious, presupposes that every canonization is already, inevitably, a choice in favor of a certain standard of selection: there are, as I said, many more saints than those who can be canonized. The opening of a process of canonization already indicates a choice among a very large number [of potential candidates]. The choice is linked to some chance events: for example, a religious order will be able to gather testimony about an individual's sanctity, and follow the canonization procedure more easily, than those who are ignorant of the process, or friends of a father or mother of a family . . . it seems legitimate to me to ask whether the standards generally in effect until now ought to be made more complete today by means of

new emphases, in order to place before the eyes of Christendom those figures who, more than anyone else, make the Holy Church visible to us, in the midst of so many doubts about Her holiness.

On the face of it, Ratzinger appeared to be saying no more than many critics of the system—including some of the saint-makers themselves—had said in the past: namely, that the promotion of candidates for canonization had long since become the province of the religious orders which, for practical purposes, are the only institutions in the church which have the time, money, and will to promote causes—including those of laymen. Had he been more candid, however, Ratzinger might have spelled out for the benefit of all who care just what standards the congregation does observe in selecting candidates to process for sainthood. The reason he did not, I suspect, is that apart from the priorities I described in chapter 3 (Third World figures, laymen, and others from underrepresented constituencies in the church), there *are* no discernible standards for choosing one candidate over another.

By now it should be clear that the congregation's *modus operandi* is, essentially, to accept all causes proposed to them by local bishops. And the more bishops who support a given cause, the better its chances of acceptance. In this sense, it is a seller's market. To be sure, some candidates are occasionally rejected, but the congregation keeps no record of rejectees nor is it evident, under the new legislation, who makes that decision or how.

In the past, it was up to the Devil's Advocate and his staff of lawyers, together with censors (like Father Lozano) delegated to examine a candidate's writings, to present objections to the introduction of a cause. The typical grounds for rejection were *doctrinal*—that is, something the candidate wrote or advocated was found to be unorthodox; *spiritual* or *psychological*, as in cases where a supposed mystic turns out to have been spiritually or emotionally unstable; *technical*, as in cases where proper procedures have not been followed on the diocesan level; and *political* or *pastoral*, as in cases where beatification of a candidate would actually harm the local church.

With the Reform of 1983, there is no single person or body charged with making these decisions. In theory, the local bishop is the first church official empowered to judge whether there are any serious objections to a cause. In practice, however, it is virtually impossible to find out why a bishop, or a national hierarchy, refuses to initiate a formal cause. Typically, causes are not rejected outright but put on indefinite hold. In controversial cases, it appears, the reasons are usually political or ideological and therefore are never formally acknowledged. For example, supporters of the Austrian Franz Jäggerstätter, who was executed by the Nazis for refusing induction into the army, have failed for years to get a forthright explanation for the lack of a formal process. The reason appears to be that some of the Austrian bishops, and not a few interested parties in Rome, feel that Jäggerstätter's canonization would be interpreted as official endorsement of pacifism—a position which conflicts with the church's "just-war" theory and an attitude with which John Paul II has shown little sympathy. Moreover, in the case of Archbishop Romero, it is clear that the pope himself, for both pastoral and political reasons, instructed the Salvadorean bishops to delay acting on Romero's obvious reputation for holiness.

Conversely, if a local bishop forwards a cause to Rome, the congregation does everything it can to oblige. Until the *positio* is presented to the consultors, no one within the congregation has the right or responsibility to question the cause. Although a relator has the freedom to turn down a cause, in fact, as we have seen, the relators' habit is to accept every candidate offered to them. If in the course of preparing the *positio* the relator should discover a major obstacle to the candidate's claim to martyrdom or heroic virtue, he is bound by his oath to the truth to make that obstacle known. But so far as I was able to ascertain, since the Reform this has never happened. A process may die for lack of sufficient evidence or because the promoters lose interest, as was the case for several years with the cause of Philippine Duchesne. Or, as is currently the situation of Pius IX, a pope may decide that proceeding to beatification or canonization is pastorally or politically inopportune. But the general principle is clear: once a cause is accepted by Rome, the expectation is that the candidate will at least be declared heroically virtuous or a martyr. And the more conventional and innocuous the candidate (typically, founders of religious orders), the better his or her chances of eventually being declared a saint.

BLESSEDS AND SAINTS: A BLURRED DISTINCTION

IN THIS CONTEXT, Ratzinger's remarks could be understood as a plea for standards for distinguishing between candidates whose life and virtues or martyrdom provide a timely message to the whole church, and those of merely local interest. When beatification was first introduced into the system, four centuries ago, its purpose was to distinguish between hometown favorites and figures deemed exemplary for Christians everywhere. Beatification (initially by the local bishop) was for the former, canonization (always by the pope) for the latter. But that geographical distinction has long since faded: the way the saint-making system has evolved, any blessed who is accredited with a second miracle of intercession is automatically eligible for canonization. As a result, the church's calendar of saints has become crowded with names, like Philippine Duchesne and Giuseppe Moscati, who have no meaning to Catholics outside their native countries and may not even be widely known within them.

In short, the division between beatification and canonization has become a theological distinction with little practical significance. Technically, only canonization carries the theological "certainty" that the Servant of God is in fact in heaven. But this guarantee means little to those Catholics who already venerate blesseds or who invoke popular figures like Padre Pio who have yet to be beatified. Similarly, the fact that restricted veneration is permitted to blesseds but universal veneration is required for the canonized no longer constitutes a real distinction. Newly canonized saints are rarely included in the liturgical calendars of the churches outside their own countries, because there is no room for them. More than two-thirds of the days on the church's liturgical calendar celebrate events in the life of Christ, the church, and the Virgin Mary. This leaves only about one hundred days open for honoring saints. Thus, for obvious reasons, the calendar of the German church, for example, does not include American saints, the French does not include African saints, etc. As a practical matter, therefore, only classic figures, like St. Francis and, more recently, Thérèse of Lisieux, are regularly included in calendars outside their native countries. In effect, then, all saints are local saints and very few attain the kind of universal cult which was originally supposed to distinguish the canonized from the beatified.

The saint-makers are well aware of this blurring of boundaries between beatification and canonization. Indeed, there has been considerable discussion among them as to whether the beatifications should be continued in their present form, modified, or dispensed with altogether. In his commentary on the legislation of 1983, Monsignor Fabijan Veraja, the sub-secretary of the congregation, notes that the new laws were formulated in such a way as to allow further changes without requiring additional legislation.

In the future, for instance, the authority for beatifying Servants of

God could be returned to local bishops or to national conferences of bishops (as Cardinal Leon Josef Suenens suggested at Vatican Council II) and papal canonizations reserved for exemplary figures chosen by the Holy See for their timely and transnational appeal. This is one scenario which has been discussed among the saint-makers. But in matters of holiness, which saints are more deserving than others of universal veneration? And who is most competent to decide? These are the substantive issues to which Ratzinger alluded when he spoke of the need to distinguish certain saints from others.

As long as John Paul II is pope, however, he is unlikely to allow the authority to beatify to revert to his brother bishops. The present system, centralized in Rome, fits his peripatetic interpretation of the pope's unique role as supreme teacher and pastor of the universal church. For this pope, making saints has become a form of ecclesiastical politics: yet another opportunity to remind Roman Catholics everywhere, but especially those in the Third World, of their unity in one fold and under one supreme shepherd. As Archbishop Crisan, the secretary of the congregation, has observed, "When he travels, the pope likes to bring a blessed in his pocket." What's more, he added, to Catholics outside Rome the elaborate beatification ceremonies are "like something from another world."

Can the church have too many saints? This question, too, lay behind the unusually spirited reaction to Ratzinger's comments. In theory, of course, everyone is called to holiness. But the canonization process, as we have seen, was developed to restrain rather than facilitate the propensity of the faithful to impute holiness promiscuously. Now, however, it appears that the church is burdened with an anomaly: a system which, for all its fastidiousness, is beatifying more people—many of them virtually indistinguishable in their stories and exemplarity from each other—than the faithful seem to want or need.

Meanwhile, John Paul II is creating an expanding pool of blesseds, some of whom, by the inexorable operation of the system, will become tomorrow's saints. On Sunday, April 23, 1989, to cite one routine occurrence, John Paul II beatified two priests and three nuns who will never be household names outside certain regions and their own religious orders. The priests were Spanish missionaries, Martin Lumberas and Melchior Sanchez, who were martyred together in Japan in 1632. The nuns were Catherine Longpré of France, who entered the convent at age twelve, was tormented by demons most of her life, and died in Canada in 1668 at the age of thirty-four; Frances Siedliska of Poland, foundress of a religious order, who died in 1902; and Maria Anna Rosa Caiani of Italy, another foundress, who died in 1921. Together, they joined a backlog of blesseds, most of them members of religious orders, who represent the likeliest candidates for future canonization.

Defenders of the present system concede that few of those who are canonized or beatified have more than local reputations. But they insist that in the aggregate all these disparate blesseds and saints, representing diverse countries and historical periods, inscribe a pattern which, like a quilt, reveals the forms that holiness has taken in the modern world. Perhaps they do. But if the purpose of canonization is to set before the faithful fresh and unique examples of Christian holiness—"prime numbers," in theologian von Balthasar's suggestive phrase—then the system needs a thorough reexamination. When one saint begins to look much like another, it is time to question how and why they are made.

MYSTERY AND MYSTIFICATION

THERE IS A TENDENCY, inside the congregation and out, to confuse the mysterious ways of God with the unnecessarily mystifying ways of the saint-making process. For members of the congregation, I suspect, this tendency is rooted in the theological assumption that they do not *make* saints, but only discover those whom God has raised up in our midst. As they view it, their work in investigating lives for proof of martyrdom or heroic virtue is merely human labor bracketed by divine action: initially, it is the Holy Spirit who moves the faithful to recognize holiness and thereby establishes an authentic reputation for sanctity (*fama sanctitatis*). At the end of the process, it is again the Holy Spirit who provides the necessary "divine signs" in the form, most often, of inexplicable physical cures.

To be sure, some members of the congregation are well aware of human failings—their own and those of the system. But in spite of this, they are convinced that if a cause is stalled or fails, it is because God wills it, not because of human or systemic errors. Time and again, I was assured that if God wants a Servant of God canonized, it will happen. The effect, then, is to assume that in spite of its manifest defects, the system—and those who operate it, including the pope—ultimately produces the saints God wants. And since the system's procedures have been, at least until now, shrouded from outside observation, devout Catholics have also been inclined to either marvel at or ridicule a process which they do not understand.

To the extent that they try to illuminate the operation of God's grace in the candidate's life, the saint-makers do indeed deal with mystery. But the way they do this is not at all mysterious. Like most bureaucratic procedures, it is complex and, as I've come to feel, at points inconsistent and confused. The complexity arises chiefly from the fact that several layers of authority and professional competence are brought to bear at different stages of the process. Like a centipede, a cause cannot move forward unless all the necessary parts are set in locomotion. Too much, I believe, is made of the pope's role in the making of saints by those who are outside the system. Similarly, too much responsibility is attributed to the faithful by those inside the system. In my judgment, the one indispensable figure is the local bishop, especially now that he has been given sole responsibility for investigating candidates' lives, virtues, or martyrdom. If the bishop does not push the cause, nothing happens locally or in Rome.

PROCESS AND PROFESSIONALISM

As LONG As the making of saints was regarded as a function of canon law and lawyers, it enjoyed the reputation, however exaggerated, for professionalism. A profession is a guild which exacts standards of knowledge, competence, and procedure of those admitted to its practice. But since the Reform of 1983 (and, I suspect, long before), it has been evident that there are no hard and clear professional standards for those who direct the Congregation for the Causes of Saints or—what is more important—those who serve as relators, postulators, and, especially, theological consultors.

Like other departments of the Holy See, the congregation is headed by a political appointee. Upon his retirement in 1989, for example, Cardinal Palazzini was replaced by Cardinal Angelo Felici, who has no particular competence—and no experience at all—in the making of saints. The relators, as we have seen, are expected to have certain theological and linguistic qualifications, but a doctorate in history—a necessary discipline, it would seem, for the appraisal of historical documents and testimony—is not required. Specialization in spiritual theology is preferred, yet not all of the relators or consultors can claim competence in the theology of the spiritual life, and not enough men have been found who have the necessary language requirements. As a result, the congregation is forced at times to turn to outsiders who have no experience in the preparation or judgment of causes.

The truth of the matter is that the congregation takes the best men it can get. Unlike the Vatican diplomatic corps, the congregation has no professional school for training saint-makers, although it does provide a *studium* or series of lectures for collaborators and officials of diocesan tribunals. For the most part, the saint-makers are men of intelligence who, like many university administrators, gain doctorates and later, by happenstance, drift into a field to which they hadn't expected to devote their labors. Competence in saint-making, therefore, is something you learn on the job, and the best practitioners are products of long experience and hard work.

None of this should be surprising. After all, corporations are filled with engineers turned salesmen, salesmen turned administrators, and chief executive officers who in their youth majored in comparative literature. But unlike a well-managed corporation, the Vatican does not always reward competence with responsibility. Moreover, in these lean years of vocations to the priesthood, Vatican congregations must make do with the talent available. There is no great competition, I discovered, for positions as relators of the congregation or as postulators general for the major religious orders.

This is not to suggest that the men who work in or consult with the congregation are second-rate. Like other arms of the Holy See, the congregation relies on a mixed bag of talent, much of it mediocre, some of it quite high. The problem, as I see it, is that all these men are working within a system which is deficient in the checks and balances expected of a profession. Too much room is left for subjective judgment, pressure, and caprice.

The major deficiency is that everyone directly involved with a cause has reason to see it succeed. This is particularly true of the postulator, who works for the promoter of the cause, and the collaborator (or collaborators) who is invariably someone who is already convinced of the candidate's holiness. Indeed, most collaborators, like Sister Elizabeth Strub, who wrote the *informatio* for Cornelia Connelly, are drawn from the religious orders which sponsor causes. Or, like Father Joseph Martino of Philadelphia, who prepared the *positio* for Katherine Drexel, they are drawn from the diocese which stands to benefit by the eventual canonization. In the case of Cardinal Newman, the author of the *positio*, Father Vincent Blehl, is a scholar who has devoted most of his adult life to editing, teaching, and promoting the candidate. As a practical matter, it seems, only the already convinced can be induced to do the work required for producing the key text on which a judgment of sanctity is made. But a genuinely professional process would require that these important duties be assigned to competent people who have no personal or professional stake in the outcome of the cause.

Another glaring deficiency is the congregation's lack of a procedure for ensuring that *positiones* are judged by a disinterested panel of theological consultors. For example, judges of the Roman Rota, which handles marriage annulments and other legal issues, are chosen by rotation, in chronological order. But in the Congregation for the Causes of Saints, the theological consultors for each cause are selected by the Promoter of the Faith. The reasons for this, I was told, are practical. The congregation prefers consultors with knowledge of the candidate's language and culture, and in any case must choose from among those who are free at the moment to take on a cause. But as we saw in the case of Pope Pius IX, the congregation ignored the one consultor on their list who was a biographer and expert on the candidate—Father Giacomo Martina—presumably because he was known to think the pope less than a saint. In this case, however, the Promoter of the Faith would have acted more professionally if he had picked a panel which included a balance of known proponents and opponents of such a controversial candidate. Indeed, the fact that he did not do so may have been one reason why John Paul II created another committee to advise him on the opportuneness of acting on the favorable verdict of the theological consultors.

Whatever the practical reasons for assigning the writing of *positiones* to proponents of a cause, and for leaving the choice of judges to the private judgment of the Promoter of the Faith, the lack of professional procedures leaves the system open to the charge of manipulation.

Imagine, for instance, a cause in which the reigning pope and a plurality of the Catholic hierarchy throughout the world are known to be supportive of the candidate's canonization. Imagine, furthermore, that the candidate is the founder of a new religious organization whose membership list is secret but whose members are bent on validating their organization by having their founder canonized a saint. Suppose, moreover, that several high-ranking officials of the congregation are openly sympathetic to the organization and the founder's cause. Imagine, then, the pressure on the relator of the cause, who is expected to be impervious to outside influences and independent in his judgment. Without a system of disinterested selection of judges, what guarantee does the church have that such a cause will be processed and the theological consultors chosen with strict impartiality—particularly since the names of the judges and their votes are held secret until long after judgment has been rendered?

Such thoughts come naturally to mind when we observe the astonishing progress of the cause on behalf of Josemaría Escrivá de Balaguer, the founder of Opus Dei. Escrivá died on June 26, 1975. To the members of Opus Dei, a worldwide association of priests and laity, he is "The Father," whose book of 999 spiritual maxims, *Camino* (*The Way*), illuminates the path to spiritual perfection and to the "Christianization" of the secular world. Long before his death, "The Father" was regarded within Opus Dei as a saint, a divinely led leader whose personal vision of the Christian calling affords those who submit to the movement's discipline a secure path to salvation. John Paul II is a devoted admirer: in 1984, the pope told an international meeting of the movement that "perhaps in this formula ("Work of God" for the Christianization of society) there is the theological reality, the essence, the nature itself of the vocation of the age in which we live and in which you have been called to the Lord."

To critics, however, Escrivá was a rather vain man who did not discourage reverence for his person (in his writings, his title of choice, "The Father" is sometimes hard to distinguish in context from "the Father" addressed by Jesus) and the leader of a quasi-sectarian movement within the church whose lay followers resemble the Mormons in their penchant for private rites and secret societies, in their meticulous preoccupation with proper dress and circumspect manners, and—above all—in their cocksure attitude that they alone have found the form that Catholicism must take in its relentless struggle with the world, the flesh, and the Devil.

Because Opus Dei does not publish the names of its members or readily identify its secular operations, it has been criticized by opponents as a conservative fifth column in the church and in society. Since Opus Dei is a personal prelature, its operatives take direction from their superior in Rome. To that extent, they function independently of local bishops. In Spain and various countries of Latin America, Opus Dei is regarded as a powerful force in politics, education, business, and journalism. Whatever the truth of these assumptions—hard facts about Opus Dei are difficult to come by—some former members have testified to the sect-like nature of their experience with the movement, especially the fellowship's tendency, in some situations, to separate younger recruits from their natural families if parents are opposed to Opus Dei. What worries parents, naturally enough, is Opus Dei's insistence that members take spiritual direction, including the confession of sins, only from priests of the movement. Since even young men and women in their twenties and early thirties are often insecure and psychologically immature, some parents are concerned about the effect of the organization on their children, particularly young adults who take vows of perpetual chastity and live as Opus Dei "families" while remaining in secular occupations.

For its part, Opus Dei denies that it is a secret society or that it has any agenda other than the spiritual perfection of its members. Opus Dei credits its founder with discovering that holiness is for everyone, not just clergy and monastics, although in fact this "revolutionary" idea is neither new nor novel. The organization has, however, aggressively recruited well-educated and career-minded lay Catholics, inspiring them—much as Jesuit high schools and colleges have traditionally done—with the notion that to be a good lawyer or businessman is as much God's work as service in the church. Opus Dei claims 76,000 lay members and 1,300 priests around the world, and as members now describe it, the organization is little more than a disciplined, ultra-orthodox society of Roman Catholics who, much like tertiaries of traditional religious orders, live a quasi-monastic life in the world while pursuing secular careers.

What actually sets Opus Dei members apart from other committed Catholics is their devotion to Escrivá and his writings. In this respect they are not unlike the Jesuits, who take their spiritual formation from the Spiritual Exercises of their founder, Ignatius Loyola. Ignatius is a canonized saint, and in light of Escrivá's determination to light the path to sainthood for Opus Dei members, it is understandable that they should do all they can to see that his life and work are validated by a declaration of sainthood. Yet to judge by his writings alone, Escrivá was an unexceptional spirit, derivative and often banal in his thoughts, personally inspiring, perhaps, but devoid of original insights. Indeed, a sampling of his 999 apodictic sayings reveal a remarkable narrowness of mind, wariness of human sexuality, and artlessness of expression, at best a Catholic Poor Richard without Ben Franklin's occasional wit:

No. 15. Don't put off work until tomorrow.
No. 22. Be firm! Be strong! Be a man! And then . . . be an angel!
No. 28. Marriage is for the rank and file, not for the officers of Christ's army. For, unlike food, which is necessary for every individual, procreation is necessary only for the species, and individuals can dispense with it.

A desire to have children? Behind us we shall leave children—many children . . . and a lasting trail of light, if we sacrifice the selfishness of the flesh.

No. 61. When a layman sets himself up as arbiter of morals, he frequently errs; laymen can only be disciples.

No. 132. Don't be such a coward as to be "brave." Flee!

No. 180. Where there is no mortification, there is no virtue.

No. 573. Thank you, my God, for placing in my heart such love of the pope.

No. 625. Your obedience is not worthy of the name unless you are ready to abandon your most flourishing work whenever someone with authority so commands.

No. 814. A little act, done for love, is worth so much!

Saints, of course, need not be eloquent. But those who offer direction to others should exhibit some keenness of spiritual perception and a discernible level of profundity. One has only to compare Escrivá's writings with, say, Dorothy Day's columns for *The Catholic Worker*, Romano Guardini's writings on the spirit of Catholicism or Simone Weil's essays in pursuit of God to recognize that Escrivá's gifts, whatever they may be, do not include a deep knowledge of the soul or of the age in which we live.

In short, there are enough questions about Opus Dei and its founder to justify the saint-makers' tradition of going slow with controversial causes. Yet, on April 9, 1990, just fifteen years after his death, Escrivá was declared heroically virtuous by John Paul II. Moreover, the postulator, Father Flavio Capucci, a member of Opus Dei, has three very promising intercessory miracles he was working on. With any luck, Escrivá will eclipse Thérèse of Lisieux, whose canonization just twenty-eight years after her death is still the modern record. Why so fast?

In 1987, when I first spoke to Father Eszer, the relator of the cause, he gave no inkling that the *positio* on Escrivá's heroic virtue was close to completion. But after Escrivá had been declared venerable, Eszer spoke somewhat less guardedly. In the first place, the formal request to open Escrivá's cause had been made at the earliest possible moment, five years after his death, by Cardinal Ugo Poletti, Vicar of Rome. Secondly, support for the cause included letters from 69 cardinals, 241 archbishops, 987 bishops—nearly a third of the Catholic episcopate—plus 41 superiors of religious orders and congregations. How many of these were also members of Opus Dei is uncertain. In any case, Opus Dei claims tens of thousands of supporters throughout the world and so a large outpouring of requests for Escrivá's cause was to be expected.

Third, the leaders of Opus Dei were primed for the process. Since they had long looked upon their founder as a saint, they had already collected every scrap of written evidence on his behalf. Altogether, the documents and testimony ran to twenty thousand pages. "My main job," Eszer said, "was to cut out repetitions. You cannot hand the theological consultors a whole library to read." As it was, the final *positio* was six thousand pages long.

"How did you manage so much work in so short a time?" I asked.

"I didn't have that much to do," he replied. "The *positio* was written by the postulator, who had four Opus Dei university professors working for him."

"I thought," I interjected, "that *positiones* were written under the direction of the relator."

"Well, I was in control. But everything was done by them. I saw only the postulator, never the other men. These Opus Dei people, they are very industrious, very discreet."

"Then the *positio* was edited by you?"

"No, I just cut out the excess testimony."

The testimony, it turns out, was taken in two processes, one in Madrid and the other in Rome. Altogether, the tribunals heard from ninety-two witnesses, forty-four of them lay people. Eszer did not know how many of them were Opus Dei members. Nor was he in a position, he said, to say how many of the witnesses—if any—had opposed the cause.

"Surely," I said, "given the highly controversial nature of the man and his movement, there must have been some opponents."

"The only criticism I have read of Opus Dei," he replied, "came from former members, people who left." These were not, he suggested, credible witnesses.

"Well, then," I pressed, "were any of the judges negative in their votes?"

"This I cannot say," he replied, meaning he wouldn't.

Eventually, the *positio* on behalf of Escrivá will become available for public scrutiny; perhaps even the votes of the judges as well. Until then, no one will know the extent to which the questionable aspects of the man and his work were given a full and proper airing. Escrivá may indeed be the great saint that Opus Dei holds him out to be. But the speed and unobstructed ease with which he was passed by the congregation raises many questions about the process itself: its toughness, impartiality, professionalism, and freedom from ecclesiastical pressure and spiritual politics.

TIMELINESS AND *FAMA SANCTITATIS*

IT IS ONE thing to assert, as I repeatedly have, that the saint is a product of a system, quite another to suppose that those who do get canonized are in fact the saints the church needs as exemplars for this or any other era. On the contrary, the very length of the process mitigates against the notion of "timeliness" in the matter of recognizing saints. Which is to say that the formal canonization process, properly understood, is not an action but a *reaction*, and in most cases a decidedly delayed reaction. To identify sainthood exclusively with formal canonization, therefore, is to overlook the populist dimension of saint-making. There can be no officially approved saints unless there are first "saints of the people," or at least of some of the people. And it is this populist action, rather than the official reaction, which constitutes the true history—the story of the stories—of the saints. *

This said, it is far from clear to me just what qualifies, in the eyes of the saint-makers, as a popular or a genuine reputation for holiness. In the past, they looked to devotional activities at tombs and shrines, and in some Catholic cultures (often, religious subcultures), these activities continue today. But as we observed in the case of Cardinal Newman, certain saints do not inspire traditional forms of cultic devotion, nor are many educated Catholics inclined to express their devotion in traditional ways. For example, for millions of people (and not only Roman Catholics), the poetry of the Victorian Jesuit, Gerard Manley Hopkins, provides not only aesthetic pleasure but a mediated experience of the Christian life and commitment. The same can be said of the writings of the late Trappist priest, Thomas Merton—a cult figure in more ways than one. I have never visited either man's grave, but I am devoted nonetheless. Yet to my knowledge, this sort of de-

---

* One of the difficulties inherent in using canonization processes as a sociological prism for examining the religious mentality of an age, as Donald Weinstein and Rudolph M. Bell do in *Saints and Society: The Two Worlds of Western Christendom, 1000–1700*, is knowing whether one is talking about the figure who inspired that process or the figure who emerged from the process. The difference reflects the gap in time between the initial reputation for holiness and subsequent investigation, and validation by the competent church authority. That is only one aspect of the problem. Another troubling aspect is the difference between the originating populist impulse to recognize someone as a saint and the later rationale for canonization, which often reflects the institutional motives of the saint-making elite. To cite an extreme example, one may ask whether Joan of Arc (1412–1431) reflects the religious mentality of fifteenth-century France, or the priorities—spiritual or political—of the Holy See in 1920, when she was finally canonized. Saints are protean figures who can acquire reputations which have little or nothing to do with their own self-understanding, or that of the age which engendered their initial reputation of holiness. For a very recent example of the remodeling of a saint, see the quasi-feminist, quasi-liberationist interpretation of Philippine Duchesne by a member of her order, Sister Catherine M. Mooney, R.S.C.J., in *Philippine Duchesne: A Woman with the Poor* (New York: Paulist Press, 1990). A comparison of this spirited biography of Duchesne with the *positio* on her behalf would demonstrate, I suspect, the difference between how saints are proved worthy of canonization and how, once canonized, they can be transformed into more contemporary exemplars of heroic virtue.

votion does not qualify as a reputation for holiness. In any case, neither priest has been put forward by their respective religious orders as a candidate for sainthood.

On the other hand, it remains a mystery to me how the congregation can ascribe a continuing reputation for holiness to a marginal nineteenth-century figure like Anne Catherine Emmerich, whose visions and prophecies have already been shown to be the conscious elaborations of an overwrought Romantic poet. The stories she told—and most of the stories told about her—are not true, but they form the basis of her once robust reputation for holiness. Apart from these apocryphal tales, what evidence is there that Emmerich continues to enjoy the sort of reputation required to justify a formal process? Like many of the saints we get today, her reputation for holiness appears to rest on little more than a memory nurtured like a slender votive candle by the remnants of her religious order. In short, *fama sanctitatis* is one of those aspects for canonization for which there are no apparent standards.

THE *POSITIO*: HEROIC VIRTUE AND THE NARRATED LIFE

I OBSERVED ABOVE that the formal canonization process is essentially a reaction to a popular movement. It is, of course, much more than that. It is also an investigation into the candidate's life and reputation for holiness. But the first fruit of that investigation is a written text, the *positio*, which is a redaction or retelling of the candidate's story based on the testimony of witnesses and on critically assessed historical documents.

The Jesuit saint-makers, Paul Molinari and Peter Gumpel, regard *positiones* as theological treasures to be mined for what they reveal about the forms of authentic Christian spirituality, and they regret that these texts are not read more often by theologians outside the congregation. I, too, would like to see more attention paid to the texts on which sanctity is judged—but for different reasons. From my own reading of *positiones*, I have come to share the dissatisfaction expressed by some of the congregation's theological consultors. In essence, their complaint is that most *positiones* do not show how the Servant of God grew in the holiness expected of a saint. In other words, the evidence for each required virtue is assembled and sanctity is proved, all too often without explaining how the subject developed the unique holiness that makes one saint different from all others.

This strikes me as a very serious objection, one worthy of wide discussion by scholars and bishops beyond the confines of the congregation. But in spite of all the doctoral degrees granted by Rome's pontifical universities, no one, so far as I have been able to discover, has subjected these texts to systematic critical examination. No one outside the congregation has asked why *positiones* take the form they do, whether the texts can and should be changed, and—in particular— how those texts relate to the larger question of why we get the saints we do. Absent such as formal study, I offer the following critical comments of a privileged observer. In doing so, I want to acknowledge the candor of the people most responsible for the writing of *positiones:* the postulators, the relators, and their collaborators. I trust they will understand why I choose to view their work in a different, though not inhospitable, light.

First, the saint-makers put too much trust in the historical-critical method as a "scientific" procedure for establishing the salient facts about a saint. Understandably, perhaps, they are reacting to Protestant charges that the stories of saints are compounded of fanciful legends. But the notion that history is an exact science is itself a fancy of the Enlightenment; historians today are more modest about their methods. They recognize that "facts" exist only in relation to an interpretive scheme, a story. I think, therefore, that the saint-makers would gain greater conceptual clarity about their craft—and its relationship to biography in general—if they would recognize that they do what all historians do: they tell a story. A documented story, to be sure, but a story nonetheless.

It is precisely this narrative element which links the texts produced for the purpose of canonization to its predecessor texts: the medieval lives of saints, the early Christian legends, the passion stories of the martyrs, and Luke's account of the martyrdom of St. Stephen. Each of these narrative forms reflects a certain culture and society, and each is shaped by literary conventions through which the action of divine grace is rendered intelligible. If it is true that saints are known only through their stories, then it behooves us to examine how sanctity is made intelligible through the conventions which govern the writing of modern *positiones.*

The saint-makers, of course, insist that their purpose is not to tell a story but to prove heroic virtue, and that the *positio* is merely an instrument to that end. Under the old juridical system that was clearly the case. As long as the saint-making *processus* was regarded as a trial, as the Latin term implies, the *positio* functioned like a legal brief on behalf of the candidate in question. Lawyers sifted the *vita* and the documents supporting it for evidence for or against the candidate's claim to the required virtues. What mattered was not the text but the legal dialectic, with all its adversarial rhetoric and bite. However tendentious the arguments may have been, the amended "text" which emerged from the exchanges between the Devil's Advocate and the defense lawyer was the story which determined the holiness of the saint. Like a jury verdict, the final "truth" about a saint was produced by the force of oral argument, not the logic of narrative.

The Reform of 1983 removed the lawyers and with them the juridical format for making saints. But it did not eliminate the requirement of proving heroic virtue: that burden fell to the authors (the relator and his collaborator) of the text. The result, as I have emphasized, is a hybrid genre in search of its proper form. The problem here is not a lack of standards, as with *fama sanctitatis*, but a confusion of purpose. On the one hand, the text is supposed to be the narrative of a unique life—the biography of one of God's "prime numbers." On the other, it is expected to satisfy the nonnarrative demands of moral theology.

John Henry Newman recognized what can happen when one text is forced to serve two masters. He could have been talking about modern *positiones* when he complained of hagiographical biographies that "do not manifest a saint but mince them into spiritual lessons." Newman understood the requirements of good literature. He recognized that the manifestation of character, even a saintly character, depends on elements of plot and characterization which cannot be organized according to a recipe for proving moral virtue. But that is exactly what the congregation now demands from a *positio*—including the one on Newman himself.

In imaginative hands, narrative and proof of virtue can be made to mesh. As we saw in chapter 8, Sister Elizabeth Strub managed to make the life story of Cornelia Connelly determine the form in which each of the required virtues were manifest. In doing so, however, Strub not only took certain liberties with the conventions by which *positiones* are usually organized, but also raised—at least in my mind—a much larger issue which needs to be addressed: are saints holy because they are virtuous—in which case proving sanctity according to a scheme of virtues makes procedural sense—or are they virtuous because they are holy—in which case telling the story of the candidate's unique transformation through the grace of God's love should be the saint-makers' primary goal.

Throughout this book I have stressed the centrality of stories to the

process of the making of saints. I have done so because man is essentially a storytelling animal. We understand ourselves, if at all, as characters in a story, and it is through stories that we come to understand
others, including saints. As we saw in chapter 2, the early Christians
recognized saints only in so far as they could be perceived as living out
the story of Jesus all over again. But alongside this narrative mode,
Christianity also developed another mode of discourse for talking
about sanctity, one that aims at describing the character or virtues
expected in a saint. It is the discourse of moral philosophers and
theologians, and it is as old as the church itself.

As citizens of a Greco-Roman culture, the early Christians inherited the language of virtue and adopted it to their own self-
understanding as members of a new community in Christ. Already in
the letters of Paul, the earliest documents of the church, we find the
Christian concept of grace refracted through the conceptual prism of
virtue: grace is manifest as faith, hope, and charity. Of these virtues,
charity or love of God is supreme because through it the soul partic-
ipates in the very life of God Himself and is united to Him. Charity,
in this view, animates and perfects the other virtues. Moreover, it is
the one virtue which continues after death: in heaven, faith and hope
are no longer necessary for the "friends of God," because they now
possess—and are possessed by—God's eternal love.

As we saw, martyrs were regarded by the early church as people
who achieved perfection of virtue by surrendering their lives like Jesus did in perfect love of the Father. Martyrdom, in other words,
presupposed perfection of faith and hope as well as of charity. In
nonmartyrs, however, perfect love of God was not so obvious. Their
claim to sanctity was not based on how they died but how they lived.
To be considered a saint, therefore, one had to develop over the course
of a lifetime perfection of character or virtue. Thus, the stories and
legends of nonmartyrs—especially ascetics—were stories of heroic virtue.

Along with the language of virtue, however, the early fathers of the
church also adopted the Greek model of the morally virtuous person.
In addition to faith, hope, and charity, the good Christian was expected to exercise the Aristotelian virtues of prudence, justice, fortitude, and temperance. To be sure, pride of place belonged to the
virtues infused by God through his grace, but this did not exclude the
moral virtues by which grace was to manifest itself in relation to
others. Thus, alongside the stories of saints, the church fathers had, by
the time of Augustine, developed the basic elements of a moral the-

ology which would eventually be used as standard for measuring saint-hood.

It was only after saint-making became a formal papal process that this scheme of virtues was invoked as a heuristic device for investigating the lives of people reputed to be saints. The term "heroic virtue" entered the church's vocabulary via the translation of Aristotle's *Nichomachean Ethics* in 1328 by Robert Grosseteste, bishop of Lincoln, and one of the witnesses to the signing of the Magna Carta. Aristotle had used the term to designate moral virtue on a heroic or godlike scale, and the phrase was eventually adopted by St. Thomas Aquinas, whose synthesis of Aristotelian and Christian ideas on virtue established the conceptual framework by which sanctity was henceforth to be judged. St. Bonaventure (1221–1274) was the first papally canonized saint whose life was investigated according to the rubric of the three theological virtues (faith, hope, and charity) and the four cardinal moral virtues (prudence, justice, fortitude, and temperance). Thereafter, heroic virtue became synonymous with holiness in the technical terminology of saint-making and was eventually enshrined as the governing concept of the congregation through the treatises on beatification and canonization by Prospero Lambertini (Pope Benedict XIV).

The issue now facing the saint-makers, as I see it, is whether they should continue to demand proof of heroic virtue in the traditional manner. There are, it seems to me, three major objections to this approach. First, proving virtue appears to be ultimately incongruent with identifying the unique holiness of the saint, as revealed through the candidate's life story. Second, the traditional scheme of virtues strikes me as rigid and arbitrary; to prove them, the candidate's life must be squeezed into a procrustean bed. Third, by identifying holiness with *perfection* of virtue, the saint-makers are forced to exclude from *positiones* any evidence of human failure; in doing so, they omit what is really exemplary in the life of a saint—the struggle between virtue and vice, or, in wider scope, between grace and nature. In short, they are reduced to writing hagiography by the historical-critical method.

These are serious charges, I realize, charges that go beyond procedural questions to the heart of the canonization process. Are they valid?

In theory, at least, there appears to be no contradiction between the church's required virtues and the narrated life of a saint. As the contemporary British philosopher Alasdair MacIntyre has shown, every system of conceiving and ordering virtues is "linked to some particular notion of the narrative structure or structures of human life." Thus, the order and understanding of the Christian virtues, with charity or love of God as center and source, is intelligible only within a story which imagines human life as a quest for unity or friendship with God. In such a scheme, for example, humility is a virtue along with justice, whereas in Aristotle's ethics, which does not envision life with God as the goal of human existence, humility is a vice.

Seen in this perspective, therefore, it would appear that there is no incongruity between the life story of a saint and the scheme of heroic virtues demanded by the canonization process. The more the saint becomes like Christ through the gift of divine love, and the more he manifests that love in his actions toward others, the more does the saint live out the Christian story. Indeed, from a theological viewpoint, we might be justified in concluding that the real subject of a saint's life is not the individual human being but the action of grace as it transforms that individual into what he or she was destined to become: a friend of God.

But if it is through cooperation with the gift of divine grace that saints become holy, why should the saint-makers demand proof of prudence, justice, fortitude, and temperance? Important as they are, these virtues are not written on stone tablets. Why not stress other virtues such as humility, patience, and mercy, which were emphasized by Jesus himself and are therefore qualities one might reasonably expect to find in a Christian saint? For that matter, why not look to the Beatitudes ("Blessed are the meek," and so on) which Jesus recommended to his followers? In sum, why not stress Gospel values alone when analyzing the life of a saint?

My point is that if the saint-makers were more flexible in the virtues they expect of saints, they would do greater justice to the variety and uniqueness of the friends of God, and privilege the telling of their stories over the proof of specific virtues. To be sure, every Christian saint should be distinguished by extraordinary charity, hope, and faith, but is it necessary that they be found exceptional in prudence, justice, fortitude, and temperance? These are qualities one expects in any morally good person and thus are not (thank goodness) exclusive to followers of Christ. Moreover, the plain truth is that saints are not always prudent or just, or temperate or courageous, and the saint-makers, in fact, do not demand anything like perfection in these categories.

The *positio* in defense of Pius IX, it seems to me, is a good example of the strengths and weaknesses of using these virtues as a heuristic device. There, the pope's conduct of his papacy was under review, and detailed analysis according to the moral virtues showed that in certain situations his moral judgment and actions were considerably less than perfect. In response, the lawyer for the defense, Carlo Snider, argued that the pope did the best he could under the circumstances. Indeed, Snider's ultimate (and ultimately successful) appeal was to narrative, not moral theology: however imprudent, unjust, intemperate, or uncourageous specific actions of the pope may have been at the time, he argued, they were ultimately validated by the unfolding "salvation history" of which Pius IX's long and stormy tenure in office was a crucial chapter.

But a more honest and accurate telling of the pope's story, it seems to me, would have obviated any appeal to "salvation history." By acknowledging his weaknesses of character, his vices—indeed, even his sins—the *positio* could have gone on to demonstrate his holiness by showing how the pope overcame his human failings and grew in the grace of God. But *positiones*, as we now know, do not focus on sins. Apart from occasional selections from the candidate's own writings, official *vitae* normally do not discuss the sorts of conflicts—the wrestling with real sins like despair, pride, envy, and such—which reveal character. Are we to believe, therefore, that saints are sinless? Because they are concerned only with virtue and its perfection, *positiones* invite the reader to do just that.

As the system now stands, the theological consultors are called upon to judge life stories in which sin has been airbrushed out of the text. The reason, it appears, is purely procedural. If serious sin is encountered anywhere along the line—in the testimony of witnesses, in the private papers of the candidate, in the archives of the Vatican's other congregations, or in the preparation of the *positio*—the cause will probably be stopped. Under the old juridical system, a defense lawyer might try to bury evidence of serious sin, and it was up to the Devil's Advocate to ferret it out. This is what happened in the case of Pius IX, whose third and final *positio* was an answer to cumulative objections. But now that the old adversarial system has been abolished, it is up to the postulator and relator, who are under oath to hide nothing, to make these judgments. Thus, by the time a cause reaches the discussion phase, the theological consultors are presented with a text which focuses only on the positive. As a result, the issues that concern them are not substantive but evidentiary: do the documents support a judgment that the candidate was virtuous to the degree of heroicity or perfection required of a saint?

In sum, I find that the current method of organizing and writing *positiones* cannot, of its very nature, do full justice to the life of the candidate. Given the present requirements of the congregation, the authors of *positiones* are constrained to build in proofs of virtues which may, in fact, be irrelevant to the way that particular candidate lived out his or her story, and to leave out contrary evidence which might be crucial for understanding the uniqueness of the candidate's holiness. I am not at all suggesting that saints should not be examined for heroic virtue, including moral virtue. On the contrary, the grounding of holiness in virtue is particularly important in an age like ours for which, in the spiritually promiscuous climate of the United States, at least, "spirituality" has become a catchall term for elevated states of feeling combined with psychological control over the nervous system and vague communings with an indeterminate and innocuous higher power—all detached from the moral choices and conduct that produce character. But I am suggesting that a focus on virtue without concomitant attention to faults fails to produce believable saints. If candidates must be screened for evidence of seven virtues, why not scrutinize their lives for traces of the seven deadly sins as well?

Saints, as I think of them, should surprise us, not confirm our moral or theological assumptions. Their stories should remind us not of the excellence of the virtuous life, but of the unpredictability of what happens when a person allows himself "to be transformed by the encompassing logic of a life lived in and through God." In this sense, to borrow Mahatma Gandhi's justly famous phrase, the life of every genuine saint is "an experiment with truth." And the purpose of the canonization process, it seems to me, is to discover whether and how that experiment turned out.

The story of a saint, as I have come to understand it, is about God and his relationship to humankind. "It is a terrible thing," Dorothy Day often observed, "to fall into the hands of the living God." The writing of a saint's life, therefore, should be an exercise in primary theology. That is, it should not be the secondary exercise of theologians anxious to prove what is already known and accepted, but the primary exercise of Christian insight and imagination brought to bear on the raw data of a human life transformed by divine grace. Saints are not people who have different experiences. Saints experience the same things as you and I, but their insight into them is different. It is this difference which distinguishes the saint from others, and one saint from another. The task of the saint-makers, therefore, should be to illuminate that specific difference, to discover what fresh and formative insight the love of God has produced in the candidate, to trace out the effect on a man or a woman who says, with Christ, "Not my will but thine be done." That is what every saint has in common, and that is what makes the every saint, in the Christian tradition, altogether unique.

The making of saints, then, is an act of the religious imagination. The saint imagines what it might be like for him or her to live as Christ did, in total obedience to the father, and does just that. The community beholds the saint and tells his or her story: this, too, is an act of the religious imagination. The saint-makers' responsibility is not simply to verify the intuition of the faithful, but to enter into the religious imagination of the candidate—the better to understand and explain the meaning of his or her particular form of holiness. And if the candidate is truly holy, his or her story will be told and retold again and again as a narrative demonstrating the power of God's grace.

Unfortunately, the church's saint-makers appear to be uncomfortable with the imagination. Since the Reformation they have taken refuge in canon law and demonstrable fact. The tendency to identify holiness with heroic virtue is, as I see it, symptomatic of the system's inability to recognize its own imaginative reconstruction of saints' lives. Every *positio* is, in fact, an interpretation of a life according to a scheme of things illuminated by the light of faith. And it is because they are unwilling to trust that light completely that the saint-makers look to miracles for divine confirmation.

Miracles: Signs of Divine Friendship

Of all the elements in the making of saints, proof of miracles is the one which most intrigues, perhaps even outrages, the secular mind. It is also the subject of one of the few real debates among the saint-makers. As we saw, the physicians on the congregation's medical board are, as a group, the ones who are most insistent that the church continue to require miracles of intercession for canonized saints. This strikes me as impressive evidence that miracles still happen. But it would be even more impressive if the president of the board, Dr. Raffaello Cortesini, were to follow through on his plan to publish the cases he has witnessed and the documents supporting them. Let him demonstrate for the scientific and medical professions the stringency of the miracle process, and the grounds on which the board has made its judgments.

But it seems to me that miracles are still in the eye of the beholder, and to limit the miraculous to what can be beheld only with the eyes of modern science and its instruments is to restrict the traditional meaning of miracles as signs of friendship with God. If tomorrow the faithful were to address their prayers for divine assistance exclusively to Christ—and thereby eliminate the possibility of intercessory miracles—would that in any way diminish the number or importance of saints? Moreover, since Catholics are not obliged to believe in the miracles officially attributed to a saint—indeed, apart from the parties involved, the details of these miracles are essentially house secrets—it seems enough that a candidate is widely evoked for blessings. As the (so far) frustrated search for a miracle on behalf of Cardinal Newman suggests, the lack of miracles in no way diminishes a candidate's reputation for holiness or inhibits an authentic cult of the saints.

As a practical matter, this or any other pope can dispense with the requirement of a miracle. And in cases like Newman's, I think he should. It is enough, I believe, that large numbers of people include Newman among those they regard as members of "the church triumphant" and pray to him for guidance and inspiration. Nonetheless, I would be disappointed if the church were to dispense altogether with miracles as a sign of divine approbation. Like grace, I relish them as gifts, and who are we to say that God no longer responds to prayer addressed to saints? Ask anyone who has ever prayed for a desperately ill friend. Not all miracles are the work of modern science. And it is only another form of faith which insists that ultimately "science" will explain everything that occurs.

What the church should consider, however, is waiving the requirement of a miracle for beatification. Let blesseds become what they once were—local saints—rather than merely candidates for higher church honors. Let the size and extent of the cult determine who is worthy of "universal" veneration, and let the church demand miracles, as they are currently understood, only of candidates for canonization.

ORTHODOXY AND SAINTHOOD

SINCE CANONIZATION IS an ecclesial process, it is understandable that saints should reflect an authentic Catholic faith. Nonetheless, it is not at all clear to me what sort of orthodoxy is required of a saint, or what form heterodoxy must take before it becomes a bar to sainthood. St. Thomas Aquinas, for instance, argued against the immaculate conception of the Virgin Mary (the belief that she was conceived without original sin) six centuries before it was defined a dogma of the faith, yet he is no less a saint for his now-unorthodox opinion. Charles Borremoo contested the temporal power of the papacy—in his day, virtually an article of faith—yet he, too, was eventually canonized. On the other hand, Meister Eckhart, the fourteenth-century Dominican theologian, mystic and preacher, was a deeply spiritual friar who died in obedience and submission to the church. Yet because some of his theological speculations were posthumously condemned by Rome, it is unlikely that he will ever be declared a saint. Much the same is true of the twentieth-century Jesuit mystic and scientist, Pierre Teilhard de Chardin, who was silenced (and therefore deprived of needed criticism) by the Vatican during a crucial period of his lifetime for his speculations on evolution, but who was known for his deep Christian spirituality, as is evidenced by "The Divine Milieu" and other writings.

As we saw in examining the case of Cardinal Newman, intellectuals are disadvantaged as candidates for canonization to the degree that they venture deeper understandings and fresh interpretations of the faith. They run the risk of being wrong, and the more they publish, the greater the risk. I do not intend a case here for either Eckhart or Chardin, but I do question a system which, it seems to me, penalizes those whose intellectual formulations do not always conform to the prevailing orthodoxy in the church. If the Christian faith were nothing more than a set of authoritative propositions to be repeated and upheld, the unorthodox would be easy to spot. But Christianity deals in truths that ultimately rest on mystery, and to relate that mystery to the changing horizons of human culture and knowledge is the task of Christian intellectuals. In any case, the nature of a vital orthodoxy is such that it is always recognized in retrospect. Paraphrasing Newman, we can say that to be faithful to the Gospel is to change, and to be orthodox is to have changed often.

But as matters now stand, the safer, the more conventional a Catholic thinker is, the more likely is he or she to be canonized. Why this should be so is not entirely clear to me. Perhaps there is a fear that to canonize a thinker is to canonize all his writings as well. But as we saw with popes, canonization of the man implies no validation of his papacy. Surely a process that investigates lives as thoroughly and at such leisure as the church takes should be able to distinguish the questing spirit behind all the thoughts, arguments, and words that an intellectual tends to produce. When confronted with a Christian thinker or mystic, it seems to me, the saint-makers would do well to heed the observation of Simone Weil, who knew a thing or two about

Christ, the Holy Spirit, and various conversations that take place among Christians. She had mystics in mind, but her words should apply, with reservations, to intellectuals as well:

> A collective body is the guardian of dogma; and dogma is an object of contemplation for love, faith and intelligence, three distinctly individual faculties. Hence, almost since the beginning, the individual has been ill at ease in Christianity, and this uneasiness has been notably one of the intelligence. . . .
>
> Christ himself who is Truth itself, when he was speaking before an assembly such as a council, did not address it in the same language as he used in intimate conversation with his well-beloved friend, and no doubt before the Pharisees he might easily have been accused of contradiction and error. For by one of those laws of nature, which God himself respects, since he has willed them from all eternity, there are two languages that are quite distinct although made up of the same words; there is the collective language and there is the individual one. The Comfortor whom Christ sends us the Spirit of truth, speaks one or the other of these languages, whichever circumstances demand, and by a necessity of their nature there is not agreement between them.
>
> When genuine friends of God—as was [Meister] Eckhart to my way of thinking—repeat words they have heard in secret amidst the silence of the union of love, and these words are in disagreement with the teaching of the Church, it is simply that the language of the marketplace is not that of the nuptial chamber.

MUST SAINTS BE CATHOLICS?

SHORTLY AFTER VATICAN Council II, a small group of Lutherans approached some of the saint-makers to inquire whether Rome might not consider canonizing Dietrich Bonhoeffer, the Lutheran pastor, theologian, and martyr who was executed by the Nazis in 1945. To do so, the visitors felt, would be a striking affirmation of the council's recognition, after centuries of condemnations of Protestants as heretics, of "real but imperfect" communion between Rome and its "separated brethren." The reply was that to canonize Bonhoeffer would be poaching. If the Lutherans regard Bonhoeffer as a saint, the visitors were told, it would be more appropriate if they did the honors themselves.

I have great sympathy with that perspective. On principle, Lutherans do not invoke the saints as Catholics do, though they do memorialize some of them, including Pastor Bonhoeffer. But it would be intrusive to submit the life and death of Bonhoeffer to Rome's investigative procedures, and very difficult to give him passing marks on Roman orthodoxy. Moreover, to canonize someone from another Christian communion would presuppose two things: that the only "real" saints are those canonized by Rome and that the differences of faith and practice which still separate the various Christian churches are of little importance.

The first supposition is decidedly false. Two centuries ago, in his treatise on beatification and canonization, Prospero Lambertini (Pope Benedict XIV) considered the case of a non-Catholic Christian who died for true faith in Jesus Christ, and concluded that such a person was a martyr in the sight of God, if not in the eyes of the church. In other words, Rome makes claims only on behalf of her own. Canonization, to repeat, is an ecclesial act, something done by and for the church. Even so, the Roman Catholic Church does appear to be groping for some kind of formula for acknowledging non-Catholic Christians who meet its standards, at least in the case of martyrs. In 1964, for example, Pope Paul VI canonized twenty-two black Ugandan martyrs who were brutally put to death in 1886, seventeen of them youthful servants of the deranged Ugandan king. Another two dozen Anglican Christians were also martyred for their faith in the sweep of persecution, and the pope acknowledged their blood witness by adding, after a pause, "And we do not wish to forget the others also, who belong to the Anglican confession, who met death for the name of Christ."

Nonetheless, real differences remain between Roman Catholic and other Christians concerning the meaning, identity, and veneration of saints—differences which gestures of ecumenical goodwill cannot overcome. During the years I was researching and writing this book, for example, scholars officially representing Roman Catholics and Lutherans in the United States were engaged in formal study and dialogue on the role of saints—and particularly Mary, the Mother of Jesus—in the life of Christian faith. In February 1990, they wrote a joint paper outlining areas of agreement and disagreement. Although both sides affirmed a common belief in Jesus Christ as the "sole mediator" between the faithful and "the Father," they recognized that after nearly five hundred years of separation, the two communions had very different attitudes toward saints.

Some of the differences were doctrinal: the Lutherans, for instance, were willing to concede (as Martin Luther readily did) that saints and their stories were pedagogically useful as virtuous examples for the faithful. But to invoke them through prayer for assistance, they insisted, was neither warranted by Scripture nor doctrinally congruent with Luther's principle that Christians are justified (saved) through faith in Jesus Christ alone. Remembering exceptional followers of Christ was one thing, but turning to them for help, they felt, was unnecessary, ineffectual, and quite likely contrary to the Gospel.

In reply to the Lutherans, the Roman Catholics insisted that to invoke the intercession of the saints in no way attributes to them the power and glory that belongs to Christ alone. Prayers to saints were not competitive with prayers to God—saints are not to be thought of as "friends in high places," they argued—since only God through Christ answers prayers. On the contrary, the Catholics maintained, invocation of the saints provides increased awareness of Christ by glorifying him through veneration of those in whom Christ has definitively triumphed over sin.

Nonetheless, the Catholics readily conceded that abuses have occurred in the veneration of the saints, particularly in the veneration of Mary, and continue to occur as a "disorder of the faith." Moreover, the Catholic scholars pointed out that while the veneration and invocation of saints is strongly urged by the church, no pope or council of the church has declared these practices obligatory. In any case, both sides agreed that their divergences in doctrine on the question of saints were not of the sort to keep the two churches forever separate.

But doctrine, in the end, is not the salient issue. It seldom is in matters of religion. Lutherans, for instance, have much more in common with Roman Catholics than do most other heirs of the Protestant Reformation. Why, then, should the invocation and veneration of saints remain a stumbling block on the road to a reunited Christianity?

The reasons have to do with religious imagination and experience. Martin Luther's resonate reiteration of Faith *alone*, Scripture *alone*, Christ *alone* bespeaks a different understanding of the Christian story from the narrative which structures the Roman Catholic experience. As the Catholic scholars put it in their concluding reflections,

> The Catholic tradition holds that Jesus Christ alone is never merely alone. He is always found in the company of a whole range of his friends, both living and dead. It is a basic Catholic experience that when recognized and appealed to within a rightly ordered faith, these friends of Jesus Christ strengthen one's own sense of communion with Christ. It's all in a family, we might say; we are part of a people. Saints show us how the grace of God may work in a life; they give us bright patterns of holiness; they pray for us. Keeping company with the saints in the Spirit of Christ encourages our faith. It is simply part of what it means to be

Catholic, bonded with millions of other people not only throughout the world, but also through time. Those who have gone on before us in faith are still living members of the body of Christ and in some unimaginable way we are all connected.

To speak of saints in the Catholic tradition, therefore, is to evoke a particular sensibility—those "unconsciously held convictions about what is real and what is not." Catholic saints make sense only within a world where the "body of Christ" is more than just a metaphor. To invoke the saints is to suppose that between the faithful on earth and those in heaven there is an organic connection "in Christ" that is stronger and more real than the biological, psychological, social, and emotional ties that sustain human solidarity in this life.

WHY MAKE SAINTS?

IN THE COURSE of preparing this book, a number of people, including several at the Vatican, asked me why I was interested in the making of saints. My initial answer was: because no one has adequately explained how and why it is done. But now that I have observed the process firsthand, I recognize another motive: because saints matter. It follows, therefore, that the way saints are made also matters—not only to those Roman Catholics who venerate them but to anyone who seriously asks, "What does it mean to be fully human?"

Holiness implies "wholeness." But as John Coleman has remarked, holiness "often shatters our ordinary notions of what makes human life whole." To aspire to holiness is to aspire to something other than a "complete" life, or even a morally "good" life. Saints disrupt conventional assumptions about what is real and worth our while and what is not. The attraction of saints, as Coleman astutely observes, "is their power to lure us beyond virtue to virtue's source." What makes saints interesting, therefore, is not what we find in them worth imitating—real saints are not the sort of people who try to "set a good example"—but rather what makes them inimitable. With each new saint, "a terrible beauty is born."

But who, today, cares about saints? To be sure, the Roman Catholic Church continues to add to its list of official saints. But few of the people they canonize are recognized or recognizable beyond circumscribed constituencies. Even in the Roman Catholic liturgy, reference to saints and their feast days is muted; Catholic theologians, for their part, rarely discuss saints.

And outside the church? It is a commonplace among religious scholars and cultural historians that the saint as a social ideal has become vestigial in modern Western societies. In this respect, the fate of a saint is no different than that of any other heroic figure: democratic societies love celebrities—that is, charismatic people who attain a brief and circumscribed notoriety—but they are inherently suspicious of figures whose lives challenge the assumption that everyone is essentially equal. Martin Luther, who insisted that even saints are also sinners in the eyes of God, was in this sense the prophet of the modern world, a world in which no one is really any better than anyone else.

"The great revolutions in human history do not change the face of the earth," writes literary historian Erich Heller. "They change the face of man, the image in which he beholds himself and the world around him. The earth merely follows suit." If this is so, what sort of society is it that cannot countenance the saint? What is missing in societies in which the saint no longer matters?

Connection: The cult of the saints presupposes that everyone who has existed, and everyone who will exist, is interconnected—that is, that there really is a basis in the structure of human existence for "the communion of saints." Otherwise, there would be no point in praying to the saints who have died or, for that matter, in praying for one another. But to assert that all human beings are radically connected over space, through time, and even beyond death is to counter the experience and assumptions of Western, free-enterprising societies which prize personal autonomy and the individuated self. In such societies, even the observable connective tissue that once held people together—of marriage, family, and community, of blood, soil, and social purpose, are experienced as arbitrary limitations on the primacy and sovereignty of the self. When traditional bonds become attenuated, individuals tend to collide, like billiard balls, rather than connect. Where natural bonds have atrophied, it is difficult to imagine a family of familiars that is prior to and independent of whatever social contracts we choose to enter into. How can we imagine and celebrate saints when, as sociologist Robert Bellah has observed of contemporary Americans, we lack "communities of memory that tie us to the past [and] also turn us toward the future as communities of hope"?

Dependency: The search for connections is a very modern, very Western experience. The thrust of contemporary Western culture is to encourage autonomous human beings who cooperate as citizens but remain essentially independent. Our prevailing ethos is individualistic, utilitarian, and self-expressive. To be free is to be in control.

Occasionally, however, a powerful movement arises and in its encompassing sweep we feel the archaic pull of primordial communion and radical interdependency. We are, we discover, part of a common story after all. In this, the last decade of the millennium, the new and paramount story of communion and interdependency, one might argue, is the story of the "environment." Through it, we recognize that we all share the fate of the planet and its diverse ecosystems. We become, with a certain humility and ecological bonhomie, "friends of the earth."

But in order to commune with the earth, we must first listen and tell her story. Evolution, in the telling, is what the earth is up to. And depending upon how the story is told, humankind is either the self-conscious species through which evolution has achieved its apex, or the random product of an impersonal process that whispers "I am all that is." Either way, evolution—can we doubt it?—is our new and necessary myth.

To be a "friend of God" is, in one respect at least, like being a friend of earth. To cite Coleman yet once more, "Saints [in all religious traditions] invite us to conceptualize our lives in terms of other than mastery, usefulness, autonomy and control. As free instruments of a higher grace and vehicles of transcendent power, they provide a vision of life that stresses receptivity and interaction." In other words, there are no self-made saints, any more than—contrary to an older American myth—there are self-made men. What makes us fully human, if saints are to be believed, are gifts: what the gift of life begins, the gift of grace completes.

To be a friend of God, therefore, one must first learn God's story. In every religious tradition, it is the saints who reveal what God is up to. Sacred texts are essential, of course, but they reveal only the central plot. In the tradition I have been inspecting, it is Jesus who reveals what God is like and up to, but Christians come to understand only when they make His story their own. For all Christians, that is the meaning of sanctity.

Particularity: Christian holiness is incarnational. Each saint occupies his own ecological niche of time, place, and circumstance. The importance that Christians have traditionally attached to tombs, shrines, and pilgrimages attests to the belief that God's providence is manifest in the local, the circumscribed—in the particular. Because grace is everywhere, the particular has eternal significance.

This scandal of the particular is manifest especially in the veneration of relics. Like all forms of religion, such veneration invites superstition and other abuses. But rightly understood, the honor accorded the bodies of saints is an affirmation that the whole person in his concrete singularity is subject to the divine embrace. Relics bespeak holiness on a fully human scale: the concrete, the physical, the tactile. It is precisely the sort of holiness one might expect in a religion that looks to a particular person, Jesus, not only as the revelation of what God is like but also as the revelation of what every person, in his own concrete humanity, is called to be.

But if the Christian idea of sanctity is to be appreciated in an age of expanding global consciousness, a new kind of saint—or at least a new awareness of what sanctity needs—is needed. Simone Weil saw this with great clarity. In her last letter to Father Jean-Marie Perrin before her death in 1943, Weil wrote of the need for saints of "genius" who could illuminate "the present moment" in ways that the saints of the past no longer can. "A new type of sanctity," she imagined, would bring "a fresh spring . . . almost equivalent to a new revelation of the universe and of human destiny. . . Only a kind of perversity can oblige God's friends to deprive themselves of having genius," she insisted, "since to receive it in superabundance they only need to ask their father for it in Christ's name."

Only God makes saints. Still, it is up to us to tell their stories. That, in the end, is the only rationale for the process of "making saints." What sort of story befits a saint? Not tragedy, certainly. Comedy comes closer to capturing the playfulness of genuine holiness and the supreme logic of a life lived in and through God. An element of suspense is also required: until the story is over, one can never be certain of the outcome. True saints are the last people on earth to presume their own salvation—in this life or in the next.

My own hunch is that the story of a saint is always a love story. It is a story of a God who loves, and of the beloved who learns how to reciprocate and share that "harsh and dreadful love." It is a story that includes misunderstanding, deception, betrayal, concealment, reversal, and revelation of character. It is, if the saints are to be trusted, our story. But to be a saint is not to be a solitary lover. It is to enter into deeper communion with everyone and everything that exists.

Notes

PREFACE
PAGE

5   The discrepancy between the number of individuals beatified or canonized and the lower number of beatifications and canonizations is explained by the fact that some martyrdom causes are group causes. Martyrs who died at the same place under the same persecution (though not necessarily at the same time) are counted as a single cause. For example, in 1988 Pope John Paul II canonized 117 Vietnamese martyrs who had previously been beatified as a single cause. *Beati* and *Sancti* belonging to a group are honored as a group and are therefore considered a single beatification or canonization. Thus, the number of beatifications and canonizations attributed to John Paul II, while a record, is not nearly as high as some media stories have reported by erroneously treating each member of a group cause as a Blessed or Saint.

6   "A controversial saint-making," *The Tablet*, May 13, 1995, p. 614.

6   "May this day mark a new beginning!" *L'Osservatore Romano*, weekly edition, no. 21, May 24, 1995, p. 2.

6   Ibid.

7   "Names of Slav saints form stupendous litany," ibid., p. 12.

7   *Tertio Millennio Adveniente*, Apostolic Letter of His Holiness John Paul II to the Bishops, Clergy and Lay Faithful on Preparation for the Jubilee of the Year 2000, Vatican City: Libreria Editrice Vaticana, 1994.

10   Kenneth L. Woodward with Christopher Dickey and Pia Hinckle, "A Questionable Saint," *Newsweek*, January 13, 1992, pp. 50–51.

11   Kenneth L. Woodward with Christopher Dickey and Pia Hinckle, "A Coming-Out Party in Rome," *Newsweek*, May 14, 1993, p. 62.

12   For a summary of recent scholarship on saints, see Lawrence S. Cunningham, "A Decade of Research on the Saints: 1980–1990," *Theological Studies*, vol. 53, no. 3, September 1992, pp. 517–33.

13   For a representative article, see Donald M. Steel, "With All God's People: Toward a Protestant Reclaiming of the Communion of Saints," *Theology Today*, vol. 51, no. 4, January 1995.

INTRODUCTION

PAGE

15   For the life of Mother Teresa, see Eileen Egan, *Such a Vision of the Street; Mother Teresa—the Spirit and the Work* (New York: Doubleday, 1986.

16   Russian Orthodox: For a concise account of the history and procedures for canonization in the Russian Orthodox Church, including a list of those canonized, see Metropolitan Juvenaly of Krutitsy and Kolomna, "The Canonization of Saints in the Russian Orthodox Church," presented to and published by the *Local Council of the Russian Orthodox Church*, held June 6–9, 1988, in the U.S.S.R. in connection with the celebration of the Millennium of the Baptism of Russia (mimeographed).

17   by others, for others: Pierre Delooz, "Toward a Sociological Study of Canonized Sainthood in the Catholic Church," *Saints and Their Cults: Studies in Religious Sociology, Folklore and History*, ed. Stephen Wilson (Cambridge, England: University of Cambridge Press, 1983). For a fuller treatment, see Pierre Delooz, *Sociologie et Canonizations* (Liege: Faculté de Droit, 1969).

19   "Formal canonization procedures ...": John A. Coleman, "After Sainthood," in *Saints and Virtues*, ed. John Stratton Hawley (Berkeley: University of California Press, 1987), p. 224.

CHAPTER ONE

All quotations from living persons are from the author's interviews unless otherwise noted.

PAGE

21   McCarrick letter to O'Connor, The Cardinal Cooke Archives.

22   Veraja-Groeschel conversation: author's interview with Groeschel.

23   "A cause of canonization ...": Fabijan Veraja, *Commentary on the New Legislation for the Causes of Saints* (Rome: Sacred Congregation for the Causes of Saints, 1983), p. 15.

24   "the perfect number-two man": Edward Tivnan, "A New Yorker Up for Sainthood: Admirers of Terrence Cardinal Cooke Start a Campaign That Could take Centuries,"*The New York Times Magazine*, November 30, 1986, p. 68.

25   Cooke's letter: reprinted in *"This Grace Filled Moment,"* eds. John Rear-

don, Robert L. Stewart, and Anne Buckley (New York: Rosemont Press, 1984), pp. 56–57.

25   from death backward . . .: James Tunstead Burtchaell, *The Giving and Taking of Life: Essays Ethical* (Notre Dame, Ind.: University of Notre Dame Press, 1989), p. 46.

29   "I was lonely . . .": Dorothy Day, *The Long Loneliness* (New York: Harper & Brothers, 1952), p. 157.

30   "It was killing . . .": ibid., p. 148.

30   "The scandal of . . .": ibid., p. 150.

30   "I loved the church . . .": ibid., pp. 149–50.

31   "effective humanitarians": Robert Coles, *Dorothy Day: A Radical Devotion* (Reading, Mass.: Addison-Wesley, 1987), p. 97.

31   "the most significant . . .": historian David O'Brien in *Commonweal* at the time of Day's death, cited in *By Little and By Little: The Selected Writings of Dorothy Day,* edited with an introduction by Robert Ellsberg (New York: Alfred A. Knopf, 1983), p. xvii.

31   O'Connor's column: "A Good Question," *Catholic New York,* January 3, 1985.

32   "a saint for our time": Father Henry Fehren, "Let's Canonize Dorothy Day," *Salt,* September 1983, pp. 4–5.

32   Hennessy letter to *Salt,* dated December 1, 1987, quoted with her permission.

33   Stier letter: published in *Salt,* November/December 1987, p. 24.

33   "If sanctity . . .": William D. Miller, *All Is Grace: The Spirituality of Dorothy Day* (New York: Doubleday, 1987), p. 102.

33   "If we imitate . . .": ibid., p. 101.

33   "all are called . . .": ibid., p. 102.

34   *The Eleventh Virgin:* cited in William D. Miller, *Dorothy Day: A Biography* (San Francisco: Harper & Row, 1982), p. 5.

35   Berrigan letter: published in slightly abbreviated form in *Salt,* November/December, 1987, p. 25.

36   "feel clean . . .": James R. Brockman, S.J., *Romero: A Life* (Maryknoll, N.Y.: Orbis Books, 1989), p. 243.

37   "No soldier . . .": ibid., p. 241.

39   Rivera y Damas's prohibition of plaque: author's interviews with Rivera y Damas and Sister Teresa of Ávila.

39   Romero's viscera: author's interview with Rivera y Damas and Ricardo Urioste.

41   Pastoral letter: Archbishop Oscar Romero, *Voice of the Voiceless: The Four Pastoral Letters and Other Statements* (Maryknoll, N.Y.: Orbis Books, 1985), pp. 85–113.

42   Incident with female Spanish journalist: author's interview with Jesús Delgado.

43   Salvadoran bishops divided over Romero: author's interview with Ricardo Urioste.

46   Romero interview: Brockman, op. cit., p. 248.

49   "his severe condemnation . . .": "Tribute to a Martyr: Archbishop Romero Praised As Pastor As Well As Prophet," *Catholic New York,* April 12, 1990, p. 33.

CHAPTER TWO

PAGE

51 The most comprehensive: *Bibliotheca Sanctorum*, published in Rome by Istituto Giovanni XXIII, nella Pontifica Università Laterense.

52 too long and too remote: among recent critics, see Lawrence S. Cunningham, *The Meaning of Saints* (San Francisco: Harper & Row, 1980), pp. 34–59.

52 "eye of the beholder . . .": Burtchaell, op. cit., p. 22.

53 "unto death": Phil. 2:8.

53 "also remembered as martyrs . . .": Burtchaell, op. cit., p. 16.

53 "I entreat you . . .": Ignatius, "Letter to the Romans," in Edgar A. Goodspeed, trans., *The Apostolic Fathers: An American Translation* (New York: Harper & Brothers, 1950), p. 222. For an expanded commentary on the concept of martyrdom in the early church, see W. H. C. Frend, *Martyrdom and Persecution in the Early Church* (New York: New York University Press, 1967).

56 "It was not . . .": quoted in Kenneth L. Woodward, "How America Lives with Death," *Newsweek*, April 6, 1970, p. 88.

56 "We can chart . . .": Peter Brown, *The Cult of the Saints: Its Rise and Function in Latin Christianity* (Chicago: University of Chicago Press, 1981), pp. 6–7.

56 " 'You keep adding . . .' ": quoted in ibid.

56 "tomb and altar . . .": ibid., p. 9.

57 "dearer to us . . .": "The Martyrdom of St. Polycarp," in *The Acts of the Christian Martyrs*, trans. Herbert Musurillo (Oxford, England: The Clarendon Press, 1972), p. 17.

57 "Here lies . . .": cited in Brown, op. cit., p. 4.

57 "all natural things . . . miracle of miracles": cited in Benedicta Ward, *Miracles and the Medieval Mind: Theory, Record and Event, 1000–1215*, rev. ed. (Philadelphia: University of Pennsylvania Press, 1987), pp. 2–3.

58 "Wherever Christianity . . .": Brown, op. cit., p. 12.

58 "abandon the Crucified": Musurillo, op. cit., p. 15.

58 "disciples and imitators . . .": ibid., p. 17.

59 "crowds of men . . .": ed. and trans. F. R. Hoare, *The Western Fathers* (New York: Sheed and Ward, 1954), p. 184.

59 "tomb containing . . .": Cunningham, op. cit., p. 9.

60 "Legend is the homage . . .": Hippolyte Delehaye, *The Legends of the Saints* (New York: Fordham University Press, 1962), p. xx.

61 "Antony 'was daily . . .' ": Athanasius, *The Life of Antony and the Letter to Marcellinus* (New York: Paulist Press, 1980), p. 66.

62 so moved the youthful: Peter Brown, "Late Antiquity," in *A History of Private Life I: From Pagan Rome to Byzantium*, ed. Paul Veyne (Cambridge, Mass.: The Belknap Press of Harvard University Press, 1987), p. 287.

63 export of relics: P. Chiovrarco, "Relics," *New Catholic Encyclopedia*, vol. 12 (New York: McGraw-Hill, 1967), p. 237.

63 On the practice of stealing relics, see Patrick J. Geary, *Futra Sacra: The Theft of Relics in the Middle Ages* (Princeton, N.J.: Princeton University Press, 1978).

66   Exchange between Lafranc and Anselm: Margaret R. Toynbee, *S. Louis of Toulouse and the Process of Canonization in the Fourteenth Century* (Manchester, England: Manchester University Press, 1929), pp. 141–42.

67   in one notable case . . .: ibid., p. 137.

67   Alexander III upbraids a local bishop: Reverend Monsignor Robert J. Sarno, *Diocesan Inquiries Required by the Legislator in the New Legislation for the Causes of Saints*. Dissertatio ad Doctoratum in Facultate Juris Canonici Pontificae Universitas Gregorianae (Rome: Tipografia Guerra, 1988), p. 41.

67   halos or rays . . .: ibid., p. 42.

68   "from Kings, Princes . . .": ibid., p. 9.

69   "who had monopolized . . .": André Vouchez, *La Sainteté en Occident aux derniers siècles du moyen âge, d'après les procès de canonization et les documents hagiographiques* (Rome: Ecole Française de Rome, 1981), p. 14. Rough translation from the French by Richard Kieckhefer.

69   "no servants of God . . .": ibid., p. 13.

69   "the identification of sanctity . . .": ibid., p. 14.

71   "preachers spread . . .": ibid., p. 21.

71   "When a toothache . . .": ibid., p. 25.

71   "as effects of . . .": ibid., p. 25.

71   "continuous, uninterrupted virtue": Innocent IV, *In quinque liborus decretalium*, quoted in Vouchez, p. 602, n. 51, and cited in Sherry L. Reames, *The Legenda Aurea: A Reexamination of Its Paradoxical History* (Madison: University of Wisconsin Press, 1985), p. 199.

72   "allows[s] us to see . . .": Vouchez, op. cit., p. 3.

72   "as a state of . . .": ibid., p. 23.

72   Thomas of Cantilupe: Reames, op. cit., p. 201.

73   "treasury of vicarious 'merits' ": Donald Weinstein and Rudolph M. Bell, *Saints & Society: The Two Worlds of Western Christendom, 1000–1700* (Chicago: University of Chicago Press, 1982), p. 249.

73   "bureaucratization of sanctity": Cunningham, op. cit., pp. 48–59.

73   advocate in heaven: Brown, op. cit., p. 58.

74   "excesses and abuses": Johan Huizinga, *The Waning of the Middle Ages* (Garden City, N.Y.: Doubleday Anchor Books, 1954), p. 163.

74   "Too large a part . . .": ibid., p. 176.

74   words replaced images . . . the symbol became merely symbolic: Eric Heller, *The Disinherited Mind* (New York: Meridian Books, 1957), pp. 263 and 265.

74   ". . . The Reformation attacked . . .": Huizinga, p. 177.

74   "a fine piece . . .": cited in Richard Kieckhefer, "Sainthood in the Christian Tradition," Richard Kieckhefer and George D. Bond, eds., *Sainthood: Its Manifestations in World Religions* (Berkeley: University of California Press, 1988), p. 7.

75   "Next to Holy . . .": ibid.

75   "Only men of irreligious . . .": John F. Clarkson et al., trans., *The Church Teaches: Documents of the Church in English Translation* (Rockford, Ill.: TAN, 1973), p. 215.

75   "from time immemorial" . . . "on the strength of": Urban VIII quoted in Burtchaell, op. cit., p. 20.

77   "The 'fierce' light...": Canon Macken, *The Canonization of Saints* (Dublin: M. H. Hill and Sons, 1910), pp. 35–36.
77   "In the processes...": ibid., pp. 49–50.
77   "The mystery of sainthood...": Jerrold M. Packard, *Peter's Kingdom: Inside the Papal City* (New York: Charles Scribner's Sons, 1985), p. 192.
79   (This wariness...: Veraja, op. cit., p. 15.
80   (as late as 1982: author's interview with Robert Sarno, official of the congregation.
80   Olier story: author's interview with Yvon Beaudoin, O.M.I., archivist and relator of the congregation.
81   only one cause: author's interview with Sarno. This tradition continues. For evidence, see Joan Carroll Cruz, *The Incorruptibles* (Rockford, Ill.: TAN, 1977) and especially Patricia Treece, *The Sanctified Body* (New York: Doubleday), 1989.
84   Frassati story: author's interview with Paul Molinari, S.J., postulator of his cause.
86   "arguably the oldest": John T. Noonan, Jr., *Power to Dissolve: Lawyers and Marriages in the Courts of the Roman Curia* (Cambridge, Mass.: Belknap Press of Harvard University Press, 1972), p. ix.

CHAPTER THREE

All quotations with members of the congregation are taken from the author's interviews.

PAGE
90   Suenens' suggestion: Sarno, op. cit., p. 18.
92   Frederick Ozaman story: author's interview with Father William Sheldon, postulator general for the Vincentians.
93   "we know nothing...": author's interview with Yvon Beaudoin.
95   As Porsi read them: For his detailed criticism, see Luigi Porsi, "Cause di Canonizzazioni e procetura nella cost. apost. "Divinus Ecclesiasticus CX, 1985, pp. 365–400.
96   "great historical enterprises": David Knowles, *Great Historical Enterprises* (London: Thomas Nelson, 1963). My account of the Bollandists is based on chapter 1, "The Bollandists," pp. 3–33, as well as on the author's interviews with four current members of the Bollandists at their center in Brussels, Belgium, in 1987.
97   destroyed the conventions: Richard Kieckhefer, op. cit., p. 33.
97   discovered a supportive speech: author's interview with Paul Molinari, S.J.
97   "for having contributed...": Veraja, op. cit., p. 3.
97   "And so with...": ibid.
111 "millions of dollars": Liz Roman Gallese, "American Saint's Cause Took Century of Work, Millions in Donations," *The Wall Street Journal*, June 25, 1975, p. 1.
111 Vincentians' reaction: author's interview with Sheldon.
112 spices, sugar, chocolate: Bernard Plongeron, "Concerning Mother Agnes of Jesus: Themes and Variations in Hagiography (1665–1963)" in Concil-

ium 129, *Models of Holiness*, ed. Christian Duquoc and Casiano Floristan (New York: Seabury Press, 1979), p. 31.

115   "canonized their former local hero": Pierre Delooz, "The Social Function of the Canonization of Saints," in Concilium 129, p. 23.

115   "Palazzini's job. . .": Peter Hebblethwaite, *In the Vatican* (London: Sidgwick & Jackson, 1986), p. 114.

118   Figures on lay saints: Delooz, op. cit., p. 21.

121   "Honor we show the saints . . .": A. E. Green, "Canonization of Saints (Theological Aspect)," *New Catholic Encyclopedia*, op. cit., p. 59.

122   "The pope cannot . . .": ibid.

122   "Should the church": ibid.

122   no pope has: Eric Waldram Kemp, *Canonization in the Western Church* (London: Oxford University Press, 1948), p. 160.

122   a sensational book: Giordano Bruno Guerri, *Povera Santa, Povero Assassino: La vera storia di Maria Goretti* (Rome: Arnoldo Mondadori, 1985).

124   a "white book": Commissione di Studio Istituta della Congregazione per le Causae dei Santi, *A Proposito di Maria Goretti, Santita e Canonizzazione* (Vatican City: Libreria Editrice Vaticana, 1985).

124   not permitted to question: this view was widely held long before Vatican I's declaration of papal infallibility. See Kemp, op. cit., p. 168.

125   notoriously unreliable: see *Butler's Lives of the Saints*, Complete Edition, edited, revised and supplemented by Herbert Thurston, S.J., and Donald Attwater, vol. 3 (Westminster, Md.: The Christian Classics, 1981), pp. 338–39.

125   debatable issue: for a careful expression of doubt, see Francis A. Sullivan, S.J., *Magisterium: Teaching Authority in the Catholic Church* (Mahwah, N.J.: Paulist Press, 1983), p. 136.

CHAPTER FOUR

PAGE

128   "It sticks in . . .": Anne Roiphe, *A Season of Healing: Reflections on the Holocaust* (New York: Summit Books, 1989), p. 128.

130   millions of Christians: for a learned survey of the literature on Jews, Catholics, and the Nazis, see Istvan Deak, "The Incomprehensible Holocaust," *The New York Review of Books*, vol. 36, no. 14., September 28, 1989, pp. 63–72.

130   "the uninhibited freedom": quoted in Anthony Rhodes, *The Vatican in the Age of the Dictators (1922–1945)* (New York: Holt, Rinehart and Winston, 1973), p. 176.

131   a single student: author's interview with Redemptorist Valabek, postulator of the cause.

132   ". . . activities endanger[ing] . . . his hostility": from the report of the arresting officer read to the author by Redemptus Valabek.

134   "We raise to the glory": Eleni Dimler, "Priest-Journalist, Victim of Nazis, Named 'Blessed' by Pope," *Religious News Service*, dispatch from Vatican City, November 4, 1985, p. 12.

135   "rationalistic prejudice": Edith Stein, *Life in a Jewish Family*, trans. Jo-

sephine Koeppel, OCD, Collected Works of Edith Stein, vol. 1 (Washington, D.C.: I.C.S. Publications, 1986), p. 260.

136   "This . . . is the truth." Sr. Renata de Spiritu Sancto, OCD, Edith Stein, trans. Cecily Hastings and Donald Nicholl (New York: Sheed and Ward, 1952), p. 64.

136   "My return to God . . .": testimony of Carmelite sisters given in process for beatification and canonization of Edith Stein and repeated in conversation with Jan Nota, S.J., as reported in Schwabisches Tageblatt (Tubingen), August 11, 1987.

136   "not only in a spiritual sense . . .": testimony of Johannes Hirschann, S.J., in Jacob Schlafke, Vice Postulator, Diocesan Process for Beatification, chap. II (Cologne, 1962), p. 27.

136   "deplore the hatred . . .": Sr. Renata de Spiritu Sancto, OCD, op. cit., p. 117.

136   "I am confident" and "I always have to think . . .": Edith Stein, Selbstbildnis in Briefen, Edith Steins Werke (Freiburg: Herder, 1977), p. 120.

136   "for the atonement . . .": Jakob Schlafke, Edith Stein: Documents Concerning Her Life and Death, trans. Susanne M. Batzdorff (New York: Edith Stein Guild, 1984), p. 5.

137   "Come, let us go": there is some question concerning the source and authenticity of this quote. The Carmelites of Holland attribute it to Maria Delsing, a lay volunteer in the extern quarters of the Carmel in Echt, where she worked with Rosa Stein, as the woman who overheard Edith saying it to her sister. It is quoted without mention of who overheard it in Romaeus Leuven, OCD, Heil im Unheil, Edith Steins Werke, vol. X (Freiburg: Herder, 1983), p. 166.

137   "Urge Swiss Consulate": ibid. The text for a telegram written in Edith Stein's hand is included in a letter intended for the Swiss consul at Amsterdam in Edith Stein, Selbstbildnis in Briefen, op. cit., p. 177. Further details on this last-minute effort forthcoming in Josephine Koeppel, OCD: Edith Stein: The Intellectual Mystic (Wilmington, Del.: Michael Glazier, 1990).

138   Testimony of witnesses: author's interview with Ambrose Eszer, relator of the cause.

139   Postulatory letters of German and Polish bishops: Ambrose Eszer, "Edith Stein, Jewish Catholic Martyr," Carmelite Studies 4 (Washington, D.C.: I.C.S. Publications, 1987), p. 312. Also Sarno, op. cit., pp. 21–22.

139   Wojtyla's thesis on Schler: George Hunston Williams, The Mind of John Paul II: Origins of His Thought and Action (New York: Seabury Press, 1981), pp. 124–40.

140   "You damned Jew . . .": author's interview with Ambrose Eszer, O.P., relator of the cause.

143   "You are, of course, free to defend . . .": quoted by Peter Hebblethwaite, "Curia Raps Scholar on Martyr's Fate," National Catholic Reporter, March 20, 1987, p. 25.

143   "allegedly exacting processes . . .": James Baaden, "A Question of Martyrdom," The Tablet, January 31, 1987, p. 108.

143   Pope's beatification homily, heard and witnessed by the author on May 1,

144   1987, in Cologne, West Germany, and reprinted in *Carmelite Studies* vol. 4, op. cit., pp. 298–306.

144   "There is no greater love . . .": John 15:13.

144   Kolbe dialogue with Fritsch: Patricia Treece, *A Man for Others: Maximilian Kolbe, Saint of Auschwitz in the Words of Those Who Knew Him* (San Francisco: Harper & Row, 1982), p. 171.

144   "The prisoners . . .": Boniface Hanley, O.F.M. *Maximilian Kolbe: No Greater Love* (Notre Dame, Indiana: Ave Maria Press, 1982), p. 70.

145   "a martyr of charity": author's interview with Peter Gumpel, S.J.

147   "And so, in virtue": "He Died a Martyr of Love, Giving His Life for Another," *L'Osservatore Romano*, no. 42, October 18, 1982, p. 12.

148   "appearance of a saint": author's interview with Beaudoin, relator of Callo's cause.

149   "prophetic sign . . .": "We Present the New Blessed as Lay Faithful, a Sign of the Church of the Third Millennium," *L'Osservatore Romano*, weekly edition, no. 41, October 12, 1987, p. 19.

150   "Human good can become . . .": cited by Leonardo Boff, "Martyrdom: An Attempt at Systematic Reflection," in Concilium 1983, vol. 163, *Martyrdom Today*, ed. Edward Schillebeeckx and Johannes-Baptist Metz (New York: Seabury Press, 1983), p. 14.

150   "solitary witness": Gordon Zahn, *In Solitary Witness: The Life and Death of Franz Jägerstätter*, rev. ed. (Springfield, Ill.: Templegate Publishers, 1986).

150   "could go beyond . . .": Sarno, op. cit., p. 35.

152   "This is not . . .": Barbara Crossette, "Sainthood for 117 Outrages Vietnam," *The New York Times*, May 29, 1988.

154   "It would be foolish . . .": Enda McDonagh, "Dying for the Cause: An Irish Perspective on Martyrdom," in Concilium 163, *Martyrdom Today*, p. 34.

155   "By its very nature . . .": Jon Sobrino, *Spirituality of Liberation: Toward Political Holiness* (Maryknoll, N.Y.: Orbis Books, 1988), p. 84.

CHAPTER FIVE

PAGE

158   "icons of agapic love": Harvey D. Egan, S. J., *Christian Mysticism: The Future of a Tradition* (New York: Pueblo Publishing Company, 1984), p. xvi.

159   "the Father and I": John 10:30.

159   "he who sees . . .": John 12:45.

159   "I live . . .": Gal. 2:20.

159   "in genuine raptures . . .": Teresa of Ávila, *The Interior Castle*. 6th Mansion, chapter 4, cited in Steven T. Katz, "The 'Conservative' Character of Mystical Experience," *Mysticism and Religious Traditions*, ed. Steven T. Katz (New York: Oxford University Press, 1983), p. 12.

159   "He is our Very . . .": Julian of Norwich, *Showings*, cited by Katz, op. cit., p. 16.

159   "espousing her soul . . .": cited in Katz, ibid., p. 16.

159   "Where have you . . .": St. John of the Cross, *The Poems of St. John of the*

Cross, 3d ed. trans., John Frederick Nims (Chicago: University of Chicago Press, 1979), p. 3.

160 "secondary mystical phenomena": for a detailed contemporary discussion of these phenomena and their relation to the mystical life, see Harvey D. Egan, S.J., op. cit., pp. 304–37.

161 "the mystical moment . . .": Katz, op. cit., p. 41.

161 "the 'conservative' character . . .": ibid., pp. 3–60.

162 "infused contemplation": for a discussion of infused versus "acquired" contemplation, an issue which long divided Dominican and Jesuit theologians, see for the Dominican side the Reverend R. Garrigou-Lagrange, O.P., *Christian Perfection and Contemplation*, 11th ed. (St. Louis, Mo.: B. Hérder, 1937), pp. 221–35. For the Jesuits, consult Augustin Poulain, S.J., *The Graces of Interior Prayer* (Westminster, Vt.: Celtic Cross Books, 1978), pp. 54–99.

164 According to one count: Egan, op. cit., p. 314. Egan's number is apparently based on a questionable study written by Dr. Antoine Imbert-Gourbeyre, *La Stigmatisation, l'Extase Divine et les Miracles de Lourdes* (Clermont-Ferrand, 1895). For an acute criticism of Imbert-Gourbeyre, see Herbert Thurston, S.J., *The Physical Phenomena of Mysticism* (Chicago: Henry Regnery, 1952), p. 49, n. I, and pp. 32–130.

166 "Wind your crown . . .": P. Stefano and M. Manelli, *Short Story of a Victim: Theresa Musco (1943–1976)*, trans. Johanna Pearson (S. Mari, Italy: Eitrice Terzo Millennio, 1984), p. 36.

166 "Theresa consecrates her . . .": ibid., p. 46.

167 Siri's letter reproduced: ibid., p. 3.

168 "When I was . . .": Prosper Lambertini (Benedict XIV), *De servorum Dei beatificatione et beatorum canonizatione*, 1734–38, vol. 3, p. 49. Cited in Thurston, op. cit., p. 17.

168 Stories of Joseph of Cupertino and quotations attributed to the saint: Thurston, op. cit., pp. 15–17.

169 Since most visions : Lambertini, *Heroic Virtue: A Portion of the Treatise of Benedict XIV on the Beatification and Canonization of the Servants of God*, vol. 3. Translated into English from the original Latin (London: Thomas Richardson and Son, 1851), p. 323.

169 "if the ecstasy . . .": ibid., p. 259.

169 "if a man . . .": ibid., p. 261.

170 "a divine ecstasy . . .": ibid., p. 265.

172 "Love, suffer, and make reparation": Francis Johnson, *Alexandrina: The Agony and The Glory* (Rockford, Ill.: TAN, 1979), p. 25.

172 "Give me your hands . . .": ibid., p. 34.

173 "scientifically inexplicable": ibid., p. 83.

173 "retained her weight . . ." ibid., pp. 83–84.

173 "the mother of the poor," etc.: ibid., p. 106.

174 All quotations from consultors' reports taken from *Beatificationis et canonizationis Serva Dei Alexandrine Maria da Costa Positio Super Scriptis*, trans. from the Italian by Father Robert Findley, S.J. (Rome: Sacro Congregatio pro Causis Sanctorum, 1977).

178 The postulator is preparing . . . : author's correspondence with the postulator, Dom Fiora, S.D.B., January 26, 1989.

180   "her distinguishing characteristic . . .": from a brief biography, author unattributed, introducing the main texts in Anne Catherine Emmerich, *The Dolorous Passion of Our Lord Jesus Christ* (Rockford, Ill.: TAN, 1983), p. 34. It is obvious that this biographical sketch is an English translation of Brentano's original book, published in 1834. For a comparable English translation of the same passage from Brentano's original German edition, see Herbert Thurston, S.J., *Surprising Mystics* (Chicago: Henry Regnery, 1955), p. 57.

180   "pretensions" . . . "history": ibid., p. xix.

181   "During the time . . .": ibid., p. 246.

182   "I was fully . . .": Very Reverend Carl E. Schmoger, *The Life of Anne Catherine Emmerich*, vol. 1, reprinted from English edition of 1885 (Rockford, Ill.: TAN, 1976), p. 12.

182   "At her baptism . . .": cited in Thurston, *Surprising Mystics*, p. 65.

182   appreciative note: Albert Schweitzer, *The Quest for the Historical Jesus* (New York: Macmillan, 1968), pp. 108–9.

182   "bringing a fresh source . . .": George Goyau, Epilogue to Jeanne Danemarie, *The Mystery of Stigmata: From Catherine Emmerich to Theresa Neumann*, trans. Warren B. Wells (London: Burns, Oates & Washbourne, 1934), p. 235.

185   "coredemptive" with Christ: Fernando of Riese Pio X, "The Mystery of the Cross in Padre Pio," Gerado Di Flumeri, O.F.M. *Padre Pio of Pietrelcina: Acts of the First Congress of Studies on Padre Pio's Spirituality* (San Giovannii Rotondo: Edizioni "Padre Pio da Pietrelcina," 1978), p. 95. See also "Padre Pio's Story," *The Voice of Padre Pio*, vol. 18, no. 5, 1988, p. 5.

186   "Go out to the fields . . .": C. Bernard Ruffin, *Padre Pio: The True Story* (Huntington, Ind.: Our Sunday Visitor, 1982), p. 150.

186   bugged his confessional: ibid., p. 285.

186   "acts that have the . . .": ibid., p. 289.

186   "an indigestible dainty": ibid., p. 286.

CHAPTER SIX

PAGE

192   "are like a . . .": "Miracles Are Messages and Signs of a God Who Is Love," *L'Oservatore Romano*,, weekly edition, nos. 51–52, Dec. 19, 26, 1987.

192   "to spend my . . .": *Story of a Soul,: The Autobiography of St. Thérèse of Lisieux*, trans. from the original manuscript of John Clarke, O.C.D. (Washington, D.C.: ICS Publication, 1976), p. 263.

193   Since 99 percent: estimate from author's interview with Raffaello Cortesini, president of the Consulta Medica (the Board of Physicians) to the Congregation for the Causes of Saints.

193   miracles were perceived: for a detailed explanation of the medieval worldview, see Ward, op. cit.

193   Louis of Anjou: Margaret R. Toynbee, op. cit., pp. 191–92.

199   According to the thin: *Canonizatonis Ven. Servi Dei Joseph Gérard (1831–1914), Posito Super Miraculo* (Rome: Congregatio Pro Causis Sanctorum, 1987).

202   In an unusual: *Canonizationis Ven. Servi Dei Juníperi Serra (1713–1784) Relatio et Vota Congressus Peculiaris Super Miro.* (Rome: Congregatio pro Causis Sanctorum, 1987).

203   the final *positio: Canonizationis Ven. Servi Dei Junípero Serra* (1713–1789) *Positio Super Miraculo* (Rome: Congregatio pro Causis Sanctorum, 1987).

205   "undifferentiated neoplasia": *Canonizationis Beatae Philippine Duchesne (1769–1852) Relatio et Vota Congressus Peculiaris Super Miro* (Rome: Congregatio Pro Causis Sanctorum, 1987), p. 6.

206   "Apparently they . . .": Mark I. Pinsky, "Nun's 1960 Recovery May Answer Prayers For Serra's Sainthood," *Los Angeles Times*, August 4, 1987, p. 3.

207   "For a long time . . .": *L'Osservatore Romano*, op. cit., nos. 51 to 52.

208   "There seems to be . . .": *L'Osservatore Romano*, ibid.

209   One such miracle: "La moltiplicazione del riso per i poveri," *Il miracolo: Relta o suggestione?: Rassegna di fatti straordinari nel cinquantennio 1920–1970* (Rome: Citta Nuova Editrice, 1981), pp. 133–41. Trans. for the author by Robert Findley, S.J. Though unsigned, this article was written by Paul Molinari, S.J., postulator of the cause, and is drawn from *Canonizationis Beati Ioannis Macías, O.P. (1585–1645), Positio Super Miraculo* (Rome: Sacra Congregatio pro Causis Sanctorum, 1974).

210   Miracle attributed to Rasoamanarvio: author's interview with Molinari, postulator of the cause.

211   "Bombers were above . . .": interview by Theresa Waldrop at author's request.

212   "We had this wonder . . .": interview by Theresa Waldrop at author's request.

213   "Suppose we call them . . ." Author's interview with Martin.

215   long and passionate essay: Paolo Molinari, "Observations aliquot circa miraculorum munus et necessitatem in causis beatificationis et canonizationis," *Periodica de re morali canonica liturgica* 63. (1974). A shorter version, in English, appears as: Paul Molinari, "Saints and Miracles," *The Way*, October 1978. pp. 287–99.

215   "in no way connected . . .": ibid., p. 289.

215   "It was a time . . .": ibid., p. 292.

215   "was not in fact . . .": ibid., p. 293.

216   ". . . We do not believe . . .": ibid., p. 299.

216   "So," he remarked: Peter Hebblethwaite, "Pope Cites Stein's Jewish Roots," *National Catholic Reporter*, May 15, 1987, p. 24.

217   equally impassioned essay: Ambrose Eszer, "Miracoli ed Altri Segni Divini. Considerationi Dommatico-Storiche con speciale riferimento alle Cause dei Santi," *Studi in onore del Card. Pietro Palazzini* (Pisa: Giardini Editori e Stampoatori, 1987), privately translated for the author by Robert Findley, S.J., p. 129.

218   "a kind of psychoanlyst . . .": ibid., p. 129.

218   " 'God makes miracles . . .": ibid., p. 131.

218   "were perfectly able . . .": ibid., p. 143.

218   "only God . . .": ibid., p. 148.

218   "a believer in grave . . .": ibid., p. 149.

NOTES † 419

CHAPTER SEVEN

PAGE

224 "No one is . . .": cited in William M. Thompson, *Fire & Light: The Saints and Theology* (New York: Paulist Press, 1987), p. 10.

224 "representative saints . . . irrefutable": ibid., pp. 10–11.

224 "Herein lies . . .": Karl Rahner, S.J., *The Practice of Faith: A Handbook of Contemporary Spirituality* (New York: Crossroad, 1983), p. 157.

225 ideal type: Richard Kieckhefer, op. cit., p. 32.

225 intellectual combat: Michael Goodich, "The Politics of Canonization in the Thirteenth Century: Lay and Mendicant Saints," in *Saints and Their Cults: Studies in Religious Sociology, Folklore and History*, ed. Stephen Wilson (Cambridge, England: Cambridge University Press, 1985), p. 183.

225 Mother Agnes of Jesus: Plongeron, op. cit., pp. 25–35.

225 "An agent of Satan . . .": Weinstein and Bell, op. cit., p. 141.

228 Born in Philadelphia: for an uncritical, popularly written but well-documented life of Drexel written by a member of her own religious order and published to further Drexel's cause, see Sister Cornelia Consuela Marie Duffy, S.B.S., *Katharine Drexel: A Biography* (Cornwells Heights, Pa.: Mother Katharine Drexel Guild, 1966).

230 that was the text: all quotations are from the vols. 1 (*Expositio et Documenta*), 2 (*Summarium Depositionum Testium*), and 3 (*Relatio Relatoris et Informatio*), *Canonizationis Servae Dei Catherinae Mariae Drexel* (Rome: Sacra Congregatio pro Causis Sanctorum, 1986).

243 "The saints have not . . .": Kieckhefer, op. cit., p. 19.

248 "It is common knowledge . . .": Peter Gumpel, S.J., "Report of the Relator," *Positio: Information for the Canonization Process of the Servant of God Cornelia Connelly* (née Peacock) *1809–1879* (Rome: Sacred Congregation for the Causes of Saints, 1987).

249 translation of a poem: for a compelling discussion of the relationship between music and message in the translation of poetry, see John Frederick Nims, *A Local Habitation: Essays on Poetry* (Ann Arbor: University of Michigan Press, 1985), pp. 30–53.

CHAPTER EIGHT

PAGE

254 All quotations are taken from *Positio for the Canonization Process of the Servant of God Cornelia Connelly* (née Peacock) *1809–1879*, 4 vols. (Rome: Sacred Congregation for the Causes of Saints, 1983, 1987).

270 "an outrage . . .": Leonard Whatmore, "Cornelia Connelly: Gold in the Fire," *The Homiletic and Pastoral Review*, June 1963. Cited in *Positio*, vol. 3, p. 12.

270 "theology of Christian marriage": Joseph H. O'Neill, "No Support Here for Mother Connelly's Cause," cited in ibid.

271 "We simply cannot . . .": Paul Molinari, S.J., "Commitment to Love: A Reply to Cornelia Connelly's Critics," ibid., p. A13.

271 "firm and indeed heroic . . .": ibid.

271 "He will also supply . . .": ibid., p. A14.

271 "the fruits in . . .": ibid., A15.

CHAPTER NINE

PAGE

280   Suenens' speech: summarized in Luigi Bettazzi, *Una Chiesa per tutti* (Rome: Editrice A.V.E., 1971), translated for the author by Robert Findley, S.J., pp. 363–64.

282   "the church would . . .": ibid., p. 364.

282   "the prophet of new structures . . .": ibid., p. 365.

283   "Under Pope John . . .": p. 369.

284   "An ad hoc . . .": ibid.

284   "Now why should . . .": ibid., p. 370.

284   stony silence: Giancarlo Zizola, *The Utopia of Pope John XXIII*, trans. Helen Barolini (Maryknoll, N.Y.: Orbis Books, 1978), p. 240.

285   "a definitive biography . . .": author's interview with the official, who requested anonymity on this episode.

286   vindicate the theological "errors": for the attitude of one of the leaders of the most reactionary faction, see Stefano M. Paci and Paolo Biondi, "Interview with Giuseppe Siri," *30 Days*, June 1988, pp. 70–74.

288   "zeal for the preservation . . .": Lambertini, vol. 2, op. cit., p. 101.

288   "There is not a more splendid . . .": ibid., p. 98.

288   footnote: J. N. D. Kelly, *The Oxford Dictionary of Popes* (New York: Oxford University Press, 1986), pp. 206–10 and 212–13.

289   Pius V and Jews: Kelly, op. cit., p. 268.

290   anti-Modernist crusade: for a detailed examination of the impact of this crusade on Catholic scholarship, especially in the United States, see Gerald P. Fogarty, S.J., *American Catholic Biblical Scholarship: A History from the Early Republic to Vatican II* (San Francisco: Harper & Row, 1989).

292   Pius XII's plan for a council: the agenda and extent of prior consultation with the bishops were much different and narrower than John's plans for Vatican II. See Peter Hebblethwaite, *Pope John XXIII: Shepherd of the Modern World* (New York: Doubleday, 1984), pp. 310–12.

295   for his "silence . . .": for a balanced view from a contemporary historian, see Deak, op. cit., p. 66.

296   chauffeur story: author's interview with Father John Lozano, who, as a censor for the congregation, reviewed documents on Pius XII.

298   His foolish play: Rolf Hochhuth, *The Deputy*, trans. Richard and Clara Winstop (New York: Grove Press, 1964).

298   "drafted by Cardinal Pacelli": some historians say that it was drafted by Cardinal Faulhaber at Pacelli's request, others that it was written at Castel Gandolfo and delayed at Pacelli's request. See Anthony Rhodes, *The Vatican in the Age of the Dictators (1922–1945)* (New York: Holt, Rinehart and Winston, 1973), p. 203.

299   work of Owen Chadwick: Owen Chadwick, *Britain and the Vatican during the Second World War* (Cambridge, England: Cambridge University Press, reprinted 1987).

300   highly critical: Gordon Zahn, *German Catholics and Hitler's War* (Notre Dame, Ind.: University of Notre Dame Press, 1989).

302   Roncalli was accused: Francis X. Murphy, C.SS.R., *The Papacy Today: The Last 80 Years of the Catholic Church from the Perspective of the*

Papacy (New York: Macmillan, 1981), pp. 34–35. Also, Hebblethwaite, *Pope John XXIII*, op. cit., pp. 52–53 and 73–74.

302   De Gaulle and the bishops: Hebblethwaite, op. cit., pp. 205–7.

303   "A Death in the Family of Mankind": Francis X. Murphy, C.SS.R., "Pope John XXIII," *Encyclopedia of Religion*, vol. 8 (New York: Macmillan, 1988), p. 110.

306   *"impulsivo":* evidence that this charge against Roncalli has been taken seriously by his friends can be seen in the defense against it made by Cardinal Giacomo Lercaro of Bologna, in Giacoma Lercaro and Gabriele De Rosa, *John XXIII: Simpleton or Saint?* trans. Dorothy White (Chicago: Franciscan Herald Press, 1965), pp. 22–26.

CHAPTER TEN

PAGE

311   "the almost mystical awe . . .": William J. Basuch, *Pilgrim Church: A Popular History of Catholic Christianity* (Mystic, Conn.: Twenty-Third Publications, 1989), p. 334.

312   he "had allowed for . . .": E. E. Y. Hales, *Pio Nono: A Study in European Politics and Religion in the Nineteenth Century* (New York: P. J. Kennedy & Sons, 1954), p. 19.

313   rejected them all: ibid., pp. 255–90.

313   a sizable minority: John Tracy Ellis, *Perspectives in American Catholicism* (Baltimore: Helicon, 1963), pp. 123–88. See also Margaret O'Gara, *Triumph in Defeat: Infallibility, Vatican I, and the French Minority Bishops* (Washington, D.C.: Catholic University of America, 1988).

313   "European tradition is . . .": Rhodes, op. cit., p. 19.

314   "The Pope is God . . .": Patrick Granfield, *The Limits of the Papacy* (New York: Crossroad, 1987), p. 42, no. 30.
       "Christ [as] if he . . . ": Basuch, op. cit., pp. 332–33.

315   Snider's *positio:* quotations, taken from *Novissima Positio Super Virtutibus Canonizationis Servei Dei PII Papae IX* (Rome: Sacra Congregatio pro Causis Sanctorum, 1984).

316   amassed a huge private fortune: Rhodes, op. cit., p. 36.

321   for a contrary view on Mastai's epilepsy, see G. Martina, "Justified Reservations on a Recent Work," *L'Osservatore Romano*, weekly edition, March 9, 1978, p. 10.

332   dissenting Catholic theologians: see, for example, Hans Kung, *Infallible? An Inquiry* (New York: Doubleday, 1971); and Most Reverend Francis Simons, *Infallibility and the Evidence* (Springfield, Ill.: Templegate, 1968).

335   "frenzy of renown": on the relationship between canonization and other forms of celebrity, see Leo Braudy, *The Frenzy of Renown: Fame and Its History* (New York: Oxford University Press, 1986).

CHAPTER ELEVEN

PAGE

337   "the Devil's gateway": Tertullian, "On the Apparel of Women"; quoted in Catherine M. Mooney, R.S.C.J., *Philippine Duchesne: A Woman*

with the Poor (New York/Mahwah, New Jersey: Paulist Press, 1990), p. 16.

337 "the body and society": Peter Brown, The Body and Society: Men, Women and Sexual Renunciation in Early Christianity (New York: Columbia University Press, 1988).

338 "at the moment . . .": Saint Augustine, The City of God, trans. Marens Dods, D.D. (New York: The Modern Library, 1950), pp. 464–65. See also Garry Wills, "The Phallic Pulpit," The New York Review of Books, December 29, 1989, pp. 20–26.

338 "there will be . . .": Matt. 22:30.

338 Adam's primitive integrity: as conceived by the Church of Jesus Christ of Latter-day Saints, however, heaven at its apex is crowned by the endless reproduction of "spirit children" between a husband and wife who attain the status of gods. See Colleen McDonnell and Bernard Long, Heaven: A History (New Haven, Conn.: Yale University Press, 1989), pp. 313–22.

338 "The more exactly . . . Marriage, then . . .": cited in Margaret R. Miles, Carnal Knowing: Female Nakedness and Religious Meaning in the Christian West (Boston: Beacon Press, 1989), p. 67.

339 The legend of Alexis: for a relatively recent retelling, see Cardinal John J. Wright, The Saints Always Belong to the Present (San Francisco: Ignatius Press, 1985), pp. 43–54.

339 hagiography itself is no longer: Kieckhefer, op. cit., pp. 33–34.

340 "and therefore their parents . . .": Peter Hebblethwaite, "Pope John Paul Canonizing Saints at Record Pace," National Catholic Reporter, no. 30, May 22, 1987, p. 7.

341 "All three are . . . a prophetic sign . . .": L'Osservatore Romano, no. 41, Oct. 12, p. 19. All quotes from the pope's beatification speech for the three blesseds are from this article. For the brief biographies of each blessed, see "Three Martyrs Beatified in St. Peter's Basilica," L'Osservatore Romano, weekly edition, no. 40, October 5, 1987, p. 20.

346 her brief autobiography: latest edition translated as Story of a Soul: The Autobiography of St. Thérèse of Lisieux. A new translation from the original manuscripts by John Clarke, OCD. (Washington, D.C.: I.C.S. Publications, 1976).

347 "the greatest of modern saints": Dr. Joyce R. Emert, OCDS, Louis Martin: Father of a Saint (Staten Island, N.Y.: Alba House, 1983), p. 44.

347 "a true model . . .": ibid., p. 180.

347 "as a daughter . . .": ibid., pp. xvii–xviii.

347 Mary and Joseph: while Mary has been a constant saint, her husband has suffered from periodic neglect or railment as a divine cuckold. See Wilson, op. cit., p. 7.

348 does not list the Martins together: Louis is on p. 181, Azélie on p. 195. Index ac Status Causarum Vatican City: Congregatio pro Causis Sanctorum, 1988).

349 "represent[s] more perfectly . . .": Emert, op. cit., p. 20.

350 "rather like a convent": Monica Furlong, Thérèse of Lisieux (New York: Pantheon Books, 1987), p. 5.

CHAPTER TWELVE

PAGE

355 "public thinker": I owe the phrase to the lectures of the late Professor Frank O'Malley of the University of Notre Dame. See Frank O'Malley, "The Thinker in the Church: The Spirit of Newman," *The Review of Politics*, vol. 21, no. 1, January 1959, pp. 5–23. Reprinted in Joseph W. Houppert, ed., *John Henry Newman* (St. Louis: B. Herder, no date given).

356 "Saints are not literary . . .": cited in Brian Martin, *John Henry Newman: His Life & Work* (New York: Paulist Press, 1990), p. 156.

356 "Whether Rome canonizes . . .": *London Times*, August 12, 1890.

357 enlisted in the battle . . .: for Newman citations at the 1987 international assembly of the Pontifical Council of the Family, see Carlo Caffarra, "Conscience, Truth and Magisterium in Conjugal Morality," *Marriage & Family: Experiencing the Church's Teaching in Married Life* (San Francisco: Ignatius Press, 1989), pp. 21–36.

357 Archbishop of Canterbury: author's interview with Canon Christopher Hill, secretary to the Archbishop for ecumenical affairs, in London.

357 His latest biography: and the most complete is Ian Ker, *John Henry Newman: A Biography* (Oxford, England: Clarendon Press, 1988).

358 "Lead, Kindly Light": *Verses on Various Occasions*, in *Newman's Works* (London: Longmans, Green, 1903), p. 156.

358 "was beginning to prefer . . .": John Henry Newman, *Apologia Pro Vita Sua* (Garden City, N.J.: Doubleday Image Books, 1956), p. 135. Cited in J. M. Cameron, "Newman the Liberal," *Nuclear Catholics & Other Essays* (Grand Rapids, Mich.; Eerdmans, 1989), p. 216.

358 Newman, "Essay on the Development of Christian Doctrine," Works, ibid., p. 423

358 described in his novel: Newman *Loss and Gain: The Story of a Convert*, Works, ibid.

359 "the true church . . ."; John Henry Newman, *Letters and Diaries*, vol. 11, ed. C. Stephen Dessain et al. (Oxford: Clarendon Press, 1976), p. 3.

359 "O how forlorn . . .": Ker, op. cit., p. 520.

360 classic work on education: Newman, *The Idea of a University*, *Newman's Works*, ibid.

360 "I see much danger . . .": cited in Cameron, op. cit., p. 225.

360 "I will either go . . .": ibid., p. 226.

361 "If a check . . .": "Guidance of Newman," *The Tablet*, June 21, 1986, p. 651.

361 "What is the province . . .": ibid.

361 "Truth for its . . .": from Kingsley's Review of Froude's *History of England*, vols. 7 and 8, in *Macmillan's Magazine*, January 1864, pp. 216–17, excerpted in *Apologia*, op. cit., p. 38.

361 "vanquish not only . . .": cited in J. M. Cameron, *John Henry Newman, Writers and Their Work*, no. 72 (London: Longmans, Green), 1956, p. 33.

361 Newman, *Grammar of Assent*, Works, op. cit.

362 "Mere error . . .": cited in Cameron, "Newman the Liberal," op. cit., p. 223.

362 "I have never . . .": Newman, *Letters and Diaries*, vol. 29, op. cit., pp. 61–62.

363   "It is not good . . .": Ker, op. cit., p. 659.

363   "Let us be patient . . .": cited in ibid., p. 660.

363   Gladstone's essay: The Right Honorable W. E. Gladstone, "The Vatican Decrees in Their Bearing on Civil Allegiance: A Political Expostulation" (London: John Murray, 1874), reprinted in *Newman and Gladstone: The Vatican Decrees with an Introduction by Alvan S. Ryan* (Notre Dame, Ind.: University of Notre Dame Press, 1962).

363   "Conscience first . . .": John Henry Newman, D.D., of the Oratory, "A Letter to his Grace The Duke of Norfolk on Occasion of Mr. Gladstone's Recent Expostulation" (London: B. M. Pickering, 1875), reprinted in ibid., p. 129.

363   "Certainly, if I am . . .": ibid., p. 138.

364   "my own perpetual residence . . .": quoted in Ker, op. cit., p. 711.

364   "Of the multitude . . .": cited in Vincent Ferrer Blehl, "Prelude to the Making of a Saint, *America*, vol. 160, no. 9, March 11, 1989, p. 214.

364   first major biographer: Wilfrid Ward, *The Life of John Henry Cardinal Newman*, 2 vols. (London: Longman's, Green, 1912).

367   "came across a book . . .": Louis Bouyer, C.O., *Newman: His Life and Spirituality*, trans. J. Louis May (New York: P. J. Kenedy & Sons, 1958).

368   bibliography of secondary Newman studies: John R. Griffin, *Newman: A Bibliography of Secondary Sources* (Front Royal, Va.: Christendom College Press, 1980).

370   "real, hidden but human life": Newman, Introduction to his "Essay on St. John Chrysostom," reprinted in Hilda Graef, God and Myself: The Spirituality of John Henry Newman (New York: Hawthorn Books, 1968), p. 185.

370   "I want to hear . . .": ibid., p. 186.

370   "I am not content . . .": ibid., p. 187.

372   "Newman carried . . .": author's conversation with Vincent Ferrer Blehl, S.J., postulator of Newman's cause.

373   Miracles attributed to Aquinas: James A. Weisheipl, O.P., *Friar Thomas D'Aquino: His Life, Thought and Work* (New York: Doubleday, 1974), pp. 347–48.

CONCLUSION

PAGE

374   "who perhaps mean . . .": Marina Ricci, "A Few False Facts and . . . The Polemics Rage," *30 Days*, Year 2, no. 5, May 1989, p. 16.

374   in *The New York Times* . . .: Alan Riding, "Vatican 'Saint Factory': Is It Working Too Hard?" *The New York Times*, April 15, 1989, p. 4.

375   "It [saint making] is like . . .": John Thavis, "Booming Saint-Making Industry Might Be Slowing," *National Catholic News Service*, March 31, 1989, p. 16.

375   "In fact, I said . . .": Marina Ricci, "I Never Said There Are Too Many," interview with Cardinal Joseph Ratzinger, *30 Days*, May 1989, pp. 18–19.

378   In his commentary . . .": Veraja, op. cit., pp. IV–6. For a fuller development, see Fabijan Veraja, *La Beatificazione. Storia, Problemi, Prospect-*

tive. Sussidi per lo studio delle Cause dei Santi 2 (Rome: Sacra Congregazione per le Cause dei Santi, 1983).

379 "When he travels . . .": John Thavis, *op. cit.*

379 On Sunday, April 23, 1989 . . . : "Pope beatifies five religious in Vatican ceremonies," *L'Osservatore Romano*, weekly edition, no. 17, April 24, 1989, p. 12.

384 book of 999 spiritual maxims: Josemaría Escrivá de Balaguer, *The Way* (Manila: Sinag-Tala Publishers, 1982).

384 "perhaps in this formula . . .": cited in *Catholic Almanac, 1985* (Huntington, Indiana: Our Sunday Visitor, Inc., 1984), p. 81.

384 For an uncritical biography of Josemaría Escrivá de Balaguer published by an Opus Dei press, see François Gondrand, *At God's Pace* (New Rochelle, N.Y.: Scepter Press, 1989). For an uncritical account of Opus Dei, originally published by an Opus Dei press, see Dominque Le Tourneau, *What Is Opus Dei?* (Dublin: The Mercier Press, 1987).

384 For criticism of Escrivá and of Opus Dei, see Michael Walsh, *Opus Dei: An Investigation into the Secret Society Struggling for Power Within the Roman Catholic Church* (London: Grafton, 1989). See also Penny Lernoux, *The People of God: The Struggle for World Catholicism* (New York: Viking, 1989).

385 "Don't put off. . . .": Escrivá, op. cit.

386 Yet on April 9, 1990 . . .: "Promulgation of Decrees," *L'Osservatore Romano*, weekly edition, no. 16, 1990, p. 2.

388 Donald Weinstein and Rudolph Bell, *op. cit.*

392 Already in the letters of Paul: 1 Cor. 13:13.

393 St. Bonaventure was the first . . .: K. V. Truhlar, "Virtue, Heroic," *Catholic Encyclopedia*, vol. 14, *op. cit.*, p. 709.

394 "linked to some particular . . .": Alasdair MacIntyre, *After Virtue* (Notre Dame: University of Notre Dame Press, 1982), p. 163.

394 "Blessed are the meek": Mt. 5:5.

396 "to be transformed by . . .": John Coleman, *op. cit.*, p. 212.

396 "an experiment with truth": Mohandas Gandhi, *An Autobiography: Or the Story of My Experiments with Truth*, trans. Mahadev Desai (Boston: Beacon Press, 1968).

396 "It is a terrible thing . . . ": Miller, *All Is Grace, op. cit.*, p. 63.

396 Saints are not people: on insight and experience, see John S. Dunne, C.S.C., *The Way of All the Earth* (New York: Macmillan, 1972). See also Kenneth L. Woodward, "What Is God? John Dunne's Life of Discovery," *Notre Dame Magazine*, vol. 9, no. 3, July 1980, and "Spiritual Adventure: The Emergence of a New Theology," a conversation with John Dunne by Kenneth L. Woodward, *Psychology Today*, vol. 11, no. 8, January 1978.

396 "Not my will . . .": Mt. 26:39.

399 Pierre Teilhard de Chardin, *The Divine Milieu: An Essay on the Interior Life*. (New York: Harper and Row Torchbooks, 1968).

4c . "A collective body . . .": Simone Weil, *Waiting for God*. (New York: Harper Colophon Books, 1973) p. 79

400 For the life of Dietrich Bonhoeffer, see Eberhard Bethge, *Dietrich Bonhoeffer* (New York, Harper & Row, 1970).

401 "And we do not . . .": Associated Press, "The First Black Saints—22 Africans Canonized," *New York Herald Tribune*, Oct. 19, 1964. p. 2.

401 a joint paper: "The One Mediator, The Saints, and Mary: Lutherans and Catholics in Dialogue." Final corrected draft to be published by Augsburg Press (Minneapolis) in 1991.

402 "friends in high places": *ibid.*, p. 143.

402 "The Catholic tradition holds . . .": *ibid.*, p. 136.

403 "unconsciously held . . .": Erich Heller, *The Disinherited Mind op. cit*, p. 263. For a discussion of the Catholic sensibility as Gothic, see Kenneth L. Woodward, "Religion, Art and the Gothic Sensibility," *Perspectives*, vol. ix, no. 1, January–February 1964, pp. 14–17.

403 stronger and more real than: for a study of emotional ties as "vital connections" based on biology, verifiable psychologically but sociologically malleable, see Arthur Kornhaber, M.D., and Kenneth L. Woodward, *Grandparents/Grandchildren: The Vital Connection* (Garden City, New York: Anchor Press/Doubleday, 1981).

403 "often shatters our . . .": Coleman, *op. cit.*, p. 211.

403 "is their power . . .": Coleman, *ibid.*, p. 220.

403 "a terrible beauty is born": William Butler Yeats, "Easter 1916," *The Collected Poems of W. B. Yeats* (New York: Macmillan, 1955), p. 178.

403 theologians rarely . . . discuss saints: Kieckhefer, *op. cit.*, p. 34.

404 "The great revolutions . . ." Heller, *op. cit.*, pp. 265–266.

404 "communities of memory . . .": Robert Bellah, Richard Marsden, William Sullivan, Ann Swindler, and Stephen Tipton, *Habits of the Heart* (Berkeley, California: University of California Press, 1985), pp. 152–153.

405 had achieved its apex . . .: see Teilhard de Chardin, *The Phenomenon of Man* (New York: Harper Torchbooks, 1959).

405 "I am all that is": Konstantin Kolenda, *Cosmic Religion: An Autobiography of the Universe* (Prospect Heights, Illinois: Waveland Press, 1989), p. 11. For a third position between Chardin and Kolenda, see Thomas Berry, *The Dream of the Earth* (San Francisco: Sierra Club Books, 1988).

405 "Saints invite us . . .": Coleman, *op. cit.*, p. 209.

406 "A new type of sanctity . . .": George A. Pinchas, ed., *The Simone Weil Reader.* (New York: David McKay Co, Inc., 1977), p. 114.

406 "harsh and dreadful love": Ellsberg, *By Little, op. cit.*, p. 264. The complete sentence, "Love in practive is a harsh and dreadful thing compared to love in dreams," was a favorite quote of Day's, and is taken from the words of Father Zosima in Fyodor Dostoyevski's *The Brothers Karamazov*.

APPENDIX

Since the Middle Ages, the canonization process has required the testimony of witnesses to the candidate's virtues or martyrdom. The following questions, typical of the genre, constitute the "Interrogatory" prepared by the Congregation for the Causes of Saints and employed by the American tribunals to elicit testimony on behalf of Mother Katharine Drexel of Philadelphia during the Apostolic (second) Process. She was beatified on November 20, 1988.

1. What is your name?

2. Have you read the Articles of Testimonial Proof of the Servant of God, Katharine Marie Drexel?

3. Do you have any other information to supply that is not contained in these Articles?

4. Have you any information concerning the early life of Katharine Drexel other than that which is supplied in the Articles? Please supply the information.

5. Do you have any knowledge, personal or otherwise, of evidence of a religious vocation on the part of Katharine Drexel? If so, kindly give this information.

6. What facts do you know concerning Katharine Drexel's formal vocation?

7. What facts do you know concerning the establishment of the Religious Congregation of the Sisters of the Blessed Sacrament and the part played in its establishment by Mother Katharine Drexel?

8. What spiritual devotions were the center of the spiritual life of the Sisters of the Blessed Sacrament?

9. When, how long, and how were you associated with Mother Katharine Drexel?

10. How often were you in contact with Mother Katharine personally?

11. What did you think of the administrative authority of Mother Katharine in handling the Sisters of the Institution?

12. Would you consider Mother Katharine Drexel just or too strict in her handling of the Sisters? What reasons do you have for these statements?

13. Do you consider that Mother Katharine Drexel gave the wisest directions in carrying out the work of the Institution? If not, why not?

14. What do you think of the relationship that existed between Mother Katharine Drexel and her sister, Mrs. Morrell? Please explain your answer.

15. Do you consider that Mother Katharine Drexel practiced well the virtues of Faith, Hope, and Charity? If not, where did she fail in the practice of a) Faith; b) Hope; c) Charity?

16. Do you consider that Katharine Drexel's life indicates that she was moved by a great love of neighbor in her activities?

17. What would you say of the methods used by Mother Katharine Drexel in treating a) the members of the Congregation; b) the sick members of the Congregation; c) the employees; d) children?

18. Do you know whether or not Mother Katharine Drexel sought guidance in making her decisions?

19. How did Mother Katharine Drexel accept the directions given to her by her superiors?

20. Would you consider Mother Katharine Drexel as prudent in handling the affairs of the Sisters of the Blessed Sacrament?

21. Did other people seek direction from Mother Katharine Drexel? If so, how often and why?

22. Was Mother Katharine Drexel concerned with the rights of others?

23. Do you think that she was too demanding of others? If so, give examples.

24. What do you think of the corrections given by Mother Katharine to the Sisters? Were they in accord with the problems? Please give examples.

25. How successful was Mother Katharine in maintaining the growth of the community in early days?

26. Do you feel that Mother Katharine exhibited courage in accepting hardships? If not, why not?

27. Did Mother Katharine show concern for the hardships of others? If not, please give examples.

28. Was Mother Katharine inclined to be a self-controlled person in her actions and works? If not, please give examples of lack of self-control.

29. Did Mother Katharine seek praise of humans or was she always humble in her actions? Please explain her actions.

30. What was Mother Katharine's attitude toward poverty? What example did she give to members of her community that would lead them to have an appreciation of the true spirit of poverty?

31. Did Mother Katharine preserve the spirit of chastity?

32. How did Mother Katharine train the members of her community in the appreciation of the true spirit of chastity?

33. Did Mother Katharine use excessive means to safeguard the chastity of others?

34. How did Mother Katharine demonstrate her true spirit of obedience?

35. Was Mother Katharine always obedient to various Church authorities to whom she was subject?

36. How did Mother Katharine accept the commands given by these authorities?

37. Do you consider that Mother Katharine always exhibited a true appreciation of the meaning of obedience? If not, why not?

38. What was Mother Katharine's attitude on the problem of segregation? How did she attack this problem?

39. How did Mother Katharine spend the last years of her life?

40. If you were associated with Mother Katharine during the time of her sufferings, did she accept them in such a way as to indicate her willingness to suffer? If not, explain your answer.

41. Did the Sisters who were in charge of Mother Katharine during her illness ever complain about this task? If so, what were their complaints?

42. Do you know anything about the death of Mother Katharine Drexel?

43. Do you think her funeral was indicative as to her being accepted as a holy and saintly woman? If not, please explain your answer.

44. Did you consider Mother Katharine to have a reputation for saintliness during her lifetime? If not, please explain your answer.

45. How many persons considered Mother Katharine to be saintly during her lifetime?

46. How many persons associated with Mother Katharine questioned her reputation for holiness? Why did they question this reputation?

47. Following her death, did Mother Katharine's reputation for sanctity grow? Please explain your answer.

48. Following her death, has any person sought Katharine Drexel's intercession for favors?

49. Do you know if any favors have been granted through the intercession of Mother Katharine since her death?

50. Would you consider that today Mother Katharine has a wide-spread reputation for sanctity?

51. Do you today consider Mother Katharine a saintly person? If not, why not?

SELECTED BIBLIOGRAPHY

DOCUMENTS

Canonizationis Servae Dei Marcelli Callo (1921–1945) Positio Super Martyrio et Super virtutibus. Rome: Congregatio pro Causis Sanctorum, 1986.

Positio for the Canonization Process of the Servant of God Cornelia Connelly (née Peacock) 1809–1879. 4 vols. Rome: Sacred Congregation for the Causes of Saints, 1983, 1987.

Beatificationis et Canonizationis Servae Dei Alexandrina Marie da Costa Positio Super Scriptus. Rome: Sacra Congregatio pro Causis Sanctorum, 1977.

Canonizationis Servae Dei Catherinae Mariae Drexel (1858–1955). Vol. I: *Expositio et Documenta.* Vol. II: *Summarium Depositionum Testium.* Vol. III: *Relatio Relatoris et Informatio.* Rome: Congregatio pro Causis Sanctorum, 1986.

Canonizationis Beatae Philippine Duchesne (1769–1852) Positio Super Miraculo. Rome: Congregatio pro Causis Sanctorum, 1987.

Canonizationis Beatae Philippine Duchesne (1769–1852) Relatio et Vota Congressus Peculiaris Super Miro. Rome: Congregatio pro Causis Sanctorum, 1987.

Canonizationis Ven. Servi Dei Joseph Gerard (1831–1914) Positio Super Miraculo. Rome: Congregatio pro Causis Sanctorum, 1987.

Canonizationis Beati Ioannis Macias, O.P. (1585–1645), Positio Super Miraculo. Rome: Sacra Congregatio pro Causis Sanctorum, 1974.

Canonizationis Servi Dei Papae IX Novissima Positio Super Virtutibus. Rome: Sacra Congregatio pro Causis Sanctorum, 1984.

Canonizationis Ven. Servi Dei Juniperi Serra (1713–1784) Positio Super Miraculo. Rome: Congregatio pro Causis Sanctorum, 1987.

Canonizationis Ven. Servi Dei Juniperi Serra (1713–1784) Relatio et Vota Congressus Peculiaris Super Miro. Rome: Congregatio pro Causis Sanctorum, 1987.

Commissione di Studio Istituita dalla Congregazione per le Cause dei Santi, *A Proposito di Maria Goretti, Santità E Canonizzazioni.* Vatican City: Libreria Editrice Vaticana, 1985.

Diocesan Process for the Beatification of Edith Stein. Cologne, 1962.

New Laws for the Causes of the Saints. trans. by Rev. Robert J. Sarno. Rome: Sacred Congregation for the Causes of Saints, 1983.

Veraja, Fabijan. *Commentary on the New Legislation for the Causes of Saints.* Rome, 1983.

BOOKS

Abbott, Walter M. *The Documents of Vatican II.* New York: America Press, 1966.

Athanasius. *The Life of Antony and the Letter to Marcellinus. The Classics of Western Spirituality.* New York: Paulist Press, 1980.

Aubert, Roger. *The Church in a Secularized Society.* Vol. 5 of *The Christian Centuries.* New York: Paulist Press, 1978.

Augustine, Saint. *The City of God.* New York: Random House, 1950.

Barwig, Regis N. *More Than a Prophet: Day-by-Day with Pius IX.* Altadena, California: The Benzinger Sisters Publishers, 1978.

Bainton, Roland H. *Here I Stand: A Life of Martin Luther.* New York: New American Library, 1950.

Bausch,William J. *Pilgrim Church: A Popular History of Catholic Christianity.* Mystic, Connecticut: Twenty-Third Publications, 1980.

Bellah, Robert, Richard Marsden, William Sullivan, Ann Swindler and Stephen Tipton. *Habits of the Heart.* Berkeley, California: University of California Press, 1985.

Bensman, Joseph and Robert Lilienfeld. *Craft and Consciousness: Occupational Technique and the Development of World Images.* New York: John Wiley & Sons, 1973.

Berman, Harold J. *Law and Revolution: The Formation of the Western Legal Tradition.* Cambridge, Mass.: Harvard University Press, 1983.

Berry, Thomas. *The Dream of the Earth.* San Francisco: Sierra Club Books, 1988.

Bethge, Eberhard. *Dietrich Bonhoeffer.* New York: Harper & Row, 1970.

Bettazzi. Luigi. *Una Chiesa per tutti.* Rome: Editrice A.V.E., 1971.

Bibliotheca Sanctorum. Rome: Istituto Giovanni XXIII nella Pontifica Universita Lateranese.

Blehl, Vincent Ferrer, S. J., and Francis X. Connolly, eds. *Newman's Apologia: A Classic Reconsidered.* New York: Harcourt, Brace & World, 1964.

Bouyer, Louis, C.O. *Newman's Vision of Faith: A Theology for Times of General Apostasy.* San Francisco: Ignatius Press, 1986.

———. *Newman: His Life and Spirituality.* trans. by J. Louis May. New York: P. Kennedy, 1958.

Braudy, Leo. *The Frenzy of Renown: Fame and Its History*. New York: Oxford University Press, 1983.

Brockman, James R., S. J. *The Word Remains: A Life of Oscar Romero*. New York: Orbis, 1983.

————. *Romero: A Life*. Maryknoll, New York: Orbis Books, 1989.

Brown, Peter. *The Cult of the Saints: Its Rise and Function in Latin Christianity*. Chicago: University of Chicago Press, 1982.

————. *The Body and Society: Men, Women, and Sexual Renunciation in Early Christianity*. New York: Columbia University Press, 1988.

Brunatto, Emanuele. *Padre Pio*. Geneva: AID, 1963.

Burtchaell, James Tunstead, C.S.C. *The Giving and Taking of Life: Essays Ethical*. Notre Dame, Indiana: University of Notre Dame Press, 1989.

Chadwick, Owen. *Britain and the Vatican during the Second World War*. New York: Cambridge University Press, 1987.

Cameron, J. M. *John Henry Newman*. London: Longmans, Green & Co., 1956.

————. *Nuclear Catholics and Other Essays*. Grand Rapids, Michigan: William B. Eerdmans Publishing Company, 1989.

Clarke, John, O.C.D., trans. *Story of a Soul: The Autobiography of St. Thérèse of Lisieux. A New Translation from the Original Manuscripts*. Washington, D.C.: ICS Publications, 1976.

Clarkson, John F., et al., trans. *The Church Teaches: Documents of the Church in English Translation*. Rockford, Illinois: TAN, 1973.

Coles, Robert. *Dorothy Day: A Radical Devotion*. Reading, Massachusetts: Addison-Wesley, 1987.

Congregatio Pro Causis Sanctorum. *Index ac Status Causarum*. Rome: Tipografia Guerra, 1985.

————. *Index ac Status Causarum*. Citta del Vaticano, 1988.

Conway, J. S. *The Nazi Persecution of the Churches 1933–45*. New York: Basic Books, 1968.

Coppa, Frank J. *Pope Pius IX: Crusader in a Secular Age*. Boston: Twayne Publishers, 1979.

Cruz, Joan Carroll. *The Incorruptibles*. Rockford, Illinois: TAN, 1977.

Cunningham, Lawrence S. *The Meaning of Saints*. San Francisco: Harper & Row, 1980.

Danemarie, Jeanne. *The Mystery of Stigmata: From Catherine Emmerich to Theresa Neumann*. Trans. by Warre B. Wells. London: Burns, Oates & Washbourne Ltd, 1934.

Daniel-Rops, Henri. *The Church of Apostles and Martyrs*. New York: E. P. Dutton. 1960.

Dawidowicz, Lucy S. *The War Against the Jews, 1933–1945*. New York: Holt, Rinehart and Winston, 1975.

Day, Dorothy. *Loaves and Fishes*. New York: Harper & Row, 1963.

————. *The Long Loneliness*. New York: Harper & Brothers, 1952.

Delehaye, Hippolyte, S. J. *The Legends of the Saints*. New York: Fordham University Press, 1962.

————. *Les Origines du culte des martyrs*. Brussels: Bureaux de la Société des Bollandistes, 1912.

————. *The Work of the Bollandists*. Princeton: Princeton University Press, 1922.

Delooz, Pierre. *Sociologie et canonisations*. Liège: Faculté de Droit, 1969.

DeNevi, Don and Noel Francis Moholy. *Junípero Serra: The Illustrated Story of the Franciscan Founder of California's Missions*. San Francisco: Harper & Row, 1985.

Dessain, C. S. *The Spirituality of John Henry Newman*. Minneapolis: Winston Press, 1977.

Dessain, C. Stephen, et al., eds. *John Henry Newman, Letters and Diaries*, vol. II. Oxford, England: Clarendon Press, 1976.

Duffy, Cornelia Consuela Marie, S.B.S. *Katharine Drexel: A Biography*. Cornwells Heights, Pennsylvania: Mother Katharine Drexel Guild, 1966.

Dunne, John S. *The Way of All the Earth*. New York: Macmillan, 1972.

Duquoc, Christian, and Casiano Floristan, eds. *Models of Holiness*. Concilium *129*. New York: The Seabury Press, 1979.

Egan, Eileen. *Such a Vision of the Street: Mother Teresa—the Spirit and the Work*. New York: Doubleday, 1986.

Egan, Harvey D., S. J. *Christian Mysticism: The Future of a Tradition*. New York: Pueblo Publishing Company, 1984.

Ellis, Msgr. John Tracy. *Perspectives in American Catholicism*. Baltimore: Helicon, 1963.

Ellsberg, Robert, ed. *By Little and By Little: The Selected Writings of Dorothy Day*. New York: Alfred A. Knopf, 1983.

Emert, Dr. Joyce R., O.C.D.S. *Louis Martin: Father of a Saint*. Staten Island, New York: Alba House, 1983.

Emmerich, Anne Catherine. *The Dolorous Passion of Our Lord Jesus Christ*. Rockford, Illinois: TAN, 1983.

Escrivá de Balaguer, Josemaría. *The Way*. Manila: Sinag-Tala Publishers, 1982.

Falconi, Carolo. *Pope John and the Ecumenical Council*. Cleveland: The World Publishing Company, 1964.

———. *The Silence of Pius XII*. Boston: Little, Brown and Company, 1965.

Farmer, David Hugh. *The Oxford Dictionary of Saints*. Oxford, England: Clarendon Press, 1978.

Feiner, Johannes, and Lukas Vischer. *The Catechism*. New York: The Seabury Press, 1975.

Flumeri, Gerardo Di, O.F.M. *Padre Pio of Pietrelcina: Acts of the First Congress of Studies on Padre Pio's Spirituality*. San Giovanni Rotondo, Italy: Edizioni "Padre Pio da Pietrelcina," 1978.

Forell, George, and James F. McCue. *Confessing One Faith: A Joint Commentary on the Augsburg Confession by Lutheran and Catholic Theologians*. Minneapolis: Augsburg Publishing House, 1982.

Fogarty, Gerald P., S.J. *American Catholic Biblical Scholarship: A History from the Early Republic to Vatican II*. San Francisco: Harper & Row, 1989.

———. *The Vatican and the American Hierarchy from 1870 to 1965*. Stuttgart, Germany: Anton Hiersemann, 1982.

Forest, Jim. *Love Is the Measure: A Biography of Dorothy Day*. New York: Paulist Press, 1986.

Foy, Felician A., O.F.M., ed. *Catholic Almanac, 1985*. Huntington, Indiana: Our Sunday Visitor, 1984.

Frend, W. H. C. *Martyrdom and Persecution in the Early Church*. Garden City, New York: Doubleday Anchor, 1967.

————. *The Rise of Christianity*. Philadelphia: Fortress Press, 1984.

Furlong, Monica. *Thérèse of Lisieux*. New York: Pantheon, 1987.

Gandhi, Mohandas. *An Autobiography: The Story of My Experiments with Truth*. Translated by Mahadev Desai. Boston: Beacon Press, 1968.

Garrigou-Lagrange, R., O.P. *Christian Perfection and Contemplation*. St. Louis: B. Herder Book Company, 1937.

Geary, Patrick J. *Furta Sacra: The Theft of Relics in the Middle Ages*. Princeton, New Jersey: Princeton University Press, 1978.

Gettleman, Marvin, Patrick Lacefield, Louis Menashe, David Mermelstein, and Ronald Radosh, eds. *El Salvador: Central America in the New Cold War*. New York: Grove Press, 1981.

Gondrand, Francois. *At God's Pace*. New Rochelle, New York: Scepter Press, 1989.

Goodspeed, Edgar J. *The Apostolic Fathers: An American Translation*. New York: Harper & Brothers, 1950.

Graef, Hilda. *God and Myself: The Spirituality of John Henry Newman*. New York: Hawthorne Books, 1968.

————. *The Way of the Mystics*. Westminster, Maryland: The Newman Bookshop, 1948.

Granfield, Patrick. *The Limits of the Papacy*. New York: Crossroad, 1987.

Griffin, John R. *Newman: A Bibliography of Secondary Studies*. Front Royal, Virginia: Christendom College Press, 1980.

Guerri, Girodano Bruno. *Povera santa, povero assassino: La Vera storia di Maria Goretti*. Roma: Arnoldo Mondadori, 1985.

Hales, E. E. Y. *Pio Nono*. New York: P.J. Kenedy & Sons, 1954.

————. *Pope John and His Revolution*. London: Eyre & Spottiswoode, 1965.

————. *Revolution and Papacy*. Notre Dame, Indiana: University of Notre Dame Press, 1966.

Hanley, Boniface, O.F.M. *Maximilian Kolbe: No Greater Love*. Notre Dame, Indiana: Ave Maria Press, 1982.

Hansen, Eric O. *The Catholic Church in World Politics*. Princeton, New Jersey: Princeton University Press, 1987.

Hawley, John Stratton, ed. *Saints and Virtues*. Berkeley: University of California Press, 1987.

Hebblethwaite, Peter. *Pope John XXIII: Shepherd of the Modern World*. Garden City, New York: Doubleday, 1984.

Heffernan, Thomas J. *Sacred Biography: Saints and Their Biographers in the Middle Ages*. New York: Oxford University Press, 1988.

Heller, Eric. *The Disinherited Mind*. New York: Meridian Books, 1959.

Hentoff, Nat. *John Cardinal O'Connor: At the Storm Center of a Changing American Catholic Church*. New York: Charles Scribner's Sons, 1988.

Hoare, F. R., trans. and ed. *The Western Fathers*. New York: Sheed and Ward, 1954.

Hochhuth, Rolf. *The Deputy*. Translated by Richard and Clara Winston. New York: Grove Press, 1964.

Holmes, J. Derek. *The Papacy in the Modern World*. New York: Crossroad, 1981.

Houppert, Joseph W., ed. *John Henry Newman*. St. Louis: B. Herder Book Company, no date.

Huizinga, J. *The Waning of the Middle Ages: A Study of the Forms of Life, Thought and Art in France and the Netherlands in the Dawn of the Renaissance.* Garden City, New York: Doubleday Anchor, 1954.

Imbert-Gourbeyre, Dr. Antoine. *La Stigmatisation, L'extase divine et les miracles de Lourdes.* Paris: Clermont-Ferrand, 1895.

Johnson, Paul. *Pope John XXIII.* Boston: Little, Brown and Company, 1974.

Johnston, Francis. *Alexandrina: The Agony and the Glory.* Rockford, Illinois: TAN, 1979.

Katz, Steven T., ed. *Mysticism and Religious Traditions.* New York: Oxford University Press, 1983.

Kelly, J. N. D. *The Oxford Dictionary of Popes.* New York: Oxford University Press, 1986.

Kemp, Eric Waldram. *Canonization in the Western Church.* London: Oxford University Press, 1948.

Kerr, Ian. *John Henry Newman: A Biography.* Oxford: Clarendon, 1988.

Kieckhefer, Richard. *Unquiet Souls: Fourteenth-Century Saints and Their Religious Milieu.* Chicago: University of Chicago Press, 1987.

Kieckhefer, Richard and George D. Bond, eds. *Sainthood: Its Manifestations in World Religions.* Berkeley: University of California Press, 1988.

Klee, Howard Clark. *Miracle in the Early Christian World: A Study in Sociohistorical Method.* New Haven: Yale University Press, 1983.

Knowles, David. *Great Historical Enterprises.* London: Thomas Nelson and Sons Ltd, 1963.

————. *The Historian and Character.* Cambridge: University Press, 1963.

Koeppel, Josephine, O.C.D. *Edith Stein: The Intellectual Mystic.* Wilmington, Delaware: Michael Glazier, 1990.

Kolenda, Konstantin. *Cosmic Religion: An Autobiography of the Universe.* Prospect Heights, Illinois: Waveland Press, 1989.

Kornhaber, Arthur, and Kenneth Woodward. *Grandparents/Grandchildren: The Vital Connection.* Garden City, New York: Doubleday Anchor, 1981.

Kselman, Thomas, *Miracles and Prophecies in Nineteenth-Century France.* New Brunswick, New Jersey: Rutgers University Press, 1983.

Kung, Hans. *Infallible? An Inquiry.* Garden City, New York: Doubleday, 1971.

Lambertini, Prosper. *De servorum Dei beatificatione et beatorum canonizatione.* 5 vols. Bologna, Italy, 1734–1738.

————. *Heroic Virtue: A Portion of the Treatise of Benedict XIV on the Beautification and Canonization of the Servants of God.* 3 vols. London: Thomas Richardson and Son, 1851.

Lercaro, Giacomo, and Gabriele DeRosa. *John XXII: Simpleton or Saint?* Chicago: Franciscan Herald Press, 1965.

Lernoux, Penny. *The People of God: The Struggle for World Catholicism.* New York: Viking, 1989.

Le Tourneau, Dominique. *What Is Opus Dei?* Dublin: The Mercier Press, 1987.

Leuven, Romaeus. O.C.D. *Heil im Unheil. Edith Steins Werke,* vol. X. Freiburg: Herder, 1983.

MacIntyre, Alystair. *After Virtue.* Notre Dame: University of Notre Dame Press, 1982.

Macken, Canon. *The Canonization of Saints*. Dublin: M. H. Hill and Sons, 1910.

Manelli, P. Stefano M. *Short Story of a Victim: Theresa Musco (1943–1976)*. Translated by Johanna Pearson. S. Mari, Italy: Editrice "Terzo Millennio," 1984.

Martin, Brian. *John Henry Newman: His Life and Work*. Mahwah, New Jersey: Paulist Press, 1982.

Martina, Giacomo, S.J. *Pio IX (1846–1850)*. *Miscellanea Historiae Pontificiae*, vol. 38. Rome: Editrice Pontificia Università Gregoriana, 1974.

———. *Pio IX (1851–1866)*. *Miscellanea Historiae Pontificiae*, vol. 51. Rome: Editrice Pontificia Università Gregoriana, 1986.

McClendon, James Wm., Jr. *Biography as Theology: How Life Stories Can Remake Today's Theology*. Nashville: Abignon Press, 1974.

McDonnell, Colleen, and Bernard Long. *Heaven: A History*. New Haven: Yale University Press, 1989.

McNamara, Jo Ann. *New Song: Celibate Women in the First Three Christian Centuries*. New York: The Institute for Research in History and the Haworth Press, 1983.

Metz, Johannes-Baptist, and Edward Schillebeeckx, eds. *Martyrdom Today*. *Concillium 163*. New York: The Seabury Press, March 1983.

Miles, Margaret. *Carnal Knowing: Female Nakedness and Religious Meaning in the Christian West*. Boston: Beacon Press, 1989.

Miller, William D. *All Is Grace: The Spirituality of Dorothy Day*. New York: Doubleday, 1987.

———. *Dorothy Day: A Biography*. San Francisco: Harper & Row, 1982.

Molinari, Paul, S.J. *Saints: Their Place in the Church*. New York: Sheed and Ward, 1965.

Mooney, Catherine M., R.S.C.J. *Philippine Duchesne: A Woman with the Poor*. New York: Paulist Press, 1990.

Morley, John F. *Vatican Diplomacy and the Jews during the Holocaust 1939–1943*. New York: KTAV Publishing House, 1980.

Murphy, Francis X., C.S.S.R. *The Papacy Today: The Last 80 Years of the Catholic Church from the Perspective of the Papacy*. New York: Macmillan, 1981.

Musurillo, Herbert, trans. *The Acts of the Christian Martyrs*. Oxford, England: Clarendon Press, 1972.

Newman, John Henry. *Apologia pro vita sua*. Garden City, New York: Doubleday, 1956.

———. *Grammar of Assent*. *Newman's Works*. London: Longmans, Green, 1903.

———. *The Idea of a University*. *Newman's Works*. London: Longmans, Green, 1903.

———. *Loss and Gain: The Story of a Convert*. *Newman's Works*. London: Longmans, Green, 1903.

———. *Verses on Various Occasions*. *Newman's Works*. London: Longmans, Green, 1903.

Nims, John Frederick. *A Local Habitation: Essays on Poetry*. Ann Arbor: University of Michigan Press, 1985.

Nims, John Frederick, trans. *The Poems of St. John of the Cross*, third edition. Chicago: University of Chicago Press, 1979.

Noonan, John T., Jr. *Power to Dissolve: Lawyers and Marriages in the Courts of the Roman Curia.* Cambridge, Massachusetts: Belknap Press of Harvard University Press, 1972.

O'Gara, Margaret. *Triumph in Defeat: Infallibility, Vatican I and the French Minority Bishops.* Washington, D.C.: Catholic University of America, 1988.

Packard, Jerrold M. *Peter's Kingdom: Inside the Papal City.* New York: Charles Scribner's Sons, 1985.

Pater, Thomas, A.B., S.T.L. *Miraculous Abstinence: A Study of One of the Extraordinary Mystical Phenomena.* Washington, D.C.: Catholic University of America Press. 1946.

Pinchas, George A., ed. *The Simone Weil Reader.* New York: David McKay Company, 1977.

The Pontifical Council for the Family. *Marriage and Family: Experiencing the Church's Teaching in Married Life.* San Francisco: Ignatius Press, 1987.

Poulain, Augustin, S.J. *The Graces of Interior Prayer.* Westminster, Vermont: Celtic Cross books, 1978.

Purcell, Mary. *Matt Talbot and His Times.* Dublin: C. Goodliffe Neale, 1976.

Rahner, Karl, S.J. *The Practice of Faith: A Handbook of Contemporary Spirituality.* New York: Crossroad, 1983.

Reames, Sherry L. *The Legenda Aurea: A Reexamination of Its Paradoxical History.* Madison, Wisconson: University of Wisconsin Press, 1985.

Reardon, John, Robert L. Stewart and Anne Buckley, eds. *This Grace Filled Moment.* New York: Rosemont Press, 1984.

Renata de Spiritu Sancto, O.C.D. *Edith Stein.* Translated by Cecily Hastings and Donald Nicoll. New York: Sheed and Ward, 1952.

Rhodes, Anthony. *The Power of Rome in the Twentieth Century.* New York: Franklin Watts, 1983.

––––––. *The Vatican in the Age of the Dictators (1922–1945).* New York: Holt, Rinehart & Winston, 1973.

Romero, Oscar. *Voice of the Voiceless: The Four Pastoral Letters and Other Statements.* Translated by Michael Walsh. Introductory essays by Jon Sobrino and Ignacio Martin-Baro. Maryknoll, New York: Orbis, 1985.

––––––. *The Violence of Love: The Pastoral Wisdom of Archbishop Oscar Romero.* Translated and compiled by James R. Brockman, S.J. San Francisco: Harper & Row, 1988.

Ruffin, C. Bernard. *Padre Pio: The True Story.* Huntington, Indiana: Our Sunday Visitor, 1982.

Ryan, Alvan S. *Newman and Glastone: The Vatican Decrees.* Introduction by Alvan S. Ryan. Notre Dame, Indiana: University of Notre Dame Press, 1962.

Sarno, Rev. Msgr. Robert J. *Diocesan Inquiries Required by the Legislator in the New Legislation for the Causes of Saints.* Dissertatio ad doctoratum in facultate juris canonici pontificae universitas gregorianae. Rome: Tipografia Guerra, 1988.

Schillebeeckx, E., O.P. *God: The Future of Man.* Translated by N. D. Smith. New York: Sheed and Ward, 1968.

Schlafka, Jakob. *Edith Stein: Documents Concerning Her Life and Death.* Translated by Susanne M. Batzdorff. New York: Edith Stein Guild, 1984.

Schmöger, Carl E. *The Life of Anne Catherine Emmerich.* 2 vols. Reprinted from the English edition of 1885. Rockford, Illinois: TAN, 1983.

————. *The Lowly Life and Bitter Passion of Our Lord Jesus Christ and His Blessed Mother, Together with the Mysteries of the Old Testament from the Visions of Venerable Anne Catherine Emmerich as Recorded in the Journal of Clement Brentano.* Translated from the fourth German edition, 1914. New York: The Sentinel Press, 1946.

Schweitzer, Albert. *The Quest for the Historical Jesus.* New York: Macmillan, 1968.

Sherman, James Edward, A.B., S.T.D. *The Nature of Martyrdom: A Dogmatic and Moral Analysis According to the Teaching of St. Thomas Aquinas.* Paterson, New Jersey: St. Anthony Guild Press, 1942.

Stein, Edith. *Life in a Jewish Family 1891–1916: An Autobiography.* Collected Works of Edith Stein, vol. 1. Translated by Josephine Koeppel, O.C.D. Washington, D.C.: I.C.S. Publications, 1986.

————. *Selbstbildnis in Briefen. Edith Steins Werke.* Freiburg, West Germany: Herder, 1977.

Sobrino, Jon. *Spirituality of Liberation: Toward Political Holiness.* Maryknoll, New York: Orbis Books, 1988.

Sugg, Joyce, ed. *A Packet of Letters: A Selection from the Correspondence of John Henry Newman.* Oxford, England: Clarendon Press, 1983.

Sullivan, Francis A., S.J. *Magisterium: Teaching Authority in the Catholic Church.* Mahwah, New Jersey: Paulist Press, 1983.

Teilhard de Chardin, Pierre. *The Phenomenon of Man.* New York: Harper Torchbooks, 1959.

————. *The Divine Milieu.* New York: Harper Torchbooks, 1968.

Treece, Patricia. *Man for Others: Maximilian Kolbe, Saint of Auschwitz in the Words of Those Who Knew Him.* San Francisco: Harper & Row, 1982.

————. *The Sanctified Body.* New York: Doubleday, 1989.

Trevor, Meriol. *Newman's Journey.* Huntington, Indiana: Our Sunday Visitor, 1985.

Turner, Victor, and Edith Turner. *Image and Pilgrimage in Christian Culture.* New York: Columbia University Press, 1978.

Underhill, Evelyn. *Mysticism.* New York: New American Library, 1974.

————. *The Mystics of the Church.* Wilton, Connecticut: Morehouse-Barlow, 1925.

Veyne, Paul, ed. *A History of Private Life I: From Pagan Rome to Byzantium.* Cambridge: Belknap Press of Harvard University Press, 1987.

Voragine, Jacobus de. *The Golden Legend.* Translated and adapted from the Latin by Granger Ryan and Helmut Riperger. London: Longmans, Green, 1941.

Vouchez, Andre. *La Sainteté en Occident aux derniers siècles du moyen âge, d'après les procès de canonisation et les documents hagiographiques.* Rome: École Française de Rome, 1981.

Walsh, Michael. *Opus Dei: An Investigation into the Secret Society Struggling for Power within the Roman Catholic Church.* London: Grafton Books, 1989.

Ward, Wilfred. *The Life of John Henry Cardinal Newman.* London: Longmans, Green, 1912.

Weisheipl, James A., O.P. *Friar Thomas D'Aquino: His Life, Thought and Works.* New York: Doubleday, 1974.

Williams, George Hunston. *The Mind of John Paul II: Origins of His Thought and Action.* New York: The Seabury Press, 1981.

Wilson, Stephen, ed. *Saints and their Cults: Studies in Religious Sociology, Folklore and History.* Cambridge: Cambridge University Press, 1983.

Wright, Cardinal John J. *The Saints Always Belong to the Present.* San Francisco: Ignatius Press, 1985.

Yeats, William Butler. *The Collected Poems of W. B. Yeats.* New York: Macmillan, 1955.

Zahn, Gordon. *German Catholics and Hitler's War.* Notre Dame, Indiana: University of Notre Dame Press, 1989.

————. *In Solitary Witness: The Life and Death of Franz Jägerstatter.* Springfield, Illinois: Templegate Publishers, 1964.

Zeno, Dr., O.F.M. Cap. *John Henry Newman: His Inner Life.* San Francisco: Ignatius Press, 1987.

Zizola, Giancarlo. *The Utopia of Pope John XXIII.* Maryknoll, New York: Orbis Books, 1978.

ARTICLES

Associated Press. "The First Black Saints—22 Africans Canonized." *New York Herald Tribune,* October 19, 1964, p. 1.

Baaden, James. "A Question of Martyrdom." *The Tablet,* January 31, 1987, p. 108.

Blehl, Vincent Ferrer, "Prelude to the Making of a Saint." *America,* vol. 160. no. 9, March 11, 1989, pp. 213–16.

Chiovaro, P. "Relics." *New Catholic Encyclopedia,* vol. 12. New York: McGraw-Hill, 1967, pp. 234–240.

Crossette, Barbara. "Sainthood for 117 Outrages Vietnam." *The New York Times,* May 29, 1988, p. 5.

Deak, Istvan. "The Incomprehensible Holocaust." *The New York Review of Books,* vol. 36, no. 14., September 28, 1989, pp. 63–72.

Dimler, Eleni. "Priest-Journalist, Victim of Nazis, Named 'Blessed' by Pope." *Religious News Service,* dispatch from Vatican City, November 4, 1985, p. 12.

"Edith Stein, Jewish Catholic Martyr." *Carmelite Studies 4* (Washington, D.C.: ICS Publications, 1987), pp. 310–327.

Editorial on the death of John Henry Newman. *London Times,* August 12, 1890.

Eszer, Ambrose. "Miracoli ed altri segni divini. Considerazioni dommatico-storiche con speciale riferimento alle cause dei santi," *Studi in onore del Card. Pietro Palazzini.* Pisa: Giardini Editori e Stampoatori, 1987.

Fehren, Fr. Henry. "Let's Canonize Dorothy Day." *Salt,* September 1983, pp. 4–5.

Fernando of Riese Pio X, O.F.M. Cap. "Padre Pio's Story." *The Voice of Padre Pio,* vol. 18, no. 5, 1988, pp. 5–7.

Gellese, Liz Roman. "American Saint's Cause Took Century of Work, Millions in Donations." *The Wall Street Journal,* June 25, 1975, p. 1.

Green, A. E. "Canonization of Saints (Theological Aspect)." *New Catholic Encyclopedia*, vol. 3. New York: McGraw-Hill, 1967, pp. 59–61.

"Guidance of Newman." *The Tablet*, June 21, 1986, pp. 650–51.

Hebblethwaite, Peter. "Curia Raps Scholar on Martyr's Fate." *The National Catholic Reporter*, March 20, 1987, p. 1.

———. "Pope Cites Stein's Jewish Roots." *National Catholic Reporter*, May 15, 1987, p. 24.

———. "Pope John Paul Canonizing Saints at Record Pace." *National Catholic Reporter*, May 22, 1987, p. 7.

"He Died a Martyr of Love, Giving His Life for Another: Canonization of Maximilian Maria Kolbe." *L'Osservatore Romano*, no. 42, October 18, 1982, p. 1.

"Homily During Mass of Beatification: We Present the New Blessed as Lay Faithful, a Sign of the Church of the Third Millennium." *L'Osservatore Romano*, Weekly Edition, no. 41, October 12, 1987, p. 19.

Interview with Jan Nota, S.J. *Schwäbisches Tageblatt* (Tübingen), August 11, 1987.

John Paul II, Pope. "Homily at the Beatification of Edith Stein (Friday, May 1, 1987, 10 A.M.)," *Carmelite Studies 4*. Washington, D.C.: ICS Publications, 1987, pp. 298–306.

Juvenaly, Metropolitan of Krutitsy and Kolomna. "The Canonization of Saints in the Russian Orthodox Church," presented to and published by the Local Council of the Russian Orthodox Church, held June 6–9, 1988, in the U.S.S.R. in connection with the celebration of the Millennium of the Baptism of Russia (mimeographed).

Martina, G. "Justified Reservations on a Recent Work." *L'Osservatore Romano*, Weekly Edition, March 9, 1978.

"Miracles are Messages and Signs of a God Who Is Love." *L'Osservatore Romano*, Weekly Edition, nos. 51–52, December 19–26, 1988, p. 16.

Molinari, Paul (unsigned). "La moltiplicazione del riso per i poveri." *Il miracolo: Realtá o suggestione?: Rassegna di fatti straordinari nel cinquantennio 1920–1970*. Rome: Città Nuova Editrice, 1981, pp. 133–41.

Molinari, Paul. "Canonization (History and Procedure)" *The New Catholic Encyclopedia*, vol. 3. New York: McGraw-Hill, 1967, pp. 55–59.

———. "Martyrdom: Love's Highest Mark and Perfect Conformity to Christ." *The Way*, Winter, 1980, pp. 14–24.

———. "Obserevationes aliquot circa miraculorum munus et necessitatem in causis beatificationis et canonizationis." *Periodica de re morali canonica liturgica*, no. 63, 1974, pp. 341–84.

———. "Saints and Miracles." *The Way*, October 1978.

———. "The Theology of Canonization." *The Way*, Winter, 1980, pp. 7–13.

Molinari, Paul, and Peter Gumpel. "Heroic Virtue: The Splendor of Holiness." *The Way*, Winter, 1980, pp. 25–34.

Murphy, F. X. "Pope John XXIII." *Encyclopedia of Religion*, vol. 8. New York: Macmillan, 1988, pp. 107–110.

O'Connor, Cardinal John J. "A Good Question." *Catholic New York*, January 3, 1985, p. 12.

O'Malley, Frank. "The Thinker in the Church: The Spirit of Newman." *The Review of Politics*, vol. 21, no. 1, January 1959, pp. 5–23.

"The One Mediator, The Saints, and Mary: Lutherans and Catholics in Dialogue." Final corrected draft to be published by Augsburg Books, Minneapolis 1991.

Paci, Stefano M. and Paolo Biondi. "Interview with Giuseppe Siri." *30 Days*, June 1988, pp. 70–74.

Pinsky, Mark I. "Nun's 1960 Recovery May Answer Prayers for Serra Sainthood." *Los Angeles Times*, August 4, 1987, p. 3.

"Pope Beatifies Five Religious in Vatican Ceremonies." *L'Osservatore Romano*, Weekly Edition, no. 17, April 24, 1989, p. 12.

Porsi. Luigi. "Cause di canonizzazione e procedura nella cost. apost. 'Divinus perfectionis Magister': Considerazioni e valutazioni." *Monitor Ecclesiasticus* CX, 1985, pp. 365–400.

"Promulgation of Degrees." *L'Osservatore Romano*, Weekly Edition, no. 16, April 16, 1990, p. 2.

Ricci, Marina. "A Few False Facts and . . . the Polemics Rage." *30 Days*, year 2, no. 5, May 1989, pp. 16–18.

———. "I Never Said There Are Too Many," interview with Cardinal Joseph Ratzinger. *30 Days*, May 1989, pp. 18–20.

Riding, Alan. "Vatican 'Saint Factory': Is It Working Too Hard?" *The New York Times*, April 15, 1989, p. 4.

Thavis, John. "Booming Saint-Making Industry Might be Slowing." *National Catholic News Service*, March 31, 1989, p. 16.

"Three Martyrs Beatified in St. Peter's Basilica." *L'Osservatore Romano*, Weekly Edition, no. 40, October 5, 1987, p. 20.

Tivnan, Edward. "A New Yorker Up for Sainthood: Admirers of Terence Cardinal Cooke Start a Campaign That Could Take Centuries." *The New York Times Magazine*, November 30, 1986, pp. 46–71.

"Tribute to a Martyr: Archbishop Romero Praised as a Pastor as Well as a Prophet." *Catholic New York*, April 12, 1990, p. 33.

Truhlar, K. V. "Virtue, Heroic." *New Catholic Encyclopedia*, vol. 14. New York: McGraw-Hill, 1967, pp. 709 –10.

Veraja, Fabijan. *La beatificazione. Storia, problemi, prospettive. Sussidi per lo studio delle cause dei santi 2*. Rome: Sacra Congregazione per le Cause dei Santi, 1983.

Wills, Garry. "The Phallic Pulpit." *The New York Review of Books*, December 29, 1989, pp. 20–26.

Woodward, Kenneth L. "Spiritual Adventure: The Emergence of a New Theology," a conversation with John Dunne. *Psychology Today*, vol. 11, no. 8, January 1978.

———. "What Is God? John Dunne's Life of Discovery." *Notre Dame Magazine*, vol. 9, no. 3, July 1980.

———. "How America Lives with Death." *Newsweek*, April 6, 1970, p. 88.

———. "Religion, Art and the Gothic Sensibility." *Perspectives*, vol. 9, no. 1, January–February 1964, pp. 14–17.

INDEX

PHOTO CREDITS